LOVAK REPU

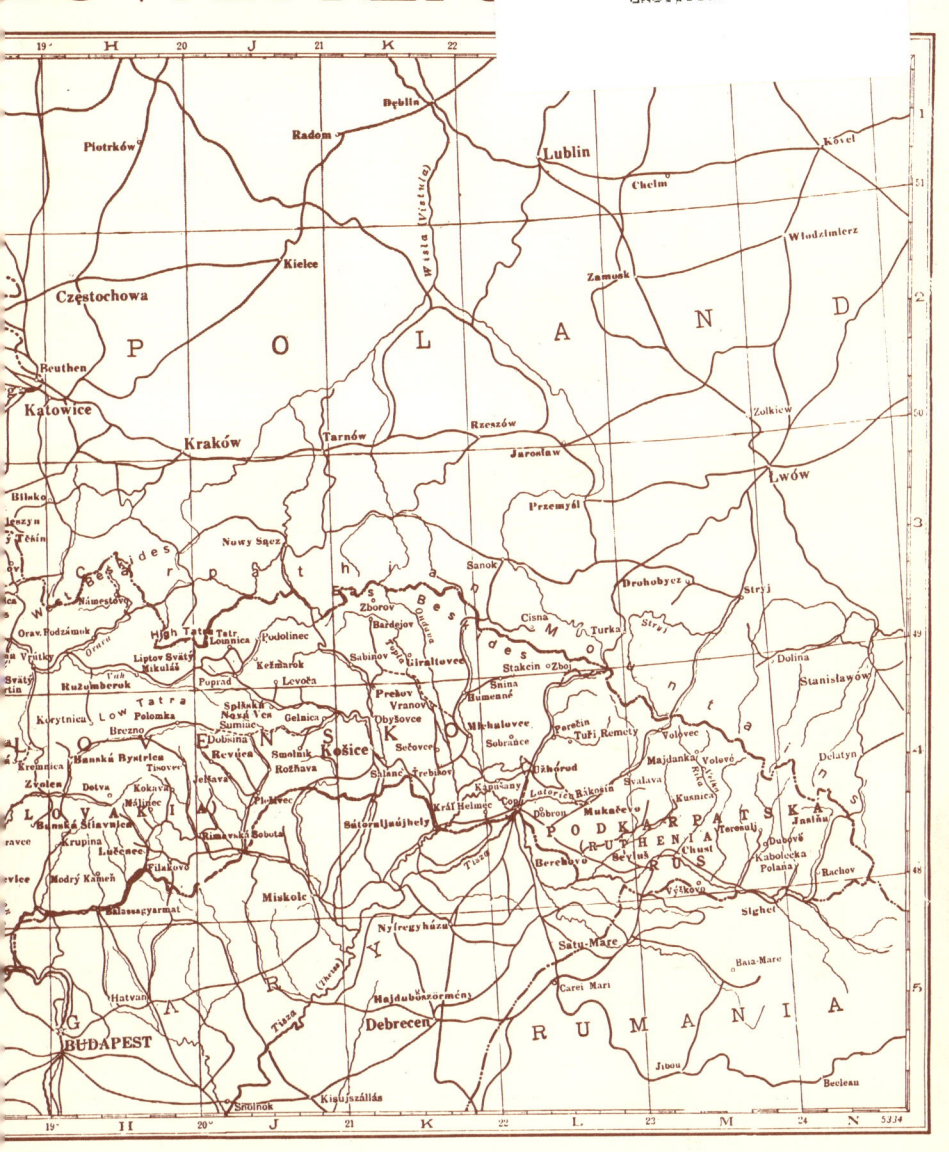

ENNÍK AND NEW-YORSKÉ LISTY
York City 28, N. Y.
ATwater 9-7320

THE JEWS OF CZECHOSLOVAKIA

THE JEWS OF CZECHOSLOVAKIA

HISTORICAL STUDIES AND SURVEYS

VOLUME III

AVIGDOR DAGAN
EDITOR IN CHIEF

GERTRUDE HIRSCHLER

LEWIS WEINER
ASSOCIATE EDITORS

5744-1984

THE JEWISH PUBLICATION SOCIETY OF AMERICA
PHILADELPHIA

SOCIETY FOR THE HISTORY OF CZECHOSLOVAK JEWS
NEW YORK

Copyright © 1984

By the Jewish Publication Society of America
and the Society for the History of Czechoslovak Jews

All Rights Reserved

First Edition

Library of Congress Cataloging in Publication Data

Main entry under title:
The Jews of Czechoslovakia.
   Includes bibliographies, illustrations, and index.
   1. Jews—Czechoslovakia—History. 2. Czechoslovakia—
Civilization—Jewish influences. 3. Holocaust, Jewish
(1939-1945)—Czechoslovakia. 4. Czechoslovakia—Ethnic
relations.
DS135.C95J45   943.7′004924   67-12372
ISBN 0-8276-0230-8 (v. 3)

Manufactured in the United States of America

Designed by Sidney Feinberg

End sheet map "Czechoslovakia in Transition"
© Rand McNally & Co. Used by permission.

End sheet "Map of Czechoslovak Republic"
© Hammond Incorporated. Used by permission.

ACKNOWLEDGMENTS FOR PICTORIAL AND OTHER MATERIAL

The Society for the History of Czechoslovak Jews gratefully acknowledges the courtesy extended to the editors of this volume by the Yad Vashem Archives in Jerusalem and by the Yitzhak Katznelson Museum at Kibbutz Lohame HaGetaot, which kindly permitted the use of pictorial material from their files as illustrations for this book.

For other illustrations the Society is indebted to Messrs. Bedřich Gruenzweig, Jan Lukas, Joseph C. Pick, Maximilian S. Spell, Karel Štern, and Erich Vogel.

Pictures were reproduced also from F. Steiner, ed., *Tragédia slovenských Židov* [The Tragedy of Slovak Jewry] (Bratislava: 1949).

The Society wishes to thank Atheneum Publishers, New York, for permission to quote excerpts from Ehud Avriel's book, *Open the Gates: The Dramatic Personal Story of "Illegal" Immigration to Israel* (New York: 1975).

TO THE MEMORY
OF THE CZECHOSLOVAK JEWS
WHO PERISHED AS VICTIMS
OF NAZI PERSECUTION.

PREFACE

Our Sages teach that whoever sets out to perform a good deed must be told, "Complete what you have begun."*

It is in this spirit that the Society for the History of Czechoslovak Jews presents the third and last volume of its series, *The Jews of Czechoslovakia: Historical Studies and Surveys,* as a capstone for its monument to Czechoslovak Jewry.

The plan to publish this series was first conceived by the Society in 1961 under the guiding inspiration of its founder and first president, Dr. Kurt Wehle, and the late Dr. Oskar K. Rabinowicz. Volume I appeared in 1968; Volume II, in 1971. These two volumes cover the history of the Jews of Bohemia, Moravia, Silesia, and Slovakia from the middle of the nineteenth century, focusing primarily on the period from 1918 to 1938, from the emergence of the Czechoslovak Republic founded by Tomáš G. Masaryk until its fall as the result of the Munich agreement and the German occupation of the "Historic Lands."

The present volume records the saddest chapter in the thousand-year history of the Jews in the region known in modern times as Czechoslovakia. Alas, this must be also the last chapter, for of the multitude of Jewish communities that studded the landscape of Czech and Slovak history for ten centuries, only a very few have survived. For the rest, all that has remained is one vast museum, a few buildings bearing historic memories—and the cemeteries. But most of the final generation of Jews who lived in Czechoslovakia until the Holocaust have left us even without the solace of graves

---

* Jerusalem Talmud, Pesahim 10:5, et al.

and tombstones. It is to the memory of this martyred generation that the Society for the History of Czechoslovak Jews wishes to dedicate the present volume, which encompasses the years of World War II, the Holocaust, and the aftermath of the Nazi terror.

Work on Volume III was begun by the Society under the presidency of Mr. Ludovit Sturc. Mr. Sturc's death in the summer of 1976 not only caused a delay in the publication of this volume but also left a keenly felt gap in the ranks of the Society. His devotion to the growth and welfare of the Society, his warm human kindness, and his eagerness to blend the memories of the past with the best of the present endeared him to all his friends and associates. His memory will always remain with us.

The interest shown by the public for the first two volumes encouraged the inner circle of the Society to continue and finish the series. To this end, an Editorial Board was formed consisting of Dr. Avigdor Dagan (chairman), Prof. Fred Hahn, Dr. Zdenka Münzer, and Mr. Lewis Weiner.

As president of the Society for the History of Czechoslovak Jews, it is my privilege to extend the Society's sincere thanks to the distinguished men and women who contributed articles to Volume III: Mr. Ehud Avriel,* Dr. Avigdor Dagan, Dr. Yeshayahu Jelinek, Mr. Erich Kulka, Dr. Zdenek Lederer,* Dr. John G. Lexa,* Dr. Ladislav Lipscher, Mr. Joseph C. Pick, Dr. Livia Rothkirchen, Dr. Hana Volavková, and Dr. Kurt Wehle.

The articles in this book, like those in the preceding two volumes, vary greatly in quality and in their approach to the subject matter. They were chosen for inclusion in this trilogy precisely because they were the work of individuals from a wide spectrum of academic, professional, political, and social backgrounds. By and large, the contributing authors in all three volumes represent a social, cultural, political, and geographic cross-section of the Jewish community of Czechoslovakia as it was prior to the Holocaust.

The task of gathering these authors and incorporating their work into the context of the present volume was performed by the Editorial Board in collaboration with its chairman, Dr. Avigdor Dagan, who resides in Jerusalem. A distinguished author and journalist, Dr.

---

* Deceased.

PREFACE   xi

Dagan has spent a lifetime in the service of the Jewish people, first as an official of the Jewish party in pre-1939 Czechoslovakia, then as a close advisor to the Czechoslovak government-in-exile in London, and during the past three decades as a member of the Israeli diplomatic corps. He graciously agreed to act as editor in chief of this volume and carried out that function with great sensitivity, consummate tact, and boundless devotion. The Society for the History of Czechoslovak Jews owes Dr. Dagan a lasting debt of gratitude.

I deem it a most fortunate coincidence that our co-publisher, the Jewish Publication Society of America, assigned Miss Gertrude Hirschler, a long-time friend of the Society for the History of Czechoslovak Jews, to work on the project. Miss Hirschler and I served together as associate editors of this volume. In addition to the literary skills of an editor, Miss Hirschler brought to this task a thorough knowledge of the subject matter and an intuitive understanding of what our Editorial Board and the contributing authors sought to accomplish. She takes pride in having acted as a link, both professionally and personally, between the Jewish Publication Society and the Society for the History of Czechoslovak Jews. We herewith acknowledge her valued aid and counsel in the preparation of this book for publication.

I also wish to express my heartfelt thanks to the following whose help and advice were invaluable in our endeavor: Mr. Joseph Abeles, Dr. Kurt Bock, Prof. John Wolfgang Brügel, Dr. Stephen S. Barber,* Mrs. Simi Eichorn, Dr. Jindřich H. Fantl, Dr. Leo Gruna, Dr. Paul Hartman, Mr. Michael Kates, Dr. Miroslav Kerner, Mrs. Sylvia Landress, Rabbi Norman R. Patz, Rabbi Dr. Hugo Stransky,* Dr. Ernest Sturc, and Miss Esther Togman.

In addition to the publication of this historical series, the Society for the History of Czechoslovak Jews has been engaged in a number of other activities designed to create an interest in the history of Czechoslovak Jewry and to maintain the bonds that link Czechoslovak Jews the world over. Notably, the Society arranged a celebration of the Millennium of Czechoslovak Jewry in New York's Town Hall on November 17, 1968. The program, in which well-known

---
* Deceased

American Jews also participated, included historical surveys, a motion picture presentation, and musical works composed in the ghetto of Terezín (Theresienstadt).

Since 1946 the Society has sponsored annual memorial services for the Jews of Czechoslovakia who perished in the Holocaust. The Joseph Popper Lodge of B'nai B'rith, which was founded by immigrants from Czechoslovakia in New York, participates in this event. The initiators of the memorial services were Prof. Guido Kisch, honorary president of the Society, and the late Dr. Frederick Fried, a member of the Society's board of directors.

The Society for the History of Czechoslovak Jews gratefully acknowledges the help received for the publication of this volume from the Joseph Popper Lodge and Chapter of B'nai B'rith, and the continued cooperation of the Jewish Publication Society of America, especially its editor, Mr. Maier Deshell, and its executive vice-president, Mr. Bernard Levinson, for their friendly interest and personal concern.

The Society for the History of Czechoslovak Jews hopes that this volume will be received in academic circles and by the general public with the same warmth and recognition as were its two predecessors. It is hoped, too, that this book will not only serve students of the Holocaust as a source of factual information but will also convey to posterity memories, values, and ideals that outlive the inhumanities of evil men and that these values can take their rightful place in building a better future for all mankind.

Lewis Weiner
President
Society for the History of Czechoslovak Jews

Contents

- ix   Preface
- xv   List of Illustrations
- xvii   Introduction
- xxiii   Note to the Reader
- xxv   Abbreviations
- xxviii   From the Munich Agreement to the Communist Takeover In Czechoslovakia: *Chronology of Events: 1938–1948.*

I. HOLOCAUST

- 3   The Jews of Bohemia and Moravia: 1938–1945
  Livia Rothkirchen
- 75   Anti-Jewish Laws and Regulations in the Protectorate of Bohemia and Moravia
  John G. Lexa
- 104   Terezín
  Zdenek Lederer
- 165   The Jews of Slovakia: 1939–1945
  Ladislav Lipscher

262 The Annihilation of Czechoslovak Jewry
Erich Kulka

II. RESISTANCE

331 Jews in the Czechoslovak Armed Forces During World War II
Erich Kulka

449 The Czechoslovak Government-in-Exile and the Jews
Avigdor Dagan

III. THE AFTERMATH

499 The Jews in Bohemia and Moravia: 1945–1948
Kurt Wehle

531 The Jews in Slovakia: 1945–1949
Yeshayahu Jelinek

551 Prague and Jerusalem: The Era of Friendship
Ehud Avriel

567 The Jewish Museum of Prague
Hana Volavková

584 The Story of the Czech Scrolls
Joseph C. Pick

611 *The Authors*

Cumulative Indexes for Volumes I-III

615 *Index of Names*

653 *Index of Places*

666 *Index of Subjects*

List of Illustrations

Between pages 164 and 165

1. Map showing plans for redistricting of the Jewish religious congregations of Bohemia and Moravia, March 1941.
2. The leaders of the Jewish Religious Congregation of Prague, May 1941.
3. Dynamiting of the synagogue at Budějovice, July 5, 1942.
4. From the minutes of the Prague conference on the "solution of the Jewish problem" (October 17, 1941).
5. Jews at the Trade Fair grounds in Holešovice, a suburb of Prague, where they were assembled for deportation to Terezín.
6. A Jewish family in Prague, wearing identification tags and Stars of David, awaiting deportation to Terezín (1942).
7. Announcement, in Czech and German, of shopping hours for Jews in Prague.
8. Children's playground on Karlovo Náměstí (Charles Square), Prague.
9. Plan of the Terezín ghetto.
10. Terezín: Ghetto currency.
11. Terezín: Voucher for clothing and shoes.
12. Terezín: Food voucher.
13. Terezín: A clothing store

14. Title page of children's Hebrew primer produced clandestinely in Terezín.
15. A children's opera performed in Terezín.
16. In the ghetto (drawing).
17. Monument erected in the Jewish cemetery of Terezín.
18. Examples of anti-Semitic Czech and German posters and graffiti in Bratislava.
19. Deportations of Jews from Slovakia: A graphic representation.
20. Jews and other partisans in the Slovak uprising, August and September 1944.
21. Auschwitz: Arrival and "selection" of victims.
22. Auschwitz: "Processing" of new arrivals.
23. Auschwitz-Birkenau: Postcard sent by the inmate Hugo Sax to a relative in the Protectorate of Bohemia and Moravia.
24. Auschwitz-Birkenau: The gas chambers (plan of ground floor).
25. Map showing movements of Czechoslovak army units in the Middle East during World War II.
26. Anti-aircraft battery manned by Czechoslovak soldiers (Jewish and non-Jewish) defending the port of Tobruk, 1941.
27. Lieutenant Otto Smik, leader of the 127th British Air Squadron.
28. The battle of Sokolovo, March 1943.
29. A partial list of Czechoslovak soldiers killed in the battle of Sokolovo, March 1943.
30. Message from Foreign Minister Jan Masaryk to the *Keren HaYesod* (Palestine Foundation Fund), October 1945.
31. Ark curtain, *Altneuschul,* Prague.
32. Chalice from the collection of Jewish ceremonial art in Prague's State Jewish Museum.
33. Holocaust memorial in the restored Pinkas Synagogue in Prague, 1959.
34. Section of wall of the Holocaust memorial in the Pinkas Synagogue in Prague.

INTRODUCTION

The two previous volumes of *The Jews of Czechoslovakia* are collections of essays discussing the role of the Jews, as a minority group and as individuals, in various aspects of Czechoslovak Jewish life prior to 1939. This, the third and final volume, encompasses the saddest period in the story of the Jews of Czechoslovakia; World War II and the Holocaust. It concludes with a survey of efforts by a cruelly decimated remnant after the war to renew Jewish life in a land where Jews had lived for over a thousand years.

The difference between the historical material included in Volumes I and II, on the one hand, and the contents of this last volume, on the other, may perhaps be likened to that between a walk through a garden in full bloom and a pilgrimage to a cemetery. Against the rich record of outstanding achievements in a variety of endeavors through which Jews once helped enhance the image of Czechoslovakia in the world arena, there now appears the gray shadow of a small community striving for bare survival.

This difference between flowering and desolation, between stability and chaos, is reflected also in the quality of the material presented in this volume. A survey of normal, peaceful developments, conducted in a methodical fashion, is one thing; the counting of the dead left after a catastrophe is quite another. A host of victims are doomed to remain missing, without a possibility of accounting for them. Accordingly, it will be noted that the statistics cited in this volume, gathered as they were from a variety of sources and at different times, do not always tally to the last fraction. If, thanks to the scrupulously responsible research and meticulous scholarship of the contributing authors, it was possible to reduce discrepancies to a minimum, this is a happy outcome deserving of special recognition.

Perhaps the greatest difficulty faced by the editors, and by the group of men and women whose essays are included in this volume, was the fact that the events which they discuss are still comparatively recent history—indeed, often part of the authors' personal lives—which, even after four decades, the writers find it difficult to view with the objectivity of historians aided by the perspective of time. The period covered by these essays cast up a multitude of problems and issues that have remained the subject of considerable disagreement to this day. The reader will therefore find marked differences among the authors in their evaluations of certain events and developments, in their diagnoses of cause and effect, and in their judgments based on hindsight. In some instances the editors attempted to elicit a common denominator from the divergent views expressed by the various contributors. In other cases it seemed more appropriate to leave these differences deliberately unresolved.

Among the subjects treated in this book that still give rise to heated debate is the relationship between Czechs, Slovaks, and Jews at various crucial moments in the Holocaust period. To what degree had anti-Semitism taken root among Czechs and Slovaks? To what extent did Czechs and Slovaks collaborate with the Germans in their attempted "final solution of the Jewish problem"? Might a greater number of Jews in Czechoslovakia have been saved if the Czech and Slovak populace had displayed a more actively helpful attitude? The Czechoslovak armies in exile that fought alongside the Allies during World War II included a large proportion of Jews. What was the attitude of the non-Jewish officers and men toward their Jewish comrades in arms?

There is a wide range of possible answers to all these questions. The attitudes and conduct of Czechs and Slovaks toward the Jews during the Holocaust reflected a wide spectrum of hues, from the outright philo-Semitism represented by the ideological heirs of Tomáš G. Masaryk to the crude hatred demonstrated by the hooligans in the uniforms of the Fascist Vlajka and Hlinka Guards. It cannot be said that the behavior of the Czechs and Slovaks toward the Jews during the war was worse than that of most other European nations under the Nazi heel. Yet there are those who suggest that one could have expected the people of Tomáš G. Masaryk to be less indifferent than other nations to the fate of their Jewish fellow citizens. It would certainly be both wrong and futile to attempt to deny that there were anti-Semitic tendencies in Czechoslovakia, or to minimize their significance. But it would be equally unjust to magnify the importance of these anti-Semitic manifestations out of proportion. Thus, it can hardly be denied that anti-Semitism did in fact exist among the officer corps of the Czechoslovak armies in exile. Yet, the many war decorations awarded to Jewish members of the Czechoslovak fighting units bear witness to the fact that the contribution of Jews to the military effort of the Czechoslovak resistance was appreciated by those in command, and that the record of Jewish officers and men fighting together with Czechs and Slovaks against the common enemy won widespread respect. That this last reality has not found expression in Czechoslovak historiography since the war is a concomitant of influences and methods of statistical study that cannot simply be ascribed to native Czech or Slovak anti-Semitism. Among other things, the questionnaires filled in by the soldiers did not include religion but only ethnic origin, and most of the Jewish men, who regarded the Czech or the Slovak language as their mother tongue, listed their ethnic origin as "Czech" or "Slovak."

With regard to the overall principles that guided the editors in the preparation of this volume, the reader is referred to the Introduction to Volume I. There, it was pointed out that the Editorial Board of the Society for the History of Czechoslovak Jews did not consider itself bound by any particular Jewish or political ideology and did not attempt to dictate the views to be set forth by the contributing authors. Beyond urging the authors to be as objective as possible in their presentations, and to view their personal reminiscences in the larger context of historical events, the editors permitted each author full freedom of expression, and it is the authors who bear the final responsibility for their contributions.

One more point should perhaps be made quite clear. Prior to World War II, the dividing line between the Zionists and those Jews who rejected Jewish nationalism and advocated assimilation was more marked in Czechoslovakia than in many other parts of the world. Czechoslovakia was one of the very few countries (Germany was another) where the proponents of assimilation were organized in a political and cultural movement. (See Egon Hostovský, "The Czech-Jewish Movement," Volume II, pp. 148–54.) Though not all of its members were practicing Jews in the accepted religious sense, the Czech-Jewish movement regarded religion, not nationality or ethnic origin, as the sole distinction between the Jews and their non-Jewish neighbors. Contributing authors in this volume have variously used the term "assimilationist" to define those who subscribed to this ideology. In view of developments since the war, the differences and tensions between the Zionists and the "assimilationists" of an earlier era have become largely irrelevant. Nevertheless, in order to avoid any misunderstanding, the editors would like to make it clear beyond the slightest doubt that this term was not intended in a pejorative meaning.

Finally, as editor in chief, I would like to render my personal thanks to all the members of the Editorial Board and all the contributing authors for their help and cooperation. Special appreciation goes to Mr. Lewis Weiner, the president of the Society for the History of Czechoslovak Jews, who, despite his heavy professional commitments, gave most generously of his time and knowledge to act as an associate editor of Volume III. Without his tireless and dedicated efforts, this volume could not have been published. The other associate editor, Miss Gertrude Hirschler, officially joined this project as the editor assigned by our co-publisher, the Jewish Publication Society of America, to work with the Editorial Board in the preparation of Volume III. In fact, however, her professional and personal ties with the Society for the History of Czechoslovak Jews go back over many years before that. She is the author of the article on "The History of Agudath Israel in Slovakia (1918–1939)" in Volume II (pp. 155–72).

As one reads the essays in this final volume of our trilogy, the impact of the tragedies recorded in them would seem to leave little room for optimism. Yet, one may take comfort in the fact that the cultural and spiritual heritage of the Jews of Czechoslovakia still survives. It lives on not merely in the showcases of museums and in a few cemeteries and empty synagogues, but through the spirit of those Czechoslovak Jews who escaped the fate of the Six Million and who found the strength and faith to build new homes and new lives for themselves and their families. It is hoped, therefore, that these three volumes of essays on the history of the Jews of Czechoslovakia will be read not merely as a pious gesture to the past of one particular segment of Jewry, but also as an inspiration to a new generation now making its own contribution to Jewish history.

AVIGDOR DAGAN

NOTE TO THE READER*

Some technical and methodological explanations seem to be necessary at the outset to guide and assist the reader.

1. The first two volumes of *The Jews of Czechoslovakia* were limited to the history of the period from 1918 to 1939. The present volume deals with the decade from 1939 to 1949. However, as in the case of the first two volumes, so in this book, too, a set chronological order could not always be strictly followed, for history is a fluid process, and the problems and events of any given period cannot be understood in isolation from earlier epochs. The bibliographies that appear at the end of most of the essays in this volume will be found useful also in this respect.

2. In a historical work of this nature, it was inevitable that more than one author should have dealt with the same event, viewing it from his particular vantage point. The free, logical flow of the narrative was given priority over the avoidance of repetitions. In order to guide the reader to other aspects of a problem discussed by several authors, the editors have introduced cross-references into the text.

3. Czech and German terms have been retained in their original spellings. Hebrew terms were transliterated according to the Sephardi pronunciation of modern Hebrew, as spoken in Israel.

4. The names of all cities and towns in Czechoslovakia were rendered in the official Czech or Slovak languages. In some instances, the German and Magyar names by which they were known were added. Only Prague was retained in the English version.

5. Some individuals mentioned in this book have changed their names, usually following their emigration to Israel. Where this is the case, the name used in Czechoslovakia is given and the new name follows in parentheses.

In other cases, where the spelling of names in the same family varied (e.g., Schulhoff and Schulhof), the rendition employed by the bearer was used.

---

* For additional information, see Volume I, pp. xxi–xxiii.

ABBREVIATIONS

AA	*Auswärtiges Amt* (German Foreign Office)
AAPA	*Politisches Archiv des Auswärtigen Amtes* (Political Archives of the German Foreign Office, Bonn).
ADAP	*Akten zur deutschen auswärtigen Politik* (Documents relating to German Foreign Policy)
AJDC	Archives of the American Jewish Joint Distribution Committee (JDC)
AUD KSČ	*Ústav dějin Kommunistické strany Československa* (Archives of the Institute for the History of the Communist Party of Czechoslovakia, Prague)
AÚDKSS	*Archív Ústavu dějin Kommunistickej strany Slovenska* (Archives of the Institute for the History of the Communist Party of Slovakia)
AVHU	*Archív Vojenského Historického Ústavu* (Archives of the Institute of Military History, Prague)
AW	Private archives of Dr. Albert (Vojtěch) Winterstein
BA	*Bundesarchiv* (Archives of the Federal Republic of Germany, Coblenz)
CBF	Central British Fund
CZA	Central Zionist Archives, Jerusalem
DGFP	Documents on German Foreign Policy (same as ADAP)
FS	*Freiwillige Schutzstaffel* (Voluntary defense squads organized by the German party in Slovakia)
HC	*Historický časopis* (Historical Journal)
HG	*Hlinkova Garda* (Hlinka Guard, Slovak nationalist paramilitary organization)
IFZ	*Institut für Zeitgeschichte* (Institute for Contemporary History, Munich).

IMT	International Military Tribunal
JDC	American Jewish Joint Distribution Committee
JNBL	*Jüdisches Nachrichtenblatt* (periodical)
JSS	*Jewish Social Studies* (periodical)
KSČ	Communist party of Czechoslovakia
KSS	Community party of Slovakia
MF	*Ministerstvo financií* (Slovak Ministry of Finance)
MV	*Ministerstvo vnútra* (Slovak Ministry for Internal Affairs)
NA	National Archives of the U.S., Washington.
ND	Documents of the Nuremberg War Crimes Trials
NG	German Foreign Ministry Papers
NS	*Narodný súd* (National Court of Justice)
PA	German Foreign Ministry Papers
POHG	*Pohotovostné oddiely Hlinkovej Gardy* (Alert Units of the Hlinka Guard)
PR	*Policajné riaditelst'vo* (Police Headquarters, Bratislava)
RFSS	German Foreign Ministry Papers
RGBL	*Reichsgesetzblatt* (Reich Law Gazette)
RSHA	*Reichssicherheitshauptamt* (Central Office of Reich Security)
SD	*Sicherheitsdienst* (Security Service)
SdB	*Sonderbericht* (Special Report)
Sipo	*Sicherheitspolizei* (Security Police)
SRP	*Svaz rasově prenásledovaných* (Organization of Victims of Racial Persecution at the Hands of the Fascist Regime)
ŠSÚA	*Štátny slovenský ústredný archiv* (Central Archives of the Slovak State, Bratislava)
SÚA	*Statní Ústřední archiv* (Central State Archives, Prague)
SSUV	Slovak State Council Papers
Tnlud	*Tribunál ľudu* (National Court of Justice)
ÚHÚ	*Ústredný hospodársky úrad* (Central Economic Office, Bratislava)

ÚPV	*Úrad predsedníctva vlády* (Slovak Prime Minister's Office)
UNRRA	United Nations Relief and Rehabilitation Administration
URO	Central Federation of Trade Unions
UŽ	*Ústredňa Židov* (Jewish Office)
VHA	*Vojenský historický archiv* (Archives of Military History, Prague)
VOBL	*Verordnungsblatt des Reichsprotektors für Böhmen und Mähren* (Official Gazette of the Reich Protector for Bohemia and Moravia)
WIZO	Women's International Zionist Organization
WJC	World Jewish Congress
YVA	Yad Vashem Archives, Jerusalem
ŽNO	*Židovská Náboženská Obec* (Jewish Religious Congregation)
ŽRS	*Židovská Rada Starších* (Council of Jewish Elders)

FROM THE MUNICH AGREEMENT TO THE COMMUNIST TAKEOVER IN CZECHOSLOVAKIA

Chronology of Events: 1938-1948

(For purposes of orientation, this chronology includes also certain key events of World War II)

1938

September 29-30: The Munich agreement signed by Germany, Italy, Great Britain, and France paves the way for the dismemberment of Czechoslovakia.

October 1: Germany occupies the Sudetenland.

October 5: President Eduard Beneš resigns and a caretaker government is formed under General Jan Syrový. František Chvalkovský is named director of foreign policy. The leading role in internal affairs is assumed by Rudolf Beran, who eventually becomes Prime Minister.

October 6: In Slovakia, politicians set up an autonomous Slovak government in Žilina. The power is in the hands of the *L'udova Strana* (People's party) founded by Andrej Hlinka and led by Dr. Jozef Tiso.

November:* The *Židovská Ústredňa Uradovňa pre krajinu Slovenskú* (Central Jewish Office for the Region of Slovakia) is formed to organize the vocational reorientation of Slovak Jews, to solve problems affecting Slovak Jewry, and to render effective assistance in the emigration of Jews from Slovakia.

---

*Note: Here and in other instances where the exact date could not be established or where the event took place over a longer period of time only the month is given.

November 2:	The Vienna award cedes part of Slovakia to Hungary. The rest of Slovakia is guaranteed autonomy within a federal state of Czechs, Slovaks, and Ruthenes replacing the Czechoslovak Republic and named Czecho-Slovakia.
November 9–10:	Kristallnacht pogroms in Germany and Austria.
November 30:	Emil Hácha is installed as president of Czecho-Slovakia.

1939

January 27:	All Jews are dismissed from the civil service of Czecho-Slovakia.
March 14:	A Slovak parliament officially proclaims the "independent" state of Slovakia.
March 15:	Germany occupies Bohemia and Moravia.
March 16:	Hitler signs decree incorporating the Czech Historic Lands into the Reich Protectorate of Bohemia and Moravia. Subcarpathian Ruthenia is ceded to Hungary.
March 18:	Baron Constantin von Neurath is appointed Reich Protector in Bohemia and Moravia. Hermann K. Frank, a Sudeten German leader, is appointed Secretary of the Protectorate.
April 18:	The Slovak state enacts its first anti-Semitic legislation. Ordinance 63 defines who is a Jew and restricts the number of Jews to be permitted in certain liberal professions.
April 27:	Emil Hácha, who has been permitted to remain in office nominally as "State President" of the Protectorate, reorganizes the cabinet and appoints General Alois Eliáš Prime Minister.
May:	Youth Aliyah training school is opened in Prague to teach young people skills needed for life in Palestine.
June 13:	First law of anti-Jewish discrimination in education is passed by the Slovak state.
June 21:	Reich Protector von Neurath proclaims comprehensive decree to eliminate the Jews from virtually all the economy of the Protectorate. The decree defines Jews in accordance with the Nuremberg racial laws of 1935.

July:	*Zentralstelle für jüdische Auswanderung* (Central Office for Jewish Emigration) is set up in Prague under the personal supervision of Adolf Eichmann, who leaves SS Hauptsturmführer Hans Günther in charge.
July 4:	Jewish students are excluded from German-language public schools and high schools in the Protectorate.
August 5:	The Protectorate enacts first laws to "protect" the non-Jewish population from contact with Jews.
August 11:	Jews in provincial areas of the Protectorate are ordered to leave their homes and resettle in Prague within one year.
August 23:	Germany and the Soviet Union sign a non-aggression pact.
September 1:	Germany invades Poland.
September 3:	Britain and France declare war on Germany: World War II breaks out.
September 17:	Soviet forces occupy the eastern part of Poland.
September 27:	Warsaw falls to German forces.
October:	Josef M. Kadlec, the Czechoslovak consul general in Jerusalem, issues a call for Czechoslovak citizens in Palestine to register as potential volunteers for service with Czechoslovak army units in exile to fight alongside the Allies. His call is answered by 1,200 Jewish refugees from Czechoslovakia.
October 19:	First transport of Jews from Moravská Ostrava arrives at "agricultural reservation" (read: concentration camp) near Nisko (German-occupied Poland), south of Lublin.
October 26:	Second transport of Jews from Ostrava arrives at Nisko camp. For lack of accommodations, some Jewish deportees are driven into the Soviet sector of Poland.
November:	*Národní výbor* (Czechoslovak National Council) is set up in Paris.
November 21:	The Federation of Evangelical Pastors of Slovakia sends a memorandum to the President, cabinet, and parliament of Slovakia protesting Hlinka Guard outrages perpetrated against Evangelical ministers and other religious functionaries, and Jews.

1940

February 16:	The authority of the *Zentralstelle für jüdische Auswanderung* is extended over the entire Protectorate.
March 15:	All Jewish religious congregations in the Prague area are placed under the jurisdiction of the Jewish Religious Congregation of Prague.
March 23:	Hermann Göring suspends deportation of Jews to Poland, apparently because of adverse reactions abroad.
April 4:	In Jerusalem, Consul General Kadlec issues a general mobilization order for Czechoslovak citizens living in Palestine to join Czechoslovak army units in exile. This order causes concern among Czechoslovak Jewish refugees who have been unable to obtain Palestine citizenship from the British mandatory authorities or who have opted to retain Czechoslovak citizenship. Eventually, thanks to the intervention of Jan Masaryk and Moshe Shertok (Sharett), the matter is quietly dropped.
April 9:	Germany occupies Denmark and invades Norway.
April 13:	For various reasons, the German authorities decide to abandon the Nisko camp. Most of the remaining inmates are sent to Silesia or to Vienna.
April 25:	The Slovak parliament enacts the "First Aryanization Law."
April 30:	The Jews in the Protectorate of Bohemia and Moravia are ordered to sell their gold, platinum, silver, pearls, and precious stones to the HADEGA purchasing agency and to deposit all their stocks, bonds, and other securities at a foreign currency bank.
May:	With the consent of Protectorate authorities, the Jewish communal leader Hanna Steiner visits Berlin and Hamburg to make arrangements with various foreign consulates and with shipping companies for the emigration of Jews from Bohemia and Moravia. Dr. Oskar Neumann is elected president of the Zionist Federation of Slovakia.
May 10:	German invasion of Western Europe begins.
May 14:	Holland capitulates to Germans.

May 20:	Two Slovak Evangelical bishops send pastoral letters to all Evangelical parishes in Slovakia condemning Jew-baiting as a violation of human justice and divine law.
May 28:	Belgium capitulates to Germans.
June 10:	Italy enters the war on the side of Germany.
June 15–17:	The Soviet Union annexes the Baltic states.
June 22:	France surrenders to Germany.
July 21:	The *Státní rada* (State Council) is set up as the provisional parliament of the Czechoslovak government-in-exile in London. The British government recognizes the provisional Czechoslovak government in London under Eduard Beneš.
July 28:	Slovak leaders meet with Hitler in Salzburg (Salzburg Conference) and agree to set up a National Socialist regime in Slovakia. Dr. Jozef Tiso, formerly Prime Minister, becomes President of the Slovak state. Former Deputy Premier Vojtech Tuka is named Prime Minister and Foreign Minister.
August 8:	All Jewish children are barred from public schools in the Protectorate.
September 2:	Last "illegal" transport bound for Palestine leaves the Protectorate of Bohemia and Moravia.
September 3:	The Slovak parliament adopts Constitutional Law 210 authorizing the government to take whatever action it sees fit in matters of Aryanization.
September 13:	Jews in the Protectorate may no longer rent vacant apartments and can move only into apartments already occupied by other Jews.
September 16:	Slovak Law No. 45 creates *Ústredný Hospodársky Úrad* (Central Economic Office), headed by Augustín Morávek and charged with the task of organizing the "solution of the Jewish problem" in Slovakia.
September 30:	Slovak Ordinance 234 provides for the establishment of the *Ústredňa Židov* (Jewish Office), which is to reorganize Jewish life in Slovakia and carry out orders of the Slovak state affecting Jews. All Zionist organizations and institutions in Slovakia are disbanded.
November:	Slovakia joins Rome–Ber'in–Tokyo "axis."

1941

April:	Palestine office in Prague is closed.
June 22:	Germany attacks the Soviet Union.
July 5:	The Nuremberg laws are introduced into the Protectorate effective retroactively as of March 15, 1939.
July 21:	British government officially recognizes Czechoslovak government-in-exile under Beneš's leadership in London. The Slovak Ministry for Internal Affairs issues first labor draft call under a law making Jews between the ages of eighteen and sixty subjects to forced labor service.
August:	Slovak government liquidates the ghetto of Bratislava.
September 1:	All Jews in the Protectorate are ordered to wear a yellow Star of David.
September 9:	Slovak state enacts Nuremberg-type "Jewish Code" (Ordinance 198/1941).
September 15:	First reports of initial experiments with gas chambers in Auschwitz.
September 27:	SS Obergruppenführer Reinhard Heydrich is appointed Acting Reich Protector in Bohemia and Moravia.
October:	Heydrich orders closing of all synagogues and other Jewish places of worship in the Protectorate.
October 7:	Catholic bishops of Slovakia draft memorandum to leading Slovak government officials rejecting the "racism" of the "Jewish Code," primarily the effect of the code on Jewish converts to Catholicism.
October 10:	First conference on the "solution of the Jewish problem" is held in Prague and is attended by Heydrich and Eichmann.
October 16:	First transport of Jews from Prague leaves for ghetto of Lodz.
October 17:	Second conference on the "solution of the Jewish problem" meets in Prague under the chairmanship of Heydrich.
October 19:	Terezín (Theresienstadt) is chosen as a ghetto.

November 12:   Vatican objects to the Slovak "Jewish Code" because of its effect on the legal status of Jewish converts to Catholicism.

November 18:   In London, Beneš names Arnošt (Ernst) Frischer, former chairman of the Jewish party in the Czechoslovak Republic, to the *Státní Rada* (State Council).

November 20:   One thousand Jewish deportees from Brno arrive in Minsk.

November 24:   First transport of young Jewish men from Prague arrives in Terezín as *Aufbaukommando* (construction detail).

November 30–December 4:   First large transports of Jews from Prague, including old people, arrive in Terezín.

December 7:   Japanese attack Pearl Harbor.

December 11:   Germany declares war on the United States.

1942

January: Refugees from Nisko in the Soviet Union are permitted to join the Czechoslovak Brigade at Buzuluk.

January 9:   First transport of Terezín ghetto inmates is sent to the ghetto in Riga.

January 10:   Nine Terezín ghetto inmates are hanged for engaging in "prohibited" activities.

January 20:   Plans for the "final solution of the Jewish problem" are unveiled at Wannsee Conference under chairmanship of Heydrich.

February 26:   Seven more Terezín ghetto inmates are hanged for engaging in "prohibited" activities.

March: "Department 14," in collaboration with Hlinka Guard and regular police, organizes deportations of Jews from Slovakia. Start of regular transports from Terezín to ghettos and labor camps in German-occupied Poland.

March 14:   Vatican sends note to Slovak government requesting cancellation of plans for the deportation of Jews from Slovakia.

March 28:   First transport of Jews from Slovakia arrives in Auschwitz-Birkenau.

April:	First transport of 1,000 from Terezín arrives in Trawniky and is ordered to proceed on foot to the ghetto of Piaski.
April 11:	First transport of entire families of Jews leaves Slovakia for Eastern Europe.
April 25:	Transport of 1,000 dispatched from Terezín to Warsaw. From there, those found fit for work are sent to the Rembertów labor camp near Warsaw. Those found unfit for work are deported in groups to Treblinka.
May 15:	Slovak parliament adopts Constitutional Law 68 "on the Evacuation of Jews," giving legal sanction to deportations.
May 15–June 30:	"Family transports" from Slovakia arrive in Lublin district.
May 17:	First transport from Terezín leaves for Maidanek.
May 27:	Heydrich is fatally wounded by Czech resistance fighters. Kurt Daluege succeeds him as Acting Reich Protector in Bohemia and Moravia.
June 10:	Special "penal transport" of 1,000 Jews is sent from Prague to Poland as reprisal for assassination of Heydrich.
June 28:	German and Italian armies in North Africa reach El Alamein; Palestine is in danger of invasion.
July:	"Working Group" underground organization is created in Slovakia; its leaders include Rabbi Michael Ber Weissmandl and Mrs. Gisi Fleischmann.
August 3:	Systematic work is begun at the Central Jewish Museum in Prague under German supervision to classify and arrange objects of Jewish cultural and historical interest from provincial areas into a permanent exhibit. The Germans view this project as a gathering of "relics of the extinct Jewish race"; the Jews see it as a means of preserving precious objects for posterity. Evangelical bishops of Slovakia issue a pastoral letter declaring that Slovak treatment of Jews is not consistent with Slovakia's supposed character as a Christian state.
August 20:	*Zentralstelle für jüdische Auswanderung* in Prague is renamed *Zentralamt für die Regelung der Judenfrage in Böhmen und Mähren* (Central Office for the Settlement of the Jewish Problem in Bohemia and Moravia); its

	main concern is the confiscation of Jewish property and its redistribution to Germans.
October 20:	Last of a series of transports leaves Slovakia for Auschwitz. After this, there are no more deportations from Slovakia for almost two years.
October 28:	First transports from Terezín are sent directly to Auschwitz and Treblinka.
November 2:	German and Italian armies defeated at El Alamein.
November 7:	U.S. and British forces land on coast of northwest Africa.
November 11:	Germany occupies southern France.
November 22:	In Jerusalem, the Jewish Agency officially confirms German plans for the mass extermination of the Jews.
December 15:	At a special session in London the *Státní Rada* (State Council) adopts a declaration condemning those responsible for barbarism against the Jews.

1943

January 20–26:	Mass deportations from Terezín to Auschwitz.
January 28:	Jewish Religious Congregation in Prague is dissolved.
February 2:	German Sixth Army annihilated near Stalingrad.
February 8:	Jewish Religious Congregation in Prague reorganized as *Ältestenrat der Juden in Prag* (Council of Jewish Elders in Prague).
March 8:	Reacting to agitation for the resumption of deportations of Jews (including converts to Christianity) from Slovakia, Slovakia's Catholic hierarchy issues a pastoral letter protesting against "measures that innocently deprive whole groups of our coreligionists and others of our fellow citizens of their personal, familial, and material rights."
April 19:	Outbreak of Warsaw ghetto revolt.
May 5:	Vatican expresses unhappiness at plan of Slovak government to resume deportations of Jews.
May 15–18:	Terezín ghetto undergoes "beautification" in preparation for visit from Danish Red Cross. At the same time, several thousands of inmates are sent from Terezín to Auschwitz to reduce the population of the ghetto.

FROM THE MUNICH AGREEMENT TO THE COMMUNIST TAKEOVER

May 16:	Last resistance in Warsaw ghetto ends.
June 23:	Danish Red Cross commission visits Terezín ghetto.
July 9:	Allies invade Sicily.
July 25:	Italy's dictator Benito Mussolini is dismissed by King Victor Emmanuel III.
August 2:	Inmates revolt in Treblinka death camp.
August 24:	Dr. Wilhelm Frick is appointed Reich Protector in Bohemia and Moravia.
September 3:	Allied troops land on Italian mainland.
September 8:	Italy surrenders to Allies.
September 11–18:	"Family transport" sent from Terezín to Auschwitz.
October 6:	Terror-stricken by reports of gassings, fifty-three children from Bialystok refuse to enter showers in Terezín. The SS thereupon deports them to Auschwitz, where they all die in the gas chambers.
December:	German Foreign Ministry sends emissary Edmund Veesenmeyer to Bratislava to speed up implementation of the "Final Solution" in Slovakia. Eduard Beneš visits Moscow.

1944

February:	Again, "beautification" of Terezín ghetto for foreign visitors under SS Obersturmbannführer Karl Rahm, the ghetto's third and last commandant.
March 19:	German army occupies Hungary, endangering 7,000 Slovak Jews who fled there from neighboring Slovakia.
April 21:	Rudolf Vrba (Walter Rosenberg) and Alfred Wetzler, two young Slovak Jews who escaped from Auschwitz, give detailed eyewitness report to "Working Group," which in turn forwards the report to individuals and organizations throughout the free world.
June 6:	D-Day; Allies land in Normandy.
June 20:	Jakub Edelstein, first *Judenältester* (Jewish Elder) of the Terezín ghetto, is shot in Auschwitz with his family. Slovak authorities reject appeal of Gisi Fleischmann to supply at least Slovak Jewish children in Nazi-occupied Hungary with Slovak passports so that they may return to the relative safety of Slovakia.

June 23:	Red Cross commission composed of two Danish officials and one Swiss from the International Red Cross inspect the Terezín ghetto.
June 25:	Report on liquidation of "family camp" of Czech Jews in Birkenau filed at British embassy in Switzerland by a representative of the Czechoslovak government-in-exile in Geneva. The report is forwarded to London and Washington along with a request that Allied air forces bomb the gas chambers and that Germany be threatened with collective reprisals.
August 25:	General Charles De Gaulle, head of the Free French forces, enters Paris.
August 29:	Slovak uprising begins. German Tatra Division moves into Slovakia to quell the revolt.
August 30:	Jewish underground members in Nováky concentration camp join the Slovak uprising.
September 5:	New Slovak government is formed under Dr. Jozef Tiso's nephew, Stefan Tiso.
September 12:	Allies enter the German heartland from the west.
September 13:	Soviet troops reach Slovak border.
September 20:	Four Jewish parachutists from Palestine British units reach area held by Slovak insurgents. Two of the parachutists make contact with "Working Group"; the other two proceed to Hungary.
September 30:	Deportations of Jews from Slovakia are resumed.
October:	Georges Dunant of the International Red Cross Committee arrives in Slovakia with funds from the American Jewish Joint Distribution Committee (JDC) and requests permission to set up shelters for Jewish children in Slovakia. The Slovak authorities refuse his request.
October 6:	Czechoslovak troops from the Soviet Union enter Czechoslovakia via the Dukla Pass.
October 17:	Last transport of Jews from Slovakia, including Rabbi Weissmandl and Gisi Fleischmann of the "Working Group," leaves for Auschwitz. (Gisi Fleischmann will die in Auschwitz; Rabbi Weissmandl will survive the war).
October 28:	Banská-Bystrica, held by Slovak insurgents, falls. Slovak uprising ends.

FROM THE MUNICH AGREEMENT TO THE COMMUNIST TAKEOVER xxxix

November:	Last deportations from Terezín and Slovakia to Auschwitz.
November 26:	Heinrich Himmler orders dismantling of gas chambers and crematoria in Auschwitz; surviving inmates are transferred to concentration camps in Germany.
December:	Transports of Jews from Slovakia arrive in Terezín.
December 15:	Following mass deportations from Terezín, the ghetto is reorganized. A new *Ältestenrat* is appointed, with Dr. Benjamin Murmelstein of Vienna as chairman and Rabbi Leo Baeck of Berlin as deputy chairman.

1945

January 10:	Prof. Carl Burckhardt, president of the International Red Cross Committee, asks Slovakia's president Jozef Tiso to stop deportations of Jews from Slovakia and to help Jews who have gone into hiding. Tiso claims he has neither the power nor the means to comply with Burckhardt's request.
January 19:	Soviet forces occupy Lodz and Auschwitz.
February 13:	Budapest falls to Soviet forces.
March:	German troops leave Slovakia.
March 5:	Another "beautification" of the Terezín ghetto is ordered because of negotiations conducted by Himmler and *Reichssicherheitshauptamt* (RSHA) chief Ernst Kaltenbrunner with International Red Cross Committee concerning inspection of concentration camps and rescue of camp inmates.
March 7:	U.S. forces cross Rhine at Remagen; Cologne falls to Allies.
April 4:	Bratislava, capital of Slovakia, liberated. In London, Beneš as president and the Communist party form a coalition government headed by Zdeněk Fierlinger, a Czech "Marxist social democrat" who served as Czechoslovak ambassador to the Soviet Union before and during World War II.
April 6:	Paul Dunant of the International Red Cross Committee, escorted by Eichmann, visits Terezín.
April 10:	Buchenwald liberated.

xl   FROM THE MUNICH AGREEMENT TO THE COMMUNIST TAKEOVER

April 13:	Soviet forces enter Vienna.
April 15:	Bergen-Belsen liberated.
April 23:	Soviet forces reach outskirts of Berlin.
April 25:	U.S. and Soviet troops meet at Elbe river south of Berlin.
April 30:	Hitler dies in his bunker in Berlin.
May 2:	Berlin capitulates; Red Cross moves into Terezín.
May 4:	"Czech Assistance Action," a group of volunteer physicians and nurses from Prague, arrives in Terezín to help quell typhoid outbreak among survivors.
May 5:	Plzeň occupied by U.S. forces.
May 7:	General Alfred Jodl signs Germany's unconditional surrender to Allies.
May 8:	V-E Day; Germans in Prague capitulate.
May 9:	Soviet troops arrive in Prague.
May 11:	Soviet troops enter Terezín.
May 16:	President Beneš arrives in Prague.
June 29:	Subcarpathian Ruthenia annexed by Soviet Union.
October:	Jan Masaryk, foreign minister in the Beneš government, provides trains for use by the *B'riha* underground Zionist organization to transport Holocaust survivors from Czech-Polish border to the West, from where the refugees can make their way to Palestine.
December:	U.S. forces complete their withdrawal from Czechoslovakia. In Prague, President Beneš and Premier Fierlinger assure Alexander L. Easterman of the World Jewish Congress that the Jews in Czechoslovakia will enjoy full freedom and equality and will be compensated for property confiscated from them during the Nazi era.

1946

May 26:	Czechoslovak constituent assembly is elected and a new government formed in which the Communists emerge as the strongest single party.
July 2:	The new government, headed by Klement Gottwald, initiates close cooperation of Czechoslovak Ministry of Social Welfare with *B'riha* outpost in Prague to aid Holocaust survivors.

1947

August 12: Conference of European Zionist Federations held at Karlovy Vary (Carlsbad) receives congratulatory messages from President Beneš and the Minister of Culture, Václav Kopecký, a Communist. Beneš urges a radical end to racism and anti-Semitism and supports the creation of a Jewish state in Palestine as the "only possible and just solution of the World Jewish question." Kopecký's message praises the Zionists "for trying to change the tool of imperialism . . . into an economically and politically independent state."

November 29: United Nations adopts resolution providing for two independent states, one Arab and one Jewish, in Palestine. Arabs refuse to abide by the resolution.

December 1: First arms deal between Czechoslovakia and the Haganah, the defense force of Palestine Jewry, concluded.

1948

February 25: Communists assume power in Czechoslovakia.

March 10: Foreign Minister Jan Masaryk dies in Prague under mysterious circumstances.

April: Czechoslovak government sells first consignment of German-made Messerschmitt aircraft to Haganah.

May 14: State of Israel proclaimed in Tel Aviv.

June 7: Beneš resigns from presidency of Czechoslovakia.

June 14: Klement Gottwald succeeds Beneš as President of Czechoslovakia; Antonin Zápotocký is named Prime Minister.

I. Holocaust

THE JEWS OF BOHEMIA AND MORAVIA: 1938–1945*

By Livia Rothkirchen

INTRODUCTION: THE AFTERMATH OF MUNICH (CZECHO-SLOVAKIA)

The grim chain of events unleashed in the short-lived rump state of Czecho-Slovakia following the Munich agreement may well be characterized as a prelude to the catastrophe that was to strike all of European Jewry. The developments of those fateful months—from September 1938 to March 1939—have been recorded by contemporary historians down to the last detail.[1]

The Munich agreement was signed on September 30, 1938. Five days later, President Eduard Beneš resigned. His successor, Emil Hácha, a distinguished jurist and former presiding judge of the Supreme Administrative Court who had no marked political profile, was sworn in on November 30. A new caretaker government was installed, headed by General Jan Syrový, a veteran of the Czechoslovak Legion of World War I and inspector general of the Czechoslovak army. However, the leading role in the internal affairs of the truncated republic was to be played not by Syrový but by Rudolf Beran, the leader of the rightist Agrarian party, who later became prime minister. A two-party system was introduced, with the politi-

---

* This study should be read in conjunction with the essays by John G. Lexa, "Anti-Jewish Laws and Regulations in the Protectorate of Bohemia and Moravia" (pp. 75–103); Zdeněk Lederer, "Terezín" (pp. 104–64), and Erich Kulka, "The Annihilation of Czechoslovak Jewry" (pp. 262–328). Though these three studies complement one another and sometimes overlap, certain repetitions were not eliminated so as not to disrupt the flow of the narrative in each essay. [Ed.]

cians of the center and the right uniting in mid-November 1938 to form the National Unity party, while the Social Democrats created the National Labor party as the "loyal opposition." From its inception, the new government was plagued by acute domestic and international problems, with the Jewish question constantly recurring on its agenda.

The frontiers dictated by Germany after her annexation of the Sudetenland cut deep into the body of the Czech Historic Lands. But this was not all. As Winston S. Churchill was to put it, "The Germans were not the only vultures upon the carcass . . . others, too, were eager to get a piece of flesh."[2] Hungary and Poland, too, made territorial claims that had to be satisfied. One of the first moves of the new government was to grant autonomy to Slovakia and Subcarpathian Ruthenia in an effort to appease the radical "separatist" elements in those territories. Thus the Czechoslovak Republic founded by Tomáš Garrigue Masaryk was replaced by a new federation of Czechs, Slovaks, and Ruthenes under the name of Czecho-Slovakia.

We know today that as early as October 1938, Adolf Hitler had decided to liquidate *"die Resttschechei,"* i.e., Bohemia and Moravia, by exploiting the minority conflicts in what was left of the Czechoslovak Republic after the amputation of the Sudetenland. All of Germany's efforts were directed to this end.

It soon became clear that Czechoslovakia, the once-admired model democracy of Central Europe, was drifting into the political, economic, military, and cultural sphere of Nazi Germany. As George F. Kennan of the American embassy in Prague poignantly observed, "Nothing was left in the popular mind but bitterness, bewilderment, and skepticism. Every feature of liberalism and democracy, in particular, was hopelessly and irretrievably discredited."[3]

The attitude of local authorities toward the Jewish population varied. It was harshest in Slovakia, where the political upheaval was accompanied by excesses of rhetoric that culminated in physical violence.[4] Nazi propaganda disseminated by the Reich's own media and by agents planted inside the rump state of Czecho-Slovakia exploited every opportunity to incite the populace against the Jews. The fact that Julius Streicher devoted an entire issue of his hate sheet, *Der Stürmer,* to the Jews in Czecho-Slovakia was an ominous portent. The influx of refugees from the Sudetenland, including many German-speaking Jews, resulted in the growth of virulent anti-Semitism in Czecho-Slovakia. A loan of £10,000,000 from Britain to the new Czecho-Slovak government was intended to ease the refugee problem. The British government hoped that this aid would promote moderation and prevent the adoption of anti-Jewish measures[5] openly advocated in Czecho-Slovakia by local *volksdeutsch* (ethnic German) rightist groups and by the younger elements within the Czech National Unity party. A demand for the large-scale expulsion of Jewish refugees had been voiced from various platforms with the argument that "a place must be found for the young Czech generation within the reduced state."[6] Thus, Sokol (the national physical culture organization) passed a resolution to the effect that "the Jewish question should on national and social grounds be so resolved that those who have emigrated [sic] into the country since 1914 should return to their original homes."[7]

The first of many anti-Jewish demonstrations in Czecho-Slovakia was organized by Fascist groups in the streets of Prague. A report sent by the Runciman mission from Prague to Britain's foreign secretary, Viscount Halifax, tells of a conversation between R. J. Stopford (an official of the British treasury and an expert on refugee problems), and Count Kinský, a member of the old Czech nobility. In that conversation Kinský reported he had heard from the Czecho-Slovak foreign minister, Dr. František Chvalkovský, that the Germans were pressing for action against the Jews. However, Kinský had added, efforts should be made to prevent such action. "There must be no pogroms before January or February [1939] in order [not to jeopardize] an Anglo-French loan."[8]

The consensus of opinion is that, despite German pressures, the government of Rudolf Beran did not go to extremes in harassing the Jews. Nevertheless, an atmosphere of apprehension prevailed among the Jewish population. During the two weeks preceding November 19, 1938, over 5,300 persons applied to the American consulate in Prague[9] for visas. The vast majority of these applicants were Jews, many of them presumably refugees from Germany, Austria, and the Sudetenland.

JEWISH REFUGEES IN CZECHOSLOVAKIA AND CZECHO-SLOVAKIA: 1933-1939

Following Hitler's accession to power in 1933, political leaders of German leftist parties and many noted German democrats were granted *bona fide* asylum by the Czechoslovak republic.[10] Two major factors had combined to make that country a haven for anti-Nazi exiles: first and foremost, its geopolitical location, set between East and West, bordered on two sides by Nazi Germany, and second, its image as a democratic, freedom-loving nation.

After the promulgation of the Nuremberg racial laws in 1935, thousands of Jews left Germany to escape persecution. Prague became a transit center for Jewish refugees awaiting immigration visas for England and overseas countries.

The Jewish leadership in Czechoslovakia made sincere efforts to provide financial and moral assistance for the refugees. A Jewish Committee of Aid for Refugees from Germany was established in Prague. It was headed by Dr. Joseph Popper, chairman of the Supreme Council of the Federation of Jewish Religious Congregations of Bohemia, Moravia, and Silesia and president of the Grand Lodge of the Czechoslovak B'nai Brith.[11] Among the members of the committee's executive board were two valiant women, Marie Schmolka, a noted social worker,[12] and Hanna Steiner, president of WIZO (the Women's International Zionist Organization) in the Historic Lands.[13] This pioneering philanthropic organization subsequently gave rise to a countrywide Jewish Aid Committee that was to play a crucial role in the lives of many Jewish refugees from Germany and later from Austria and the Sudetenland.

There were in Prague also several nonsectarian committees that dealt with refugee problems. The Social Democrats, the Social Democratic Relief Committee, the Communists, the Central Association to Aid Refugees, and the Czech Intellectuals (Šalda Committee, named after the well-known Czech writer and critic F. X. Šalda) each had refugee aid organizations of their own. But the scope and activities of the Jewish Aid Committee were far broader.[14] At the suggestion of the Czechoslovak government all these relief committees merged to form a "National Coordinating Committee." In 1936 Marie Schmolka, the chairman of this committee, was nominated to represent Czechoslovakia at a conference of the member states of the League of Nations called in July of that year by Sir Neill Malcolm, the League of Nations High Commissioner for the Refugees from Germany.

As the situation of the Jews in Central Europe deteriorated, Marie Schmolka's manifold functions expanded still further. The American Jewish Joint Distribution Committee (JDC) entrusted her with responsible tasks, the Jewish Colonization Association (ICA) recognized her as the representative of Czech relief work, and HICEM, a composite of HIAS (the Hebrew Immigrant Aid Society), ICA and Emig-direkt, appointed her director of its Prague office.[15]

The lion's share of the funds for refugee aid in Czechoslovakia came from wealthy individuals and public figures, religious and relief organizations, from England, and from the Quakers in the United States. The Freemasons and even the "Red Help" in Moscow sent donations regularly. Generous donations were made by President Tomáš Garrigue Masaryk and his successor, Eduard Beneš.[16]

During the second half of the 1930s the Czechoslovak authorities, under pressure from Nazi Germany, abandoned their lenient attitude toward the entry of Jewish refugees and instructed the border police to tighten its controls. In 1937, the Ministries of Internal Affairs and National Defense announced plans to transfer refugees from the border area and Prague to eight districts of the Czech-Moravian highlands (Česko-Moravská Vysočina). In an effort to prevent this step, Marie Schmolka lodged a protest on behalf of the Supreme Council of the Federation of Jewish Religious Congregations.[17]

As of October 1, 1938 (the day after the signing of the Munich agreement), there were in Czechoslovakia at least 5,000 refugees from Germany and Austria. After the detachment of the Sudetenland a cable dispatched on November 23, 1938, from the American Legation in Prague refers to 91,625 registered refugees from the Sudetenland; of these, approximately 6,700 were Jews.[18] The number of unregistered refugees was estimated at between 10,000 and 15,000. Altogether, some 17,000 Jews from the Sudetenland (out of the 20,000 to 22,000 Jews who had originally lived there) had moved into the interior of Czechoslovakia.[19]

The option of "choice of residence" set forth in the Munich

agreement was not honored by the authorities. Notwithstanding representations made to General Syrový by High Commissioner Sir Neill Malcolm and by General Faucher of the French military mission in Prague, newly arrived Jewish refugees from German-occupied areas were expelled.[20] In the hasty implementation of this expulsion order many families were broken up. The whole problem had arisen so suddenly that no organizations were prepared to take charge of these refugees; the police registered them and gave them forty-eight hours to return to their original homes. Some were caught at railroad stations and turned back then and there. The tribulations of these unfortunates were recorded in reports and cables sent by Wilbur J. Carr, the U.S. minister in Prague: "The suicide toll amongst refugees mounts but it is impossible to convey the figures as the Czech radio station has stopped mentioning these cases unless the dead are prominent citizens, such as the editor of the *Prager Tagblatt*."[21]

In response to the plight of the refugees, the Lord Mayor's Fund was set up in London. A campaign launched by the London *News Chronicle* raised £20,000 to help resettle refugee families. The committee in charge of this campaign was headed by the former British minister in Prague, Maclay. Its members included representatives of the Czechoslovak Red Cross and of the Czechoslovak government; Wenzel Jaksch, the leader of the Sudeten German Social Democrats, who represented the German Aid Committee (formed to help anti-Nazi refugees from the Sudetenland); and Marie Schmolka, who spoke for the Jewish refugees. Most of the refugees found shelter in Prague, Brno, Moravská Ostrava, and Olomouc, but some landed in smaller places, where shortages of food and housing were attributed to the newcomers and created fertile ground for anti-Semitic propaganda.

After the German forces marched into the Sudetenland, expulsions of Czechs and Jews from that region took place daily.[22] Human beings were treated like hunted animals. The German authorities drove groups of refugees from the Sudetenland to the Czech frontier; some of these managed to pass into Czech territory illegally and proceeded to Prague or Brno, but others, both Jews and gentile anti-Nazis, were turned back by Czech border guards. Since they also could not reenter the German-occupied territory they had left, they remained stranded in no-man's land.

The relief organizations were no longer able to cope with the situation. Marie Schmolka worked tirelessly, visiting the border areas where refugees were concentrated, gathering evidence with a view to mobilizing public opinion, and sending appeals and reports to foreign ambassadors in Prague and to Jewish social and philanthropic agencies in other countries. Her apartment in one of the ancient buildings of Old Prague, with its arched ceilings and recesses (Max Brod was to describe it as "a dark, mighty castle whence battling ghosts were sent out to the world"),[23] became the heart of the rescue campaign. It was upon Schmolka's suggestion that Milena Jesenská, the noted Czech writer and journalist, traveled to the Slovak-Hungarian border and wrote a moving report for the Czech press on the plight of the refugees in no-man's land.[24] Jesenská's protest was one of the very few made by Czech non-Jews during those months of misery and agony.

At last, early in March 1939, as a result of British representations to Berlin, the expulsions stopped and most of the refugees from the Sudetenland were granted temporary asylum in Czecho-Slovakia.[25] But this reprieve was hardly relevant, for on March 15, Hitler's armies marched into Bohemia and Moravia.

THE CZECHS AND THE JEWS: JANUARY 1933–MARCH 15, 1939

As already indicated, the Czechoslovak Republic of Tomáš G. Masaryk from its very inception gained worldwide esteem as the most enlightened state in Central and Eastern Europe because of its democratic parliamentary rules safeguarding personal liberties and, in no small measure, because of its liberal attitude toward the Jews. The image of Masaryk, with his historic role in the Hilsner ritual murder trial,[26] served to endorse the general trust and belief vested in the young democracy by Jews in general.

During the 1930s, while the Nazi ideology on the Jewish problem infiltrated Central Europe and was steadily gaining ground, Czech public opinion, apart from minor Fascist groups, remained aloof from active anti-Semitism.

It soon became clear that the Nazi *Weltanschauung* and policy of territorial expansionism posed a real threat to the sovereignty of Czechoslovakia, and Czechs began campaigning actively against the inroads of Nazi ideology, including the Hitler brand of anti-Semitism. The first organization formed to combat the virulent anti-Jewish propaganda reaching the country through mass media inspired and financed by foreign nationalist factors was the Czechoslovak League against Anti-Semitism.[27] The leadership of the League included outstanding political figures and men of letters, and it was in the bulletin of this group that the writer F. X. Šalda made his profound observation on the innate Czech attitude toward Jews: "A strange phenomenon—we do not have in our country a political party, not even the smallest, advocating in its program anti-Semitism, racial hatred, or animosity. This is often described as our great political advantage over other countries and our Republic is regarded in Central Europe as an explicitly philo-Semitic country. Yet, there must exist, hidden in the depths of the soul of our people, a kind of hatred toward Jews, which bursts out at a certain moment and casts its shadow over a case which otherwise would be as clear as [the fact] that two and two makes four."[28]

The final months of Masaryk's Czechoslovak Republic were marked by a mood of apprehension and confusion. This atmosphere is reflected in an editorial written by the renowned Czech intellectual and liberal journalist Ferdinand Peroutka. Entitled "Comments on the Czech People and the Jews,"[29] it evoked a heated discussion in the Jewish press.[30] In the late summer of 1938, a Sunday issue of *Národní Politika,* then the newspaper with the largest circulation in Czechoslovakia, carried an article entitled "Židé mezi námi" [The Jews in Our Midst], accusing the Jews of "exploiting other races," "lacking consideration [for others]," "lusting for power," and even of "spreading unrest and revolt wherever they may be."

Following the Munich agreement, most of the Jews in Czecho-Slovakia felt perplexed and abandoned. In November 1938, a small but vocal group of Bohemian Jews committed to the ideal of Czech-Jewish assimilation (the Svaz Čechů-Židů or "Czech-Jewish movement")[31] convened a press conference declaring their full support for a Czech ethnic state, in the hope that such a statement might help overcome the difficulties of the Jews and pave the way for their fuller integration into what was left of Czechoslovakia.[32] The predominant mood of the Jews during the months preceding Germany's occupation of Bohemia and Moravia may be seen from the statistics of suicide and conversion among the Jews. Of the total of 709 conversions of Jews to Christianity reported for the year 1938, 506 were recorded during the three months following the Munich agreement.[33]

The Zionist movement, which included a small representation of Bohemian Jews (though the bulk of its membership came from Moravian Jewry, which was more traditional), experienced a rise in popularity. Young people from both left and right, seeking a new concept of living and pinning their hopes on emigration to Palestine, joined its ranks. Some even ventured along the dangerous road of "illegal immigration" organized by Betar (*B'rit Trumpeldor*), the youth movement of the Revisionist party.[34] They sailed in dilapidated chartered boats and, as often as not, were intercepted by the British, who forced them to turn back or took them to internment camps. The tragic fate of the S.S. *Patria,* which sank in Haifa Bay late in November 1940 with over 200 passengers, mostly Jews from Czechoslovakia, has been described by a survivor of the disaster.[35]

The drain of Jewish capital and Czecho-Slovakia's increasing difficulties with her export trade were instrumental in maintaining a moderate attitude in official circles. Occasionally, sober views were voiced in the Prague parliament. On December 14, 1938, a conservative deputy, Dr. Ladislav Rašín (son of former Minister of Finance Alois Rašín), praised the prime minister for not yielding to "gutter demagogy" on the Jewish problem.[36] He warned that "the result of anti-Jewish excesses would only be that markets would be closed to Czecho-Slovakia's export trade, the promotion of which was the chief task of the government. For economic reasons the Jewish concerns and the Jews themselves must be given legal security as soon as possible."[37] It was reported that many members of assimilated Czech-Jewish families who had married into the upper strata of Czech society enjoyed favorable treatment.[38]

It is interesting to note that when he visited Hitler's headquarters on January 21, 1939, Foreign Minister Chvalkovský was reprimanded by the Führer: "Jews inside our Reich are being destroyed but inside Czechoslovakia they still persist, poisoning the whole nation."[39] The ethnic Germans in Czecho-Slovakia, who presumably spoke for official Reich circles, also voiced their dissatisfaction with the moderation shown by the government toward the Jews and insisted on far more radical measures to eliminate "the Jewish influence."

As for the Czechs, their resentment now focused mainly on German-speaking Jews: "It is characteristic of Bohemia, where nationality is a matter of language rather than of blood, that the distinction between friend and foe is made on the basis of language rather than ethnic origin. Thus, such resentment of Jews as existed among the Czech populace of Bohemia centered largely on the Jews who spoke German rather than Czech—particularly those who had settled in Bohemia only after World War I."[40]

From the time that the situation of the Jews first became precarious, Czech official circles encouraged the emigration of Jews, both individually and in groups. On January 13, 1939, a "transfer agreement" was signed between the Czecho-Slovak ministry of finance and the Jewish Agency for Palestine,[41] which provided for the emigration of 2,500 Czechoslovak Jews and the transfer of £500,000 via the Bank of England to the British Mandate of Palestine. This amount was part of a loan of £18,000,000 which the British government had just extended to Czechoslovakia. The terms of the agreement were set out in a letter from Dr. Josef Kalfus, the Czecho-Slovak minister of finance, to Dr. František Friedmann, the Jewish Agency's representative in Prague. Clause 3 of the letter stipulated: "The Jewish Agency shall see to it that the sum provided in the above manner shall be used exclusively for the purpose of the permanent settlement in Palestine of the refugees for whom they are [sic] intended."[42]

The initiator of the scheme was the veteran Zionist leader, Dr. Leo Herrmann. It was he who, with the help of the Prague Transfer Committee (consisting of Dr. František Friedmann, Dr. Franz Kahn, Jakub Edelstein, Dr. Pavel März, and the engineer Otto Zucker) and of the Czecho-Slovak and British governments, brought the project to a successful conclusion.[43] Most of the immigration certificates issued by the Palestine government to the refugees from Czecho-Slovakia were so-called "capitalist" certificates; i.e., immigration permits for individuals with assets of £500 or more. The first group of these "transfer" immigrants arrived in Palestine in March 1939; the second, during the first months of the war, in October 1939 and January 1940.

During its brief life-span the Czecho-Slovak parliament passed only two laws that were commonly viewed as directed primarily against the Jews: two decrees of January 27, 1939, calling for a review of the naturalization proceedings through which certain individuals had obtained Czechoslovak citizenship after 1918 and for the deportation of certain aliens. These individuals were required to register with the provincial authorities no later than April 30, 1939.[44] The purpose of these decrees obviously was to oust the refugees who had come from Germany and Austria and who, along with the new influx of refugees from the Sudetenland, presented an acute ethnic problem. The government of Czecho-Slovakia wanted to forestall the possibility of having a German-speaking majority in the country. Paradoxically, in this atmosphere of depression and antagonism, Jews who claimed German nationality were blamed by the Czechs for the loss of the Sudeten territories and there was a general tendency to discriminate against them as "Germans"! (According to the census of 1930, of the 117,551 Jews who then lived in Bohemia, Moravia, and Silesia, 36.44 percent claimed Czech nationality, 31.40 percent Jewish nationality, and 30.45 percent, German nationality. The remaining 1.71 percent professed allegiance to other ethnic groups.)

During the period immediately preceding the end of Czechoslovak independence, there occurred in Czecho-Slovakia a development unparalleled in any other country: Leading Jewish circles were "unofficially" approached by government officials and given to understand that the authorities would welcome their proposals for the "solution of the Jewish problem."[45] In response, early in January 1939, the Supreme Council of the Federation of Jewish Religious Congregations submitted a detailed memorandum to the government and the presidium of the parliament touching upon the most essential issues raised and requesting clarification of future official policy toward emigration in general and of the status of the Jews under the new conditions in particular. The Supreme Council offered its full cooperation in rebuilding the economy of the state, while underlining the significance it attached to the safeguarding of equal rights in the republic. The memorandum ended with a statement to the effect that the Jewish problem in Czecho-Slovakia could be materially eased by the vocational reorientation of the Jews, along with the gradual emigration of those Jews who desired to leave the country for economic reasons.[46]

In February 1939, British and American diplomats stationed in Prague and closely observing developments in Czecho-Slovakia reported that the situation of the Jews in the country was unmistakably deteriorating.[47] Some Jews in public service were being notified that their services were no longer required; others were "encouraged" to resign voluntarily from their posts. Since only very few Jews had served in the government during the era of the republic, the effect of these dismissals was not too widespread; nevertheless, it was estimated that, as a result, some 1,000 individuals lost their means of livelihood. The report referred specifically to the particularly flagrant case of Dr. Julius Friedmann, head of the Economic Section of the Ministry for Commerce and of Foreign Affairs, who had rendered inestimable services to the country. Jewish physicians were asked to leave their posts at public hospitals, and leading Czech athletic clubs dropped their Jewish members. About forty-five Jewish professors at the German University of Prague were pensioned off. "Purges" had taken place also in German-language theatrical establishments and German-language newspapers,[48] mostly upon the direct instigation of Karl Freiherr von Gregory, the press attaché of the German legation in Prague.

But though clouds were gathering on the horizon, the vast majority of Jews in Bohemia and Moravia still remained unmolested as late as the beginning of March 1939. Once the initial shock and anxiety following the Munich agreement had subsided, many Jews, deeply rooted in the Czech Historic Lands, tried to adjust to the new climate, hoping that the tide would turn in their favor.

THE CZECHS AND THE JEWS: AFTER THE GERMAN OCCUPATION

Chauvinism and narrowmindedness became more perceptible and vociferous after the German occupation of Bohemia and Moravia, and the proclamation of a Nazi puppet state in "independent" Slovakia. Then profound demoralization and cynicism gained the upper hand among the Czech populace, and the relationship between the Czechs and the Jews in what was now the Reich "Protectorate of Bohemia and Moravia" reached its lowest point.[49] In the name of Hitler's New Order, radical Jew-baiters voiced their desire to free the Protectorate from the vestiges of "Benešism," Bolshevism, and freemasonry, all of which, of course, were associated in their minds with liberal attitudes toward the Jews.[50]

However, the promulgation of the extreme anti-Jewish ordinances drawn up by the National Unity party met with opposition from the Catholic clergy. Cardinal Karel Kašpar of Prague, even though he was ill at the time, warned that if the measures were to be enforced, he would issue a pastoral letter condemning them. As a consequence, the ordinances were withdrawn.[51]

Meanwhile, anti-Semitic agitation continued in the Protectorate of Bohemia and Moravia. At a meeting of the National Aryan Cultural Union at Pardubice on July 29, 1939, the speaker, one František Drázda, advocated the complete exclusion of Jews and "Jewish freemasons" from national life, going so far as to suggest extermination as a means toward that end. *Arijsky boj* [The Aryan Struggle], a bulletin issued by Vlajka, the most extreme among the Fascist organizations in the Protectorate of Bohemia and Moravia (with a membership of about 13,000), called for the ghettoization of the Jews. In eastern Moravia, Fascist circles received support from the National Socialist Czech Workers party and the Agrarian party.[52]

The outbreak of World War II engendered a more optimistic mood among the Czechs, who now hoped for a speedy defeat of the Germans and the restoration of Czechoslovak independence. Religious pilgrimages as well as theater and concert performances were exploited for outbursts of Czechoslovak patriotism. A climax was reached with mass student demonstrations on Czechoslovak Independence Day, October 28, 1939,[53] in which a number of students were killed. Over a thousand Czechs were then sent to concentration camps, and all Czech universities and institutions of higher learning were closed.

These developments produced a certain change in the feelings of many Czechs toward their Jewish fellow citizens. Manifestations of sympathy toward Jews became one of the outlets of Czech hatred for foreign rule.

The Nazis employed every possible means of intimidation to bring about the isolation of the Jews.[54] Czech gentiles caught at Jewish homes or at the offices of the Jewish Religious Congregation during police raids were taken to Gestapo headquarters for interrogation.[55] However, while the German citizens in the Protectorate of

Bohemia and Moravia, even those who were known as liberals, were cautious about coming into contact with Jews, some Czechs continued to visit their Jewish friends, mostly during the evening hours, trying to render them small services and to save them the harassments of everyday life.[56] Eyewitnesses recorded that the Star of David pinned to the breast of Jews was generally regarded with sympathy by the Czech populace. Some localities even openly protested when Jewish doctors were barred from practice.[57]

On the whole, however, there is no evidence of a far-reaching will on the part of the Czech populace to help the Jews during the era of German occupation. Many Jew-baiters denounced fellow Czechs who had received possessions and valuables from Jewish friends or acquaintances for safekeeping. Offenses of this kind were severely punished. Other Czechs became *Treuhänder,* official custodians of Jewish property, in cases of Aryanization. (But significantly, according to a German intelligence report from Prague to Berlin, the Czechs at one point made it widely known that "anyone who became rich from Jewish property was a traitor to his people.")[58]

A few well-known Czech writers and artists made it possible for their Jewish colleagues to produce some of their works under pseudonyms, thus enabling them to earn a living and raising their morale.[59] Thus, thanks to the benevolence of some friendly editors and publishers, the young and gifted poet Jiří Orten (Ohrenstein) was able to publish his first volumes of poetry between 1939 and 1941 under various pseudonyms (Karel Jílek, Jiří Jakub, etc.) But on August 30, 1941, his twenty-second birthday, Orten was run over by a Nazi vehicle on Prague's Rašín embankment and died the next day of his injuries. Yet, as late as 1941 the noted humorist Karel Poláček could publish his "Restaurant at the Stone Table" under the name of the Czech painter Vlastimil Rada,[60] and in this manner was able to support himself. That year, too, František Zelenka[61] still worked under a wide range of pseudonyms creating settings for Shakespearean comedies for Prague's Vinohrady Theater. Jiří Weil escaped from prison with the aid of a Czech police official and disappeared. The word was spread that he had "committed suicide," but in fact he went underground.[62]

During the initial period of German occupation the clandestine left-wing socialist home resistance organization, the so-called

PVVZ—Petiční výbor Věrni Zůstaneme (Petition Committee "We Remain Faithful"), regularly sent messages and situation reports to Beneš, who was then head of the Czechoslovak National Council in London. These reports contain constant references to the persecution of the Jews. The nucleus of the executive of this organization who compiled the reports was composed of three Jewish intellectuals: Josef Fischer (a university lecturer), Dr. Karel Bondy, and Dr. Victor Kaufmann.[63] Fischer played a major role in the drafting of the committee's program and by-laws.[64] Eventually, all three were arrested and, following their trial by the *Volksgericht* (People's Court) in Berlin, were found guilty of underground activity and executed on November 11, 1944. (That same court tried and sentenced the valiant Czech-Jewish actress Anna Polertová, née Baumová, of Prague, who was executed in January 1945.)[65] It should be noted that later reports sent by the Czechoslovak resistance organizations to the Czechoslovak government-in-exile in London contained hardly any references to the plight of the Jews in the Protectorate.[66]

With the arrival of SS Obergruppenführer Reinhard Heydrich as Acting Reich Protector in Bohemia and Moravia and the first deportations of Jews in the fall of 1941, a new and more severe intimidation campaign was launched against Czechs suspected of pro-Jewish sympathies. The minutes of Heydrich's conference of October 17, 1941, on "the solution of the Jewish problem"[67] tell of a proposal to deport, along with the Jews, a number of Czechs who were known to have befriended Jews. Heydrich's report of February 4, 1942, spoke frankly of the decimation of the Czech intelligentsia; it referred to 4,000-5,000 individuals who had been tried or executed on charges of resistance activity. Heydrich stressed that these people had been leading figures in the underground movement, "men of high intellectual qualities," not merely fellow travelers.[68] On May 27, 1942, when the deportations of Jews to Terezín (Theresienstadt) and to the East had reached a peak, Heydrich was fatally wounded by Czech resistance fighters. The terror, the mass arrests, and the daily executions that followed this act paralyzed all Czech resistance activity for some time.

The Czech-language broadcasts of the BBC from London, consisting mainly of appeals from Jan Masaryk, the foreign minister of the Czechoslovak government-in-exile, and Jan Stránský, the liberal newspaper publisher, urged listeners in Czechoslovakia to do everything in their power to help the Jews, "the most wretched of the wretched,"[69] so that when they would be liberated they would be able to tell the world that "we remained decent people" even during the horrors of the German regime.[70]

Notes of a conversation between a representative of the International Red Cross and the German Red Cross in Berlin on July 7, 1943,[71] reveal that about 3,000 gift parcels were sent each month from the Protectorate of Bohemia and Moravia to the ghetto of Terezín. However, it can be assumed that most of the senders were not gentiles but Jewish partners in mixed marriages.

Opinions have been divided with regard to the attitude of the Czechs toward their Jewish fellow citizens during the period of Nazi rule. France's ambassador Coulondre in Berlin claimed that "the Czechs even after Munich maintained a decent attitude and accepted anti-Semitic measures merely as one of the sad necessities which had befallen the Republic."[72] In a report from Prague to Berlin dated October 15, 1940, Ziemke, the representative of the German foreign ministry to the Reich Protector, wrote: "Up to now the Czech has refrained from dealing on his own accord with the Jewish problem. Apart from the members of the rightist opposition groups, he is friendly toward Jews (*judenfreundlich*), although basically not because of [personal] attachment but for reasons of political expediency. Our enemy is his friend, and our behavior toward the Jews augurs their own treatment by us in the future. . ."[73]

The sad fact, however, remains that during the height of the deportations the prevailing attitude among the Czech populace was a tacit acceptance of the disappearance of the Jews from the country. The seeming Czech indifference to the plight of the Jews may be explained largely by the immense risks entailed in helping Jews. The life of the "offender's" whole family was at stake. Press reports of early November 1943 tell of eight persons, including two women, who were sentenced to death in Prague for helping Jews cross the border and for giving them food and shelter.[74]

Anti-Semitism was proliferating even within Czechoslovak army units formed to fight alongside the Allies on the eastern and western fronts, and within the home resistance organizations. A message sent by the latter via Ankara, Turkey, to the government-in-exile in London in 1943 makes blunt reference to the subject:

> Anti-Semitism will probably be the only thing we shall partially adopt from the Nazi ideology. Our people do not agree with the bestial methods of the Germans; nevertheless, they are of the opinion that most of the Jews deserve just what is happening to them now. After the war, in the new republic, our people hope that the Jews will not be able to hold the same positions [as before], profiting from our labor. They do not think that the property taken from them during the German rule should be returned at all.
>
> [Such a return] would be considered [contrary to the wishes of Czech] public opinion.[75]

It is true that we cannot define Czech anti-Semitism as "bestial." Such conduct was alien to the Czech mentality. But at the same time we cannot say that many Czechs sacrificed themselves to protect Jews or to save them from deportation.[76] We know of no cases of Czech families giving shelter to Jewish children in their homes.

In all fairness, however, it must be mentioned that during the final winter of the war, hundreds of concentration camp inmates passing through the Protectorate in "death marches" to the heartland of Germany encountered kindhearted men and women in the Czech countryside who gave them food and other succor.[77]

INITIAL PHASES OF PERSECUTION: 1939–1941

The German occupation of Bohemia and Moravia on March 15, 1939, brought about a basic change in the life of the Jews in the Historic Lands.[78] Together with the occupying forces, the Gestapo marched in, too, and immediately launched a wave of arrests under the code name *Aktion Gitter* (Operation Bars).[79] The first to be arrested were emigrés from Germany, politicians of the *ancien régime*, known public figures, and, of course, Jews. The roundup was carried out by the Czech gendarmerie, which apparently had prepared its own lists well in advance.[80] During the first week of the German occupation, 1,000 persons were arrested; before long, 4,639 were behind bars. Among those arrested were Marie Schmolka and Hanna Steiner, who were taken to the Pankrác prison. Most of these early prisoners were subsequently released, except for the German-Jewish refugees, who were sent to concentration camps. Marie Schmolka was released through the intervention of Senator Františka Plamínková,[81] who had once served as president of the Czechoslovak Women's Council. Schmolka managed to leave the country and settled in London, where she died on March 27, 1940. Steiner was also released but eventually was to die in Auschwitz.

On March 16, 1939, Hitler himself came to Prague, staying at the historic Hradčany Palace. There, he signed the decree incorporating the Czech Historic Lands into the Reich under the euphemistic designation "Reich Protectorate of Bohemia and Moravia."[82] Germany took charge of the Protectorate's defense and foreign relations. However, internal administration was left in the hands of the Czech authorities. Formalities were preserved. Emil Hácha was permitted to retain the title of president; however, he himself, along with the cabinet ministers appointed by him, was responsible to the Reich Protector, Baron Constantin von Neurath, who was appointed to his position on March 18, 1939. Karl Hermann Frank, one of the leaders of the former Sudeten German party, was appointed secretary of the Protectorate. All other key positions were filled by Reich officials. Although the Beran government was not immediately dismissed, all vestiges of Czech sovereignty were abolished *de facto*. The parliament was replaced by a fifty-member *Národní Souručenství* (Committee of National Solidarity) appointed by the president.

On April 27 Hácha reorganized his cabinet, appointing as the new prime minister General Alois Eliáš, who once had been a prominent figure in the Beneš administration. Eliáš was to maintain secret contacts with the Czechoslovak government-in-exile in London and to play a leading role in the Czech resistance movement.[83] He considered it his task to work for the survival of the Czech people at a minimum sacrifice of Czech lives. However, opinions differ regarding his attitude toward the Jews.

During the first few weeks of the occupation, the Germans seemed to follow an ambiguous policy toward the Jews. They disseminated anti-Semitic propaganda but did not openly engage in anti-Jewish activities. They left that task, and particularly the initiative in anti-Jewish measures, to the Czech Fascists. As a matter of fact, Nazi party members in the Protectorate received orders from party headquarters in Munich to abstain from fraternizing with Czech Fascists and from molesting Jews, for fear of anti-Fascist uprisings.[84]

However, anti-Jewish excesses began at an early stage. The synagogue in Vsetín was burned down on the day the Germans marched in. The synagogue of Jihlava (Iglau) was set on fire on March 30. In Roudnice and Klatovy Jews were forbidden to use sidewalks and were forced to walk in the middle of the street. Jews suffered particularly harsh treatment in localities with large German populations.[85] Under the pretext of a reprisal for a "provocation" allegedly committed on April 24 by Jews on a trolley car in Plzeň (Pilsen) against thirty German soldiers, 150 "Marxists" and 150 Jews were rounded up in cafés and from their homes.[86] Among those arrested were Mayor Pik of Plzeň, several members of Beneš's party, and Jewish doctors and lawyers. During the spring of 1939 several pogroms took place at Příbram, and the synagogue of Dobříš was damaged. Between May 19 and 28, Fascist groups organized violent demonstrations; Jews in Brno were dragged out of cafés and attacked in the streets.[87] The Fascists clamored for the enforcement of the Nuremberg racial laws and for the creation of a Czech secret police, to be called "Czestapo." The Fascist groups in Moravia produced the most active and zealous anti-Semites: a number of synagogues in the area—in Brno, Olomouc, and Uherský Brod—were burned down.

It seems that the first attempt to destroy the historic *Altneuschul* in Prague was made as early as March 20, 1939.[88] Miraculously, the wind put out the flames. The second attempt, several months later, during the *Shavuot* holiday, was an abortive bomb thrown from a neighboring building. From that time on, the Jewish Religious Congregation of Prague employed a security guard, who, for several months, was in charge of guarding the city's Jewish historic sites and monuments.[89] On May 25 and 26, Fascists staged an anti-Semitic demonstration in the streets of Prague, but were ignored by the public.[90]

The first sectors of the Czech population to yield to Nazi anti-Semitic propaganda were the merchants, followed by the bar and medical associations. Also, groups of citizens recruited mainly from Fascist ranks appealed to the National Unity party and to the Czech government to oust the Jews from economic and public life.

Jobless Czech government officials and professional men, former residents of the Sudetenland, Slovakia, and Subcarpathian Ruthenia, who had moved into Bohemia and Moravia in search of new employment and were the first to participate in the Aryanization process,[91] only served to exacerbate the "Jewish problem."

While drafts for a series of anti-Jewish measures were shaped and reshaped by the Eliáš government, the Reich Protector published, on June 21, 1939, a comprehensive decree eliminating the Jews from virtually all economic life and forcing them to register all their assets with the authorities.[92] This decree, effective retroactively as of March 15, 1939, defined Jews in accordance with the Nuremberg laws. This act was, of course, intended to show the Czechs who was master in their country, and it took the Eliáš government by surprise. It became clear that the placement of the Jews under German jurisdiction abolished the original quasi-independence upon which the "autonomous" Protectorate of Bohemia and Moravia had been based. Apart from this, it was understood that the main purpose of the decree was to transfer the expropriated Jewish property into German hands and thereby to strengthen the German ethnic presence in the Protectorate in line with the overall policy of Germanization.[93]

The prevailing mood in Czech official circles at the time was succinctly described by George F. Kennan: "The members of the government continue to toy with the idea of resigning voluntarily, as a gesture. . . . But whether this resignation will be voluntary seems increasingly doubtful. Being Czechs, they have a remarkable capacity for delay, and in all probability they will keep on putting things off until they find themselves thrown out by the Germans. . . . They almost—but not quite—decided to make an issue out of the imposition of the [anti-] Jewish law in the middle of June."[94] It is typical of the Czech government and its puppet character that even a relatively minor side issue, such as the preparation of a list of forty families whom President Hácha wished to have exempted from laws affecting Jewish property (with each case to be carefully examined by the Czech authorities), was dragged out until the fall of 1940, when it was rejected out of hand by the Reich Protector.[95]

The SS had its own methods for handling the Jewish problem; those who agreed to "entrust" their property to German banks were promised exit permits. In June 1939, Adolf Eichmann arrived in Prague from Vienna to set the emigration process into motion. To this end the *Zentralstelle für jüdische Auswanderung* (Central Office for Jewish Emigration) was set up,[96] characteristically enough in a villa located in Prague's elegant Střešovice district and confiscated from a Jew, Marc Rosenthal. The *Zentralstelle* was directly subordinate to the *Reichssicherheitshauptamt* (RSHA; Central Office of Reich Security), the central intelligence office of the Reich government; the official in charge of the *Zentralstelle* until the end of the war was SS Hauptsturmführer Hans Günther.

The segregation of the Jewish population proceeded quickly. Through the *Landräte*—the German administrative bodies set up in all the regions and districts of Bohemia—[97]and through the Gestapo the Germans quickly acquired control over local Czech administration in the provinces. Jews were required to register all their property and business enterprises with the *Landräte,* which in turn were authorized to appoint a *Treuhänder* (custodian) and then to decide whether to "Aryanize" this or that enterprise or to liquidate it outright. When the deportations began, these agencies were most instrumental at every level in clearing the provinces of their Jewish population.

Soon after his arrival in Prague, Eichmann issued an order for the concentration of all Jews from the provinces in the capital.[98] At the beginning of August 1939, the leaders of several Jewish Religious Congregations in the provinces met in České Budějovice to discuss the implementation of Eichmann's order and ways of calming the panic-stricken Jews.[99] The first orders limiting the movements and personal freedom of Jews were issued by the police of Prague, but the Jews in the provincial towns were exposed to harsher treatment than those living in the capital.

There is evidence that various Czech government authorities intervened with the Germans in an attempt to repeal the order expelling the Jews from the provinces. On August 25, for instance, the Czech ministry of internal affairs appealed to Eichmann, asking him to amend the Gestapo order in Německý Brod with a provision to the effect that "those Jews [in the provinces] wishing to emigrate from the country with the aid of the *Zentralstelle* should not be prevented from doing so, and should not be forced to move to

Prague before leaving the country."[100] Thus, in order not to antagonize the general public, Eichmann decided not to implement the planned concentrations of the Jews from the provinces in Prague. However, with the outbreak of the war in September 1939, the Germans cast off every semblance of leniency towards the Jews in the Protectorate. A reign of terror was unleashed; ordinance followed ordinance limiting the freedom of movement of Jews and dismissing them from employment in private industry. Other regulations were aimed at isolating the Jews from the general population. A campaign of harassment was waged against the Jews, denying them certain food rations, sugar, tobacco, and items of clothing.[101]

There was a new wave of arrests. Hostages taken in the countryside included numerous prominent Jews from all walks of life.[102] František Parkus of Nymburk, Filip Polak of Benešov, Messrs. Blama and Frischmann, Rabbi Dr. Hoch of Plzeň, and Rabbi Dr. Grünfeld of Jihlava were taken as hostages and perished in concentration camps.[103]

As early as mid-September 1939, the Jews of the Ostrava and Frýdek-Mistek districts were singled out by Eichmann and Günther (the latter had been promoted to the rank of Sturmbannführer) for special treatment.[104] They were ordered to register with the Jewish Religious Congregation and simultaneously to apply for admission to a so-called *Umschulungslager* (vocational retraining camp). On October 17, 1939, all the males were ordered to leave for an unknown destination; they were permitted to take with them only a limited quantity of personal belongings. Entire Jewish communities were left without their menfolk. The first transport of 1,000 men left Moravská Ostrava in sealed railroad cars, arriving at Nisko in German-occupied Poland on October 19.[105] They were soon followed by 1,500 others. They detrained at a camp located on barren land southwest of Rozwadow. There were no accommodations of any sort for the new arrivals. They were ordered to build living quarters on the muddy ground without proper materials or tools. Two leading members of the Jewish Religious Congregation of Prague, Jakub Edelstein[106] and Richard Friedmann (the latter had come to Czechoslovakia from Vienna), were attached to the Nisko transport in order to help the deportees "resettle," and then to return to

Prague to report their progress to the Jewish Religious Congregation. Their encounter with the Nazi "resettlement plan" was to have great significance in subsequent developments. Upon his return to Prague, Edelstein consulted his Zionist associates in the Jewish Religious Congregation and together, they decided to inform the authorities that "no threat of punishment could prevail upon them to lend a hand to this kind of emigration: even if the Zionist Federation were to be dissolved and its leaders sent to Dachau, they would have no part in this horror." [107]

The sufferings of the men in the Nisko camp have been described by some survivors of the transports. Part of the group was detached from the main body and driven eastward, pursued by rifle shots, to the border between the German and Soviet sectors of Poland. Many were killed by the Germans, by Polish and Ukrainian bandits in the woods, or by Russian border guards while trying to cross the Bug river into the Soviet sector. Those who did succeed in entering the Soviet sector were recruited into labor battalions and sent to the Donetz region and other remote places in the Russian hinterland. [108]

During that winter, some groups from the Nisko camp were put to work building roads and clearing away the ruins of bridges nearby. On March 23, 1940, Hermann Göring suddenly suspended deportations of Jews to the *Generalgouvernement* (as the central district of German-occupied Poland was called). Apparently the "evacuation" as carried out during the winter months had provoked criticism abroad. [109] It seems that the Nisko project also met with the disapproval of Governor General Hans Frank, who was eager to see his territory *judenrein* (clear of Jews). Furthermore, there is evidence that Soviet protests against the shunting of Jews across the demarcation line between the German and Soviet sectors of Poland [110] may have been a consideration when the Germans decided to liquidate the camp. [111]

Reports of the Nisko transports leaked into the local press in Moravská Ostrava, and although the Germans attempted to deny them and deceive the public with false explanations, the Jews had now become aware of what was in store for them.

Only the young and exceptionally hardy survived the Nisko experience. In January 1942, those who had fled from Nisko into the Soviet Union were permitted to join the Czechoslovak brigade at

Buzuluk. Eventually, these men were to take part in the battles of Sokolovo, Kiev, Belaya Tserkev, at the Dukla pass, and in the liberation of Slovakia.[112]

THE CONFISCATION OF JEWISH PROPERTY

From the very outset one of the main objects of Nazi policy was to secure control over all Jewish property. It has been estimated that before World War II, approximately one third of all industrial and banking capital in Czechoslovakia had been in Jewish hands.[113] The greater part of these enterprises was owned by ten wealthy families.[114]

The largest metallurgical combine in the country, the Vítkovice Iron Works in the Moravská Ostrava district, was controlled by the Viennese branch of the Rothschild family. The most important coal field in the Ostrava-Karvinna area was initially developed by the Gutmann family. A number of mines in Kladno were also owned by Jews. The Petschek family owned a banking house in Prague and coal mines in northern Bohemia, in Most (Brüx), Falknov (now Sokolov) and Duchcov (Dux). The Weinmann family of Ústí nad Labem (Aussig) also owned coal mines in northern Bohemia. Jews were prominent in the timber industry and trade, the glass industry, hat-making, hosiery manufacture, textiles, and other branches of industry.[115]

By means of negotiations, both "voluntary" and forced, entailing blackmail and threats, the Germans gained control of the assets of these Jewish families. Most of the assets were incorporated into the Hermann Göring Werke. A noteworthy case was that of the Böhmische Escompte Bank (Bohemian Discount Bank; "BEBCA") in Prague,[116] which was taken over by the Dresdner Bank in February 1939, a month before the German occupation. This was accomplished by means of pressures and other devices on the part of the Germans. The bank subsequently became the main instrument for the Aryanization of large Jewish capital holdings. Its three directors, Dr. Feilchenfeld, Dr. Löb, and Dr. Kantor, were killed by the Nazis.

Following the occupation of Czechoslovakia and the outbreak of the war, the Germans suspended negotiations with Jewish owners of business and manufacturing concerns: they chose to disregard their obligations, and the terms of the Aryanization agreements were never honored. However, many members of the wealthy families were able to emigrate overseas and so escaped the Holocaust. The Germans negotiated only with the largest industrial companies because many of them had connections with West European countries (thus, the Rothschilds had managed to convert the Vítkovice Iron Works into a British enterprise as early as February 1937).

Jewish property in general was subject to Aryanization under the decree of June 21, 1939, issued by Reich Protector Von Neurath.[117] The aim of this decree was to transfer Jewish property directly into German hands, thus forestalling efforts of the Protectorate government itself to gain control of the Jewish assets. Von Neurath did not even bother to notify the Czech authorities in advance of his intentions. The decree stipulated that the transfer of Jewish business enterprises was permissible only by special written authorization. In addition, the Reich Protector assumed the authority to appoint *Treuhänder* at his own discretion. The technical aspects were handled by the *Zentralstelle für jüdische Auswanderung*. The *Treuhänder* could, with the approval of the authorities, sell the property in his custody to other *Volksgenossen* (ethnic Germans).[118] Proceeds from such sales were forwarded to the German *Winterhilfe* (Winter Relief Fund).

Under the decree of June 21, 1939, Jews were ordered to register, and subsequently (on April 30, 1940) to sell gold, platinum, and silver articles, precious stones, and pearls in their possession to a special public purchasing agency, HADEGA, and to deposit all their stocks, bonds, and securities at a foreign currency bank.[119]

The law concerning "Jewish enterprises" was formulated in such a way that non-Jewish property was also affected, since Jewish business enterprises in Bohemia and Moravia were widely linked with the assets of non-Jewish Czech investors.

The sale of Jewish-owned real estate was conducted in the most fraudulent manner possible. First, the *Zentralstelle* prepared sales contract forms with a stipulated price already filled in; the market price had to be paid only after the property had been resold. The Jewish owner was summoned by the Nazis and was handed this form, which he had to return, signed and notarized, within two hours. These contracts were then transferred to the so-called *Auswanderungsfond* (Emigration Fund).[120] A further refinement was added to this procedure by the Protectorate's ministry of finance, which issued an order requiring the Jewish party to the contract to pay a sales tax.

By the end of 1940, nearly half a million Germans had moved from the Reich to the Protectorate of Bohemia and Moravia. Approximately 120,000 of them lived in Prague. Many worked as supervisors in various Czech institutions or acted as Aryanizers, making fat profits from taking over Jewish firms.[121] One instance of such sudden wealth was that of two German women who were appointed managers of a small hat shop formerly owned by Czech Jews. The two women commissars, who had no previous experience in the field and performed no function except that of supervision, drew monthly salaries totaling 6,000 crowns, as against a monthly total of no more than 5,000 crowns paid to all the eight employees of the shop.[122]

With the beginning of deportations from the Protectorate, Czech Fascists, especially members of the National Unity party, made claims on the property confiscated from the deportees and pressured the Protectorate government to negotiate on their behalf with the Reich authorities. A marginal note in a letter on this subject, written in November 1941,[123] refers to a meeting between Ježek, the Protectorate's minister of internal affairs, and Horst Böhme, the German chief of the Protectorate's police and security services, regarding measures to be taken against the Jews. The letter explained that "all measures taken against the Jews are within his [i.e., the German's] jurisdiction, and the possibility of isolating the Jews from the rest of the Aryan population is being given due consideration."[124]

The total value of Jewish assets expropriated by the Germans in the Protectorate of Bohemia and Moravia has been estimated at "at least half a billion dollars."[125]

THE MASS DEPORTATIONS

In the wake of the German onslaught on the Soviet Union in June 1941, Nazi policy against the Jews entered a new phase. While Heydrich's instructions to the *Einsatzgruppen* (mobile killing units) in Poland on September 21, 1939, only made vague mention of the *Endziel,* the "final objective," the order issued to Heydrich by Göring on July 31, 1941, frankly spoke of a *Gesamtlösung,* a "total solution," which was to be implemented in all areas under German influence.[126] The secrecy of the "operation" was scrupulously guarded; all correspondence relating to what became known as the *Endlösung* ("Final Solution") was classified as "top secret." Sophisticated methods of deception—fraud, camouflage and circumlocutory, innocuous language—were employed to mask the true intentions of the Germans.

Early in September 1941, Hans Günther, the chief of the *Zentralstelle* in Prague, ordered the city's Jewish Religious Congregation to prepare a statistical breakdown of the Jewish population of the Protectorate of Bohemia and Moravia according to age, ability to work, family status, health, etc. On October 1, 1941, the Jewish Religious Congregation of Prague was ordered to register 1,000 Jews per day. Individuals and whole families were summoned for registration.[127] As of that date, the total Jewish population of the Protectorate numbered 88,105 persons, distributed as follows:

Prague	46,801
Brno	11,102
Olomouc	4,015
Moravská Ostrava	3,903
Zlín	3,335
Plzeň	3,106
Kolín	2,588
Tábor	2,352
Kladno	2,079
Jihlava	1,721
Pardubice	1,554
Hradec Králové	1,554
Klatovy	1,529
Mladá Boleslav	1,315
České Budějovice	1,151
Total	88,105

In a letter dated September 18, 1941, Heinrich Himmler referred to Göring's order of July 31, 1941, stressing its urgency: "The *Führer* demands that the Reich and the Protectorate, from West to East, be liberated from the Jews as soon as possible."[128] The first transports of Jews to the "East," composed of men, women, and children and directed to Lodz and Minsk, left Prague on October 16, 1941. By November 18, a total of five transports had been sent from Prague to Lodz and one from Brno to Minsk and Riga. These deportees were to share the fate of hundreds of thousands of Polish and Russian Jews; the greater part were annihilated in the most notorious extermination centers set up in Belzec, Chelmno, Treblinka and Lublin (Maidanek).[129] Some were massacred at the Ninth Fort of Kovno, Latvia.

Late in September 1941, SS Obergruppenführer Reinhard Heydrich was appointed Acting Reich Protector; he took office in Prague on September 27. Two weeks later, on October 10,[130] he called a meeting at Hradčany Palace, attended by Karl Hermann Frank, Horst Böhme, Eichmann, Maurer, Hans Günther, Wolfram, and Dr. Karl Freiherr von Gregory, to discuss the "solution" of the "Jewish problem" of the Protectorate. It was decided to concentrate the Jews in Terezín and then (after their numbers had been considerably depleted by death) to send them on to the East. About 5,000 Jews were to be "evacuated" from the Protectorate within the next few weeks. At the press conference held after the meeting, Heydrich made his first reference to the resistance movement in the Protectorate, warning the Czech populace against having anything to do with underground groups. He also explained that the anti-Jewish measures taken were an integral part of a planned step-by-step policy leading to the *Endziel,* the "final goal." In Heydrich's words, Terezín was meant to be only an *Übergangslösung* ("interim solution"). In fact, he did not even mention the name of the ghetto to the assembled newsmen. From that point on, events moved swiftly. Two days after the conference, Heydrich issued an order authorizing the *Zentralstelle für jüdische Auswanderung* to take over all the property of deported Jews that was listed on the forms signed by each Jew prior to his deportation. The *Auswanderungsfond* took charge of the expropriated Jewish assets which then, in fact, passed into German possession.

Following this crucial meeting, Günther, the head of the *Zentralstelle,* summoned the representatives of Prague's Jewish Religious Congregation to his office. He ordered them to submit plans for one or more "labor ghettos,"[131] to investigate which towns in Bohemia and Moravia would be suitable for such ghettos, and eventually to consider the organization of ghettos with appropriate housing and labor facilities on the outskirts of some of these cities.

Another top secret meeting took place a week later, on October 17.[132] The deliberations at this session dealt with the speedy deportation of 5,000 Jews to Lodz, Minsk, and Riga, where the authorities "have already expressed agreement to accept fifty thousand Jews each."[133] Among other items on the agenda were the tactics to be employed in assembling Jews for the transports, the intimidation of the Czech populace, and the evacuation of the original inhabitants of Terezín to make room for the Jews. On behalf of the Jewish Religious Congregation, a committee of fourteen experts immediately set to work to draw up plans for "labor ghettos."[134] A number of places were suggested, mostly industrial towns such as Kyjov, Ivančice (Eibenschütz), Německý Brod, Beroun, Čáslav, Hlinsko, Choceň, Turnov, and Roudnice nad Labem. However, all of these were rejected by the SS on some pretext or other; Čáslav, for example, was "too beautiful."[135] The Jewish leadership—mainly Dr. František Friedmann, Otto Zucker, and Jakub Edelstein—favored cities located in the heart of overwhelmingly Czech-populated areas. Finally, the Germans informed the Jewish leaders that they had decided upon Terezín (Theresienstadt), a fortress city located near Litoměřice (Leitmeritz), sixty kilometers northwest of Prague. Various objections raised by the Jewish community officials were swept aside, and the date for the departure of an *Aufbaukommando* (construction detail) to help set up the ghetto was fixed for November 24, 1941. The task of this work detail was to prepare the town, which had been cleared of its resident population, for the Jewish deportees. The SS knew precisely what awaited the Jews at their destination. The minutes of the infamous meeting at Hradčany Palace contained their ambiguous description of the new living accommodations: *"Die Juden haben sich die Wohnungen in die Erde hinab zu schaffen"* (The Jews will have to build their dwellings under the ground).[136]

In conformity with the multifaceted policy of Nazi deception, the real function assigned to Terezín—that of transit station on the way to Auschwitz—was carefully concealed from the leaders of the Jewish Religious Congregation.

Between November 24, 1941, and March 16, 1945, a total of 122 trains, with a total of 73,608 persons aboard, was dispatched from the Protectorate of Bohemia and Moravia to Terezín.[137]

The agony of the deportees began with the summons from the Jewish Religious Congregation that stated the day and hour at which they were to report at the assembly points. In Prague, this function was filled by a group of wooden shacks on the Trade Fair grounds, with dirty walls and no sanitary facilities except for outdoor latrines located some distance away.[138] The area was guarded by Czech police outside and by SS units inside.

Initially, certain categories (children of mixed marriages, Jewish spouses of non-Jews, families of persons employed by the Jewish Religious Congregation, etc.) were exempted from deportation. The selection of the "passengers" to go aboard each train began with an administrative step: From the enormous card file of registered Jews, the SS men at the *Zentralstelle für jüdische Auswanderung* in Prague would pick out about 1,200 to 1,300 names and hand them over to the Prague Jewish Religious Congregation, which then sent the summonses to the individuals thus chosen for deportation. Summonses were usually delivered at night, along with a sheet giving instructions about how and when to report.[139] On the initiative of Hanna Steiner, teams of young people organized voluntarily to help the aged and sick prepare for the transport and to carry their luggage to the assembly point.[140]

Upon arrival on the Trade Fair grounds, each person was allotted "living space," a tiny piece of bare ground in one of the shacks on which to sleep. He was then called to the desks to fill in numerous forms, including a *Vermögenserklärung* (declaration of personal assets) and hand over his house keys, ration cards, home fuel ration certificate, valuables, cash, and personal documents. This processing took about three days.[141] Escorted by SS guards, German police, or even Czech gendarmes, most of the transports left Prague before dawn or late at night, marching to the Holešovice railroad station, which was near the Trade Fair grounds, under cover of darkness in order to avoid a public spectacle in the capital. The reaction of the public when one group of deportees from Prague was marched to the station in broad daylight was described by a woman who survived one of the first transports sent from Prague to Lodz. The column of deportees—the old, the young, and little children—making its way to the station, escorted by SS men and gendarmes, was watched by Czech crowds on the pavements on both sides of the street, "the men ostentatiously taking off their hats, many of the women weeping." [142]

Many of the deportees were subjected to exhaustive questioning, during which standard SS methods were employed. Those who collapsed under the torture were taken to Prague's Jewish hospital, which was forced to certify that they had died of some illness. [143]

On the eve of one transport, the Prague Jewish Religious Congregation dispatched a team of transport department workers headed by a Viennese Jew, Robert Mandler, to assist in the registration of the deportees, the placement of the deportees aboard the train, and other matters connected with the departure of the transport. This team was ironically known among deportees as the "circus," because of the "traveling show" it helped put into motion. . . .

In the provincial towns the assembly points were large halls, mainly community centers, schools, or synagogues. There, the abuses reported were similar to those perpetrated in Prague.

The boarding of the deportation trains took several hours. At first, passenger cars were provided for the deportees; later, they rode in freight cars fitted with benches, and finally in bare boxcars. The trip from Prague to Bohušovice, the railroad station nearest to Terezín, took two to three hours. At Bohušovice, the deportees were received by an SS unit, Czech gendarmes, and a team of ghetto inmates. The first inspection of the new arrivals took place under chaotic conditions, to the accompaniment of shouts and beatings. After this checkup was completed, the deportees set out on the two-mile march to Terezín.

The number of Jews in the Protectorate of Bohemia and Moravia diminished steadily. Neither Germany's difficulties on the battlefront nor wartime exigencies within the Protectorate slowed down the deportations. Each week, beginning on November 16, 1941, transports left for Terezín from Prague, Plzeň, Brno, and other cities. The press said nothing about the steady decline in the Jewish population of the Protectorate. The shrinking number of physicians and dentists advertising their services in the weekly bulletin of Prague's Jewish Religious Congregation provided the only indication of what was happening. [144]

Heydrich's work in Prague was guided by three principal aims:

laying the ground for the Germanization of the Protectorate of Bohemia and Moravia, wiping out pockets of Czech resistance, and, as far as the Jews were concerned, launching the "Final Solution." Heydrich's handling of the Czech population was intended to take two directions: to cajole the working classes into submissive and diligent labor for the war effort, and to stamp out the intelligentsia and Czech patriotic elements in accordance with the concept voiced by Hitler himself:

> I therefore need peace in this region so that the workers, the Czech workers, may make full use of their labor to support the German war effort . . . This means, of course, that the Czech workers must be given the grub (*zum Fressen*) . . .[145]

Thus, Heydrich's campaign of intimidation was aimed at "bending the Czechs, not breaking them."

The terror which accompanied Heydrich's rapid rise to power culminated in savage reprisals following his assassination on May 27, 1942. The Germans launched an unprecedented *Grosszähmung* ("dragnet operation," lit., "taming operation") against the population of Bohemia and Moravia.[146] Over 45,000 members of all available German police and military units were hastily dispatched to the Protectorate. They searched and questioned hundreds of thousands of persons, detaining 13,119, many of them Jews. Mass executions became the order of the day; the names of those executed were announced over the radio and in the press. The official announcements account for 1,331 executions between May 28 and July 3, 1942. Among those executed were 201 women.[147] In retaliation for having given temporary asylum to the parachutists responsible for Heydrich's assassination, the entire male population of the villages of Lidice and Ležáky was shot by German SS squadrons. On June 10 a special penal transport of 1,000 Jews was dispatched from Prague to Poland. They were taken to Ujazdowo, where they were ordered to dig their own graves before they were executed.[148]

Although the state of emergency was lifted on July 3, the reign of terror continued. Kurt Daluege, who replaced Heydrich as Acting Reich Protector of Bohemia and Moravia, issued an order establishing the death penalty for anyone aiding, or failing to report, persons engaged in activities hostile to the Reich, including giving shelter to Jews.[149] Additional restrictions on the movements of Jews (use of public transportation, etc.) were issued, which made the life of the Jews still left in the Protectorate totally unbearable.

On August 20, 1942, the *Zentralstelle für jüdische Auswanderung* was renamed *Zentralamt für die Regelung der Judenfrage in Böhmen und Mähren* (Central Office for the Settlement of the Jewish Problem in Bohemia and Moravia). The office's main concern now was the confiscation of Jewish property and its redistribution to Germans as well as the thorough exploitation of whatever Jewish self-administration still existed.

In September, a special internment camp was set up at Svatoboŕice near Hodonín (Göding) for relatives of prominent political emigrés in exile and of resistance members living abroad.[150] Among the internees were some Jews who received especially harsh treatment from the camp guards; many of them were beaten and died in the camp.

Daluege's tenure as Acting Reich Protector marked a change in the legal status of the Jews in the Protectorate of Bohemia and Moravia. Until July 1, 1943, legal cases involving Jews had been handled by German courts; after that date, under Paragraph 13 of the "Reich Citizenship Law," Jews accused of a crime were tried and sentenced by the Gestapo.[151]

On August 24, 1943, Dr. Wilhelm Frick was appointed Reich Protector of Bohemia and Moravia, and Karl Hermann Frank, secretary of the Protectorate, received the official title of "German Minister of State for Bohemia and Moravia," thus becoming the head of the Protectorate at last.

The situation of the Jews who still remained in the Protectorate during the crucial period of the mass deportations was described by Dr. Arnošt Neumann, a member of the *HaShomer HaTzair* (left-wing Labor Zionist) movement, who, aided by the Czech leftist underground, succeeded in escaping from the Protectorate and reached his native Slovakia at the end of August 1943. In a report sent to Geneva, dated September 5, he related that there were still three labor groups working outside Terezín: one at Oslavany near Brno, another on Heydrich's estate in Panenské Břežany, and a third in the coal mines at Kladno. Neumann's letter deals primarily with the enforced registration and the response of the Jewish Religious Congregation and of the *HeHalutz* (pioneering Zionist youth) organization to the deportation transports:

During the period of registration, the members of *HeHalutz* were attending training courses, and there they registered together, hoping to be included in a transport as a group. We supported this approach. Naturally, parents fought to have their children with them and wanted to enter the transport as a family unit. The main concern among the Jews was to make sure that the transports would be carried out smoothly. Though prompted by the desire to aid the victims in their plight, they caused, in fact, harm, since they gave those about to be deported the impression that the transport did not spell danger to their lives. . . . The transports were carried out with unprecedented efficiency, in an orderly fashion, with Jews themselves helping to organize them. Thus, even the *halutzim,* led by the best of intentions in extending their services, became the helpers of the executioners. All this created an atmosphere which discouraged the will to resist. Only a few tried to escape the transports by seeking employment either on the staff of the Jewish Religious Congregation or in other [exempt] capacities. Only later, when the horrifying news trickled back about hunger, terrible housing conditions, and complete helplessness did our stand toward the transports begin to change.

At first, our comrades did not report for the transports and demanded that the others who still remained do likewise. What did refusal to report for a transport entail? First of all, one had to hide and the problem was where. . . . Only very few gentiles were ready to extend help in this respect. You must remember that there was a horrible reign of terror. So, for instance, following the Heydrich affair, they shot everyone who was hiding and had not registered. Secondly, it must be borne in mind how difficult it was under the prevailing regime to "legitimize" the comrades as "Aryans.". . . We have established contact with Communists who are fighting against our common enemy, and they have recognized our political integrity. Consequently, for the time being, they regard debates on ideological issues as academic and they have promised to lend us their support within the framework of their regional organization. They advised us not to report for transports and provided us with a source of baptismal certificates which made it possible for us to live [in this country]. Our friend Benzion Feuerstein[152] acted as liaison between them and ourselves.[153]

In fact, however, only a very few Jews were saved by failing to report for deportation. As Neumann's account implies, only individuals of great daring chose to evade registration and to live in hiding, and even some of these were caught, brought to trial, and sentenced to death by hanging. During 1944 and the early part of 1945, Jewish partners in mixed marriages and small groups of employees of the *Ältestenrat* (Council of Jewish Elders) who until then had been exempted from deportation were also shipped to Terezín. And so the uprooting of the Jews from the Protectorate of Bohemia and Moravia was nearing completion.

THE ROLE OF THE JEWISH RELIGIOUS CONGREGATIONS: 1939–1945

On the eve of the German occupation, there were in Bohemia and Moravia a total of 136 Jewish Religious Congregations.[154] The Supreme Council of the Federation of Jewish Religious Congregations of Bohemia, Moravia, and Silesia (*Nejvyšší Rada Svazů Náboženských Obcí Židovských v Čechach, na Moravě a ve Slezsku*) in Prague constituted the highest authority to which the autonomous religious congregations in the provinces turned for advice and guidance on many questions.

The Jewish population figures registered on October 1, 1939, with the Jewish Religious Congregation in Prague were as follows:[155]

Place of Residence	Number of Jews	% of total Jewish population	Number Professing the Jewish Religion	% of total Jewish population
Prague	46,170	51.22	39,871	49.64
Other places in Bohemia	18,318	20.32	16,234	20.21
Brno	9,726	10.79	9,020	11.23
Moravská Ostrava	4,185	4.64	4,130	5.14
Other places in Moravia	11,748	13.03	11,064	13.78
Totals	90,147		80,319	

The German occupation radically altered the situation of the religious congregations. Abandoned and isolated, with no avenue of appeal, they became subordinate to the *Zentralstelle für jüdische Auswanderung*, which in turn reported directly to the *Reichssicher-*

heitshauptamt (RSHA) in Berlin. However, interference by the Prague Gestapo, motivated mostly by internal rivalries with the *Zentralstelle*, was not a rare occurrence.

Aryanization started a steady process of pauperization among the Jews. The load placed upon the Jewish communal organizations was immense and unprecedented. Given the spate of regulations issued daily by the various authorities, and the rapidly changing conditions, it was obvious that these Jewish organizations would have to undergo modifications if they were to cope with the new realities.

On April 7, 1939, the chairman of the seven Jewish religious congregations which functioned independently in various parts of Prague [156] agreed to unite and to centralize their activities. The next day, a meeting was held in the ancient Jewish Town Hall of Prague, with the participation of twenty provincial delegates, representing eleven localities, to discuss several pressing issues. The reports of the representatives from the provinces were alarming: "Wherever the German population is large, the situation is bad." [157]

During the first weeks following the German occupation, thousands of Jews, mostly refugees from the Sudetenland, fled to England. The majority of these were able to proceed to England thanks to the assistance of the British Committee for Refugees from Czechoslovakia. [158] Among the refugees who reached England were some active members of various political parties, journalists, intellectuals, and former high officials of the Czechoslovak republic. Another category of escapees, consisting mostly of Zionist-oriented public figures, managed to emigrate to Palestine at the outbreak of the war, partly under the terms of the transfer agreement signed between the Czechoslovak Ministry of Finance and the Jewish Agency for Palestine in January 1939. [159] Others crossed the "green" border into Poland.

At the outset, the Jewish Religious Congregation of Prague was led by two members of the assimilationist "Czech-Jewish movement," Dr. Emil Kafka, the chairman, and Dr. František Weidmann, the secretary (who, after Kafka's departure for London, was appointed chairman by the *Zentralstelle*). Jakub Edelstein, the noted Zionist leader and director of the Palestine Office in Prague, was appointed deputy chairman. [160] Another Zionist officer of the Jewish Religious Congregation was Otto Zucker, chairman of *Keren HaYesod* (The Palestine Foundation Fund), who directed the cultural activities of the Religious Congregation and was later associated with a special relief fund.[161]

The German occupation and the events that followed broke down existing barriers and brought about a truce among the various factions of the Czech Jewish leadership. They were united in one common aim: to save what still could be salvaged. This attitude is reflected in the reminiscences of the veteran Zionist Dr. Karel Stein:

> Most of the Jews were assimilated linguistically and culturally and regarded themselves either as Germans or as Czechs. Only a minority claimed Jewish nationality and had a Zionist outlook. Another group, neither assimilated nor Zionist, that of the Orthodox Jews, was influential not because of its numbers but rather because of its activities. The assimilated Jews must have constituted almost seventy percent of the entire community. German-speaking Jews lived in Prague, Brno, Moravská Ostrava, Opava, Plzeň, and many other communities. It should be emphasized that during the occupation the assimilated Jews proudly proclaimed their Jewish origin; [the chorus was] led by individuals who had been imbued with Czech culture and thoroughly alienated from Judaism, which had hitherto given them only pain. Now, however, they began to study Jewish history and Jewish values. The dispute among the factions came to an end and everyone was anxious to contribute to the common effort to save what still could be salvaged. The intellectual leaders of the assimilated Czech Jews, Edvard Lederer and Dr. Otakar Guth, called upon their followers, especially the "Kapper" Student Organization, to cooperate fully on behalf of the Jewish cause. Ideological differences were overcome and replaced by mutual trust and reliance. There was not one who acted as an informer or became a traitor.[162]

As chairman of the Prague Jewish Religious Congregation, Dr. Kafka convened a meeting in Prague of the representatives of the Jewish Religious Congregations of Bohemia and Moravia in order to discuss their impending transfer to the capital. The delegates made the journey to Prague with the permission of the *Zentralstelle*.

Another meeting took place on August 13, 1939, in the ancient Jewish Town Hall; this meeting was attended by 128 persons and an observer from the police, who duly reported the proceedings to the authorities.[163] At this conference both Dr. Kafka and Dr. Weidmann, the chairman and, respectively, the secretary of the Jewish Religious Congregation, recalled the thousand-year history of Czechoslovak Jewry and the milestones of Jewish achievements, particularly in the struggle for Jewish rights, witnessed by the historic chamber. Kafka and Weidmann also expressed their feelings for Czechoslovakia, the land "to whose soil most of us are attached with all our hearts and souls, which our forefathers helped to cultivate, in which they are buried, and in which the traditions of ancient Jewish families are deeply rooted."[164]

The most important issue at that point was emigration, which was then still openly encouraged by the German authorities. The latter part of July 1939 saw the creation of the *Zentralstelle für jüdische Auswanderung* under the personal supervision of Adolf Eichmann and under the directorship of Hans Günther. Working under the direction of the *Zentralstelle* was the emigration department of the Jewish Religious Congregation, with a staff of about ninety individuals headed by the well-known writer Hanus Bonn. Leading figures of the Jewish Religious Congregation, including Marie Schmolka, Hanna Steiner, Jakub Edelstein, Dr. František Friedmann, and Dr. Emil Kafka were given official permission to visit foreign countries for the purpose of raising funds and negotiating with Jewish organizations such as HICEM, ORT, and mainly the American Jewish Joint Distribution Committee (JDC), with a view to organizing mass emigration. These efforts yielded a total of $1,062,199, most of which was contributed by the JDC or "the Joint," as it was popularly known among European Jews.[165]

Hanna Steiner, Friedmann, and others maintained contacts with foreign consulates, attended to passport and visa formalities, and helped make travel arrangements.

At the end of August 1939, a special department of records (*Zentralmatrik*) was set up to house the registers of births, marriages, and deaths of all the Jewish religious congregations in the Protectorate of Bohemia and Moravia.

The education department of the Jewish Religious Congregation organized a large-scale vocational reorientation program geared to conditions in the countries to which Czech Jews were most likely to emigrate. Statistical reports for the year 1940 listed courses in agriculture, handicrafts, industrial arts, innkeeping, and foreign languages. The recorded attendance at these courses was as follows:

```
1939 . . . . . . . . . . . . . . . . . . 1,825
1940 . . . . . . . . . . . . . . . . . . 6,952
1941 . . . . . . . . . . . . . . . . . . 8,382
```
[166]

These courses were held regularly until the end of September 1941, when they were suspended by order of the *Zentralstelle.*[167]
During the crucial year of 1939, a total of 19,016 Jews emigrated from Czechoslovakia.[168]
The Palestine Office was still functioning in Prague, engaged primarily in encouraging and arranging emigration to Palestine and in training prospective emigrants in skills they would need in the Jewish Homeland. The executive of the Palestine Office in Prague consisted of the following prominent Zionist personalities: Jakub Edelstein, who maintained contacts with the authorities; Dr. Franz Kahn, who was in charge of youth and *halutzim* (pioneers); Dr. František Friedmann, who handled the practical details of transfer and emigration; Jacob Reiss; and Otto Zucker, who acted as treasurer. The information and legal department was headed by Dr. A. Beneš and Dr. Leo Janowitz.[169]

Within a period of a year and a half, the *HeHalutz* pioneering organization succeeded in registering 3,000 young people with a view to preparing them for emigration to Palestine. Of these, 1,908 were engaged in *hakhsharah,* i.e., practical training to prepare them for a life as pioneers. They were assigned in small groups to jobs on the lands of Czech farmers. As late as the fall of 1940 a "vocational retraining camp" was established in Česká Lípa, southern Bohemia, on an estate once owned by Jews. Initially the 530 young *halutzim,* men and women, worked in that camp under relatively favorable conditions. Later, however, these conditions deteriorated and eventually the place in some respects came to resemble a concentration camp.

The outbreak of the war put an end to mass emigration from the Protectorate of Bohemia and Moravia and made it difficult, if not virtually impossible, for individuals to leave. Nevertheless, the *Zentralstelle* ordered all wealthy Jews to submit an emigration file (*Auswanderungsmappe*)[170] indicating Shanghai or some other place as a fictitious "destination." Staggering taxes were imposed on these potential emigrants, although it was obvious that the land and sea routes by which these plans could have been carried out were now closed.

The isolation of the Jews in the Protectorate due to the war began to take its economic and psychological toll. A report to the JDC, dated September 20, 1939, and signed by Hanna Steiner and Dr.

Weidmann, describes the burdens placed upon the Jewish Religious Congregation in Prague:

> The Jewish Congregation has to carry on all the social work for Jewry (in Prague) and in the provincial towns . . . it has to manage Jewish educational work, relief for the sick and the aged, the care of young people, vocational training, and so on. A detailed report was given [to you] at your last conference in Paris . . . This letter is to [impress upon you] the necessity to enable us to take up negotiations with the American [Jewish Joint] Distribution Committee in Europe.[171]

As late as May 1940 Hanna Steiner made trips to Berlin and Hamburg with the consent of the authorities for negotiations with shipping companies and consulates of neutral countries in a desperate attempt to arrange for the emigration of a group of children and adults. She conferred with the consuls of Santo Domingo, Venezuela, and Ecuador in Germany and maintained steady contacts with representatives of the JDC. In December 1940 she was in Berlin to discuss emigration possibilities with leaders of the *Reichsvereinigung der deutschen Juden,* the Nazi-sanctioned representative body of German Jewry.[172] Edelstein, who in May 1939 had actually spent several days in Palestine to discuss possibilities for the resettlement of Czech Jews and then returned to Prague, now concentrated on organizing the emigration of groups of children from the Protectorate of Bohemia and Moravia to neutral countries. To this end he visited Geneva, Trieste, Berlin, Budapest, and Bratislava (Slovakia was then still nominally independent), leaving members of his family in Prague as hostages to ensure his return.[173]

On Friday, November 24, 1939, there appeared the first issue of a bilingual weekly, *Jüdisches Nachrichtenblatt—Židovské Listy,* which served as the official organ of the Jewish Religious Congregation in Prague and was censored by the Gestapo. Since Jews were not permitted to subscribe to, or to purchase, other newspapers, this was, in fact, the only newspaper available to the Jews in the Protectorate.[174] Initially, the Czech branches of *Keren HaYesod* (the Palestine Foundation Fund) and *Keren Kayemet LeYisrael* (the Jewish National Fund) acted as co-sponsors of the paper, but after the disbanding of all Zionist organizations and institutions in the Protectorate in September 1940, the Jewish Religious Congregation was left to bear sole responsibility. Edited by Dr. Oscar Singer, the paper gave employment to a number of prominent journalists who had been dismissed from their former positions. Among the free-lance contributors were the composer Karel Reiner, the poet Jiří Orten (Ohrenstein), Emil Faktor (formerly the editor of the *Berliner Tageblatt*), the cartoonist Fritz Taussig (Fritta), and many others well-known to Jewish and gentile readers in the Czech Historic Lands. Initially, this new organ was to fill two principal functions: to encourage emigration and to inform the Jewish population of all anti-Jewish laws and regulations enacted in the Protectorate. It was replete with advertisements offering vocational training and courses in foreign languages and with information about prospective countries of emigration, including Latin America and even Africa. It featured letters written by recent emigrants from their new homes and descriptions of kibbutz life in Palestine. Some of the editorials appealed for calm and discipline, urging still-affluent Jews to help their less fortunate brethren.[175] Other editorials indulged in soul-searching and recalled the glories of past Jewish history with the aim of preserving Jewish self-respect and faith in a better tomorrow. Still others sounded somber warnings: "Under certain circumstances the conduct of any individual can bring disaster upon the entire Jewish community. For this reason it is incumbent upon us to avoid any action that might endanger all Jews. This applies [particularly] to all political or pseudo-political activities."[176]

In the fall of 1941, the weekly newspaper shrank to a two-page bulletin. Apart from classified advertisements—lists of physicians and dentists, and visiting hours at Jewish cemeteries (the only "recreation grounds" still open to Jews in Prague)—most of the space in the *Nachrichtenblatt* was now devoted to newly promulgated anti-Jewish laws. There were no references to mass deportations or to the disintegration of the Jewish communities in the provinces. During the last two years of its existence—1943 and 1944—emphasis shifted to such trivialities as helpful hints on how to economize on gas, electricity, and other scarce goods and services.

Under a decree enacted by the Reich Protector on March 5, 1940, the Jewish Religious Congregation of Prague was given jurisdiction over all Jewish religious congregations in the Protectorate of Bohemia and Moravia,[177] and also over all individual Jews, including those of "non-Mosaic faith"; i.e., non-practicing Jews or converts to Christianity. The Jewish Religious Congregation in turn was subject to the authority of the *Zentralstelle für jüdische Auswanderung* in Prague and of the *Sicherheitsdienst* (SD; the intelligence branch of the SS) in Brno.

Following the German occupation, the functions of the Jewish Religious Congregation in Prague were divided into three spheres: welfare, service to the *Zentralstelle,* and liquidation of Jewish assets. In subsequent ordinances, the activities of the Religious Congregation were redefined as follows: (1) collection of fees and taxes imposed upon Jews; (2) aid for needy Jews; (3) gathering Jewish statistical data; (4) emigration; (5) implementation of German orders for forced labor, and assistance to deportees.[178]

In order to cope with these new functions, a huge bureaucratic apparatus—thirty-two sections with a total of approximately 2,600 employees—was set up. The main activities of the staff centered around the welfare department, which had fourteen subdivisions. By that time, most of the Jews were without gainful employment and were forced to live from their savings or the proceeds of the enforced sale of their businesses, or had to accept assistance from the Jewish community. By July 1940, the welfare department of the Jewish Religious Community had cared for more than 8,000 persons.[179]

Bank accounts owned by Jews were blocked; only small amounts (500 crowns) could be withdrawn each month. Eventually the Germans approved the creation of a special fund, launched by Otto Zucker with the slogan, "Give! Build! Live!",[180] which the more affluent Jews could endow with money transferred from their personal bank accounts. This new fund made it possible for the Jewish Religious Congregation to care for its needy members, to provide them with clothing, to open soup kitchens and infirmaries, and to run vocational retraining classes and foreign language courses for those who still hoped to emigrate. Official fund-raisers, mostly former lawyers, were engaged by the Jewish Religious Congregation. They visited provincial areas to solicit contributions from affluent Jews. The noted Czech-Jewish writer Norbert Frýd, who participated in this campaign, relates his fund-raising experiences in his memoirs.[181] During his visit to Mladá Boleslav, he first came face to face with the misery of Jews who had been turned out of their homes and crowded into a dilapidated old castle outside the city.[182]

His admiration for these unfortunates knew no bounds when, on his second visit, he found they had organized a group that had succeeded in making the castle habitable, complete with plumbing, showers and bathrooms. Frýd describes Otto Zucker's fund-raising and winter relief campaign as a "formidable project" aimed at keeping the desperate Jewish community above water.[183]

The German authorities issued an order to register all Jewish-held apartments in the Protectorate. Jews in Prague were forced to leave elegant apartments in better, modern residential neighborhoods and to move into old, inferior tenements in the city's First, Second, and Fifth districts. Their former homes were assigned to Germans who had moved to Prague from the Reich.

The various departments of the Jewish Religious Congregation gradually were turned into the unwilling tools of the German authorities so that arguments and appeals were impossible. Nevertheless, the officials of the Jewish Religious Congregation did all they could to help their unfortunate brethren, sometimes at the risk of their own lives, for any obstruction of German authority was regarded as sabotage, punishable by death. Indeed, some officials of the Jewish Religious Congregation were deported on charges of "sabotage" long before the mass deportations began. On the wall of the *Zentralstelle* office in Prague there was a bulletin board bearing photos and personal data of the leading officials of the Jewish Religious Congregation. The Jews themselves ironically called it the *Sterbetafel* (death board). In the summer of 1941, prior to the start of the mass deportations to the East, Obersturmbannführer Karl Rahm, who was then Günther's deputy at the *Zentralstelle,* learned that the first 1,000 Jews due for registration had not reported in full number. Furious, he tore the pictures of Hanuš Bonn (the head of the emigration department) and of his deputy Erich Kafka from the bulletin board and ordered the deportation of both men to Mauthausen. According to another account, Bonn and Kafka were deported for arguing that the registration of Jews could not be carried out with the dispatch expected by Rahm. At any rate, death certificates for both men were sent by the SS to the Jewish Religious Congregation, with the warning that a similar fate would be in store for anyone else attempting to "sabotage" German orders.[184] Dr. Neuwirth, an official of the Jewish Religious Congregation's administrative department, and his deputy were also sent to a concentration camp, never to return, on charges of having unlawfully purchased goods with the intention of sending them to the Terezín ghetto. Late in September 1941, the organized emigration that had gone on from the beginning of July 1939 with the help of the Jewish Religious Congregation in Prague came to a standstill. That fall, the registration of Jews ordered by the German authorities was carried out by the Jewish Religious Congregations of Prague and Brno. Each Jew was assigned a serial number, which he had to report in person at the *Zentralstelle*.[185]

According to the official report submitted by the Jewish Religious Congregation to the *Zentralstelle*, the total Jewish population of the Protectorate of Bohemia and Moravia at the end of the first half of 1940 was 103,389.[186] In addition, as of March 31, 1941, there were in the Protectorate of Bohemia and Moravia 12,680 Jews of "non-Mosaic faith," of whom 5,611 professed no religion whatsoever.[187] These individuals were registered and cared for by the department for "Jews of non-Mosaic faith" (*B-Juden*), which the Jewish Religious Congregation in Prague had been ordered to set up on March 16, 1940.[188]

Eventually, the Jewish Religious Congregation was forced to function also as a labor exchange, and a so-called Central Labor Office was set up for this purpose. Initially, Jews were employed for day labor, such as shoveling snow at the airports and in the streets, and for agricultural and other menial tasks. Later, they were drafted also for roadbuilding and other heavy work. According to the register of the Central Labor Office, a total of 7,132 Jews was engaged in such menial work at the turn of the year 1939/40. On January 1, 1942, 12,907 Jews were doing forced labor.[189]

It should be noted that an ordinance concerning the segregation of, and the forced labor to be performed by, Jews was actually cited as the "legal" basis for the deportation of the Jews of the Protectorate. The sternest measures connected with the deportations were ordered and carried out by the *Zentralstelle* itself. They were not publicized over the radio or through the official law gazette but were transmitted verbally to representatives of the Jewish Religious Congregation. Early in October 1941, the Jewish Religious Congregation began to help prepare the deportees for their "evacuation" to

Terezín, preceded by the *Aufbaukommando* of 365 young men to set up basic living conditions for the ghetto inmates.

The apartments, furnishings, and other valuables left behind by the Jews were assessed by the "Krämer department" created within the Jewish Religious Congregation for this purpose. Known by the name of its director, Salo Krämer, former chairman of the Jewish Religious Congregation of Moravská Ostrava, this department alone employed several hundred individuals.[190] In the summer of 1943, most of the members of this team were deported to Terezín; others were sent directly to Auschwitz. The loot processed by the department was transferred to Germany proper, or sold to Nazi chieftains and clerks in Prague who were more than eager to appropriate for themselves furniture and other household goods formerly owned by Jews. A document dated May 20, 1942, and signed by Horst Böhme, chief of the police and security services in the Protectorate, takes the German population of Prague to task for exploiting the *Zentralstelle* as a "warehouse agency" from which to take Jewish property,[191] while at the same time deriding the SS men for having to "negotiate" with the Jews. Possessions left behind by the deportees were efficiently "processed." Books were carefully cleaned, bookplates removed and the former owners' names erased. Monograms on silverware and table linen were removed. The items were then turned over to the SS, who stored them under lock and key. The expensive furniture thus confiscated was sufficient to furnish 110 apartments, which were reserved for prominent officials or exhibited as "model homes." As of January 14, 1944, there were in Prague a total of fifty-four large warehouses (which had once housed synagogues or assembly rooms of Jewish organizations) in which textiles, furs, rugs, furniture, glassware "abandoned" by the deportees were stored.[192]

Meanwhile, the Jews on their own initiative gathered items from religious institutions that had been closed. These objects were collected, classified, and registered by a team of experts and eventually became the nucleus for the postwar collection of the State Jewish Museum in Prague. The Klaus, Pinkas, and High Synagogues were made available to house these objects and in this way were saved from being used by the Germans as warehouses for other Jewish property.[193] The synagogues were no longer used for worship because the Germans had issued an order in the fall of 1941 forbidding Jews of the Protectorate to worship in public. (Clandestine services were conducted daily at the home of Dr. Aladar Deutsch, chief rabbi of Prague.)

In the provincial areas the registration of Jews for deportation began in January 1942[194] and proceeded according to the following schedule:

Plzeň	1/5–14/42
Kladno	2/6–11/42
Budějovice	3/30–4/3/42
Tábor	4/7–14/42
Kolín	4/17–25/42
Jihlava	4/29–5/5/42
Olomouc	5/8–15/42
Pardubice	5/18–24/42
Hradec Králové	5/28–6/2/42
Mladá Boleslav	6/4–6/42
Klatovy	6/16–19/42
Moravská Ostrava	6/25–7/4/42
Prague	9/3–4/42
Zlín	1/11–20/43

On February 19, 1942, a month after the Wannsee Conference (at which plans for the "Final Solution" had first been unveiled), Eichmann summoned representatives of the Jewish Religious Congregation of Prague (along with those of Vienna and Berlin) to brief them on the forthcoming mass deportations from the "Greater Reich" to the East or to Terezín.[195] On May 29, 1942, two days after the assassination of Heydrich, Eichmann summoned them once again and, upon their arrival, subjected them to his own brand of humiliation. He made them line up against a wall and stand there for about six hours. He then announced to them that the *Sowjetparadies* ("Soviet Paradise") exhibition arranged in Berlin for Nazi propaganda purposes had been disturbed by an anti-Nazi demonstration in which five Jews had allegedly participated. As a punishment for this offense, Eichmann said, 500 Jews had been arrested; of these, 250 had been shot then and there, and the rest shipped to concentration camps. He then threatened the communal leaders with similar measures if any Jews were to participate in "sabotage" activities in the future.[196]

Before the deportation of Jews from the provinces began on March 27, 1942, all Jewish religious congregations in the provinces were dissolved.[197] The *Oberlandräte* (whose functions included supervising local Czech agencies) were reorganized into *Aussen-oder Ortsstellen* (branch offices). These branch offices were then charged with organizing the transports of the Jews to be deported from their localities.

The minutes of the Wannsee Conference had made a point of stressing that the Jews had to be deported from the Protectorate because of "housing and other socio-political needs," and Terezín was described as an "old-age ghetto." Prior to the establishment of the Terezín ghetto, the *Zentralstelle* had agreed that the Jewish Religious Congregation in Prague should act as an intermediary agency to provide the ghetto with the most essential items, partly from its own stores and partly by purchase from other sources. In reality, however, no personal contact was permitted between the ghetto and the Jews in the outside world, and most of the assistance from the Jewish Religious Congregation had to be sent clandestinely.

Thanks to several courageous officers and staff members of the Jewish Religious Congregation, funds obtained from various sources were channeled for the purchase of essential supplies for the ghetto. From letters and reports smuggled out to the *HeHalutz* center in Geneva[198] it is clear that funds reached the Prague Jewish Religious Congregation from Jewish organizations in neutral countries (e.g., the Rescue Committee in Istanbul and the JDC and *HeHalutz* organizations in Geneva) and that they were used for the purchase of food and other necessities which were then sent by various ways and means to "Jakobstadt" or "Ir Jakov" (German and Hebrew, respectively, for "Jacobtown"; i.e., the town of Jakub Edelstein), the code names used for Terezín in clandestine Jewish correspondence.[199]

The heart and soul of one unique mutual assistance project was Heinz Prossnitz, a lad of sixteen.[200] Because his father had headed the financial department of the *Ältestenrat der Juden in Prag* (Council of Jewish Elders in Prague), the successor organization of the Jewish Religious Congregation, Heinz was among the last Jews to be deported from Prague. Aided by two friends, Erika Wolf[201] and Edita Březina, he initiated correspondence with Jewish organizations and individuals (Dr. Fritz Ullmann and Nathan Schwalb) in neutral countries and with their help sent hundreds of parcels to the ghettos of Lodz (Litzmannstadt) and Lublin and to the camps of Auschwitz and Sachsenhausen. Other contacts in Slovakia, Hungary, Sudetenland, and even in Germany proper helped him acquire money and goods for parcels destined for Terezín. Prior to his own deportation to Terezín in the late summer of 1944, Heinz made arrangements for the continuation of this assistance to concentration camp inmates.[202]

It is interesting to note that until March 1, 1943, through arrangements made jointly by the JDC and the Jewish religious congregations of Budapest, Nagyvárad (Grosswardein), and Subotica in Hungary and Bratislava in Slovakia, the Jewish religious congregations in the Protectorate were regularly supplied with canned kosher meat, with matzot for the Passover holidays and with the traditional *lulav* (palm branches) and *etrog* (citron) for the festival of Sukkot (Tabernacles).[203]

On January 28, 1943, the tenth anniversary of the establishment of the Third Reich, the Jewish Religious Congregation of Prague (along with its counterparts in Berlin and Vienna) was abolished as an independent religious body. Its top officials, among them Richard Israel Friedmann, Dr. Franz Kahn, and Dr. Weidmann, were deported to Terezín.[204] They all died in Auschwitz in 1944. Weidmann was savagely beaten by an SS man at the Bohušovice railroad station before boarding the train for Auschwitz; Friedmann was shot under the pretext that he had attempted to escape.[205]

On February 8, 1943, the Jewish Religious Congregation in Prague was reorganized as the *Ältestenrat der Juden in Prag*,[206] initially headed by Salo Krämer and his deputy, Herbert Langer. The last *Judenälteste* (from July 1943) was Dr. František Friedmann. His deputy in charge of administration was Erich Kraus.[207] Both men belonged to a "privileged" category because they had gentile wives. Both survived the Holocaust, but Friedmann died shortly after the war.

EPILOGUE

The last mass transports of *Volljuden* (full Jews) left Prague during the summer of 1943. Aside from the small circle of members of the

Ältestenrat and their families, only Jewish partners in mixed marriages (the so-called *Arisch versippten;* i.e., close kin of Aryans) were left in the Protectorate. These individuals, too, had been required to register (October 27, 1942)[208] and were required to show proof periodically that their Aryan spouses were still alive and that they were still married to them. Another category who still remained in the capital were the "disputable cases," 1,081 individuals unable to produce all the documents required to prove their Aryan origins.[209]

According to the central records, there were, as of August 31, 1943, still 8,606 Jews left in the Protectorate. Of these, 7,490 maintained contact with the Jewish community. The rest were either under arrest or in hiding. On September 30, 1944, there were still 7,890 Jews in the Protectorate, including 844 persons recorded as being under arrest or of unknown whereabouts.[210] By December 31, 1944, the total number of those maintaining contact had diminished to 6,795:

City or Town	Total
Prague	4,824
Plzeň	242
Kolín	251
Tábor	206
Kladno	279
Jihlava	121
Pardubice	194
Hradec Králové	203
Klatovy	148
Mladá Boleslav	182
České Budějovice	145
Total	6,795

The greater part of these were partners in mixed marriages, who as a rule were permitted to stay on in their own apartments but were entitled to restricted food rations only.[211]

During the fall of 1944 smaller groups of Jews, mainly Jewish partners in mixed marriages who had lost their "privileged" status due to divorce or by the death of their Aryan spouses, were shipped to Terezín. That summer Czech partners in mixed marriages from all over the Protectorate had been sent to labor camps in Bystřice near Benešov and to Postoloprty. Their Jewish spouses were transferred to Prague and billeted and put to work in barracks that had once housed the Hagibor Jewish Athletic Club.

Late in January and early in February 1945, a total of 4,243 persons were sent to Terezín.[212] These last groups of deportees included the officials of the *Ältestenrat der Juden*. We know the details concerning these final transports[213] from a report dated February 9, 1945, and prepared for the *Zentralamt für die Regelung der Judenfrage in Böhmen und Mähren* (Central Office for the Settlement of the Jewish Problem in Bohemia and Moravia, the successor organization of the *Zentralstelle für jüdische Auswanderung*) by the chairman of the *Ältestenrat*.[214]

One category of Jews who escaped deportation altogether were the so-called "submarines," who had "gone underground," living in hideouts or with forged Aryan documents. Among these were some members of *HeHalutz* who lived mostly in Prague with Aryan papers.[215] They were working at various jobs; some even taught German at the Institute for Modern Languages while maintaining contacts with underground cells.[216] Their day-to-day lives and harrowing experiences have been poignantly depicted in short stories by Arnošt Lustig.[217] The total number of Jews who survived "underground" in this manner in Bohemia and Moravia was 424.[218]

At the end of the war, most of the once-flourishing 325 localities in Bohemia and Moravia where Jews had resided for many centuries were *judenrein*. As of May 5, 1945, the total number of officially registered Jews left in the Protectorate of Bohemia and Moravia was 2,803.[219] Of the 350 Jewish cemeteries, old and new, many had been desecrated. Some of the 313 synagogues had been converted into depots for confiscated Jewish property or into public warehouses.

In Prague and a few other localities, Jewish survivors created small communities. Most of these, however, gradually declined in numbers, due partly to natural attrition, but mostly to emigration.

APPENDIX 1

Note: Statistics cited in these Appendices are based on reports available at the Yad Vashem Archives (Collections 07/10-1, 0-64, E 11292) and on a list of transports compiled by Karel Lagus and Josef Polák and cited in their work *Město za mřížemi* [City Behind Bars] (Prague, 1964), pp. 334–37, 346–47. Another report submitted by the *Ältestenrat der Juden in Prag* to the *Zentralamt* refers to 25,977 persons, YVA, E 1237. According to the statistics compiled by Josef Polák, the total number of those who emigrated after March 15, 1939, was 26,111 (see Appendix 5).

EMIGRATION STATISTICS
FROM MARCH 15, 1939, TO JUNE 19, 1944

Country	3/15/39 to 7/27/39	7/28/39 to 12/31/39	1940	1941	1942	1943	6/19/44	Total
U.S.A.	1,029	3,398	2,225	174	—	—	—	6,826
Other overseas countries not including Palestine	180	1,401	2,748	56	—	—	—	4,385
Palestine	720	1,348	49	—	—	—	—	2,117
Overseas	1,929	6,147	5,022	230	—	—	—	13,328
England	5,769	1,105	—	—	—	—	—	6,874
France	341	116	—	—	—	—	—	457
Slovakia	76	164	623	166	19	1	2	1,051
Generalgouvernement (German zone of Poland)	—	1,985	—	—	—	—	—	1,985
Hungary	150	236	162	89	250	96	—	983
Rest of Europe	504	494	369	50	4	—	—	1,421
Unknown destination	—	—	—	—	—	—	1	1
Europe	6,840	4,100	1,154	305	273	97	3	12,772
Totals	8,769	10,247	6,176	535	273	97	3	26,100

APPENDIX 2

JEWISH POPULATION IN THE PROTECTORATE OF BOHEMIA AND MORAVIA AS OF APRIL 30, 1945

Brno	804
České Budějovice	121
Jihlava	112
Mladá Boleslav	168
Kladno	272
Klatovy	145
Kolín	273
Hradec Králové	190
Moravská Ostrava	294
Olomouc	368
Pardubice	178
Plzeň	203
Prague	4,356
Tábor	185
Zlín	215
	7,884
These include: Half-Jews	6,621
"Disputable" cases	90
Foreign nationals	1
Others	12
	6,724

APPENDIX 3

LIST OF TRANSPORTS FROM THE PROTECTORATE TO THE EAST AND TO TEREZÍN*

No.	Designation of Transport	Point of Origin	Date of Departure	Total
1	A	Prague	10/16/41	1,000
2	B	"	10/21/41	1,000
3	C	"	10/26/41	1,000
4	D	"	10/31/41	1,000
5	E	"	11/3/41	1,000
6	F	Brno	11/16/41	1,000
7	AK-1	Prague	11/24/41	365
8	G	"	11/30/41	1,000
9	H	Brno	12/2/41	1,000
10	J	Prague	12/4/41	1,000
11	K	Brno	12/5/41	1,000
12	L	Prague	12/10/41	1,000
13	M	"	12/14/41	1,000
14	N	"	12/17/41	1,000
15	R	Plzeň	1/17/42	1,000
16	S	"	1/21/42	1,000
17	T	"	1/25/42	604
18	U	Brno	1/28/42	1,000
19	V	Prague	1/30/42	1,000
20	W	"	2/8/42	1,000
21	X	"	2/12/42	1,000
22	Y	Kladno	2/22/42	800
23	Z	"	2/26/42	823
24	Ac	Brno	3/19/42	1,000
25	Ad	"	3/22/42	1,000
26	Ae	"	3/27/42	1,000
27	Af	"	3/31/42	1,000
28	Ah	"	4/4/42	1,000
29	Ai	"	4/8/42	923
30	Ak	České Budějovice	4/18/42	909
31	Am	Prague	4/24/42	1,000
32	Ao	"	4/28/42	1,000

* According to Polák, JB II and JB III left from Panenské Břežany and Cv II from Plzeň-Bory.

No.	Designation of Transport	Point of Origin	Date of Departure	Total
33	At	"	5/7/42	1,000
34	Au	"	5/12/42	1,000
35	Au-1	"	5/15/42	1,000
36	Av	Třebíč	5/18/42	720
37	Aw	"	5/22/42	650
38	AAa	Brno	5/26/42	81
39	AAb	Kolín	6/5/42	744
40	AAc	"	6/9/42	724
41	AAd	"	6/13/42	734
42	AAe	Prague	6/20/42	1,000
43	AAf	Olomouc	6/26/42	900
44	AAg	"	6/30/42	900
45	AAh	Prague	6/10/42	1,000
46	AAl	"	7/2/42	1,000
47	AAm	Olomouc	7/4/42	900
48	AAn	Prague	7/6/42	1,000
49	AAo	Olomouc	7/8/42	745
50	AAp	Prague	7/9/42	1,000
51	AAq	"	7/13/42	1,000
52	AAr	"	7/16/42	1,000
53	AAs	"	7/20/42	1,000
54	AAt	"	7/23/42	1,000
55	AAu	"	7/27/42	1,000
56	AAv	"	7/30/42	1,000
57	AAw	"	8/3/42	1,000
58	Ba	"	8/10/42	1,460
59	Bd	"	9/4/42	1,000
60	Bf	"	9/8/42	1,000
61	Bg	"	9/12/42	1,000
62	JB	"	9/14/42	51
63	Bh	Moravská Ostrava	9/18/42	860
64	Bi	"	9/22/42	860
65	Bl	"	9/26/42	860
66	Bm	"	9/30/42	862
67	JB II*	Prague	10/17/42	10
68	Bz	Tábor	11/12/42	650
69	Ca	Prague	10/24/42	1,000
70	Cb	Tábor	11/16/42	617
71	Cc	Prague	11/20/42	1,000
72	Cd	Klatovy	11/26/42	650

THE JEWS OF BOHEMIA AND MORAVIA: 1938-1945

No.	Designation of Transport	Point of Origin	Date of Departure	Total
73	JB III*	Prague	11/26/42	3
74	Ce	Klatovy	11/30/42	619
75	Cf	Pardubice	12/5/42	650
76	Cg	"	12/9/42	606
77	Ch	Hradec Králové	12/17/42	650
78	Ci	"	12/21/42	548*
79	Ck	Prague	12/22/42	1,000
80	Cl	Mladá Boleslav	1/13/43	550
81	Cm	"	1/16/42	491
82	Cn	Uherský Brod	1/22/43	1,000
83	Co	"	1/26/43	1,000
84	Cp	"	1/30/43	837
85	Cv	Prague	3/6/43	1,021
86	Cv II*	"	3/8/43	13
87	Cw	"	3/9/43	84
88	Cx	"	3/22/43	51
89	Cy	"	4/9/43	149*
90	Cz	"	4/30/43	47
91	Da	"	5/7/43	9
92	Db	"	5/13/43	56
93	Dc	"	6/9/43	175
94	Dd	"	6/12/43	15
95	De	"	7/5/43	603
96	Df	Moravská Ostrava	6/29/43	72
97	Dg	Brno	6/30/43	60
98	Dh	Prague	7/8/43	485
99	Di	"	7/13/43	838
100	Dk	"	7/15/43	30
101	Do	"	9/11/43	53
102	Dn	Lípa	9/14/43	84
103	Dp	Prague	10/29/43	17
104	Dq	"	12/8/43	18
105	Dt	"	1/9/44	148
106	Dt-II	"	1/10/44	14
107	Du	"	1/28/44	26
108	Dv	"	2/25/44	18
109	Dw	"	3/24/44	17
110	Dy	"	4/26/44	20
111	E	"	5/17/44	24*
112	Ed	"	6/16/44	25

No.	Designation of Transport	Point of Origin	Date of Departure	Total
113	Ea	"	7/21/44	17
114	Ef	"	8/18/44	51
115	Ei	"	9/8/44	13
116	Eu	"	10/28/44	18
117	Fa	"	11/17/44	40
118	Ec	"	1/26/45	13
119	Ez	Various localities		292
120	AE1	Prague	1/31/45	1,056
121	AE2	"	2/4/45	895
122	AE3	"	2/14/45	761
123	AE5	Lípa	3/15/45	55
124	AE4	Prague	2/25/45	520
125	AE6	Moravská Ostrava	3/4/45	53
126	AE7	Olomouc	3/7/45	53
127	AE8	Prague	3/15/45	122
128	AE9	"	3/16/45	139
				80,626

Of these 80,626, a total of 73,608 left for Terezín between November 24, 1941, and March 16, 1945. The list does not include the deportees to Nisko on October 17 and 26, 1939, of whom 460 returned to Ostrava in 1940, and 123 who returned with the army of General Ludvík Svoboda after the liberation.

APPENDIX 4

JEWS DEPORTED FROM BOHEMIA AND MORAVIA TO TEREZÍN VICTIMS AND SURVIVORS

Point of Origin	Number of Prisoners	DIED			SURVIVED		
		In Terezín	In other camps	At Gestapo headquarters or as fugitives	In Terezín	Elsewhere	Released Abroad
Prague	39,395	2,946	28,763	146	5,564	1,918	58
Brno	9,064	998	7,357	25	311	349	24
Moravská Ostrava	3,567	193	3,114	9	152	94	5
Olomouc	3,498	269	2,943	6	173	105	2
Uherský Brod	2,837	314	2,321	2	75	122	3
Plzeň	2,617	274	2,123	18	110	92	
Kolín	2,202	165	1,894	5	88	49	1
Kladno	1,623	137	1,362	4	46	74	
Třebíč	1,370	135	1,176	1	35	18	5
Klatovy	1,269	141	1,055	1	30	42	
Tábor	1,267	148	1,044	2	38	35	
Pardubice	1,256	153	1,012	1	43	47	
Hradec Králové	1,198	144	946	2	45	59	2
Mladá Boleslav	1,041	102	896		33	10	
České Budějovice	908	79	799	1	15	12	2
Česká Lípa	139	—	51	1	63	24	
Panenské Břežany	64	3	42	—	5	14	
Individuals	293	12	185	12	49	32	3
Total	73,608	6,213	57,083	236	*6,875	3,096	105

* About 3,500 of these had been in the "workers transports" AE 1-9, "protected," until January–February 1945 because they were married to Aryans.

APPENDIX 5

SURVEY OF THE "FINAL SOLUTION" IN THE PROTECTORATE OF BOHEMIA AND MORAVIA

Number of "Jews by race" (so classed under the Nuremberg laws) as of March 15, 1939		118,310	
Emigrated before the start of deportations		26,111*	
Number remaining		92,199	92,199
Deported to Terezín	73,608		
Deported directly to the East from Prague, Brno and Moravská Ostrava	7,849		
Arrested, caught in hiding, suicides	7,939	89,396	
Left in Protectorate (not deported)		2,803	
Returned after the war:			
From Terezín	6,900		
From transports to the East	3,371		
From prisons and hideouts	848		
From Nisko camp (with army of General Ludvík Svoboda)	123	11,242	14,045
Number of Survivors		14,045	
Total Number of Victims			78,154

* This survey does not include individuals who left the Protectorate prior to the beginning of the Nazi persecution or returned with various Czechoslovak army units organized abroad.

Recapitulation: Of an original total Jewish population (before the start of deportations) of 92,199 in Bohemia and Moravia, 78,154, or 84.8 percent, perished in the Holocaust.

NOTES

1. For the most relevant sources on this subject, see Documents on British Foreign Policy 1919-1939, 3d Series, vols. III-IV (hereafter referred to as DBFP); Documents on German Foreign Policy 1918-1945, Series D, vol. IV (hereafter referred to as DGFP); British Public Record Office (hereafter referred to as PRO); Hubert Ripka, *Munich: Before and After* (London: 1939); George F. Kennan, *From Prague After Munich, Diplomatic Papers 1938-1940* (Princeton, N.J.: 1968); Heinrich Bodensieck, "Das Dritte Reich und die Lage der Juden in der Tschecho-Slowakei nach München," *Vierteljahreshefte für Zeitgeschichte,* no. 9 (Stuttgart: 1961), pp. 249-61.
2. Winston S. Churchill, *The Second World War,* vol. I, *The Gathering Storm,* 7th ed. (London: 1965), p. 289.
3. George F. Kennan, *From Prague After Munich,* p. 7.
4. N. Aronovici, "Victims of Fate. Expulsion of Jews from Slovakia," in *Report of American Jewish Joint Distribution Committee* (JDC), November 28, 1938. Personal files of Mr. Moshe Ussoskin, Jerusalem.
5. DBFP, vol. III, pp. 380-81, 559-60, 631-33 (1907-1968).
6. Cabled report from Wilbur J. Carr to the U.S. Secretary of State, Prague, November 25, 1938, National Archives, Washington, D.C., 860 F.4016/61 (NA).
7. Letter from the British minister in Prague, B. C. Newton, to British foreign secretary Lord Halifax, October 26, 1938, PRO No. 366, C 13068/1667/62.
8. Record of a conversation between Count Kinský and R. J. Stopford, reported by J. M. Troutbeck, first secretary at the British Legation in Prague, to Foreign Secretary Lord Halifax, November 15, 1938, PRO No. 397, C 14 188/2475/12 (Enclosure).
9. Report from Wilbur J. Carr. . . .
10. Bohumil Černý, *Most k novému životu; Německá emigrace v Čechách v letech 1933-1939* [A Bridge to New Life: German Emigration to the Czechoslovak Republic 1933-1939] (Prague: 1967); Kurt R. Grossmann, "Refugees to and from Czechoslovakia," in *The Jews of Czechoslovakia: Historical Studies and Surveys,* vol. II (Philadelphia: 1971), pp. 565-81; Manfred George, "Refugees in Prague, 1933-1938," *ibid.,* pp. 582-88.
11. Popper settled in Palestine in 1940 and died in Jerusalem in 1943. The Dr. Joseph Popper Lodge of B'nai B'rith in New York City, founded by refugees from Czechoslovakia, is named after him.
12. See *In Memoriam Marie Schmolka* (London: 1944); 2d ed. (Tel Aviv: 1970).

13. Hanna Steiner remained in Prague until June 1943, when she was deported to Terezín along with other leaders of the Jewish community of the Protectorate of Bohemia and Moravia. She died in Auschwitz in 1944.
14. See also Kurt R. Grossmann, "Refugees to and from Czechoslovakia." ...
15. See also Chaim Yahil, "Social Work in the Historic Lands," in *The Jews of Czechoslovakia*, vol. II, pp. 393–400.
16. Černý, *Most k novému životu*, pp. 23–24.
17. Černý, *Most k novému životu*, p. 178.
18. Cable from Wilbur J. Carr to the U.S. Secretary of State, Prague, November 23, 1938, NA, 840.40. According to the British representative on refugee matters, there were 91,959 refugees, but this number did not include those from the Reich and from Austria, estimated at 5,000, equally divided between Jews and Germans. R. J. Stopford's MS, "Prague 1938/39," part II, Central Zionist Archives (hereafter referred to as CZA), Jerusalem.
19. JDC report, November 28, 1938.
20. Cable from Wilbur J. Carr to the U.S. Secretary of State, October 12, 1938, NA 860 F.918/13.
21. *Ibid.* It was Rudi Thomas, the "live wire and stimulant" of the *Tagblatt* (see vol. II, p. 584), who committed suicide.
22. Report by Marie Schmolka, in charge of HICEM, Prague, on her visit to Camp Mischdorf near Bratislava, November 27, 1938, and other reports on "no-man's land," PRO F.O. 371/21588.
23. See Brod's reminiscences, "A Home in Prague," *In Memoriam Marie Schmolka*, p. 14.
24. *Přítomnost* (The Present), Prague, December 12, 1938.
25. Cable from Wilbur J. Carr to the U.S. Secretary of State, Prague, March 19, 1939, NA 860 F.48/50: Aide Mémoire 860 F.48/51.
26. For Masaryk's attitude toward the Jews see *Masaryk a židovství* (Prague: 1931); German edition: *Masaryk und das Judentum* (both volumes edited by E. Rychnovsky in cooperation with O. Donath and Friedrich Thieberger). For an account of the Hilsner trial, see Hans Kohn, "Before 1918 in the Historic Lands," in *The Jews of Czechoslovakia*, vol. I, p. 17.
27. *Věstník čsl. ligy proti antisemitizmu* [Bulletin of the Czechoslovak League Against Anti-Semitism], vol. II, no. 5, May 1937.
28. *Ibid.*
29. *Přítomnost,* January 19, 1938.
30. *Židovské Zprávy,* Prague, November 11, 1938; *Selbstwehr,* Prague, January 28, 1938, February 25, 1938.

31. For a survey of this group, see Egon Hostovský, "The Czech-Jewish Movement," in *The Jews of Czechoslovakia,* vol. II, pp. 148-54.
32. *Židovské Zprávy,* November 11, 1938.
33. *Věstník židovské obce náboženské v Praze* [Bulletin of the Jewish Religious Congregation in Prague], February 17, 1938, June 23, 1938, November 1, 1938.
34. Fini Brada, "Emigration to Palestine," in *The Jews of Czechoslovakia,* vol. II, pp. 589-98; *Sefer HaMaapilim* (The Book of "Illegal" Immigrants), ed. Moshe Basok (Jerusalem: 1947).
35. G. A. Steiner, *Patria* (Tel Aviv: 1946). The story of the S.S. *Frossula* and her 700 passengers was described by Robert Weil, Yad Vashem Library, 75-209 VIII.
36. B. C. Newton to Lord Halifax, Prague, October 20, 1938, PRO C 15720/2475/12.
37. *Ibid.*
38. George F. Kennan's report to the U.S. Secretary of State on "The Jewish Problem in the New Czechoslovakia," Prague, February 17, 1939, NA 860 F. 4016/68.
39. Kennan, *From Prague After Munich,* p. 62.
40. Kennan's report to the U.S. Secretary of State, February 17, 1939, p. 4.
41. CZA (Central Zionist Archives), Z 4/20. 377 I. See also Fini Brada, "Emigration to Palestine."
42. *Ibid.* Certified English translation of the agreement, CZA, Z 4/20. 377 II.
43. For further details, see Livia Rothkirchen, "The Czechoslovak Government-in-Exile: Jewish and Palestinian Aspects in the Light of Documents," in *Yad Vashem Studies* (YVS), vol. IX, pp. 157-99.
44. *Sbírka zákonů a nařízení Československé Republiky* [Book of Laws and Statutes of the Czechoslovak Republic], vol. I, no. 14-15/39, February 10, 1939; DBFP, IV, p. 8.
45. JDC report, November 28, 1938, p. 16.
46. *Ibid.,* p. 23 (1935-1939).
47. J. M. Troutbeck to Lord Halifax, February 9, 1939, PRO No. 63 C 1868/5/62; Kennan's report to the U.S. Secretary of State, February 17, 1939, p. 4.
48. Kennan's report to the U.S. Secretary of State, February 17, 1939, p. 7. See also *Pariser Zeitung,* December 27, 1938; *Frankfurter Zeitung,* January 12, 1939.
49. The most virulent hatred of the Jews was voiced by the newspapers *Arijský boj, Štít národa,* and *Arijský útok.* See Tomáš Pasák, "Česky antisemitismus na počátku okupace" [Czech Anti-Semitism at the Be-

ginning of the Occupation], *Věda a život* [Life and Science], Brno, March 1969, pp. 147-151. According to a report in *Štít národa,* the Ministry of Internal Affairs, by its Ruling No. 27680, approved the founding of the *Národní arijská kulturní jednota* (National Aryan Cultural Union).
50. *Ibid.*
51. Detlef Brandes, *Die Tschechen unter deutschem Protektorat,* 2 vols. (Munich and Vienna: 1969), vol. I, p. 119.
52. Tomáš Pasák, "Vstup německých vojsk na české území v roce 1939" [The Entry of the German Army into Czech Territory in 1939], *Československý časopis historický* (CCH) [Journal of Czechoslovak History], vol. XVII, no. 2, Brno, 1969.
53. Brandes, *Die Tschechen . . . ,* vol. I, pp. 81-82; Vojtěch Mastný, *Czechs Under Nazi Rule: The Failure of National Resistance 1939-1942* (New York: 1971), p. 88.
54. See the British Vice-Consulate in Prague to the Foreign Secretary, PRO F.O. No. 52/39 (C 11116/5/62).
55. Evidence to this effect in the files of the Olomouc Gestapo, record of November 14, 1941, Yad Vashem Archives (YVA), 0-64; Livia Rothkirchen, "Czech Attitudes Toward the Jews During the Nazi Regime," in *Yad Vashem Studies,* vol. XIII, 1979, pp. 287-320.
56. Brandes, *Die Tschechen . . . ,* vol. I, p. 79.
57. The inhabitants of Horousany and Horouśanky in the district of Český Brod appealed to the Protectorate government on behalf of Dr. Jan Skála Rosenbaum on April 15, 1939; see Karel Lagus and Josef Polák, *Město za mřížemi* [City Behind Bars] (Prague: 1964), photo reproduction of the appeal facing p. 48.
58. Brandes, *Die Tschechen . . . , vol. I, p. 79,* relies on the secret report of the Prague *Sicherheitsdienst* for the period from March 13, 1939, to March 15, 1940.
59. See Pavel Eisner, "Jinoch Exodus" [The Exodus of Youth], in *Židovská ročenka, Rada Židovských náboženských obcí* [Jewish Yearbook, Council of Jewish Religious Congregations] (Prague 5719 [1958/59]), pp. 79-93.
60. Article on Karel Poláček by Václav Vondra in *Práce,* Prague, October 19, 1974.
61. Hana Volavková, "Jewish Artists in the Historic Lands," in *The Jews of Czechoslovakia,* vol. II, p. 489.
62. For a "Who Was Who" in cultural life in the Terezín ghetto, see *Terezín,* eds. F. Ehrmann, O. Heitlinger, R. Iltis (Prague: Council of Jewish Communities in the Czech Lands, 1963).

63. A detailed account of the activities and the fate of these men in the MS by Jan Marek, "Zápisky z boje" [Notes from the Struggle], written in Děčin in 1968, is now in my possession.
64. Brandes, *Die Tschechen*..., vol. I, p. 60.
65. Jan Marek MS, p. 174; Livia Rothkirchen, "The Defiant Few: Jews and the Czech 'Inside Front' (1938–1942)" in *Yad Vashem Studies*, vol. XIV, 1981, pp. 35–88.
66. Jan Marek MS. Apart from some scattered information on Terezín in the years 1934–1944, the published material of the Czech home resistance (Acta I, II) contains no references to the deportations of Jews from the Protectorate.
67. Václav Král, ed., *Lesson from History:* Documents Concerning Nazi Policies for Germanization and Extermination (Prague: 1961), pp. 125–30.
68. Brandes, *Die Tschechen*..., vol. I, p. 243.
69. Jan Masaryk, *Speaking to My Country* (London: 1944), p. 119.
70. *Ibid.,* p. 141; Masaryk's appeal to the Czech people on the occasion of the Jewish New Year 5704 (1943).
71. H. G. Adler, *Die verheimlichte Wahrheit* (*Theresienstädter Dokumente*) (Tübingen: 1958), p. 305.
72. *Two Years of German Oppression in Czechoslovakia* (London: Czechoslovak Ministry of Foreign Affairs, Department of Information, 1941), p. 80.
73. See J. W. Brügel, *Tschechen und Deutsche 1939–1946* (Munich: 1974), p. 121.
74. *Der Neue Tag,* November 7, 1943, listed their names as follows: František Kučera (born Prague, 1909); Petr and Thomas Řiháček (both of Străsnice); Jan Sedloň (born Radiow, 1904); Jaroslav Klemeš (born Sudoměřice, 1896); Elsa Taussig (born Leipzig, 1885); František Šedivý (born Prague, 1896); Marie Pospíšilova (born Prague, 1917). See National Archives, OSS, November 25, 1943.
75. Quoted in Pasák, "Vstup německých vojsk...," p. 151.
76. This subject merits a separate study. It is worth noting that the files of the Yad Vashem Department of Righteous Gentiles contain acccunts of Czechs aiding Jews in their plight (Files 426/705; 1361/624).
77. At the end of the war 325 localities in Bohemia and Moravia where flourishing Jewish communities had existed for many centuries were *judenrein*. For an account of the revival of Jewish religious congregations in Bohemia and Moravia and the reconstruction of Jewish communal life, see Kurt Wehle, "The Jews in Bohemia and Moravia: 1945–1948," in the present volume, pp. 499–530.
78. See Pasák, "Vstup německých vojsk..."

79. Mastný, *Czechs Under Nazi Rule,* p. 88.
80. Ladislav Feierabend, *Ve vládě protektorátu* [In the Government of the Protectorate] (New York: 1962; in Czech), p. 14.
81. Plamínková was executed during the Heydrich terror in February 1942. See *Heroes and Victims* (London: Czechoslovak Ministry of Foreign Affairs, Information Service, 1945), p. 110.
82. For the text of the decree, see Gerhard Jacoby, *Racial State* (New York: 1944), pp. 318-22.
83. Mastný, *Czechs under Nazi Rule,* pp. 60, 154-55.
84. *Ibid.,* p. 87; Brandes, *Die Tschechen* . . . , pp. 45-46.
85. Report on Bohemia and Moravia, File Czechoslovakia 1939-1940, American Jewish Joint Distribution Committee Archives (JDCA), New York.
86. Report of Josef Fischer, May 21-28, 1939, on the internal political and economic situation, sent from Prague by the underground *Politické Ústřední-PU* (Political Center) to the Czechoslovak government-in-exile in London. See Acta II, p. 428.
87. *Ibid.,* p. 435.
88. Testimony of Franz Fischof, September 17, 1945. From the collection of the postwar Prague Documentation Project (*Dokumentační Akce*), now at YVA, Jerusalem, DA collection, Zeev Shek collection in Yad Vashem, YVA 0-64.
89. *Ibid.*
90. Report of Josef Fischer, May 29, 1939, Acta II, pp. 433-39.
91. See Moses Moskowits, "The Jewish Situation in the Protectorate of Bohemia and Moravia," *Jewish Social Studies* IV, January 1942, p. 18.
92. See *Verordnungsblatt des Reichsprotektors in Böhmen und Mähren* [Gazette of the Reich Protector in Bohemia and Moravia] (VOBL R. Prot.); Jacoby, *Racial State,* p. 212. See also John Lexa, "Anti-Jewish Laws and Regulations in the Protectorate," in the present volume, pp. 75-103.
93. For details on the Germanization scheme, see Král, *Lesson from History.*
94. Kennan, *From Prague After Munich,* pp. 192-93.
95. Lagus and Polák, *Město za mřížemi,* p. 41.
96. After February 1940, the jurisdiction of the *Zentralstelle* was extended over the whole territory of the Protectorate. (VOBL R. Prot. No. 21, March 5, 1940). On August 20, 1942, the *Zentralstelle* was renamed *Zentralamt für die Regelung der Judenfrage in Böhmen und Mähren* (Central Office for the Settlement of the Jewish Problem in Bohemia and Moravia).

97. For a map showing the Jewish religious congregations according to this new district administrative division, see appendix, "Die neuen Sprengel der Kultusgemeinden in Böhmen und Mähren," from personal files of Maximilian Spell (Spiegel), Jerusalem.
98. Ordinance of June 21, 1939, VOBL R.P., 1939, pp. 45-49; Mastný, *Czechs Under Nazi Rule,* p. 91; documents pertinent to Eichmann's evacuation campaign emanating from the Central State Archives in Prague (*Státní Ústředni Archiv-SÚA*) were published by O. D. Kulka in *Yalkut Moreshet,* no. 18, November 1974, Tel Aviv, pp. 170-182.
99. O. D. Kulka, *ibid.* See also *Wochenberich der Jüdischen Kultusgemeinde in Prag,* July 30-August 5, 1939, YVA 07/10-1.
100. SÚA documents, see note 98.
101. Jacoby, *Racial State,* p. 237.
102. Richard Feder, *Židovská tragedie, dějstvi poslední* [The Jewish Tragedy: The Final Act] (Kolín: 1947), p. 22; Acta II, p. 428.
103. Feder, *Židovská tragedie,* p. 29; testimony of Margit Galat (née Hutter), YVA, E 2.
104. For the documentation of the Gestapo in Moravská Ostrava, see *Nazi-Dokumente Sprechen* (Prague: 1966), and the file of the *Reichssicherheitshauptamt* (RSHA) on the Nisko campaign in YVA, DN/30-1.
105. See J. Zehngut, *Dějini Židovstva ostravského* [The History of the Jews of Ostrava], 1952.
106. Edelstein's report was recorded in the diary of Moshe Sharett (Shertok), entry for February 2, 1940, CZA, S25/198/4: 192/3, quoted in Livia Rothkirchen, "The Zionist Character of the Self-Government of Terezín, A Study in Historiography," in YVS, vol. xi, 1976, pp. 67-70.
107. Rothkirchen, "The Zionist Character . . . ," p. 69.
108. For the testimonies of some of these individuals, see YVA 0-59; E/69-2-3; 0-3/2640; 0-33/1132.
109. H. G. Adler, *Der verwaltete Mensch, Studien zur Deportation der Juden aus Deutschland* (Tübingen: 1974), p. 140.
110. Memorandum by State Secretary Ernst Freiherr von Weizsäcker on a conversation with Colonel General Wilhelm Keitel, December 5, 1939, DGFP, vol. VIII, Doc. 419, p. 487.
111. Of 1,291 men sent to Nisko from Moravská Ostrava, 460 returned to Ostrava when the camp was dissolved in April 1940. Two years later these were deported to Terezín and from there to the East. See Lagus and Polák, *Město za mřížemi,* p. 300.
112. Erich Kulka, "Jews in Czechoslovak Armed Forces During World War II," in the present volume, pp. 389-426.

113. Leopold Chmela, *The Economic Aspects of the German Occupation of Czechoslovakia* (Prague: 1948), p. 104.
114. For a detailed account, see Raul Hilberg, *The Destruction of European Jews: A Documented Narrative History* (Chicago: 1961), pp. 66–81. According to the assessment of Walter Utermöhle and Herbert Schmerling of the Office of the Reich Protector, there were in the territory of Bohemia and Moravia about 30,000 establishments, factories, and shops in Jewish ownership with a total value of about 17 billion crowns. For a systematic survey of anti-Jewish legislation enacted up to August 15, 1940, compiled by these two officials, see *Právní postavení Židů v Protektorátu Čechy a Morava* [The Legal Status of the Jews in the Protectorate of Bohemia and Moravia] (Prague: 1940), p. 13.
115. The occupational structure of this Jewry conformed to that of the Jews in the western part of Europe. In 1930 about fifty-eight percent of all Jews in Bohemia and Moravia-Silesia were classified as gainfully employed; this category comprised 67,168 persons, of whom 47,334 were males and 19,834 females. The largest group (30,021) earned their livelihood in commerce, banking, insurance, communications, and transportation, in that order. Second in importance were those engaged in manufacturing industries (12,520), particularly in clothing (2,955) and foods (2,017). A total of 7,486 Jews were classified in the category "professions and public service"; of these, all but a small number were practicing professionals. See Moses Moskowits, "The Jewish Situation . . . " *Jewish Social Studies* IV, January 1942, p. 34. See also Joseph C. Pick, "The Economy," in *The Jews of Czechoslovakia*, vol. I, p. 359.
116. See report of the Böhmische Escompte Bank in Prague on Aryanizations carried out in Bohemia and Moravia from March 1939 to April 1941 (Prague, August 1941) in *Trials of War Criminals Before the Nuremberg Military Tribunals,* vol. XIII, pp. 671–74 (NID-13463).
117. VOBL. R. P., p. 45; Jacoby, *Racial State,* pp. 203–20.
118. Jacoby, *Racial State,* p. 218. See also Karel Kratochvíl, *Bankéři* [Bankers] (Prague: 1962).
119. Kratochvíl, *Bankéři,* pp. 213–14.
120. Ordinance of March 5, 1940; Jacoby, *Racial State,* p. 234.
121. Kennan, *From Prague After Munich,* p. 233.
122. *Ibid.*
123. Pertinent documents from the Central State Archives in Prague (SÚA) quoted in Miroslav Kárný, "Terezínský koncentrační tábor v plánech nacistů" [The Terezín Concentration Camp in the Plans of the Nazis], CCH, vol. XXII, no. 5, 1974, p. 685.

124. *Ibid.*
125. Kennan, *From Prague After Munich,* p. 189; Chmela, *The Economic Aspects . . . ,* pp. 64–65.
126. Göring to Heydrich, PS-710.
127. Jewish Religious Congregation (JKG), *Jahresbericht* [Annual Report] *1941,* see *Věstník* No. 51/52, 1951; H. G. Adler, *Theresienstadt 1941–1945: Das Antlitz einer Zwangsgemeinschaft* (Tübingen: 1960), pp. 64–65, 753.
128. In this letter, Himmler entrusted Heydrich with the task of carrying out the proposed evacuations. See Himmler's letter addressed to Reichsstatthalter Greiser, Himmler files, No. 94, MS Division, U.S. Library of Congress, Washington, D.C.
129. For a list of concentration camps, see Lagus and Polák, *Město za mřížemi,* pp. 356–61.
130. *Věstník,* no. 7, 1958; Adler, *Theresienstadt 1941–1945,* pp. 720–22.
131. Lagus and Polák, *Město za mřížemi,* p. 61.
132. For notes on the discussion on future planning in the Protectorate of Bohemia and Moravia, see Král, *Lesson from History,* pp. 125–30.
133. *Ibid.*
134. The Jewish Religious Congregation presented an elaborate scheme entitled "Ghettoisierung der Juden im Protektorat;" see Adler, *Theresienstadt 1941–1945,* p. 31.
135. Adler, *ibid.*
136. See note 20; Lagus and Polák, *Město za mřížemi,* p. 60.
137. See Appendices. See also Zdeněk Lederer, *Terezín,* in the present volume, pp. 104–64.
138. Feder, *Židovská tragedie,* p. 36.
139. Lagus and Polák, *Město za mřížemi,* pp. 71–73.
140. Adler, *Theresienstadt 1941–1945,* p. 44.
141. A detailed graphic illustration of the timetable and procedure, "Abfertigungsvorgang bei Abwanderung der Juden nach Tagen und Arbeitsstellen," undated, in the files of Maximilian Spell (Spiegel), Jerusalem.
142. Testimony of Margit Galat (nee Hutter), YVA E/2.
143. Feder, *Židovská tragedie,* p. 35.
144. E.g. *Jüdisches Nachrichtenblatt* (JNBL), No. 52, December 25, 1942, advertised thirty-two physicians and nine dentists; in No. 24, December 15, 1944, there were only ten physicians and three dentists.
145. Král, *Lesson from History,* pp. 119–20.
146. *Abschlussbericht. Attentat auf SS-Obergruppenführer Heydrich am 27.5. 1942 in Prag,* p. 10, Occ E7(a)5, YIVO, New York; Jaroslav

Drabek, "The Assassination of Reinhard Heydrich," in *Czechoslovakia Past and Present*, ed. Miloslav Rechcigl, vol. I (The Hague and Paris: 1968), p. 766.
147. Rechcigl, *ibid.* See also *Heroes and Victims* (London: 1945).
148. Feder, *Židovská tragedie;* Lagus and Polák, *Město za mřížemi,* pp. 310-11.
149. Jacoby, *Racial State,* p. 257.
150. J. Grnová, *Svatobořický tábor* [The Svatobořice Camp] (Brno: 1948).
151. Jacoby, *Racial State,* pp. 245-46.
152. Feuerstein headed a group of young people who were caught and executed; see *Sefer HaShomer HaTzair* [HaShomer HaTzair Book] (Merhavia: 1956), vol. I, p. 758.
153. This report, a unique document of some 2,000 words written in German, is quoted here only in part. It was sent abroad anonymously; the author's identity was confirmed by the testimony of Heda Türk and Moshe Leshem (Arnošt Lemberger) (YVA E/199).
154. For a comprehensive survey, see Gustav Fleischmann, "The Religious Congregations 1918-1938," in *The Jews of Czechoslovakia,* vol. I, pp. 267-329.
155. The Jewish community embraced all Jews, *Glaubensjuden* (individuals who considered themselves Jews) and *Geltungsjuden* (individuals who did not consider themselves Jews but were classed as such by others), regardless of whether or not they practiced any religion. See *Jüdisches Nachrichtenblatt* (JNBL), No. 2, December 1, 1939.
156. *Report on Bohemia and Moravia 1939-1940,* American Jewish Joint Distribution Committee (JDC) Archives, New York, File Czechoslovakia 1939-1940 (JDCA).
157. *Ibid.*
158. This committee was set up in 1938. Other organizations established to aid refugees in England were the Federation of Czechoslovakian Jews, the HICEM Group at the Czech Refugee Trust Fund, the Maccabi Aid Committee, the Self-Aid Association of Jews from Bohemia, Moravia, and Slovakia in England. In October 1939 all these joined to form a Joint Committee of Jews from Czechoslovakia in England. See files CZA, Z4/20376 I.
159. See Chapter I, CZA, Z4/20. 377 I.
160. Most of our information on the activities of the Jewish Religious Congregation during that period is based on the weekly reports (*Wochenberichte*) and the overall situation reports (*Lageberichte*) which the Jewish Religious Congregation in Prague submitted to the *Zentralstelle* between July 1939 and December 1942. *Wochenbericht* No. 12, March 16-22, 1940. YVA, 07/10-1.

161. Other leading personalities in the Jewish Religious Congregation during the initial period of German occupation were the Zionists Dr. Franz Kahn and Dr. František Friedmann and the representatives of the Czech-Jewish movement, Dr. O. Guth, Dr. Neuwirth, and the architect Bittermann.
162. "Die Juden zur Zeit des Protektorates in Böhmen und Mähren-Schlesien," recorded by Friedrich Thieberger after a series of interviews with Dr. Karel Stein, chairman of the Jewish Religious Congregation of Prague after the war. Stein emigrated to Israel in 1949 and died in Jerusalem in 1961. (Stein MS, 22 pp.).
163. Jewish Religious Congregation (JKG) *Wochenbericht* No. 4, August 13–19, 1939, YVA, 07/10-1.
164. *Ibid.*
165. Jewish Religious Congregation (JKG) *Lagebericht,* April 1, 1941, YVA, 07/11-2.
166. Report sent by Jakub Edelstein from Prague to Eliyahu Dobkin, Jewish Agency, Jerusalem, December 12, 1939, CZA, S25/2379. The breakdown of these totals is as follows: Agriculture, 844 (Bohemia: 387, Moravia: 457); handicrafts, 3,025 (Bohemia: 2,224, Moravia: 801); industrial arts, 1,354 (Bohemia: 661, Moravia: 693); innkeeping, 871 (Bohemia: 456, Moravia: 415); foreign languages, 858 (Bohemia: 533, Moravia: 325). See "Die jüdische Kultusgemeinde und das Palästinaamt," Prague, December 31, 1940, pp. 5–6, Yad Vashem Library, sign. 10.154.
167. Jewish Religious Congregation (JKG) *Lagebericht,* April 1, 1941, YVA, 07/11-2.
168. See Statistical Tables in Appendices.
169. Report sent by Jakub Edelstein to Eliyahu Dobkin, December 12, 1939, CZA, S25/2379.
170. Jewish Religious Congregation (JKG) *Lagebericht,* April 1, 1941, YVA, 07/11-2.
171. American Jewish Joint Distribution Committee Archives (JDCA), File Czechoslovakia 1939–1940.
172. Report of December 9, 1940, YVA, DA collection.
173. Edelstein sent letters and postcards from his trips to Dr. Fritz Ullmann in Geneva. See CZA, A-370/44.
174. Most of the issues of this weekly are available at the Yad Vashem Library and Archives. The role of the weekly is discussed in an indepth study, "Židovské Listy v letech 1939–1944" [The Jewish Weekly During the Years 1939–1944], an unpublished dissertation by Zdeněk Jirotka at the Faculty of Journalism, Charles University, Prague.

175. One such editorial was entitled "Mit dem Herzen denken" [Thinking with One's Heart], JNBL, October 17, 1941.
176. JNBL, November 24, 1939.
177. JNBL, March 15, 1940, April 4, 1941; Jacoby, *Racial State,* pp. 233–34; Philip Friedmann, "Aspects of the Jewish Communal Crisis in the Period of the Nazi Regime in Germany, Austria, and Czechoslovakia," in *Essays on Jewish Life and Thought (Presented in Honor of Salo Wittmayer Baron),* ed. J. L. Blau (New York: 1959), p. 214.
178. The chairman of the Jewish Religious Congregation and his deputy were assisted by the Central Secretariat, the Control Department, and the Legal Department. The Central Secretariat was in charge of the office for contacts with authorities, the office dealing with Jewish religious congregations outside Prague, the Personnel Department, the Statistical Office, the Organization Department, and the Press Department (the latter was closed in 1941). After 1943, statistical and legal matters were transferred to a newly created Record Department. The administration was divided into two branches: the Finance Department and the Economic Administration. Other departments were the Department for Religious Affairs, the Social Welfare Department, the Department for Culture and Schools, the Emigration Department, the Central Labor Office, the Department for Jews of Non-Mosaic Faith, the *Treuhandstelle* (a trusteeship office created by order of the *Zentralstelle* for the purpose of registering and gathering Jewish property), the Information Department, and the so-called "H" Department, a small special department that worked directly under the orders of the *Zentralstelle,* to check and verify declarations made by Jews concerning their assets.
179. JNBL, July 26, 1940.
180. Czech: *"Darovat-budovat-žít!"* German: *"Opfern-Aufbauen-Leben!",* JNBL, November 24, 1939.
181. Norbert Frýd, *Lahvová pošta, aneb konec posledních sto let* [The Bottle Post, or The End of the Last One Hundred Years] (Prague: 1971), pp. 116–17.
182. *Ibid.,* p. 119.
183. *Ibid.,* p. 116.
184. *Ibid.,* p. 113; this incident was recorded in the trial of Karl Rahm, see *Věstník,* IX, nos. 12, 17, 1947.
185. Report of the *Ältestenrat der Juden in Prag* to the *Zentralamt* on emigration and deportations from the Protectorate, Prague, June 19, 1944. Documents submitted at the Eichmann trial, YVA, E 1237.
186. Jewish Religious Congregation (JKG) *Lagebericht* for the first half of 1940, YVA, 07/10-3. But see also *Bericht über das Jahr 1943,* in which

the *Ältestenrat der Juden* states that the Jewish population of Bohemia and Moravia was 97,961 at the end of 1939 and only 90,041 at the end of 1940.
187. Jewish Religious Congregation (JKG) *Lagebericht* for the first quarter of 1941, YVA, 07/10-3.
188. *Ibid.*
189. "Die jüdische Kultusgemeinde und das Palästinaamt," p. 6. See also Lagus and Polák, *Město za mřížemi,* p. 38.
190. For an account of the activities of this department, see Adler, *Die verheimlichte Wahrheit,* pp. 77-85.
191. *Ibid.,* pp. 84-85.
192. Lagus and Polák, *Město za mřížemi,* pp. 65-75; see also "Standmeldung zum 21. September, 1943" [Situation Report as of September 21, 1943], in Adler, *Die verheimlichte Wahrheit,* pp. 77-81.
193. See Hana Volavková, "The Jewish Museum in Prague," in the present volume, pp. 567-583.
194. YVA, E 1237.
195. MS Josef Löwenherz, Vienna, 1945. See Adler, *Die verheimlichte Wahrheit,* p. 11; YVA, E T/1156.
196. *Ibid.* See also Adler, *Theresienstadt 1941-1945,* p. 774.
197. Franz (František) Friedmann, *Rechtsstellung der Juden im Protektorat Böhmen und Mähren, I, Stand zum 31.7.42. (Für internen Gebrauch der Jüdischen Kultusgemeinde in Prag),* YVA 0-64.
198. Many of the letters that reached Jewish organizations abroad during 1942 and 1943 are now in the archives of the Labor Zionist movement (ALM) in Tel Aviv, and in the CZA and YVA in Jerusalem.
199. Letter of Heinz (Schuster) and Lazar (Moldavan) sent from Prague on May 19, 1943, to Geneva, YVA, JM/1698.
200. Some entries from Prossnitz's diary and some of his extensive correspondence with Terezín and the outside world have been salvaged. See YVA, 07/18; 0/19.
201. Erika Wolf's testimony given in Prague after the war has been preserved in the YVA 0-64.
202. For Prossnitz's correspondence, see YVA 07/18-1.
203. Testimony of Franz Fischof, YVA, 0-64.
204. Adler, *Theresienstadt 1941-1945,* p. 740.
205. *Ibid.,* p. 741.
206. *Ibid.,* pp. 739-40.
207. See YVA, 10-64.
208. See report of Jewish Religious Congregation (JKG) to the *Zentralstelle,* June 19, 1944, YVA, E 1237.
209. *Ibid.*

210. There are minor discrepancies in the various statistical sources. According to an official German estimate of January 31, 1945, the number of part Jews (the so-called *Arisch versippten Juden*) was 7,046. Of these, 3,060 were in Prague and 3,386 in the provinces; a total of 3,902 were males and 3,144 females. See YVA, 0-64.
211. Feder, *Židovská tragedie*, p. 92.
212. Report of the *Ältestenrat der Juden in Prag* to the *Zentralamt für die Regelung der Judenfrage in Böhmen und Mähren*, prepared on the order of Obersturmführer Girczik, YVA, 0-64.
213. *Ibid.*
214. Survey compiled by the *Ältestenrat der Juden in Prag*, YVA, DA collection.
215. The report of Dr. Arnošt Neumann sent from Bratislava (September 5, 1943) to Geneva mentions the following members of *HeHalutz* as living in hiding: Heda Türk, Jonah Farkas, Ernst Kruh, Arnošt Lemberger, Chaja Roth, Narzissenfeld, Elie Friedmann, Raffi Fischer; see ALM.
216. This information is based on the testimony of Heda Türk (YVA, E 199) and on information given to me personally by Moshe Leshem (Arnošt Lemberger) of Jerusalem, who, together with his colleague, was employed as a teacher at the School of Modern Languages in Prague and maintained contact with the Czech underground. I am grateful to Mr. Leshem for confirming some of the data and identity of *HeHalutz* members.
217. E.g., "The Return," in *Night and Hope* (Iowa City: 1973).
218. Adler, *Theresienstadt 1941–1945*, p. 15.
219. Eight hundred and twenty of the survivors were of the Jewish faith; of these, thirty-eight percent were children of mixed marriages under the age of fourteen, who were just about to be deported when the war ended. See Peter Meyer, *et al.*, in Chapter 1, "Czechoslovakia," in *The Jews in the Soviet Satellites* (Syracuse: 1953), p. 62.

ANTI-JEWISH LAWS AND REGULATIONS IN THE PROTECTORATE OF BOHEMIA AND MORAVIA

John G. Lexa

A survey of anti-Jewish laws and regulations during the Nazi occupation of Bohemia and Moravia in 1939–45 can give only a partial insight into the conditions under which Jews lived during that period. It can provide only an inkling of the day-and-night regime of terror of which many aspects are not at all reflected in the official legislation: from the early orders commanding Jews to shovel snow at Ruzyně airport, to the manner in which Jews were forced to collaborate in the systematic inventorying, storage and delivery to German authorities of furniture and other personal property left behind by Jews deported to Terezín or to the extermination camps. The laws make no reference to the organization of "transports" and to the individual and wholesale killings, nor to the manner in which the Nazi authorities, dispensing with formal confiscation procedures, compelled Jews to surrender their property "voluntarily," first piecemeal in individual cases and then wholesale by the thousands, when Jews prior to their deportation had to sign over to the Nazi authorities whatever was left of their assets. The persecution and harrassment reflected in the official legislation were, in fact, merely the tip of the iceberg.

Since the present study is to deal with conditions in the Protectorate of Bohemia and Moravia only, it will not cover conditions in the German-speaking border areas occupied by Nazi forces as early as October 1938, as an immediate result of the Munich agreement signed the month before. At that time the majority of Jews residing in the border areas fled to the central parts of Bohemia and Moravia, which then still belonged to the post-Munich Republic of Czecho-Slovakia. Those who were able to do so, emigrated. Those few who remained in the border areas which became known as the Sudetenland soon discovered they had made a mistake. In November 1938, following the Grynszpan affair,* they were rounded up and sent to concentration camps.

By the time Bohemia and Moravia (or what was left of them after the incorporation of the Sudetenland into the Reich) were occupied by the Germans on March 15, 1939, anti-Jewish legislation had been developing in Germany for six years.[1] It is no wonder, therefore, that Hitler's order establishing the Protectorate of Bohemia and Moravia[2] made specific reference to the Nuremberg Laws of 1935.[3] The First Regulation implementing the Nuremberg Citizenship Law[4] was the first in which the Nazi definitions of Jews and "persons of mixed (part-Jewish) blood" were legally codified.

DEFINITION AND IDENTIFICATION OF JEWS AND *MISCHLINGE* (PERSONS OF MIXED BLOOD OR JEWISH "HALF-CASTES")

The Nazi definitions of who was, and who was not, a Jew were officially promulgated in the Protectorate, with "retroactive effect to March 15, 1939," in the Regulation concerning Jewish Property, issued by the Reich Protector in Bohemia and Moravia on June 21, 1939,[5] followed by the Government Regulation of the Protectorate Government dated July 4, 1939, but actually issued only on April 24, 1940,[6] and reiterated by a regulation of the Protectorate government dated March 7, 1942.[7] Although Nazi doctrine claimed the existence of basic racial differences between Jews and "Aryans," the statutory definition of Jews found itself compelled in part to specify religious differences[8] in the case of both Jews and *Mischlinge;* i.e., persons of mixed blood or Jewish "half-castes."[9] On March 1, 1940,

---

* Herschel Grynszpan, a boy of seventeen, was deeply affected by the sufferings of his parents, who were among the Jews deported from Germany to a no-man's land on the Polish frontier. As an act of protest, he shot Ernst vom Rath, secretary of the German embassy in Paris, in November 1938. The *Kristallnacht* pogroms were the German "revenge" for the shooting.

all persons who were regarded as Jews under these definitions were ordered to report to police headquarters for the purpose of having the first page of their identification cards (*občanská legitimace, Bürgerlegitimation*) stamped with a large capital "J."[10]

Eighteen months later this identification of Jews was no longer considered conspicuous enough. Under a police regulation issued by Reinhard Heydrich, then head of the German Security Police, and dated September 1, 1941,[11] all Jews above the age of six were ordered to wear in public a large yellow Star of David with the lettering *Jude* (Jew) in black. This badge had to be permanently sewn to the left front of all outer garments. Section 3 of this police regulation exempted the following "privileged Jews" from wearing the yellow star: (a) Jewish men married to German "Aryan" women, provided they had children who were not considered Jews or (b) Jewish women married to German "Aryan" men. (However, these wives were exempt from wearing the yellow star only for the duration of the marriage, regardless of whether or not there were children.) The non-Jewish spouse in each case had to be a German citizen of German ethnicity. Jews married to non-Jews who were Czechs or members of other non-German ethnic groups were not exempt from wearing the star.

SEGREGATION OF JEWS FROM THE NON-JEWISH POPULATION

While persecution and harassment of individual Jews started in the Protectorate from the very first day of the German occupation, March 15, 1939, systematic and official efforts to "protect" the non-Jewish population from the "dangers" of any contacts with Jews did not begin until the summer of 1939. In the meantime, the Gestapo was busy issuing exit permits (*Durchlassscheine*)[12] to Jews who were able to emigrate, leaving their property behind. Also, the elimination of Jews from certain professions had begun[13] and the first measures concerning Jewish property[14] were enacted. On July 21, 1939, Reich Protector Constantin von Neurath issued an order organizing a *"Zentralstelle für jüdische Auswanderung"* (Central Office for Jewish Emigration),[15] hereafter referred to as the *Zentralstelle*, headed by the commander of the Security Police of the Reich Protector's office. This *Zentralstelle* became the center for the persecution and harassment of Jews throughout the period of German occupation. The campaign to "protect" the non-Jewish population from any contact with Jews opened in August 1939. On August 5, restaurant owners were ordered to serve Jews only in separate rooms reserved for Jewish patrons.[16] Shortly thereafter, police headquarters in Prague issued a proclamation[17] prohibiting the admission of Jews to specified restaurants. Restaurants or parts thereof which were declared off limits to Jews had to be conspicuously marked as such. The presence of Jews in areas marked "Off Limits to Jews" was prohibited and punishable. Jews were no longer allowed to use municipal and other public swimming and bathing areas; hospitals, homes for the aged, and similar institutions were ordered to segregate Jewish patients from non-Jewish patients and to see to it that Jews and non-Jews should not use their facilities at the same time. Six months later, Jews were excluded from access to theaters and motion picture theaters.[18] In May 1940 this prohibition was extended to public parks and gardens in Prague,[19] and in July 1940 to river steamboats.

In August 1940 the harassment was intensified by the imposition of restricted shopping hours for Jewish shoppers in non-Jewish stores.[20] At the same time the separate "Jewish areas" in restaurants and other public places were discontinued and the establishments were ordered to cater either to Jews or to non-Jews only.[21] The next month Jews were excluded from access to hotels in Prague, except for two, the "Fiser" and the "Star."[22]

Jews were prohibited to enter any wooded areas owned by the municipality of Prague[23] and were permitted to travel on city streetcars only in the second car. If the second car had a second door in the center, they were allowed to use only the rear section.[24] In December 1940 Prague police headquarters started a new line of harassment—Jews were forbidden to set foot in certain streets, in this case in the vicinity of the Produce Exchange, on the days when the exchange was open for business.[25] The idea caught on. Jews were not permitted on the banks of the river Vltava (Moldau),[26] in the vicinity of Hradčány Palace,[27] and on public thoroughfares which ran through some small parks in the center of the city.[28] In June 1942 certain main thoroughfares, too, were declared off limits to Jews from 3 P.M. on Saturdays until 8 A.M. on Mondays.[29] In June 1941 service for Jews in barber shops was limited to the hours from

8 to 10 A.M.[30] In September public libraries and lending libraries were declared off limits to Jews.[31] Later that month Jews were informed that they could no longer enter any post offices in Greater Prague except for the one on Ostrovní Street in the city's Second District, and even that only between the hours of 1 and 3 P.M.[32] Further restrictions of the use by Jews of railroads, streetcars, and buses followed.[33] In December 1941 the prohibition barring Jews from libraries was extended to include museums, exhibitions, galleries, archives, and auction sales.[34] In February 1942 Jews were excluded from all laundries and cleaning establishments.[35] In May 1942 Jews were barred from all barber shops and beauty parlors, and barbers and hairdressers were prohibited to go to serve Jewish patrons at their homes.[36] The Protectorate Government Regulation of March 7, 1942, dealing with the relations between Jews and the non-Jewish population[37] prohibited female citizens of the Protectorate under the age of forty-five to accept employment in households that included a Jewish adult. Those already employed in such households could remain if they had reached the age of thirty-five by July 1, 1942. In June 1942 additional restrictions on the use of railroads by Jews were issued.[38] In August 1942 Jews were forbidden to visit non-Jewish cemeteries.[39] Treatment of Jewish patients by non-Jewish physicians and the admission of Jews to hospitals were limited to emergencies, with Jewish and non-Jewish patients kept strictly segregated.[40] A decree issued on October 7, 1942, prohibited Jews from using taxicabs or other passenger vehicles.[41] Access by Jews to streetcars in Prague was further limited effective November 1, 1942.[42]

A curfew for Jews, in force every night from 8 P.M. until the next morning, was imposed in September 1939.[43] Effective November 1, 1940, Jews were forbidden to leave their places of residence (either permanently or temporarily) except by special permission of the *Zentralstelle*.[44] In January 1941 Jews residing within Greater Prague or Brno (Moravia) were required to turn in their driver's licenses; driving schools were forbidden to accept Jews as students.[45] Under the terms of Heydrich's police regulation of September 1, 1941,[46] which required Jews to wear the yellow star, Jews wishing to go anywhere outside the immediate neighborhood of their homes had to carry with them a written permit from the local police. Such a permit could be issued only by the *Zentralstelle*. In January 1941 residential telephones of Jews were disconnected, except for those of Jewish attorneys, physicians, midwives, and hospitals, and those of the offices of the Jewish Religious Congregation. Other exceptions were made upon certification by the Jewish Religious Congregation and with the consent of the local police.[47] A year later Jews were forbidden to use public telephones of any kind[48] and a few weeks thereafter even telephones of non-Jewish subscribers sharing a household with Jews were disconnected.[49]

JEWISH PROPERTY AND BUSINESS CONCERNS

Though the sale or transfer of Jewish property, including Jewish business enterprises, had already been prohibited shortly after the occupation of Bohemia and Moravia and the establishment of the Protectorate,[50] comprehensive provisions were issued, partly with retroactive effect to March 15, 1939, in a regulation issued by the Reich Protector under date of June 21, 1939.[51] All sales and transfers of Jewish-owned real property, businesses, and interests therein as well as of securities now required prior written permission.[52] All agricultural and forest lands owned by Jews had to be reported to the office of the *Oberlandrat* (County Administration) by July 31, 1939.[53] Jews were forbidden to acquire real estate or interests in business enterprises or securities.[54] All gold, silver, platinum, pearls, and other jewelry owned by Jews had to be reported by July 31, 1939, along with art objects valued (per piece or per collection) in excess of Kč 10,000.[55] The Reich Protector could appoint *Treuhänder* (custodians) for the administration of Jewish property. Under a *Durchführungserlass* (implementing decree) of the same date[56] the authority to grant permission for the sale or transfer of businesses employing less than 100 persons or whose annual sales did not exceed Kč 3,000,000 (except banks and insurance companies) was transferred to the offices of the *Oberlandrat*.[57] In September 1939 all radio sets owned by Jews were confiscated.[58] On October 4, 1939, the German government issued a "Regulation concerning the Confiscation of Property in the Protectorate of Bohemia and Moravia."[59] This law was not explicitly limited to Jewish property,[60] but it was widely implemented in the confiscation of property owned by Jews.[61] In November 1939 the Treasury Department of the Protectorate decreed that rentals for real property owned by Jews had to be paid into frozen bank accounts from which funds could be withdrawn only with the consent of the local tax administration.[62] In January 1940 this arrangement was extended to all payments into bank accounts owned by Jews. Transfers of savings accounts or securities owned by Jews required the consent of the Treasury Department, as did withdrawals from Jewish-owned safe deposit boxes. Banks had to report to the Treasury Department all Jewish safe deposit boxes rented after March 15, 1939. Without a special permit from the Treasury Department Jews could withdraw no more than Kč 1,500 per week from their frozen accounts for use by themselves and their families.[63] In March 1940 all these restrictions were extended also to non-Jews married to Jews.[64] Within two weeks all Jewish-owned securities, gold, silver, and platinum objects, jewelry, and pearls had to be placed into sealed safe deposit boxes from which they could be withdrawn only by special official permission. The same obligation was applicable also to the property of non-Jews merely kept by Jews for their use and vice versa.

In January 1940 the Reich Protector issued a "Regulation concerning the Elimination of Jews from the Economy of the Protectorate." Pursuant to Section 2 of this regulation, Jewish business concerns could be forbidden to conduct economic activities of any kind.[65] An implementing regulation of the same date made this prohibition applicable to all Jewish retail businesses dealing in textiles, footwear, and leather goods, effective April 30, 1940.[66] Jews were "permitted" (read "forced") to sell their gold, silver, platinum, pearls, and jewelry to the HADEGA Company on Hybernská 32, Prague II, upon prior "written permission."[67] Pursuant to a regulation dated February 7, 1940, Jewish businesses had to report all the property (including property located in foreign countries) which they owned as of December 31, 1939. All real property and all shares and other interests in business enterprises owned by Jews or their non-Jewish spouses had to be reported by March 13, 1940.[68] In March 1940 the prohibition under the Reich Protector's "Regulation concerning the Elimination of Jews from the Economy of the Protectorate" was extended, effective April 15, 1940, to the entire motion picture industry.[69] In July 1940 the Reich Protector decreed that any contract for the assumption of the management of Jewish property was subject to approval by and registration at the Office of the Reich Protector.[70] Exceptions could be made in the case of properties with a gross value not in excess of Kč 100,000. In September 1940 new regulations were issued for the reporting of valuables [71] and securities owned by Jews or their non-Jewish spouses. [72] A proclamation by the Treasury Department of the Protectorate in November 1940 ordered Jews to transfer all their savings deposits into frozen (non-interest-bearing) current accounts by December 31, 1940; if the depositor failed to submit the savings book for such transfer by that time, the bank was required to do so automatically by January 31, 1941. Jews were not permitted to make savings deposits. [73] In December 1940 the amounts Jews were allowed to withdraw from their frozen (current) accounts were further reduced. [74] Starting in January 1941 Jews were "requested to offer" their deposits of valuables and securities for sale to the HADEGA, subject to a 20 percent deduction in the case of debentures, payable initially to the Reich Protector's office and later to the *Auswanderungsfond für Böhmen und Mähren* (Emigration Fund for Bohemia and Moravia), hereafter referred to as the *Auswanderungsfond.* In the case of shares, the owner received no more than the rate as of April 1, 1938; the difference between that rate and the current rate of the shares had to be turned over to the same office. On January 10, 1941, a new implementing regulation for the elimination of Jews from the economy of the Protectorate prohibited Jews from engaging in virtually any kind of economic activity. [75] All stamp collections owned by Jews had to be deposited with a bank by March 15, 1941, or an application for approval of its sale had to be submitted to the Treasury Department of the Protectorate by that date. [76] The Second Regulation of the Reich Protector in Bohemia and Moravia concerning the Welfare of Jews and Jewish organizations dated October 12, 1941, was typical of Nazi hypocrisy. [77] It authorized the *Zentralstelle* in Prague to liquidate the properties of "emigrating" Jews if the owner had signed a written application for that purpose. [78] An additional regulation one month later canceled the claims of Jewish creditors. However, the creditor could obtain some compensation from the *Auswanderungsfond* provided an application for such compensation was filed no later than July 31, 1942. [79] Any necessary entries in land registers and other public registers had to be made by the registrars free of charge on motion by the *Zentralstelle.* To make sure that no Jewish property should escape them, the Germans forbade Jews to dispose of any property (including furniture and objects for personal use, accounts receivable, etc.) without an official permit. This prohibition included also the delivery of furniture and personal effects to any other persons (i.e., non-Jews) for safekeeping and any waivers of accounts receivable or other transactions that would reduce the value of the property. Any sales of furniture, personal effects, and other personal property after October 18, 1940, had to be reported to the *Zentralstelle*.[80] In July 1943 the estates of deceased Jews were declared forfeit in favor of the German Reich.[81]

JEWISH EMPLOYEES DEPRIVED OF THEIR RIGHTS AND POSITIONS

Many non-Jewish employers did not wait for formal legislation to dismiss their Jewish employees but took action soon after March 15, 1939, either voluntarily or upon the informal "suggestion" of other non-Jews. However, the office of the Reich Protector did not turn its attention to this matter until October 1939. Then it decreed that employment contracts of any kind with Jewish employees could be terminated on six weeks' notice, with all claims of the employee, including pension claims, null and void, regardless of any prior contract or statutory provisions to the contrary. Lump sum severance payments to Jews could not exceed half a year's salary.[82] Any "loopholes" that might have remained were closed in September 1940 when an additional regulation reduced to the 1939 limit any severance pay granted or contracted for prior to the effective date of the 1939 regulation. The provisions of the regulation were applicable also to Jewish survivors of Jewish or non-Jewish employees and excluded Jewish employees from all private pension and insurance funds; they were applicable also to former employees who had already retired.[83] A Protectorate regulation of November 1940 placed limits on the pensions of retired Jewish public employees and on benefits for their survivors.[84]

Starting early in 1941 the emphasis of the legislation shifted from the dismissal of Jewish employees to the employment of Jews under the direction of the labor exchanges. In May and again in August 1941 the Protectorate's Department of Health and Social Welfare, based upon a Protectorate government regulation of January 1941,[85] issued directives to the labor exchanges concerning the employment of Jews.[86] A further directive issued in October 1941[87] required employers to consult with the *Zentralstelle* before hiring Jewish employees. A regulation issued by the German government[88] declared that Jews employed at work assigned by the German authorities were "employees *sui generis*"; the implementing regulation pursuant to this regulation[89] listed a number of employee protection laws not applicable to Jews and ruled that under this new law Jews were not entitled to overtime or holiday pay, vacation pay, family or child support payments, bonuses or severance pay. An employer no longer had to give notice to Jewish employees before dismissing them. He could terminate the employment of a Jew at any time as of the end of the following working day, while Jews had to accept any job assigned to them by the labor exchange and could not change jobs without permission. Jews had to be segregated from other employees. Similar provisions were promulgated by the Protectorate government during 1942.[90]

DISCRIMINATION AGAINST JEWS IN THE PROFESSIONS

On March 16, 1939, Jewish attorneys were deprived of the right to practice except to serve Jews.[91] Soon thereafter, Jews were dismissed from all positions in public administration, at official agencies and institutions, in the courts, and at schools. Due to the delaying tactics typical of Czech bureaucracy, the comprehensive Protectorate Government Regulation concerning the Position of Jews in Public Life dated July 4, 1939, was not promulgated until nine months later, in April 1940.[92] This regulation excluded Jews from all positions in the courts and in the public administration, on representative bodies and commissions, and in education (as teachers, professors, lecturers, researchers, etc.). Jews could no longer work as notaries public, translators, consultants, civil or mining engineers, stockbrokers, veterinarians, pharmacists, performing artists, or editors. They were also debarred from membership in clubs and social, cultural, or economic organizations, etc. Jewish physicians, like Jewish attorneys, were permitted to practice only if they confined their ministrations to Jews, but the number of Jewish doctors and lawyers in any case could not exceed 2 percent of all licensed attorneys or physicians, respectively, in the Protectorate. A similar regulation applicable to Jewish dentists followed in September 1940.[93]

HARASSMENT OF JEWISH CONSUMERS

In October 1940 the municipal administration of Prague announced that Jews would not receive any clothing ration cards.[94] They were told that if they needed clothes, they should buy them from old clothes dealers. Jews were not issued ration cards for apples;[95] they were excluded from special rations of sugar,[96] vegetables,[97] tobacco products,[98] preserves and jellies,[99] and shaving soap, from special soap rations for children over one year of age,[100] all fruits (fresh, dried or canned), nuts, cheese, candies, fish and fish products, poultry, venison,[101] carp, wine and liquor,[102] onions,[103] garlic,[104] pork,[105] oranges, and tangerines.[106] They were not permitted to buy new caps,[107] suitcases, knapsacks, briefcases, bags, shopping bags, purses, or leather straps.[108] They were not entitled to consumer identification cards for the distribution of unrationed provisions.[109] Fishing licenses of Jews were revoked.[110] In 1942 the sale of newspapers to Jews was prohibited.[111] In the summer of 1942 the *Zentralstelle* ordered all Jews to surrender their cameras, typewriters, adding machines, calculators, bicycles, portable musical instruments, furs, ski boots, skis, and ski poles, and house pets such as dogs, cats, and birds. In August 1942 the prohibitions against the sale to Jews of the items and products mentioned earlier were reiterated and reinforced; now not only the sale but even the supplying of such goods to Jews free of charge (as gifts) was prohibited.[112] The list of prohibited goods was enlarged by the addition of all meats, eggs, rolls, and cakes as well as white bread. Milk rations were limited to children under six years of age.[113] The list was further "amended" by the addition of honey[114] and yeast[115] to the foods which Jews were no longer permitted to have.

TAXATION

Anti-Jewish discriminatory provisions were not introduced into the tax laws of the Protectorate of Bohemia and Moravia until December 1942. Under a regulation concerning property taxes (introduced in the Protectorate effective January 1, 1943) Jews were no longer entitled to personal income tax exemptions. Jews (and non-Jews married to Jewish women) were required to file property tax returns on assets which were not otherwise classed as taxable.[116]

The Withholding Tax Regulation of 1943 discriminated against Jews, Poles, and gypsies by placing them into the highest income tax bracket (Group I for single taxpayers) regardless of their marital status. They could no longer claim exemptions for children or other dependents.[117] At the same time a 15 percent surtax was added to income taxes payable by Jews, Poles, and gypsies, as a "social equalization."[118] The Income Tax Regulation of August 1943 also explicitly placed married Jews into Group I for tax purposes. Married couples filing joint returns were treated as Jews if the husband was Jewish.[119]

HARASSMENT OF JEWISH TENANTS

Under a decree issued by the *Zentralstelle* and dated September 13, 1940, Jews were no longer permitted to rent vacant apartments. They were forced to move into apartments already occupied by other Jews. Shortly thereafter the Reich Protector issued a regulation under which apartments occupied by Jews could, upon termination of the lease, be rerented only with the consent of the *Zentralstelle*.[120] Such apartments were not subject to rent controls applicable to non-Jewish tenants.[121] Legal protection against the termination of leases to which non-Jews were entitled could not be invoked by Jews.[122] In February 1943 the *Zentralamt für die Regelung der Judenfrage in Böhmen and Mähren*[123] (Central Office for the Settlement of the Jewish Problem in Bohemia and Moravia; formerly the *Zentralstelle für Jüdische Auswanderung*), hereafter referred to as the *Zentralamt,* ruled that henceforth Jews who had been forced to move out of apartments in Prague could move only into apartments in the First, Second, or Fifth districts of Prague which were still occupied by Jewish tenants.[124]

EDUCATIONAL DISCRIMINATION AGAINST JEWS

In July 1939 the Department of Education of the Protectorate of Bohemia and Moravia issued a decree excluding Jewish pupils from all German-language public schools and high schools. The number of Jewish students in Czech-language schools was limited to 4 percent of the total enrollment.[125] By a regulation of the German government under the date of August 2, 1939, all German universities in the Protectorate were taken over by the Reich effective September 1, 1939. This meant that whatever Jewish students were still left at these universities were now to be barred from continuing their studies. There was no need for legislation to dismiss Jews from Czech universities, because all Czech universities in the Protectorate had already been closed down on November 17, 1939. In the summer of 1940 even the 4 percent *numerus clausus* still permitted in 1939 seemed too much: under legislation dated August 7, 1940, no Jewish students whatsoever could be admitted to Czech-language schools, public or private, for the academic year of 1940/41.[126] For some time after March 1939 various training courses sponsored by the Jewish Religious Congregation had flourished in Prague, mainly to prepare prospective Jewish emigrants for jobs as skilled laborers. In March 1941 those courses were prohibited.[127] But all this was still not considered enough. In July 1942 all Jewish schools were closed and all public or private education for Jewish children was prohibited.[128] What still remained to be done now was to bar *Mischlinge,* Jewish "half-castes," from educational institutions. Such legislation was not long delayed. Under a law dated September 8, 1942, *Mischlinge* of the first degree (i.e., half-Jews who were descended from two Jewish grandparents but did not profess the Jewish religion and were not married to Jews) could no longer be admitted to German-language or Czech-language institutions of higher learning. They could be admitted only to vocational, agricultural, or art schools, and even that only by special permission of the Department of Education. Under this new law all *Mischlinge* at teachers' colleges had to be promptly dismissed, without exception.[129]

RESTRICTIONS ON JEWISH ORGANIZATIONAL ACTIVITY

In March 1939 all activities of Jewish organizations were prohibited effective immediately. Later all these organizations were officially dissolved by the *Zentralstelle.* Previously existing separate Jewish religious congregations in the various districts of Prague were merged into the Jewish Religious Congregation of Prague. All Jewish religious congregations throughout the Protectorate were "reorganized" by a regulation of the Reich Protector concerning the

"Welfare of Jews and Jewish Organizations" in March 1940.[130] The stated purpose of all Jewish religious congregations was to help Jews emigrate, though other functions could be assigned to them by the Reich Protector. Jewish religious congregations throughout the Protectorate had to comply with instructions issued through the Jewish Religious Congregation of Prague, in accordance with instructions from the *Zentralstelle,* which was to supervise all Jewish religious congregations, foundations, and funds, and had the authority to dissolve them. Jewish property taken over by the *Zentralstelle* was transferred to the *Auswanderungsfond* in Prague. Under a regulation issued in August 1941 the Jewish religious congregations were charged with the welfare and support of indigent Jews who formerly had been entitled to support from public welfare.[131] Under a decree of October 1941 all synagogues in the Protectorate were closed.[132] In March 1942 all Jewish religious congregations in the Protectorate, except for the Jewish Religious Congregation of Prague, were dissolved and their assets transferred to the *Auswanderungsfond.*[133] In August 1942 the name of the *Zentralstelle* (Central Office for Jewish Emigration) was changed to *Zentralamt fur die Regelung der Judenfrage in Böhmen und Mähren* (Central Office for the Settlement of the Jewish Problem in Bohemia and Moravia), and in February 1943 the name of the Jewish Religious Congregation of Prague was changed to *Ältestenrat der Juden in Prag* (Council of Jewish Elders in Prague).

BAN ON JEWISH ARTISTIC ACTIVITIES

By a decree of September 1941[134] all public performances or mechanical reproductions of musical works involving Jews as composers, arrangers, librettists, or performing artists were prohibited. The distribution of sheet music or recordings of such works, even free of charge, and the use of such works or recordings for teaching purposes were likewise forbidden.

EMIGRATION

Possibilities for emigration from the Protectorate and the official attitude toward Jewish emigration varied during several distinct periods following the German occupation of Bohemia and Moravia. In the initial period from March 15 to early June 1939 it seemed that the authorities (both German and Protectorate authorities) were genuinely interested in supporting Jewish emigration. *Durchlassscheine* (exit permits) could be obtained from the Gestapo with relative ease and emigrants were able to take along personal effects and furniture as well as valuables. The first "tightening of the screws" followed the issuance on June 23 of a regulation covering, among other things, the "export of personal effects and valuables of emigrants."[135] Prospective emigrants needed an ever-proliferating number of official certificates from various agencies and offices.[136] The *Zentralstelle für jüdische Auswanderung* (Central Office for Jewish Emigration) set up on July 21, 1939, was[137] in sole charge of all matters connected with the emigration of Jews. In November 1939 the Protectorate government imposed an emigration tax[138] payable by all persons emigrating from the Protectorate after March 14, 1939, if the value of their property was in excess of Kč 200,000 or if their taxable income in 1938 or later amounted to not less than Kč 140,000. The tax rate was 25 percent of the net property value. This tax was collected by Protectorate authorities. The March 1940 regulation of the Reich Protector concerning the "Welfare of Jews and Jewish Organizations"[139] imposed an additional, separate "Jewish tax" (*Židovská dávka, Jüdische Abgabe*) to be collected by the *Zentralstelle*.[140] Perhaps as a result of the long lines of applicants at the Treasury Department, a decree was issued in January 1940 authorizing local tax offices to issue tax waivers for emigrants at their discretion.[141] Following the outbreak of war between Germany and the Soviet Union in June 1941 emigration from the Protectorate became increasingly difficult. It virtually came to an end with the start of deportations from the Protectorate in November 1941 and the entry of the United States into the war a month later. Nevertheless, as late as January 1943 the Protectorate's Treasury Department issued a proclamation[142] to the effect that Jews traveling to foreign countries could carry with them only articles absolutely necessary for their personal use! All other articles to be carried by the travelers required an export permit from the Treasury Department. Applications for such export permits had to be submitted to the Treasury Department of the Protectorate through the *Zentralamt für die Regelung der Judenfrage in Böhmen und Mähren*. In the meantime, deportations to Terezín and Auschwitz and the "Final Solution" of the Jewish problem had begun. The removal of the Czech population from Terezín was ordered by a regulation of the Reich Protector dated February 16, 1942,[143] which authorized the commandant of the Security Police of the Reich Protector's office to take the necessary steps for the establishment of a Jewish settlement (ghetto) by administrative measures independent of the laws of the Protectorate.[144]

A list of the many ghetto regulations issued by the Jewish administration in Terezín under Nazi command is given under note 145 at the end of this chapter.[145]

NOTES

1. April 7, 1933, *Reichsgesetz zur Wiederherstellung des Berufsbeamtentums* [Law for the Reorganization of the Professional Civil Service], *Reichsgesetzblatt (RGBl;* Reich Law Gazette), p. 175; September 22, 1933, *Reichskulturkammergesetz* [Law Concerning the Reich Chamber of Culture], *RGBl.* I, p. 661; October 4, 1933, *Schriftleitergesetz* [Law Concerning Editors], *RGBl.* I, p. 713; September 15, 1935, *Reichsbürgergesetz* [Reich Citizenship Law], *RGBl.* I, p. 1146; *idem, Gesetz zum Schutze des deutschen Blutes und der deutschen Ehre* [Law for the Protection of German Blood and German Honor], *RGBl.* p. 1146; November 14, 1935, *Erste Verordnung zum Reichsbürgergesetz* [First Regulation to Implement the Reich Citizenship Law], *RGBl.* I, p. 1333; April 26, 1938, *Verordnung über die Anmeldung des Vermögens von Juden* [Regulation concerning the Registration of Jewish Assets], *RGBl.* I, p. 414; November 12, 1938, *Verordnung zur Ausschaltung der Juden aus der deutschen Wirtschaft* [Regulation concerning the Elimination of Jews from the German Economy], *RGBl.* I, p. 1580; November 28, 1938, *Reichspolizeiverordnung über das Auftreten der Juden in der Öffentlichkeit* [Reich Police Regulation Concerning the Appearance of Jews in Public], *RGBl.* I, p. 1675, etc.

All these anti-Jewish laws and regulations became effective also in the territories ceded to the Reich under the Munich agreement in October 1938. However, they did not become effective in the area of Těšín (Teschen, northeastern Moravia, bordering on German Silesia and Poland) until October 26, 1939, pursuant to decrees enacted by Hitler on October 8 and November 2, 1939: *Erlass des Führers und Reichskanzlers über die Gliederung und Verwaltung der Ostgebiete vom 8. Oktober 1939* [Decree of the Führer and Reich Chancellor Con-

cerning the Organization and Administration of the Eastern Territories, October 8, 1939], *RGBl.* I, p. 2042; *Erlass des Führers und Reichskanzlers über das Inkrafttreten des Erlasses über die Gliederung und Verwaltung der Ostgebiete vom 20. Oktober 1939* [Decree of the Führer and Reich Chancellor concerning the Effective Date of the Decree concerning the Organization and Administration of the Eastern Territories, October 20, 1939], *RGBl.* I, p. 2057.
2. *Erlass des Führers und Reichskanzlers* dated March 16, 1929, *RGBl.* I, p. 485, March 16, 1939.
3. The new law conferred citizenship in the German Reich upon all ethnic Germans in the Protectorate of Bohemia and Moravia in accordance with the *Reichsbürgergesetz* [Reich Citizenship Law] of September 15, 1935, and extended to them the "rules for the protection of German blood and German honor."
4. *RGBl.* I, p. 1333.
5. *Verordnungsblatt des Reichsprotektors in Böhmen und Mähren* [Collection of Regulations issued by the Reich Protector in Bohemia and Moravia], 6/39.
6. *Sbírka zákonů a nařízení Protektorátu Čechy a Morava* [Collection of Laws and Regulations of the Protectorate of Bohemia and Moravia], 136/40.
7. *Sbírka zákonů a nařízení Protektorátu Čechy a Morava* [Collection of Laws and Regulations of the Protectorate of Bohemia and Moravia], 85/42.
8. A person was deemed to be a Jew (a) if he had three grandparents who were "full Jews" by race, a grandparent being deemed a "full Jew" if he or she was, or had ever been, a member of a Jewish religious community; (b) a person of "mixed blood" with only two "fully Jewish" grandparents was deemed to be a Jew if (1) said person had been a member of a Jewish religious community on or after September 15, 1935, or (2) had been married to a Jew on or after that date, or (3) was the offspring of a mixed marriage contracted after that date, or (4) was the offspring of extramarital relations with a Jewish party and had been born after July 31, 1936. (Regulation of the Reich Protector, note 5 above; in the Protectorate Regulations, notes 6 and 7 above, the date under items (b) (1) and (2) was changed to September 16, 1935; the date under item (b) (3), to September 17, 1935).
9. A *Mischling* (Jewish "half-caste") was any descendant of one or two Jewish grandparents who was not deemed to be a Jew under any of the above definitions (*Dritte Verordnung zur Ausführung des Gesetzes zum Schutze des deutschen Blutes und der deutschen Ehre* [Third Regulation for the Implementation of the Law for the Protection of Ger-

man Blood and German Honor], July 5, 1941, *RGBl.* I, p. 384 and Protectorate Regulation 85/42, note 7 above). Protectorate Regulation 137/42 dated April 9, 1942, further distinguished between *Mischling* of the first degree (a descendant of two Jewish grandparents) and of the second degree (a descendant of only one Jewish grandparent).
10. This order was communicated to the Jewish Religious Congregation of Prague, which was made responsible for informing those affected.
11. *RGBl.* I, p. 547, promulgated September 3, 1941, effective fourteen days later. Later that month, Heydrich was named Acting Reich Protector in Bohemia and Moravia.
12. Issued pursuant to a decree of Heydrich as "Reich Minister of Internal Affairs" dated April 14, 1939, validating Czechoslovak passports issued prior to March 16 subject to exit or entry visas issued "by the competent German passport office," published in the *Verordnungsblatt des Reichsprotektors in Böhmen und Mähren* [Collection of Regulations issued by the Reich Protector in Bohemia and Moravia.]
13. The greatest rush to get rid of Jewish competition seems to have prevailed among attorneys at law: a prohibition against further practice by Jewish attorneys was issued by the attorney's chamber, the bar association, and the Justice Department as early as March 15, 1939. A Protectorate Government Regulation dated July 4, 1939, actually excluding Jews from the professions (attorneys at law, notaries public, pharmacists, physicians, performing artists, teachers, researchers, etc.) was not promulgated until April 24, 1940, under No. 136/40.
14. During the second part of March 1939 the heads of the German civil administration in Brno (Moravia) and Prague (Bohemia) issued wholesale bans on the sale of Jewish business concerns, real property, or Jewish property in general. The Regulation concerning Jewish Property, issued by the Reich Protector (note 5 above), followed on June 21, 1939. Two days later a regulation of the Protectorate Government concerning the "export" of personal effects and valuables of emigrants was issued as part of the currency regulations (Protectorate Regulation 155/39 of June 23, 1939).
15. This order was published in the daily newspapers.
16. Order of the Presidium of the Provincial Administration (*Zemský úřad, Landesbehörde*) in Prague.
17. Proclamation of Prague police headquarters dated August 14, 1939, published in the daily newspapers.
18. Order of the Provincial Administration in Prague dated February 20, 1940.
19. Proclamation of Prague police headquarters dated May 17, 1940.

20. Store owners were ordered to limit shopping hours for Jews to the hours between 11 A.M. and 1 P.M. and between 3 P.M. and 4:30 P.M. A proclamation of the Protectorate Department of Internal Affairs dated February 10, 1941, made these restrictions applicable also to non-Jews doing shopping for Jews.
21. Proclamation of the Presidium of the Provincial Administration in Prague dated August 15, 1940; Order of Prague police headquarters dated August 16, 1940.
22. Proclamation of Prague police headquarters dated September 10, 1940; later changed to "Tatra" and "Fiser," then only "Fiser." Finally on December 1, 1942, the use by Jews of this last hotel, too, was prohibited.
23. Proclamation printed in the daily newspapers on September 4, 1940; on July 17, 1941, police headquarters in Prague extended the prohibition to all wooded areas, public or private, within Greater Prague.
24. Proclamation of Prague police headquarters dated September 4, 1940; in the city of Brno (Moravia) Jews were restricted to the front platform of the rear car as early as January 1, 1940.
25. Order of Prague police headquarters dated December 9, 1940. The city of Brno followed suit with a similar order on January 16, 1941.
26. I.e., on both banks of the river between the railroad bridge and the Hlávka bridge: Order of Prague police headquarters dated July 29, 1941.
27. Order of Prague police headquarters dated October 31, 1941.
28. Order of Prague police headquarters dated January 2, 1942.
29. Proclamation of Prague police headquarters dated June 5, 1942, covering Wenceslas Square, Příkopy, Národní Třída, Hybernská Street, and the streets leading to the main railroad station and the zoo.
30. Order of Prague police headquarters dated June 26, 1941.
31. Order of Prague police headquarters dated September 6, 1941.
32. Proclamation of the Postal Administration in Prague dated September 24, 1941.
33. Decree of the Protectorate Department of Transportation dated October 14, 1941: Jews were permitted to use only the most inferior class of railroad accommodations (wooden benches), were forbidden to travel on through or express trains, could not be issued platform admission tickets, and had to be turned away from, or ordered to leave, trains that were overcrowded. The use by Jews of sleeping or dining cars had been prohibited by the *Zentralstelle für jüdische Auswanderung* (Central Office for Jewish Emigration) as early as August 7, 1940. In November 1941 the issuance to Jews of reduced-fare multiple-trip streetcar tickets was prohibited, except for one- or two-line

commuters' tickets for trips from home to work upon submission of a written certificate by the employer that the trips were necessary. By decree of the *Zentralstelle* dated November 22, 1941, Jews, except for disabled war veterans and blind persons, were barred from buses; even the blind and disabled were allowed to use seats only if all non-Jews in the vehicle had found seats. Jews were excluded from trolleys without exception. Effective January 23, 1942, Jews were excluded from all streetcars and buses between 3:00 P.M. Saturdays and 1:00 A.M. Mondays; otherwise the use of streetcars and buses by Jews was limited to trips to and from work upon certification by the employer, to sick persons upon attestation by a physician, persons over the age of sixty upon presentation of an age statement, and school children for trips to and from school. An order of the Prague Electric Works dated May 8, 1942, required streetcar conductors to eject Jews from streetcars if the car was filled up or if there was no space in the car for non-Jews waiting at a streetcar stop.

34. Order of Prague police headquarters dated December 4, 1941.
35. Order of Prague police headquarters dated February 21, 1942.
36. Decree of the *Zentralstelle* dated May 29, 1942.
37. Note 7 above.
38. Decree of the Protectorate's Department of Transportation and Technical Matters dated June 23, 1942, Ref. D 43, 584/42—15 H 1; Jews could occupy only the rearmost compartment of the last car in the train, could not hire railroad porters, and were barred from waiting rooms and restaurants of railroad stations.
39. Internal memorandum of Prague police headquarters.
40. Proclamation of the Medical Association in Bohemia dated August 26, 1942, published in the *Journal of Czech Physicians,* September 4, 1942. This proclamation was based upon a decree of the Protectorate's Department of Internal Affairs dated August 4, 1942.
41. Internal decree of the Presidium of the Provincial Administration of Bohemia dated October 7, 1942, File No. 51356.
42. Decree of the *Zentralstelle* dated October 10, 1942. Streetcar passes could be issued only to the following Jews: licensed physicians, leading employees of the Jewish community, holders of positions essential to the war effort (if their place of work was more than forty-five minutes' walk from their home), and, only in exceptional cases, to sick persons. Jewish children and individuals over the age of sixty were no longer permitted to use streetcars.
43. Order of the Gestapo, Prague, dated September 1939, to the Prague Jewish Religious Congregation, which had to inform all Jewish individuals concerned.

44. Proclamation of Prague police headquarters dated November 1, 1940, relating to Jews residing within Greater Prague. District Administration Offices (*Okresní úřady*) throughout the Protectorate issued similar proclamations for their respective districts.
45. Proclamations of Prague police headquarters dated January 23, 1941, and Brno police headquarters dated January 24, 1941. The issuance of driver's licenses to Jews was prohibited.
46. Note 11 above.
47. Decree of the Protectorate Department of Transportation (Postal Administration) dated January 7, 1941.
48. Decree of the Protectorate Department of Transportation and Technical Matters (Postal Administration) dated January 31, 1942.
49. Idem, dated February 25, 1942.
50. Note 13 above.
51. Note 5 above.
52. Sec. 1.
53. Sec. 3.
54. Sec. 4.
55. Sec. 5.
56. Sec. 9.
57. First Implementing Decree (*Durchführungserlass*) issued by the Reich Protector in Bohemia and Moravia dated June 21, 1939, *Verordnungsblatt des Reichsprotektors in Böhmen und Mähren 45/39.*
58. By order of the *Zentralstelle* all radios owned by Jews had to be surrendered on September 23 and 24, 1939.
59. *Verordnung über die Einziehung von Vermögen im Protektorat Böhmen und Mähren* (signed by Reich Minister of Internal Affairs Wilhelm Frick and Reich Minister of Finance Count Schwerin von Krosigk), *RGBl* I, p. 199.
60. Sec. 1: The Reich Protector in Bohemia and Moravia or any agencies designated by him were authorized to confiscate on behalf of the Reich the property of persons or of associations of persons who had supported activities hostile to the Reich as well as objects or rights which were used or destined for the furtherance of such activities. The Reich Minister of Internal Affairs was to determine, after consultation with the Reich Protector in Bohemia and Moravia, what activities were to be classed as hostile to the Reich.
61. See, e.g. *Erste Beilage zum Deutschen Reichsanzeiger und Preussischen Staatsanzeiger* (First Annex to the German Reich Gazette and Prussian State Gazette) dated April 27, 1942, containing among other publications a proclamation of the Prague Gestapo dated April 24, 1942, whereby, based on the regulation of October 4, 1939, the assets

of the Waldes families of Prague and Dresden, the Rindler, Wolfner, Löwidt, Fuchs, Hesky, Fischl, Rie, Hajsman, Pick, and Politzer families as well as the assets of the Comenius Clubs (Spolek Komenský) throughout Bohemia were confiscated.

62. Decree of the Treasury Department of the Protectorate dated November 11, 1939, File No. 18,753/1939-VI.
63. Decree of the Treasury Department of the Protectorate dated January 23, 1940, Official Gazette of the Protectorate of Bohemia and Moravia, 22/1940.
64. Decree of the Treasury Department of the Protectorate dated March 9, 1940. Fifth Implementing Decree of the Reich Protector dated March 2, 1940, *Verordnungsblatt des Reichsprotektors 81/40.*
65. Regulation of the Reich Protector in Bohemia and Moravia dated January 26, 1940, *Verordnungsblatt des Reichsprotektors 41/40.*
66. First Implementing Regulation to the Regulation of the Reich Protector in Bohemia and Moravia concerning the Elimination of Jews from the Economy of the Protectorate dated January 26, 1940, *Verordnungsblatt des Reichsprotektors 43/40.*
67. Third Implementing Regulation of the Reich Protector dated January 26, 1940, *Verordnungsblatt des Reichsprotektors 44/40.*
68. Fourth Implementing Regulation of the Reich Protector dated February 7, 1940, *Verordnungsblatt des Reichsprotektors 45/40.*
69. Second Implementing Regulation dated March 19, 1940, *Verordnungsblatt des Reichsprotektors 89/40.*
70. Seventh Implementing Regulation of the Reich Protector dated July 10, 1940, *Verordnungsblatt des Reichsprotektors 299/40.*
71. Proclamation of the Protectorate's Treasury Department dated September 16, 1940, File No. 63,048/40-VI concerning objects of gold, silver, or platinum, jewels, and pearls, also other jewelry and art objects and collections of any kind, of a value in excess of Kč 10,000. Reports as of September 15, 1940, were to be filed with the Treasury Department of the Protectorate by October 15, 1940.
72. Eighth Implementing Regulation of the Reich Protector dated September 16, 1940, *Verordnungsblatt des Reichsprotektors 507/40.* Reports as of November 1, 1940, were to be filed by November 15, 1940.
73. Proclamation of the Treasury Department of the Protectorate dated November 15, 1940, File No. 70,822/40-VI, Official Gazette of the Protectorate dated November 18, 1940.
74. Proclamation of the Treasury Department of the Protectorate dated December 6, 1940, File No. 73,537/40-VI: Single persons or widowers could withdraw Kč 2,000 per month; married couples living in a joint household, Kč 3,000 per month. For any additional Jewish indi-

vidual in the household of the owner of the account, Kč 500 could be withdrawn each month. Withdrawals from frozen accounts owned by non-Jews married to Jews were still permitted up to Kč 1,500 per week.

75. The Third Implementing Regulation of the Reich Protector in Bohemia and Moravia for the Elimination of Jews from the Economy of the Protectorate dated January 10, 1941, effective March 31, 1941, covered retail and wholesale businesses, restaurants, and hotels, insurance, shipping, forwarding and storage concerns, travel agencies, tourist guides, transportation and car rental firms, banking and foreign exchange businesses, pawn shops, credit information and debt collection firms, security guards, vending machine operators, advertising agencies, real estate brokerage firms, mortgage brokers, employment agencies, marriage brokers, and other brokerage and commercial representatives.

76. Proclamation of the Treasury Department of the Protectorate dated February 5, 1941, File No. 51,919/41-VI.

77. *Zweite Verordnung des Reichsprotektors in Böhmen und Mähren über die Betreuung der Juden und jüdischer Organisationen, Verordnungsblatt des Reichsprotektors 51/41.*

78. "Niederschrift" (Protocol). Shortly thereafter, the first deportations from the Protectorate started and Jews by the thousands were forced to sign such "applications."

79. Regulation of the Reich Protector in Bohemia and Moravia concerning the Welfare of Jews and Jewish Organizations dated November 19, 1941, *Verordnungsblatt des Reichsprotektors 61/41.* For properties taken over after June 30, 1942, this deadline was extended by a further regulation dated June 30, 1943, *Verordnungsblatt des Reichsprotektors 89/43.*

80. Proclamation of the *Zentralstelle für jüdische Auswanderung* dated October 25, 1941.

81. *Dreizehnte Verordnung zum Reichsbürgergesetz* dated July 1, 1943, *RGBl* I, p. 372, promulgated also in *Verordnungsblatt des Reichsprotektors* of July 31, 1943, No. 20, p. 103/43.

82. Regulation of the Reich Protector of Bohemia and Moravia dated October 23, 1939, concerning the Dismissal of Jewish Employees in the Protectorate of Bohemia and Moravia, *Verordnungsblatt des Reichsprotektors 281/39.*

83. Regulation of the Reich Protector concerning the Legal Status of Jewish Employees dated September 14, 1940, *Verordnungsblatt des Reichsprotektors 475/40.*

84. Protectorate Government Regulation dated November 7, 1940, Protectorate Code of Laws and Regulations 130/40.
85. Protectorate Government Regulation concerning Measures for the Direction of the Labor Force dated January 23, 1941, Protectorate Code of Laws and Regulations 46/41, dealt with labor assignments for the population of the Protectorate, including Jews.
86. Directives of the Protectorate Department of Health and Social Welfare dated May 9 and August 29, 1941.
87. Directive of the Protectorate Department of Health and Social Welfare dated October 14, 1941.
88. *Verordnung über die Beschäftigung von Juden* (Regulation concerning the Employment of Jews) dated October 3, 1941, promulgated in *RGBl* of November 4, 1941, No. 124/41, *RGBl* I, p. 675.
89. Regulation for the Implementation of the Regulation concerning the Employment of Jews, dated October 31, 1941, *RGBl* I, p. 681.
90. Government Regulation dated December 18, 1941, concerning Measures for the Direction of the Labor Force, promulgated February 24, 1942, Code of Laws and Regulations 21/42; Proclamation of the Protectorate Department of Economy and Labor dated June 30, 1942, Official Gazette No. 159 of July 9, 1942; Government Regulation concerning the Employment of Jews dated July 17, 1942, Code of Laws and Regulations dated July 28, 1942, No. 122/42.
91. Note 12 above.
92. Protectorate Government Regulation 136/40, promulgated April 24, 1940.
93. Protectorate Government Regulation dated September 10, 1940, No. 421/40.
94. Proclamation No. 60 of the Municipal Administration of Prague dated October 10, 1940. The Protectorate Department of Commerce followed suit with a similar proclamation (March 1941) with added details: Jews could buy notions for sewing worth up to Kč 2.00 per quarter. In exceptional cases, Jews who were emigrating could obtain clothing ration cards sufficient to obtain half a year's clothing rations before their departure. An additional proclamation of the Protectorate Department of Commerce dated November 4, 1941, authorized the issuance of clothing ration cards to Jews who had been wounded in military service during World War I.
95. Proclamations of the Protectorate Department of Agriculture dated January 18, 1941, November 8, 1941.
96. Proclamations of the Protectorate Department of Agriculture dated June 13, 1941, July 26, 1941.

97. Proclamation of the Protectorate Department of Agriculture dated August 29, 1941.
98. Decree of the Treasury Department of the Protectorate dated October 1, 1941.
99. Proclamation of the Protectorate Department of Agriculture No. 864 dated October 16, 1941.
100. Decree of the Protectorate Department of Commerce dated October 10, 1941.
101. Proclamation of the Protectorate Department of Agriculture No. 362 dated October 23, 1941, Protectorate Code of Laws and Regulations 126/41 and Proclamation of the Protectorate Department of Agriculture dated November 21, 1941.
102. Proclamation of the Protectorate Department of Agriculture No. 406 dated November 27, 1941.
103. Proclamation of the Protectorate Department of Agriculture No. 384 dated November 8, 1941.
104. Proclamation of the Protectorate Department of Agriculture dated January 8, 1942.
105. Proclamation of the Protectorate Department of Agriculture dated January 15, 1942.
106. Proclamations of the Protectorate Department of Agriculture dated December 8, 1941, and January 27, 1942.
107. Order of the Protectorate Department of Economy and Labor dated January 23, 1942.
108. Decree of the Protectorate Department of Economy and Labor dated April 3, 1942.
109. Proclamation of the Protectorate Department of Agriculture and Forestry dated May 27, 1942.
110. Proclamation of the President of the Provincial Administration of Bohemia dated February 8, 1941.
111. Published in Czech-language newspapers on January 12, 1942, German-language newspapers on May 1, 1942; by decree dated May 7, 1942, the sale of all periodicals to Jewish *Mischlinge* and non-Jews living in a joint household with them was prohibited.
112. Proclamation of the Protectorate Department of Agriculture and Forestry No. 284 dated August 10, 1942, Protectorate Code of Laws and Regulations 133/42. Further tightening followed by Proclamation of the same department dated December 2, 1942, Code of Laws and Regulations 405/42.
113. Circular of the Protectorate Department of Agriculture and Forestry to all district offices dated December 1, 1942, File No. 136,485-IV A/4.

114. Proclamation of the Protectorate Department of Agriculture and Forestry dated December 12, 1942, Official Gazette No. 293 of December 12, 1942.
115. Effective April 4, 1943; also Proclamation of the Protectorate Department of Agriculture and Forestry dated June 26, 1943, Official Gazette No. 148 of June 28, 1943.
116. Protectorate Government Regulation concerning the Property Tax dated December 22, 1942, Protectorate Code of Laws and Regulations 410/42.
117. Protectorate Government Regulation concerning the Income Withholding Tax of Employees dated April 22, 1943, Protectorate Code of Laws and Regulations 105/43, effective June 1, 1943.
118. Protectorate Government Regulation concerning the Imposition of a Social Equalization Tax in the Protectorate of Bohemia and Moravia dated May 3, 1943, Protectorate Code of Laws and Regulations 119/43.
119. Protectorate Government Regulation concerning the Income Tax dated August 9, 1943, Protectorate Code of Laws and Regulations 233/43.
120. Regulation of the Reich Protector in Bohemia and Moravia concerning the Renting of Jewish Apartments dated October 7, 1940, *Verordnungsblatt des Reichsprotektors 511/40.*
121. Protectorate Government Regulation concerning Special Measures of Communities regarding the Procurement of Living Quarters dated February 26, 1941, Protectorate Code of Laws and Regulations 177/41.
122. Protectorate Government Regulation concerning the Protection of Tenants against the Termination of Leases dated June 26, 1941, Protectorate Code of Laws and Regulations 248/41.
123. Note 14 above and note 139 below.
124. Order of the *Zentralamt* dated February 15, 1943.
125. Decree of the Protectorate Department of Education and Popular Culture, *Verordnung zur Überführung der Deutschen Hochschulen im Protektorat Böhmen und Mähren in die Verwaltung des Reichs* (Regulation for the Transfer of German Institutions of Higher Learning in the Protectorate of Bohemia and Moravia to the Administration of the Reich), August 21, 1939, *RGBl* I, p. 1371.
126. Regulation of the Protectorate Department of Education and Popular Culture dated August 7, 1940.
127. Order of the *Zentralstelle* dated March 14, 1941.
128. Order of the *Zentralstelle* dated July 24, 1942. Three days later, on July 27, 1942, the Protectorate Department of Education issued a

decree prohibiting the giving of instruction to Jewish children even in private groups or by private lessons, by teachers, paid or unpaid.
129. Decree of the Protectorate Department of Education dated September 8, 1942, File No. 92269/II.
130. Regulation of the Reich Protector in Bohemia and Moravia concerning the Welfare of Jews and Jewish Organizations dated March 5, 1940, *Verordnungsblatt des Reichsprotektors* 11/40.
131. Regulation of the Reich Protector in Bohemia and Moravia dated August 25, 1941. Pursuant to this regulation, Protectorate Government Regulation dated November 20, 1941, published on January 8, 1942, under No. 2/42, stated that inasmuch as responsibility for the support of indigent Jews had been taken over by the Jewish religious congregations, the local community had no further obligation to aid such Jews.
132. Decree of the Acting Reich Protector in Bohemia and Moravia.
133. Decree of the *Zentralstelle* dated March 27, 1942.
134. Decree of the President of the Provincial Administration in Prague dated September 10, 1941.
135. Protectorate Government Regulation 155/39, Sec. 22, note 13 above.
136. Long lines of prospective emigrants at all such offices indicated growing bureaucratic difficulties. Applicants were often sent away with instructions to return another day. (Ironically, the last name of one official who was in charge of issuing tax waivers to prospective emigrants at the Treasury Department of the Protectorate was Nechvátal, literally, "One who was in no hurry.") Such delays forced many Jews who might still have been able to leave the country in the summer of 1939 to remain until the outbreak of the war made emigration impossible.
137. Note 14 above. The jurisdiction of the *Zentralstelle* was extended to the entire Protectorate on February 16, 1940. (Originally it had been limited to the city of Prague and vicinity.)
138. Protectorate Government Regulation concerning the Emigration Tax, dated November 23, 1939, Code of Laws and Regulations 287/39.
139. Originally this tax was imposed temporarily for a period ending in December 1941. It was extended for another year by Regulation 46/42 of December 18, 1941, and indefinitely by Regulation 55/43 dated January 29, 1943.
140. On May 29, 1942, the Treasury Department of the Protectorate advised the emigration tax department of the Tax Administration of Brno that this tax collected from Jewish emigrants pursuant to the regulation of March 5, 1940, was deemed a public fee or tax and

should, therefore, be deducted in computing the Protectorate emigration tax. File No. 42,025/42-III/9a.
141. Decree of the Treasury Department of the Protectorate dated January 17, 1940.
142. Proclamation of the Treasury Department of the Protectorate dated December 14, 1942, published on January 16, 1943, in the Code of Laws and Regulations under No. 13/43.
143. Regulation of the Reich Protector in Bohemia and Moravia dated February 16, 1942, *Verordnungsblatt des Reichsprotektors 9/42* dated February 28, 1942.
144. Ibid. Sec. 14.
145. In addition to general concentration camp regulations (*allgemeine Ordnung der jüdischen Selbstverwaltung—besondere Lagerordnung*) the following regulations were enacted for the Terezín ghetto: *Verordnung über die Schlichtungsstellen* (Regulations concerning Courts of Arbitration) dated February 9, 1942; *Verhaltungsvorschriften für die Strafgerichte* [Rules for Criminal Courts] dated January 5, 1943; *Dienstordnung der Detektivabteilung* [Official Regulations for the Detective Division], dated March 14, 1943; *Dienstvorschrift für Mitarbeiter der Verwaltung* [Official Regulations for Members of the (Jewish) Administration], dated March 21, 1943; *Ordnung zur Sicherung der Arbeitsdisziplin* [Rules for the Maintenance of Discipline at Work], dated March 21 and April 4, 1943; *Jugendgerichtsordnung* [Juvenile Court Procedure] dated April 14, 1943; *Strafordnung der Detektivabteilung* [Criminal Procedure for the Detective Division], dated May 22, 1943; *Berufungs-und Beschwerdeverfahren in Jugendstrafrechtsfällen* [Criminal Appeals Procedure in Juvenile Court Cases], dated October 27, 1943; *Verordnung über Nebenstrafen* [Regulation concerning Supplemental Punishments], dated March 26, 1944; *Verordnung über Versorgungsvergehen und Durchführungsvorschriften zur Verordnung über Versorgungsvergehen* [Regulations concerning Supply Misdemeanors and Implementing Regulations pertinent to the Regulation concerning Supply Misdemeanors], dated April 26, 1944; *Zuständigkeit der Detektivabteilung bei kleineren Eigentumsvergehen* [Competence of the Detective Division in Cases of Petty Larceny], dated June 2, 1944; *Verwaltungsstrafordnung* [Administrative Criminal Procedure], dated November 27, 1944; *Rundschreiben betreffend Ergänzung und Vereinfachung der strafrechtlichen Vorschriften* [Circular Supplementing and Amending Criminal Law Provisions], dated March 10, 1945, containing new provisions relevant to libel and slander cases and amendments of regulations concerning supply misdemeanors,

criminal procedure in juvenile court cases, the maintenance of discipline at work, administrative criminal procedure, official regulations for members of the Jewish administration, and supplemental punishments.

BIBLIOGRAPHY

Friedmann, Dr. Franz. *Rechtsstellung der Juden im Protektorat Böhmen und Mähren* [The Legal Status of Jews in the Protectorate of Bohemia and Moravia], mimeographed, Part I (as of July 31, 1942), Part II (as of March 31, 1943), Part III (as of September 22, 1943).

Baum, Karl. *Nazi Anti-Jewish Legislation in the Czech Protectorate: A Documentary Note in Soviet Jewish Affairs: A Journal of Jewish Problems in the USSR and Eastern Europe,* No. 3, London: ed. J. Miller, published by Institute of Jewish Affairs, Ltd., May 1972.

Reichsgesetzblatt (RGB1) [Reich Law Gazette], in annual volumes, cited by page numbers.

Verordnungsblatt des Reichsprotektors in Böhmen und Mähren—Regulations issued by the Reich Protector in Bohemia and Moravia.

Sbírka zákonů a nařízeni Protektorátu Čechy a Morava [Code of Laws and Regulations of the Protectorate of Bohemia and Moravia].

Úřední list Protektorátu Čechy a Morava (Amtsblatt des Protektorates Böhmen und Mähren)—Official Gazette of the Protectorate of Bohemia and Moravia.

Mimeographed chronological listing of "Decrees Governing and Regulating Living Conditions of Jews in the Protectorate," from 4/7/43 through 11/6/44.

Copies of circulars of the Secretariat of the Council of Jewish Elders in Prague concerning the ghetto administration in Terezín (Theresienstadt).

TEREZÍN

by Zdenek Lederer

From its beginning in November 1941 to its end in May 1945 the history of the ghetto in Terezín (Theresienstadt) was determined by two contending, though admittedly unequal, forces. The first and more crucial of these was the Nazi plan to exterminate European Jewry; the second, the efforts of the Jewish leadership to save at least some part of the community.

The Nazi extermination plan, euphemistically called the "final solution of the Jewish problem in Europe," has been amply documented since the end of World War II. Its four phases were: to deprive the Jews in Nazi-held lands of all their civil and personal rights, to isolate the Jews from the non-Jewish population, to deport the Jews to Nazi-conquered territories in Eastern Europe, and, finally, to annihilate them. Once decided upon in principle, this plan underwent modifications but it never diverged from its basic aim. This is also clearly apparent from the history of the Terezín ghetto in its various phases, from that of a "labor ghetto" for Jews from the Protectorate of Bohemia and Moravia, to an "old people's ghetto" for the "privileged," to a "model ghetto" for display to foreign visitors in order to counteract rumors circulating in Germany and elsewhere about what was being done to the Jews under Nazi rule.

It must be understood that plans for the "Final Solution" were kept secret and for a long time remained completely unknown not only to the public at large but also to the intended victims. Indeed, when the Terezín ghetto was first established in November 1941 the Nazis themselves were not sure how to fulfill Hitler's promise that a world war would end in the "liquidation of the Jewish race in Europe."[1]

The first German "experiment" with Jews in the Protectorate of Bohemia and Moravia was the deportation of almost 1,300 people from Moravská Ostrava to Nisko on the River San in Poland in October 1939. The Nazis had a vague plan for deporting all the Jews from German-occupied territories into the area between the Vistula and Bug rivers. However, this plan was soon cancelled and the Nisko camp liquidated in April 1940.[2]

On October 10, 1941, a conference on "the solution of the Jewish problem" took place in Prague. It was attended by Reinhard Heydrich, the chief planner of the extermination program; Karl Adolf Eichmann, the head of the *Zentralstelle für jüdische Auswanderung* (Central Office for Jewish Emigration) in Vienna and chief executor of Heydrich's plans; Karl Hermann Frank, who was then the State Secretary for the Protectorate, and several other high officials.[3]

The records of that conference[4] include a decision to send transports of Jews from the Protectorate to Lodz, Minsk, and Riga. The conference also "considered the possibility of ghettoization in the Protectorate." The records mention "one ghetto in Bohemia and one in Moravia" but finally conclude that "it would be best if the *Zentralstelle* took over Theresienstadt." The document continues: "The number of Jews in this temporary *Sammellager* (assembly center) would be substantially reduced. Evacuation to Eastern territories would follow and then the whole area might be used for a model German settlement."

Six days later the first transport of Jews left Prague for Lodz. Five more transports followed, totaling 6,000 persons. In November another transport left Brno for Minsk, Belorussia.* At the same time, the Prague branch of the *Zentralstelle* ordered the Jewish Religious Congregation of Prague to submit the names of small towns which would be suitable for the "ghettoization" of Jews and to work out a model plan for Jewish settlements in these places. It was stressed that only inferior housing could be contemplated. The Jewish Religious Congregation, which in the summer of 1941 had set up a

---

* For statistics of transports to and from Terezín see Livia Rothkirchen, "The Jews of Bohemia and Moravia: 1939-1945," and Erich Kulka, "The Annihilation of Czechoslovak Jews," in the present volume, pp. 55-59 and 320-322, respectively.

special "Department G" (i.e., Ghetto Department) to deal with plans for ghettos and camps for Jews in the Protectorate, suggested over a dozen small towns in Bohemia and Moravia but the *Zentralstelle* rejected them all as being "too good for the Jews," "too close to Prague," or "too large." In the end, the *Zentralstelle*—obviously acting on the recommendation of the Prague conference—chose Terezín, a small garrison town about forty miles north of Prague. At the same time the *Zentralstelle* promised the Jewish leaders that no more deportations of Jews to Eastern Europe would take place.

Although Terezín had not been their choice and they had tried—in vain—to have the decision changed, the Jewish leaders of Prague considered the German promise to stop deportations to the East an important achievement. Two years earlier, Jakub Edelstein, who was to become the first chairman of the *Ältestenrat der Juden* (Council of Jewish Elders)—that is, head of the ghetto administration in Terezín—had been ordered by Eichmann as the representative of the Jewish Religious Congregation of Prague to travel to Nisko, where he spent several weeks. The chaos, misery, and utter disregard for human life he saw at Nisko had convinced Edelstein that anything would be better than deportation to the East. Thus he and his circle in Prague viewed the establishment of a ghetto in the Protectorate above all as a chance to prevent the dreaded deportations. Edelstein and his associates hoped to create in Terezín a self-governing Jewish community, where the inhabitants, though they would be forced to do hard work and to undergo many hardships, would at least be spared the dangers to which the Jews in the Protectorate were constantly exposed. The Jewish leaders were firmly convinced that the Germans would eventually lose the war and so they tried to play for time.

In the light of what we know today, those hopes were wildly optimistic, but at the time they were supported by arguments that seemed quite logical and realistic. Edelstein believed that the Nazis were interested in obtaining cheap industrial labor, which a Jewish settlement such as that contemplated in Terezín would amply provide. He also counted on the personal interests of the SS in Prague. If all the Jews were to be deported from the Protectorate, there would be no more need for a *Zentralstelle* in Prague, which provided the SS men with easy jobs far away from the battlefront. Moreover, Edelstein pointed out, the gradual "ghettoization" of the

Jews with all of their property left behind and the establishment of a satrapy in Terezín would offer the SS officers great opportunities for acquiring personal wealth.

All these were rational arguments. However, the Jewish leaders had not comprehended the irrational element in the Nazi hatred of Jews. They were in no position to do so. They had no way of knowing then that Hitler considered the extermination of European Jewry one of his principal war aims and that he and his henchmen would create a vast bureaucratic and military machinery solely for this purpose.

Theoretically, it is true that the Jewish leaders had two other alternatives to accepting "ghettoization": they could have organized armed resistance, or they could have refused to participate in the implementation of the Nazi schemes. Armed resistance against an infinitely stronger enemy is no doubt to be admired under certain circumstances. But such an action presupposes a military organization and some access to weapons. The Jewish community in the Protectorate, and later in Terezín, had neither. Martyrdom would have been an act of personal heroism, but no responsible leader of a community which included many old people as well as women and children could even have thought in terms of active resistance—certainly not in 1941.

A refusal to participate in the implementation of the Nazi order would have been no more than an individual resolution of a personal dilemma. Some Jewish leaders did indeed retire into private life in order to escape the responsibility, but this did not help matters. The Germans simply replaced the old leaders with new ones ready to do business with the SS. To refuse such an appointment by the German authorities would have been tantamount to suicide. Even in 1941 no one could have doubts that the SS was capable of killing Jews for much less serious offenses.[5]

As for Edelstein and his close associates, they considered resignation out of the question. Edelstein never doubted that in this desperate situation it was the duty of a Jewish leader to stand between the SS and his community, to exploit every possible opportunity for alleviating its burdens, and to leave no stone unturned in order to save as many Jewish lives as possible. Edelstein and his first deputy in Terezín, Otto Zucker, had opportunities to emigrate as late as 1941, but they chose to remain with their people.

Seen in retrospect, Edelstein's policy was an oversimplified attempt to solve an onerous and complex problem. But Edelstein was not a complicated person. Born in a Polish Hasidic family, he had the natural astuteness as well as the sentimentality of the East European Jew. His personal requirements were modest, his cultural needs simple. He had a great capacity for work and he also demanded a great deal from those who worked with him. He was a man of genuine courage. Each time he had to negotiate with the SS—which was almost daily—he was literally sick with fear: nevertheless, in his negotiations he appeared completely calm and capable of talking to SS officers as an equal. He belonged to *Po'ale Zion*, the Labor Zionist movement. His public manner had all the idealistic conviction, and also a little of the demagogy, of a people's tribune. Far from being dictatorial, Edelstein sometimes procrastinated in enforcing unpopular measures and regarded his own Jewish community as the sole qualified judge of his actions.

Otto Zucker, the former head of the Palestine Office in Prague and head of the Jewish Religious Congregation of Brno, was in many respects Edelstein's opposite. An architect and construction engineer by profession, Zucker was a highly cultured individual. Though a man of pronounced views and strong emotions, he was reserved and did not like to be in the limelight. Sometimes he involuntarily betrayed the impatience of one who had no illusions left. Edelstein was basically an optimist and instinctively believed for a long time that the Jews would somehow manage to survive this period just as they had always survived persecution in the past. Zucker was more pessimistic. The more he surmised the dangers and, indeed, the hopelessness of the situation, the more convinced he became that resistance would be the only way to survival. In his dealings with the SS Zucker lacked Edelstein's outward aplomb and ready wit but he inspired respect. He scarcely attempted to disguise his contempt for the Nazis.

Edelstein and Zucker, both in their forties, were the two principal figures in the first phase of "Ghetto Theresienstadt." They helped create this ghetto in the hope that it would afford a chance for Jews from Bohemia and Moravia to survive the war there. But for people in a desperate situation hope is not only an indispensable source of strength; it is also one of the best allies of self-deception. It must be said that from the start it was the SS who called the tune, relentlessly pursuing the Nazi aims. It is clear from the records of the Prague conference that the Germans never seriously contemplated Terezín as a permanent labor ghetto for the Jews from the Protectorate. Their promises to the Jewish leaders that deportations to the East would stop were made merely to assure the smooth course of subsequent deportations. All subsequent developments in the Terezín ghetto, too, were determined mainly by decisions and organizational changes made by the SS, with the Jewish leadership becoming increasingly powerless to act.

The Nazis chose Terezín because it was eminently suited for their purposes. Terezín had been built in 1780 as a garrison town by order of Emperor Joseph II, ruler of Austria and Bohemia. It was named Theresienstadt for his mother, the Empress Maria Theresa. Its ramparts formed a twelve-pointed star, broken by six gates. Within the ramparts, too, the town was arranged in a rigid geometric pattern. The streets were straight, intersecting at right angles. Huge blocks of barracks dwarfed all the other buildings. On the opposite bank of the River Ohře (Eger), which flowed not far from the walls of Terezín, there was another fortification complex called the Little Fortress.

Originally built to prevent Prussian incursions into Bohemia, Terezín must have been in its day a formidable work of military architecture. As things turned out, its strength as a fortress was never put to the test. At the end of the nineteenth century it ceased to be used as a fortress. From that time on, Terezín stood still. Technical progress and urban development passed it by, just as hostile armies had ignored it in the past. It remained a small, dreary garrison town. The Little Fortress was used as a prison during the remainder of Austro-Hungarian rule and during the era of the Czechoslovak Republic. Soon after the German occupation of Czechoslovakia it became a notorious Gestapo prison, which was to remain outside the ghetto jurisdiction. Though some Jews were also transferred there from the ghetto for "punishment" and others were brought there directly after their arrest without passing through Terezín, most of its inmates were non-Jews. In 1940 the town of Terezín had 3,700 inhabitants living in 219 buildings. The average total complement of the garrison was about 3,500 soldiers.

From this brief description it should be obvious why the SS chose Terezín. The town had only a small number of inhabitants. Once these had been resettled elsewhere, it could be sealed off and controlled with ease by a small military detachment. The barracks provided ready-made housing for large numbers of deportees.

BEGINNINGS OF THE GHETTO

On November 24, 1941, the first transport of some 350 young men from Prague arrived at Bohušovice, the railroad station nearest Terezín. Over 75,000 Jews from Czechoslovakia were to follow. For the overwhelming majority of these Terezín became the last but one stage on their way to death.

The first and second transports (the second arrived from Prague a few days after the first) were called *Aufbaukommandos* (construction details) I and II. These were young and able-bodied individuals who were supposed to prepare Terezín for the arrival of subsequent transports. But the men, women, and children deported in haste from Prague and Brno filled the barracks more quickly than the construction details could work. As a result, nothing was ready for the newcomers: there were no bunks, few pallets, no medical equipment, and no kitchens.

The Jewish administration of the ghetto was set up according to plans prepared in Prague and was headed by Edelstein and Zucker.[6] From the very start, their task was immensely difficult. They had almost no resources with which to work, the inmates whom they had to organize were bewildered, and the SS command, headed by *Lagerkommandant* (camp commander) Dr. Siegfried Seidl,[7] was very harsh. Soon the Jewish sector of Terezín, which consisted of barracks, took on the character of an internment camp. The women were separated from the men and all contact between them was strictly forbidden. The gates of the barracks were guarded by Czech gendarmes. Inmates were allowed to leave their barracks only in escorted work details or with a special pass countersigned by the *Lagerkommandant*. All correspondence with the outside was forbidden under penalty of death.

Before long the strict rules claimed their first victims. During the first two months of 1942 sixteen male inmates were executed by hanging, nine on January 10 and seven on February 26. One of them was a boy of eighteen. They had been sentenced to death for "crimes against the dignity of the German Reich"; namely, trying to smuggle letters out of Terezín and attempting to make purchases at stores in Terezín's "Aryan" sector.

On January 9, shortly before the first executions, a transport of 1,000 inmates left Terezín. A second transport followed a few days later. Both were bound for Riga.[8] It was now clear that Terezín had never been intended as a "labor ghetto." In accordance with the SS plans, Terezín had become an assembly center for transports to the ghettos and death camps of Eastern Europe. These deportations became the most important feature of life in Terezín.

Between January 1942 and October 1944, sixty-three transports, totaling almost 87,000 people, left for the East. Dispatched at irregular intervals, they struck terror in the hearts of the inmates of Terezín.

A transport to the East was usually ordered three or four days before its actual departure date. The SS command stipulated the age groups, and later also the nationality groups, from which the deportees were to be chosen and specified which categories or groups were to be exempted from deportation for the time being. As a rule the exemption of an individual meant that his family, too, was temporarily safe from deportation. But in most cases this protection was not permanent; sometimes a group exempted from one transport was expressly assigned to one that followed. The general instructions from the SS command were followed by a list of the names of individuals to be deported under *Sonderweisungen* (special orders) of the command.

The cards bearing the names of people belonging to "protected categories" were removed from the card index kept by the Central Registry. Then the Transport Commission, which was composed of members of the ghetto's *Ältestenrat* (Council of [Jewish] Elders) and representatives of all the administrative departments, had to compile, from the remaining cards, the actual transport lists according to the age or nationality requirements announced by the SS command. It was a terrible task; sometimes the number of deportees amounted to one-half the "unprotected" population of the ghetto. Those selected for deportation had the right to appeal to the Transport Commission, but once one's name had been placed on the list it was difficult to have it removed.

Each administrative department had its own exemption list based on specific qualifications. Ghetto bigwigs tried to protect their relatives and friends. Under an agreement made at the time of the first transports each political group—the Zionists, the assimilationists, and the Communists—could draw up a list of individuals to be exempted from deportation. Thus, Otto Zucker always kept a list of artists, writers, and other cultural personalities whom he tried to save.

By accepting at least partial responsibility for the composition of the transports from Terezín to the East, the Jewish leaders in Terezín continued to follow the policy they had begun in Prague. However, their dilemma was more difficult now and they had even less room for maneuvering. Refusal to obey an order from the SS command meant certain death. It could be argued that the SS might not have been able to find replacements for leaders who would have chosen the path of passive (or active) resistance. But this would not have stopped the deportations. Instead of permitting the Jews to make up their own list of deportees, the SS men could simply have surrounded one or two of the Jewish barracks at a time and herded their occupants into the trains. They had done this elsewhere. Moreover, the Jewish leaders in Terezín felt that as long as they remained at their posts there was still hope for a partial success of their policy in terms of saving Jewish lives.

It would be hypocritical to pretend that the ordinary inmate in Terezín did not tacitly endorse this policy which, baldly stated, meant that as long as others went to their death, he would be able to survive. Human nature being what it is, it is highly improbable that under the circumstances any other group of people would have felt or acted differently. Nor is it surprising that most of the inmates of Terezín should have taken refuge in self-deception and wishful thinking. For a long time, almost until the end, people tried to convince themselves that the transports were really going to "other ghettos and labor camps in the East," where, they said, they might be able to survive the war, even though, admittedly, it might be under conditions much worse than in Terezín.

Hindsight, of course, is always easy. But to put this mentality into the proper historical perspective, it must be remembered that the inmates of Terezín did not know about the extermination camps in Poland and Belorussia any more than they had known about the Nazi plan for the systematic extermination of the Jews. The thought that millions of human beings could be slaughtered in cold blood was still beyond their imagination. It is true that a few individuals eventually received reliable information about what was really happening in the East but they kept their knowledge to themselves. It is doubtful that even they could believe these reports sufficiently to make them credible to others. It is strange but true that by 1942 the West already knew about the gas chambers in Auschwitz (without, however, taking appropriate action), while the future victims in Terezín still knew nothing.

During the first six months of 1942 transports from Bohemia and Moravia kept arriving in Terezín. The ghetto's Jewish population, crammed into the barracks, rose to 20,000. During that same interval some 16,000 inmates were deported from Terezín to the East. By order of the SS, the deportees during that period were all under the age of sixty-five. Consequently, by May 1942, 27 percent of the ghetto's population was already sixty-five years of age or older. This made the task of assuring tolerable living conditions for the inmates increasingly difficult. But worse was yet to come.

By this time the Nazi extermination plan had advanced one stage further. Terezín's role in the plan had been defined in more precise terms. In January 1942 another conference "on the final solution of the Jewish problem" took place, this time at Wannsee (a suburb of Berlin) under the chairmanship of Reinhard Heydrich.[9] According to the minutes of that conference,[10] plans were outlined at Wannsee for the "resettlement" (read: liquidation) of all European Jews. With regard to Terezín the document stated: "It is intended not to evacuate Jews above the age of sixty-five but to remove them to an *Altersghetto* [old people's ghetto]. Theresienstadt is under consideration [for this purpose]. Taken to the old people's ghetto along with these. . . . will be Jews who were seriously wounded during the war [i.e., World War I] and Jews holding war decorations (Iron Cross, First Class)."

Earlier, the Jewish leaders in the Protectorate of Bohemia and Moravia had been deceived by promises of a "labor ghetto." Now those interceding on behalf of elderly Jews in Austria and Germany were to be deceived by an equally false impression of an "old people's ghetto." They were told variously that the elderly would be "resettled" at a "Reich Home for the Aged," or at the "Theresienstadt Spa," etc. As a result, they even paid considerable amounts in advance for their board and lodgings.

The decision of the Wannsee conference initially to present Terezín as a haven for the aged, disabled war veterans, and holders of war decorations was an example of what Hitler had once called "a propaganda adjustment of a war aim, necessary from a psychological point of view." While, of course, the original aim—the plans for the "Final Solution"—remained unaltered, the inmates of Terezín were to be given a semblance of "self-government."

At the end of 1942 Terezín was emptied of its indigenous non-Jewish population. The inmates of the ghetto were relieved of some of the most severe restrictions; the gendarmes withdrew to the gates of the town, and the ghetto inmates were free to move about within the town after work until the curfew.[11] However, men and women were still segregated in the barracks and in the additional buildings made available to them following the departure of the gentile population. A few days later, the entire town was formally handed over to the *Ältestenrat*, the Council of [Jewish] Elders, who constituted the leadership of the ghetto. Now Terezín was inhabited only by its Jewish inmates and their Nazi jailers. A new phase in the ghetto's history had begun.

THE GHETTO STRUCTURE

The structure of the Jewish administration in Terezín bore the bureaucratic imprint of the Nazi state. (Since its basic lines were dictated by the SS, this could hardly have been otherwise.) There was too much red tape, too much futile bureaucratic activity, and, of necessity, some abuse of power. But the principle which underlay the activities of the *Ältestenrat,* though not always effectively implemented on every level, was still to wage a struggle with the SS in order to ease the lot of the inmates. All eight departments of the administration contributed, in varying degrees, toward this aim.

It is not within the scope of this essay to describe the organization of "Ghetto Theresienstadt" in detail. We will merely outline the character of the individual departments and their basic function.

Within the limitations imposed by the SS command, the office of the chairman of the *Ältestenrat* and his deputy (later two deputies) who comprised the *Leitung* (administration) of the ghetto, was the most powerful body in Terezín. Its executive organ was the Central Secretariat, which controlled the central registry and the security services, notably the *Ghettowache* (ghetto police). The ghetto police in Terezín never achieved the position of power attained by similar organizations in some other camps and ghettos.

The Economic Department controlled food supplies and food distribution in the communal kitchens. It was here that, not unexpectedly, most of the abuses occurred, particularly on lower levels. Without condoning the abuses, one should perhaps point out that they were no worse in the ghetto of Terezín than among the populace in most German-occupied countries which was not subjected to the harsh pressures of ghetto life. Certainly they were no worse than in the German heartland, with its black market, its war profiteers, and its general lowering of moral standards. The Economic Department also controlled several ghetto workshops which produced goods for "export." The output of these workshops never became as significant as the Jewish leaders had hoped but the important thing was that the workers in some of them were exempted from deportation.

The Department for Internal Administration included, most importantly, a housing section, which allocated living quarters, [12] and a post office. The role of the post office assumed some importance after the stringent ban on correspondence with the outside world was lifted and inmates were allowed to write a limited number of censored letters and cards and to receive a limited number of food parcels.

The Technical Department operated under a perpetual shortage of essential materials, but it was able to do a remarkable amount of work. It substantially increased the output of the local electric power plant, tripled the water supply, expanded the kitchens, improved sanitary installations, etc. Its engineers and workers even built a two-mile railroad line from Terezín to Bohušovice, three kilometers away.

The Health Department was efficiently organized. Its slender resources were impossibly strained by the high proportion of aged and infirm among Terezín's ghetto population. Most of the doctors and nursing staff devotedly carried out their tasks, which often seemed hopeless. There were health centers, infirmaries, and surgeries in each of the larger barracks. Later there were even homes for the blind, the aged, and the infirm. Even during the "best" period, mortality in Terezín was eight times higher than had been normal for Jews in the Historic Lands before the war. During the worst period it was as much as thirty times higher.

The Youth Welfare Office received every possible assistance from the *Ältestenrat*. Most of the children were housed in special billets with their own kitchens, which were better supplied than those of the adults. A dedicated staff acted as teachers for the young—an activity which had to be concealed from the SS. There were elementary and secondary school courses and a high school course for young people of outstanding ability whom the ghetto administration managed to exempt from labor assignments.[13]

Work was compulsory for all able-bodied inmates between the ages of fourteen and sixty-five. All new arrivals were registered by the Labor Department. They were required to work for at least six weeks in the so-called mobile force, which was organized in groups of 100 each according to age and sex. These were labor details directed by the Labor Department to go wherever they were needed from day to day. Afterwards newcomers could choose either to remain in the mobile force or, preferably, to apply for a "permanent" job with one of the other departments. Applications were supported by proof of qualifications for the job or, more often, by personal connections. If an employee lost his job, which happened rarely, he reverted to the control of the Labor Department. The official working week was fifty-two hours for manual laborers and fifty-seven hours for office employees, but in fact the average working week was much longer. The Sabbath was a normal working day.

The Cultural Department was established at the end of 1942, when the SS decided to create a semblance of "normal life" in Terezín. Until then cultural activities had been pursued only in secret. Once officially permitted, they reached a scope and intensity far beyond the original intentions of the SS. The department remained purely administrative in character, permitting cultural life to develop without official interference. There were several theater and cabaret groups, a number of orchestras, performances by soloists, a mixed choir that performed operas, a children's choir, and lectures on a wide range of subjects. Books, mainly from liquidated Jewish households and institutions, were gathered in Terezín to form a large lending library.

The Finance Department kept records of transactions with suppliers and customers outside the ghetto and later set the wage rates in the ghetto currency, which was almost worthless.

THE *MUSTERGHETTO* (MODEL GHETTO)

The takeover of Terezín by the Jewish administration meant only very short reprieve. Transports of aged Jews from Germany and Austria began to arrive at an increasing pace. Between July and September 1942 these transports brought to Terezín a total of 41,000 people whose average age was over seventy. At the same time another 24,000 people were brought in from Bohemia and Moravia. The population of Terezín trebled from 20,000 at the beginning of July to 60,000 by the end of September. At the same time, Terezín was losing its labor force as inmates from the Protectorate under the age of sixty-five were deported to the East. Before long, the labor force in Terezín plummeted to a mere thirty percent of the original total.

There was not nearly enough medical and nursing staff to take care of all the helpless old people. As a result these unfortunates spent the last weeks or days of their lives in misery. When they arrived, most of their luggage was confiscated at the checkpoint, the so-called *Schleuse* (literally "lock" or "floodgate"), in one of the barracks, through which each arriving transport had to pass. The buildings were filled very quickly and the newcomers had to be lodged under most primitive conditions in the vast, badly lit lofts of the barracks. It was impossible to delouse them properly and the scant food rations often reached them further diminished through theft.

Before long, the so-called "privileged resettlers" were dying by the hundreds of enteritis and pneumonia; 1,000 in July, over 2,000 in August, and almost 4,000 in September. Corpses remained unburied for days because the gravediggers were unable to cope with the demand for their services. This, no doubt, was one of the most appalling periods in the history of Terezín.

By September 1942 even the SS realized that the ghetto could not continue much longer in this fashion. They had achieved their "propaganda adjustment of a war aim" by establishing the concept of an "old people's ghetto." It no longer mattered how many old people actually stayed in Terezín. The age limit was now reversed; the SS command ordered the deportation of nine transports, comprising 18,000 people over the age of sixty-five, to the East. This time the selection was made solely by the SS, without any reference to the ghetto leadership. Old people about whom inquiries might be made by influential relatives or friends abroad were kept in Terezín. Others—many of them only half-alive—were herded into the deportation trains. Their destination given in the "order of the day" was: "Transfer to another ghetto."[14]

During this period of horror, the SS, consistent with their dual policy, began introducing measures designed to give Terezín some semblance of a normal town. They proceeded to develop an idea already implicit in the concept of the "old people's ghetto." Terezín was to become a *Musterghetto,* a "model ghetto" to be shown, if necessary, to visitors from abroad to counter the rumors of atrocities which were beginning to spread in the West and elsewhere.

This policy brought a relaxation of some earlier restrictions. Inmates now were permitted to carry on a limited, censored postal correspondence and to receive food parcels from relatives and friends outside. Cultural life was permitted; eventually, even a café was opened on the main square, where patrons could listen to the "municipal band" (which, however, was forbidden to play works by German composers). Soccer games were permitted and fervently pursued. Special ghetto currency was issued by the "Bank of the Jewish Administration in Terezín," at which every working inmate had to deposit fifty percent of his wages. Inmates who did not work received a uniform allowance smaller than the wages earned by the workers. This "ghetto money" could be used only for purchases in several newly opened stores, which were stocked mainly with the shoddiest trash taken from the confiscated luggage of the inmates themselves.

With the arrivals from Germany and Austria continuing, Jews from Czechoslovakia soon ceased to be the main element in the population of Terezín. This change in the population brought changes also in the composition of the *Ältestenrat.* By October 1942 six Jews from Czechoslovakia had been replaced in the Council by six Jews from Germany and Austria, but Edelstein remained as chairman and the administration continued largely unaltered. In January 1943 senior officials of the Jewish *Kultusgemeinden* (official

Jewish religious communities) of Berlin and Vienna were deported to Terezín. By the order of the SS, Dr. Paul Eppstein, a former lecturer in sociology from Mannheim, was named to replace Edelstein as chairman of the *Ältestenrat.* Edelstein became Eppstein's first deputy; his second deputy was Dr. Benjamin Murmelstein, who before the war had been a rabbi in a suburb of Vienna and a member of the executive board of the Vienna *Kultusgemeinde.* Gradually Jews from Germany and Austria were appointed to posts also in the ghetto's administrative departments.

THE GHETTO TRIUMVIRATE

From this point on, we note a lack of unity in the Jewish leadership of Terezín. Besides feeling slighted as a pioneer who had been demoted, Edelstein realized that sharing power with individuals who did not agree with his ideas would make any attempt at resistance more difficult. Relations within the Eppstein-Edelstein-Murmelstein triumvirate remained strained as long as the arrangement lasted. Murmelstein kept in the background, but Eppstein lost no time in asserting his leading position. He regarded Edelstein's bold attitude toward the SS as adventurous and his attempts to influence the development of the ghetto as rather futile. Eppstein had neither Edelstein's tough optimism nor Zucker's stubborn will to resist. His spirit had been broken in a Gestapo prison some time before his deportation. Although blameless in many respects, he lacked the essential qualities of leadership which Edelstein, despite his shortcomings, possessed to a high degree.

Dr. Murmelstein was the only member of the triumvirate to survive the Holocaust. Born in Poland, he had studied philosophy and became a rabbi and later also a lecturer at the University of Vienna. In Vienna he had projected the image of a domineering, harsh individual. This reputation followed him to Terezín and did not improve there. But it should be pointed out that allegations made against him could not be substantiated when subjected to an impartial scrutiny.[15] Murmelstein was an extremely ambitious man of considerable scholarly attainments and organizing ability. His policy, especially later in the history of the Terezín ghetto, when he came more to the foreground, was one of subtle stratagems. Sometimes he appeared close to a point where it seemed that his personal fear of the SS might outweigh his sense of responsibility toward the ghetto community.

EVERYDAY LIFE IN "GHETTO THERESIENSTADT"

By the beginning of 1943, most Bohemian and Moravian Jews were either in Terezín or had been deported to the East. The flow of "privileged resettlers" from Germany and Austria had diminished, though smaller transports were still arriving. In April yet another nationality group was added to the ghetto: the first transport of Jews from Westerbork (Holland) passed through the checkpoint of Terezín.[16] In February and March additional transports left Terezín for the East. Then, there was a pause until September. Those seven months were the only period in the history of the Terezín ghetto which permitted some respite and stabilization.

Except for the initial period, Terezín did not have the character of a concentration camp. Its horrors were of a different order. Vestiges of civilian life remained and the degree of comfort (or privation and suffering) depended largely on whether one was in a position to obtain extra comforts. Naturally, the main problem was food. Official rations from communal kitchens and food depots in the barracks and blocks of houses, especially the reduced rations for the non-working inmates, were insufficient.[17] They consisted mainly of soup made of synthetic lentil or pea powder and of potatoes, boiled groats, millet, noodles, and some root vegetables with a negligible amount of meat, all ladled out once a day, at lunchtime. Small amounts of sugar, margarine, and jam were doled out in the various buildings and barracks. Bread rations varied. Individuals engaged in hard physical labor received more; those who did not work received less. In the morning there was a mess full of *ersatz* coffee. In the evening there was either more of the same, or soup. To depend solely on this diet meant starvation. Such was the fate of many old people from Germany and Austria who had no relatives in the ghetto to help them or who had nothing to barter for food and did not receive parcels from the outside. Official welfare did not amount to much. In the morning, at noon, and before nightfall, these old people, clutching their pans or mugs, patiently lined up for their food. They literally begged for the watery soup and were glad to get a few gulps of the vile coffee.

Others, more fortunate, had additional sources of food. Some had managed to bring in money or jewelry to sell for food. There was a good deal of smuggling because the SS never succeeded in completely severing contacts between the ghetto and the world outside. Others received food parcels sent regularly by friends or relatives. Groups working at the nearby SS farm smuggled vegetables into the ghetto. Stealing from public property, as opposed to private theft (which was comparatively rare), was called *schleusen* ("sluicing"). This included all sorts of goods, such as coal, wood, and clothing from the German central depot, or simply any article that could be exchanged for food or cigarettes.

Although smoking was a major offense, often punished by deportation, cigarettes were the universal currency. They were brought in by black marketeers with "Aryan" contacts. Whenever the SS organized searches of the barracks or when a new transport to the East was announced, the price of cigarettes would go up. Employees of the ghetto workshops took orders from individual inmates on a barter basis. The privilege of more frequent access to the public laundry and the bathhouse, and even preferential medical treatment, could be purchased. Artists sold their pictures or painted portraits for fees payable in cigarettes or food. The only commodity not for sale at any price was exemption from deportation to the East.

Understandably, young people had a better chance of survival than the elderly. Family relationships were often reversed, with children becoming the supporters and protectors of their elders. In most cases, familial ties remained intact with families keeping close together. It was common for young people to volunteer for a transport to the East in the hope that by doing so they would be able to help their parents who might follow them there. On the whole, it can be said that under the constant stress of ghetto life in Terezín, bonds of genuine family affection were strengthened, often by acts of self-sacrifice. On the other hand, relationships which had been superficial or shaky to begin with disintegrated more quickly in the ghetto than they would have under normal circumstances. This was particularly true in the case of married couples, who, with the exception of a privileged few, were not permitted to live together in Terezín. Husbands and wives could meet only for a brief period at the end of the working day, before the curfew, when they had to part again.

Younger inmates reacted to the atmosphere of impending doom by trying to enjoy what pleasures they could find. The past was a dim memory, the future dubious, to say the least. Only the present was real. In a kind of desperate innocence, many conventions were thrown overboard and lack of privacy did not necessarily inhibit sexual relations. Marriages were permitted, but the number of births was small and, for obvious reasons, pregnancies were usually interrupted.

Overcrowding made privacy almost unattainable; this made for additional tension and friction. Most of the living accommodations, whether barracks or other buildings, were, in fact, designed for sleeping only. These were also the only places where inmates could store their personal possessions, eat, and spend their free time after the curfew. Living accommodations for each inmate consisted simply of a bunk and a narrow space which divided it from the next bunk and was shared by six other inmates. Most of the bunks were arranged in two tiers; in some large rooms in the barracks, originally used for storage, three-tier bunks were erected. Small comforts such as a bunk near the stove or near the window assumed disproportionate importance. Under these conditions many people became irritable and quarreled bitterly, but if there was pettiness there was also generosity and a spirit of comradeship.

The ingenuity of some people in turning their bunk space into a home of sorts was amazing. Women did the impossible with their rations, supplementing them with whatever they could get. They prepared meals for their men on small electric rings, which they had installed illegally and which had to be hidden quickly whenever a search warning went out.[18] Day-to-day life was difficult; even the acquisition of a needle or of a pair of shoelaces presented a problem.

On the whole, the Jews adapted easily to social conditions in Terezín. Former lawyers, businessmen, traveling salesmen, and professional people took to manual work with good humor and without much grumbling. A surprising number of artisans worked well in all fields but, except for idealists in some of the ghetto services, the rule was to work as slowly as possible.

There were no mechanical means of transportation in the ghetto, nor were there horses. The universal vehicles were hearses taken from disbanded Jewish communities, with the elaborate superstructure usually removed. Each day these vehicles could be seen in the streets, hauled by a group of workers and laden with loaves of bread, wooden planks, luggage of new arrivals, or old people on their way to a delousing station or to medical treatment.

CULTURAL LIFE IN TEREZÍN

The scope and intensity of cultural life in "Ghetto Theresienstadt" has already been mentioned. It developed after the SS, for propaganda purposes, had decided to give Terezín the semblance of a normal town. Before long, cultural activities became an essential part of ghetto life. For the older inmates they were a solace, helping them forget the dreary present and conjuring up memories of a better past. Younger people saw cultural programs not only as welcome entertainment but also as a source of strength and a link with the world outside. With admirable devotion, young and old rehearsed plays and concerts after a day's work. They gave lectures and arranged performances and recitals at the ghetto's hospitals and homes for the aged. At one time inmates were offered a choice of ten different theater and cabaret performances, numerous musical events, and up to forty lectures on a wide range of topics each week. Performances were given in uninhabitable lofts and in the courtyards of houses and barracks. Later, two former cinemas and the former *sokolovna* (gymnasium) were used for this purpose. Hundreds of prisoners wrote poetry and painted or drew pictures. It was a form of inner resistance, a way to spiritual freedom.

But this flowering of culture in the Terezín ghetto was not without its ambiguities. Compared to the rest of Nazi-occupied Europe, one could almost say that the inmates of Terezín enjoyed freedom of speech and expression. The SS did not concern itself with controlling what was said on the stage or in the lecture halls. Although later some Czech plays were banned, supervision remained perfunctory. One is forced to conclude that the SS tolerated the fervent cultural life in the ghetto in the sure knowledge that it would be short-lived. It did not matter much what the inmates wrote or said; in the end they would all be exterminated. In the meantime cultural life (in any case something alien to SS men) was a useful means to help the SS create the false impression of a normal town. It also helped lull the inmates into a false sense of security.

No important literary work was produced in Terezín, perhaps because the creation of genuine literature needs a certain detachment which was understandably lacking in the ghetto. Established authors such as the well-known novelist Karel Poláček or the gentle poet and translator Kamil Hoffman kept silent but there were many others who tried to express what they felt in prose and verse. Their poetry is of psychological interest. Witnessing apocalyptic events, their lives under almost constant stress, most of the writers in Terezín expressed sentiments that were purely conventional. The older generation wrote in the style of the liberal nineteenth-century poets. Younger versifiers used the hackneyed phrases of the socialist poets of the 1920s. Some showed talent (chiefly lyrical, in the tradition of Czech poetry) but most of them could not find words to convey their own shattering experiences and the harsh realities of the ghetto.

With a few exceptions this characteristic is common to all poetry written in, or even about, concentration camps by people who under normal circumstances might never have taken up the pen. The poetry composed in Terezín by non-Zionist Czech Jews has one conspicuous feature: an almost total absence of Jewish motives. Most of these assimilationists avoided Jewish problems altogether. They identified completely with the Czech nation, its loss of independence, and its hopes for the future. They saw their plight not as another chapter in the long history of Jewish suffering but as a sudden political calamity. In other words, even though they were being persecuted not as Czechs but as Jews, they still felt as Czechs, whose sufferings in the war were incomparably less harsh and certainly less clearly defined than those of the Jews. Seen from this point of view, the largely undistinguished poetry of Terezín attains a tragic dimension.

Terezín's best achievements were in music. Despite the enthusiasm shown both by the performers and the public, the theater rarely reached truly professional standards. The two important figures of the Czech theater in Terezín were František Zelenka and Gustav Schorsch, both from Prague. Zelenka (born in 1904) was an experienced stage designer who before the war had worked for the Osvobozené Theater owned by the playwrights and actors Jiří Voskovec and Jan Werich in Prague and for other Czech theaters. In Terezín Zelenka designed sets and costumes for various stage productions such as the baroque folklore play *Esther,* a children's opera entitled *Brundibár,* and for *Karussel,* a cabaret production by another inmate, the actor Kurt Gerron of Berlin. Zelenka's designs showed skill, great inventiveness, and wit in using the limited materials available. He also successfully directed Molière's play *Georges Dandin.*

Schorsch (born in 1918) was a graduate of the Prague Academy of Dramatic Art. He exercised great influence, particularly among young people, through the sheer moral force of his personality. In Terezín he lectured on literature and philosophy and held nightly seminars on acting and the theater. He also organized numerous poetry recitals and directed several plays. He had the makings of a great director or teacher. A man of wide erudition, he could explain his ideas lucidly and was able to inspire his actors, who were largely inexperienced amateurs. Completely selfless, he seemed unaware of his grim surroundings, devoting himself singlemindedly to the work he thought important. His production of Gogol's *Marriage* was perhaps the best theatrical performance staged in Terezín.

Competent entertainers catered for more popular tastes. Musicals, operettas, and cabarets were greatly appreciated. The most popular among the latter was a cabaret by Karel Švenk (born in 1908), a self-taught musician and born Chaplinesque comedian from Prague. Švenk wrote the music, the dialogue, and also the lyrics for his two principal plays, *Ať žije život* (Long Live Life) and *Poslední cyklista* (The Last Bicyclist), both mildly satirical and vaguely socialist in content. His optimistic Terezín march ("Where there's a will, there's a way . . . we'll laugh upon the ruins of the ghetto in the end") was sung throughout Terezín.[19]

While no work of lasting literary significance was written in Terezín, things were different in the visual arts, on which reality always has a more direct impact. True, of the hundreds of pictures drawn or painted in Terezín, many do not rise above the level of dilettante or commercial art. But some are competently done or are of topographical interest. It is in the surviving works of three artists, Bedřich Fritta (Fritz Taussig), Otto Ungar, and Peter Kien that we find the ghetto depicted with veracity and vision.

All three men were employed in the *Zeichenstube* (drafting room) of the Technical Department, which, in addition to purely technical drawings, produced graphs, charts, and illustrations for the numerous reports demanded by the SS. Fritta was the head of the drafting office and Kien his deputy. With the full knowledge of the Jewish leadership, they sheltered in the *Zeichenstube* a number of fellow artists, giving them not only access to utensils and materials they could not have obtained otherwise but also ample time for private work.

Fritta, who was born in Ivančice in 1907, was a cartoonist and illustrator before the war. In Terezín he grew in stature. Immediately after his arrival there in the winter of 1941, he began to work on a series of pen-and-ink drawings. He attempted to put on paper as a kind of artistic testimony the things he saw each day in the ghetto. His cycle, *Horrors of Terezín,* faithfully reflects the terrible present: the haunting appearance of emaciated old men and women with huge yellow stars on their breasts; the grim faces of the workers; deportees to the East dragging their pathetic bundles on their way to the railroad station; the bleak vistas of Terezín's streets; the sordid barracks and courtyards; the general atmosphere of decay, and the hollowness of all the German attempts at "beautifying" the ghetto for the benefit of foreign visitors. The people who crowd Fritta's highly stylized nightmarish drawings are not individuals. In sharp, economical lines he attempted to portray the sufferings of mankind as a whole. Fritta was not an impartial witness. Though he drew only the tortured masses and rarely the torturers, he was a stern accuser. His narrow but powerful vision was derived from a deep inner conviction which is lacking in the works of other artists using identical themes. Even now his pictures convey the dread of Terezín. His art has withstood the test of time.

Otto Ungar, who was born in 1901, came to Terezín in the early days of the ghetto from his native Brno, where he had taught drawing and mathematics at a secondary school. His job in the *Zeichenstube* allowed him enough time to wander through the ghetto, observing and sketching. His work has a wider range than that of Fritta, partly because he was basically a painter, not a draftsman. In Terezín he produced mainly water colors but also some oils. His subject matter is similar to Fritta's but the treatment is different. His pictures reflect more sadness than sheer horror, greater maturity, and more interest in purely visual themes. His heavy figures of old men and women painted in somber colors and wide brush strokes convey a religious Old Testament feeling reminiscent of Rouault. The few trees in Terezín which Ungar so lovingly painted express a landscape artist's longing for nature and for wider, free horizons beyond the walls.

Peter Kien, the youngest of the three, born in 1919, was only twenty-two when he came to Terezín with one of the *Aufbaukommandos* from Prague. He had studied with Professor Willy Nowak at the Prague Academy of Arts. The three years he spent in Terezín were all the time that was given him for the development of his wide-ranging and genuine talent. As if he knew that his time was so short, Kien drew and painted like a man obsessed. He never went anywhere without his sketchbook, and with an amazing dexterity he recorded in pencil, or in pen and ink, anything that attracted his interest. Hundreds of his sketches, hidden by his friends, have survived. They all show Kien's observant eye, his surprisingly sure hand, his almost uncanny gift of characterization. Unlike Fritta, Kien broke out of the narrow confines of the ghetto. He did not shun the horrors he encountered each day, but he did not attempt to reduce them to symbols. He did not want to make a committed statement. He was interested in basic things and qualities—in movement, light, color, textures, and in features of the human face. Even in Terezín he sought beauty and found it. He used as many techniques as he could, experimenting and discovering. He made witty, elaborate caricatures of well-known personages and friends. He painted portraits in chalk and oil. He tried landscapes and still-lifes and even produced a stage backdrop for the performance of his play, *Puppets*. (He wrote poetry, too, and a libretto for an opera by Viktor Ullmann). In October 1944 Kien volunteered for a transport to the East into which his parents had been placed. He died in the gas chambers of Auschwitz.

Fritta and Ungar also went to Auschwitz. In July 1944 they were arrested together with three other artists (Felix Bloch, Leo Haas, and Norbert Troller), their families, and the aged art collector František Strass. First they were taken to the SS command and were interrogated by the commandant, SS Obersturmbannführer Karl Rahm; Ernst Möhs, the liaison officer between Berlin and Terezín who conveyed deportation orders and other directives from Berlin to the *Lagerkommandant;* and Rolf Günther from Berlin, who had some of their drawings and accused the artists of "disseminating hostile propaganda."[20] Later they were taken to the Little Fortress, where they were handed over to the Gestapo. Bloch was beaten to death; the others were sent to Auschwitz, one by one. Fritta died shortly after his arrival in Auschwitz; Ungar survived the evacuation of the camp to Buchenwald in the winter of 1944–45, only to die in a hospital near Weimar in July 1945. Strass died in Auschwitz. Haas (who was born in Opava in 1901 and treated the same themes as Fritta) and Troller survived the war.

A few other Terezín artists should also be mentioned. Karel Fleischmann, who was born in České Budějovice in 1897, was a physician whose sketches of the old and infirm show compassion and sometimes even an understanding humor. Malvína Schalková, who was born in Prague in 1887, was a sensitive painter of realistic scenes from everyday life in the ghetto. Adolf Aussenberg, who was born in Prague in 1917, painted sunny dreams of southern landscapes that adorned the walls of dormitories in the children's quarters.

A moving document of children's art in Terezín is the collection of 4,000 drawings, paintings, and collages which was preserved by the teachers of the Youth Welfare Office and donated by one of them to the State Jewish Museum in Prague after the war. The themes had been either assigned by their teachers or chosen freely. The pictures are in pencil, crayon, and water color on tinted or colored paper. The collages were made with all sorts of materials that happened to be at hand. Most of these young artists perished in Auschwitz; only a few were lucky enough to survive the war in Terezín.

Looking through the children's drawings one gradually becomes aware that their work was basically unaffected by the horrors of their surroundings. In the context of Terezín art they chose the way of Peter Kien rather than that of Fritta. In the drawings on themes chosen freely they depicted what they saw around them—food lines, barred windows, stretcher bearers, ghetto policemen, and freight trains filled with people. But their tendency is to soften rather than to stress the depressing scenes, and they paid a lot of attention to things which children might have drawn also under normal circumstances. Girls depicted ballerinas, flowers, and pretty cottages. Boys painted such "manly" subjects as detectives, battle scenes, and so forth. In other words, the children tried to create a complete, undistorted world of their own. A collection of drawings and poems by children in Terezín was published by the State Jewish Museum in Prague in 1962. In the epilogue, Jiří Weil aptly notes that the children saw everything the grownups saw:

> They saw the endless queues in front of the canteens, they saw the funeral carts used to carry bread and the human beings harnessed to pull them. They saw the infirmaries which seemed like a paradise to them and funerals which were only a gathering-up of coffins. They saw executions too, and were perhaps the only children in the world who captured them with pencil and paper . . . They heard the shouts of the SS men at roll call and the meek mumblings of prayer in the barracks where the grown-ups lived.
> But the children saw too what the grown-ups didn't want to see—the beauties beyond the village gates, the green meadows and the bluish hills, the ribbon of highway reaching off into distance and the imagined road marker pointing toward Prague, the animals, the birds, the butterflies . . . They saw things too that the grown-ups cannot see—princesses with coronets, evil wizards and witches, jesters and bugs with human faces, a land of happiness where for an admission of one crown, there was everything to be had . . . They saw too the rooms they'd lived in at home, with curtains at the window and a kitten and a saucer of milk. But they transported it to Terezín . . . All this they drew and painted, and many other things besides . . . [21]

RELIGION, MORALE, AND POLITICS IN TEREZÍN

What about religion, that other great support of the persecuted through the ages? What was the place of religious faith in the life of the Terezín community?

Officially, Jewish holidays were treated as ordinary working days in Terezín. However, religious services were held on those days before and after working hours. Some of the Jewish communities had brought with them their Scrolls of the Law, their *megillahs* (the Scrolls of Esther, which told the story of a miraculous deliverance of Jews from another foe, the evil Haman of Persia), ceremonial cups for the *kiddush* wine, and the *menorah* on which the Hanukkah lights were kindled. Services were held in a hall in one of the barracks and in improvised *shtibels* (prayer rooms) in lofts and attics. Each *shtibel* had its own rabbi and cantor. Dr. Zikmund Unger of

Brno acted as chief rabbi of the ghetto, assisted by Dr. Erich Weiner from Plzeň and Dr. Vojtěch Schoen from Brno. Religious marriage ceremonies were performed for practicing Jews; non-practicing or converted Jews were required to declare before the registrar that they would have their marriages legalized at the first opportunity.

The Jews from Germany and Austria, and later from Denmark, congregated around their own rabbis who had been deported to Terezín with them.[22] But most of the Jews from Czechoslovakia, particularly the younger generation, were indifferent to religious ideas and observances. Many of them celebrated Christmas in the traditional nonsectarian fashion to which they had been accustomed at home. Jewish history was taught at the children's homes in Terezín but more emphasis was placed on Jewish survival and national aspirations than on the purely religious aspects of Judaism. The only Jewish rites observed universally in the ghetto were those associated with death and burial: the washing of the dead before burial, funeral orations, and the mourners' *kaddish*.[23] Catholics and Protestants, whose number rose considerably during the final months of the war as children of mixed marriages arrived in Terezín, held services of their own.

The official language of "Ghetto Theresienstadt" was German, but even after the Jews from Czechoslovakia had been outnumbered by the Jews from other lands Czech was still mostly used and it was the Czechoslovak Jews who remained the principal active element in Terezín and gave the ghetto its character. Initially there was friction, both within the Jewish leadership and among the ordinary inmates, between the two main political groups into which the Jews in Terezín were divided: the Zionists and the assimilationists. Many of the latter considered themselves more Czech than Jewish. Zionists held leading positions in the office of the *Judenälteste* (the chairman of the *Ältestenrat*) and of his deputy, in the latter's secretariat, in the Labor Department, at the Youth Welfare Office, and also on some lower levels. The assimilationists were predominant in the Economic Department and in some other less influential offices. The Zionists were the only important group with a consistent political program and a closely knit organization. This also helped to strengthen their position in Terezín. A few Zionist activists saw their experience in Terezín as a kind of endurance test for their future life in an independent Jewish state. Many others felt that the

Jews in their enforced community should show a spirit of defiance and prove both to themselves and to the Germans that they would be able to overcome even the most difficult situations. This feeling was shared by a number of non-Zionists.

The assimilationists in Terezín had no leader comparable to Jakub Edelstein or Otto Zucker and no postwar aims other than to return to their homes where they had lived before their deportation. However, they formed the bulk of Terezín's working population and their strength lay in their sheer numbers, as well as in their cultural ascendancy, based on the living Czech culture which a great part of Czechoslovak Jewry, Zionists and non-Zionists alike, held in common.

In the later phases of the Terezín ghetto, the differences between Zionists and non-Zionists subsided and in the end even the assimilationists regarded Edelstein and Zucker as their representatives who defended their interests against the growing German-Jewish element. There was also a gradually dawning awareness that they were all in the same boat drifting in a sea of perils.

The hatred which the inmates felt for all Germans sometimes extended also to the German Jews in the ghetto, who were often accused of being pedantic and officious. Their position was, naturally, much more difficult because they could identify only with the German past, not with the German present.

The number of Communists among the Jews from Czechoslovakia in Terezín was insignificant compared with that of Zionists and assimilationists. Their activities were largely limited to mutual support (they were even represented, though not openly, of course, in the *Ältestenrat*) and to meetings at which they "analyzed the situation."

No one in Terezín ever doubted that the Germans would eventually lose the war, but the question was when. It was clear that the fate of the ghetto was closely bound up with the fortunes of the German armies. News supplied by incoming transports and by some friendly Czech gendarmes and other contacts who regularly listened to foreign broadcasts was quickly spread by word of mouth. "What's the news?" was the common greeting when people met.[24] At one time copies of the official German newspaper in the Protectorate of Bohemia and Moravia were posted on several billboards in the ghetto but this practice was discontinued after the magnitude of the German defeat at Stalingrad (February 2, 1943) had become obvious. Nevertheless, newspapers were smuggled in, avidly read, and thoroughly discussed. Many "absolutely reliable" rumors found ready acceptance but caused great disappointment when they proved to be unfounded. Political debates turned mainly on war events, and, as always, there were optimists and pessimists. The optimists maintained that before long the Germans would not be able to spare railroad lines and rolling stock for deporting Jews to the East. The pessimists, however, feared that even on the verge of their final defeat the Germans would drag the Jews down with them.

THE TIDE TURNS

In the summer of 1943 the tide of war began to turn in favor of the Allies. There had been no deportations to the East in four months and optimism was gaining ground. People began to believe in earnest that the reason for the deportations of Jews from Terezín to the East really had been "lack of space" in the ghetto and that, with the Germans otherwise occupied, the ghetto would now enjoy a modicum of peace. But they were soon to be tragically disillusioned.

In June 1943, Siegfried Seidl, the first SS commandant of Terezín, was replaced by Obersturmführer Anton Burger, a former Austrian schoolteacher.[25] Burger was not only a fanatical Nazi but also a sworn enemy of the Czechs and particularly of the Czech Jews, whom he suspected of underground activities. He was convinced that his predecessor had been on far too familiar terms with Jakub Edelstein. As a consequence, Edelstein's position became even more difficult than it had been before.

In July the SS ordered the workers' barracks cleared to make room for the archives of one of the departments of the *Reichssicherheitshauptamt* (RSHA; Central Reich Security Office), the Nazi government's main security department. These archives were transferred from Berlin to the Terezín ghetto because the Germans felt that there they would be safe from Allied bombings.[26] The barracks had to be cleared within thirty-six hours; this meant that new accommodations had to be found for almost 6,000 inmates in the already overcrowded ghetto.[27] Two months later, in September 1943, the SS cited this overcrowding as a pretext for dispatching a transport of 5,000 Czechoslovak Jews to the East. The lull in the deportations from Terezín had come to an end.

The list of persons to be included in this transport by express order of the SS command was clearly aimed at weakening the Czech group. Among the deportees was one of Edelstein's most trusted assistants, the able head of the Central Secretariat, Leo Janowitz. The *Lagerkommandant,* Anton Burger, also made a personal "selection" from the members of the two Czech *Aufbaukommandos* (construction details), AK I and II, who until then had been exempted from deportation in accordance with a promise given when they first arrived in Terezín late in 1941. The transport which left Terezín in September was officially described as a "labor transport" in order to foster the myth that the Germans were now running short of manpower and were using Jews as workers in their factories.[28]

Some six months later, postcards arrived in Terezín from these deportees. The return address on each card was "Labor Camp Birkenau near Neu-Berun" (a name which until then had been completely unknown). The cards all stated that living conditions at the "labor camp" were fair. The optimists in Terezín rejoiced. These cards seemed to confirm their hopes. But some of the messages contained ominous hints. The senders of the cards mentioned the names of people known to have been killed by the Gestapo a long time before and wrote that these people were now "together" with them. This message was a warning, and also literally true: the cards had been postdated, having been written on SS orders about a week before their senders entered the gas chambers of Auschwitz.

But on the whole, these hints went unheeded in Terezín. Some of the inmates even interpreted the messages in the cards as "good news," indicating that the people mentioned in the cards as "being together" with the senders had not been killed after all but were alive in the Birkenau "labor camp." Others, in their pathetic need for hope, suppressed their misgivings, but even they, of course, had no idea that Birkenau was identical with the death camp of Auschwitz.

Another indication of what awaited the Jews in the East came with the arrival of a transport of about 1,300 Jewish children from Poland late in August 1943. This heartbreaking tattered procession was taken to the delousing station. There the children panicked and refused to go under the showers. Finally, some Jewish medical orderlies gained the children's confidence. A boy of twelve, who acted as "spokesman" for the young arrivals, surreptitiously explained that they had come from the ghetto of Bialystok in Poland. At Bialystok their parents had either been shot in the town square or gassed inside a building which had been marked "Baths." Since the Germans had threatened death to anyone who talked to the children, this story did not spread widely and even those who heard it found ways to disregard it. After all, they told themselves, Terezín was, thank God, not in Poland . . . and so on. The Jewish leadership realized that these reports were true and confirmed their worst fears of what was happening to the deportees in Poland, but even they did not fully connect the fate of the Jews in the Polish ghettos with the fate of transports from Terezín to the East.

Early in October the children from Bialystok were placed into wooden barracks outside the town, where they were kept in strict isolation in the care of a voluntary staff of fifty inmate nurses. The reason for this arrangement remained a mystery, but the optimists in Terezín noted reports that the nurses had been ordered to take off their yellow Stars of David and to sign a declaration that they would not under any circumstances discuss their experiences in Terezín. From these reports the optimists concluded that the children, accompanied by the nurses, would be sent to neutral Switzerland.[29]

"BEAUTIFICATION"

At about the same time (in October 1943) the first transport of Jews from Denmark arrived in Terezín. Two more such transports followed, bringing the total of deportees from Denmark to about 450. This was the smallest national group in Terezín, but its arrival was to have a remarkable impact on the life in the ghetto.

The story of the Danish Jews during the Holocaust is one of the few examples of a successful Jewish struggle against persecution. When in October 1943 the *Zentralstelle für jüdische Auswanderung* (Central Office for Jewish Emigration) decided to round up the Jews in Denmark and deport them, the German naval attaché, George Ferdinand Duckwitz, secretly informed the Danish underground and the Swedish government. Most of the Jews in Denmark, with the active assistance of the Danes, succeeded in escaping to Sweden before the roundups for deportation began, so that the SS were able to deport only a fraction of Denmark's Jewish population. Almost immediately after the arrival of Danish Jews in Terezín, Danish authorities requested that representatives of the Danish and Swedish Red Cross be permitted to visit them. Pressure was kept up and though the *Zentralstelle* was furious, the German Foreign Office did not wish to reject the Danish request, because it was supported by neutral Sweden. Negotiations dragged on, with the Danes persisting and Berlin vacillating. Meanwhile, the Danish Jews in Terezín acquired a truly privileged status. They were allowed to receive and write letters almost without restrictions. Food parcels, generously supplied by the Danish and Swedish Red Cross, made them practically independent of the ghetto food rations. They were better housed, and last, but certainly not least, they were strictly exempt from deportation to the East.

Finally, in April 1944, following the intervention of King Christian X of Denmark, the bishop of Copenhagen, and the chancellors of Danish universities, Berlin gave in. The date for the Red Cross visit to Terezín was set for June. As early as December 1943 a special program of improvements, much more far-reaching than previous "normalization" measures, had been ordered in Terezín. The new scheme was given the name *Stadtverschönerung* ("city beautification") and Dr. Benjamin Murmelstein of the ghetto triumvirate was put in charge.

The announcement of the impending "beautification" coincided with the departure from Terezín of two transports consisting of 5,000 Jews from Czechoslovakia. The destination of this transport was Auschwitz. Traveling in the guard's car attached to one of the deportation trains was Jakub Edelstein, the first *Judenälteste* of Terezín. Edelstein had been arrested on November 9, 1943, along with the head of the central registry and two of his clerks, after *Lagerkommandant* Burger had raided the registry and seized a part of its records. Charged with having abetted the escape of fifty-five inmates from the ghetto,[30] Edelstein was taken to the cellar of the SS command and kept there in strict isolation until the departure of the next transport to the East. In Auschwitz he was taken to the main camp and placed into an underground prison while his family went to Birkenau with the rest of the transport. On June 20, 1944, they were all shot in the crematorium building in Auschwitz. According to eyewitnesses, Edelstein died as manfully as he had lived.[31]

In Terezín, Otto Zucker took Edelstein's place both as Paul Eppstein's first deputy and as the acknowledged spokesman of the Jews from Czechoslovakia.

In February 1944 the "beautification" began in earnest when Burger was relieved of his post and SS Obersturmbannführer Karl Rahm, originally a lathe operator by trade, was appointed *Lagerkommandant* in his place. Like his predecessors, the third and last *Lagerkommandant* of Terezín was an Austrian.[32] He harbored the half-envious dislike which some of his fellow Austrians felt for the Germans. He vented his prejudice on Eppstein, the German Jew in the triumvirate, whose position consequently became increasingly precarious. As director of the "beautification" program, Rahm took up the idea with great zeal and thoroughness. In the first phase, general improvements were carried out. In the second, Rahm concentrated on details of the actual route which the visiting Red Cross commission would take through the ghetto.

In May 1944, in the midst of the "beautification" efforts, three transports left Terezín—a total of 7,500 people, of whom one-third were Jews from Czechoslovakia. The reality of the extermination plan was not to be sacrificed to the fiction of "beautification." All the same, the "beautification" measures, thoroughly pursued and given every priority, greatly increased the self-deception among many of the inmates. They saw these activities as another proof that despite everything, the status of "Ghetto Theresienstadt" was unique. Moreover, Germany was clearly on the road to defeat and the end of war seemed much nearer. Such was the prevailing view among the optimists.

The pessimists, on the other hand, feared that the "beautification" program had a specific purpose and that it would stop once that purpose was achieved. They also pointed out that though Paris had been liberated by the Allied armies, Terezín and the whole of the Protectorate of Bohemia and Moravia were still firmly in the hands of Germans.

The much-expected, oft-rehearsed visit of the Red Cross commission took place on June 23, 1944. Two senior Danish officials and one Swiss from the International Red Cross Committee arrived in Terezín, attended by a number of high SS officers, including Rolf Günther and Ernst Möhs. Except for Rahm, the commandant, none of the SS officers was in uniform. Accompanied by Eppstein, the commission was escorted along the scheduled route. For the occasion, Eppstein had been given a car driven by an SS chauffeur from the SS command, who took off his cap and opened the car door with a flourish for his "boss." Other staged effects were duly displayed along the route. They were set off by signals from orderlies who raced ahead of the commission. Eppstein, as chairman of the *Ältestenrat,* was ordered to act as the guide for the visitors, with the SS remaining in the background. In a lecture prepared for him by the SS command, he "enlightened" the visitors on "Jewish Self-Government in Terezín."[33] The guests visited the Danish Jews in their apartments, which had been specially furnished and decorated for the occasion.

Terezín, as presented to the visitors on that beautiful summer day, was not unlike a posed photograph. It was frozen in the present of its false image. It had no past and, as far as the SS were concerned, no future. From their point of view the visit had gone off satisfactorily. They had "beautified" Terezín to such an extent that it could safely be shown to the visitors during the eight hours they spent there; everything had gone according to plan. True, the commission noted that many of the improvements seemed to be of recent date but they expressed admiration for the achievements of Jewish self-government in the ghetto. The Danish member of the commission emphasized in his report that "it must be presumed that the morale of the population . . . will depend to a not inconsiderable extent on the belief that their stay in Theresienstadt is merely temporary."[34]

Surprisingly, the "beautification" was not discontinued immediately after the departure of the visitors. The SS decided to exploit their laboriously achieved asset by producing a film about Terezín for propaganda use in Germany. It was to show the pleasant life the Jews in Terezín were enjoying while German cities were being bombed. The film was made by Aktualita, a private company in Prague specializing in documentary films, and produced and directed by the Terezín inmate Kurt Gerron, who had been a cabaret actor in Berlin before the war. Many of the inmates, especially those with pronounced Jewish features, were ordered to join the cast of the production. A crude piece of propaganda, the film was never used as intended because it was not ready for showing until March 1945. By that time even the much-vaunted Nazi propaganda machine was grinding to a halt.

In mid-September 1944, immediately after the end of the filming, rumors of impending new deportations to the East began to spread through Terezín and were soon confirmed by an announcement that two transports were about to be sent eastward.

LIQUIDATION

As the German armies were driven back into the German heartland on all fronts, the *Zentralstelle* began to speed up the extermination of the Jews. Hungarian and Slovak Jews were sent to Auschwitz by the thousands. The last remaining Polish ghetto, that of Lodz (where a small number of Jews deported from Prague during the winter of 1941 had survived), was liquidated during August and September. The turn of Terezín, the last major Jewish community in Central Europe with the exception of Budapest, had come.

The first announcement was made on September 23, 1944, and was couched in cautious terms. Five thousand male workers were to leave Terezín and travel "in the direction of Dresden" to set up "a new labor camp under the direction of Otto Zucker." Families of the departing workers who were left in Terezín were told they would be fully exempt from deportation. They were promised, among other things, that there would be frequent postal communications with the new camp.

By deporting more than half of Terezín's total male working population of about 8,000, the SS were attempting to insure themselves against the possibility of an open revolt in the ghetto, which would have been dangerous for them in the strategically important Protectorate amidst the repressed but increasingly hostile Czech population. After the uprisings that had taken place in Warsaw and in Slovakia in the summer and early fall of 1944 they were taking no chances. This deportation also dealt effectively with the most active element in Terezín, the Jews from Czechoslovakia and their leader, Otto Zucker.

Four days after the announcement of the Dresden "project," Eppstein was placed under arrest by *Lagerkommandant* Karl Rahm and charged, under a transparent pretext, with attempting to escape. On the same day he was escorted to the Little Fortress, where he was shot in the back by one of the guards immediately after his arrival.[35] It has been suggested that Eppstein was executed because he had refused to organize the transports "in the direction of Dresden" but there is no evidence to support this assertion. In fact, at the time of his arrest, the first two transports had already been put together. Most probably the SS killed him in order to increase confusion in the ghetto by depriving it of its executive head. It may be assumed that the decision had been made in Berlin and brought to Terezín by Ernst Möhs, the harbinger of deportations, who was present at Eppstein's arrest. Eppstein's death remained unknown in the ghetto; Rahm even accepted underwear and food from his wife for delivery to him. The announcement that Eppstein had been deported was not made until a month later.

The first train, with 2,500 men, left Terezín on September 27, 1944; the second, two days later. At the station, Zucker and Karl Schliesser (a Czech who had been head of the Economic Department and had been ordered to join the transport as an "expert") were separated from the other deportees so that they might be able to "travel in comfort and receive instructions." Zucker tried to protest, but to no avail. The two men were seen once more when the train arrived at Auschwitz in the early hours of the next morning. Handcuffed, they were taken "to the other side" and shot.

The third transport of workers was augmented by families of men who had already left or were now leaving Terezín. They were told that they would be "permitted to join" their loved ones at their destination. As a result, many volunteered for the transport.

Until then, many of the inmates still believed that the deportations would be of limited character and, to a certain extent, that the deportees were really being sent to set up a new labor camp. This soon changed. Only two hours after *Lagerkommandant* Rahm had given assurances that no further deportations would take place, another transport was ordered to leave Terezín. Thereafter, the departure of one transport was closely followed by an order to dispatch the next. There was no respite. With the hard core of the ghetto gone, the SS dropped all pretense. Until that point, such individuals as physicians and artisans who were considered essential for the smooth operation of the ghetto had been exempted from deportation. But now exemptions were limited to individuals above the age of sixty-five. The old were allowed to remain in Terezín while their children left. The SS singled out certain groups which were still to be exempted from deportation, such as the Jews from Denmark and a small group of Dutch Jews in whom international organizations might be expected to take a special interest. But the list of inmates to be deported by order of the SS command grew steadily longer. Handed out at every transport, these lists methodically included higher and lesser officials of the administration, political suspects, former army officers, and so forth. Finally, all those inmates under sixty-five years of age who were still left in Terezín were paraded before Rahm and Möhs, who "selected" each individual case on the spot.

The eleventh and last transport left Terezín on Czechoslovak Independence Day, October 28, 1944. The last two cars of this train had been "reserved" for most of the members of the *Ältestenrat* and other important personages. When they arrived in Auschwitz these passengers were taken directly to the gas chambers.

Thus, within a month, over 18,000 people, or about two-thirds of the population of "Ghetto Theresienstadt," had been deported. Of those who stayed behind, over seventy percent were women. The ghetto administration was totally disrupted. Maintenance almost came to a standstill and the future of the ghetto was very uncertain.[36]

This near-liquidation proved to be the last successful strike of the *Zentralstelle* against Terezín. Beginning in the summer of 1944, dissidents who were opposed to the extermination plan were at work in Germany. In time these trends became more powerful. Hitler was determined to the very end to achieve at least one of his war aims, that of exterminating European Jewry, but communication with him became more and more difficult. It was clear that he was fast losing control of the situation. Some of his closest collaborators, including SS chief Heinrich Himmler, the overlord of concentration camps and of the *Reichssicherheitshauptamt,* began to act on their own. Negotiations regarding the fate of the surviving Jews opened between a number of international and Jewish organizations and certain SS officers and groups. The negotiations were protracted, difficult, and confused. Nevertheless, they saved lives during the final months of the war and they saved the Jews who were still left in Terezín at the time.

Although some of its staff took part in these negotiations, Eichmann's *Zentralstelle* still tried to continue implementing the extermination plan. But as the end of the war drew nearer, the adherents of the "Final Solution" were losing the means, if not the will, to carry it out. Due to these opposing tendencies the final phase of Terezín's existence as a ghetto was marked by repeated efforts to save the remaining inmates side by side with actions intended to destroy them. The former efforts did not gain the upper hand until shortly before the end of the war.

During November and December 1944 Terezín slowly recovered from the shock and trauma of the mass deportations. The SS ordered several alterations in their living quarters, as if they were intended to stay there forever. The work had to be done by a greatly reduced labor force, which now consisted mainly of women and children from the age of ten upward.

Early in December 1944, an SS commission inspected the town to see if there was any purpose it could still serve. Several days later, a program of stabilization was launched. On December 15, a new *Ältestenrat* was appointed. Benjamin Murmelstein, who had run the ghetto alone since Eppstein's arrest, now became the *Judenälteste*, the sole head of the ghetto. Dr. Leo Baeck, the highly respected rabbi from Berlin, was named his deputy. In the new *Ältestenrat* each of the nationalities in the ghetto was represented,[37] but the reorganized administration to all practical purposes remained in the hands of Murmelstein.

In December 1944, a transport of some 400 Jews arrived from the transit camp of Sered, Slovakia. During the months that followed, three others arrived, bringing the total number of Jews from Slovakia in Terezín to about 1,400.[38] The newcomers brought a great deal of information about Auschwitz. The true character of the camp had been known to Jews in Slovakia since the spring of 1944.[39] Nevertheless, people in Terezín were still reluctant to believe that most of the transports that left the ghetto had been marked for Auschwitz.

At the end of January 1945, a transport of about 1,000 people reached Terezín. These were Jewish partners in mixed marriages who until then had been exempt from "ghettoization." They were now brought to Terezín in nine transports from Prague and other cities—a total of over 3,500 persons. The *Zentralamt* machine was also still operating in Germany and kept dispatching transports to Terezín right up to the middle of April 1945.[40]

But on February 3, to the great surprise of the inmates, the SS issued an order for a transport of 1,200 people to go not to the East but to Switzerland. This was the result of negotiations conducted with the Germans by the former president of the Swiss Confederation, Jean-Marie Mussy, supported by the Agudath Israel and the Union of Orthodox Rabbis of the United States and Canada. The Terezín inmates, of course, had no knowledge whatsoever of these negotiations. At first they regarded the new transport with suspicion, especially since the Danes, who were still exempt from deportation, were excluded. But eventually a group of volunteers assembled and left on February 5. They found themselves traveling in a comfortable express train. A few days later, postcards arrived in Terezín from Switzerland. This development set off a wave of optimism among the remaining inmates because it now seemed that there had been a definite, drastic change in SS policy.

At about the same time construction work was begun on two bastions of the old Terezín fortifications. The purpose of the work was a mystery. Both sites were inspected by high-ranking SS officers, including Rolf Günther. The Jewish engineers who had been watching the projects closely concluded that a passage in one of the bastions was being converted into a gas chamber and that a moat in the other was being altered to serve as a trap where inmates could be mowed down by machine-gun fire from above. The engineers pressed Murmelstein to make representations to *Lagerkommandant* Rahm, but Rahm ridiculed their fears, explaining that the passage was to serve as a food store and the moat as a "duck pond." Work on both projects continued, though at a much slower pace, to be stopped only after the second "beautification" of Terezín had been ordered on March 5, 1945.

THE SECOND "BEAUTIFICATION"

The renewed "beautification" effort was set off by negotiations between the International Red Cross Committee, Heinrich Himmler, and the chief of the *Reichssicherheitshauptamt,* Ernst Kaltenbrunner, on the wider issue of concentration camp inspections and the rescue of camp inmates. Once again a Red Cross delegation was permitted to visit Terezín, which, once again, had to serve as a "model camp." Installations from the first "beautification" of the year before were overhauled and even improved. All documents and statistics referring to the period prior to January 1945, including mortality figures and transport lists, were collected and incinerated. The SS went through all the photographs in Terezín and destroyed them, including photographs of deportees in the possession of relatives who had remained behind in the ghetto. The wildly unrealistic purpose of all these arrangements was to present Terezín as a model Jewish settlement without any unpleasant past.[41]

On April 6 a three-man delegation, led by Paul Dunant, the International Red Cross delegate for "Ghetto Theresienstadt," arrived in a white car marked with a large red cross. Accompanied by Adolf Eichmann and other SS officers, Dunant toured the ghetto and met Benjamin Murmelstein. Afterwards he left for Prague to continue negotiations with Karl Hermann Frank,[42] the State Secretary for the Protectorate of Bohemia and Moravia. The Red Cross emblem displayed on the visitors' car brought some reassurance to the people in Terezín even though they had no certainty that the SS might not launch a sudden desperate last-ditch operation against them. The mood in the ghetto improved considerably when, on April 15, the Swedish Red Cross, having negotiated the release of the Danish Jews, came to call for them with a convoy of buses.

LIBERATION

Lagerkommandant Karl Rahm did not leave Terezín until May 5 or 6, but the authority of the SS began to break down after Dunant's visit and the departure of the Danish Jews. The inmates were becoming impatient. During the night of April 17, rumors spread through the ghetto that the Germans had capitulated and that the SS had fled. The inmates cheered, embraced one another in the streets, and sang. In the midst of the rejoicing Rahm appeared with an armed detachment in one of the barracks, where the inmates had already began to pack their belongings. It was a tense moment, but the tension subsided with the first word of Rahm's address to the crowd: "Gentlemen . . ." He urged the inmates to keep calm because the end of the war was at hand. Then he turned and marched away.

However, Eichmann and Günther made two more—admittedly feeble—attempts to use the inmates of Terezín for their purposes. On April 19, a new transport was announced, allegedly bound for Switzerland. The inmates at first did not suspect foul play but soon there were misgivings. Participation in this transport was not voluntary and the SS command stressed that the transport should be kept secret from Paul Dunant. The *Ältestenrat* succeeded in sending a message to Dunant in Prague. Dunant returned to Terezín on April 21 with a firm promise from State Secretary Frank that there would be no more deportations from Terezín. Dunant assured the Council of the "continuous support of the International Red Cross in every respect." But several days after Dunant's second visit, the SS, despite Frank's promise, tried to organize another transport. This time the transport was to be one of workers and artisans for "the construction of barracks in Germany." Neither transport materialized; both attempts probably reflected the Nazi plan to make a last stand in the Bavarian Alps, holding hostages for negotiations.

This last-ditch effort on the part of the SS was overshadowed by other events. On April 20, 1945, the first transports from concentration camps evacuated before the advancing Allied armies arrived in Terezín.[43] The prisoners had been dragged through the now chaotic German heartland, in some cases for several weeks, some in railroad cars, others on foot. Often they had gone without food for days. Once they reached Bohemia, they were directed to Terezín. The first train brought 2,000 men and women in the last stages of exhaustion. Among them were some men who had been deported from Terezín the previous October. Their own mothers were unable to recognize them.

These last arrivals were appalling harbingers of even more horrifying news. At last, the remaining inmates of Terezín were brought face to face with the truth about the "other ghettos and labor camps in the East" and the "labor camp of Birkenau" to which their loved ones and friends had been deported. Any illusions they still might have harbored were now shattered. The fate of European Jewry became terribly clear at last.

The history of the ghetto in Terezín began with executions. It ended with a typhoid epidemic. Discovered in the last days of April among new arrivals, the disease spread quickly. It was impossible to take effective measures and altogether some 3,000 cases occurred, 500 of them fatal. The main burden of caring for the patients fell to the Jewish medical service. On the eve of liberation, some forty doctors, nurses, and orderlies gave their lives for their fellow Jews. The arrival of the Czech Assistance Action, a group of volunteer doctors and nurses from Prague, on May 4, 1945, did little to alleviate the critical situation. They attended almost exclusively to the non-Jewish prisoners from the Little Fortress, who had been brought to Terezín after Dunant and the Red Cross had taken over in the ghetto. The former ghetto now had a total population of over 30,000 people. Many were in urgent need of medical attention but the ghetto had been left to its own devices. Decisive action against the epidemic had to await the arrival of medical units of the Red Army. The Russians entered Terezín on May 11, set up a new delousing station and five hospitals, and ordered a strict quarantine. By the middle of June they had succeeded in quelling the outbreak.

Thus, the chaotic transitional period following the breakup of the SS authority gradually and painfully merged into freedom. May 2 should be considered the actual day of liberation, the day on which "Ghetto Theresienstadt" as such ceased to exist. On that day the SS flag was hauled down from the abandoned SS headquarters and replaced by the flag of the International Red Cross. Murmelstein resigned, and for a few days Terezín was nominally run by a council headed by Dr. Leo Baeck. With the arrival of the Russians, Dunant, his mission accomplished, handed over the command. Jiří Vogel, a Czech Communist and former member of the *Ältestenrat,* was appointed as the temporary head of the administration in the name of the Czechoslovak Republic. After two weeks of quarantine the repatriation of inmates began and did not end until August.

For several months thereafter, Terezín remained empty, suspended between its past and its future. German inscriptions faded on dirty and peeling walls, wooden huts slowly disintegrated, and the tracks over which the deportation trains had traveled to the East became overgrown with grass. In 1946, former inhabitants of the town began to return and soon the barracks were occupied by units of the Czechoslovak army.[44]

In conclusion, a few general observations remain to be made:

As we have shown, "Ghetto Theresienstadt," contrary to the wishful thinking of some of its inmates, was not unique. It merely represented an "adjustment of a war aim" within the framework of the Nazi plan for the extermination of the Jews. Thus, while the Nazi deceit took the form first of a "labor ghetto," then of an "old people's ghetto," and finally of a "model ghetto," the most relevant feature always was the railroad line which led from Terezín to Auschwitz.

History will recall Terezín as a gateway through which most of the Jews of Bohemia and Moravia, members of a once vigorous and flourishing community, passed on the way to their death.

Though history may regret what did not come to pass, it can record only what actually happened. It must be admitted that the efforts of the Jewish leadership had only a limited success. True, they helped make the lives of Terezín's inmates easier. To some extent the leaders of the ghetto helped delay deportations to the East and so were instrumental in saving those few who were permitted to remain in the ghetto. Jakub Edelstein, Otto Zucker, and others may have failed to fulfill the expectations of their posterity, but this does not detract from their claim to our respect and admiration. They could not win their struggle because they attempted the impossible. Yet their motives were noble and we must remember that they paid with their lives for their endeavors on behalf of their fellow Jews.

NOTES

1. Hitler's address to the Reichstag on January 30, 1939.
2. On their arrival at the Nisko camp, the deportees from Moravská Ostrava, later joined by Jews from Vienna and from several Polish cities, found that there were not even huts to sleep in; they had to build these themselves. When the camp was liquidated, some of the inmates were driven by armed guards across the Soviet frontier; others were taken back to Ostrava, from where they were deported, first to Terezín and subsequently to the East. See Erich Kulka, "The Annihilation of Czechoslovak Jews," in the present volume, pp. 265–68.
3. Eichmann's office, the *Zentralstelle für jüdische Auswanderung* (its Prague branch was later renamed *Zentralamt für die Regelung der Ju-*

denfrage in Böhmen und Mähren, Central Office for the Solution of the Jewish Problem in Bohemia and Moravia) was to all practical purposes identical with Sub-department IV b 4 of the Gestapo which, under Heinrich Mueller, formed Department IV of the *Reichssicherheitshauptamt* (RSHA; Central Reich Security Office), headed by Reinhard Heydrich until his assassination in May 1942, and afterwards by Ernst Kaltenbrunner. The Berlin *Zentralstelle* had branches in the occupied countries, among them the *Zentralamt* (or *Zentralstelle*) in Prague, headed by Hans Günther. The *Lagerkommandatur* of Terezín was a *Dienststelle* (field office) of the Prague *Zentralamt.* Eichmann's aide-de-camp Ernst Möhs acted as liaison between the Berlin *Zentralamt* and its branches. Günther was allegedly killed in a skirmish near Prague in May 1945; Mueller and Möhs disappeared and as of this writing have yet to be brought to justice.

4. Records of the Conference on the Solution of Jewish Problems, published in Czech in *Věstník židovské náboženské obce v Praze* [Information Bulletin of the Jewish Religious Congregation of Prague], No. 11, 1961. See Illustration 4.
5. Thus, at the beginning of the deportations, when two officials of the Prague Jewish Religious Congregation, Hanuš Bonn and Erik Kafka, merely suggested that they could not cope with the pace of registrations ordered by the *Zentralstelle,* they were charged with sabotage and sent to Mauthausen, where they died twelve days after their arrest.
6. It consisted of the office of the *Judenälteste* (chairman of the Council of Jewish Elders) and his deputy, their Central Secretariat, and five, later eight, administrative departments. The *Ältestenrat* (Council of Jewish Elders) consisted of the *Judenälteste,* his deputy, the head of the secretariat and heads of the departments and their deputies. The *Judenälteste* and his deputy were appointed directly by the SS. Members of the council were chosen by agreement among Jewish political groups, or on the basis of their expertise in certain fields. The first council consisted of the following: Jakub Edelstein, Otto Zucker, Rudolf Bergmann, Erwin Elbert, Rudolf Freiberger, Julius Gruenberger, Leo Hess, Leo Janowitz, Erich Klapp, Erich Munk, Egon Popper, Karl Schliesser, and Jiří Vogel.
7. Seidl, a native of Vienna, was apprehended after the war, sentenced to death, and hanged in Vienna in February 1947.
8. This was the only time that the true destination was given in a transport order. Subsequent transport orders spoke merely of "destination East," "another ghetto," "territory of the Reich," etc. For detailed information on the fate of transports from Terezín see: Zdeněk Lederer, *Ghetto Theresienstadt* (London: 1953), pp. 199–242.

9. Four months later, on May 27, 1942, Heydrich was assassinated in Prague by Czechoslovak parachutists from Britain. A few days after he died, all 20,000 inmates the Terezín were ordered to sign a statement that they knew nothing about the origin of a suitcase, a bicycle, and other articles allegedly found on the spot where Heydrich had been ambushed. Apparently the SS did this in order to be able to report that the ghetto offered no leads to the assassin. On June 10, thirty workers from the Terezín ghetto were driven by truck to the village of Lidice, which had been razed as a reprisal for Heydrich's assassination. There, they were ordered to dig a mass grave to bury the villagers murdered by the SS.
10. *Trials of War Criminals before the Nuremberg Military Tribunals,* (Washington: 1952), vol. XIII, HG-2586, pp. 210–17.
11. Sometimes, as a collective punishment, the SS command extended the curfew so that no one was allowed to leave the barracks after 6 P.M. Such a punishment was usually combined with a ban on the use of electric lights that evening.
12. For most of the time living space per head did not exceed two square meters, compared with the minimum of eight square meters required by prewar Czechoslovak law. The density of population in the Terezín ghetto per square kilometer varied from almost 170,000 in 1942 to 80,000 in 1944.
13. Approximately 15,000 children passed through Terezín; of these, only 100 survived the war.
14. The first 10,000 most probably went to the Minsk region of Belorussia. There are no reliable reports because there were no survivors from these transports. The four October transports (8,000 people from Bohemia and Moravia) were killed off in Treblinka, with the exception of the last, which became the first transport from Terezín to arrive in Auschwitz, where the gas chambers had been in operation since September 1941. Auschwitz became the destination of all transports which left Terezín for the East. The last deportees from Terezín arrived in Auschwitz at the end of October 1944.
15. After the war, Dr. Murmelstein spent six months in custody in Prague while charges of collaboration made against him were investigated by the Czechoslovak authorities. The charges were found to be unsubstantiated and Murmelstein was released.
16. Westerbork was a transit camp for Dutch Jews on their way to the East set up by the *Zentralstelle* in 1942 along lines resembling those of Terezín. Most of the inmates were sent to their death at Sobibor and Auschwitz. But inmate officers and several other "privileged" inmates were sent to Terezín instead. The last transport of 2,000 Dutch Jews

arrived in Terezín in August 1944. Their total number reached almost 5,000. Many of them were refugees from Germany who had been trapped in Holland when the Nazis invaded that country in the spring of 1940.
17. There were different rationing classifications. In order to receive the standard rations (Category N) one had to be registered as working. Rations were lower for the non-working population (Category K), and higher for those engaged in hard physical labor (Category S).
18. Searches became less frequent as Terezín evolved from a quasi-internment camp into a "self-governing" ghetto community. The SS rarely visited the ghetto except on official occasions and to supervise transports to the East. (However, Edelstein and his successors reported to the SS command daily.)
19. Zelenka and Schorsch as well as Švenk were deported to Auschwitz in October 1944. All three perished.
20. It has never been discovered how the SS got hold of the pictures. Strass was an avid art collector who continued his avocation in Terezín. He had good contacts with the outside world and succeeded in smuggling out some of the drawings he had bought from Fritta and other artists. According to Haas (*Terezín* [Prague: 1965], p. 158) some of these works reached Switzerland. Oddly enough, the SS only searched for other pictures much later, toward the end of the war. After the liberation of the ghetto, Fritta's drawings were taken out of their hiding place. Together with the works of Ungar and other Terezín artists they are now in the State Jewish Museum in Prague. The pictures have been exhibited several times and reproduced both in Czechoslovakia and abroad.
21. *I Never Saw Another Butterfly: Children's Drawings and Poems: Terezín 1942–1944,* ed. Hana Volavková (Prague: 1962), Eng. trans. Jeanne Nemcova.
22. Among them were Dr. Leo Baeck and Dr. Martin Salomonski of Berlin, Dr. Leopold Neuhaus of Frankfurt on Main, and Dr. Max Friediger of Copenhagen. One of the most popular rabbis preaching in Czech was Dr. Richard Feder of Kolín.
23. Initially the dead were buried in paper shrouds; the use of textiles was strictly forbidden. They were interred in mass graves in a cemetery outside the walls of the town. Starting in the fall of 1942, they were cremated in a newly erected crematorium near Terezín and their ashes kept in cardboard urns. In October 1944, 25,000 urns were emptied into a disused quarry and into the nearby river in an attempt on the part of the SS to destroy all evidence of the high mortality among the Terezín inmates.

24. The news of the Allied landing in Normandy became known in Terezín on the same day, June 6, 1944.
25. After the war, Burger escaped from an American internment camp. He has not been apprehended to date.
26. The archival material included Gestapo papers dealing with concentration camps, thousands of index cards, and files. They were burned before Department No. VII, *Konzentrationslagerpapiere,* also referred to as *Berliner Dienststelle* (Berlin Office), left Terezín in April 1945.
27. The population of the Terezín ghetto in July 1943 was 46,000.
28. Eventually, things indeed came to this point, but only after May 1944, although the gas chambers in Auschwitz did not stop operating until November of that year. The September transport went to the Jewish part of Auschwitz, called Birkenau, where the deportees from Terezín spent the next six months. On March 7, 1944, those still alive, with the exception of thirty-seven people (mostly twins used for medical experiments), were killed in the gas chambers.
29. This might really have happened. In May 1943 the Swiss embassy in Berlin transmitted to the German Foreign Office an offer from the British government to admit to Britain 5,000 children from Poland, Lithuania, and Latvia. The offer was never officially rejected but it was sabotaged by Eichmann's *Zentralstelle.* And so the children and their nurses, including Franz Kafka's favorite sister, Otla Davidová, went from Terezín to Auschwitz, directly to the gas chambers.
30. There had always been discrepancies in the registry, partly due to errors in transport lists, which were subsequently papered over, and partly because the Jewish administration tried to cover up as many escapes as possible. In any event, escapes were not numerous. Though it was not particularly difficult for an active man to escape, it was very hard, once outside, for a ghetto inmate to find a hiding place or to obtain forged Aryan papers. In the entire span of the ghetto's existence only about forty people were reported as missing from the ghetto.
31. Deposition made in 1945 in Prague by A. Schoen with the "Documentation Action" of the Jewish Agency. See H. G. Adler, *Theresienstadt 1941–1945,* 2d ed., (Tübingen: 1960), p. 810.
32. After the war, Rahm was extradited from Austria and sentenced to death in Litoměřice, Czechoslovakia. He was hanged in April 1947.
33. Many of the "beautification" measures were merely semantic. The words "ghetto" and "camp" were eliminated. The "Order of the Day" was renamed "Bulletin of the Local Administration." Streets marked only by letters and figures were given pleasant-sounding names such as South Street, Lake Street, etc.

34. Hvass, Frants: *Besog i Theresienstadt den 23 Juni 1944,* MS., Copenhagen; Adler, *Theresienstadt 1941-1945,* pp. 752-53.
35. Deposition by Hochaus, a former SS guard at the Little Fortress, during the trial of *Lagerkommandant* Rahm in April 1947; Lederer, *Ghetto Theresienstadt,* pp. 150-51.
36. On September 27, 1944, there were about 30,000 inmates in Terezín. On October 29 there were slightly over 11,000; of these about 3,500 came from Czechoslovakia. No more than 1,400 men under the age of sixty-five were left.
37. Rabbi Dr. Max Friediger represented the Danish Jews; Dr. Heinrich Klang, the Jews from Austria; Prof. Eduard Meijers, the Dutch Jews; Dr. Alfred Meissner, the Czechoslovak Jews. Meissner (d. 1952) had been one of the principal authors of the democratic constitution adopted by the Czechoslovak Republic in 1920, was a long-time member of the prewar Czechoslovak parliament, and served as minister of justice in 1920 and again from 1929 to 1934.
38. This was still a "privileged resettlement" of inmate officers of the Sered camp, through which Slovak Jews had passed on their way to Auschwitz.
39. See Rudolf Vrba and Alan Bestic, *I Cannot Forgive* (London: 1963; New York: 1964), Vrba (Walter Rosenberg), a young Jew from Slovakia, escaped from Auschwitz with another inmate, Alfred Wetzler, in April 1944 and wrote a detailed report, which was handed, along with others, to the papal nuncio in Slovakia and passed on to the International Red Cross Committee and the American and British governments. (See also bibliography.)
40. The last transport from the Protectorate arrived in Terezín from Prague on March 16; the last Jews from Slovakia arrived on April 7. The very last Jews deported by the *Zentralstelle* were seventy-seven people from Vienna who were "ghettoized" on April 15, 1945, two days after the fall of the Austrian capital to the Red Army.
41. Much attention was given to the cemetery and crematorium outside the town. Earthenware urns were deposited in a hall decorated with flowers and two monuments, made to look "old," were hastily put up. The staff was impressively instructed to say that the crematorium had been used only for those who had died of contagious diseases and, when asked about the death rate in the ghetto, to give only a very low figure.
42. Dunant was not deceived. After spending the evening of his visit with Eichmann, who tried to convince him that the Jews in Terezín were better off than the Germans in the Reich, Dunant wrote in his report to Geneva . . . "More interesting than the actual living conditions and

installations in the Ghetto of Theresienstadt was the question whether it had indeed served merely as a transit camp for the Jews and how many deportations to the East had taken place [from there]." In *Documents sur l'activité du Comité international de la Croix-Rouge en faveur des civils detenus dans les camps de concentration en Allemagne (1939-1945),*" (Geneva: 1946).

43. A total of nearly 15,000 concentration camp inmates, both Jews and non-Jews, arrived in Terezín during the last two weeks of the war. About 1,500 of them died shortly after their arrival.
44. The following statistics should be mentioned here. Between November 1941 and April 1945 almost 140,000 Jews were deported to Terezín; over 75,000 of these came from Czechoslovakia. Between January 1942 and October 1944 over 88,000 Jews were deported from Terezín to the East; about 60,000 of these had come from Czechoslovakia. Of these 60,000, some 3,000 returned at the end of the war. More than 33,000 people died in Terezín; over 6,000 of these were Jews from Czechoslovakia. About 9,000 Jews from Czechoslovakia survived the war in Terezín; of these, some 3,000 had come to Terezín from the Protectorate of Bohemia and Moravia prior to 1945. These figures include deportees from the Sudetenland.

BIBLIOGRAPHY

The most complete bibliography on Terezín published to date is that by H.G. Adler in the second augmented edition of his book *Theresienstadt 1941-1945. Das Antlitz einer Zwangsgemeinschaft* [. . . The Face of an Enforced Community]. The following is a selection of books, articles, manuscripts, and documents on the subject of Terezín in general and the Jews from Czechoslovakia in particular. Standard works on extermination camps in Poland, on the SS organization, and on related subjects have been included. *Věstník židovské náboženské obce v Praze* [Information Bulletin of the Jewish Religious Congregation of Prague] is referred to as *Věstník*.

Adler, H. G. *Theresienstadt 1941-1945. Das Antlitz einer Zwangsgemeinschaft,* 1st ed. Tübingen: 1955; 2d rev. ed., Tübingen: 1960.

The definitive work in the German language dealing in detail with the history of Terezín, its sociology, and psychology.

———. *Die verheimlichte Wahrheit* [The Concealed Truth]. Tübingen: 1958.

Collection of documents supplementing the author's first book on Terezín. With reproductions of drawings by Terezín artists.

――――. *Der Kampf gegen die "Endlösung der Judenfrage"* [The Struggle Against the "Final Solution of the Jewish Problem"]. Bonn: 1960.

A systematic survey of the efforts to save European Jewry from total annihilation.

――――. *Der verwaltete Mensch: Studien zur Deportation der Juden aus Deutschland* [Man under Administration: Studies on the Deportation of Jews from Germany]. Tübingen: 1974.

A monumental work on the techniques of deportation with sociological conclusions. The Nazi and the Soviet systems compared.

――――. "Ideas Towards A Sociology of the Concentration Camp," *The American Journal of Sociology,* Chicago, March 1958.

Arendt, Hannah. *Eichmann in Jerusalem.* New York: 1963.

Auředníčková, A. *Tři léta v Terezíně* [Three Years in Terezín]. Prague: 1946.

Personal reminiscences; information about the religious life of Roman Catholics. The author arrived in Terezín in the summer of 1942.

Bacon, Yehuda. *Eyewitness Report,* MS. Jerusalem; Yad Vashem Archives, 1949.

An eyewitness report. The author came to Terezín from Ostrava in September 1942 and was deported from Terezín to Auschwitz in December 1943. Information about life at the children's homes, about Edelstein's execution, and about the so-called "family camp" in Auschwitz.

Baeck, Leo. "A People Stands Before Its God." In *We Survived: The Stories of Four Hidden and Hunted in Nazi Germany.* New Haven: 1949.

The experiences of Rabbi Baeck in Berlin during the Hitler era and in Terezín, where he arrived in January 1943.

Blumental, N. *Obozy* [The Camps]. Lodz: 1946.

This first volume of *Dokumenty i materiały do dziejów okupacji niemieckiej w Polsce* [Documents and Material on the German Occupation of Poland] describes life in Auschwitz, Treblinka, Maidanek, Sobibor, etc.

Bondy, Ruth. *Edelstein neged ha-z'man* [Edelstein Against Time]. Tel Aviv: 1981.

Bor, J. *Opuštěná panenka* [The Deserted Doll]. Prague: 1961.

A semi-fictional story from Terezín.

――――. *The Terezín Requiem.* London: 1963.

A semi-fictional account of the performance of Verdi's *Requiem* in Terezín. Translated from the Czech.

Broszat, Martin, ed. *Kommandant in Auschwitz* [Commandant in Auschwitz]. Stuttgart: 1958.

A publication of the *Institut für Zeitgeschichte* containing notes by Rudolf Hoess, the first *Lagerkommandant* of Auschwitz, written in 1946/47, while he was in Polish custody awaiting execution.

Bubeníčková, R., with L. Kubátová and I. Malá. *Tábory utrpení a smrti* [Camps of Suffering and Death]. Prague: 1969.

Caro, Klara. *Stärker als das Schwert,* MS., 1946, Wiener Library, London.

A survivor's report. The author arrived in Terezín in June 1942 and left with the transport to Switzerland in February 1945. She particularly describes Zionist cultural life at Terezín, in which she took a leading part.

———. "Die Persönlichkeit Jakob Edelsteins" [The Personality of Jakob Edelstein], In *Allgemeine Wochenzeitung,* Düsseldorf, February 13, 1959.

A tribute to Edelstein.

Cohen, David. *The Russians in Terezín.* London: 1946.

Dormitzer, Else. *Theresienstädter Bilder* [Pictures of Terezín]. Hilversum: 1945.

Poetry written in Terezín (in German), 1943-45.

———. *Drei Berichte über Theresienstadt* [Three Reports on Terezín], MS., 1945, 1946, 1955, Wiener Library, London.

Three eyewitness accounts.

The author arrived in Terezín in April 1943 and worked at the post office there.

Ehrman, F., ed. *Terezín.* Prague: 1965.

A collection of articles on various aspects of life in Terezín written by several authors. Published by the Council of Jewish Congregations in the Czech Lands in Czech, English, and German. With reproductions of paintings and drawings by Terezín artists.

Eisenbach, A. *Getto Lodzskie* [The Lodz Ghetto]. Warsaw: 1946. Volume III of *Dokumenty i materialy do dziejów okupacji niemieckiej w Polsce* [Documents and Materials on the German Occupation of Poland].

An important work on the Lodz ghetto; includes a description of the arrival of Jews from Czechoslovakia in the fall of 1941.

Feder, Richard. *Židovská tragedie—dějství poslední* [The Jewish Tragedy: The Final Act], Kolín: 1947.

A well-informed account of life in the Protectorate of Bohemia and Moravia and in Terezín by the rabbi of Kolin (1942-1945). Rabbi Feder survived Terezín and after the war became chief rabbi of the Czech Lands. He died in Brno in 1970 at the age of ninety-five.

Fischl, A. J. "Er bewahrte viele vor dem Tod" ["He Saved Many from Death"], *Allgemeine Wochenzeitung,* Düsseldorf, September 24, 1954.

An article on Georg Ferdinand Duckwitz, the German naval attaché in Copenhagen, who helped save the majority of Danish Jews from deportation by informing the Danish resistance of the intentions of the SS.

Frankl, Viktor E. "Psychologie und Psychiatrie des Konzentrationslagers" [Psychology and Psychiatry of the Concentration Camps]. In *Psychiatrie der Gegenwart, Forschung und Praxis,* III, Berlin; 1961.

Franková, H. and Hyndráková, A. "Die jüdische Selbstverwaltung im Ghetto von Terezín (Theresienstadt) 1941-45: Ihre Organisation, Tätigkeit und Rechtsbefugnis" [Jewish Self-Government in the Ghetto of Terezín: Organization, Activity and Legal Authority], *Judaica Bohemiae,* VIII, 1., Prague: 1972.

Friediger, Max. *Theresienstadt.* Copenhagen: 1946.
   An account by the chief rabbi of Copenhagen, who arrived in Terezín in October 1943 and left in April 1945. (In Danish.)

Friedmann, C. *Deposition,* MS., Prague, 1945.
   A report given to the "Documentation Action" of the Jewish Agency by the widow of Richard Israel Friedmann, a high official of the Vienna *Jüdische Kultusgemeinde.* Friedmann went with Edelstein to Nisko in October 1939; he was later transferred to Prague and in March 1941 he accompanied Edelstein to Holland to help the *Joodsche Rat (Judenrat)* there. After the establishment of the ghetto in Terezín Friedmann remained in Prague in charge of supplies for the ghetto. He did his best, often resorting to illegal means at great personal risk in order to help his fellow Jews. In January 1943, he was arrested and deported to Terezín, where he refused to accept any office because he had grave misgivings about the policies of the Jewish leadership there. In May 1944 Friedmann was sent to Auschwitz, where he was shot shortly after his arrival.

Friedmann, Franz. *Die Rechtsstellung der Juden im Protektorat Böhmen und Mähren, I. Teil: Stand am 31.7.1942; II. Teil: Stand am 31.3.1943* [The Legal Status of the Jews in the Protectorate of Bohemia and Moravia . . .], MS., Prague.
   Internal reports compiled for the Prague Jewish Religious Congregation.

Friedmann, Philip. "The Lublin Reservation and the Madagascar Plan." *YIVO Annual of Jewish Social Science,* VIII, New York, 1953.

———. "Aspects of the Communal Crisis in the Period of the Nazi Regime in Germany, Austria and Czechoslovakia." *Essays on Jewish Life and Thought,* New York, 1959.

Frýd, Norbert. "Kultura v předposlední stanici" [Culture at the Last But One Stop]. *Plamen,* no. 9, Prague, 1964.

Goldschmidt, Arthur. *Geschichte der evangelischen Gemeinde in Theresienstadt* [Story of the Evangelical Congregation in Terezín]. Tübingen: 1946.

Green, G. *The Artists of Terezín.* New York: 1969.
   An appreciation, with reproductions of paintings and drawings.

Grossman, Frances G. "The Trees of Terezín: A Psychological Study of Art by Children in Concentration Camp." *Israel Horizons,* New York, nos. 7 and 8, May-June, 1973.

Gutfeld, Alexander. "Die Sterblichkeit in Theresienstadt in Ihrer Beziehung zur Dauer des Aufenthaltes" [The Mortality Rate in Terezín Linked to Duration of Stay]. *Allgemeines Statistisches Archiv,* XXXV/1., Munich, 1951.

Hirsch, G. "Von Theresienstadt in die Schweiz" [From Terezín to Switzerland]. *Der Neue Weg,* Vienna, nos. 15, 16, 1946.

———. "Der Galgen von Theresienstadt" [The Gallows of Terezín]. *Das freie Wort,* Düsseldorf, January 12, 1952.

An article on the occasion of the tenth anniversary of the January executions in Terezín.

Hořec, J., ed. *Deníky dětí* [Children's Diaries]. Prague: 1961.

Excerpts from war diaries of children. Helga Weiss (born in 1929), who arrived in Terezín in December 1941, was deported to Auschwitz three years later and passed through several concentration camps. She was liberated in Mauthausen.

Iltis, Rudolf, ed. *Nazidokumente sprechen* [Nazi Documents Speak]. Prague: 1955.

Collection of documents published by the Council of Religious Congregations in the Czech Lands and the Central Association of Jewish Communities in Slovakia.

———. "Karel Rahm před svými soudci" [Karl Rahm Facing His Judges]. *Věstník,* nos. 10–14, 16–19, 23, 25/6, 1947, and no. 18, 1948.

Report on the trial in Litoměřice of the last *Lagerkommandant* of Terezín.

———. "Hasičský sbor v terezínském ghettě [The Terezín Ghetto Fire Brigade]. *Věstník,* no. 2, 1947.

An otherwise unconfirmed report on clandestine activities of the Terezín fire brigade.

———. "Jak došlo k založení terezínského ghetta" [How the Ghetto in Terezín Was Founded]. *Věstník,* no. 48, 1948.

———. "Přelíčení s Rudolfem Haindlem" [The Trial of Rudolf Haindl]. *Věstník,* nos. 40–41, 1948.

Report on the trial in Litoměřice of a member of the Terezín SS.

———. "SS Hauptsturmführer Seidl konal svou povinnost" [SS Hauptsturmführer Seidl Did His Duty]. *Věstník,* no. 12, 1946.

Report on the Vienna trial of the first *Lagerkommandant* of Terezín.

———. "Statečný zachránce důležitých listin" [The Courageous Rescuer of Important Documents]. *Věstník,* no. 18, 1946.

The story of Josef Polák, a clerk in the Central Registry in Terezín, who collected statistical and documentary material, probably at the risk of his life. Several books on Terezín are partly based on his collection.

Jacobson, Jacob. *Terezín. The Daily Life, 1943–45.* London: 1946.

Jacot, M. *The Last Butterfly.* New York: 1974.
   A novel with its plot in Terezín.
Kárný, M., "Svědectví Josefa Taussiga" [The Testimony of Josef Taussig]. *Terezínské listy,* Ústí nad Labem, no. 2, 1971.
   An article on the work of Josef Taussig, a Communist journalist deported to Terezín in December 1942 and from there to Auschwitz in October 1944. He died in Flossenburg.
Kermisz, J. *Akcje i Wysidlenia* [Raids and Liquidations]. Warsaw: 1946.
   An important work on the persecution and extermination of Polish Jewry.
Kersten, Felix. *The Memoirs of Doctor Felix Kersten.* New York: 1947.
   Toward the end of the war, Dr. Kersten, Himmler's personal physician, mediated between his patient and several groups and individuals who were trying to save Jewish prisoners in concentration camps. Among the results of these negotiations was the transport from Terezín to Switzerland in February 1945 and the departure of the Danish Jews from Terezín in April of that year.
Klang, Heinrich. "Rechtsordnung in Theresienstadt" [Law and Order in Terezín]. *Der Bund,* Berne, June 8, 1946.
Kogon, Eugen. *Der SS-Staat: Das System der deutschen Konzentrationslager* [The SS State: The System of the German Concentration Camp], 2d ed. Berlin: 1947.
   The most exhaustive study on the subject to date.
Kopecký, J., ed., *Nevyúčtován zůstává život* [Life's Unsettled Accounts]. Prague: 1948.
   A tribute to the poet and theater director Gustav Schorsch.
Král, Albert. "Epidemic of Encephalitis in the Concentration Camp of Theresienstadt during Winter 1943-1944." *Journal of Nervous and Mental Diseases.* Chicago, vol. 105, April 1947.
Kraus, F. R. "Výstava archívních dokumentů na Pražském hradě" [Exhibition of Archival Documents at the Prague Castle]. *Věstník,* no. 7, 1958.
   The exhibition included the first document to mention Terezín as a prospective camp for Czech Jews: the records taken at the Prague conference on the "Solution of the Jewish Problem" in October 1941 (*Notizen aus der Besprechung am 10.10.1941 über die Lösung der Judenfrage*). This document is now in the Czechoslovak State Archives.
Kraus, Ota and Kulka, Erich. *The Death Factory.* Oxford: 1966.
   Information about the fate of the Jews from Czechoslovakia in Auschwitz. Includes two poems written by deportees from Terezín shortly before their death in the gas chambers. Translated from the Czech original, *Továrna na smrt.* Prague: 1959. Also in Hebrew.

Křížková, M. "Stálá musejní exposice Památníku Terezín" [Permanent Exhibit at the Terezín Memorial]. *Terezínské listy,* Ústí nad Labem, no. 2, 1971.

A survey of exhibits held at the former Little Fortress in 1949, 1954, 1962, 1965, and 1971. All exhibits except that of 1965 were devoted primarily to the concentration camps of the Little Fortress and Litoměřice (Richard). In 1968 the Czechoslovak government announced that an independent ghetto exhibit would be installed in the town of Terezín itself.

Kryl, M. "Nový pramen k dějinám terezínského ghetta" [A New Source for the History of the Terezín Ghetto]. *Terezínské listy,* Ústí nad Labem, no. 1, 1970.

Discussion of the diary of Egon Redlich (see under Redlich's name in this bibliography).

―――. "Nad jednou studií o terezínském ghettě" [About A Study on the Ghetto in Terezín], *Terezínské listy,* Ústí nad Labem, no. 2, 1971.

A polemical review of S. Schmiedl. *Hechaluz in Theresienstadt: Its Influence and Educational Activities* (see under Schmiedl's name in this bibliography).

Kulišová, T. and Tyl, O. *Terezín. Malá pevnost-Ghetto* [Terezín, the Little Fortress Ghetto . . .], Prague: 1960.

An official publication with emphasis on the Little Fortress concentration camp. Numerous photographs (twelve from the ghetto after liberation).

Kypr, P., ed. *Malá pevnost Terezín* [The Little Fortress of Terezín]. Prague: 1950.

A well-documented history of the camp, but non-Communist inmates are largely disregarded. Reference to the execution of Paul Eppstein.

Lagus, Karel and Polák, Josef. *Město za mřížemi* [City Behind Bars]. Prague: 1964.

A semi-official publication of the Union of Anti-Fascist Fighters, based on the documentary collection of Josef Polák. The first comprehensive work in Czech (1964: *sic*).

Las, V. "Vzpomínáme na 10. června 1942" [We Remember June 10, 1942]. *Věstník,* no. 24, 1951.

An eyewitness account by a member of the group of workers sent from Terezín to Lidice to bury villagers murdered by the SS in reprisal for the assassination of Heydrich.

Lederer, Zdenek. *Ghetto Theresienstadt.* London: 1953.

The first detailed study on the subject and the only comprehensive work published in English to date. The Czech original was suppressed by the Czechoslovak authorities after the 1948 Communist take-over.

Loewenstein, Karl. "Minsk. Im Lager der deutschen Juden" [Minsk. In the Camp of the German Jews], *Ius, Politik und Zeitgeschichte*, vol. XLV/56; Supplement to the weekly *Das Parlament*, Bonn, November 7, 1956.

Before World War I Dr. Karl Loewenstein was an officer in the German navy and for many years an aide-de-camp to the German Crown Prince Friedrich Wilhelm. In November 1941 he was arrested in Berlin and deported to the ghetto of Minsk. As the result of intervention with top German circles he was released after six months and sent via Vienna to Terezín, where he was kept in prison while the SS command awaited further instructions from Berlin. In September 1942, Loewenstein was appointed chief of the Terezín ghetto police, which he reorganized along military lines. He also created control groups to fight corruption in the communal kitchens. After getting into conflict with the Jewish leadership he was deposed by the SS command but survived the war in Terezín.

Lustig, Arnošt. *Night and Hope, Day and Night*. London and New York: 1963.

Translation of selections from two separate Czech volumes published in Prague: *Diamanty noci* [Diamonds of the Night] (1956) and *Noc a naděje* [Night and Hope] (1958). Short stories of Terezín by the author, who arrived in Terezín as a youth.

Mannheimer, M. E. *Theresienstadt and From Theresienstadt to Auschwitz*. London: 1945.

A survivor's report. The author was taken to Terezín from Westerbork and left in September 1944.

Murmelstein, Benjamin. *Geschichtlicher Überblick* [Historical Survey], MS., Terezín, 1945. Wiener Library, London.

A historical review written by the last *Judenälteste* of Terezín shortly after the war.

———. *Terezín, Il ghetto-modello di Eichmann* [Terezín: Eichmann's Model Ghetto]. Milan, 1961.

Apologia by the author; important for a study of the final period of the Terezín ghetto.

Neumann, Jirmejahu Oskar, *Im Schatten des Todes. Ein Tatsachenbericht vom Schicksalskampf des slovakischen Judentums* [In the Shadow of Death: A Factual Report of the Fateful Struggle of Slovak Jewry]. Tel Aviv: Olamenu, 1956.

An informative account of the persecution and resistance of Slovak Jewry.

Oppenheim, Ralph Gerson. *The Door of Death. Theresienstadt Diary*. London: 1948.

Semi-fictional account of the deportation of the Danish Jews to Terezín and of their life there. Translation from the Danish (*Det skulde saa* vaere: Marianne Petits dagbok fra Theresienstadt, Copenhagen, 1945); also in German (*An der Grenze des Lebens,* Hamburg, 1961).

Ornsteinová, Edith. "Vzpomínka na Jakuba Edelsteina" [Remembering Jakub Edelstein]. *Věstník,* no. 3, 1945.

A tribute by one of Edelstein's intimates.

Pick, J., Polák, Richard and Pacovský, Josef. *Terezín očima hygienika* [Terezín as seen by a Health Officer]. Prague: 1948.

Pokorná, Lilly. *Eine Ärztin erlebt das "Musterlager" Theresienstadt* [A Woman Physician Experiences the "Model Camp" of Terezín]. MS., Sao Paulo, 1948, Institute für die Zeitgeschichte (Munich).

A valuable account by a woman who worked as chief radiologist in Terezín from January 1941 until August 1945. A wealth of detail about the medical aspects of life in Terezín.

———. "Die Lungentuberkulose im Konzentrationlager Theresienstadt im Vergleich mit der bei Häftlingen in anderen Konzentrationlagern" [Pulmonary Tuberculosis in the Terezín concentration camp compared with that in Inmates of Other Concentration Camps]. In *Der Tuberkulosenarzt.* Marburg: 1950.

Poláček, Karel. *Se žlutou hvězdou* [With the Yellow Star]. Havlíčkův Brod: 1961.

A posthumously published work by a well-known Czech Jewish novelist.

Poláček, O. "Výročí hrdinství českých žen" [Anniversary of the Heroic Act of Czech Women]. *Věstník,* no. 28/29, 1948.

An article describing the liquidation of the "family camp" of Auschwitz in July 1944, when 600 women from Terezín voluntarily followed their young children into the gas chambers.

Prochnik, Rudolf. *Juden in Theresienstadt. Ein statistischer Bericht* [Jews in Terezín. A Statistical Report], MS., Terezín, 1945. Wiener Library, London.

A valuable statistical report by the last head of the secretariat of the Jewish administration in Terezín under Benjamin Murmelstein.

Redlich, Egon. *Diary of Egon Redlich,* MS., Terezín 1942/44, Czechoslovak State Archives.

An active Zionist and leader in the *HeHalutz* movement, Redlich was the head of the Youth Welfare Office in Terezín. According to the news bulletin of the International Council of Jews from Czechoslovakia in London, which quotes from the Czech press, the diary was discovered during repairs to roofs in Terezín in 1967. Passages taken out of context were used in a series of crudely anti-Zionist articles published in the Prague weekly *Tribuna* in January 1974. See also S. Schmiedl, *Hechaluz in Theresienstadt: Its Influence and Educational Activities* (see under Schmiedl's name in this bibliography).

Reitlinger, Gerald. *The Final Solution.* London: 1953.

> One of the most comprehensive accounts of the Jewish tragedy.

Schmiedl, S. *Hechaluz in Theresienstadt: Its Influence and Educational Activities.* Jerusalem: 1968.

> A serious study. Includes passages from the diary of Egon Redlich.

Shek, Y. Zeev. "Zum 10. Jahrestag der Befreiung von Theresienstadt" [On the Tenth Anniversary of the Liberation of Terezín]. *MB Mitteilungsblatt,* Tel Aviv, May 20, 1955.

> The commemoration of the anniversary at Givat Hayyim.

Simonsohn, Berthold. "Sein Andenken wird weiterleben" [His Memory Will Live On]. *Jüdische Sozialarbeit,* Frankfort a.M., nos. 3/4, 1959.

> A short laudatory biography of Dr. Paul Eppstein.

Singer, J. *Erinnerungen aus Wien und Theresienstadt* [Reminiscences of Vienna and Terezín], MS., London, 1955. Wiener Library, London.

> An interesting eyewitness account. The author arrived in Terezín from Vienna in September 1942 and worked at one of the "export" workshops. She stayed on after the liberation, helping with the repatriation of inmates until October 1945.

Spies, Gerty. *Theresienstadt.* Munich: 1946.

> Poetry written in Terezín.

Spilka, B., ed. *Terezín Ghetto.* Prague: 1945.

> Report of the Repatriation Department of the Czechoslovak Ministry of Social Welfare.

Springer, Erich. "Zdravotnictví v terezínském ghettě" [Medical Services in the Ghetto]. *Věstník,* no. 5, 1950.

> An article by the chief surgeon of Terezín. Part of a larger work. Dr. Springer came to Terezín with one of the first transports and stayed there until the end of the war.

Taussig, J. "O terezínských kabaretech" [Terezín Cabarets], *Terezínské listy,* Ústí nad Labem, no. 2, 1971.

> Text of a lecture given in Terezín in July 1944. The author was in Terezín from December 1942 until October 1944, when he was deported to Auschwitz. He died in Flossenburg.

Trunk, Isaiah. *Judenrat: Jewish Councils in Eastern Europe under Nazi Occupation.* New York: 1972.

Tůma, Mirko. *Ghetto našich dnů* [The Ghetto of Our Time]. Prague: 1946.

> The first brief, hastily written account of this subject published in Czech. Tůma was in Terezín from November 1941 until the liberation.

Utitz, Emil. *Psychologie des Lebens in Theresienstadt* [The Psychology of Life in Terezín]. Vienna: 1948.

Largely personal reminiscences with an emphasis on cultural life in Terezín. The author, formerly professor of psychology and esthetics at the German University of Prague, arrived in Terezín in the summer of 1942 and was appointed chief librarian of the central library that had just been set up at the time.

———. "Ústřední knihovna koncentračního tábora Terezín" [The Central Library in the Terezín Concentration Camp]. *Věstník,* no. 47, 1950.

A concise report on the Central Library of Terezín. The books came from liquidated households of Jews or from the libraries of Jewish organizations that had been abolished. The number of volumes in the library reached well over 200,000. In addition, the SS directed to Terezín 60,000 volumes of Hebraica to be catalogued by a group of Jewish scholars, probably for a museum "of the extinct Jewish race" which the Nazis planned to establish after the war.

Volavková, Hana, ed. *I Never Saw Another Butterfly: Children's Drawings and Poems From Terezín 1942–1944.* New York, Toronto, and London: 1959, 1962.

Contains twenty-two poems and forty-eight paintings, drawings, and collages by thirty-nine children in Terezín. The title is taken from a poem by twelve-year-old Pavel Friedmann.

Vrba, Rudolf and Bestic, Alan. *I Cannot Forgive,* London: 1963; New York: 1964.

After escaping from Auschwitz in April 1944, Vrba (Rosenberg) made his way back to his native Slovakia and wrote a detailed report which he handed over to the papal nuncio in Bratislava. The report was eventually published by the War Refugee Board in Washington.

Weber, Ilse. *Gedichte* [Poems], MS., Terezín, 1942–44, Yad Vashem Archives, Jerusalem.

Contains fifty-nine poems on camp themes. The author, who worked for two and a half years as a nurse in one of the Terezín hospitals, was deported in October 1944 to Auschwitz, where she perished. Several of her poems, including the often-published *Schafe von Lidice* [Sheep of Lidice], were translated into Czech.

Weil, Jiří. *Život s hvězdou* [Life with the (Jewish) Star]. Prague: 1949.

A novel about the life of Jews in the Protectorate. The hero decides not to report for transport to Terezín but to go underground.

———. *Žalozpěv za 77,297 obětí* [Elegy for 77, 297 Victims]. Prague: 1958.

———. "Literární činnost v Terezíně" (Literary Life in Terezín). *Židovská ročenka* [Jewish Yearbook]. Prague: 1955/56.

A report on literary documents from Terezín (in Czech and German) in the collection of the State Jewish Museum in Prague.

Weiss, A. *Le typhus exanthématique pendant la deuxième guerre mondiale en particulier dans les camps de concentration* [Exanthematous Typhus During World War II, Particularly in the Concentration Camps]. Geneva: 1954.

The author of this medical study was deported from Hungary to Auschwitz in 1944 and was taken from there via several concentration camps to Terezín, where he arrived in April 1945. Describes the fight against the typhus epidemics.

Yahil, Leni. *The Rescue of Danish Jewry: Test of Democracy.* Philadelphia: 1969.

A detailed scholarly account of successful Danish and Swedish efforts to save the Jews of Denmark from deportation and to bring them back home from Terezín.

Zehngut, J. "Nisko." *Věstník,* nos. 7–10, 13, 26/7, 1949.

A survivor's report on the first transport from Moravská Ostrava to Nisko (October 1939) and on living conditions at the camp.

Zucker, Otto. *Geschichte des Ghetto Theresienstadt zum 31.12.43* [History of Ghetto Theresienstadt as of 12/31/43]. MS., Terezín, 1944.

A valuable document written by one of the Jewish leaders in the Terezín ghetto.

* * *

Aktenvermerke (Notes from files), MSS., Prague, October–December, 1941.

Twenty-six documents concerning the prehistory of Terezín, mostly notes taken by representatives of the Jewish Religious Congregation of Prague after meetings with the *Zentralstelle* SS. This was the indirect form in which the SS issued all their orders and instructions to the Jewish Religious Congregation throughout the war.

Bericht über den Status des ehemaligen Konzentrationslagers Theresienstadt [Report on the Status of the Former Concentration Camp of Terezín], MS., Terezín, June 18, 1945.

An inventory of the property and assets (including investments) taken over by the local administration of Terezín after the war.

Bilag til beretning til folketinget [Supplement to the Report to the Folketing]. Copenhagen: 1954 and 1955.

Documents on the deportation of Danish Jews to Terezín and on the Danish intervention with the Germans including (II/18) the report written by F. Hvass, director of the Political Department of the Danish Foreign Office, after his visit to Terezín in June 1944.

Catalogue of Camps and Prisons in Germany and German-Occupied Countries, 2 vols. and supplement. Arolsen: 1949/51.

Catalogue of Records held by the International Tracing Service at Arolsen, 4 vols. Arolsen: 1954.
Documents on Terezín in vol. I: Deportation lists, lists of the transports to Switzerland and to Sweden (Danes), etc.

Documents sur l'activité du Comité International de la Croix-Rouge en faveur des civils detenus dans les camps de concentration en Allemagne (1939–1945) [Documents on the Activity of the International Red Cross Committee on Behalf of Civilians Interned in the Concentration Camps in Germany (1939–1945)], 3d. ed. Geneva: 1946.

Eichmann Trial Papers, MS., Jerusalem, 1961, Wiener Library, London.

German Crimes in Poland, Warsaw, 1946/7. (No author listed)

Note sur l'activité du Comité International de la Croix-Rouge au camp de Theresienstadt [Note on the Activity of the International Red Cross Committee in the Theresienstadt Camp]. Geneva: 1945.

Documents concerning Terezín, particularly the negotiations and the visits of the International Red Cross representatives in 1944/45.

Notizen aus der Besprechung am 10.10.41 über die Lösung von Judenfragen [Notes of the Conference of 10/10/41 on the Solution of Jewish Problems], MS., Prague, 1941, Czechoslovak State Archives.

A key document on German policy toward the "Jewish problem" in the Protectorate of Bohemia and Moravia; predecessor of the *Wannsee Protokoll.* Full text in H. G. Adler, *Theresienstadt 1941–1945* (2d ed.).

Trial of Major War Criminals, Nuremberg, 1946/49.

Trials of War Criminals before the Nuremberg Military Tribunals, Vols. XIII, XXVII, XXXI, Washington, 1952.

"Wannsee Protokoll" zur Endlösung der Judenfrage [The "Wannsee Protocol" on the Final Solution of the Jewish Problem]. Düsseldorf: 1952.

The most important German document (January 22, 1942) on the extermination policy. It specifies the role of Terezín as an "old people's ghetto."

Zpráva evidenčního oddělení RŽNO [Report of the Registry Department of the Prague Council of Jewish Religious Congregations]. Věstník, nos. 23/4, 1947.

Data on emigration from the Protectorate of Bohemia and Moravia, deportations to Terezín and from Terezín to Auschwitz, the number of survivors in Terezín, etc.

　　　　　　　·········· Old borders of congregational districts
　　　　　　　────── New borders of congregational districts
　　　　　　　⊙　　Seat of religious congregation
　　　　　　　◎　　Seat of congregational district

1. Map showing plans for redistricting of the Jewish religious congregations of Bohemia and Moravia, March 1941. The purpose of this plan was to concentrate the Jews in the principal cities of the districts for more expeditious deportation.

2. The leaders of the Jewish Religious Congregation of Prague, May 1941. (Left to right, from top to bottom): *Top row* (1) Dr. Franz Weidmann, Director; (2) Jakob Edelstein, Deputy Director and Director of the Central Zionist Federation and Palestine Office; *2nd row* (3) Dr. Karl Fleischmann, Central Secretary; (4) Herbert Langer, Deputy Central Secretary; (5) Dr. Adolf Beneš, Deputy Central Secretary; *3rd row* (6) Dr. Oskar Singer, *Jüdisches Nachrichtenblatt* (publication); (7) Dr. Karl Stein, Department for Provinces; (8) Erich Kraus, Organization Office; (9) Dr. Erwin Ziemlich,

Personnel Office; (10) Dr. Otto Fischer, Bureau of Statistics; (11) Richard L. Friedmann, Relations with Authorities; *4th row* (12) Friedrich Prossnitz, Financial Management; (13) Emil Metzl, Financial Controller, Provinces; (14) Engineer Rudolf Ehrmann, Economic Management; *5th row* (15) Dr. Hans Bonn, Emigration Department; (16) Hanna Steiner, Promotion of Emigration; (17) Dr. Franz Friedmann, Office of Transfer and Information and Counseling Department; (18) Emil Kafka, Procurement of Emigration Papers; (19) Abraham Fixler, Relations with Central Office for Jewish Emigration; *6th row* (20) Dr. Franz Kahn, Organization of Central Zionist Federation and Palestine Office; (21) Alois Fischl, Administration of Palestine Office; (22) Dr. Leo Janowitz, Department of Certificates (for Emigration to Palestine) and Deputy Director of *Opfern-Aufbauen-Leben* ("Sacrifice-Build-Live") Fundraising Campaign; (23) Dr. Erich Munk, Emigration of Children and Adolescents; (24) Engineer Otto Zucker, *Opfern-Aufbauen-Leben* Fundraising Campaign; Director of the Jewish Religious Congregation of Brno; (25) Joseph Lichtenstern, Labor Transports; *7th row* (26) Dr. Wilhelm Katz, Social Service Department; (27) Dr. Kurt Heller, "Open" Relief and Care of the Poor; (28) Miroslav Körper, Administration of Care of the Sick; (29) Dr. Karl Klein, Physicians' Service; (30) Dr. Viktor Müller, Institutions of "Closed" Social Services; (31) Engineer Franz Fuchs, Department of Housing; *8th row* (32) Heinz Schuster, Labor Office; *9th row* (33) Dr. Josef Pollak, Department of Culture and Education; (34) Willy Schönfeld, Vocational Counseling; (35) R. Freiberger, Dr.Eng., Vocational Reorientation Courses; *10th row* (36) Dr. Aladar Deutsch, Chief Rabbinate; *11th row* (37) Dr. Franz Sander, Department for Non-Mosaic Jews (individuals professing another religion but regarded as Jews under Nuremberg Laws).

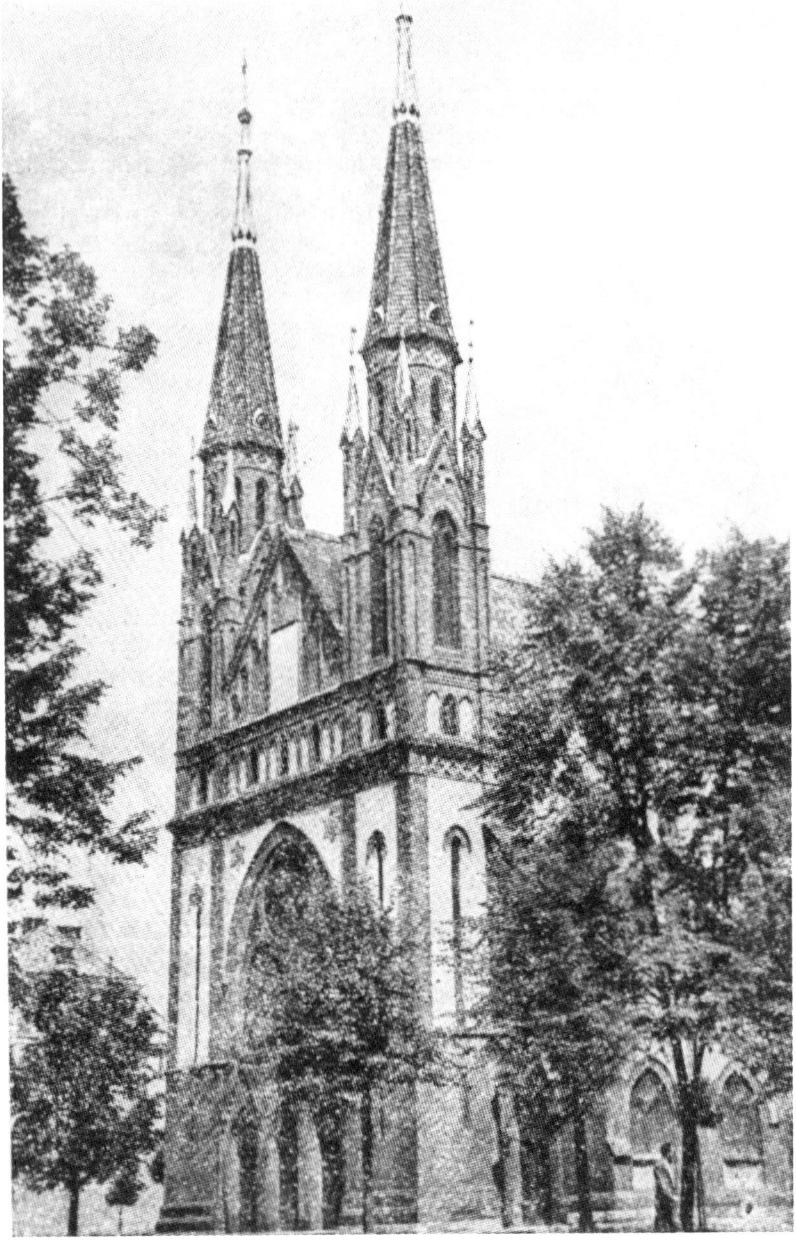

3. Dynamiting of the synagogue at Budějovice, July 5, 1942.

Notizen aus der Besprechung über künftige Planungen im Protektorat Böhmen und Mähren am 17. Oktober 1941, um 16,00 Uhr.

Teilnehmer:

SS-Obergruppenführer Heydrich
SS-Gruppenführer F r a n k
SA-Brif. Dr. v. B u r g s d o r f f
SS-O'Stubaf. B ö h m e
SS-O'Stubaf. Dr. G e s c h k e
SS-O'Stubaf. S o w a
SS-O'Stubaf. v. G r e g o r y
SS-Stubaf. J a c o b i
Min.Dirigent Dr. B e r t s c h - II -
Min.Dirigent Dr. F u c h s - I -

Zur Judenfrage:

Zunächst wird ein Transport von 5.000 Juden nach Litzmannstadt evakuiert. Ein Teil ist bereits fort. Wenn alle 5.000 fort sind, soll eine kurze Presse-Notiz darüber in die Zeitung kommen, aber in geschickter Weise, es muss darin zum Ausdruck kommen, wie schnell die reichsdeutsche Arbeit abrollt. Dann soll eine kurze Pause erfolgen, um die Vorbereitungen zur weiteren Evakuierung bzw. Ghettoisierung nicht zu stören.
Inzwischen werden die Juden aus Böhmen und Mähren in je einem Übergangslager gesammelt für die Evakuierung. Für diesen Zweck ist von dem Wehrmachtsbevollmächtigten beim Reichsprotektor Theresienstadt von allen Wehrmachtsteilen völlig freigemacht worden. Den Tschechen ist nahegelegt, anderswohin zu ziehen. Falls der Grund und Boden nicht sowieso schon Reichseigentum ist, wird er von der Zentralstelle für jüdische Auswanderung aufgekauft und damit deutscher Grundbesitz. In Theresienstadt werden bequem 50-60.000 Juden untergebracht.
Von dort aus kommen die Juden nach dem Osten. Die Zustimmung von Minsk und Riga für je 50.000 Juden ist bereits eingegangen.
Theresienstadt wird dann nach vollständiger Evakuierung aller Juden in einer tadellosen Planung deutsch besiedelt und somit zu einem Kernpunkt deutschen Lebens. Es liegt äusserst günstig dafür. Somit wird ein weiterer Vorposten mustergültig nach den Gedankengängen des Reichsführers-SS als Reichskommissar für die Festigung deutschen Volkstums geschaffen.
Über diese Planungen darf keinesfalls auch nur die geringste Kleinigkeit in die Öffentlichkeit dringen. Sämtliche Teilnehmer an der Sitzung wurden eindringlich darauf hingewiesen.
B.d.S. legt im Einvernehmen mit Abteilungsleiter IV die Pressenotiz vor, die über die Evakuierung der Juden berichtet, evtl. mit der Warnung an die Tschechen, sich nicht mit Juden gleichzustellen, da sie sonst ebenfalls mit evakuiert werden und als Juden anprangert. Es wäre zu überlegen, ob nicht zwei oder drei bekannte Tschechen, die sich mit Juden gemein gemacht haben, propagandistisch herausgestellt werden.

4. From the minutes of the Prague conference on the "solution of the Jewish problem" (October 17, 1941), with Reinhard Heydrich as chairman. The agenda included secret Nazi plans for a ghetto in Terezín (Theresienstadt).

Re: The Jewish Problem

To begin with, a *transport of 5,000 Jews* will be evacuated to *Lodz*. A part of this transport has already left. After all 5,000 have left, a brief report should appear in the press, but it must be done in a clever manner. It should show how efficient the Germans are in their work. Then there should be a brief pause so as not to disturb preparations for additional evacuations (ghettoization).

In the meantime the Jews of Bohemia and Moravia will be gathered for evacuation in one *transit camp* each. For this purpose the authorized *Wehrmacht* representative at the Reich Protector's Office has cleared *Theresienstadt* completely of all *Wehrmacht* units. The Czechs have been urged to move elsewhere. In case the landed property is not already the property of the Reich, it will be purchased by the Central Office for Jewish Emigration and will thus become German property. Theresienstadt could easily accommodate 50–60,000 Jews.

From there the Jews will be sent to the East. Minsk and Riga have already agreed to accept 50,000 Jews each.

After all the Jews have been evacuated, Theresienstadt will be settled by Germans under impeccable planning, and the city will thus become a nucleus of German life. Its location is eminently suited for this purpose. This will create a model outpost for the consolidation of German ethnicity according to the ideas of the Reichsfüerer SS as Reich Commissar.

In agreement with the Head of Department IV, B.d.S. will submit the press release reporting the evacuation of the Jews, perhaps with a warning to the Czechs not to identify with the Jews, since they will then be evacuated along with them and labeled as Jews. It would be worth considering whether one might not expose, for propaganda purposes, two or three prominent Czechs who have made common cause with the Jews.

5. Jews at the Trade Fair grounds in Holešovice, a suburb of Prague, where they were assembled for deportation to Terezín (1942).

6. A Jewish family in Prague, wearing identification tags and Stars of David, awaiting deportation to Terezín (1942).

Laut Verordnung der Polizeidirektion in Prag vom 5. August 1940, G. Z. 19.040 präs. ist

Juden der Einkauf

nur in der Zeit 15–17

von ~~11 bis 13 u. von 15 bis 16.30~~ Uhr gestattet.

Židům dovolen nákup

7. Announcement, in Czech and German, of shopping hours for Jews in Prague: "By order of Police Headquarters in Prague, dated August 5, 1940 ... Jews will be permitted to shop only between the hours of 3 and 5 P.M." Original hours, crossed out, were from 11 A.M. to 1 P.M. and from 3 to 4:30 P.M.

8. Children's playground on Karlovo Náměsti (Charles Square), Prague. Sign on top, in German and Czech, reads: "Jews not admitted."

TO LITOMEŘICE

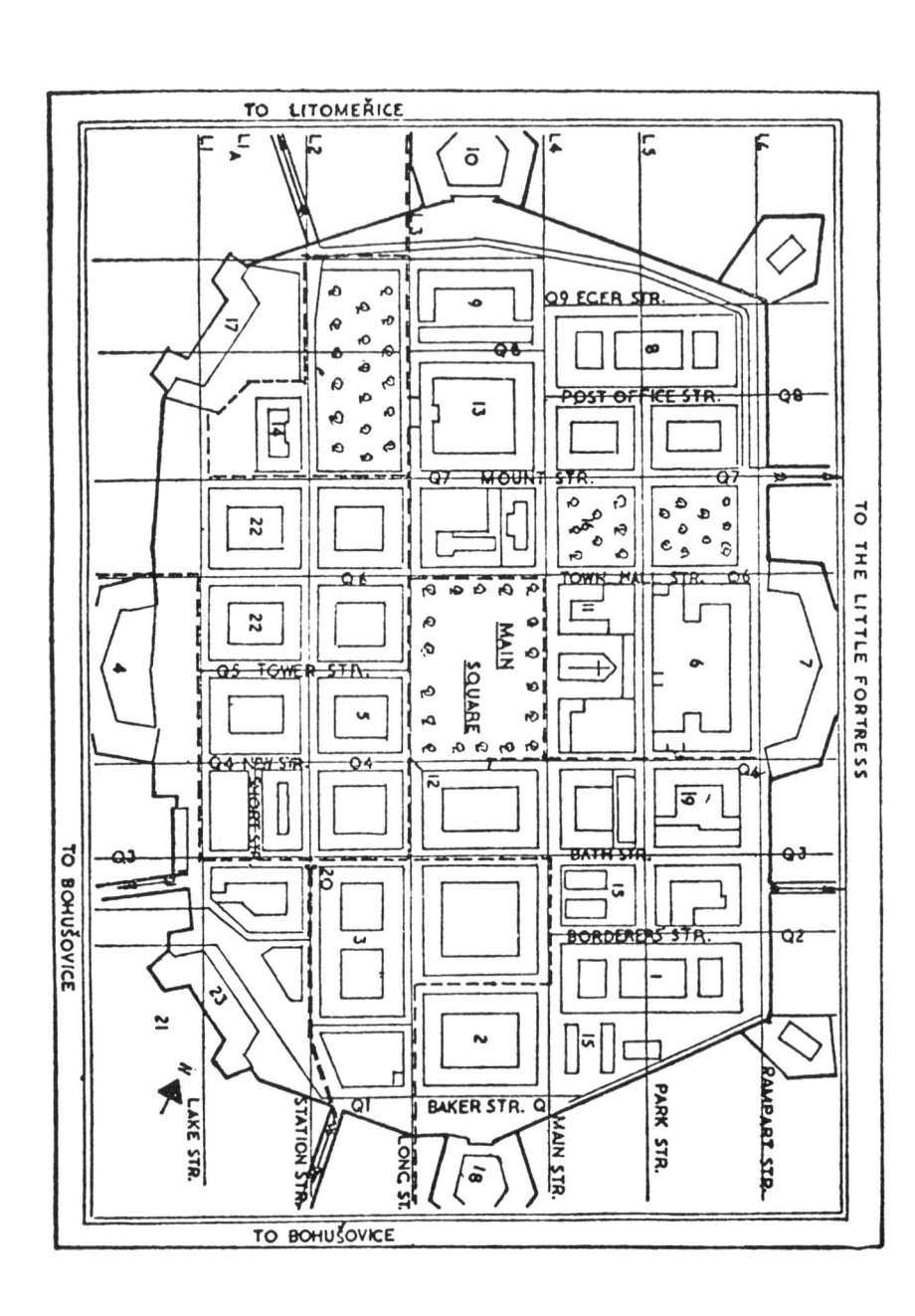

L1 L1A L2 L3 L4 L5 L6

10

Q9 ECER STR.

9

Q8

8

POST OFFICE STR. Q8

17

14

13

Q7 MOUNT STR. Q7

22

Q6

TOWN HALL STR. Q6

22

Q5 TOWER STR.

5

MAIN SQUARE

6

7

TO THE LITTLE FORTRESS

Q4 NEW STR. Q4

SHORT STR.

12

19

BATH STR. Q3

Q3

20

3

15

BORDERERS STR.

1

Q2

23

21

2

15

TO BOHUŠOVICE

N LAKE STR. STATION STR. Q1 BAKER STR. Q LONG ST. 18 MAIN STR. PARK STR. RAMPART STR.

4

TO BOHUŠOVICE

9. Plan of the Terezín ghetto.

Legend to the Plan of the Ghetto in Theresienstadt.

1—Magdeburg Barracks; seat of the Jewish Administration.
2—Hanover Barracks.
3—Hamburg Barracks.
4—Sudeten Barracks; later used to house German Archives.
5—Engineers' barracks.
6—Vrchlabí Barracks; the Central Hospital.
7—Kavalírka Barracks.
8—Dresden Barracks.
9—Podmokly Barracks; later German billets.
10—Usti Barracks; checking station, and German stores in the later period.
11—SS headquarters during the early period; later used as post office.
12—SS headquarters and prison in the later period.
13—SS billets.
14—Gendarmes' billets.
15—Five wooden maintenance sheds.
16—Children's pavilion during "beautification."
17—Building yard.
18—Central bakery and central stores of the Ghetto.
19—Delousing station.
20—Rail terminus in the later period.
21—Rampart III called The Southern Hill.
22—Quarters used for prominent internees during the later period.
23—Last checking station.

——— Inner ramparts of the ghetto.
- - - - Rail side-line to Bohušovice.

List of Streets in the Ghetto
with names given for purposes of "beautification"

L6—Rampart Street (Wallstrasse).
L5—Park Street (Parkstrasse).
L4—Main Street (Hauptstrasse).
L3—Long Street (Lange Strasse).
L2—Station Street (Bahnhofstrasse).
L1A—Short Street (Kurze Strasse).
L1—Lake Street (Seestrasse).

Q9—Eger Street (Egergasse).
Q8—Post Office Street (Postgasse).
Q7—Mount Street (Berggasse).
Q6—Town Hall Street (Rathausgasse).
Q5—Tower Street (Turmgasse).
Q4—New Street (Neue Gasse).
Q3—Bath Street (Badegasse).
Q2—Hunters' Street (Jaegergasse).
Q1—Baker Street (Baeckergasse).

10. Terezín ghetto currency. These notes were issued by the *Ältestenrat* (Council of Elders) of the Terezín ghetto and bear the signature of the *Judenälteste* (chairman of the *Ältestenrat*), Jakub Edelstein. The design was the work of a ghetto inmate, the architect and graphic artist Maximilian Spell (Spiegel), who copied the motif of Moses and the Ten Commandments from the amulet given to him by his mother before he left for Terezín (*left*). Spiegel survived the war and settled in Israel.

12. Terezín: Food voucher. Daily bread rations in Terezín were issued in three categories. Inmates performing hard physical labor received three quarters of a pound of bread each day. Those engaged in administrative work received half a pound. The sick and others unable to work received one third of a pound. In addition, each inmate received one small piece of margarine and one spoonful of granulated sugar once in ten days.

11. Terezín: Voucher for clothing and shoes. All luggage brought to Terezín by the deportees was confiscated on arrival and inspected by other inmates working under the supervision of an SS officer. "Good" items were sent directly to Germany. Items considered less valuable were left to the inmates or placed into a central depot to be distributed among the inmates from time to time. By the beginning of 1943 the SS had set up make-believe stores in the ghetto to create an impression of normal city life. Inmates were given an "opportunity" to buy clothes and shoes from these stores, but only once a year at the most. Often, inmates found themselves buying back the clothes that had been taken from their own luggage at the time of their arrival. They paid for their purchases with this voucher, with a coupon detached for each purchase.

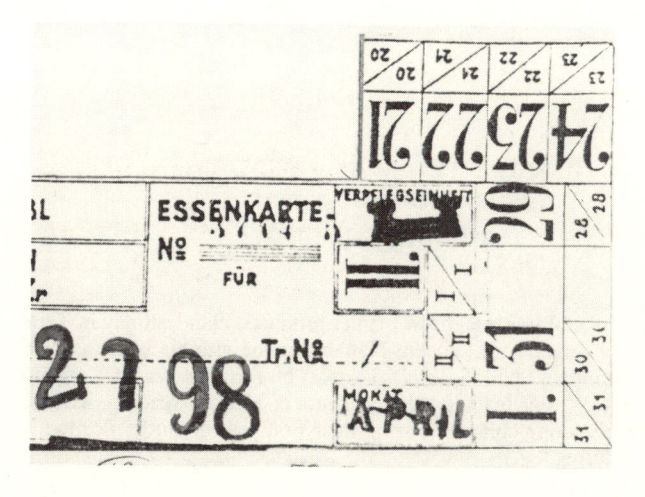

13. Terezín: Men's clothing store. One of the make-believe stores set up by the Germans in the Terezín ghetto. Intended to impress visiting Red Cross representatives, this store was featured in a propaganda film, complete with a cast of well-dressed "salespersons" and "customers."

לְתִינוֹקוֹת

מִקְרָאָה צְעִירָה

לְרֵאשִׁית לִמוּד הַקְּרִיאָה הַכְּתִיבָה וְהַשָּׂפָה
לְתִינוֹקוֹת בִּשְׁנַת הַלִּמּוּדִים הָרִאשׁוֹנָה
בְּאוֹתִיּוֹת מְאִירוֹת עֵינַיִם

14. Title page of children's Hebrew primer produced clandestinely in Terezín. The author was Dr. M. Voskin-Nahartabi; the graphic work was executed by Maximilian Spell (Spiegel). The text on this page reads: " . . . For young children . . . For teaching the elements of Hebrew reading, writing, and language to young children during their first year of study. Printed in large, clear lettering."

15. A children's opera performed in Terezín. The cast of *Brundibar*. The music was composed by Hans Krása, who, along with many of these young actors, perished in a death camp.

16. *In the Ghetto.* Pen and ink drawing by an inmate of the Terezín ghetto, Karel Fleischmann, a physician.

17. Monument erected in the Jewish cemetery of Terezín after the war in memory of the sixteen inmates executed by the Germans in the ghetto on January 10 and February 26, 1942 for "crimes against the dignity of the German Reich," i.e., attempting to smuggle letters out of Terezín and attempting to make purchases at stores in Terezín's "Aryan" sector.

18. Examples of anti-Semitic Czech and German posters and graffiti in Bratislava. The Jews are described as "bloodsuckers" and "slavedrivers."

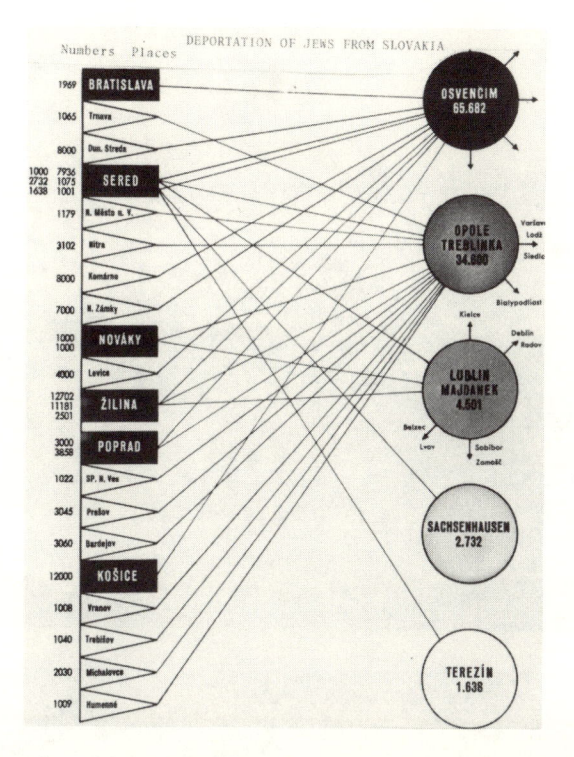

19. Deportation of Jews from Slovakia: a graphic representation (Osvencim = Auschwitz).

20. Jews and other partisans in the Slovak uprising, August and September 1944.

21. Auschwitz: Arrival and "selection" of victims.

22. Auschwitz: "Processing" of new arrivals, from street clothes (*top*) to prison garb (*bottom*).

23. Auschwitz-Birkenau: Postcard (front and back) sent by the inmate Hugo Sax to a friend in the Protectorate of Bohemia and Moravia: "Am here with wife and daughter; [we] are in good health and doing well. Expect to hear from you soon also, and send our love. Hugo Sax and family. Birkenau, September 17, 1943." Inmates of the Czech "family camp" were ordered to send such postcards in German to counteract reports of what was happening to Jews in the camp. Post office stamp next to postage stamp with Hitler's picture (*top*) reads: "Mothers, keep matches away [from children]."

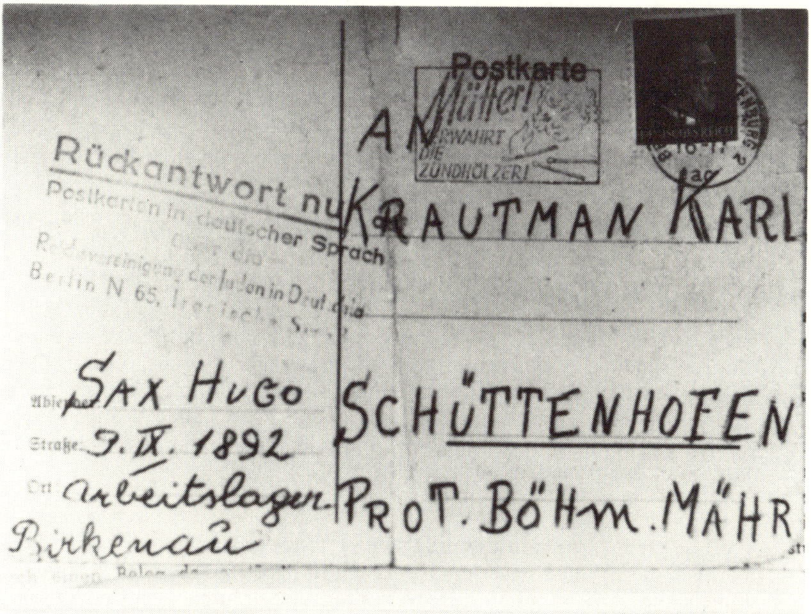

Postkarte

Rückantwort nur ...

Postkarten in deutscher Sprache

Berlin N 65, ...

AN
KRAUTMAN KARL
SCHÜTTENHOFEN
PROT. BÖHM. MÄHR

SAX HUGO
9. IX. 1892
Arbeitslager-
Birkenau

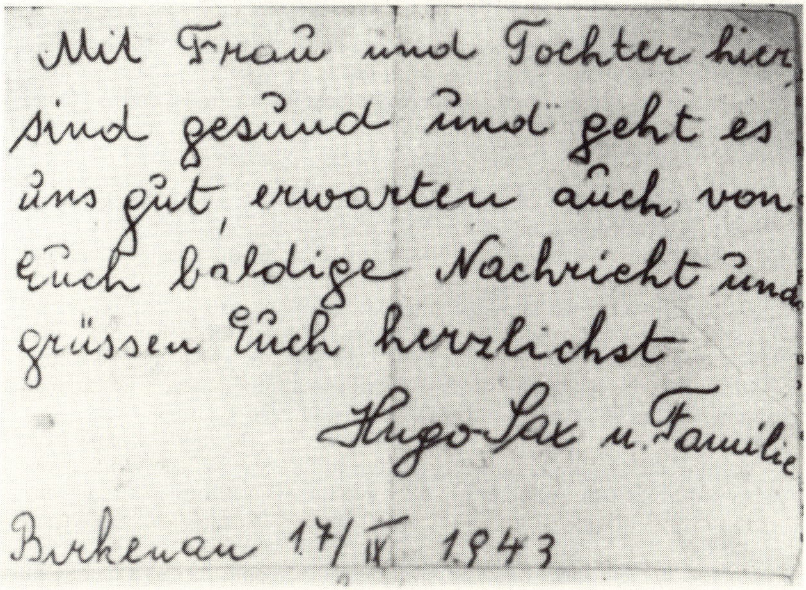

Mit Frau und Tochter hier
sind gesund und geht es
uns gut, erwarten auch von
Euch baldige Nachricht und
grüssen Euch herzlichst

Hugo Sax u. Familie

Birkenau 17/IX 1943

24. Auschwitz-Birkenau: The gas chambers (plan of ground floor). This was one of the plans (with English captions added later) smuggled out of the SS office building by the inmate Vera Foltýnova, an engineer from Czechoslovakia.

FIG. 2.

Crematoria I and II

These crematoria were about 340 ft long by 170 ft across.

Basement

The basement consisted of two main rooms: the undressing-room, which also served as a mortuary, and the gas chamber. Able-bodied persons went down the steps into the basement; the old, the sick, the half-dead and the dead were pushed down a concrete slide. The gas chamber (about 269 square yards) looked like a large communal bathroom, but the showers in the roof emitted cyclon gas instead of water. Up to 2000 people could occupy the gas chamber at the same time. Normally death took place after 20 to 30 minutes, but sometimes after several hours. The basement also contained a furnace for melting down the gold plundered from the corpses, a small mortuary and an office.

Ground floor

After gassing, the corpses were taken up to the ground floor by a lift and burnt in the 15 three-stage furnaces. Each furnace consumed not less than three bodies in 20 minutes. There were altogether 30 furnaces in Crematoria I and II, capable of burning 6500 bodies every 24 hours, or 2,000,000 in a year.

Adjoining the furnace-room was the engine-room, a large fuel-room, and other smaller rooms for various purposes.

There was also an execution room and post mortem room on the ground floor.

Crematoria III and IV

These crematoria were about 220 ft long and 42 ft across. All the equipment was on the ground floor.

The victims entered the undressing-room from the entrance hall and went into the three gas chambers. As in Crematoria I and II, these gas chambers were fitted up like communal bathrooms except that cyclon gas came out of the showers in the roof instead of water. More than 200 people could be accommodated in the three gas chambers which covered a total area of nearly 300 square yards. Normally death took place after 20 to 30 minutes, but sometimes not for two or three hours.

After gassing, the corpses were transferred to the mortuary and from there to the furnace-room which contained 8 furnaces. Each furnace consumed at least three bodies every 20 minutes. The 16 furnaces in Crematoria III and IV were capable of burning up to 3500 corpses in 24 hours, or 1,000,000 in a year.

Next to the furnace-room were various other rooms, such as a fuel-room, wash-room and store.

All the crematoria were surrounded by well-trimmed lawns.

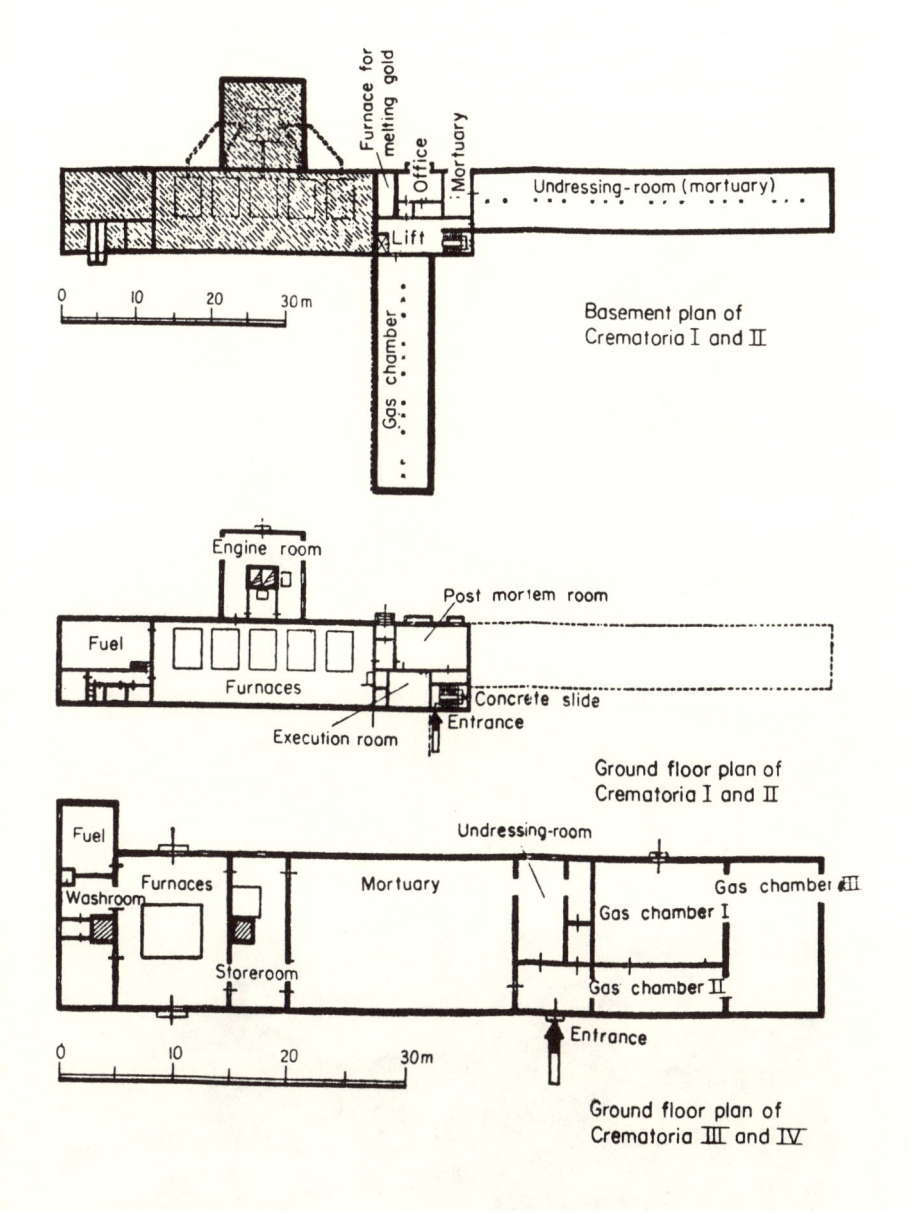

Basement plan of Crematoria I and II

- Furnace for melting gold
- Office
- Mortuary
- Undressing-room (mortuary)
- Lift
- Gas chamber

0 10 20 30 m

Ground floor plan of Crematoria I and II

- Engine room
- Post mortem room
- Fuel
- Furnaces
- Execution room
- Entrance
- Concrete slide

Ground floor plan of Crematoria III and IV

- Fuel
- Washroom
- Furnaces
- Storeroom
- Mortuary
- Undressing-room
- Gas chamber III
- Gas chamber I
- Gas chamber II
- Entrance

0 10 20 30 m

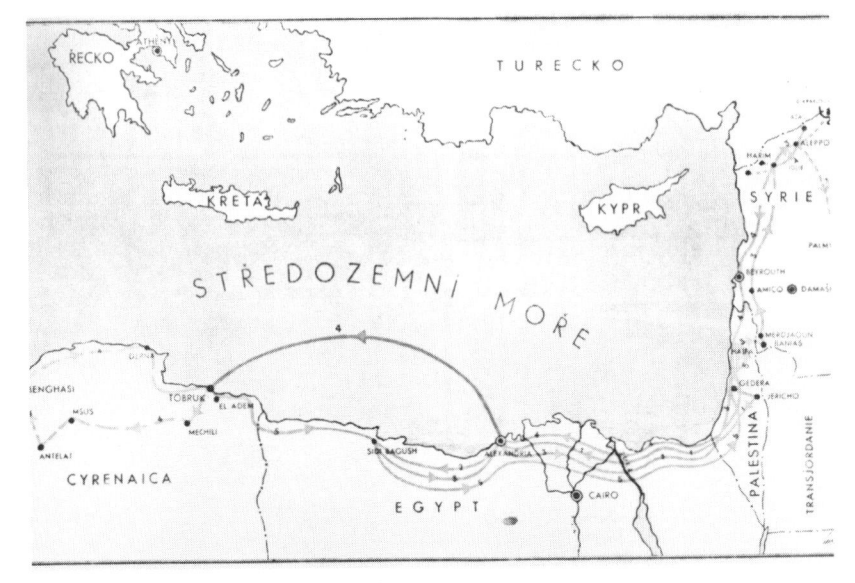

25. Map showing movements of Czechoslovak army units in the Middle East during World War II.

26. Anti-aircraft battery manned by Czechoslovak soldiers (Jewish and non-Jewish) defending the port of Tobruk, 1941.

27. Lieutenant Otto Smik, leader of the 127th British Air Squadron, was awarded five Czechoslovak War Crosses, the Czechoslovak Medal of Honor, and the British Flying Cross. Only his closest comrades in arms knew that Smik was Jewish. He was killed on a bombing mission over Holland on November 28, 1944.

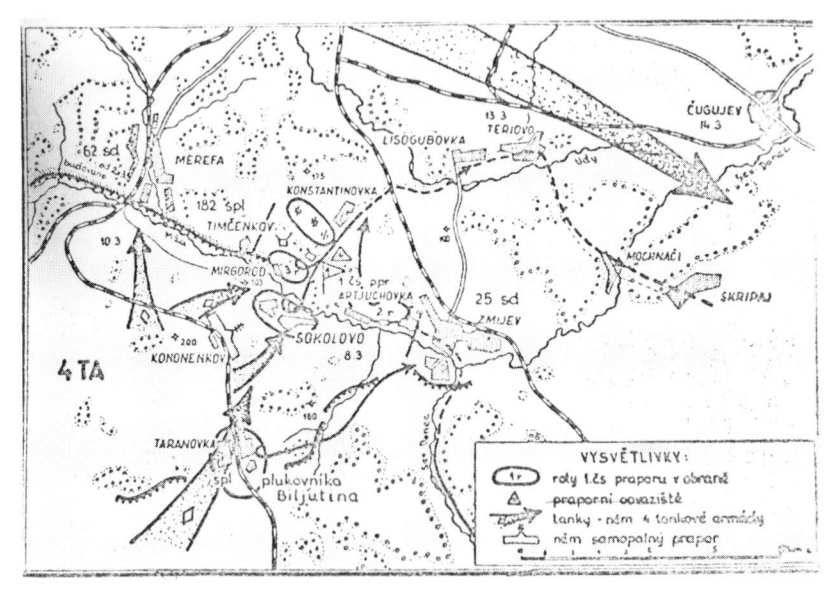

28. The battle of Sokolovo, March 1943.

Key

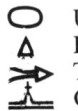

○ Units of First Czechoslovak Battalion in defensive positions
△ Battalion Field Hospital
➤ Tanks of the 4th German army
⊥ German machine gun battalion

29. A partial list of Czechoslovak soldiers killed in the battle of Sokolovo, March 1943. Names of Jewish soldiers are marked with "X".

30. Message from Foreign Minister Jan Masaryk congratulating the Keren Hayesod (Palestine Foundation Fund) on its twenty-fifth anniversary (October 1945).

31. Ark curtain donated to the *Altneuschul* in Prague by Salomon Perlsticker and his wife in the year 1592, one of the oldest dated exhibits in Prague's State Jewish Museum.

32. From the collection of Jewish ceremonial art in Prague's State Jewish Museum. According to tradition, this chalice originally belonged to the famous Rabbi Judah Löw ben Bezalel (Maharah of Prague; c. 1520–1609). Prior to World War II it was owned by the Jewish community of Mikulov (Nikolsburg), Moravia.

33. Holocaust memorial, completed in 1959, in the Pinkas Synagogue in Prague. Names of Nazi concentration camps are inscribed on the eastern wall on either side of the ark. (These inscriptions have been destroyed by water damage).

34. Section of a Prague wall of the Holocaust memorial in the Pinkas Synagogue inscribed with the names of 77,297 Czechoslovak Jews killed during the Nazi regime. (This section was also marred by water damage.)

THE JEWS OF SLOVAKIA: 1939-1945

By Ladislav Lipscher

I.
ANTI-JEWISH MEASURES ADOPTED AFTER THE ESTABLISHMENT OF THE INDEPENDENT STATE OF SLOVAKIA
(March 14, 1939–July 27, 1940)

Definition of Jewish Identity, Restrictions on Civil Rights of Jews in Slovakia

Before it could begin drafting laws to deal with the "Jewish problem," the government of the newly proclaimed independent Slovak state felt it necessary to determine who, in fact, should be considered a Jew. Already on April 18, 1939, the government issued Ordinance 63. Under Section I of this ordinance, a Jew was one who:

1) ... professed Judaism even if he had converted to one of the Christian faiths sometime after October 30, 1918;
2) ... had no official religious affiliation but had at least one Jewish parent;
3) ... had one parent who was a Jew in accordance with definitions (1) or (2) (except if he himself had converted to one of the Christian faiths prior to October 30, 1918);
4) ... one who contracted a marriage with an individual who was a Jew in accordance with definitions (1) to (3) if such marriage took place at any time following the effective date of this Ordinance and as long as he (or she) remained married to such an individual;
5) ... one who was living in an extramarital relationship with an individual who was a Jew in accordance with definitions (1) to (3) at any time

following the effective date of this Ordinance, as well as any issue resulting from this relationship.

The second part of Ordinance 63 was entitled "Restrictions on the Numbers of Jews in Certain Liberal Professions." The number of Jewish attorneys or candidates for the bar to be permitted to practice law was restricted to 4 percent of the total number of attorneys registered at the bar association of the locality involved. Jewish attorneys were permitted to represent only Jewish clients.[1] Jews could not become notaries nor could they serve as newspaper editors, except for Jewish publications.

The Slovak government adopted similar regulations with regard to Jewish participation in other professions. The number of Jewish physicians permitted to practice was also restricted to 4 percent of the total membership of the Chamber of Physicians. However, the government did not enforce these regulations as strictly as it did the anti-Jewish restrictions in the legal profession.[2]

ANTI-JEWISH MEASURES IN BUSINESS AND INDUSTRY

1. *Liquidation and Aryanization of Jewish Concerns*

The government's determination to enforce its anti-Jewish measures in the economic sphere did not meet with opposition from the population. There is no report that any of the political figures in responsible positions at the time disagreed with these measures. The economic difficulties of the newly established state led many politicians and professionals in responsible positions to proceed with caution in this very sensitive field.[3] It was felt that if the Slovak government were to insist on the speedy elimination of the Jews from the country's economy, there would be a danger that the vacancies would be filled not by Slovaks but by Germans. These fears were freely voiced in the official Slovak press.[4]

Considerations which would have dictated a more moderate approach in the implementation of anti-Jewish measures—particularly in the economic sphere—were, however, offset by the political necessity to allay the dissatisfaction that prevailed among the population. Many felt that one such remedy would be the "Aryanization" of Jewish property at the earliest possible moment.

It was under these two opposing pressures that the Slovak government took the first steps leading to the elimination of the Jews from the economy of the Slovak state. The process of restricting the role of Jews in the Slovak economy was begun with legal steps based on what was euphemistically termed "voluntary Aryanization." Under this arrangement, Jewish owners of businesses and manufacturing concerns had to take on an Aryan partner, with the term "voluntary" implying that each Jewish owner was free to choose his own Aryan partner. While the government did not explicitly dictate the terms of these partnership contracts, the general rule was that the Jewish partner could not retain more than 40 percent, or, in exceptional cases, 49 percent, of the net profits of the concern.

On April 25, 1940, the Slovak parliament enacted Law No. 113 regarding businesses owned by Jews and the employment of Jews in Aryan business concerns. This law, a landmark in the evolution of anti-Jewish economic measures, was known as the "First Aryanization Law."

The first part of Law No. 113 dealt with businesses owned by Jews and with the question under what conditions they should be liquidated or Aryanized. If the decision called for Aryanization, it could be either "voluntary" (as described above) or "compulsory." "Compulsory" Aryanization was effected under the authority of an official decree calling for "the sale of the concern to a qualified Christian applicant." In the case of large concerns, particularly in certain special branches of the economy, Aryanization with Jews still participating in the management of the concern was permitted. The second part of the Aryanization Law dealt with the number of Jews who could be employed in any one business.

A study of the complete text of the First Aryanization Law shows that it reflected a compromise between the two opposing views which prevailed in policy-making circles at the time regarding the elimination of the Jews from the country's economic life. The implementation of the law was meant to satisfy and bolster small and middle-sized gentile businesses and thus win their owners for the new regime. At the same time, the law did not intend to disrupt the country's economy by precipitately depriving it of all its Jewish workers, and especially not of all the investments it had obtained from Jews. Jewish manufacturing concerns were exempted from Section 3 of the law in order to prevent the "invasion" of the country by German capital.

Agrarian Reform and Jewish Ownership of Land and Landed Property

As of February 1940, Slovak Jews owned a total of 101,473 hectares (or about 250,625 acres) of the country's arable and forest land.[5]

On February 29, 1940—eight weeks prior to the passage of the First Aryanization Law—the Slovak parliament enacted Law 46/1940 on agrarian reform. This law not only contained provisions for Aryanization and nationalization but also sought to effect a more equitable distribution of landed property as such. A total of 1,619,-008 hectares (or slightly over 4 million acres) was subject to Law 46/1940. Of all this land, only about 6.5 percent was owned by Jews. Yet, as subsequent developments were to confirm, it was the Jewish landowners, practically to the exclusion of all the others, who suffered the most from the implementation of the law. That this would happen was already obvious from the speeches of the two reporters on the bill, who stressed the position of the Jews as owners of landed property but made no mention of the non-Jewish landowners, although the gentiles owned 90 percent of the land to which the new law was to apply.

The views which influenced the method and extent of Aryanization in the case of Jewish business concerns were reflected also in the deliberations on the implementation of anti-Jewish measures in agriculture. It was stressed that the transfer of agrarian property from Jews to gentiles had to be done without harming the economy of the country and with the assurance that the people would continue to have an adequate supply of food.

Initial Reaction of the Victims

There is little documentation available on which to base a thorough study of the reaction of Slovak Jewry to the first anti-Jewish laws passed by the Slovak government. Our most important sources of information consist of oral testimonies and written recollections from several leading figures of the wartime Slovak Jewish community.[6]

During this early stage, the Jewish community of Slovakia, like Jews in many other countries under Nazi domination, clung to an unrealistic optimism which turned out to be fatal. They were convinced that the services of Jewish businessmen and professional people were, in the long run, indispensable to the Slovak economy. They hoped that before long the anti-Semitic zeal of the new regime would abate because they were convinced that the anti-Jewish measures adopted by the Slovak government had been enacted chiefly for propaganda purposes, to appease the radicals at home and to satisfy the rulers of the Third Reich. An even more dangerous illusion prevalent among Slovak Jews was that the Third Reich would lose the war in a short time.

Aside from these psychological factors, a brief review of the organizational structure of Slovakia's Jewish community may aid our understanding of its internal situation at the time.

The religious affairs of Slovak Jewry were supervised by two separate central bodies—one representing the general Jewish religious community and the other those strictly Orthodox congregations which considered themselves as a separate, autonomous entity.[7]

After the abolition of the Jewish party,[8] the official spokesmen of Slovak Jewry proposed the establishment of a central unified body which would be authorized to protect all the interests of the Jewish population. This proposal was approved by the government and resulted in the formation in November 1938 of a *Židovská Ústredná Úradnovňa pre Slovenskú krajinu* (Central Jewish Office for the Region of Slovakia). Among the most important functions assigned to this body were the organization of vocational reorientation courses to train Jews as artisans and agricultural workers, the solution of various problems affecting Slovak Jewish youth, and a program of effective aid for Jewish emigration.[9]

From the very outset, the Central Jewish Office for the Region of Slovakia had to cope with unexpected difficulties, not from the Slovak government but from the Jews themselves. The Central Bureau of Autonomous Orthodox Jewish Religious Congregations in Slovakia categorically refused to cooperate with the new roof organization. At a conference of chairmen of the country's major Orthodox Jewish communities held on December 19, 1938, the "autonomous Orthodox" wing of Slovak Jewry founded the Executive Committee of Orthodox Jews in Slovakia, which was essentially intended to advise the Central Bureau of Autonomous Orthodox Jewish Religious Congregations on economic affairs.

These conflicts within Slovakia's Jewish community were based not only on purely ideological differences but also on political considerations. The immediate reason for the refusal of the "autonomous Orthodox" group to work with the new national Jewish roof organization was the fear that an overall Jewish body which would include non-Orthodox and non-religious Jews might not give sufficient attention to the religious needs of the strictly Orthodox Jews.[10]

For the sake of unity and effective cooperation the representatives of the Central Jewish Office were ready to make a number of concessions. In the end, they proposed the establishment of a joint body consisting of representatives from both the Central Jewish Office and from the two central religious communal organizations. But the Orthodox were not willing to cooperate even on such a basis.[11]

One of the important achievements of the Central Jewish Office for Slovakia was its successful intervention in a matter of large-scale rescue. Following the conquest of Poland, the German occupation authorities set up a concentration camp in Sosnowiec-Bedzin, Upper Silesia, for Jews of various nationalities who had been living in the Protectorate of Bohemia and Moravia at the time of its annexation by Germany. However, the Germans made it known that they would be willing to release those internees who would be able to prove that they could gain entry into another country. The Central Jewish Office for the Region of Slovakia went into action immediately and obtained Slovak entry permits for all the internees. Upon their arrival in Slovakia on February 10, 1940, the newcomers were placed into a camp in Vyhne (Žiar nad Hronom district) which had been set up especially for them.

A role of particular importance was played during that period by Jewish organizations that sought to save Jews by helping them emigrate to other countries, notably Palestine.

After the collapse of the Czechoslovak Republic, it became necessary for the Zionists in Slovakia to create their own central body in order to deal with such major international Jewish organizations as the American Jewish Joint Distribution Committee (JDC) and HICEM. The Palestine Office (the agency of the World Zionist Organization that supervised the practical aspects of Jewish emigration to Palestine) also set up a separate branch in Slovakia. In May 1940 a national Zionist convention was held at Liptovský Sv. Mikuláš, at which it was decided to widen the Zionist organizational network in the country, and Dr. Oskar Neumann was named chairman of the Zionist Federation.

The Federation and its local branches were faced with serious challenges. One result of the systematic civil and political degradation of the Jews in Slovakia was that the latter turned in increasing numbers to Zionism. Accordingly, the Federation set itself a dual task: to train its members vocationally and intellectually for life as pioneers in Palestine, but also to keep them from succumbing to defeatism and lethargy while waiting for the possibility to emigrate to the Jewish Homeland. With these aims in mind, the Federation set up *hakhsharot* (training centers for pioneer life in Palestine) [12] and, at the same time, the Central Jewish Office organized vocational retraining courses for those who intended to settle in countries other than Palestine.

However, at this point it was not simple for Slovak Jews to emigrate, not only because most countries rejected a large influx of immigrants but also because the middle- and low-income groups in Slovak Jewry did not have sufficient funds to make the move.

As for Palestine, the British Mandate authorities set stringent limits to the number of immigration certificates they were willing to issue. Efforts of influential Zionists in Slovakia to obtain a larger number of certificates were of little avail.[13]

The Central Jewish Office was particularly anxious to get at least the young people out of the country, and it proceeded to organize groups for *Aliya Bet,* or "illegal immigration," into Palestine. The Office managed to send small groups of young men and women from Slovakia to the Protectorate of Bohemia and Moravia to join Palestine-bound transports there. Some fortunate individuals were able to leave for Palestine thanks to special immigration certificates issued by the British Mandate authorities to persons with independent means or to students with assured means of support. Finally, the Central Jewish Office attempted a mass emigration project of its own. On April 8, 1940, 736 young Jewish men and women, mostly from Slovakia, met at the port of Bratislava where they filed aboard two Yugoslav Danube steamers, the *Vojvoda Mišić* and *Princezna*

Jelena. However, the project came to nothing; after spending two weeks aboard the boats, the passengers were ordered to disembark. Some blamed the failure of the plan on Yugoslav authorities who, supposedly in response to British pressures, had forbidden the transit; others insisted that it was the Germans who had prevented the boats from sailing.

That summer, another "illegal" transport to Palestine was organized by Betar (*B'rit Trumpeldor*), a Revisionist Zionist youth group, but this attempt, too, ended in failure. The S.S. *Pencho*, with 366 prospective emigrants aboard, ran aground on a reef near the island of Kalymnos in the Aegean Sea. The passengers were taken off the boat and transferred to the island of Rhodes.

During this period, the Slovak government had no objections to Jews leaving the country. However, those Jews who sought permission to take with them even only a small part of their assets frequently encountered great difficulties, for the Slovak state did not have an adequate reserve of foreign exchange. In an effort to overcome this problem, the Jewish organizations proposed to the government a scheme by which Jewish emigrants would be permitted to take with them part of their money while at the same time not depleting Slovakia's foreign exchange reserves. In cooperation with the European central headquarters of the JDC, Slovak Jewry created a special JDC branch which was named *Ústredný výbor pre sociálnú starostlivosť Židov na Slovensku* (Central Committee for the Social Welfare of the Jews in Slovakia) and which received direct subsidies from the JDC. Half of these JDC monies was turned over to the prospective emigrants; the other half was used for welfare purposes, mainly the maintenance of the refugee camp in Vyhne and two other camps which had been opened in Bratislava for Jewish refugees from Nazi-occupied Bohemia and Austria. Under this arrangement Jewish emigrants from Slovakia were able to take with them at least part of their money.

However, in spite of a detailed agreement, the Ministry of Internal Affairs after March 1940 stopped approving applications for the transfer of funds, thus again causing a stagnation in Jewish emigration from Slovakia.

Available documents do not permit the formulation of accurate statistics on Jewish emigration from Slovakia. The emigration statistics compiled by the Jewish Office record the total number of Jews who left the country, but they do not indicate whether these figures represent only "legal" emigrants or whether they also include individuals who left Slovakia without official permission.

According to the statistics of the Central Jewish Office, a total of 7,116 Jews left during the period from March 14, 1939, to the end of 1941. Of these, 6,194 were Slovak citizens; the remaining 922 were nationals of other countries who had been temporarily staying in Slovakia. Of the 7,116, 3,776 went to Palestine, 1,462 to Great Britain, 1,500 gave no destination, and the rest were dispersed among twenty-three other countries.[14]

II.
CHANGES IN THE POLITICAL REGIME OF SLOVAKIA: THE TOTAL ELIMINATION OF JEWS FROM THE SOCIAL AND ECONOMIC LIFE OF SLOVAKIA
(August 1940–December 1941)

A More Stringent Authoritarian Regime and Acceptance of National Socialist Doctrines

The terms imposed by the Third Reich on the new Slovak state set definite limits to the sovereignty of the country both in military matters and in the determination of its foreign policy. Thus, it was only natural that before long the Reich should have sought a decisive role in Slovakia's internal affairs as well.

The pretext for the Reich's initial intervention in the domestic policies of Slovakia was a crisis within the Slovak government. This internal development represented a threat to the political positions of Slovak cabinet members, who had been among the most obsequious flunkies of the Third Reich.

In the summer of 1940 a Slovak delegation headed by President Dr. Jozef Tiso met in Salzburg first with Germany's foreign minister, Joachim von Ribbentrop, and then with Hitler himself. On July 28, 1940, the Slovaks accepted the Reich's terms for the settlement of the crisis. As a result, appropriate changes were made in the highest government posts, with the most important positions going to the most servile supporters of the Reich.

Basic and conspicuous changes were soon noted in the anti-Jewish policies of the Slovak government. In his first public appearance as prime minister and minister of foreign affairs, Dr. Vojtech Tuka stressed the necessity for a radical intensification of anti-Jewish restrictions.[15]

At the recommendation of Adolf Eichmann, SS Hauptsturmführer Dieter Wisliceny, who had been working in Eichmann's department, was appointed advisor on Jewish affairs to the Slovak government.[16]

The first practical results of the intensified anti-Jewish policies soon became evident in a spate of anti-Semitic legislation. On September 3, 1940, the Slovak parliament adopted Constitutional Law 210, which authorized the government to take whatever action it deemed necessary in matters of Aryanization. This law was to be a milestone in the evolution of anti-Jewish legislation in Slovakia.

The Slovak government was now empowered to deal with all Aryanization problems by ordinances that required only the signature of the premier and the minister of the department directly concerned.

This law tended to expand the authority of the government at the expense of both the parliament and the chief of state, Dr. Tiso. Politically, it strengthened the positions of Premier Tuka and of Alexander (Šáno) Mach, the minister of internal affairs.

CENTRALIZATION OF ANTI-JEWISH ADMINISTRATIVE FUNCTIONS

Another task which the Slovak government set out to fulfill was the centralization of the administrative agencies that were to implement the anti-Jewish laws.

So far the enforcement of anti-Jewish policies and legislation had been split up among several government agencies, and the lack of a central authority to coordinate these activities had been the cause of much overlapping and bickering over competence.

A thorough change in the entire system was made by Ordinance 222/1940, providing for the establishment of the *Ústredný hospodársky úrad* (Central Economic Office), which was given the status of a "central authority" within the Prime Minister's Office. The powers of this new agency were defined as follows:

> The Central Economic Office, on the basis of specific legislation, shall carry out whatever steps are necessary for the elimination of the Jews from the economic and social life of Slovakia and for the transfer of Jewish property to Christian ownership.

The authority of the *Štátny pozemkový úrad* (State Office for Landed Property) in matters of Aryanization and other anti-Jewish measures remained unchanged. Later, in 1941, as the anti-Jewish activities of the government increased still further, the Minister for Internal Affairs set up within his office the notorious "Department 14" to handle these matters.

A share in the implementation of anti-Jewish measures was given also to the native Fascist Hlinka Guard and the *Freiwillige Schutzstaffel*, the voluntary militia organization of local Germans, both of which had acquired notoriety for their atrocities against defenseless Jews. These atrocities were legalized by Proclamation 545/1941 from the Ministry for Internal Affairs, which explained that the two organizations had to see to it that the anti-Jewish measures adopted by the government were indeed carried out.[17]

For the sake of efficiency, steps were taken to create a central authority, also within the Jewish community, to coordinate the enforcement of government orders. To this end, a central Jewish organization was set up that eventually became part of a system developed by the Third Reich for Jewish communities throughout Nazi Europe: those who were doomed to liquidation were forced to help execute the sentence pronounced upon them. Ordinance 234 of September 30, 1940, provided for the establishment of the *Ústredňa Židov* (Jewish Office).[18] This organization was to be a

> public law corporation based on common interests; all persons who were classed as Jews under the prevailing legislation must be members of said corporation. The Central Organization of Jews is to be the sole organization of Jews residing in the Slovak Republic, with exclusive authority to represent the interests of the Jews.

All other Jewish organizations, except the Jewish Religious Congregations, were dissolved.

The principal function of the Jewish Office—aside from the unconditional enforcement of government ordinances—was, as already mentioned earlier, to retrain Jews for physical work and, at the same time, to promote their emigration. It was also put in charge of all Jewish schools and Jewish charities. It was headed by a *Starosta* (Jewish Elder), who was appointed by the Central Economic Office, to which he was personally responsible for the work of his organization.[19]

Further Deterioration of Personal Status of Jews and Systematic Expropriation of Jewish Assets

Constitutional Law 210/40 became the basis for a series of anti-Jewish laws that reached into every sphere of Slovak social and economic life.

It would go too far to make a seriatim study of all the laws by which the Jews of Slovakia were systematically deprived of the civil liberties and human rights to which they had been entitled even under the new Slovak constitution. These laws were faithfully patterned upon German prototypes which did not spare one single facet of the Jew's personal life. The most comprehensive of all these laws was Proclamation 510/1941 by the Ministry for Internal Affairs regarding specific police measures against Jews.[20]

The laws affecting the education and school attendance of Jewish students constituted a particularly severe hardship. A decree enacted on June 13, 1939, restricted the number of Jewish students at public schools to 4 percent of the total student body. Later, a law was passed excluding Jews altogether from the country's schools. Jews were also barred from training schools for apprentices, and they could no longer have the Slovak authorities validate report cards or certificates issued to them by schools or other educational institutions outside the country.

Eventually, Jewish children of school age were permitted to attend only Jewish elementary schools or classes, which had to be maintained by the Jewish religious communities. These laws were eloquent proof that the Slovak government meant to subject the Jews to a general process of attrition starting from early childhood.

In order to restrict the "economic influence" of the Jews once and for all, the Slovak government needed to know the amount and total value of property belonging to individuals classed as Jews, and the liabilities with which these Jewish assets were encumbered. Under Ordinance 203/1940 all Jewish assets had to be registered. The law covered all property or other assets owned by Jews in Slovakia or abroad as of September 2, 1940.

1. *Business and Manufacturing Concerns*

Those political forces whose spokesmen had been given key positions in the Slovak government under German pressure felt that the elimination of the Jews from the country's economy was not proceeding quickly enough.

The government therefore amended the First Aryanization Law by Ordinance 303/1940 Regarding Jewish Enterprises. The operative portion of the new regulation was Section 5, which was referred to as the "Aryanization Section." Under this ordinance the Central Economic Office was authorized to arrange for the mass liquidation of Jewish enterprises, and "voluntary" Aryanization was abolished.

Table 1 shows the results of the gradual elimination of the Jews from the Slovak economy:

TABLE 1

Specialized Branch	Total No. Trade Concessions as of March 14, 1939	No. Trade Concessions owned by Jews as of March 14, 1939		Jewish Concerns Aryanized as of Dec. 31, 1941	Jewish Concerns Liquidated as of Dec. 31, 1941
		No.	% of Total		
Hardware	7,098	1,173	16.5	199	508
Lumber	6,286	863	13.6	201	522
Groceries	30,256	7,457	24.6	637	4,460
Textiles	9,057	3,233	35.7	459	1,884
Leather Goods	6,344	832	13.1	89	530
Building and Construction	3,830	335	8.9	57	376
Other	16,395	3,381	20.6	245	1,655
Totals	79,266	17,274	21.0	1,887	9,935

As shown above, the tendency was to liquidate Jewish enterprises rather than merely to Aryanize them. To begin with, liquidation was a much simpler—and thus also a politically more effective—way of eliminating the Jews from the country's economy. By liquidation, unwanted Jewish competition was eliminated completely, while in Aryanization there always was a chance that the former Jewish owner might remain active in the concern. Also, there simply were not enough Slovak gentiles capable of running the Aryanized concerns.

The basic intent of Aryanization was the desire of Slovak capital to alter the existing distribution of property in its favor. When the Slovak state was first established, most of the factories and mines in the country were owned by Czech and foreign capital. Following the German occupation of Bohemia and Moravia, German banks and other concerns took over the investments of Czech capital in Slovakia without encountering any resistance. Throughout the life of the Slovak state, additional German capital was systematically pumped into the country. Under these circumstances, opportunities for Slovak capital expansion remained strictly circumscribed. The state utilized these limited possibilities all the more consistently and aggressively in the fight against those who had been reduced to political and social impotence as a result of the anti-Jewish measures enacted by the government.

Besides increasing the efficacy of Slovak capital, Aryanization benefited the Slovak lower middle class, which took over stores, workshops and other small concerns formerly owned by Jews. These events had a decisive influence not only on the Slovak economy but also on the political attitude of the well-to-do classes, including even those who had not been in sympathy with the puppet regime. "The fact that the Slovak middle class as a whole increased in extent, strength and wealth during the war years is of immense significance for a proper understanding of political developments in Slovakia during and after the war. [For] in most of the other countries under Nazi German control the opposite had happened; the domestic middle class was crudely repressed and all but dispossessed in favor of German enterprises. In Slovakia, by contrast, we know of almost no instance in which an enterprise of any consequence passed from the hands of the Slovak middle class into those of German finance.[21]

2. *Agriculture*

Those elements in official Slovak life who were anxious to speed up the Aryanization process objected to the narrow construction of the Agrarian Reform Law. They particularly criticized the practice of the *Štátny pozemkový úrad* (State Office for Real Property) to require non-Jewish purchasers of Jewish-owned land to deposit the full purchase price with the courts before they could receive official title to the property. These considerations led to new agrarian reform laws. Under Ordinance 93/41, the State Office for Real Property was authorized to designate by simple fiat what properties were to be taken over by the state for redistribution among interested parties.

However, the enactment of the new legislation was not followed by precipitate action such as occurred in the Aryanization of other branches of the economy. A more circumspect approach was called for here, due to the unique place of agriculture in the Slovak economy, particularly in wartime. Also, the agricultural enterprises owned by Jews were, on the average, larger and better organized than those owned by non-Jews, and they were relatively well mechanized. The authorities therefore constantly urged the competent local agencies to consider carefully in each case whether a Jewish-owned estate should be Aryanized and, if so, to whom it should be assigned or whether it would not be more expedient to redistribute it among several owners in order to prevent a decline in the country's agricultural production through loss of efficiency. Nevertheless, quite a few Slovak functionaries managed to buy or otherwise receive Jewish holdings of land.

Eventually, the implementation of the agrarian reform law was permitted to lapse with the tacit approval of both the government and the Slovak People's party. Larger estates formerly owned by Jews were simply taken over by the *Fond pre správu polňohospodárskych majetkov* (Fund for the Administration of Agricultural Property), which was set up in 1942.

3. *Houses, Savings Accounts, and Valuables*

According to the survey made by the *Štátny Štatistický Úrad* (State Bureau of Statistics), buildings owned by Jews in Slovakia represented a total value of Ks. 1,250,697,000 or 29 percent of the total Jewish assets reported. These buildings were not new; therefore, their yield was not high. This was the main reason why the government did not conduct the takeover of Jewish-owned buildings with the same dispatch as it did the Aryanization of other Jewish property.

The initial phase of the confiscation of Jewish-owned buildings ended with the official transfer of the latter to the state, effective

November 1, 1941.[22] One half of the net revenue from buildings taken over by the state was to be deposited into a *Fond pre podporu vysťahovalectva Židov* (Fund for Jewish Emigration), which was to be part of the Central Economic Office.

Among the legal measures indirectly affecting Jewish home ownership were procedures which arbitrarily excluded Jewish tenants from the protection of rent control and thus further worsened the social position of Slovakia's Jewish population. Effective July 1, 1940, rent-control laws were no longer applicable to apartments or workshops rented by Jews. Jews were forbidden to live on streets or squares anywhere in Slovakia named for Andrej Hlinka or Adolf Hitler.[23] This prohibition covered fifty-two larger towns or cities with a total of 10,931 apartments classified as "Jewish." These apartments held a total of 43,124 tenants, or about half the Jewish population of the country. It fell to the Jewish Office to find new housing for the unfortunates, a most difficult task because the housing shortages already existing in many of these cities had been further aggravated by the arrival of Jewish families who had been expelled from Bratislava.

Other property owned by Jews was classed in the official inventory as "capital assets" and assessed at a total value of Ks. 1,458,003,000.

The government ordered all cash payments made by Aryans to Jews for any purpose whatsoever to be deposited into a closed account established for this purpose at a bank selected by the authorities. In addition, Jews were required to deposit with the authorities all securities and valuables in their possession.

4. *The Fund for Jewish Emigration and the Special Levy on Jewish Property*

At one point the Germans contemplated the forced resettlement of all European Jews on the island of Madagascar. The Slovak authorities endorsed this plan and for this purpose the Fund for Jewish Emigration was set up at the Central Economic Office to cover the expenses that would be entailed in the project.

In addition to its main purpose—the forced resettlement or, euphemistically termed, "emigration"—of Jews, the Fund for Jewish Emigration was to be used to pay the salaries and other expenses of the Central Economic Office. This meant that, in effect, the Jews themselves were to be forced to pay for the upkeep of an institution which had been set up as an instrument to harass them.

To add to the income of the Fund, the banks were ordered to turn over to it 50 percent of the money still remaining in the accounts of Jewish depositors. This was the Fund's largest source of revenue; [24] according to official statistics, the total value of bank accounts kept by Jews in Slovakia at the time was Ks. 245,004,858.80.

On August 25, 1941, Premier Tuka held a closed session with his advisors, including the highest government officials concerned with the country's economy. At this session, grave concern was expressed about the rapid deterioration of Slovakia's economy since the country had entered the war against the Soviet Union. The minister of finance reported that by the end of 1941 the national budget would show a deficit of almost Ks. 600,000,000. The government decided to make up for most of this deficit by making available Ks. 500,000,000 through a special 20-percent levy on Jewish property (Ordinance 199, September 9, 1941).

The government had expected this 20-percent levy on Jewish property to yield a total of Ks. 536,000,000. But the total received by January 31, 1942, was no more than Ks. 9,204,113. In a situation report which is undated but was obviously issued sometime after January 31, 1942, the Treasury Department conceded that:

> Most of the Jews no longer possess the property they reported [for the official inventory of Jewish assets], and they do not have the liquid assets to pay the required total through the special levy. [25]

Ordinance 198/1941 on the Legal Status of the Jews, known as the "Jewish Code" (September 9, 1941)

Leafing through the Official Gazette of Slovakia for the years immediately following the changes in the Slovak government that took place following the Salzburg Conference of July 28, 1940, one could get the impression that the Slovak government during that period had nothing more important to do than to concoct anti-Jewish laws.

The anti-Jewish measures enacted in Slovakia multiplied so rapidly that the government itself could no longer keep track of them. Sometimes laws were passed that were in contradiction to each other. One of the factors in the adoption of Ordinance 198/1941 was that the step-by-step confiscation of Jewish property practiced until that time had benefited only a small and for the most part wealthy element of Slovak society. This could not be expected to satisfy the less privileged classes, particularly the more radical plebeian elements represented by the Hlinka Guard. Petitions on this subject were the center of attention at a meeting of Hlinka Guard commanders held in August 1941 under the chairmanship of Šano Mach, the minister for internal affairs, who was also the commander of the Hlinka Guard. At this meeting a resolution was passed calling for the introduction of the Nuremberg Laws in Slovakia.

The Ordinance on the Legal Status of the Jews, which was known as the *Judenkodex,* or "Jewish Code," and contained 270 articles, was one of the most voluminous pieces of legislation passed during the existence of the Slovak state; it was longer than the constitution itself.

The very first article of the code announced substantial changes in the legal status of the Jews. It set down a new definition of the term "Jew," which was the basic theme of the entire code. Generally, a Jew, for purposes of the code, was one who had at least three Jewish grandparents. A Jewish grandparent was defined as one who professed the "Israelite" faith.

The code recognized the "racial" principle of Jewishness and accordingly adopted the concept of *Mischling* or "half-caste," which it defined as applicable to an individual who had only one or two Jewish grandparents. All *Mischling* were considered non-Jews and were subject only to explicit provisions of the Jewish Code.

Some four decades earlier, Vienna's notoriously anti-Semitic mayor, Dr. Karl Lueger, had pronounced a principle which had become a classic in the history of anti-Semitism: "It is for me to decide who is a Jew." This attitude was taken over in Section 255 of the Jewish Code in Slovakia:

> The President of the Republic shall have the right to exempt individuals [of his choosing] from the provisions of this code. Such exemptions may be complete, or partial, and may be subject to [specific] conditions.

By introducing the "racial" principle into its concept of Jewishness, the code became applicable to individuals who had not been subject to anti-Jewish laws before, including those who had been baptized prior to October 30, 1918.

Except for those immediately affected, the adoption of the Jewish Code brought no particular reaction, positive or negative, from the population. However, it did provoke the first instance of opposition from the Catholic bishops to an anti-Jewish law. At a conference in Nitra on October 7, 1941, the Catholic bishops of Slovakia drafted a memorandum which was sent to leading officials of the government, pointing out that the Jewish Code was based on the ideology of racism, a doctrine rejected by both the Church and its bishops. The prelates further protested against the ban on marriages between Christians and Jewish converts to Christianity; they demanded that young Jews who had been baptized should be permitted to attend lower-grade secondary schools and institutions of higher learning and called for the abolition of the provision under which baptized Jews were required to wear the Jewish badge even when they were attending Mass in a Catholic church.

In a similar vein, Msgr. Dr. Giuseppe Burzio, the Vatican's diplomatic representative in Bratislava, made representations to President Tiso; Cardinal Luigi Maglione, the papal secretary of state, expressed the Vatican's objections to the code in a note (November 12, 1941) to Karol Sidor, once a leading figure in the Slovak People's party, who had become Slovakia's ambassador to the Holy See.

A careful perusal of these documents of protest makes it clear that the Church was not opposed to the basic intent of the code. The Church was concerned only about the legal status of those Jews who had converted to Roman Catholicism. The bishops spoke out not in behalf of the Jews but only in the interest of those Catholic families who would be affected by the provisions of the Jewish Code. "We wish to stress that we concern ourselves with this law solely from the ecclesiastical point of view, since it will affect several thousands of our [own] believers . . ."

The Slovak government paid no attention to these protests. But the bishops did not take any action. They meekly accepted a noncommittal promise from President Tiso that he would assert his prerogative to grant exemptions under Section 255 whenever he would find it proper to do so.

Aside from minor divergences, the Jewish Code was a faithful replica of the Nuremberg Laws.

Official Reich sources welcomed the enactment of the Jewish

Code with undisguised gratification, nor did they fail to stress the fact that the code had been enacted in a state headed by a member of the Catholic clergy. This fact was considered particularly significant by the Reich because it could serve as a cogent means of persuasion for those satellite states that until then had shown no special interest in solving the Jewish problem in the National Socialist manner.

VISIBLE IDENTIFICATION OF JEWS: THE EXPULSION OF JEWS FROM BRATISLAVA

Under the Jewish Code, all Jews above the age of six were required to wear a yellow Star of David, to be sewn onto the left side of outer garments. This order took effect on September 22, 1941, which that year happened to be the date of *Rosh Hashanah,* the Jewish New Year. Under the proclamation of the Ministry for Internal Affairs, the residences of Jews, too, had to bear a prescribed identifying mark.

Section 28 of the Jewish Code authorized the Central Economic Office, with the approval of the Ministry for Internal Affairs, to expel Jews from any city or community and to resettle them elsewhere in the country. Soon after the enactment of the code, the chairman of the Central Economic Office issued an order expelling most of the Jews from Bratislava by the end of 1941. All expenses entailed in this "resettlement" had to be paid by those directly concerned.

The enforcement of the order was assigned to the Jewish Office, which created an *Oddelenie pre zvláštne úkony* (Department for Special Tasks) for this purpose.

The first transport of Jews from Bratislava left the city during the night of October 27, 1941. By March 1, 1942, 6,720 Jews from Bratislava had been "resettled."

According to the official census of December 15, 1940, a total of 30,690 Jews had already been living in the towns which had been designated as "relocation centers" for the Jews of Bratislava. If the evacuation of Jews from Bratislava had been carried through in the volume originally contemplated, these towns before long would have held nearly half the Jewish population of Slovakia. Such a concentration of Slovakia's Jews in specified areas suited the intentions of the Slovak government, which contemplated the possibility of the Jews being deported from Slovakia altogether; at the time there still was talk of a forced resettlement of all European Jews on the island of Madagascar.

THE ACTIVITIES OF THE ÚSTREDNĂ ŽIDOV (JEWISH OFFICE)

The authority of the *Ústredně Židov* (Jewish Office) as a purely law-enforcing body was derived from the content and scope of the orders issued by the authorities of the Slovak state. This circumstance of necessity limited the freedom of action of the various officials and functionaries of the Jewish Office. But much depended also on the personal attitudes of the Jewish officials, attitudes which were influenced by such factors as the official's ability to understand his responsibility in this complex and difficult situation, and his personal integrity and courage. However, these qualifications had little significance in the selection of officials for the Jewish Office. Appointments were not made by Jews but by the Slovak authorities, namely, the Central Economic Office, which had no special interest in selecting individuals with high personal qualifications. As a result, there were among the staff also some dangerous elements—fortunately only a small minority—who were ready to do anything to safeguard their own lives or livelihoods.

Much of the justifiable criticism of the role of the Jewish Office should be leveled at the Department for Special Tasks, which was to assume just as crucial a role in the deportation of Slovak Jews to the death camps as it did earlier in the evacuation of the Jews from Bratislava.

However, thanks to the efforts of certain responsible functionaries, some departments of the Jewish Office were able to give effective aid to their fellow Jews. One notable case in point was the help they gave to the young, who were hit the hardest by the anti-Jewish restrictions breaking off their schooling.

In this respect, much useful work was done by Department II of the Jewish Office, which supervised the vocational retraining of the young. This department, under the direction of Dr. Oskar Neumann, provided young Jews with training by experienced instructors in two fields of work still permitted them: agriculture and trades.

The success of this vocational retraining program, of course, depended basically on the availability of employment for the trainees. A number of Jewish landowners put trainees to work on their estates. It was not so easy to find places for trainees in the trades; nevertheless, Department II eventually succeeded in organizing 147 retraining courses in the trades with a total enrollment of 2,047 trainees.

In addition to vocational retraining, there was the problem of finding employment for able-bodied Jews who had been eliminated from the economy of the country. A proclamation issued by the Ministry for Internal Affairs on April 2, 1941, called for the creation of special labor centers for Jews, to be supervised by the labor subdivision of the Jewish Office.

Jewish workers assigned to labor centers received much lower wages than those set in collective contracts; they were not permitted to work in the same places with gentiles and were not covered by the compulsory national insurance program.

ASSIGNMENT OF JEWS TO FORCED LABOR

Though in time, the Slovak approach to "the solution of the Jewish problem" lost both its economic and political motivation, it grew into a serious and burning social problem. Official circles feared that the presence of a mass of pauperized Jews would stir compassion rather than hatred among the Slovak populace, and thus, in turn, strengthen the hand of opposition forces. To forestall this eventuality, the Slovak government drew up plans to concentrate the Jews in specified areas of the country where they would live in physical isolation from the non-Jewish population and where they would be assigned to forced labor.

1. *The Military Labor Service*

The earliest organized efforts at forced labor assignments for Jews took shape following the enactment of National Defense Law 20/1940, under which Jews were exempted from military service but were required to do manual work at military labor camps instead.[26]

"*Robotník Žid*" (literally, "Work Jews"), as these Jews were officially termed, were given distinctive blue uniforms, and dark blue berets instead of the regulation forage caps. "Work Jews" were subject to the same legal restrictions as Jewish civilians.

"Work Jews" were assigned to the Sixth Labor Battalion, which consisted of five companies. Of these, three (21, 22, and 23) consisted entirely of Jews, one (24) of gypsies, and one (25) of convicts who had been transferred to the battalion from the regular army.

Jewish recruits who entered the labor service were assembled at Čemerné (Vranov district) in eastern Slovakia, where they received several weeks of basic military training, using spades instead of rifles for drill. After basic training, the Jewish labor companies were assigned to forced labor in various parts of the country.

In the spring of 1942, when the deportations of Jews from Slovakia to the death camps first began, most of the Jewish labor groups were transferred to the western part of the country. They were placed into three labor camps—Sv. Jur, Láb, and Zohor in the Bratislava district—and were put to work on drainage projects. This arrangement was expedient both politically and economically. Since most of the non-Jews in that particular area were known to be loyal to the regime, there was little likelihood that they would sympathize with the Jews. Secondly, there was not enough gentile civilian manpower available for so large and important a work project. And finally, the Jewish inmates of the labor camps represented cheap labor that did not even require social insurance coverage.

Once mass deportations were in full swing, the position of the Jews in the labor camps was relatively better than that of other Jews in the country. Jews who had been drafted for forced labor were less likely than other Jews to be deported from Slovakia to the death camps. First of all, the Jewish labor camps were under the supervision of the Ministry of Defense, which did not have a particularly good relationship with the Ministry for Internal Affairs. Thus, on several occasions, when the Ministry for Internal Affairs sought to have the Jews discharged from military labor service, the Ministry of Defense refused the requests, explaining that the Jews in the labor service were doing essential work. Secondly, there was the strong influence of the engineer Blahút, the general manager of the Moravod Company, which was in charge of the drainage project. Since he was anxious not only to complete the drainage project at hand but also to go on to other, more extensive construction assignments, this official did not want to lose so many cheap workers. Since he was prominent in the inner circles of the Slovak People's party, he was able to save nearly 1,000 young Jews at least temporarily from deportation.

On May 31, 1943, the military labor camps for Jews were disbanded and most of the inmates were moved to civilian concentration camps or concentration centers.

2. The Preparation of Concentration Camps

Ordinance 153/1941 made all Jews in Slovakia between the ages of eighteen and sixty subject to draft for forced labor,[27] except for those who had not yet been eliminated from the economic and social life of the country and those who were already employed at manual work.

The first draft call was issued on July 21, 1941, by the Ministry for Internal Affairs. Work assignments and working conditions were set by the Central Economic Office.

This draft call and the creation of the special labor centers for Jews were preliminary steps leading to the total physical isolation of the Jews from the general population. According to an official statement from the government, the physical isolation of the Jews was intended as "one step in the solution of the Jewish problem in Slovakia."

Initially, the decision to set up concentration camps for Jews in Slovakia, along with statements from individuals in responsible positions, supported the assumption that, at least for the time being, the Slovak government wanted to isolate the Jews physically from the general population, but not to expel them from the country.

This assumption seemed to be borne out by at least one significant event. On July 9 and 10, 1941, a delegation of Slovak government officials toured the concentration camps that had been set up for Jews in Upper Silesia. The group, accompanied by SS *Sturmbannführer* Albert Smogon, advisor on social problems to the Slovak government, and Dieter Wisliceny, the advisor on Jewish affairs, inspected the ghettos and the workshops in Sosnowice and Gross-Strelitz. Following their return, two of the Slovak officials in the group reported their impressions.

According to a report which the branch of the *Sicherheitsdienst* (Security Service, the intelligence branch of the SS) that had jurisdiction over Slovakia sent to the *Reichssicherheitshauptamt* (Central Office of Reich Security, the central security office of the Reich government), Dr. Izidor Koso, director of the prime minister's office and of the Ministry of Internal Affairs, supposedly remarked in the presence of two other members of the delegation that ". . . the system of forced labor for Jews as implemented in Upper Silesia is un-Christian and inhumane; we will have to find another way in Slovakia."[28] In a similar vein, Július Pečúch, the Slovak government commissioner for Jewish labor camps, said that there was no way of surviving in these camps; the Jews, he declared, were forced to exist there under conditions which would eventually kill them.[29]

The remarks of these two officials are of extraordinary significance because they indicate that at least some influential figures in the Slovak government must have realized what fate would befall the Jews if they were to be deported to Nazi-occupied Poland.

III.
THE FINAL PHASE: THE DEPORTATIONS (1941–1943)

Negotiations between Slovakia and Germany regarding the Deportation of the Jews

The aim of the Nazis in each occupied or satellite country was to make the Jews appear as a burden to the local government by turning them into pariahs and stripping them of all their possessions. This was the classic method of Reinhard Heydrich, and it was subsequently adopted also by Adolf Eichmann. After the war, Dieter Wisliceny was to describe this approach to the "Jewish problem" as follows: "My plan for solving the Jewish problem in Slovakia was to strip 90,000 Jews of their income and their property. This would create a Jewish problem which could be solved only by forcing the Jews to emigrate."[30]

Once this stage had been reached in Slovakia, the Reich put out its initial feelers on the subject of deportation. "*The Reichssicherheitshauptamt* telephoned to inquire whether the Jews of Slovakia and Croatia could be included in the planned deportation of Jews from Germany to the East [of Europe] . . . For reasons of courtesy, it is suggested that this question should be discussed with the governments of Slovakia and Croatia through the good offices of the German legations in Bratislava and Zagreb, respectively."[31]

The German envoy in Bratislava wanted to know what the Slovak government would have the German authorities do with Slovak Jews who were living in the Reich. Would the Slovak government recall them to Slovakia within a reasonable interval, or would it agree to have them deported from Germany straight to the ghettos of Eastern Europe? On December 2, 1941, the Slovak government replied that it would consent to the second alternative.[32]

The course of the German-Slovak negotiations that followed was smoothed and accelerated by an event which had nothing to do with the planned "final solution of the Jewish problem." Under agreements signed by Slovakia and Germany on December 8, 1939, and June 19, 1941, respectively, the Slovak government had agreed to provide Germany and the Protectorate of Bohemia and Moravia with a Slovak labor force as Slovakia's contribution to the German war effort. Early in 1942, the Germans asked Slovakia for additional workers. On January 21, 1942, the Slovak government declared that it was in no position to supply the additional manpower.

In his testimony at his trial after the war, Wisliceny recalled the developments that followed. In the course of the talks, the representative of the Slovak government, with the consent of Dr. Koso, suggested to Herr Sager, the representative of the Reich's Ministry of Labor in Bratislava, that 20,000 Jewish workers should be sent to Germany in place of Slovaks. When Eichmann learned of this offer, Wisliceny was summoned posthaste to Berlin, where Eichmann instructed him to notify the Slovak government that Germany was willing to accept the 20,000 Jewish workers offered by Slovakia.[33] At the same time Eichmann informed Wisliceny that these Jews would not be turned over to the Reich Ministry of Labor as workers but would be shipped—by personal order of Heinrich Himmler—into closed factories and camps under the administration of the *Reichssicherheitshauptamt.*

On his return to Bratislava, Wisliceny communicated Eichmann's instructions to Dr. Koso and to Augustin Morávek, the chairman of the Central Economic Office. Koso, along with Premier Tuka and Minister for Internal Affairs Mach, agreed to the proposal. Dr. Tuka only requested that it should be conveyed to him formally through diplomatic channels so that he would be able to discuss it with the cabinet. Thereafter, the German legation in Bratislava informed Berlin that "the Slovak government [had] seized upon the proposal with alacrity . . ."[34]

The first official indication from Slovakia that the deportation of Jews was being discussed came in the form of an announcement by the Slovak government on March 3, 1942:

> The Prime Minister has announced that representatives of the government of the *Reich* have indicated their willingness to accept all [Slovak] Jews under the condition that they be stripped of their [Slovak] citizenship. The Minister of Internal Affairs has submitted a detailed report on the deportation of the Jews, which report has been duly noted by the government.[35]

According to the minutes of the March 6, 1942, session of the Council of State, officially one of the highest authorities in the Slovak puppet state,[36] Premier Tuka reported to the council on the deportation of Jews from Slovakia to the Ukraine. He stated that Slovakia would pay the Reich 500 *Reichsmarks* for every deported Jew to cover the expenses of "resettlement." The deportations were to begin in March 1942, and would be completed by August of the same year. The Council of State duly noted Tuka's report, adding that the baptized Jews among the deportees should be placed into settlements of their own, apart from the other Jews, and provided with priests and churches to meet their religious needs.

Information which shed added light on the negotiations was supplied by Minister of Education Dr. Jozef Sivák in his testimony in court after the war. According to Sivák, Mach reported at a cabinet meeting on March 3, 1942, that the Germans had been putting pressure on Slovakia to effect a "radical solution of the Jewish problem," implying that if the Slovak government would not take steps to deal with the problem on its own, they, the Germans, would do it for them. This would have run counter to the interest of Slovakia. Unable to come to a decision, the government had decided to turn over the matter to its Committee of Economic Advisors. At the committee meeting, Dr. Peter Zaťko, secretary-general of the Central Association of Slovak Industry, and Dr. Imrich Karvaš, governor of the Slovak National Bank, pointed out that if the deportation of the Jews were to be carried out according to plan, it would result in serious damage to the Slovak economy. The committee finally decided to send a delegation to communicate their misgivings to President Tiso and to Mach. Tiso told them that he had no detailed information on the question and referred his visitors to Mach and Premier Tuka. Mach did not concur with the decision of the committee.[37]

Another important documentary source is the court testimony of Dr. Martin Sokol, chairman of the Slovak parliament, who described the subsequent developments during his trial after the war. As soon as he had learned that preparations for the deportation of Jews were under way, he called on President Tiso and suggested that Tiso call a meeting of the expanded presidium of the Slovak People's party at once because this was a very serious matter. The presidium, Sokol recalled, had met on March 17, 1942, and decided to solve the Jewish problem in Slovakia in a manner that would be in keeping with Christian ethics; i.e., that families would not be separated. In practical terms, this meant that concentration camps were to be set up in Slovakia and that a special tax would be levied on Jewish property.[38]

Preliminary Measures and Decision of the Slovak Authorities on the Deportation of Jews

Although the final decision about the future of the Jews had not yet been made, the Ministry for Internal Affairs adopted a series of organizational measures to prepare for their deportation.

The Ministry for Internal Affairs registered all Jewish males between the ages of sixteen and forty-five and then ordered them to report to their district boards for physical examination. This procedure was to be completed not later than February 28, 1942.

At the same time, orders were issued for the registration of all single, divorced, or widowed Jewish females between the ages of sixteen and forty-five who were self-supporting and had no dependent children below the age of sixteen.[39]

These preliminary steps were followed by the second phase: the concentration of the Jewish population at specified concentration points. This operation was officially described as "the concentration and transport of Jews presently in the labor force."

The following concentration points were set up for Jews: the Institution for Invalids in the Patronka district of Bratislava; the concentration camps for Jews in Novaky and Sered, and the military barracks in Poprad and Žilina. Each of these concentration points was placed under the supervision of a commandant. Both the commandant and the guards were selected from among the membership of the Hlinka Guard and the *Freiwillige Schutzstaffel.*

In order to forestall resistance on the part of the internees, which would have caused trouble not only among the Jews but also among the general populace, the Ministry for Internal Affairs issued the following directive to the commandants of the concentration points:

> The authorities concerned should, first of all, employ the psychological approach with the Jews, explaining to them that they will be put to work at places where they are needed and where their efforts will benefit the Slovak state. The persuasion tactics should have a calming and relaxing effect and all excitement should be avoided so that the entire operation may proceed without upsets.
> Should this approach of gentle persuasion not be successful, then, if need be, proceed with firmness and, by way of last resort, in the sternest manner possible.[40]

All the work connected with the deportations was accomplished with such dispatch and extraordinary punctiliousness that it was completed by the second part of March 1942. At no time during the existence of the Slovak state did the authorities manage to complete any of their other tasks in the same volume, or with the same speed and accuracy, as those linked with the deportation of the Jews.

On March 26, 1942, 1,000 Jewish girls were deported from the concentration point in Poprad to the death camp of Auschwitz. That same day the deportations appeared once again on the agenda of the Slovak Council of State. Although this body did not then play a decisive role in the structure of the Slovak government, its debate on the deportations is worthy of mention, for most of the council's members belonged to the moderate wing of the Slovak People's party and the minutes of this debate constitute the only surviving written document on the attitude of that segment in official Slovak politics toward the deportation of the Jews.

The debate was opened with the reading of a written motion submitted by Dr. Ján Balko, deputy governor of the Slovak National Bank, long-time member of the executive of the Slovak People's party and one of the government's experts on economic problems. Balko said he had been shocked into action by the atrocities which the members of the Hlinka Guard and the organizers from the *Freiwillige Schutzstaffel* had openly committed against the Jews who had been assembled for deportation. He requested Dr. Viktor Ravasz, the chairman of the Council of State, to have his motion considered at the earliest possible moment. Ravasz's initial reaction had been to advise Balko to recall his motion because "the people were afraid of the Germans and did not want to get involved in the Jewish problem." No member of the Council, Ravasz had said, would be willing to assume the role of reporter for the official reading of the motion. However, one of the members of the Council, Msgr. Jan Pösténvi, a Roman Catholic priest, volunteered for the task.

Balko's motion, which was addressed particularly to the president and the government of Slovakia, represented a singular act of courage; it dealt with the ethical and moral aspects of the deportation of Jews from Slovakia. "Is it justifiable," Balko asked, "that entire families, even if they are Jews, should be torn apart and deprived of family life, and that they should be treated in this manner despite the fact that it is a violation of Article 86 of our constitution and that it is also contrary to natural and divine law? As a state based on law and order and founded on the moral principles of Christianity, can we permit this violation of the laws of nature and God?"

Balko condemned these excesses also from the strictly juridical point of view, asserting that it was unlawful to abolish the rights of Jewish citizens of Slovakia who had acquired their citizenship in a legal manner.

The Council of State also heard a petition from the Jewish office. This document was framed in purely economic terms. It presented a thorough analysis of possibilities for the employment of Jews on public construction projects, as well as in agriculture, gardening, and forestry. Pointing to the labor shortage from which the country was then suffering, the Jewish office stated that these jobs could provide employment for 30,000 to 40,000 persons—corresponding roughly to the total number of able-bodied Jews in Slovakia.

The debate which followed the reading of the Balko motion and the petition reflected the dilemma in which a large sector of Slovak society found itself. Most of the speakers in the debate were aware that the harsh anti-Jewish measures which had been enforced in Slovakia by that time were not only at variance with their own original concepts of how to "solve the Jewish problem" but also violated the fundamentals of the Catholic interpretation of natural law, to which they themselves adhered.

This inconsistency between inner awareness and public posture which bedeviled many Slovaks in official life was attributable to several factors: first, lack of personal courage to take up the cause of the persecuted Jews at a time when anti-Semitic passions ran high. Individuals who spoke up in defense of the Jews risked being branded as "white Jews" or "Jew-lovers." Secondly, many felt helpless in the face of the question how the Jews, who had been pauperized, would support themselves if they were to remain in Slovakia. Also, it was feared that cheap Jewish labor might pose a threat to gentile workers in search of jobs. More and more questions were raised for which there was either no way, or no will, to find an answer. All the factors which we have mentioned, along with some others not specified here, and which kept the politicians of the moderate wing of the Slovak People's party, save for isolated exceptions, from taking an outspoken stand against the deportation of Jews, may be reduced to one common denominator: an inability to overcome the traditional anti-Jewish prejudices which were ingrained even in the so-called moderates. This was the reason why, at the crucial moment, these politicians accepted the deportation of Jews from Slovakia as an inescapable fact which had been imposed by the Reich and could not be altered.

A special position was represented by Ján Vojtaššák, the Catholic bishop who was vice chairman of the Council of State. He neither supported nor opposed the deportations. He was concerned exclusively with the fate of those Jews who had been baptized in the Catholic Church. The minutes of the debate record the bishop's comment:

> We have been told that special consideration would be given to such individuals [i.e., baptized Jews], but that they would be deported nevertheless. [It was understood that] they will live apart [from the Jewish deportees] and they will have schools and priests of their own. But whether this will really be done, I cannot say. However, we may take comfort [from these promises] because this is what we have been told.

After the debate, the Council of State adopted the following resolution which was duly communicated to the government:

At its session on March 26, 1942, the Council of State resolved to recommend that, in its step-by-step selection of Jews for deportation, the government should give due consideration to the vital economic interests [of the country].[41]

THE COURSE OF THE DEPORTATIONS

After all the preparations had been completed, the authorities turned to the task of assembling the Jews at the specified concentration points for deportation. On June 7, 1942, the daily *Gardista* carried a brief news item which was obviously intended to set public opinion at ease:

Both at the time of their departure and after their arrival at the camps, all the Jews are treated in such a manner that they cannot possibly have cause for complaint.

However, even a brief glance at the actual facts gives the lie to this claim. The barracks that had been prepared for the Jewish internees were totally unfit for human habitation. Once the new arrivals had passed through the gates of the camp they were greeted with kicks and blows from the Hlinka Guard overseers. At camp headquarters they were subjected to body searches during which the Hlinka Guardists on the scene stripped them even of those belongings which they had been officially permitted to take with them. In many instances the inspectors destroyed personal documents of the inmates, including the passports of Jewish naturalized citizens of the United States who had returned to visit the "old country" and had been stranded there by the outbreak of the war.[42] Each inmate was then given a number as a first step in his depersonalization.

Before boarding the trains, the deportees were forced to sign a "gift contract," by which they "voluntarily" ceded "all their property, wherever situated, irrevocably and forever, to the Central Jewish Office in Bratislava." The deportees were then divided into groups of forty and herded into freight cars that had no sanitary facilities and that were tightly sealed so that no one might be able to escape. At Zwardoń station, on the Polish border, the Slovak escorts turned the transports over to the German *Sicherheitspolizei* (Security Police).

The first eight transports that left Slovakia during the period from March 26 to April 5, 1942, contained only young men and women—a total of a little over 8,000 persons. The fact that, with these transports, Slovak Jewry lost the preponderant part of its youth should be particularly relevant to any discussion of whether or not the remaining Jews of Slovakia could have offered active resistance when they, too, were faced with deportation.

The Slovak authorities holding jurisdiction over the deportations—particularly Premier Tuka, Mach (the minister for internal affairs) and Dr. Koso (the director of the Prime Minister's Office and of Mach's ministry)—demanded that the immediate families of individuals deported for forced labor should be sent along with them. At first Eichmann, due to opposition from Wisliceny, rejected the proposal, claiming that there were no accommodations available for the families. However, he was soon to reconsider his decision and, in accordance with the change in plans, it was decided to use not only concentration camps but also certain major cities (to be selected by the Ministry for Internal Affairs) as assembly points for deportation transports.

The first deportation transport of entire families from Slovakia left on April 11, 1942, from Trnava. Once it had been decided to deport entire families together, the Ministry for Internal Affairs announced which categories of Jews would be permitted to remain on Slovak territory until further notice. Exemptions from deportation were based on specific objective criteria[43] or on exemption papers arbitrarily issued to certain individuals. Names of those exempted were placed on special lists which were sent by the Ministry for Internal Affairs to its subordinate agencies. The immediate families of these individuals were also exempted. Eventually, all those exempted received special "letters of protection" issued by the Ministry for Internal Affairs and known as *žltá legitimácia* ("yellow passes").

However, "letters of protection" did not always afford effective protection to their holders, and many such individuals were deported by mistake. When the holder of a "letter of protection," along with his immediate family, found himself in a concentration center, he had to appeal his case to the Ministry for Internal Affairs through the Jewish Office. If his appeal was accepted, Department 14 would send a telephone message to the commandant of his concentration camp ordering the discharge of the inmate concerned—provided that he had not been sent on to Poland in the meantime. Once Jews were moved directly to Poland from towns designated by the authorities, a change was made in this procedure. Officials of the Jewish Office would be dispatched to the town where the individual had been sent, to intercede for him on the spot with the local deportation commissioners.

CONSTITUTIONAL LAW 68 (MAY 15, 1942) ON THE EVACUATION OF JEWS

In order to give legal sanction to the deportation of Jews, the Ministry for Internal Affairs submitted (March 25, 1942) a draft deportation law to the Slovak parliament, but even before the legislative body could take up the bill, transports of deportees had already begun to move out of Slovakia. The scenes which took place on these occasions shocked not only the Slovak public but also many members of the country's parliament.[44] After several unsuccessful attempts to intercede with top government officials on behalf of the deportees, Dr. Martin Sokol, the speaker of the parliament, called a group of deputies to a private conference. First, this group considered the possibility of having the parliament simply refuse to take up the draft law, thus shifting the onus of guilt to the government, from which the bill had originated. However, one of the participants in the conference pointed out that this would not help the intended victims of the bill. In the end, the group decided that the bill should be submitted to the full session of parliament, but with a number of modifications.[45]

The basic intent of the proposed modifications was to reduce deportations by providing a legal foundation for exempting specified groups of the Jewish population from deportation.

The full session of the parliament on May 15, 1942, adopted the draft law, together with a resolution calling upon the government to "provide special accommodations for those baptized Jews who have already been evacuated and to make it possible for them to practice their [Christian] religion and to engage undisturbed in their religio-ethical educational work."

Briefly summarized, the most important provisions of Constitutional Law 68 on the Evacuation of Jews were as follows:

The law gave official sanction to the Slovak Republic to expel or deport its Jews. But it also specified those who would not be subject to the new law: individuals who had been baptized on or before March 14, 1939, and Jews who were legally married to non-Jewish spouses, provided that said marriage had been contracted prior to September 10, 1941, the effective date of the Jewish Code. Certain other individuals could be declared temporarily exempt for as long as a ministry of the government considered their services essential to the social or economic life of the country. Others could be exempted by special orders from the president of the Slovak Republic. Generally, when an individual was exempted from deportation, this exemption was extended also to his spouse and his minor children, and in many instances to his parents as well.

The law further stated that Jews who would be deported from Slovakia or who had left the country of their own accord would lose their Slovak citizenship and that their property would be confiscated by the state. The first to be affected by these provisions were the 38,169 Jewish citizens of Slovakia who had been deported prior to May 18, 1942, the day on which Constitutional Law 68 was promulgated. This law was retroactive.

Many members of the Slovak parliament subsequently claimed they had voted for the law because they had believed that by subjecting the deportations to legal controls they were, in fact, helping those Jews who were still in Slovakia. It cannot be denied that these deputies may have been sincere in their motivations. However, in evaluating the consequences of the legislation providing a basis for the deportations, one must consider not subjective, personal motivations but the objective situation that had been created even before the enactment of Constitutional Law 68. Accordingly, the declared good intention of Slovak deputies to help the Jews by voting for this law must, in many instances, be considered as an act of belated penitence or perhaps an attempt to protect a limited group of individuals in whom the legislators may have been interested.

On the whole, neither the Slovak parliament nor its members can be absolved of the charge of having had a direct share in the physical annihilation of Slovakia's Jewish population.

SLOWDOWN IN DEPORTATIONS

The slowdown in deportations which resulted from the exemptions granted under Constitutional Law 68 displeased the Reich so greatly that Adolf Eichmann paid a personal visit to Bratislava (May 26-28, 1942) in an attempt to straighten out matters. However, it appears that not even he was able to speed up the deportations, for in negotiations on June 12, 1942, between the Slovak and German authorities it was agreed that Germany would be satisfied as long as one transport of Jewish deportees would be sent out of Slovakia each week.

By June 26, 1942, a total of 53,000 of Slovakia's total Jewish population of 89,000 had been deported. It must be pointed out that of these original 89,000, many had fled illegally to Hungary prior to the start of the deportations or were living in Slovakia with forged "Aryan" documents, or had managed to obtain baptismal certificates bearing dates prior to March 14, 1939, thus making them legally exempt from deportation.

Under a governmental decision of August 11, 1942, agencies authorized to issue "letters of protection" were required to make monthly reviews of all exemptions and to revoke work permits granted to Jews. However, this governmental decision did not produce the hoped-for results. On the contrary, the ministries were not only slow and cautious in revoking exemptions but also insisted on the release of individuals who had been rounded up for deportation despite their exempt status.[46]

The government further decided that deportation dates were no longer to be scheduled in advance, but that transports were to be dispatched whenever a group of 1,000 Jews had been assembled at one of the concentration points. No transports left Slovakia during August 1942; two transports left in September, and only one in October. The final transport in the series, which included invalids and incurables, left Slovakia on October 20, 1942. From then on, there were no more deportations until the German occupation of Slovakia following the Slovak uprising in the summer of 1944.

Some Statistical Data on the Deportations

It is not easy to obtain reliable data on such an extensive operation as the deportation of the Jews from Slovakia. Above all, there are no comprehensive figures available from any one official documentary source. In order to compile a statistical summary of the most important developments of the period, we had to draw on data published in various sources, mindful that they were not based on unified criteria. Accordingly, Tables 2 and 3 below must be regarded as the closest possible approximation of the true figures.

TABLE 2 CHANGES IN SLOVAKIA'S JEWISH POPULATION DURING PERIOD FROM DECEMBER 16, 1940, TO JUNE 1, 1943

Total Number of Jews					
As of Dec. 15, 1940		As of Jan. 31, 1942		As of June 1, 1943	
Total	Baptized Jews included in this total	Total	Baptized Jews included in this total	Total	Baptized Jews included in this total
88,951	2,861	89,456	3,214	18,648	no figures available

If we subtract the number of Jews still in Slovakia after the temporary cessation of deportations from the number of Jews who lived in Slovakia on the eve of the first deportations (89,456 minus 18,648), it would appear that a total of 70,808 Jews had been deported from Slovakia by 1943. In fact, however, the total number of Jews actually deported up to that time was only somewhere between 58,000 and 59,000. The discrepancy of about 12,500 represents those Jews who managed to escape deportation by fleeing to Hungary or going underground. There were minor discrepancies among various official reports. A comparison of the various data available (see Table 3 below) will help give a picture of the probable totals.

It would have been possible to obtain fairly accurate statistical data on the number of Jews deported from Slovakia if copies of the lists of all the transports sent from Slovakia to the death camps had been available. These lists, which were verified by the German Security Police at the Polish border, contained such important information as the date and place of departure from Slovakia, the destina-

TABLE 3

Documentary Source	Number of Deportees		
	As of Dec. 31, 1942	1st quarter of 1943	Total
1) Letter from the Minister for Internal Affairs to the Ministry of Finance, Nov. 11, 1942	57,628	—	57,628
2) Report of the Slovak Railroad Administration on the execution of "Operation Da," January 14, 1943	57,752	—	57,752
3) Findings of the National Court of Justice in Bratislava in the criminal case against Dr. Anton Vašek (Director of Department 14) based on extant documents	57,837	—	57,837
4) *The Final Solution of the Jewish Problem in Europe*, by Dr. Richard Korherr, Inspector-General of Statistics for the SS, April 19, 1943	56,691	854	57,545
5) *The Destruction of Slovak Jewry: A Documentary History*, Livia Rothkirchen, Jerusalem: 1961			59,485

tion, and the names of the deportees in the transport. No such complete lists have yet been discovered in archives accessible to us in Czechoslovakia or elsewhere.

According to data supplied by the Slovak Railroad Administration, altogether 57 transports were sent out of Slovakia; of these, 19 had been earmarked for Auschwitz and 38 for Lublin.[47] However, it sometimes happened that the German authorities in Poland changed the destination of a transport at the last moment or that, on arrival at their official destination, the deportees would not be taken to the ghetto or camp in that place but would be distributed among several ghettos or concentration camps elsewhere. Such changes were often made particularly in transports originally marked for the Lublin ghetto; deportees in these transports were rerouted mainly to Treblinka and Lublin-Maidanek.

THE QUESTION OF JEWISH RESISTANCE TO THE DEPORTATIONS. THE *NEBENREGIERUNG* OR "WORKING GROUP"

The question of whether or not the Jews of Slovakia could or should have resisted deportation cannot be discussed without reference to the external pressures which had a direct bearing on their lives. As Slovakia submitted increasingly to the dictates of the Third Reich, her government intensified its anti-Jewish policies. Due to the repressive measures of the government, coupled with the hostility or indifference of most of Slovak public opinion, the Jews felt increasingly powerless to avert the fate that lay in store for them.

The relatively passive attitude of the Jews in Slovakia during the early days of the satellite state can be judged only in the context of their situation at the time, and not in terms of developments that came only much later. Initially, not only the Jews but also the non-Jews were simply unable to believe that when the Nazis declared their intention to destroy the Jews, they meant it in the most literal sense of the term.

The same attitude of disbelief prevailed also among the Jews in other Nazi-dominated countries. As Zivia Lubetkin Zuckerman, who was to be one of the leaders in the Warsaw ghetto revolt in the spring of 1943, testified at the Eichmann trial in Jerusalem:

> We just could not imagine that a nation would in this century pass a death sentence on a whole people. We kept asking ourselves: They humiliate us, they suppress us, but do they really intend to kill us all? We did not believe it.[48]

What efforts, if any, did the Jews of Slovakia make to prevent the deportations?

The Jewish Office first learned about the plans for the deportation of Jews sometime late in February 1942. The officers of the organization arranged a conference with other Slovak Jewish leaders who were not part of the Jewish Office to decide what course to take. The group agreed on the following three steps to forestall the deportations: (1) A memorandum on the matter would be submitted to top Slovak government officials and to all members of the Slovak parliament; (2) rabbis would be requested to make contacts with the Christian clergy; and (3) Jews with connections in government circles would be asked to intercede with these personages.[49]

The "Jeschurun" Federation of Jewish Religious Congregations in Slovakia and the Central Bureau of Autonomous Orthodox Jewish Religious Congregations in Slovakia addressed a joint memorandum, dated March 5, to President Tiso.[50] The next day Tiso was handed a similar memorandum by a delegation from the Federation of Rabbis in Slovakia. The trouble with both memoranda was that they were not relevant to the Slovak state. The arguments of the petitioners were of a purely legalistic character. It was pointed out that if a country were to deport a group of its own citizens to a place outside its own territory, this would be a crass violation of the basic principles of international law. It was also stressed that the Jews were deeply involved in the economic life of the country, and that they could always be assigned to those branches of the Slovak economy where there was a perceptible shortage of gentile workers or where the technical or professional skills of the Jews might be useful.

Following these purely objective arguments, the memoranda cited the human aspects of the problem, particularly the inevitable effect of deportation on women, children, the old and the sick, "for whom the hardships involved in mass deportation and resettlement in a new environment under extremely unfavorable conditions would mean certain death." Both groups addressed Tiso not only as president of the Slovak state but also as a priest who might be presumed to believe in the fundamental virtues of mercy and compassion.

Tiso's reaction was unexpected. Instead of making an official reply to the memoranda, he instructed the police in Bratislava to find out how the plans for the deportation of the Jews, which had been classified as top secret, could have leaked out to the leaders of Slovak Jewry. Several representatives of the Jewish Office were summoned to central police headquarters for questioning in connection with the full-scale investigation.

Only a few days later, at a meeting called especially for that purpose, Augustín Morávek, chairman of the Central Economic Office, and Dieter Wisliceny, the German advisor on Jewish affairs to the Slovak government, personally appeared before the presidium of the Jewish Office in order to break the news officially to the Slovak Jewish leadership. This meeting must have taken place sometime before March 16, 1942, because on that date the Jewish Office already had found it necessary to petition the Central Economic Office to release confiscated Jewish funds in the amount of Ks 1,000,000 for the purchase of food and other essential supplies for destitute deportees.

The petition was rejected. The Jewish Office thereupon initiated a drive in the Jewish community to collect clothing and other needed supplies for the deportees.

Since the Jewish leadership had been unable to persuade the Slovak government to abandon its plans, it had no alternative but to redirect its efforts toward saving as many Jews as possible from deportation and eventually bringing about a slowdown or even a cessation of transports.

However, it was clear that an officially sanctioned Jewish organization such as the Jewish Office would be in no position to initiate the drastic countermeasures demanded by the desperate situation of Slovak Jewry. As a result, there was formed within the legally recognized Jewish Office an "illegal" group of officials who were known as the *Nebenregierung* (literally, "other government") or the "Working Group." Among the members of this elite group were Mrs. Gisi Fleischmann, former president of the Women's International Zionist Organization (WIZO) in Slovakia; Rabbi Armin Frieder; Dr. Oskar Neumann; Dr. Albert (Vojtech) Winterstein; the Orthodox leader Rabbi Michael Ber Weissmandl; and finally three men who were new to organized Jewish life: Viliam Fuerst, Dr. Tibor Kováč, and Ondrej Steiner.

The immediate object of the "Working Group" was to do everything possible to stop the deportations. This was of desperate urgency for, as early as at the end of April 1942, some deportees who had managed to escape from the camps made their way back to Slovakia and contacted trustworthy officials of the Jewish Office with reports that Jewish deportees were being killed *en masse*. Written records of these eyewitness reports were sent to top Slovak government officials and also to individuals and institutions abroad.[51]

Since appeals to humane or religious sentiments and remonstrations regarding the basic rights of Jews as citizens had proven futile, it seemed that the most effective way of influencing the officials in charge of the deportations would be that of bribery—not an unusual phenomenon in the Slovak state. As soon as a substantial amount of cash had been raised, a way had to be found of approaching the one official who played a crucial role in the deportations: Dr. Anton Vašek, director of Department 14 of the Ministry for Internal Affairs.[52] Of course, it was necessary to gain the favor also of those ranking below Vašek in the official hierarchy and of a few of his superiors as well.

The "Working Group" sought to persuade Vašek and his associates in Department 14 not to insist on a continuous movement of deportation transports. Attempts were made to create all kinds of snags in the deportation process so that time might be gained for the group to take up the offensive with other authorities. Since it was impossible to gain direct access to Mach, the minister for internal affairs, contacts were made with Dr. Koso at the Prime Minister's Office. The crucial voice, however, was that of Dieter Wisliceny, the German advisor on Jewish affairs. Only if Wisliceny could be persuaded not to press the Slovak government for new trainloads of deportees and to intercede with Eichmann himself to this effect could there be any hope for even a temporary cessation of the deportations. The "Working Group" decided to offer Wisliceny a bribe of 40,000 U.S. dollars, an enormous amount if one considers the funds available to the "Working Group" at the time. The best contact to Wisliceny was through Karol Hochberg, the director of the "Department of Special Tasks" of the Jewish Office. Hochberg, who eagerly seized any chance to appear important, acceded to Rabbi Weissmandl's request that he talk to Wisliceny. His mission was successful.[53]

Thanks to the efforts of the "Working Group," several thousands of Slovak Jews who otherwise would have been delivered to certain death were saved.

As soon as the conditions which prevailed in the death camps became known in Slovakia, the "Working Group" initiated extensive efforts to establish contacts with the deportees in Poland and to send them help. Secret messengers—reliable gentiles who knew Polish and were familiar with the territory in which the camps were located—were employed to make the contacts and to take letters and valuables to the camps.

The Jewish youth organizations in Slovakia also did outstanding work in saving Jews from deportation. After the deportations had begun, the leaders of the left-wing Labor Zionist *HaShomer HaTzair* made plans to set up contact points on the Slovak-Hungarian border to help young Jews cross illegally into neutral Hungary, where Jews were then still relatively secure.[54] A number of these contact men crossed into Hungary themselves and made their way to Budapest, where they became active co-workers of the *Vaadat Ezra VeHatzalah* (Committee for Help and Rescue) in Budapest which helped non-Hungarian Jews from Slovakia find a refuge in Hungary.[55]

In all fairness, however, it must be pointed out that the efforts of the "Working Group" and its associates to save at least a part of Slovak Jewry succeeded in large measure only because, by that time, certain changes had taken place in the political configuration of the Slovak regime and also because certain Slovak gentiles had begun to help their Jewish fellow citizens.

Factors in the Decision to Discontinue Deportations (1942-44)

Slovakia had been one of the first satellite states of the Third Reich to deport Jews. Late in 1942 it became the first country under Nazi domination to discontinue the deportations before the last of its Jews had gone. There were several reasons for this.

First of all, by the end of 1942, there had been a basic change in the attitude of Slovak public opinion toward the Jews. This was a development of momentous significance, for only the year before, when the deportations had first begun, the Slovak public had shown no concern whatsoever for the fate of their persecuted Jewish fellow citizens. As the deportations went on, however, the picture gradually began to change. The way in which the anti-Jewish legislation was being enforced shocked the Slovak public into giving increasingly articulate expression to their disapproval of what was going on. A well-known Slovak historian described this public change in mood as follows:

> The deportation of the Jews represented a severe moral shock. It was a concrete watershed . . . which forced not only the politicians but even the lowliest citizens to review their moral and political principles. . . . Participation in this mass crime forged yet another link that inextricably bound up the destinies of the leaders of the Slovak state with the fate of German National Socialism and the final outcome of the war.[56]

Many non-Jewish elements, particularly within the Catholic Church, persistently demanded that the deportations be stopped. Premier Tuka, who was determined to continue the deportations, called on the German envoy in Bratislava to arrange for support from the Reich in the form of strong "diplomatic pressures" in favor of deportations. But all that the German envoy received from Berlin was a directive to the effect that, "at the proper opportunity," he should explain to President Tiso that the cessation of the deportation of Jews from Slovakia would create an unfavorable impression in Germany.[57]

Another determining factor in the subsequent evolution of Slovakia's policy toward the Jews was the ongoing change in the political constellation of the Slovak regime. As early as March 1942, the constant disagreements between the "moderates" and the "radicals" in the Slovak government, reflected also in the personal rivalry between President Tiso and Premier Tuka, caused considerable unrest in Slovak politics. One of the main issues in the dispute between the two wings was the deportation of the Jews, which had been consistently and fervently advocated by Tuka. The outcome of the struggle was not favorable for Tuka and his "radicals." On the insistence of the Reich, Tuka was permitted to remain premier but was forced to resign from the leadership of the Slovak People's party.

This substantial reduction of Tuka's influence triggered yet another development which was to affect the subsequent implementation of anti-Jewish laws: In July 1942, Tuka's protegé, Augustín Morávek, was forced to resign from the chairmanship of the Central Economic Office.

This shift in the political balance, along with the changes in public opinion, meant concrete support for those elements in Slovak politics which took a distinctly negative view of the deportation of Jews from Slovakia. Among the opponents of the deportations were several politicians who not only held high positions in the government but were also veteran functionaries in the Slovak People's party. Outstanding among them was the Minister of Education, Dr. Jozef Sivák.

As soon as he learned of the plans for the deportations, Sivák actively sought to prevent their being carried out. At the time, he had been working very closely with several leading figures in the Jewish community, notably Rabbi Armin Frieder, whom he had known for some time. Sivák made a point of calling the rabbi to his office in order to inform him of all cabinet plans for future anti-Jewish measures before anyone else knew of them. He personally interceded with top officials in an effort to forestall the deportations or to have them discontinued. When the Ministry for Internal Affairs requested him to revoke a substantial number of "letters of protection" issued by his office, Sivák immediately gave the Jewish community a complete list of individuals who were to be deprived of their exempt status, thus enabling the community to take appropriate action on their behalf before it was too late.

In his capacity as minister of education, Sivák protected Jewish schoolteachers from deportation as long as he could. According to regulations, teachers ceased to be exempt from deportation as soon as the number of students in their classes had fallen below the specified minimum—an inevitable development as more and more children were deported along with their parents. But Sivák never revoked a "letter of protection" issued to any Jewish schoolteacher. He was equally solicitous of the officials and employees of the Jewish Religious Congregations, whose exempt status also derived from his ministry.

When Sivák first learned the full truth about what was happening to the Jews who had been deported, he wanted to resign from the government, but the leaders of the Jewish community persuaded him to remain.

Two other highly placed officials who, though perhaps not so prominently as Sivák, attempted to mitigate the implementation of anti-Jewish laws were Minister of Justice Dr. Gejza Fritz and Minister of Finance Dr. Mikuláš Pružinský. The German authorities frequently complained that the courts under Fritz were too soft on political offenders and on the Jews. Among the members of the Slovak parliament who were concerned about the plight of the Jewish deportees were Dr. Sokol (the speaker), Dr. Gejza Medricky (Minister of Economics and deputy speaker), and men like Dr. Eugen Filkorn and Dr. Vojtech Tvrdý.

One group in the Slovak parliament which had become increasingly critical of anti-Jewish laws after the enactment of the racist Jewish Code was that which had been under the sway of Karol Sidor, a leader in the Slovak People's party who, however, was eventually to fall from grace. Among the individuals in this group were Pavel Čarnogurský, Moravčík, and others. After his removal from active politics Sidor, as already noted earlier, was named Slovakia's ambassador to the Vatican. His political activities had given no previous indication of any personal love for Jews on his part. However, he realized before long that aping Nazi patterns, particularly in dealing with the Jewish problem, would only serve to harm his country, and it was this realization that impelled him to protest against the deportation of the Jews.

In addition to the above-named politicians there were also leading figures in the Slovak economy who took up the cause of the Jews for reasons of their own. Many important positions in the country's economy had been assigned to experts who not only had never been members of the Slovak People's party but who had actually opposed its ideology. Prominent among these were Dr. Imrich Karvaš, governor of the Slovak National Bank, and Dr. Peter Zaťko, secretary-general of the Central Association of Slovak Industry. They saved many Jews not only from deportation but also from losing their jobs by insisting that these Jews were performing functions essential to the Slovak economy. Both men urged the Minister of Economics, Dr. Gejza Medrický, not to revoke the many "letters of protection" which his ministry had issued (the Ministry of Economics had issued more such documents than any other agency of the Slovak government) and in general to adopt a more liberal policy toward the Jews.

The argument that the retention of Jews in their positions was essential to the smooth progress of the country's social and economic life was based on fact and therefore had a persuasive impact on the officials directly concerned. Thus, the Ministry of Finance did not dismiss any of its Jewish key officials; the director of one of its most important departments, the appellate division for direct taxes, was a Jew, Dr. F. Singer. The Department of Health within the Ministry for Internal Affairs issued 360 "letters of protection" to Jewish physicians and another 256 to Jews who were pharmacists or engaged in related health professions. The country's Jewish veterinarians were all permitted to continue their work. The *Fond pre správu polňohospodárskych majetkov* (Fund for the Administration of Agricultural Property), which managed the landed property confiscated from Jews, had 550 Jewish employees, including agronomists, who were permitted to work in their profession.

At the request of the Central Association of Slovak Industry, the Ministry for Internal Affairs instructed its subordinate divisions not to dislocate or deport former Jewish owners or partners of industrial, business, or manufacturing concerns who were still active in those concerns as employees or as consultants to the "Aryanizers."

It must be remembered, however, that if government agencies which initially had insisted on the scrupulous enforcement of deportation orders subsequently agreed to discontinue the deportations, they were not necessarily motivated by pangs of conscience. In most cases, the apparent change of heart derived simply from a desire to keep German experts, those "imported" from the Reich as well as those who had been living in Slovakia all along, from gaining too firm a foothold in the inner structure of the Slovak state. In addition, it was an undeniable fact that many of the "Aryanizers" of once-Jewish business concerns relied heavily upon the help and advice of the former Jewish owners.

Any study of the factors which led to the cessation of the deportations must take into account also the role of the Catholic Church, which had always held an important place in Slovak life and whose influence became even greater during the era of the Slovak state.

When the Jews in Slovakia received the first authentic reports of what was happening at the death camps, they passed them on first of all to the Slovak episcopate. Hearing these reports, the Church for the first time realized that if it did not protest against the crimes perpetrated upon the Jews, it, too, might eventually end up as a victim of Nazi brutality. No less than its political leaders, the country's Catholic hierarchy, too, began to examine its principles in the light of these horrifying events. Many Church dignitaries had been opposed to the deportations from the outset; now, as the deportations continued, they were joined by a steadily growing number of colleagues who interceded with the Slovak authorities on behalf of the Jews. Even the Vatican, through its nuncio in Bratislava and through the Slovak representative at the Vatican, exerted a steady pressure on the Slovak state to stop the deportations.

It is interesting to note, however, that the other Christian denominations in Slovakia, though small in membership and without significant political influence, preceded the mighty Roman Catholic Church in voicing articulate protests against the anti-Jewish measures enacted by the Slovak state. As early as November 21, 1939, the Federation of Evangelical Pastors submitted to the president, to the parliament and to the cabinet a memorandum deploring not only the outrages perpetrated by the Hlinka Guard against ministers and other functionaries of the Evangelical Church but also the injustice committed against the Jewish citizens of the state.

In a pastoral letter sent on May 20, 1942, to all Evangelical parishes in the country, the two bishops who signed the document described Jew-baiting as obnoxious and absolutely unjustifiable conduct which violated human sensitivities, human justice, the law of God, and Christ's teachings of loving kindness. The church could not countenance but only condemn such excesses of bigotry. If any members of the Evangelical Church had participated in such acts, the bishops continued, such individuals would have to be condemned in no uncertain terms.[58]

On August 3, 1942, the Evangelical bishops of Slovakia held a meeting which once again dealt with the Jewish problem. This conference issued a pastoral letter declaring that the treatment meted out to the Jews by the Slovak government was not consistent with the supposed character of Slovakia as a Christian state. Although the Evangelical bishops of Slovakia had already protested against the Jewish Code, that code had neither been abolished nor modified but had, in fact, been made even harsher.[59] The letter further quoted a statement from one of the most respected Evangelical newspapers in the country to the effect that "the things which have been happening of late to the Jews in our country cannot be considered to be in conformity with the fundamentals of humaneness and even less with the basic principles of true Christianity."[60]

Such protests, coming from so many influential quarters, could not fail to have some effect on the regime. First of all, they influenced the subsequent decisions of President Tiso. But even the racist, pro-Nazi faction led by Tuka and Mach could no longer ignore the reports that emanated from the death camps. Accordingly, Premier Tuka requested Wisliceny to permit an official Slovak delegation to visit the "areas of resettlement" into which the Slovak Jewish deportees had been sent. During an official visit in Berlin late in July or early in August 1942, Wisliceny conveyed Tuka's request to Eichmann, citing reports that the Jews were being annihilated in Poland. Eichmann refused Wisliceny's request. "When I asked him why [he turned me down]," Wisliceny was to recall at his trial after the war, "he replied that most the of Jews [in those places] were no longer alive."[61]

Tuka's sudden interest in the Jewish deportees and the increasingly obvious negative attitude of Slovak public opinion forced the German authorities to be a little more cautious in their pressures on the Slovak government to continue the deportations. But there was also something else that caused the Germans to modify their tactics. Himmler expected to derive material benefits from a temporary cessation of deportations. He very obviously had a "financial" interest in Slovak Jewry. In the fall of 1942, he met with SS *Obergruppenführer* Gottlob Berger, the commander of the SS forces in Slovakia who happened to be visiting Slovakia at the time, to discuss how proceeds from the sale of emigration permits to wealthy Slovak Jews might help pay for the establishment of an SS division in Hungary.[62]

IV.
SLOVAK JEWRY FROM THE CESSATION OF DEPORTATIONS UNTIL THE SLOVAK UPRISING
(October 20, 1942–August 29, 1944)

Partial Changes in the Functions of Slovak Concentration Camps

Those Jews who were still in Slovakia when the deportations stopped late in 1942 could be divided into two distinct categories.

The first category, which was more numerous than the second, consisted of those Jews (and their immediate families) who had been exempted from relocation to concentration points and eventual deportation by special order of President Tiso or by virtue of "letters of protection." They and their families were permitted to live in their own apartments and hence had a certain amount of personal freedom, at least in the immediate environs of their places of residence. As of June 1, 1943, this category comprised a total of 15,626 Jews.

The second category of Jews still in Slovakia after the cessation of the deportations was those living in the localities which had been designated as concentration points for Jews and which originally took one of the following three organizational forms: (1) concentration (labor) *camps;* (2) concentration (labor) *centers;* or (3) military labor units. The concentration camps and centers were civilian units under the jurisdiction of the Ministry for Internal Affairs, whereas the military labor battalions were organized under the Ministry of Defense.

However, this formal division was no longer strictly observed after May 31, 1943, when the military labor camps for Jews were disbanded and their inmates were transferred either to already existing concentration camps or to concentration centers which had been newly organized under the jurisdiction of the Ministry for Internal Affairs. The essential difference between the concentration (labor) *camps* and the concentration (labor) *centers* was that the former were larger independent communities which had their own workshops and manufacturing enterprises, whereas the latter were smaller entities whose inmates were sent to work at places of private employment or public works projects outside.

Because they represented concentrations of large numbers of people in a few specific localities, the camps, particularly those in Nováky and Sered, became a much more important factor in subsequent developments than the "exempted" Jews of the first category. True, the "protected" Jews represented the majority of what was then left of Slovak Jewry, but they did not live together in communities; they existed for themselves as individuals or family units scattered in widely dispersed areas throughout the country.

By March 1942, the erection of the camps had progressed sufficiently to permit the start of productive work there. Thus, carpentry shops began to operate in Sered, and a tailor's workshop was started in Nováky. In the Vyhne camp, the main industry was construction work on state-operated baths nearby; later, chemicals were manufactured there as well.

Thus there came into existence, within the concentration camps, labor camps where the Jews were still effectively isolated from the rest of the population but where they and their immediate families were at least temporarily safe from deportation because they were engaged in essential work. Following the cessation of deportations late in 1942, the labor camps in Nováky, Sered, and Vyhne not only remained in operation but increased their physical capacity and production volume.

As of July 1, 1943, the Jewish labor camps and labor centers had a total of 3,653 inmates; of these, 1,552 were in Nováky; 1,095 in Sered; 352 in Vyhne; 69 in Ilava; 80 in Degeš; 41 at the Nitra Brick Works; 46 in Žilina; 189 in Sväty Jur; 113 in Láb; 71 in Devinská Nová Ves; and 45 in Zohor.

The labor camps were organized with a view to fulfilling the government's basic requirement that neither the camps as such nor their inmates, the Jews, should be a burden to the state or to its institutions. Each camp represented an autonomous, self-supporting economic unit in its own right.

Separate workshops for handicrafts, knitting, and embroidery were set up to utilize the work capacity of females, the elderly, and adolescents. A central Jewish home for the aged was established in Nové Mesto nad Váhom to relieve the camps of the burden of caring for the old who were not able to work.

Most of the products manufactured in the labor camps were delivered to the state on orders from individual ministries and their subordinate agencies. Thus, in setting up the labor camps for Jews, the Slovak state had created its own manufacturing enterprise operating exclusively under its own orders. Outstanding among the labor camp workshops were the carpentry shop in Sered which, with its superior technical equipment and capacity, was one of the most modern and productive in the country, and the ready-to-wear clothing factory in Nováky. In addition, inmates of Jewish labor camps were prominently active in construction work.

Notwithstanding the constant anxiety, the physical hardships, and the humiliation of slave labor which they had to endure, the inmates of the camps did not neglect the spiritual and cultural aspects of individual and communal life. As early as September 1942, the Jewish Office had set up elementary schools at the camps. In addition to their regular academic studies, pupils above the age of ten spent two hours of each school day in the workshops to learn a trade. Academic and vocational courses were organized for inmates between the ages of 14 and 18. Each camp had its own library.

While one is bound to marvel at the efficiency and high production volume of the Jewish labor camp industries, one might ask in retrospect whether it would not have been proper for the Jews to offer passive resistance to their taskmasters instead of working so diligently. Seen from the vantage point of the resistance movement, such a question is entirely justified, but resistance would not have been possible for every group of Jews and at every time and place during the Nazi era, particularly not during the period when Jews were being deported *en masse* from Slovakia to the death camps. It must be remembered that the labor camps, which saved thousands of Jews from deportation and death, would not have been permitted to survive if their production volume had not justified their continued existence.

But beyond ensuring their own survival, the Jews in the labor camps rendered a signal service also in the reeducation of Slovak public opinion: their performance at work gave the lie to the popular misconception, nurtured by official anti-Semitic propaganda, that the Jews were incapable of doing physical work.

The Progress of the War and Its Effect on Official Slovak Attitudes and Policies Toward the Jews

On February 2, 1943, the German armies on the Eastern front had surrendered to the Soviets on the banks of the Volga river. From that time on, Slovak government circles became increasingly aware that the very survival of the Slovak state was in jeopardy. Particularly those elements which had participated in and had reaped personal benefits from the enforcement of anti-Jewish measures feared for their future. As a result, some of them became more cautious in their behavior, attempted to cover up their past anti-Semitic activities and cast about for excuses to justify their past conduct toward the Jews. Others, however, had been so inextricably compromised in their collaboration with the Reich that they felt they had no other alternative but to adhere all the more strenuously to their original course. In line with this attitude, they made every effort to bring about a resumption of the deportations.

Several days after the Slovak public first learned of the German surrender on the Eastern front, the Hlinka Guard held a convention of district and elite unit commanders in the town of Ružomberok. The principal speaker on this occasion was Šaňo Mach, the Minister for Internal Affairs and commander of the Hlinka Guard. The main point on the agenda was, once again, the Jewish problem. Mach categorically declared that the deportation of Jews from Slovakia would have to be resumed and carried through to completion. His blunt threat that "March will come, April will come, and the transports will roll again"[63] sounded a warning not only for the Jews but also for all gentiles who had openly opposed the continuation of the deportations. That Mach was in dead earnest may be seen from a document that was found in the official files of the Slovak Ministry for Internal Affairs. It is entitled, "Plan for a Further Step-by-Step Solution of the Jewish Problem." Although this document is undated and unsigned and does not name the author of the "plan," its text and style clearly indicate that it originated from the ministry's Department 14. The plan called for the deportation of four transports of 1,000 Jews each, to be dispatched between April 18 and 22, 1943.

The agitation by the radicals for a renewal of the deportations had set off a wave of open protests. On March 8, 1943, the Catholic hierarchy in Slovakia issued a pastoral letter which was signed by all the Catholic bishops in the country and which instructed the faithful with regard to the attitude they were expected to take in the matter of the Jewish problem. The most important passage of this document reads as follows:

> Mindful of our responsibility before God and mindful of our duty to preserve the natural and revealed laws of God, we must emphatically raise our voice in warning against measures which innocently deprive whole groups of our coreligionists and others of our fellow citizens of their personal, familial, and material freedoms.[64]

On May 5, 1943, the Vatican handed to the Slovak ambassador a note expressing its unhappiness with the Slovak government's plan to resume the deportations.⁶⁵ On June 5, 1943, the papal nuncio in Bratislava informed the Vatican of his assumption that preparations for renewed deportations had been stopped.

The downfall of Fascism in Italy in July 1943 sent shock waves through the Slovak political landscape. As it became obvious that the end of Nazism might not be far off, increasing numbers of Slovak political leaders realized that they had been directly responsible for the crimes which had been committed against their Jewish fellow citizens.⁶⁶ That led to an event quite unusual at the time. On September 3, 1943, three committees of the Slovak parliament met jointly under the chairmanship of its speaker, Dr. Martin Sokol, to discuss two proposals for amendments or modifications of the anti-Jewish laws. Although the proposed changes did not in themselves contain provisions that would have materially improved the situation of the Jews, they provided an opening for a frank and thorough debate not only on the Jewish Code in particular but on anti-Jewish legislation in general. The principal report was delivered by Dr. Vojtech Tvrdý, who called attention to the effect which Slovakia's anti-Jewish laws and their consequences would have on the country's international image:

> The Jewish problem in Slovakia is an important component of the image of our state and our regime abroad. Political common sense demands that we should have respect for public opinion in neutral states, beginning with the Holy See, where the diplomatic activity of the [European] continent is centered at present . . . .
> We must realize that the question of Jewish assets will be solved once and for all at the peace conference, and if you believe that acts based on the violation of international law will be permitted to stand before world opinion, you are sadly mistaken.⁶⁷

Tvrdý then strongly called for a thoroughgoing review of the Jewish Code. In the debate that ensued, Eugen Filkorn frankly asserted that since the parliament had authorized the government to enact anti-Jewish measures, the parliament was responsible for the results and therefore obligated to explore possibilities for making amends to the Jews. Dr. Sokol said that when it debated Constitutional Law 68 on the Evacuation of Jews, the parliament had already been aware that the Jewish Code represented a violation of the Slovak constitution. However, in view of the overall situation at the time, the parliament had been unable to act upon this realization.

Not one of the deputies at this meeting voiced any objections to the statements made by Tvrdý, Filkorn, and Sokol.

This joint session of three parliamentary committees reflected the desire of the Slovak parliament to make an attempt at the civic rehabilitation, as it were, of the Jews. Naturally, the only Jews who stood to benefit from such action were those who had not yet been deported from Slovakia.

The protests from the Catholic episcopate of Slovakia and its pastoral letter of March 8, 1943, opposing the resumption of the deportations were duly reported to the German government by its representatives in Slovakia. In one such report, the German envoy in Bratislava mentions a conversation with Premier Tuka in which Tuka informed him that the episcopate had knowledge of the atrocities which the Germans had been committing against the Jews. Accordingly, Tuka had asked permission to have an official Slovak delegation visit one of the concentration camps in Germany.

Foreign Minister Joachim von Ribbentrop ordered the resumption of attempts, on an unofficial basis, to persuade the Slovak government to resume the deportations. He instructed SS Oberführer Edmund Veesenmayer, who was later to become Reich Plenipotentiary in Budapest following the German occupation of Hungary, to visit President Tiso. A brief report from Veesenmayer indicates that he personally informed Ribbentrop of the results of his interview with Tiso. Ribbentrop finally decided that, for the time being, he did "not intend to exert official pressures on Dr. Tiso regarding the final solution of the Jewish problem in Slovakia."[68]

Veesenmayer's second interview with Tiso took place on December 18, 1943. According to Veesenmayer's detailed report on the conference, he met on that occasion also with Premier Tuka, who promised him complete support. But despite an alleged promise from Tiso himself that the deportations would be resumed, roundups of Jews still in Slovakia were not.

The German Foreign Office conveyed to the chief of the *Sicherheitspolizei* (Security Police) the wish of the Slovak government to have a commission of its own choosing visit a concentration camp where there were Jewish deportees from Slovakia. Naturally, Eichmann's department could hardly have permitted such an inspection.

For this reason, it devised all kinds of subterfuges to put off action on the request. One of Eichmann's ways of diverting the Slovak government's attention was to produce a spate of correspondence from the deportees to relatives and friends in Slovakia. Thus, in August 1943, on direct orders from Eichmann, a total of 2,499 letters and postcards from the concentration camps reached Slovakia all at the same time, a quantity substantially in excess of any correspondence that had arrived there during previous months. All the letters contained the same report: "We are working and we are well."[69]

However, the Slovak government considered Eichmann's response unsatisfactory. In the end, Eichmann agreed to have a Slovak delegation inspect the concentration camp in Terezín (Theresienstadt). But at that stage Terezín had no Jews from Slovakia among its inmates.

In March 1944, neighboring Hungary was occupied by German forces. The following month, Hungary began to deport the Jews in her territory. As a result, the Slovak Jews who had fled to Hungary when that country had still been neutral and relatively safe were now in grave peril. There were about 7,000 Slovak Jews in Hungary at the time. On the urging of Gisi Fleischmann of the "Working Group," efforts were made to save at least the children with valid Slovak passports and enable them to return legally to Slovakia. However, this appeal was rejected by the Slovak authorities following a consultation meeting on June 20, 1944.

Many Slovak Jewish adults who were living in Hungary managed to escape deportation. Some returned illegally to Slovakia. But most of them owed their lives to the selfless efforts of Dr. Ján Spišiak, the Slovak ambassador in Budapest.[70] Even those Jews who had left Slovakia illegally and had thereby forfeited their Slovak citizenship could count on Spišiak's help. Defying law and instructions, he gave them Slovak passports and issued thousands of "letters of protection."

Meanwhile, in Slovakia, the Jews were alarmed by a decision of the Slovak government, made at the request of the German military command, to evacuate all Jews from the district of Šariš-Zemplín, in the eastern part of the country, by May 13, 1944. This decision was of ominous import because its consequences were unforeseeable and a relatively large number of Jews were living in the area.

The Jews who were evacuated from Šariš-Zemplín were not concentrated in any one locality; instead, most of them were assigned to forced labor in various areas outside the district. The operation involved a total of 2,597 Jews.[71]

The "Working Group" and Its Further Rescue Efforts

The "Working Group" and its associates did not confine their rescue efforts to Slovak Jews but gave effective assistance also to Jews of other countries, particularly Polish Jews who had fled to Slovakia from Nazi-occupied Poland.

In August 1942, a young girl escaped from the ghetto of Sosnowiec-Bedzin and made her way from Poland into Slovakia. She had been entrusted with the mission of contacting Jewish organizations in Slovakia and of informing them about the situation of the Jews in the Polish ghetto. Arriving in Žilina, she met with the Jewish underground fighter Ervin Steiner. The girl herself was persuaded not to attempt to return to Poland; instead, a message was sent from her to Chaim Tennenwurzel, the head of the committee of youth movements in the ghetto, suggesting that he, too, should try to escape and come to Žilina. Before long, Tennenwurzel, also known as "Janek," arrived in Žilina. It was agreed that young people should be smuggled out of the ghetto in small groups and guided across the Polish border into Slovakia. A total of thirty-nine young men and women were eventually moved from Slovakia to the relative safety of Hungary—all but Tennenwurzel himself, who was caught and executed by the Germans.

After the deportations of Jews from Slovakia had stopped, the "Working Group" was in a position to expand its rescue efforts on behalf of the Jews in Nazi-occupied Poland who had begun to cross the border into Slovakia in large numbers during 1943. The number of Jews who arrived in Slovakia from Poland during that year was estimated at about 2,500; most of them had come from the ghetto of Bochnia. The "Working Group" took measures, under the leadership of Rabbi Weissmandl, to organize help for the transients.[72] The refugees were shepherded into reception centers set up near the border, and their subsequent movement through Slovakia to Hungary was managed in various ways, depending on the situation at the moment. One of these methods was particularly ingenious; it required the cooperation of local Slovak authorities and involved the least risk for the refugees. The district board of the area would report to *Ústredňa štátnej bezpečnosti* (State Security Headquarters), the Slovak counterpart of the Gestapo, that a number of individuals, presumably of Hungarian nationality, had been apprehended in Slovakia on various charges of financial misdemeanor. The State Security Headquarters would thereupon issue an order to the effect that, after due investigation, the offenders should be "expelled" from Slovakia and "deported" to Hungary.[73] The "offenders" would then be taken under police escort to Prešov and from there south to the Hungarian border, where they crossed illegally into Hungary.[74]

When it became obvious that the deportation of Jews from German-occupied countries was continuing unabated, the "Working Group" renewed its contacts with Dieter Wisliceny. They made him a proposal which became known as the "Europa Plan" under which the Jews in occupied Europe would be saved in return for a ransom to be paid to the Reich. The "Working Group" asked that the deportations of Jews and their physical liquidation in the death camps cease, and that permission be given for the dispatching of food packages and medical supplies to the camps and ghettos under the supervision of the International Red Cross. In return for these concessions, the "Working Group" was ready to make available certain goods and foreign currency to the German Reich. In the negotiations which ensued, Wisliceny asked for a total of 2,000,000 U.S. dollars, with the provision that Poland was not to be included in the deal. Poland, he insisted, had to become *judenrein*. The "Working Group" also attempted to gain permission from Wisliceny to send a large group of children to Palestine.

Wisliceny promised to communicate the Jewish proposals to Himmler himself through Eichmann. The representatives of the "Working Group" then turned to major Jewish organizations abroad, notably to Saly Mayer, the representative of the American Jewish Joint Distribution Committee (JDC) in Switzerland, for the needed funds.[75] But in August 1943, Wisliceny was summoned to Berlin by Eichmann, who forced him to sign an undertaking to break off all contacts with the JDC.

Seven months later, on March 19, 1944, Hungary was occupied

by German forces. Almost immediately, Eichmann made it his personal task to enact and enforce anti-Jewish measures there. Wisliceny, who had been transferred to Hungary, arrived in Bratislava on March 24, 1944, to study the anti-Jewish measures that were in force in Slovakia, with a view to their subsequent application in Hungary. During his visit in Bratislava, several members of the "Working Group" met with Wisliceny to discuss with him conditions under which he might be willing to prevent the deportation of Jews from Hungary. Through Wisliceny, they sent letters to leading spokesmen of Hungarian Jewry. In one of these letters, which was written in Hebrew, Rabbi Weissmandl advised the Jewish leaders in Hungary to initiate contacts with Wisliceny at once, because it might be possible to make financial arrangements which would save the Jews of Hungary from deportation.[76]

On April 21, 1944, exactly one week before the first trainload of deportees left Hungary, two young Slovak Jews who had managed to escape from Auschwitz crossed the border into Slovakia. After the war, during the trial of the Auschwitz murderers, one of these two young men, Rudolf Vrba, was to explain why he and his companion, Alfred Wetzler, had chosen to risk their lives to escape from Auschwitz:

> On April 7, 1944, I escaped from Auschwitz together with my friend Wetzler. We had made up our minds to tell the world about what was happening in Auschwitz, and particularly to prevent the Hungarian Jews from allowing themselves to be transported to Auschwitz without offering resistance.[77]

The detailed eyewitness accounts of Vrba and Wetzler were recorded by the "Working Group" and were sent to various individuals and organizations in the free world.[78] The copy of the report that was sent to the *HeHalutz* Center in Geneva was accompanied by an appeal from Rabbi Weissmandl that the Allies begin at once to bomb the deportation routes, along with the gas chambers and crematoria of Auschwitz. This, he explained, would help save the Jews of Hungary. The World Jewish Congress and the Jewish Agency for Palestine made representations to this effect to the governments of the United States and Great Britain, and to the Polish and Czechoslovak governments-in-exile, but to no avail.

V.
SLOVAK JEWS IN THE RESISTANCE MOVEMENT (1940–1945)

Agreement on the Necessity for Resistance

Some Jews in Slovakia joined the resistance movement organized by the Communist party in Slovakia (KSS), which had been the first to establish an extensive "illegal" party network in the Slovak state. (This does not mean that the Communists were the only ones to put up armed resistance or that they were the leading force in the uprising, but the Jews found that they could gain access more easily to the Communists than to other resistance groups.) The Slovak Jews who had joined the KSS subscribed completely to the official Communist party line of that period with regard to the solution of the Jewish problem. They viewed the development and dissemination of "socialism" as a guarantee for the gradual disappearance of all anti-Jewish prejudice and for the eventual complete equality of all citizens, regardless of nationality, race or creed. For this reason, prior to the deportations, the KSS made no mention of the Jewish problem either in its program or in its statements of principles.

Other Slovak Jews joined non-Communist underground organizations such as the "Demec" group, which gathered information on military, political, and economic developments and forwarded these reports to Czechoslovak organs abroad.

On the other hand, the Zionists, who regarded the establishment of a Jewish national home in Palestine as the only true solution of the Jewish problem, sought to participate in the armed resistance movement not as individuals but as a distinct group.

As early as January 1940, the role of Zionist youths in the coming struggle for freedom had been the subject of discussion among the leadership of the left-wing Labor Zionist *HaShomer HaTzair*. These deliberations had yielded the following conclusions: A war would eventually break out between the Reich and its satellites on the one hand and the Soviet Union, on the other. Armed resistance would then erupt in the German-occupied countries. Slovak Jewish youths were in duty bound to participate in this resistance and would therefore have to be prepared for the struggle. The most heated debate centered on the question of the manner in which Jewish youths were to participate in the expected armed uprising. *HaShomer HaTzair* held that separate Jewish fighting units should be formed, then together declare themselves as a Jewish national entity.[79] *HaShomer HaTzair* was anxious to strengthen not only its own position but also the overall Slovak "anti-Fascist" resistance force. This last question was first raised at a meeting of the leadership of *HaShomer HaTzair* at Radvaň n/Hr (Banská Bystrica district), in August 1940. One of the crucial decisions made at that meeting was that the organization should contact the Slovak Communist party and coordinate certain resistance activities with the latter.[80]

Those Slovak Jews who had been able to leave the country had opportunities for resistance activities at a much earlier date than those who had remained in Slovakia. Their participation, together with the Jews from Bohemia and Moravia as well as from Subcarpathian Ruthenia in the Czechoslovak military units formed in France, Britain, the Soviet Union and the Middle East, is the subject of a special study included in this volume[81] and is therefore not treated here.

As the war continued, it became clearer that the method best suited for the resistance struggle within countries subjugated by Hitler's Germany was that of underground partisan warfare. As early as the spring of 1942, a number of partisan groups had been formed; among their members there were also Slovak Jews. However, attempts to establish bases which would have made partisan operations possible already at that time had ended in failure.

The failure of these early attempts suggest the question whether it would have been possible at all for the Jews of Slovakia to fight deportation by organizing large-scale resistance operations. One positive contribution to the debate about this problem which continues even today—after the Eichmann trial it took the character of a dispute between the postwar generation and its elders—would be to determine whether it would have been at all practically possible for the Jews to put up a large-scale resistance.

The first prerequisite for such resistance would, of course, have been timely and adequate preparations. In Slovakia, no early action was taken, mainly because no one had been able to believe that a catastrophe such as foreseen in the Nazi plan for the "Final Solution" could in fact come to pass. Then, the very first wave of deportations had taken away most of the young, the very ones who could perhaps have been expected to have the stamina to put up a fight. As already mentioned, the situation at this stage was not yet ripe for the establishment of partisan bases equipped for organized armed resistance. Neither were there propitious conditions for Jewish mass action against deportation within the general framework of increasing Slovak resistance to the Tiso regime, because at this point the Slovak public was not yet fully aware of the impact of the anti-Jewish measures and, in fact, certain segments of Slovak society even stood to benefit from the deportations. Finally, many Slovak Jews did not attempt to muster their energies for mass resistance because they were lulled into a false sense of relative security by the hope of gaining "legal exemption" from anti-Jewish measures.

Nevertheless, a change in the attitude of Slovak Jews became clearly apparent soon after the departure of the first deportation transports. Logically, this change was most conspicuous in those parts of Slovakia where Jews lived together in large numbers and in isolation from the rest of the population. This was true particularly in Nováky and Sered, the largest of the Slovak concentration camps. Although the inmates of these camps disagreed on many social and political issues, the conditions under which they now had to live together brought them close enough to one another to enable them to unite into one solid community. This development eventually provided a starting point first for mutual defense and later for armed resistance. In the case of the camp in Nováky, this was due in a large degree to the fact that this camp contained a large number of energetic young people, later augmented by most of the Sixth Labor Battalion.[82]

These young people took a lead not only in laying plans for mobilizing the camp community for defense against immediate threats to its survival but also in organizing a mass movement of partisan fighters within the camp.[83]

The partisans at Nováky were aided in their activities by the environment in which the camp was located: in a region populated by miners and tenant farmers who had no sympathy for the Slovak regime. As a result, the inmates of this camp were not entirely isolated from the outside world but were able to make contacts with underground bases beyond the camp limits during the night hours, once they could get past the Hlinka Guard sentries.

The first task at hand was to prepare for armed resistance. To this end, two parallel organizations—one small inner circle and one broad outer group—were set up. The inner circle was composed of raiding units of three to four men each who, in an emergency, would quickly evacuate those unable to fight and take them to the Basková valley in the Vtáčnik mountain region. The outer group was organized on a military basis. All inmates who were capable of fighting were divided into companies and task forces. The problem, of course, was that most of these people had never had any previous military training and that it was naturally impossible to engage in large-scale training, complete with real weapons, in the camp, under the eyes of the Hlinka Guard. Nevertheless, drills with actual weapons were secretly conducted in small groups.[84]

In the summer of 1944, representatives of the "Working Group" called on Father Augustin Pozdech,[85] a Roman Catholic priest in Bratislava who belonged to the resistance movement. Father Pozdech had contacts with Slovak army officers in the Ministry of Defense who were opposed to the government. The "Working Group" asked him to convey the following requests to his friends: (1) To see to it that the supervision of the concentration camps for Jews in Slovakia be turned over to the Ministry of Defense, because this would afford the inmates a better chance to escape deportation than if they remained under the surveillance of the Ministry for Internal Affairs, and (2) that weapons be found for those Jews who had decided to join the armed resistance. The resistance cell replied that it would not be possible to effect the change in supervision, but that the agents of the resistance movement within the various military garrisons had been instructed, in case of an emergency, to come to the aid of the Jews in labor camps near their own bases and to supply them with weapons.

This may have been the reason why, even before the general Slovak uprising in the summer of 1944, the Nováky concentration camp received an interesting visitor—a representative from a well-organized military resistance cell that was operating at an army technical and chemical center in nearby Zemianské Kostolány (Prievidza district). He had come to the camp to determine the numbers and the skills of able-bodied inmates who might be relied upon to participate in a large-scale resistance operation.

The Sered camp also harbored an underground movement which

made preparations for armed resistance, but these preparations could not be as extensive as those made at Nováky because conditions in Sered were not as favorable for such activities.

To begin with, the overlords in Sered were much more brutal in the exercise of their power than those in Nováky. Secondly, the number of young inmates in Sered was much smaller than that in the Nováky camp. Also, due to the location of this camp, the underground organization in Sered was not able to establish such close contacts with the outside and with the emerging partisan movement as its Nováky counterpart. Finally, the underground in the Sered camp was not able to secure the cooperation of the Jewish inmate government as had been the case in Nováky.

Despite all these handicaps, however, steps were taken also at Sered to prepare the inmates for participation in a possible armed uprising. In accordance with a decision made at a meeting of the *HaShomer HaTzair* leadership in Nové Mesto nad Váhom on January 1, 1944,[86] several members of *HaShomer HaTzair* in Sered left the camp to build a bunker in the Little Tatra mountain region. They also set up two clandestine stores at a farmstead near Sered where they hid food, supplies, and tools against the chance that the camp might have to be evacuated at a moment's notice.

Another Zionist youth group active in Sered was the *halutz* (pioneering) organization *Maccabi HaTzair*.

HaShomer HaTzair and *Maccabi HaTzair* became embroiled in a dispute about what action would be appropriate for the Jews in the camps to take in the event of a general Slovak uprising. *HaShomer HaTzair* insisted that the struggle of the Jews would have to be waged within the framework of the anti-Fascist front that was emerging in Slovakia, and that therefore the Jewish resistance fighters would have to join forces, in the literal sense of the word, with the partisan movement. The leaders of *Maccabi HaTzair,* on the other hand, felt that instead of squandering Jewish lives on activities not directly related to the Zionist cause, as many Jews as possible should be saved for settlement in Palestine after the war. They therefore decided not to participate in armed resistance operations; however, when the time came, they did what they could to help the Jews who, unable to fight, had hidden out in bunkers, particularly in Bratislava, to escape arrest and deportation.

Among the young Jews who had been drafted into labor service and had thereby been saved from deportation to the death camps there were also numerous members of Jewish youth movements.

The beginning of 1944 saw substantial changes in the preparations for armed revolt in Slovakia; resistance was now organized on a broad basis. Between May and July 1944, the partisan movement in eastern and central Slovakia spread, notably to the Great Tatra mountains and the upper Nitra valley.

In eastern Slovakia, partisan groups were organized which later merged to form the Chapayev Partisan Fighters' Brigade and which subsequently accepted also Jewish members.

On August 28, 1944, the day before the official start of the Slovak uprising, the leaders of the underground movement in Nováky assumed authority over the concentration camp without resort to violence. They declared all the inmates to be free and called upon the able-bodied among them to join the uprising that was about to begin.

On August 30, 1944, the underground movement at the camp in Sered also decided to join in the uprising. The Jewish inmate government immediately announced that the camp commandant was ready to turn over all the weapons under his supervision to the inmates. The inmates thereupon joined the uprising in a body.

On September 1, 1944, the partisans liberated the concentration camp in Vyhne, whose able-bodied inmates also joined the revolt.

JEWS IN THE SLOVAK UPRISING

When the Slovak uprising erupted on August 29, 1944, Jews participated in the revolt as soldiers and officers in the Czechoslovak insurgent forces and as members of partisan units.

The insurgent forces included one all-Jewish unit composed of former inmates of the Nováky concentration camp as part of the Fourth Tactical Group of the Czechoslovak insurgent forces. On August 30, the Nováky group and the Upper Nitra Partisan Brigade occupied Handlová, a town populated mostly by members of the German minority in Slovakia. This was done because some of the town's inhabitants, active Nazis, had launched operations against the insurgents. On September 2, after they had occupied Handlová, the Naváky group encircled the village of Sklené and entered into a heavy exchange of fire with armed Germans there. In the end, the Nováky group, together with the constabulary unit from Turčianské Teplice, captured all the weapons in Sklené and appointed a "Revolutionary National Committee" to administer the village.

On September 3, 1944, the Nováky group was ordered to a very important sector, Malé Uherce-Baťovany, which formed a part of the defense line of the Nitra valley and thus was of vital strategic and economic significance for the revolt. The Third Shock Troop Company, as the Nováky group was called at this stage, was then divided into two sections. The second, which defended Baťovany, is worthy of special mention. In an order of the day from the military front-line command, it was cited for bravery and for its determined resistance to the regular German troops, who enjoyed vast technological superiority over the freedom fighters and had attacked the insurgents with tanks.

The fighting spirit shown by this all-Jewish unit in the encounter with the Germans at Baťovany obviously made a deep impression on the commander of the sector, as evidenced by his words of appreciation to Lieutenant Imrich Mueller-Milén, the commander of the Nováky group: "I am—no, I had better say, I *was*—an anti-Semite," he told the Jewish officer. "I want to thank you for your men, both living and dead."

After heavy fighting in the Baťovany sector, the exhausted Nováky group was relieved by order of the high command and sent behind the lines for a brief respite. Meanwhile, regular German troops succeeded in breaking through the defense lines, occupying the Nitra valley and thus considerably reducing the area controlled by the insurgents.

A report on the resistance operations at the army technical and chemical center in Zemianské Kostolany also makes mention of the activities of the Nováky group: "Thus the only company to remain intact was the one from the Jewish camp . . . which is deserving of praise."[87] On the second anniversary of the uprising, Dr. Pavel Nemec, chief of staff of the Upper Nitra Partisan Brigade, was to pay special tribute to the Nováky group, explaining that

> We have already celebrated the anniversary of the uprising twice, but until now no mention has been made of the role of the volunteers from

Nováky. It would be an injustice to permit their part in the Czechoslovak struggle for liberation to become forgotten. . . . Our attention was engaged particularly by the so-called Mueller Company [i.e., the company under the command of Lt. Mueller-Milén]. From the very first moment that we made contact with the enemy, it held its positions without any outside aid until the breakthrough at the front lines on September 6, 1944.[88]

The Nováky group crossed the Vtáčnik mountains and moved toward Hradel (Banská Bystrica district), and on September 20, 1944, it occupied the village of Horná Štubňa (Martin district). Having accomplished this objective, it joined the J. V. Stalin First Partisan Brigade as an independent company. On September 24, it was transferred to the eastern sector of the front line to take up positions in Gasderská Dolina, the Gader valley.

The movements of large partisan units, including also part of the Nováky group, soon drew the attention of enemy forces. In the fighting around Valašská Belá, the Nováky group lost six men, including four who had been seriously wounded and taken prisoner by the Germans. These four were tortured and publicly hanged in Valašská Belá. On November 18, 1944, the group was again attacked by German forces; in this encounter, eight partisans were killed and many others so seriously wounded that they could not participate in subsequent operations.

What now remained of the Nováky group split up once again. The one part fought its way into the Vtáčnik mountains, while the other regrouped under the command of Lieutenant Mueller-Milén and joined the Jan Žižka Partisan Brigade.

Reports of the activities of the Nováky group have permitted more detailed studies of its role in the uprising than has been possible in the case of other Jewish partisans who were dispersed among various non-Jewish units. But the principal reason why the Nováky group deserves special attention from historians evaluating the role of the Jews in the Slovak uprising is that, notwithstanding constant partitions and regroupings, this group survived as the only partisan unit consisting exclusively of Jews.[89]

A special place among the Jewish fighters in the Slovak uprising was held by the four Palestine Jewish parachutists who had been dropped over the liberated area in Banská Bystrica. Haviva Reik, Zvi Ben Ya'akov, Rafael Reiss, and Haim Chermesh had joined the

British army in Palestine. Immediately after the outbreak of the Slovak uprising, all four volunteered for the special mission which the British high command planned to parachute into Slovakia. Haviva Reik had to put up a fight to be allowed to participate, for British army regulations at the time did not permit women to engage in military operations behind enemy lines. However, her perseverance and resolution won out over the dead letter of the law and she received permission to proceed. She landed on Tri Duby (Three Oaks) airfield near Banská Bystrica. The others were dropped over other territory also controlled by insurgent forces. The British military mission had only one stated objective: to establish contact between the British military command and the high command of the insurgents in Slovakia. If the four members of this mission had wanted to do no more than carry out that order, they would have returned to Palestine after the uprising had been suppressed. But they chose, instead, to remain in Slovakia even after the insurgents had retreated to the mountains, because they saw it as their duty to give whatever help they could to their fellow Jews. Haviva Reik, together with Dr. Tibor Tiroler, chairman of the local Zionist organization in Banská Bystrica, and other local Jewish leaders organized an inner actions committee for this purpose.

After the insurgents' territory had been occupied by German troops, the parachutists, with a group from HaShomer HaTzair, retreated to the mountains, from where they intended to continue their struggle, and proceeded to set up a camp in the woods just above the village of Bukovec in the Lower Tatra mountains. They were attacked and encircled by German troops but managed to escape and dispersed into the mountains, then regrouped and attempted to move east over the mountain ridge of the Little Tatras to join the partisans there. Suddenly they heard shouts in Russian and ran in the direction of the sounds. Unfortunately the Russians turned out to be men under the command of Lieutenant General Andrei Andreyevich Vlasov, who had defected to the German side. Vlasov's men captured a number of the fighters, including the parachutists, and turned them over to the German high command. Three of the four parachutists—Zvi Ben Ya'akov, Haviva Reik, and Rafael Reiss—were shot. Only Chermesh escaped. He joined another partisan unit and in 1945 returned to Palestine.[90]

By far most of the Jewish partisans other than the Nováky group fought in smaller or larger groups within mixed partisan units. A total of about 46 partisan units of substantial size were active in Slovakia; the rosters of 32 of these include Jewish names. The total number of Jews known to have fought in Slovak partisan units was 1,566.[91] Because of their youth, at least 698 of these could not have received previous military training.

It seems appropriate to conclude this chapter with a few more statistics. It is estimated that, as of early September 1944, a total of 16,000 partisans were active in the resistance in Slovakia. This means that the 1,566 Jews comprised almost 10 percent of all the partisan forces in the country. Of a total number of 2,100 partisan fighters killed or missing, 269 were Jews. This means that about 17 percent of all the Jews who fought in the partisan forces were killed. It might be added here that 166 Jews who had participated in the revolt subsequently received the Order of the Slovak Uprising.

It can be safely said that the participation of Jews in the Slovak uprising may be favorably compared with Jewish participation in the European resistance movement in general, not only quantitatively, but also in terms of fighting spirit and intensity of activities.

VI.
THE DISINTEGRATION OF THE SLOVAK STATE AND THE ROLE OF THE SLOVAK GOVERNMENT IN THE "FINAL SOLUTION"
(September 1944–April 1945)

THE GERMAN OCCUPATION OF SLOVAKIA AND THE RESUMPTION OF DEPORTATIONS

The Slovak government found itself incapable of suppressing the growing partisan movement on its own. On the eve of the uprising, entire garrisons of the Slovak army deserted and joined the resistance movement. On August 28, 1944, the German envoy in Bratislava informed President Tiso that it had become necessary to send German troops into Slovakia at once to deal with the partisans.

On August 29, the German Tatra Division crossed the Western frontier into Slovakia. Behind the advancing army, the organs of the SS and *Sicherheitsdienst* began their activities. In each of the occupied areas Jews were concentrated and then herded into the former labor camp of Sered, which had been transformed into a German concentration camp. At a cabinet meeting on October 2, 1944, the Slovak government decided to ask the German authorities to use the Jews only for labor in Slovakia, as previously agreed between the Slovak Minister of Defense and SS *Obergruppenführer* Gottlob Berger. Himmler turned down this request.

The first transport in the new wave of deportations left Sered on September 30, 1944. During the remaining months of German rule in Slovakia, altogether 11 transports, carrying a total of 12,306 Jews, left the country. Of these deportees, 7,936 were taken to Auschwitz, 2,732 to Sachsenhausen, and 1,638 to Terezín.[92] Another 3,500 Jews were shot on the spot following their arrest by the German security agencies.[93]

Rescue efforts mounted by the Jewish organizations were beset with practically insurmountable difficulties. Since the German authorities had now taken almost exclusive charge of anti-Jewish measures, the contacts which the Jews had established with Slovak authorities had become irrelevant. The German authorities categorically refused to honor "letters of protection" issued by Slovak government agencies. The leading officials of the Jewish community were arrested or forced to go into hiding. Alois Brunner, the SS commandant of the concentration camp in Sered, ordered the immediate liquidation of the Jewish Office, entrusting this task to two of its members, Mrs. Gisi Fleischmann and Dr. Tibor Kováč, both of whom, however, happened also to be members of the underground "Working Group." Another member of the "Working Group," Rabbi Weissmandl, who had been arrested and taken to Sered, attempted to plead with Brunner to stop the deportations, but to no avail. Eventually Mrs. Fleischmann was also arrested and sent to Sered. She died in the gas chambers of Auschwitz.

Nevertheless, the spokesmen of Slovak Jewry were able to inform certain Jewish institutions in Budapest and Switzerland at once of what was going on in Slovakia. These bodies had already been negotiating for some time with highly placed SS officials on possibilities of stopping the deportations and easing the conditions in the concentration camps. Dr. Rezsö (Rudolf) Kasztner, representing the *Vaadat Ezra VeHatzalah* in Budapest, and Saly Mayer, the representative of the American Jewish Joint Distribution Committee in Switzerland, had been conducting negotiations to this end with

Himmler's assistant, SS Standartenführer Kurt Becher. Kasztner arrived in Bratislava with Becher's adjutant, Grüson, to initiate contacts with local top officials of the German Security Police. However, the two sides could not come to an agreement, and the deportations of Jews from both Hungary and Slovakia continued.

Before long, protests from abroad against the resumption of the deportations began to reach Slovakia. All that the Slovak government was able to do in response at that stage was to note these protests and pass them on to the German envoy in Bratislava. On October 24, 1944, the Swiss consulate in Bratislava handed to the Slovak government an *aide-mémoire* expressing concern that Slovakia's anti-Jewish measures might have an adverse effect on relations between Switzerland and Slovakia.[94] In a letter to President Tiso which, like all the other protests, was passed on to the German envoy in Bratislava, the archbishop of Uppsala, Sweden, interceded "on behalf of the unfortunate Jewish brethren." Since the Slovak state was apparently in no position to ensure that these unfortunates would be given humane treatment, the archbishop pleaded for their transfer to neutral territories.[95] The Vatican, too, instructed its representative in Bratislava to call on Tiso and to let him know that what was being done to the Jews in his country would harm the image of the Slovak state.[96] On January 2, 1945, Georges Dunant, the delegate of the International Red Cross, sent President Tiso a letter from Professor Carl Burckhardt, president of the International Red Cross Committee, asking Tiso to stop the deportations and to help those Jews who had gone into hiding. In his reply, dated January 10, Tiso stated that he had neither the power nor the means for complying with Burckhardt's request.

In connection with the activities of the International Red Cross in Slovakia, it must be pointed out that representatives of that organization had been barred from the country until late October 1944, when Dunant arrived in Bratislava. During the early part of November, Dunant first approached the German envoy in Bratislava with the request to stop the arrests of Jews, not to deport those who had already been placed into concentration centers, or at least to exempt from deportation women, children, the sick, and others unable to work. The German envoy referred Dunant to the *Reichssicherheitshauptamt* (Central Office of Reich Security).

Dunant did not give up. In January 1945, he again turned to the

German envoy in Bratislava and also to the Slovak Foreign Ministry with a request that a shelter be established for Jewish children and the Jewish aged and sick. However, the German envoy made it plain to him that "there was hardly any likelihood of a shelter for Jews being set up."[97]

Dunant was more successful in his efforts to give direct material aid to Jews who had gone into hiding to escape arrest and deportation. In Bratislava alone, some 2,000 Jews, including about 250 children, were living clandestinely in bunkers. Dunant was contacted by a small group of young Jews who had been providing these people with money, clothing, and food.[98] He gave the group a substantial amount of cash, which they distributed among their "clients." Eventually, however, the Gestapo discovered the group, arrested its members and placed them into the last transport of deportees to leave Slovakia; the destination of that transport was Terezín. Dunant himself was summoned to Gestapo headquarters, where he was charged with giving aid to the Jews, and the Red Cross representative narrowly escaped being placed under arrest himself.

The only Jews left in Slovakia at the end of the war were those who had lived clandestinely in bunkers and those who had joined the partisans in their fight for freedom.

The Principle of *Ad Majora Mala Vitanda* and the Implementation of Anti-Jewish Policies in Slovakia

Even though the "moderate" wing, led by President Tiso himself, constituted the majority of the Slovak regime, it made no effort to stop the implementation of anti-Jewish measures. After the war the leaders of the Slovak state claimed that they had been in no position to assert their more "moderate" views regarding the "solution of the Jewish problem" because they had been intimidated by the initial military and political victories of the Third Reich and by crude pressures from the German government. They claimed that if they had offered any resistance to Germany's demands with respect to the Jews, Slovakia would have lost her independence, because Germany would have sent in her forces at once to occupy the country.[99]

Although these arguments cannot be dismissed out of hand, they are simplistic and hence in need of closer study. To what extent was the Slovak regime (meaning, Tiso's "moderate wing") truly under direct pressure from the Reich to enact and enforce anti-Jewish laws? To what extent were Slovakia's anti-Semitic measures the direct result of German demands and to what degree were they the outgrowth of initiatives originating from elements within Slovakia herself? How could a state based on Christian principles and headed by a Catholic priest [100] have shown such determination in effecting the "final solution" of the Jewish problem as did Slovakia? The reasons may be found at least partly in factors which already existed long before the time when the Reich first began to exert direct pressures on the Slovak state.

Ever since its founding in 1918, the Slovak People's party had been outspokenly anti-Semitic. The subsequent development of the party clearly shows that long before its rise to power it had already cherished its own ideas, albeit in somewhat vague terms, about the possible elimination of the Jews from the social and economic life of the country. [101]

When Slovakia became an independent state, the Slovak government on its own initiative devised and implemented a number of anti-Jewish measures which had highly negative social and economic consquences for their victims. This happened during the very early days of the Slovak state, when the influence of the Third Reich on Slovakia's internal affairs in general and on the "solution of the Jewish problem" in particular was not so marked as it was to become later on.

What course the subsequent development of anti-Jewish policies in Slovakia would have taken without direct pressure from Germany can only be surmised in retrospect. However, it may be assumed that even if Germany had not intervened, the Slovak government would not have deviated materially from the path on which it had set out when Slovakia was first established as an independent state.

It has already been stated elsewhere that official Slovak circles regarded the Jews as an element foreign to Slovak society and accused them of being enemies of the Slovak people. [102] It is significant that even the "moderate" wing of the government, along with the Catholic hierarchy, accepted this proposition without qualifications and preached it at every opportunity. [103] Thus it may be seen that Slovak governmental circles helped foment anti-Semitism long before the Third Reich began to intervene with force in the internal affairs of Slovakia. The anti-Jewish propaganda disseminated in this fashion made it easier for the government to enact additional anti-Jewish laws and finally served to silence public opposition to the deportations—at least when the transports first began.

In its efforts to justify its anti-Jewish attitudes and policies, the Slovak government was able to cite in its support the authority of at least a part of the Catholic hierarchy. Aside from those members of the hierarchy who were active in Slovak political life, other noted Slovak Church dignitaries also advocated, with various degrees of candor and in the name of the Catholic Church, the exclusion of the Jews from Slovak society and the "solution of the Jewish problem."[104]

The "radical" wing of Slovak governmental circles was strengthened by the Salzburg conference of July 1940. Nevertheless, the attempt to make Nazism the controlling ideology in Slovakia failed. Despite the expressed dissatisfaction of the Reich, Christian principles continued officially to dominate public life in Slovakia. Many important positions both in the government and in the ruling party remained in the hands of the "moderates." Tiso was able to pursue his clericalist political line in the face of opposition not only from "native" Slovak Nazis but also from the Reich. During his trial after the war, Tiso was able to quote a number of instances in which he had successfully withstood German pressures.[105]

But neither Tiso nor the spokesmen of his "moderates" went out of their way to resist German pressures when it came to the treatment of the Jews. The "moderates," and particularly Tiso, showed no interest in slowing down the stream of anti-Jewish legislation or mitigating its effects. The first timid protests from certain circles within the government were concerned only with hardships which the Jewish Code might impose upon Jews who had been baptized. The government's sole concession to the protestors was the insertion into the code of an article (Article 255) authorizing the president of the Slovak state to exempt individuals of his choosing from the provisions of the code. However, Article 255 was not invoked in any substantial measure; only about 300 presidential letters of exemption were issued.

It may be argued that once the Third Reich had decided to bring about a "final solution of the Jewish problem," the Germans would have certainly forced the Slovak government to follow suit. But the fact remains that the Slovaks did not even attempt to offer resistance; indeed, they anticipated the Germans by offering to send to Germany a total of 20,000 able-bodied Jews instead of the 20,000 Slovak workers originally demanded by the Reich. By making this offer, the Slovaks saved the Reich the trouble of exerting pressure on Slovakia. Indeed, the Slovak initiative may have hastened the Reich's decision to begin deporting Jews from Slovakia.[106]

It may be argued, of course, that the Slovak authorities might not have realized at the time that their offer to the Germans would be a prelude to the annihilation of Slovak Jewry. But the fact that the Reich so readily accepted the 20,000 Jews in place of the Slovak workers should have given the Slovak regime an inkling of what would happen to these unfortunates, for by that time it was a matter of fairly general knowledge that Jews had been deported from the Reich and German-occupied areas to the ghettos and concentration camps of occupied Poland. Only about half a year earlier (July 9 and 10, 1941), a delegation of Slovak government officials had visited some of the concentration camps in Upper Silesia and noted the inhuman conditions under which the deportees were living there.

After the war, Hans E. Ludin, Germany's last envoy in Bratislava, claimed that if Tiso had personally interceded with Hitler in the matter of the deportation of Jews from Slovakia, he might have been able to help the Jews.[107] According to Ludin, Tiso's supreme place in Slovak political life was given due respect not only in the top ruling circles of the Reich (except for SS Chief Himmler) but even by Hitler, who allegedly regarded Tiso as a *persona grata*.

However, there is no evidence that Tiso ever attempted, officially or unofficially, to intercede on behalf of the Jews. When it came to helping the Jews, Tiso remained silent and passive. Tiso was not stirred to action even when the Slovak representative to the Holy See personally handed him a note from Cardinal Luigi Maglione, the papal Secretary of State, requesting him to intervene to have the deportations stopped. He did not reply to the memorandum from the rabbis of Slovakia citing the devastating effect of the deportations on the Jews.[108]

Eventually, Tiso was persuaded to receive Rabbi Armin Frieder at a secret audience. Oskar Neumann relates that

> the young rabbi made a passionate appeal to the Christianity and humanity of Tiso . . . begging him—in the name of the faith—to have mercy upon his people. . . .

But Tiso's reply had been

> curt, cool, and reserved. He used noncommittal phrases. And then this audience, which had been very brief, was at an end. It had not accomplished anything.[109]

Testifying before the National Court of Justice on January 30, 1947, Dr. Michal Buzalka, suffragan bishop of Bratislava, recalled a remark made by the papal legate to the effect that Tiso and the Slovak government could have offered resistance to German demands for harsh measures against the Jews, because Slovak public opinion was opposed to the deportations. But, as another witness, Archbishop Dr. Karol Kmeťko, stated in hs testimony, Tiso had opted for the easy way out. When Dr. Kmeťko told Tiso about the tragic fate of the Slovak Jews who had been deported, Tiso replied: "The Germans declare that the Jews are being accorded humane treatment and that is enough for me." The archbishop recalled his surprise that Tiso should have had such implicit trust in the Germans even after he, Kmeťko, had informed him in detail about the sufferings of the Jewish deportees.[110]

Only after most of the Jews in Slovakia had been dispatched to the death camps did President Tiso finally break his silence. In one of his public addresses, he set forth his views on the deportations. Coolly he declared that the deportations had his full approval. He explained:

> God commands us to love ourselves, and this love in turn commands us to eliminate everything that may harm us, that imperils our lives. I do not think that anyone here still needs to be persuaded that the Jewish element has been a menace to the lives of the Slovaks. . . . Thus, in deporting the Jews we have simply acted in accordance with the command of God: Slovak, get rid of your enemy! It is in this spirit that we are putting things right and shall continue to do so . . .[111]

Tiso made this statement at a time when the brutal conduct of the Slovak authorities toward the Jews had stirred great indignation among the Slovak populace. Apparently, he had intended his remarks to appease public opinion which was alarmed at the treatment which the Christian regime of Slovakia was meting out to the Jews.

The Catholic bishops of Slovakia had not remained silent. Just before the deportations began, they released an official statement on the Jewish problem, but their comments cannot possibly be construed as a condemnation of the "Final Solution":

> The tragedy of the Jewish people lies in the fact that they did not accept the Savior but prepared for him a horrible and ignominious death upon the cross. The Jews had at no time and at no place blended with any other people, but have always remained in isolation as an alien element. They have never given up their hostile attitude toward Christianity. . . . In our country, too, the Jews have been a pernicious influence. . . . not only in our economy, but also in the realm of culture and ethics. Consequently the Church can have no objections if the authorities of the State adopt legal measures to impede this pernicious influence of the Jews.

Only at the end of their statement, apparently in a feeble attempt to soften these patently untrue accusations, did the bishops add that of course

> the Jews, too, are human beings and care must be taken in dealing with them that the law of the land, and natural and Divine law, should not be violated.

This official statement from the highest dignitaries of the Catholic Church in Slovakia was received with great satisfaction by the anti-Jewish agitators, who interpreted it as an endorsement from the Church for their intention to carry through the deportations.[112]

The Catholic bishops of Slovakia not only failed to condemn the deportations with an outspoken *non licet* but even omitted to recall the statement which they themselves had made in a pastoral letter issued on March 8, 1943, to the effect that "the violation of any natural law must sooner or later lead to the destruction of the social order."

However, the foregoing should not be construed to mean that there were in Slovakia no Catholic clergymen who wanted to help the Jews. Most of these rescuers were ordinary parish priests serving in small towns and villages. They hid Jews in their rectories, gave them baptismal certificates bearing dates prior to the legal "deadline" so as to make them exempt from anti-Jewish restrictions, and interceded on their behalf with the authorities.[113]

However, the official statement of the Catholic episcopate of Slovakia was not an isolated phenomenon in Church circles. It was in character with the general attitude of the Vatican toward the anti-Jewish measures that were being implemented in Slovakia and other countries under Hitler's domination.

Those who point out that the Vatican had expressed its disapproval of the deportations from Slovakia cite in their support the fact that the papal Secretariat of State had protested on several occasions against the deportations. On the other hand, the Vatican did not take practical action to lend force to its protests. There are no known indications that the Vatican had ever advised the president of Slovakia or other members of the Catholic hierarchy active in Slovak politics to resign their government positions, warning them that if they remained in office they would come into conflict with the basic teachings of the Catholic Church.

In a letter to the bishops of Berlin, dated April 30, 1943, Pope Pius XII explained his failure to take a public stand against Nazi atrocities. He said he had refrained from openly condemning the Nazis *ad majora mala vitanda* (in order to avoid greater evils). The Third Reich was a powerful and militant state which, for ideological reasons, regarded believing Catholics as its enemies. It may be argued, however, that that consideration cannot be cited as a justification for the Vatican's failure to take action in Slovakia, for unlike Nazi Germany, Slovakia was a state founded on the principles of Catholicism.

The passive attitude of President Tiso, and the infelicitous statement—to say the least—of the Catholic bishops of Slovakia did much to lull public opinion to sleep and thus helped make it possible for the "radicals" and their supporters to bring about the "final solution of the Jewish problem" quickly and unhampered by significant resistance.

Eventually, the Slovak government decided to discontinue the deportations temporarily. It is known that although Germany continued to press the Slovak government to resume the deportations, she essentially acquiesced in the Slovak decision, and Slovakia withstood the German pressures to do so.

The fact that the Reich did not attempt to force Slovakia to resume the deportations refutes the argument of Tiso and his associates that they had only agreed to the tightening of anti-Jewish legislation and to the deportations out of fear that Germany would otherwise have occupied Slovakia and turned her into a "protectorate" as she had done with Bohemia and Moravia. It also refutes the contention that the Church and Tiso had no other choice but to remain silent *ad majora mala vitanda.* [114]

It seems that, quite aside from the "radicals," Dr. Tiso and the other leading officials of the Slovak state deliberately overstressed this element of fear in order to play down their own share in the guilt.

NOTES

1. By June 3, 1940, a total of 443 Jewish attorneys had been barred. (Speech by Minister Ferdinand Durčanský, reported in *Slovák,* June 6, 1940.)
2. As of May 31, 1939, the total number of practicing physicians in Slovakia was 1,414; of these, 621, or 44 percent, were Jewish. During the three years of Slovakia's existence as an independent state, the shortage of physicians became worse. By April 15, 1942, the total number of physicians in Slovakia had dropped to 1,215; of these, some 290 were Jews, who were permitted to practice their profession without restrictions even at this late date. Report by Dr. Humburský, director of the Health Department in the Ministry for Internal Affairs to the Slovak Council of State on May 27, 1942. (ŠSÚV-ÚPV A/9-02309/70-61.K.242.)
3. In an address on February 15, 1940, Minister of Economics Dr. Gejza Medrický advocated a solution that would not upset Slovakia's economy (*Slovák,* February 18, 1940). A similar view was set forth also by Dr. Ján Balko, deputy governor of the Slovak National Bank, in his article, "Židovstvo v priemyselnom podnikní na Slovensku" [The Jews in the Industrial Enterprises of Slovakia], *Slovák,* October 8, 1939.
4. "Niekoľko zásad arizačných" [Some Basic Principles of Aryanization], *Slovák,* January 25, 1940. These views did not escape the re-

sponsible German authorities. In a report to Berlin, the German envoy in Bratislava wrote:

> The Slovak government has taken the position in this matter that it is not necessary to oust the Jews quickly at all costs, particularly with German assistance, since the Jewish problem can be solved at any time depending on the general situation . . . but it would not be possible to oust the Germans who might replace them . . .

Report SdB-RFSS, Bratislava, Oct. 18, 1939. BA-R 70 Slovakia/35; Report of the German envoy in Bratislava to the German Foreign Office. PA.AA-Pol. IV, No. 2, Vol. 1, Bratislava Legation.
5. Report by Dr. Bálko to the Council of State, Feb. 12, 1941. ŠSÚA-NS. Dr. Jan Balko, Tnĺud 46/46-25; Vlastislav Bauch, *Poĺnohospodárstvo za slovenského štátu* [Agriculture in the Slovak State] (Bratislava: 1958), p. 33.
6. The best insight into the situation of Slovak Jewry during the era of the Slovak state is given in Jirmejahu Oskar Neumann's book, *Im Schatten des Todes* [In the Shadow of Death] (Tel Aviv: Olamenu, 1956). (See entry in bibliography for full title.)
7. These central bodies were the "Jeschurun" Federation of Jewish Religious Congregations in Slovakia and the Central Bureau of Autonomous Orthodox Jewish Religious Congregations in Slovakia. Both organizations had their headquarters in Bratislava.
8. The Slovak government liquidated several political parties, including the Jewish party and the Socialist-Zionist Labor party. The activities of these parties were stopped by order of the Provincial Administration as early as November 25, 1938.
9. *Židovské Noviny,* November 24, 1938.
10. The Orthodox Jews were particularly concerned at the time that *shehitah* (the kosher slaughtering of animals for meat) might be forbidden by law and they were anxious to forestall such an eventuality.
11. Jirmejahu Oskar Neumann, *Im Schatten des Todes,* pp. 16, 32.
12. As of August 16, 1940, there were in Slovakia thirty-seven *hakhsharot* with a total membership of 618. Report of the Central Jewish Office for the Region of Slovakia. ŠSÚA-MV 12115/40. K. 1149. At a cabinet meeting on April 10, 1940, the Slovak government had given its consent to the establishment of "vocational reorientation groups" for Jews.
13. Neumann, *Im Schatten des Todes,* p. 21. See also *The Jews of Czechoslovakia,* I (New York: 1968), p. 118.
14. The total of 7,116 is given in *Prehĺad židovského vysťahovalectva po 14.III.1939* [Survey of Jewish Emigration Subsequent to March 14,

1939] issued by the *Ústredňa Židov* (Jewish Office). See also Emil Knieža, "The Resistance of the Slovak Jews," in Yuri Suhl, ed. and trans., *They Fought Back: The Story of the Jewish Resistance in Nazi Europe* (New York: 1967), p. 177.
15. *Slovák,* August 1, 1940.
16. The advisor on Jewish affairs was a *pro forma* member of the German diplomatic mission. However, he was in fact on the staff of Department IV B 4 headed by Eichmann and was responsible directly to him.
17. "The authorized members of the Hlinka Guard and the FS are hereby empowered to apprehend Jews and to turn them over to the authorities, to confiscate articles used in the perpetration of a crime, and to identify any Jew or non-Jew who has violated the anti-Jewish laws. They shall have access to all public facilities and, in the prosecution of a Jew, or if said Jew has moved away, they shall have access also to the premises of Jewish business enterprises or private residences in order to perform a body search of the Jewish individual concerned."
18. The *Ústredňa Židov* (Jewish Office) was modeled on the *Reichsvereinigung der Juden in Deutschland* (Reich Association of Jews in Germany), which had been set up in Germany under the Tenth Regulation to implement the *Reichsbürgergesetz* (Law on Reich Citizenship) issued on July 9, 1939 (*Reichsgesetzblatt,* Part I, p. 1097), and on the *Zentralstelle für Jüdische Auswanderung* (Central Office for Jewish Emigration), which was already operating in Vienna at the time.
19. The first individual to hold the position of *starosta* ("Head Jew") for Slovakia was Heinrich Schwarcz, a leading functionary of the Central Bureau of Autonomous Orthodox Jewish Religious Congregations. After he fled to Hungary, the Central Economic Office appointed Arpád Sebestyén to succeed him (September 11, 1941). The last "Head Jew" was Dr. Oskar Neumann.
20. Jews were forbidden to own fishing gear or bicycles, to use the telephone, to visit in non-Jewish homes, to have social dealings with Aryans, to be in the streets or in public places after 9 P.M., to make purchases other than from officially approved business enterprises, etc. Additional anti-Jewish measures included Ordinance 215/1940, under which Jews were required to surrender their passports; Ordinance 216/1940, under which Jews were forbidden to operate motor vehicles; Proclamations 467/1941 of the Ministry of Economics and 488/1941 of the Ministry for Internal Affairs regarding the classification of petitions submitted by Jews; Proclamation 509/1941 of the Ministry for Internal Affairs regarding travel restrictions for Jews, etc.

21. Lubomír Lipták, *Ovládnutie slovenského priemyslu nemeckým kapitálom 1939-1945* [The Control of Slovak Industry by German Capital, 1939-1945] (Bratislava: 1960), p. 153.
22. Outside of Bratislava, 8,872 apartment buildings in Slovakia were owned entirely by Jews; another 143 were partly owned by Jews. *Štatistika židovských domov a bytov na Slovensku podľa stavu K. 28.2.1942* (Statistical Survey of Jewish-owned Buildings and Apartment Dwellings in Slovakia as of February 28, 1942), compiled by the Jewish Office.
23. In Bratislava this prohibition applied also to Štefánik Street and to all new buildings.
24. The Fund also received the net income from formerly Jewish-owned houses confiscated by the state; fees for work permits issued to Jewish employees; 20 percent of the liquidation value paid by Aryanizers into the blocked accounts of former Jewish owners after all outstanding obligations had been paid; and one-half of the price paid by non-Jewish purchasers of household articles confiscated from Jews.
25. ŠSÚA-ÚHÚ 1-D 469/1-1943.K.295
26. The Ministry of Defense set March 3, 1941, as the date for the draft into military labor service. A photostatic copy of the proclamation of January 10, 1941, is in the author's files.
27. When this ordinance was subsequently incorporated into #22 of the Jewish Code, the minimum age was lowered from eighteen to sixteen.
28. Report of the *Leitabschnitt,* Security Service, Vienna, to the *Reichssicherheitshauptamt* (Central Office of Reich Security). BA-R 70, Slovakia/35.
29. Testimony of Dr. Tibor Kováč, wartime functionary in the Central Jewish Office and also member of the "Working Group." ŠSÚA-NS. Dr. Anton Vašek, TnĽud 17/46-72.
30. Wisliceny's testimony, May 6, 1946. ŠSÚA-NS. Dr. Anton Vašek, TnĽud 17/46-72.
31. Memorandum by Dr. Franz Rademacher, head of the Jewish division in the Reich Foreign Ministry, October 28, 1941, for State Secretary Ernst von Weizsacker. ND-Document NG-182.
32. Memorandum by Under State Secretary Martin Luther, head of the *Deutschland* division in the Reich Foreign Ministry, August 21, 1942. ND-Document NG-2586 J.
33. Wisliceny's testimony, May 6, 1946. ŠSÚA-NS. Dr. Anton Vašek, TnĽud 17/46-72.
34. Memorandum by Under State Secretary Luther, August 21, 1942. ND-Document NG-2586 J.
35. ŠSÚA-ÚPV 25/42. K. 235.

36. The powers of the Council of State included the determination of presidential disability, the institution of criminal proceedings against the president or members of the government, and decisions on the elimination of parliamentary mandates.
37. Information from Dr. Peter Zaťko, December 27, 1969. Dr. Imrich Karvaš, governor of the Slovak National Bank, testified in a similar vein in court on February 16, 1946.
38. ŠSÚA-NS. Dr. Sokol, Tnľud 11/47-2.
39. The high command of the Hlinka Guard confiscated the statistical register of all Slovak Jews which had been kept by the *Ústredňa Židov* (Jewish Office); it thus was in a position to supply the authorities with the most accurate information available on the Jewish population of the country. Testimonies by A. Slezák of the Jewish Office and Otomar Kubala, chief of staff of the Hlinka Guard. ŠSÚA-NS. F. Málek, Tnľud 28/46-34, 36.
40. Circular letter sent out by the Ministry for Internal Affairs, March 24, 1942. ŠSÚA-MV 700/42.K.208.
41. ŠSÚA-PSV 2890/42.K.35.
42. Testimonies by Ervin Steiner, Juraj Spitzer, Dr. Kunstadt, etc. ŠSÚA-NS. Dr. Anton Vašek, Tnľud 17/46-36, 53, 72. The commandant of the concentration camp in Žilina admitted in court that he had been forced, in gradual stages, to discharge sixty-six of the seventy-five camp guards because of their cruelty to the inmates. ŠSÚA-NS. Dr. Anton Vašek, Tnľud 17/46-72.
43. Among these objective criteria were: baptism prior to September 10, 1941; legal marriage to a non-Jewish spouse; exemption granted by the President of the Republic, etc.
44. "On Green Thursday, April 3, 1942, I returned from Poprad to Bratislava. In the station of Žilina I saw a long freight train consisting of closed, covered cattle cars. The small air vents had been barred with barbed wire netting. Behind these air vents I could see the faces of children who had been lifted up by their mothers so that they might be able to get some fresh air. I was shocked at the sight." Information given to the author from Pavel Čarnogurský, who had acted as secretary general of the Deputies' Club of the Slovak People's party in the Slovak parliament (November 3, 1969).
45. Testimonies by Dr. Eugen Filkorn, Dr. Martin Sokol, and Dr. Peter Zaťko, all former members of the Slovak parliament, before the National Court of Justice. ŠSÚA-NS Dr. Filkorn, Tnľud 26/46-24; NS Dr. Sokol, Tnľud 11/47-2.
46. Dr. Ferdinand Klinda, director of the office of the Ministry of Economics, and Dr. Karvaš, governor of the Slovak National Bank, sub-

mitted to Mach a list of individuals who had been deported even though they held legitimate "letters of protection." Mach promised not to permit such infringements in the future. ŠSÚA-NS Dr. Ferdinand Klinda, Tnľud 58/45-8. At one cabinet session, Jozef Sivák, Minister of Education and Culture, also categorically demanded that the deportation of such individuals stop. Testimonies by Jozef Sivák and Benjamin Šimkovič, ŠSÚA-NS Dr. Anton Vašek, Tnľud 17/46-27, 32.

47. Rabbi Armin Frieder testified in court that altogether 58 deportation trains had been dispatched from Slovak territory. ŠSÚA-NS Dr. Anton Vašek, Tnľud 17/46-25.
48. Gideon Hausner, *Justice in Jerusalem* (New York: 1966), p. 195.
49. Michael B. Weissmandl, *Min HaMetzar* [Out of the Depths] (New York: 1960), p. 18.
50. ŠSÚA-MV 697/42.K.207.
51. Testimonies of Ondrej Steiner and several Jewish deportees who had escaped from the death camps. ŠSÚA-NS Dr. Anton Vašek, Tnľud 17/46-26, 68, 72; NS Otomar Kubala, Tnľud 13/46-11. For data on the escape of Slovak Jews from the death camps of Auschwitz and Maidanek, see Tatiana Berenstein and Adam Rutkowski, "Żydzy w obozie koncentracyjnim Majdanek (1941-1944)" [The Jews in the Concentration Camp of Maidanek, 1941-1944], in *Biuletyn żidowskiego instytutu historycznego* [Bulletin of the Jewish Historical Institute], Warsaw: no. 58 (1966), pp. 50-51; Alfonz Bednar, *Dvojník Šimon ide do Povstania* [Double Šimon in the Uprising] (Bratislava: 1964); Betsalel Mordowicz, "Twice in Auschwitz," in *Yalkut Moreshet*, no. 9 (1968), pp. 7-20 (in Hebrew); Rudolf Vrba and Alan Bestic, *I Cannot Forgive* (New York: 1964); *Die Judenausrottung in Polen, Augenzeugenberichte. Dritte Serie. Die Vernichtungslager* [The Extermination of the Jews in Poland, Eyewitness Reports, Third Series, The Extermination Camps] (Geneva: 1944). Personal record of Dionys Lenard about his flight and conditions at the death camp at Maidanek (45 typewritten pages) submitted to F. Hoffmann-Dvorin, official of the Jewish Office. Parts of this record are in the author's files. Published under the title of *Reshimah shel Yehudi Almoni MiSlovakia she-nimlat mimahane Lublin-Maidanek be-Juni, 1942* [Testimony of an Anonymous Jew from Slovakia Who Escaped from the Camp of Lublin-Maidanek] in Livia Rothkirchen, *The Destruction of Slovak Jewry: A Documentary History* (Jerusalem: 1961), pp. 166-204.
52. Vašek received a monthly income of 100,000 Slovak crowns; in addition, he received bribes, jewelry, and other valuables. The cash he received alone totaled about Ks. 2,500,000. He received from Ks.

10,000 to 20,000 for the release of one Jewish individual from a concentration camp. Also, no work or travel permit or "letter of protection" could be validated without Dr. Vašek's authorization. Testimony by Rabbi Armin Frieder. ŠSÚA-NS Dr. Anton Vašek, Tnľud 17/46-25.

The first successes soon became apparent. No transports at all were sent off during the month of August, and only three during September and October. Another indication of the change in the attitude of the Slovak authorities may be seen from Dr. Vašek's report to his immediate superior (August 7, 1942), *"Úvahy o odložení poťažne o predbežnom zastavení vysťahovania Židov"* [Observations on the Delay or Temporary Cessation of the Evacuation of the Jews]. This report did not even touch upon the question of whether or not the deportations should be stopped; on the contrary, Vašek stressed that the Jewish problem would be solved in the best way possible under the circumstances. ŠSÚA-MV 637/42.K.206.

53. In his testimony on May 6, 1946. Wisliceny insisted that he had received no more than 20,000 U.S. dollars. In other respects, his statements on the course of the negotiations agree with the information given by Karol Hochberg to the "Working Group." ŠSÚA-NS Dr. Anton Vašek, Tnľud 17/46-72; Neumann, *Im Schatten des Todes,* pp. 140–41.
54. Reminiscences of Akiba Nir, in *Sefer HaShomer HaTzair, Kerekh Alef. HaTnuah me-reshita v'ad l'ahar mered haGetaot* [HaShomer HaTzair Book, Vol. I, The Organization from its Beginnings Until After the Ghetto Revolts] (Merhavia: 1956), p. 752.
55. Alex Weissberg, *Die Geschichte von Joel Brand* (Cologne and Berlin: 1956), p. 36. (English version: *Desperate Mission: Joel Brand's Story*) (New York: 1958).
56. L. Lipták, "Slovenský štát a protifašistické hnutie v rokoch 1939–1943" [The Slovak State and the Anti-Fascist Movement, 1939–1943], in *HČ* XIV (1966), vol. 2, p. 195.
57. On June 26, 1942, the German envoy in Bratislava reported to the German Foreign Office that "Many quarters among the Slovak populace take a very negative view of the evacuation of Jews. In recent days this attitude has been strengthened by a heavy barrage of British counterpropaganda. . . ." PA, AA-*Büro des Staatssekretärs, Slowakei* (Slovakia), vol. 2; The "British counterpropaganda" to which the envoy refers were the daily Slovak-language programs broadcast by the BBC in London that included a regular analysis of the policies of the Slovak government by Dr. Vladimír Clementis, who was to become foreign minister of Czechoslovakia in 1948. See Vladimír Clementis,

Odkazy z Londýna [Reports from London] (Bratislava: 1947). The report of the *Leitabschnitt* of the Security Service in Vienna to the RSHA (August 30, 1942) was couched in similar terms. "With the beginning of the evacuation the mood in general came to a head. . . . All of a sudden the Slovaks have begun to feel sorry for their Jews and for their harsh fate at the hands of the Germans. . . . The evacuations are being characterized not merely as inhuman but also as illegal. . . . The Jewish problem is not being viewed from the racial standpoint. Slovak circles have always viewed the racial issue with a certain distaste, for they have regarded it as a purely German idea with unacceptable consequences for Slovakia and the Slavs." BA-R 70, Slovakia/35.

58. *"Politizovanie s náboženstvom"* [Politicking With Religion], in *Gardista,* June 2, 1942.
59. Cf. Report of *Leitabschnitt* of Security Service, Vienna, August 8, 1942. IfZ, Microfilm MA 588, No. 1151-52.
60. *Evanjelický posol spod Tatier* [The Evangelical Messenger from Below the Tatra Mountains], no. 7 (1942).
61. Wisliceny's testimony, January 3, 1946, IMT, vol. IV, pp. 396-97.
62. Evidence from the *Institut für Zeitgeschichte* [Institute for Contemporary History] (Stuttgart, 1966), vol. 2, pp. 67-68; ND-Document NO-2408.
63. *Gardista,* February 9, 1943.
64. From "Katolicki biskupi na Slovensku a rasizmus" [The Catholic Bishops of Slovakia and Racism], in *Nové prúdy* [New Trends], November 18, 1945, no. 2. German translation of the pastoral letter in AAPA-Inland IIg 205 K 213045, 477195, *Die Judenfrage in der Slowakei* [The Jewish Problem in Slovakia].
65. On April 7, 1943, the papal representative in Bratislava visited Premier Tuka to communicate to him the displeasure of the Vatican. See F. Cavalli, "La Santa Sede contro le deportazioni degli Ebrei dala Slovacchia durante la seconda guerra mondiale" [The Holy See In Opposition to the Deportation of Jews from Slovakia During World War Two], in *La Civiltà Cattolica,* vol. 112, no. 14.
66. Čarnogurský describes the situation as follows: "The Jewish problem was a source of great concern in Slovak politics. In comparison, other problems, including those linked with the imminent end of the war and even the future of the state, were relegated to second place. The responsibility for Slovakia's declaration of war on the Soviet Union and for the deportation of Jewish fellow citizens. . . . weighed heavily on the president, the government and the parliament." Communication to the author, February 11, 1970.

67. ŠSÚA-SSR, *Zápisnice zo zasadnutí snemovných výborov* [Minutes of Parliamentary Committee Meetings], K.272.
68. Letter to Envoy Hans E. Ludin, July 21, 1943. PA, AA–Inland II g 205, K 209046, E 024714, *Die Judenfrage in der Slowakei* [The Jewish Problem in Slovakia].
69. ŠSÚA-ÚHÚ III/A 1732/2/14-1943. K.434.
70. Dr. Spišiak explained that his sympathy for the Jews had been motivated by feelings of personal gratitude toward Jews he had known. He had come from a poor family and had early lost his father. A Jewish teacher had taken a special interest in him. "For the first time in my life, I experienced human warmth and kind treatment. . . . Many of my subsequent actions can be explained in terms of my subconscious feelings of profound gratitude." After completing his law studies, he had taken a position in the law office of Dr. Julius Reisz, who then represented the Jewish party in the Czechoslovak parliament. "I remained in that position while the parliamentary election campaign was going on, and I witnessed at first hand the conflicts between the various groups within Jewry. I met many important personalities. This later enabled me to find more effective ways of protecting our emigré fellow citizens than I could have done without that experience. . . ." ŠSÚA-NS Dr. J. Spišiak, Tnľud 10/47/15.
71. ŠSÚA-MV 14/44.K.582.
72. The financial assistance for these operations came from the Rescue Committee in Istanbul and the Swiss headquarters of the American Jewish Joint Distribution Committee (JDC).
73. The Jews had been able to make the necessary official contacts because some of the country's best-known Jewish business firms had been taken over by highly placed State Security officials. Dr. Jozef Beňuška, director of the *Ústredňa štátnej bezpečnosti* (State Security Headquarters), was a board member of a leather manufacturing concern in Liptovský Mikuláš which formerly had been owned by Jews (Haas Brothers). His deputy, Dr. Peter Komendák, had "Aryanized" a business formerly owned by a fellow-countryman named L. Rosenzweig. Through the former Jewish owners of these firms the representatives of what was left of Slovak Jewry were now able to make contacts with these and other Slovak public officials.
74. Source: Dr. Wohlstein-Voldan (December 10, 1967), a member of the Central Jewish Office, who had taken a prominent role in these activities. At the same time rescue operations were begun on behalf of Jewish children whose parents' whereabouts were unknown and who had been left with non-Jewish families in Poland.

75. Cf. letters from Mrs. Gisi Fleischmann of May 7 and August 19, 1943, to the *HeHalutz* Center, Geneva. Archives of Moreshet Givat Haviva, Israel–D 1-470, D.626; letter from Rabbi Weissmandl (in Hebrew), to the *HeHalutz* Center. Archives of the Labor Movement, Tel Aviv; Cf. Neumann, *Im Schatten des Todes*, p. 174.
76. *Kastner-Bericht über Eichmann's Menschenhandel in Ungarn* [Rezsö Kastner's Report on Eichmann's Trading in Human Lives in Hungary] (Munich: 1961), p. 72.
77. H. Langbein, *Der Auschwitz-Prozess. Eine Dokumentation* [The Auschwitz Trial. A Documentary Report], vol. I (Vienna: 1965), p. 122.
78. These accounts were published in *Die Judenausrottung in Polen. Augenzeugenberichte. Dritte Serie. Die Vernichtungslager.* [The Extermination of the Jews in Poland. Eyewitness Reports. Third Series. The Extermination Camps] (Geneva: 1944), pp. 77 ff.
79. Report on meeting of expanded executive of *HaShomer HaTzair*, January 1940, *"Trpeli a bojovali"* [They Suffered and Fought], in *Tribuna*, August 29, 1947.
80. Reminiscences of Akiba Nir, in *Sefer HaShomer HaTzair*, p. 750.
81. See Erich Kulka, "Jews in the Czechoslovak Armed Forces during World War II," in the present volume, pp. 331–448.
82. Following the disbanding of the military labor camps for Jews at the end of May 1943.
83. *Správa o činnosti partizánskej skupiny z koncentračného tábora v Novákoch v Slovenskom národnom povstaní* [Report of the Partisan Unit of the Nováky Concentration Camp During the Slovak People's Uprising], AÚDKSS-F.6, 125.
84. Another vital component of resistance activities in the camp, though it did not require the use of weapons, was the production of forged "Aryan" papers which were issued to prospective members of the projected partisan units to protect them in case they were captured.
85. Father Pozdech was known for the help he extended to Jews. He arranged a meeting for the representative of the Jewish community with the papal representative in Bratislava and used his good relations with the Slovak episcopate to help the Jews. He also saw to it that the written record of the reports by Walter Rosenberg (Rudolf Vrba) and Alfred Wetzler on conditions at the death camps were sent on to the Czechoslovak government-in-exile in London. Neumann, *Im Schatten des Todes*, p. 205.
86. David Goldstein, "Tafkidim" [Tasks] in *Sefer HaShomer HaTzair*, pp. 754–55.
87. AÚDKSS-F.9, 63/1.

88. Pavel Nemec, "Spomienky z bojov v Nitrianskej doline" [Recollections of the Battle in the Nitra Valley], in *Tribúna,* August 29, 1947.
89. After the war, the combat activities of the Nováky group were described also in another report entitled *Bojové akcie partizánskej skupiny z koncentraćného tábora v Novákoch* [Combat Activities of the Partisan Unit from the Concentration Camp in Nováky]. AÚDKSS-F 6, 125. Other publications are František Hagara, *História partizánskych bojov: I. Hornonitrianská partizánska brigáda* [History of the Partisan Fighting: The First Upper Nitra Partisan Brigade] (Bratislava-Prievidza: 1946), pp. 27, 37, 43, 46; Boris Tartakowskij, *Smert i žizn rjadom* [Death and Life in One Column] (Moscow: 1963), pp. 117, 191, 201, 213, 229.
90. On the Palestine parachutists, see D. Goldstein, ed., *Haviva* (Prague: 1947); "Osudy jednej vojenskéj misie na povstaleckom Slovensku" [The Fate of a Military Mission in Insurgent Slovakia], in *Tribúna,* August 29, 1947; Dorothy and Pessach Bar-Adon, *Seven Who Fell* (Tel Aviv: 1947) (in Hebrew).
91. Cf. Lists of individual partisan units. AÚDKSS-F.8.
92. Testimony by Dr. F. Steiner at the Eichmann trial in Jerusalem, May 24, 1961. *Eichmann-Prozess, Sitzungsprotokolle, Nr. 50* (Records of the Eichmann Trial, No. 50); Yad Vashem, Jerusalem-M 5/57; *Dokumentačná akcia Bratislava* [Documentation Project, Bratislava].
93. After the war, mass graves containing many bodies of Jews who had been shot were discovered in Kremnička and Nemecká (Banská Bystrica district). AÚDKSS-F.6, 353.
94. Telegram from Envoy Ludin to the German Foreign Office, November 11, 1944. AA PA.–Inland II g 205 477151-477153, *Die Judenfrage in der Slowakei* [The Jewish Problem in Slovakia].
95. Telegram from Envoy Ludin to the German Foreign Office, January 3, 1945. AA PA.–Inland IIG 205, *Die Judenfrage in der Slowakei* [The Jewish Problem in Slovakia].
96. Cavalli, *La Santa Sede . . .,* p. 17.
97. Telegram from Envoy Ludin to the German Foreign Office, January 20, 1945. AA PA.–Inland II g 205 K 213010, 477164, *Die Judenfrage in der Slowakei* [The Jewish Problem in Slovakia].
98. The leader of this group was Arnold Lazar. During the daytime, these young people either stayed in hiding or went to work under assumed names. See Arnold Lazar, "Reminiscences of Fascist Slovakia," in *Yad Vashem Bulletin,* no. 18, (1966), pp. 17–25.
99. Tiso seized on this thought in his defense in court. He said: "Thus, in order to forestall intervention or perhaps even the occupation of Slovakia by the Germans, we strove to eliminate any situation which

they might have been able to use against us . . . For this reason we . . . dissolved the Communist party and attempted also to solve the Jewish problem in our own way so as not to give the Germans cause for intervention." Josef Tiso, *Die Wahrheit über die Slowakei (The Truth About Slovakia)*, defense statement before the National Court in Bratislava, March 17 and 18, 1947.

100. Of a total of sixty-three deputies in the Slovak parliament, sixteen were priests. There were priests also in the Council of State, whose deputy chairman was Bishop Jan Vojtaššák. Two out of six regional chairmen and thirteen out of sixty district chairmen of the Slovak People's party were Catholic priests. D. Hudec, ed., *Slovenská ročenka* 1943 [Slovak Yearbook, 1943] (Bratislava); *Krajinský vestník pre Slovensko* [Provincial Gazette for Slovakia] (February 1, 1939).

101. K. Čulen, *Boj Slovákov o slobodu* [The Slovak Fight for Freedom] (Bratislava: 1944), p. 71.

102. In this connection, Dr. Jozef M. Kirschbaum, former secretary general of the Slovak People's party, wrote: "In this respect we do not find ourselves in conflict with our conscience and with the teachings of Christianity, which make a clear distinction between reward and punishment. Thus, if we move against the Jews with legal methods, we punish the crimes of members of their race, without, however, punishing individuals . . ." *Slovák*, March 5, 1940.

103. Note a statement made by Dr. Tiso even before the establishment of the Slovak state: "The Jews will be excluded from our national life once and for all, because they have always acted as a subversive element and as the principal bearers of Marxist and liberal ideas in Slovakia. This people represents a serious moral problem because of its usury, trickery, and its debauchery. That is why the Christians during the Middle Ages locked them up in the ghetto and would not permit them to leave it." *Slovák*, February 28, 1939.

104. Thus, Rudolf Mikus, Provincial of the Jesuits of Slovakia, said: "The Church has always insisted that the Jews should not dwell together with the Christians, that every city should have a ghetto, and that the Jews should have to wear identifying badges. The Church advocates the elimination of the Jews." *Slovák*, February 10, 1939.

105. Tiso was able to prevent the relocation of the German population of Spiš (northern Slovakia) to the western part of the Slovak state, i.e., the Slovak-German border area (Záhorie), and the relocation of the original Slovak population of the latter area to Spiš. He also thwarted the effort of the Germans to participate directly in his government, rejecting the demand of Franz Karmasin, chief of the ethnic Germans in Slovakia, that he assign certain government positions to "refugees"

from Germany. Thanks to Tiso's intervention, the German High Command abandoned its plan to evacuate the entire population of Eastern Slovakia when the battle lines moved closer to the area. Tiso, *The Truth About Slovakia,* pp. 35 f., 158.
106. Dieter Wisliceny, the German advisor on Jewish affairs, stated in court that the deportations of Jews from Slovakia in 1942 would definitely not have occurred if the Slovak state had not made its offer. Testimony by Wisliceny, May 6, 1946. ŠSÚA-NS Dr. Anton Vašek, Tnľud 17/46-72.
107. Testimony by Ludin before the prosecutor of the National Court of Justice on October 23, 1946. ŠSÚA-NS H. E. Ludin, Tnľud 56/46-8. Ludin's characterization of Hitler's attitude toward Tiso was confirmed, albeit in somewhat modified terms, by Fritz Fiala, the former editor of the Bratislava *Grenzbote.* Fiala allegedly had been in a position to obtain authentic reports direct from Hitler's immediate entourage. In one of these reports he told how, supposedly, Hitler had found it necessary, prior to a visit from Dr. Tiso, to persuade Ernst Kaltenbrunner and other high-ranking SS officials at his headquarters to behave civilly and with dignity in the presence of the "fat padre." Cf. A. Rašla, "Šujan kontra Hoffmann" [Šujan vs. Hoffmann], in *Kultúrny život* [Cultural Life], August 2, 1968.
108. Karol Sidor, *Šesť rokov pri Vatikáne* [Six Years at the Vatican], p. 142.
109. Neumann, *Im Schatten des Todes,* p. 162.
110. ŠSÚA-NS Dr. Tiso, Tnľud 6/46. K.57.
111. Address by Dr. Tiso in Holíč (Western Slovakia), August 16, 1942. *Slovák,* August 18, 1942, no. 186.
112. *Gardista,* April 30, 1942: "This [i.e., the statement of the bishops] means that the responsible circles in the Catholic Church in Slovakia are definitely not opposed to our effecting a complete solution of the Jewish problem. This had to be said, so that it may be perfectly clear to public opinion both here and abroad, so that the public will know with what they are dealing. At the same time, it indirectly answers those who constantly refer to the Church [i.e., in their arguments against anti-Jewish excesses]. . . . It is true that the statement contains passages indicating certain reservations [i.e., regarding the situation of baptized Jews], but on closer examination we will see that these merely have reference to certain rights of the Catholic Church, rights of which we, too, are aware and which we respect."
113. The following are known instances of personal courage displayed by Catholic priests. Father Hatiar, a priest in Svit, wrote to his immediate superior, explaining his refusal to take the oath of allegiance to the Slovak state: "I shall take this oath only with the reservation that

I will not accept the laws enacted against the Jews." He said that he considered the anti-Jewish laws to be at variance with his interpretation of Catholic doctrine. In reply, he was simply told that his interpretation was not correct. (From records of the trial of the Slovak Bishops Ján Vojtaššák, Dr. Th. Michal Buzalka, and Pavel Gojdič, Prague, 1951, pp. 53-54). Another Catholic priest, Father N. Bardoš in Sučany (Martín district), publicly condemned the anti-Jewish measures and openly helped Jews. As a result of his activities he was eventually arrested and taken to the concentration camp of Ilava. (ŠSÚA-NS Dr. F. Starinský, Tnľud 49/45-23.) The Catholic orphanage "In Mary's Keeping," Bratislava, gave shelter to Jewish children without the knowledge of its board of trustees, which included some members of the German ethnic minority group. ŠSÚA-NS Dr. K. Koerper, Tnľud 17/45-58. The Catholic parish priest of Kremnica and his Evangelical counterpart paid a personal visit to the courtyard of the rabbi's domicile, to express their sympathy with the Jews who had been "concentrated" there. (Report of the District Administrator, July 10, 1942.) ŠSÚA-Alexander Mach, Tnľud 6/46.

114. At his trial Tiso said that he had been mindful of this maxim throughout his political career. "I have always employed every possible means to fight evil; only when the nation was menaced by an even greater evil did I give way in order to avoid that greater evil." Tiso, *The Truth About Slovakia,* p. 101. In its official statement (April 23, 1947) on the court verdict against Tiso, who had been condemned to death and hanged, the Vatican broadcasting station refuted Tiso's argument as follows: "There are certain laws which must be obeyed no matter how much one loves his country. The rights conferred by God upon the individual and the commandment of Christian charity must be placed above love of country, and for the sake of these alone . . . [he would have had to] resign from his office." *Dr. Jozef Tiso o sobe (Obhajobná reč pred tzv. Narodným súdom v Bratislave dňa 17 a 18, marca 1947).* A Slovak version of Tiso's defense at his trial, with notes and annotations, has been edited by J. Pauco, Passaic, New Jersey, 1952. See p. 340.

BIBLIOGRAPHY

Arendt, Hannah, *Eichmann in Jerusalem: A Report on the Banality of Evil.* New York: 1963.
Bar-Adon, Dorothy and Pessach, *Seven Who Fell.* Tel Aviv: 1947.

Bauch, V., *Poľnohospodárstvo za slovenského štátu* [Agriculture in the Slovak State]. Bratislava: 1958.

Bednár, A., *Dvojník Simon ide do Povstania* [Double Agent Simon in the Uprising]. Bratislava: 1964.

Bludný, Peter, "*Saša a ostatní*" [Sasha and the Others], *Tribúna,* Bratislava, August 29, 1947.

Bodensieck, Heinrich, "*Das Dritte Reich und die Lage der Juden in der Tschechoslowakei nach München*" [The Third Reich and the Situation of the Jews in Czechoslovakia after Munich], in *Vierteljahreshefte für Zeitgeschichte* [Contemporary History Quarterlies]. Munich: 1961, pp. 249-61.

Bojarski, Ladislaus, *Die Ausschaltung der Juden aus dem slowakischen Wirtschaftsleben und die Arisierung im Lichte der slowakischen Gesetze* [The Elimination of the Jews from Slovak Economic Life and the Aryanization in the Light of Slovak Law], Diss., Vienna, n.d.

Borský, František, *Rok pracovného zboru MNO* [A Year of the Labor Corps of the Ministry of Defense]. Bratislava: 1942.

Brod, T. *Tobrucké krysy* [The Rats of Tobruk]. Prague: 1967.

Cavalli, Fiorello, S. J., "*La Santa Sede controle deportazioni degli Ebrei dalla Slovacchia durante la seconda guerra mondiale*" [The Holy See in Opposition to the Deportation of Jews from Slovakia during World War II], *La Civiltà Cattolica,* no. 112 (1961), pp. 3-18.

Cedry Libanonu, Vydané na nehynúcu pamiatku umučených velikášov židovstva a 110,000 občanov židovského vyznania zo Slovenska 1942-1945 [The Cedars Of Lebanon: In Everlasting Memory of Jewish Leaders and 110,000 Citizens of the Jewish Faith Who Died as Martyrs, 1942-1945]. Published by *Jüdische Kultusgemeinde,* Nitra, 1960-61 (5721). Mimeographed book.

Clementis, Vladimír. *Odkazy z Londýna* [Reports from London]. Bratislava: 1947.

Čulen, K., *Boj Slovákov o slobodu* [The Slovak Fight for Freedom]. Bratislava: 1944.

Czech, D., "*Kalendarz wydarzén w obozie koncentracyjnym Óswiecim-Brzezinka*" [Calendar of Events at the Concentration Camp of Auschwitz-Birkenau], *Zeszyty Oswiecimskie* [Auschwitz Pamphlets], 1960, no. 4.

D. R., "*La Slovacchia e gli Ebrei*" [Slovakia and the Jews], *Relazioni Internazionali* 88 (1942), no. 34.

Dostal, Ludwig A., ed., *Der slowakische Judenkodex* [The Slovak Jewish Code]. Bratislava: 1941.

Dunand, Georges, *Ne perdez pas leur trace!* [Do Not Lose Track of Them]. Neûchatel: 1950.

Ďurica, Milan Stanislav, "Dr. Joseph Tiso and the Jewish Problem in Slovakia," *Slovakia,* VII (1957), no. 3-4, pp. 1-22.

Dzugas, Jozef, *"Postavenie židovského obyvateľstva v normotvorbe slovenskeho štátu v rokoch 1939-1945"* [The Situation of the Jewish Population in the Legislation of the Slovak State], *Právnicke štúdie,* Bratislava: 1967, pp. 349-91.

Fundárek, Jozef, *"Nariadenie o židovských podnikoch vo svetle platného práva, najmä obchodného"* [Ordinance on Jewish Business Concerns in the Light of the Law of the Land, Particularly Commercial Law], *Právny obzor,* Bratislava, XXIV (1941).

Galbavý, Tibor, *"O arizačných nariadeniach"* [The Aryanization Ordinances], *Politika.* Bratislava: 1940.

Goldstein, David, ed., *Chaviva.* Prague: 1947.

Gryzlov, G., *Gardistické inferno* [The Guardist Inferno]. Bratislava: 1958.

Gutachten des Instituts für Zeitgeschichte [Evidence of the Institute for Contemporary History], I, Munich: 1958; II, Stuttgart: 1966.

Hagara, F., *História partizánskych bojov: I. Hornonitrianská partizánská brigáda* [History of the Partisan Fighting: The First Upper Nitra Partisan Brigade], Bratislava-Prievidza: 1946.

Hammer, Oskar; Ziman, Ladislav; and Harmann, Viktor, *Die Rechtsstellung der Juden* [The Legal Status of the Jews]. Bratislava: 1941.

Hausner, Gideon, *Justice in Jerusalem.* New York: 1966.

Holotik, Ludovit, "The Jewish Problem in Slovakia," *East European Quarterly,* 1967, pp. 31-37.

"Jahaduth Czechoslovakia" [Czechoslovak Jewry], *Gesher: Quarterly Review of the Nation's Problems.* Jerusalem: September 1969.

Jelinek, Yeshayahu, "Lochamim Yehudim b'makhaneh Nováky" [Jewish Fighters in Camp Nováky], *Yalkut Moreshet,* 1963, no. 1, pp. 47-67.

———, "The Role of the Jews in Slovak Resistance," *Jahrbücher für Geschichte Osteuropas* 15 (1967), vol. I, pp. 415-22.

"Jews in Czechoslovakia," Reprint from *The Governments in Exile and Their Attitude Towards The Jews,* ed. Z. H. Wachsmann. New York: 1944.

Die Judenausrottung in Polen. Augenzeugenberichte. Dritte Serie. Die Vernichtungslager [The Extermination of the Jews in Poland, Eyewitness Reports, Third Series: The Extermination Camps]. Geneva: 1944.

Kamenec, Ivan, "Vznik a vývoj židovských pracovných táborov a stredísk na Slovensku v rokoch 1942-1944" [The Establishment and Development of the Jewish Labor Camps and Labor Centers in Slovakia], *Nové obzory,* 1966, pp. 15-38.

———, "Židovská otázka a spôsoby jej riešenia v čase autonómie Slovenska" [The Jewish Problem and Methods of Its Solution During the Period of Slovak Autonomy], *Nové obzory,* 1968, pp. 155-80.

———, "Snem Slovenskéj republiky a jeho postoj k problému zidovskeho obyvateľstva na Slovensku v rokoch 1939-1945" [The Parliament of the

Slovak Republic and Its Attitude Toward the Problem of the Jewish Population of Slovakia, 1939-1945], *Historický časopis.* Bratislava: 1969, pp. 329-62.

Kempner, W., *Eichmann und Komplizen* [Eichmann and His Accomplices]. Zurich: 1961.

Kirschbaum, J., *Slovakia: Nation at the Crossroads of Central Europe.* New York: 1960.

Kizlink, K., and Ralis, O., "Príspevky k výkladu zákona o židovských podnikoch 113/1940 Sl.z." [Articles Explaining the Law on Jewish Business Concerns], vol. VII, *Hospodárstvo a právo,* Bratislava.

Knieža, Emil, "The Resistance of Slovak Jews," in Yuri Suhl, ed., *They Fought Back: The Story of the Jewish Resistance in Nazi Europe.* New York: 1966, pp. 176-81.

———, "Hapraklitut hamamlachit maishima" [Indictment of the Public Prosecutor's Office], *Yalkut Moreshet,* 1966, pp. 107-14.

Langbein, R., *Der Auschwitz-Prozess: Eine Dokumentation* [The Auschwitz Trial: A Documentation], vol. I. Vienna: 1965.

Lazar, Arnold (Bumi), "Reminiscences from Fascist Slovakia," *Yad Vashem Bulletin,* no. 18 (1966), pp. 17-25.

Lettrich, J., *The History of Modern Slovakia.* New York: 1955.

Lévai, Eugene, *Black Book on the Martyrdom of Hungarian Jewry.* Zurich: 1948.

Lipscher, Ladislav, "Ein Evangelischer Pfarrer—Retter der verfolgten jüdischen Kinder in der Slowakei während des 2. Weltkrieges" [An Evangelical Pastor, Rescuer of Persecuted Jewish Children in Slovakia during World War II], *Leben und Glauben,* Laupen (Bern), June 26, 1971.

———, "La participation des Juïfs slovaques à la lutte armée pendant la deuxième guerre mondiale" [The Participation of Slovak Jews in the Armed Struggle during World War II], *Le monde juif,* no. 62, (1971), pp. 14-19.

———, "Die Einflussnahme des Dritten Reiches auf die Judenpolitik der slowakischen Regierung" [The Influence of the Third Reich on the Policy of the Slovak Government Toward the Jews], *Das Jahr 1945 in der Tschechoslowakei. Internationale, nationale und wirtschaftlich-soziale Probleme* [The Year 1945 in Czechoslovakia. International, National and Socio-economic Problems], ed. Karl Bosl. Munich: 1971, pp. 139-57.

Liptak, Lubomír, *Ovládnutie slovenského priemyslu nemeckým kapitálom 1939-1945* [The Control of Slovak Industry by German Capital, 1939-1945]. Bratislava: 1960.

Magyar, Viktor, *Slovenské židovské zákony a ich vysvetlenie* [The Slovak Anti-Jewish Laws and their Explanation]. Nitra: 1939.

Morávek, Augustín, *Príručka pre dôverníkov, dočasných správcov a arizátorov* [Handbook for Custodians, Temporary Administrators and Aryanizers]. Bratislava: 1940.

Mordowicz, Betsalel, "Twice in Auschwitz," *Yalkut Moreshet,* no. 9 (1968), pp. 7-20.

Nemec, Pavel, "Spomienky z bojov v Nitrianskej doline" [Reminiscences of the Fighting in the Nitra Valley], *Tribúna,* Bratislava, August 29, 1947, no. 17.

Neumann, Jirmejahu Oskar, *Im Schatten des Todes: Ein Tatsachenbericht vom Schicksalskampf des slowakischen Judentums* [In the Shadow of Death: A Factual Report of the Fateful Struggle of Slovak Jewry]. Tel Aviv: *Olamenu,* 1956.

———, *Gisi Fleischmann: The Story of A Heroic Woman.* Tel Aviv: 1970; German edition: *Gisi Fleischmann, die Geschichte einer Kämpferin.* Tel Aviv: 1970.

Nir, Akiba, *Shvilim b'maagal haEsch* [Paths Within A Ring of Fire]. Merhavia: 1967.

"Osudy jednej vojenskej misie na povstaleckom Slovensku" [Fate of A Military Mission in Insurgent Slovakia], *Tribúna,* Bratislava, August 29, 1947.

Pillon, Cesare, "Keď sa ticho podobá spoluvine. Pius XII. a Tiso. Milovaný syn deportuje židov" [When Silence Is Tantamount to Complicity. Pius XII and Tiso. The "Beloved Son" Deports the Jews], *Predvoj,* Bratislava, April 1, 1965.

Pohl, O., "Die Slowakei löst die Judenfrage" [Slovakia Solves the Jewish Problem], *Nation und Staat* 15 (1941-1942).

Pokorný, Ctibor, *Židovstvo na Slovensku* [Slovak Jewry]. Martin: 1940.

Polakovič, S., *K základom slovenského štátu* [On the Basic Principles of the Slovak State]. Martin: 1939.

———, *Slovenský národný sozializmus* [Slovak National Socialism]. Bratislava: 1941.

Process Dr. J. Tisom, Dr. F. Durčanským and A. Machom v Bratislave v dňoch 2. decembra 1946-15. aprila 1947 [The Trial of Dr. Jozef Tiso, Dr. Ferdinand Durčanský and Alexander Mach, December 2, 1946, to April 15, 1947], vol. 5. Bratislava: 1947.

"Rapport du Dr. Frederic Steiner, Bratislava" [Report of Dr. Frederick Steiner, of Bratislava], *Les Juifs en Europe (1939-1945). Rapports présentés à la première conférence européenne des commissions historiques et des centres des documentations juifs* [The Jews in Europe, 1939-1945. Reports presented at the First European Conference of Jewish Historical Commissions and Documentation Centers]. Paris: 1949.

Rašla, Anton, *Tiso a povstanie. Dokumenty* [Tiso and the Uprising: Documents]. Bratislava: 1947.

Reitlinger, Gerald, *The Final Solution.* London: 1968.

Riedler, Gejza, *Zakon o židovských podnikoch a o židoch zamestnaných v podnikoch a iné predpisy o arizácií* [The Law on Jewish Business Concerns and Jewish Employees in the Concerns and Additional Laws on Aryanization]. Bratislava: 1940.

Rothkirchen, Livia, *The Destruction of Slovak Jewry: A Documentary History* [Hebrew and English sections]. Jerusalem: 1961.

————, "Vatican Policy and the Jewish Problem in 'Independent' Slovakia (1939-1945)," *Yad Vashem Studies on the European Jewish Catastrophe and Resistance,* VI (1967), pp. 27-53.

Sedláková, M., *Krycie meno Jozef, O zločinoch príslušníkov POHG. Reportáže, proces, dokumenty* [Pseudonym: Joseph. On the Crimes of the Members of the POHG. Reports, Trial, Documents]. Bratislava: 1958.

Sefer hapartisanim hayehudim [The Book of the Jewish Partisans]. Merhavia: 1958.

Sefer HaShomer HaTzair. Kerekh Alef. HaTnuah Me-reshita v'ad l'ahar mered hagetaot [HaShomer HaTzair Book, Vol. I, The Organization from its Beginnings Until After the Ghetto Revolts]. Merhavia: 1956.

Senčak, Michal, *Súpis židovského majetku podľa nariadenia s mocou zákona c. 203/40 Sl.z.* [The Levy on Jewish Property in Accordance With Law Ordinance Z. 203/40 Slovak Law Gazette]. Bratislava: 1940.

Sidor, Karol, *Šest rokov pri Vatikáne* [Six Years in the Vatican]. Scranton, Pa.: 1947.

Steinberg, Lucien, "Le rôle des Juïfs de Tchecoslovaquie dans la guerre antinazi" [The Role of the Jews of Czechoslovakia in the Anti-Nazi War], *Le monde juïf,* no. 11 (1967), pp. 17-22.

Steiner, Bedrich, ed., *Tragedia slovenských Židov. Fotografie a dokumenty* [The Tragedy of the Slovak Jews. Photographs and Documents]. Bratislava: 1949.

Tartakowskij, B., *Smert i žizň rjadom* [Death and Life in One Column]. Moscow: 1963.

Vašek, Anton, *Protižidovské zákonodarstvo na Slovensku* [Anti-Jewish Legislation in Slovakia]. Bratislava: 1942.

Vnuk, F., *Neuveriteľné sprisahanie. Vojenské politicke akcie proti Slovenskéj republike v roku 1944* [The Incredible Conspiracy: Military and Political Activities Against the Slovak Republic in 1944]. Middletown, Pa.: 1964.

Vrba, Rudolf and Bestic, Alan, *I Cannot Forgive.* London: 1963; New York: 1964.

Weissberg, Alex, *Desperate Mission: Joel Brand's Story.* New York: 1958.

THE ANNIHILATION OF CZECHOSLOVAK JEWRY*

Erich Kulka

After the fall of the Czechoslovak Republic the now truncated state came under the jurisdiction of three new masters. Each of them proceeded—at least for some time—in a different measure to bring about the "Final Solution of the Jewish problem."

Those Jews who still lived in the Sudeten areas ceded to Germany after the Munich agreement became subject to the Nuremberg racial laws immediately after the annexation of these territories by the Reich. After the occupation of the rest of Bohemia and Moravia on March 15, 1939, the government of the Protectorate of Bohemia and Moravia attempted to solve its "Jewish problem" by enacting its own discriminatory legislation. Soon, however, the ruling personages in the Protectorate had to learn that in this, as in everything else, the framing of decisions and policies was to be a prerogative of the German overlords, who soon took over every phase of planning and carrying out the removal and decimation of the 118,000 Jews who were then living in the Protectorate.[1]

Of the 136,000 Jews living on the territory proclaimed on March 14, 1939, as the independent Slovak state, about 40,000 found themselves under Hungarian jurisdiction following the "Vienna award" of November 1938 as did also the 102,000 Jews of Subcarpathian Ruthenia, the easternmost part of Czechoslovakia. The 96,000 Jews who remained under the jurisdiction of the Slovak state became

---

* The research for this article was made possible by a grant from The Memorial Foundation for Jewish Culture, New York.

subject to a Jewish Code, which was adopted by the Slovak government and which in some respects was even more stringent and cruel than the laws then in force in Germany proper. Though given greater freedom of action than some other Nazi satellites, the Slovak government cooperated very closely with the German authorities in all matters connected with the deportation of the Jews. The Hungarian government, on the other hand, resisted for a long time the German pressures demanding the deportation of Hungarian Jews to the East, and limited its cooperation with Germany to the drafting of Jewish men into forced labor units used in Hungarian labor camps and on the battlefront. Only in April 1944 was the Hungarian government finally forced to accede to the German demands for the concentration of Jews in camps and ghettos, from where they were to be deported, with the assistance of Hungarian gendarmes, to Auschwitz.[2]

THE PROTECTORATE OF BOHEMIA AND MORAVIA

Emigration

Three months after the proclamation of the Protectorate of Bohemia and Moravia, SS Hauptsturmführer Adolf Eichmann came to Prague. He represented the Department for Jewish Affairs in the *Reichssicherheitshauptamt* (RSHA, the central security office of the Reich government) in Berlin, and his task was to organize the "solution of the Jewish problem" in Bohemia and Moravia. His first official act was to establish a branch of the *Zentralstelle für jüdische Auswanderung* (Central Office for Jewish Emigration), which began to function on July 22, 1939, in the district of Střešovice in Prague. The declared aim of the *Zentralstelle* was the registration of Jews for purposes of emigration, and the entire apparatus of the Jewish Religious Congregation in Prague was to be at the disposal of the *Zentralstelle* in the fulfillment of this task.

During this initial period, the purpose of deporting the Jews was not yet to exterminate them but merely to remove them from the German *Lebensraum* (living space). But the ever-increasing radicalization of the steps taken against Jews was, in fact, a chain of actions which logically led to a "final solution" through physical annihilation.

In the fall of 1940, an *Umschulungslager* (vocational retraining camp) was established under the supervision of the SS on a large country estate at Česká Lípa in southeastern Bohemia. Jews who had been dismissed from their former places of employment were sent to this estate, which had been confiscated from its former Jewish owner. Initially, conditions in this camp were relatively tolerable. However, after the outbreak of war with the Soviet Union in the summer of 1941 the regime at Česká Lípa became as tough and inhuman as that in the concentration camps. Some of the inmates were assigned to work on the estate of Panenské Břežany, then the residence of Reinhard Heydrich, who had been appointed acting Reich Protector for Bohemia and Moravia in September 1941. In 1943 the Česká Lípa camp was liquidated and its inmates—totaling about 550—were deported to Terezín.[3]

Outside Prague, the *Zentralstelle* exercised pressure on the Jewish population through the Gestapo apparatus. Two cases in point were recorded in detail. These records were eventually discovered in the archives of the Czechoslovak Ministry for Internal Affairs in Prague. Both cases bear eloquent witness to the manner in which the expulsion of Jews from areas outside Prague began:

On August 22, 1939, the Chairman of the Jewish Religious Congregation in the district of Pelhřimov received oral instructions from the Gestapo in Německý Brod to arrange without delay the liquidation of all Jewish property within a fortnight and the removal of the Jews and their families from the district to Prague within the same time limit. The District President (*okresní hejtman*) contacted the *Oberlandrat* [county administrator] in Německý Brod and was informed that the *Oberlandrat* would intervene personally with the Gestapo, that the time limit would probably be extended, and that the Gestapo would receive detailed instructions about how to liquidate Jewish property . . .

On August 6, 1939, a meeting took place on the premises of the Jewish Religious Congregation of České Budějovice, during which Rabbi Dr. Ferda informed those present that on the morning of August 5 he had been summoned to the Gestapo and had been ordered

1) to arrange for the emigration of all Jews to other countries;

2) to arrange for the removal (of all Jews) to Prague immediately, within twenty-four hours;

3) to see that every Jew would report at the Gestapo headquarters before his or her departure.

When the rabbi objected, explaining in detail why emigration in such haste would be impossible, Gestapo Commissioner Zimert insisted that the order had to be obeyed unconditionally.

Frightened and intimidated, the persecuted Jews desperately cast about for possibilities of emigration. By October 1941 about 20 percent of the total Jewish population of the Protectorate had left.* The efforts of the majority, however, were frustrated by the fact that they had no possibilities of securing immigration visas to other countries. The Evian conference called on the initiative of the United States in July 1938 had already shown the unreadiness of the free countries to receive Jewish refugees from Nazi terror.[4]

Immediately after the outbreak of war, in September 1939, many officers and board members of the Jewish Religious Congregations in the Protectorate were taken hostage. Most of them were transferred to the concentration camp of Buchenwald. In 1942 those who were still alive were deported to Auschwitz.

Nisko

By their conquest of Polish territory, the Germans gained space in which to concentrate the masses of Jews. On the basis of Hitler's order "to carry out, first of all, the *Umschichtung* ["regrouping"] of 300,000 destitute Jews from the Ostmark [i.e., Austria] and the Protectorate,"[5] Heinrich Himmler on October 8, 1939, ordered the deportation of Jews to an area between the rivers Bug and Vistula in the German sector of Poland. The implementation of this order was begun by Adolf Eichmann, as head of the *Zentralstelle für jüdische Auswanderung*. Already on October 9, Eichmann had met in Katowice with Fitzner, the head of the civil administration, and Wehrmacht General von Knobelsdorf and negotiated with them the creation of an "agricultural reservation" near Nisko, a small town on the river San, south of Lublin.[6] Before the deportations began, Jakub Edelstein, as the representative of the Jewish Religious Congregation of Prague, was summoned to Nisko to be told there by Eichmann that the Jews from the Protectorate would be transferred to that depopulated area.[7]

On October 12, 1939, a train carrying construction material left Moravská Ostrava for Nisko. The Jewish Religious Congregations of Ostrava and Frýdek were ordered by the Gestapo to register

---

* Since March 15, 1939.

without delay all Jewish males between the ages of sixteen and seventy. This registration order was published in the local press, along with a summons to all the registered individuals to report on October 17 at the Ostrava Hippodrome, from where they would be sent to a "retraining center." That same evening a transport of 1,000 men was dispatched from Ostrava. It arrived at Nisko on October 19. The deportees were met at the railroad station by a unit of the *Totenkopfverbände* (Death's Head Units) and escorted from Nisko to the hamlet of Zarcze, about ten kilometers from Nisko, where a group of German engineers and artisans had started to build a camp. Also working on the camp site were Jews who had been deported earlier from Vienna. Guarded by SS men, they were preparing the grounds and putting up barracks and barbed-wire fences. Nevertheless, the new arrivals found that no accommodations were ready for them, nor was there material from which to build them. As a result, they had to sleep in the nearby woods in the cold and rainy fall weather. Confronted by 1,000 deportees without accommodations, the SS commanders at Nisko wanted to rid themselves of this unwanted surplus humanity. Since the river San, on which Nisko was located, was then part of the demarcation line between the German and Soviet sectors of Poland, the SS bigwigs selected about 600 men from the transport who were then driven by SS guards with whips and at gunpoint to the Soviet border. Many were killed, others died of exhaustion. Those who managed to reach the Soviet zone were interrogated and registered by the Soviet authorities. Most of the deportees were allotted places to stay in Galicia and Volhynia, where they were put to work on farms. Some volunteered for work in mines.

On October 26, 1939, a second transport, numbering 291 men, was sent to Nisko from Ostrava. This transport included fifty Jews who had been brought to Ostrava from the Spielberg Gestapo prison in Brno.[8] However, the camp at Nisko was not yet ready for them, so, once again, a part of the transport was driven over the demarcation line into the Soviet zone. One such group came, via Lwow, to the village of Vítkov, where employment and shelter were arranged for them by members of the local Jewish community.[9] The inhuman toil and brutal treatment drove additional inmates of the Nisko camp to seek asylum in the Soviet sector. They escaped individually and in groups whenever they saw an opportunity to do so. On the Russian side of the river San many of these escapees were caught by Soviet patrols and handed over to the NKVD. After harsh interrogations, which in some cases dragged out over many months, they were sentenced to terms of three to eight years at hard labor for "illegal entry" or "suspected espionage" and sent to labor camps in Siberia, the Ural mountains, and the Archangelsk area. In the spring and summer of 1940 most of the escapees from Nisko who had been placed by the Soviets into Galicia and Volhynia were also deported to those labor camps.[10] Following Hitler's attack on the Soviet Union and Moscow's entry into the war on the side of the Allies, an amnesty was proclaimed for Czechoslovak citizens imprisoned in the Soviet Union. Those who had survived the hardships of the Soviet labor camps were eventually given an opportunity to join Czechoslovak armed units which had been formed in the Soviet Union early in 1942. Among those who helped to form the First Czechoslovak Field Battalion at Buzuluk there were some 300 who had escaped from Nisko. They participated in the battles for the liberation of Czechoslovakia and about 130 of them returned to Czechoslovakia after the war.[11]

The Nazi "resettlement project" at Nisko failed. On April 13, 1940, the camp was abandoned and most of the remaining inmates were sent back to truncated Silesia and to Vienna. One reason for Eichmann's failure at Nisko was that the Nazis had been unable to clear the area of its original non-Jewish population. Opposed to the influx of Jewish deportees, these "old-timers" had lodged protests with Gestapo headquarters in Lublin. The Gestapo found the protests to be consistent with the aims of Dr. Hans Frank, the governor general of Poland's German sector, who did everything to make his *Generalgouvernement judenrein* as soon as possible. Also, Eichmann's "resettlement" project did not have sufficient support from Heydrich, who from the very beginning advocated a radical liquidation of the Jews.

A total of approximately 4,000 Jewish men from Vienna, the Těšín area, Katowice, Bielsko, and the Protectorate of Bohemia and Moravia had been brought to Nisko. Some of these had perished in the camp. Others had been driven or had escaped into the Soviet sector and the rest sent back to their homes after the camp had been liquidated. About 400 men from the two transports returned to Ostrava in April 1940. They were assigned to hard labor in the

Ostrava region, and in 1942 they were transported first to the Terezín ghetto and finally to the extermination camps in Eastern Europe.

GHETTOIZATION: TRANSPORTS TO LODZ AND MINSK

The outbreak of war with the Soviet Union in June 1941 signaled the end of any inhibitions the Germans might have felt initially regarding the implementation of Hitler's threats to exterminate the Jews of Europe.[12] The decisive step was Herman Göring's order of July 31, 1941, to Reinhard Heydrich, then chief of the *Sicherheitspolizei* (Security Police), saying explicitly:

> As supplement to the task which was entrusted to you in the decree dated January 24, 1939, to solve the Jewish question by emigration and evacuation in the most favorable way possible, given by present conditions, I herewith commission you to carry out all necessary preparations with regard to organizational, substantive, and financial viewpoints for a total solution of the Jewish question in the German sphere of influence in Europe. Insofar as the competencies of other central organizations are hereby affected, these are to be involved. I further commission you to submit to me promptly an overall plan showing the preliminary organizational, substantive, and financial measures for the execution of the intended final solution of the Jewish question.[13]

This order practically put an end to all possibilities for emigration, both legal and "illegal." Nevertheless, the *Zentralstelle für jüdische Auswanderung* kept increasing pressures to hasten the registration of the Jewish population. In Poland, where pogroms were not infrequent, Jews were expelled from the cities to small towns and villages. They were concentrated mainly in the Lublin region where the first transports of Jews from other German-occupied countries had already begun to arrive. A similar fate awaited the Jewish population of Bohemia and Moravia.

The decision to effect the "Final Solution" was set forth at a conference held in Prague on October 17, 1941, under the chairmanship of Heydrich. The records of this conference, which were classified as *"Geheime Reichssache"* (Reich Secret), include the following note on the "Jewish problem":

> In the meantime the Jews of Bohemia and Moravia are being gathered in a transit camp for evacuation. For this purpose, the representative of

Reichswehr assigned to the Reich Protector has cleared Terezín completely of all units of the German army. The Czechs have been told to move elsewhere. Terezín can comfortably absorb 50–60,000 Jews. From there they will be transported to the East. Minsk and Riga have already agreed to take 50,000 Jews each. After the complete evacuation of all Jews, Terezín will become a faultlessly-planned German settlement and a center of German life . . . Under no circumstances must even the smallest detail about these plans reach the public . . .

Elsewhere, the records mention the start of the deportation of 5,000 Jews from Prague to Lodz, Poland, pursuant to a decision taken at an earlier conference on October 10, 1941.[14]

On November 6, 1941, in an attempt to avert the deportation of Jews from the Protectorate to Eastern Europe, representatives of the Jewish Religious Congregation in Prague submitted to Eichmann a detailed memorandum concerning a suggested "ghettoization of Jews within the Protectorate of Bohemia and Moravia." Eichmann accepted the plan with certain modifications, and on November 24 a hand-picked group of 342 Jewish men left Prague for Terezín with a transport marked A.K. for *Aufbaukommando* (Construction Detail).[15]

Between October 16 and November 3, 1941, even before the creation of the Terezín ghetto, five trainloads with 5,000 men, women, and children had been sent from Prague to the East. Of these 5,000, only 253 survived.[16] The transports went to the ghetto of Lodz, the well-known center of Poland's prewar textile industry. The new arrivals from Prague were permitted to keep their luggage and valuables and were placed into dilapidated buildings in a suburb of Lodz which became part of the ghetto. Several families lived together in one apartment, sometimes as many as thirty persons in one room. Initially the Jews from Prague were not assigned to productive work and, as a consequence, their food rations were minimal. Only those who had money were able to buy additional food for exorbitant prices on the black market. Sanitary facilities were primitive, medical aid was very limited, medicines and drugs were scarce, and hospitals were overcrowded. Typhoid fever patients were often left in one room together with healthy people. Of the 5,000 deportees from Prague more than 1,200 died within six months of their arrival at Lodz.[17]

When the five transports from Prague first arrived, the ghetto of

Lodz had a population of 145,000. There were 10,000 Jews from Germany and 5,000 from Austria; all the others were Polish Jews, who held all the leading positions in the ghetto. The inmates were placed into about sixty different workshops, where they were engaged in the production of linen, ready-made dresses, footwear, leather goods, carpets, and small parts for equipment used by the German army.

The ghetto of Lodz was founded in February 1940 and liquidated in the fall of 1944. The highest number of inmates in Lodz at any one time was 170,000. They were guarded by about 600 SS men, commanded by *Amtsleiter* Hans Biebow, who was in charge of the ghetto and who in turn was responsible to the German mayor of Lodz. Both men profited financially from the ghetto, and so, thanks to Biebow's machinations, did the SS. Biebow had an excellent reputation among the Nazi bigwigs and it is known that Heydrich intended to appoint him commandant of the Terezín ghetto.[18]

Internally, however, the ghetto of Lodz was ruled by a Jewish dictator, Mordechai Chaim Rumkowski, who before the war had been the director of a Jewish orphanage. He proved to be a reliable tool of Biebow and managed to remain chairman of the Lodz *Judenrat* ("Council of Jews," literally, "Jew Council") during the entire period of the ghetto's existence. While displaying devotion and absolute subservience to Biebow, Rumkowski kept searching for ways of staving off the threatening catastrophe of liquidation. He succeeded in organizing production in the ghetto so that its maintenance should become a matter of vital interest to the German army. He was supported in this effort by Biebow, who had his own vested interest in ghetto labor, and whenever the SS renewed its pressure for the liquidation of the ghetto, Biebow used the Wehrmacht's influence to obtain a postponement.

Rumkowski enjoyed special personal privileges. He lived in a villa, had a car, and was authorized to handle special funds. The currency of the Lodz ghetto bore his signature, and the ghetto stamps were engraved with his portrait. He was the recognized and feared "king" of the ghetto. But in the end he, too, perished, together with his family, in the gas chambers of Auschwitz. Rumkowski was the only one to be shot by the SS in the courtyard in front of the crematoria after being forced to look on while the bodies of the gassed inmates from Lodz were cremated in the cremation ditches. Biebow ended on the gallows in the ghetto he had ruled for years through Rumkowski.

Gradually, about 1,500 men and women from the Prague transports were integrated into the labor force of the Lodz ghetto. From time to time, smaller labor details were assigned to jobs entailing hard physical work outside the ghetto. In one such group, which drained swamps near Poznaň under the constant supervision of SS guards, there were fifty men from Prague. Only one of these fifty survived.

Those ghetto inmates not assigned to work in the ghetto industry were registered separately along with children, the aged, and the sick. From time to time, inmates in this category were "evacuated." In the spring of 1942, some 7,000 of them were taken by train to the railroad station of Kutno, from where they were driven in sealed trucks in the direction of the Chelmno extermination camp. While still on the way to Chelmno, they were all killed by exhaust fumes let into the trucks from the truck motors.

At the end of August 1942, a *Generalsperre* (embargo) was imposed upon the Lodz ghetto. All production was stopped for a week and food rations were sharply reduced. SS mobile killing squads entered the ghetto and raided workshop after workshop, house after house. All the inmates, including children, had to appear before a special "selection committee." Women and children tried to flee into the fields or to hide in the cellars of dilapidated buildings but SS men pursued them, using dogs to ferret them out, and shot them on the spot. About 17,000 prisoners who were classed as unfit for work were loaded onto trucks and taken to the extermination camps of Chelmno and Maidanek. Among them were over 1,000 men, women, and children who had come to Lodz from Prague.

After this bloody purge, the Lodz ghetto lived through a period of comparative quiet until the spring of 1944. In May of that year, about 14,000 men and women were sent to work in munitions plants inside Germany proper. In one transport of 1,000 women sent to work in a munitions plant of HASAG (Hugo Schneider Aktiengesellschaft) there were about 100 women from Prague. One of the few who survived this experience testified about the inhuman conditions under which these women worked and died.[19] Early in June 1944, six hundred men were sent to work in the iron works of Czestochowa; of these, fifty were from the Prague transports.

The final liquidation of the Lodz ghetto began at the end of June 1944. The Germans wanted to keep the ghetto from falling into the hands of the advancing Red Army, as had already been the case with the Lublin ghetto and the Maidanek camp. At that time the population of the Lodz ghetto was still approximately 70,000, some 1,200 of whom had come with the transports from Prague. Between July and the beginning of September, the deportation trains from Lodz to Auschwitz followed one another in rapid succession. The railroad siding at Birkenau led straight to the crematoria. On arrival in Auschwitz, all the prisoners went through a strict "selection." Three-quarters of those who came to Auschwitz from Lodz ended up in the gas chambers.[20]

Within two weeks those who had not been "selected" for death in the gas chambers were transported to Germany proper for hard labor. Among these were some 300 men and women from the Prague transports. Only 870 prisoners were left in the Lodz ghetto to liquidate the ghetto industries and to help in preparations for the shipment of unused raw materials and products to Germany so that they should not fall into the hands of the Soviet army. Lodz was occupied by Soviet forces on January 19, 1945. Among those liberated in the ghetto there were also nine men from Prague. An additional 244 men and women from the Prague transports were liberated at the camps of Dachau, Kauferring, Mauthausen, Bergen Belsen, and Oranienburg. The personal accounts of some survivors have been preserved.[21] The life and sufferings of Czech Jews in Lodz found literary expression in a novel by František Kafka, one of the ghetto inmates, who after the war was to become president of the Jewish Religious Congregation of Prague.[22]

In many respects the autonomous internal administration of the Lodz ghetto was similar to that known in Terezín.[23] Wages were paid with specially printed ghetto bank notes which were used as currency inside the ghetto. There were a bank, a post office, a Jewish ghetto police, and a prison. There were also cultural activities, though on a much more limited scale than in Terezín. The transports from Prague included artists, such as the conductor Kurt Beer, the opera singer Rudolf Bandler, and the writer Oskar Singer. Singer, who worked on the Lodz ghetto newspaper, was killed in Auschwitz. The economist Bernhard Heilig worked in the ghetto archives. Lectures were delivered by such academicians as the mathematician Ludwig Berwald, formerly professor at the German University in Prague, and Dr. Emil Krakauer, the rabbi of Mikulov (Nikolsburg), Moravia.[24]

STATISTICS OF DEPORTEES FROM PRAGUE TO LODZ

Date of Transport	Men	Women	Children	Total No. Deportees	Total No. Survivors
10/16/1941	473	390	137	1,000	25
10/21/1941	520	393	87	1,000	76
10/26/1941	429	487	84	1,000	52
10/31/1941	448	482	70	1,000	60
11/3/1941	442	468	90	1,000	40
Total	2,312	2,220	468	5,000	253 (= 5 percent)

The five transports from Prague had been ordered by Lieutenant General Kurt Daluege, the chief of the *Ordnungspolizei* (regular German police).[25] Daluege also signed the deportation order for a sixth transport, which consisted of 1,000 Jews from Brno and was sent not to Lodz but to Minsk. This transport—376 men, 515 women, and 109 children—arrived in Minsk on November 20, 1941. The day before, there had been a bloody pogrom in the Minsk ghetto. When war broke out between Germany and the Soviet Union, Minsk, the capital of Belorussia, had a Jewish population of over 80,000. The Germans created two ghettos in Minsk. Ghetto No. 1 held over 100,000 Polish and Russian Jews, who were systematically liquidated by SS killing squads. Ghetto No. 2 was much smaller; it consisted of deportees from Germany, Vienna, and Brno, about 7,500 men, women, and children. The SS command established an autonomous Jewish administration headed by the *Judenälteste* (Jewish Elder) Edgar Frank, a deportee from Hamburg. Men, women, and children all lived under one roof. Each person had a living space of about three square meters; there were neither beds nor pallets so that all the inmates had to sleep on the floor of the barracks. There was no electricity and a dire shortage of water and doctors. As a result of these conditions, 700 persons died within two weeks after their arrival.

Time and again the two ghettos were surrounded by SS units, which after "selecting" their victims would drive them in trucks to an open area outside the town and shoot them there. Later, SS men would load inmates onto hermetically sealed trucks and drive them to a wooded area outside Minsk. In these trucks, which became known as *dušegubky* ("soul-destroyers"), the inmates were killed on the way by exhaust gases piped into the vans. In the woods, the bodies were removed from the trucks by an inmate burial detail, dumped into ditches which had been dug in advance, and covered with earth.

These killing operations caused a rapid decrease in the number of inmates in Ghetto No. 1. For some time, Ghetto No. 2 was spared from a similar fate thanks to an SS officer, Wilhelm Kube, who, having learned from Edgar Frank that the Jews deported to this ghetto included men who held decorations for bravery from World War I, reported this fact to Berlin. Kube also saved many Jews by assigning them to jobs with German production firms that worked for the German army and maintained workshops near Minsk. However, the situation deteriorated after a visit to Minsk from Reinhard Heydrich. Heydrich reprimanded Kube for having sent him a list entitled "Jews Deported From Germany In Violation of The Law."[26] After Heydrich's departure, mass killing operations were begun also in Ghetto No. 2. About 2,600 men and women survived—mostly those who happened to be on work assignments outside the ghetto while the killing operation went on. At the end of November 1943 the Soviet army was approaching the Minsk region. Both of the ghettos were liquidated. Of all the inmates of Ghetto No. 2 the only survivors were 200 men who had been sent from Minsk to Warsaw to help clear away the rubble left by bombing raids. These men were subsequently dragged from one concentration camp in Germany to another. The few who survived these horrors were eventually liberated by the British in Bergen Belsen. Of the 1,000 men, women, and children who had been brought to Minsk from Brno, only eleven survived the war.

The adoption of the plan for the ghettoization of Terezín put a temporary stop to direct transports to the East. By order of the Gestapo, Jews from Bohemia and Moravia were concentrated in the larger towns and cities of the Protectorate. From there they were sent by train to Bohušovice to be escorted by gendarmes to Terezín, two kilometers away. The total number of Jews deported to Terezín from Bohemia and Moravia was 73,608. After June 1942 transports began to arrive in Terezín also from Germany, Austria, and Holland. A total of 139,654 Jews were deported to Terezín from various parts of Nazi-held Europe.

A separate study in this volume deals with life in Terezín.[27] The present study deals only with Terezín inmates who were deported from Terezín to the East.

It should be noted that one more transport was sent to the East, even after the establishment of the Terezín ghetto. This transport left not from Terezín but from Prague, on June 10, 1942. One thousand Jews were mercilessly snatched from their homes during the night as "punishment" for the assassination of Reinhard Heydrich by Czech resistance fighters on May 29, 1942. The transport passed through Lublin, where men between the ages of sixteen and fifty were taken off the train. The rest were taken to the extermination camp of Sobibor, where they were killed in the gas chambers. Of the men "selected" in Lublin, 120, the hardiest in the group, were sent to Ujazdow, one of the many JULAGs[28] (*Judenarbeitslager*, or labor camps for Jews) in the area of the Lublin "reservation" for Jews. At the time there were in Ujazdow about 2,000 Jews from Germany, Holland, Slovakia, and Prague who were working on swamp drainage projects in the vicinity. At the camps they had to sleep on the floor of their barracks, without blankets, their clothes often soaked by rain. Exhausted by the long daily journey from the camp to the swamps and back, many of them collapsed at work and were brought back to the camp by their fellow inmates at the end of the day, more dead than alive.

At the beginning of October 1942, a typhoid epidemic broke out at Ujazdow. The sick were moved into a special barrack, where they were left to die without medical help. One of the inmates overheard an SS officer reporting to the SS command post over the telephone that preparations for the transport of inmates to the Sobibor extermination camp were about to be completed. That night this inmate escaped from Ujazdow. He was the only one in the final transport from Prague to survive the war and to testify about the fate of all the others.[29]

With this final transport, the number of Jews deported from the Protectorate of Bohemia and Moravia directly to the East reached 7,000. Of these, 265, or 3.8 percent, survived.

Deportation from Terezín to the Baltic Region

As part of the preparations ordered by Göring's letter of July 31, 1941, Heydrich worked out a general plan for the deportation of Jews from German-dominated areas. It turned out that the manpower and facilities at the disposal of the SS formations and the police were no longer sufficient for mass liquidations. Help had to be secured from most of the other official agencies whose involvement in the "Final Solution" up to that point had been only indirect. To this end, Heydrich called a conference for December 8, 1941. However, this meeting had to be postponed for a month because one of the officials invited, whose presence Heydrich regarded as particularly important, had been unable to arrive in time. This was SS Sturmbannführer Fritz Lange, commander of the security police in Lithuania, who was then busy directing the first mass killing operations against 30,000 Jews concentrated in the ghettos of Riga and Kovno. The conference took place on January 20, 1942, at the central office of Interpol in the Berlin suburb of Gross-Wannsee. It was attended by representatives of nine ministries and five main branches of the SS and police.

In his opening address, Heydrich reviewed the progress of Jewish emigration since 1933 and plans for the "forced emigration" of the Jews. He pointed out that these projects had been affected by various developments and that the war with the Soviet Union had opened new possibilities "for the final solution of the Jewish problem in the German sphere of influence." He formulated these possibilities as follows:

> Under appropriate direction, in the course of the final solution, the Jews are now to be suitably assigned to labor in the East. In big labor gangs, with the sexes separated, Jews capable of work will be brought to these areas, employed in roadbuilding, in which task a large part will undoubtedly disappear through natural diminution.
>
> The remnant that may eventually remain, being undoubtedly the part most capable of resistance, will have to be appropriately dealt with, since it

represents a natural selection and in the event of release is to be regarded as the germ cell of a Jewish renewal. (Witness the experience of history).

In the course of the practical implementation of the final solution, Europe is to be combed from west to east. The Reich area, including the Protectorate of Bohemia and Moravia, will have to be handled in advance, if only because of the housing problem and other socio-political necessities.

The evacuated Jews will first be brought, group by group, into so-called transit ghettos, to be transported from there farther to the East.[30]

Even if Heydrich did not spell it out explicitly, it must have been clear to all participants at the Wannsee conference that they were in fact being introduced to a plan for the complete physical extermination of the Jewish people, and that they would be expected to play an active part in its implementation. Heydrich concealed, especially from the representatives of various ministries, the fact that the extermination of Jews had already been going on since the fall of 1941 at ghettos and camps set up in the German-occupied territories of Poland, the Baltic states, and the Soviet Union. At the time of the Wannsee conference hundreds of thousands of Jews were already being massacred by SS *Einsatzgruppen* (mobile killing squads) and asphyxiated by exhaust fumes in sealed trucks and at Chelmno, the first of the extermination camps. At the same time work on the erection of four other extermination camps and four up-to-date "liquidation projects" at Auschwitz-Birkenau was in full swing.[31]

The deportations first mentioned by Heydrich at the Wannsee conference had already begun during the first half of January 1942, when the first 2,000 prisoners from the ghetto of Terezín left for Riga in two transports. The first transport consisting of 1,000 men, women, and children had arrived at Riga's Skirotava railroad station on January 13. They were all taken to the Riga ghetto. The original ghetto, with a population of about 40,000 Jews, had been liquidated in November and December 1941. The new ghetto was divided into two sectors. One sector held some 6,000 Lithuanian Jews who had survived the massacre of the old ghetto. The second sector contained, at the end of January 1942, about 9,000 Jews who had been deported from Germany, Austria, and the Protectorate of Bohemia and Moravia. Two days after their arrival in Riga, 400 men and women from the Terezín transport were "selected" as fit for physical labor and taken in trucks to the concentration camp of Salaspils, about twenty-five kilometers from Riga. The inmates in that camp were exterminated by hard labor, starvation, and mistreatment. For the slightest infraction of camp discipline they were tortured and hanged on the gallows of the camp.

When the second transport arrived at Skirotava station on January 19, 1942, seventy-six men were "selected" as fit for hard labor and taken to Salaspils. The remaining 942 men, women, and children were driven in trucks to the woods outside Riga, where they were gunned down by SS killing squads and dumped into ditches that had been prepared for this purpose. The digging and the subsequent re-covering of the mass graves was the work of Salaspils inmates who had been assigned to this task by the SS and who were later also killed.[32]

Another killing operation took place in the Riga ghetto in February 1942. About 2,000 inmates were taken in trucks to the woods on the banks of the river Dvina, where they were shot. According to one survivor of this massacre, Jews who had come from Terezín and Vienna attempted to resist the executioners. Some of the victims were taken from Riga to Kovno and executed there at Fort No. 9. Among these were also Jews from the Protectorate of Bohemia and Moravia.[33]

The second Riga ghetto was liquidated early in November 1943. About 500 men and women were sent to the labor camp of Kaiserwald, about fifteen kilometers north of Riga. There the inmates were put to work in the woods, building roads and railroad lines for the German army. Kaiserwald was evacuated by the Germans in May 1944 as Soviet army units were advancing into the area. The surviving inmates were transported to the concentration camp of Stutthof near Danzig and from there to the labor camp of Gottenhof, where they arrived in January 1945. Some of them managed to escape across the Baltic Sea to Denmark and Sweden. Gottenhof was liberated by the Soviet army on March 10, 1945. Of the two transports from Terezín only 117 persons survived. What is known about life in the Riga ghetto was conveyed by the testimony given by some of these survivors.[34]

After the war, the bodies of over 60,000 Jews who had been executed were discovered in mass graves near Riga. Among the bodies that could be identified were those of some who had been deported from Bohemia and Moravia. The liquidation of the ghetto in Riga and elsewhere in the Baltic states was organized by Heydrich's trusted SS Sturmbannführer Fritz Lange. Lange was caught in the British occupation zone of Germany and handed over to German authorities in 1949. However, in the course of his interrogation, he succeeded in escaping from prison in 1951. The execution squads had been under the command of two officers of the *Sicherheitsdienst* (SD; Security Service), the intelligence branch of the SS. In 1950 one of these officers, Martin Weiss, was tried and sentenced in Würzburg to life imprisonment.[35]

The third and final transport from Terezín to the Baltic region left Terezín on September 1, 1942. The 1,000 men, women, and children passed through Riga; on September 5 they arrived at Raasiki railroad station, about twenty-five kilometers from Tallin, the capital of Estonia. Immediately upon their arrival, 120 men and seventy-five women were "selected" as fit for hard labor. All others were driven in buses to the wooded hill of Kalegi-Liiva, stripped of all their personal property, and then shot. The SS men brought to this execution site a group of prisoners who buried the dead in prepared mass graves, where thousands of bodies were discovered after the war. The exhumed bodies were identified partly as those of Soviet prisoners of war and partly as those of Jews who had been deported from Germany, Austria, and the Protectorate.[36]

Both the commander of the execution squad, SS Sturmbannführer Erwin Mere, and his deputy, Adolf Viks, have escaped justice thus far. It is known that they are alive and free; Mere is in England and Viks in Australia.

Those "selected" at Raasiki for work were taken to the Jagala concentration camp. This camp, which consisted of four large wooden barracks, was situated in a wooded area, fenced in by barbed wire and guarded by Estonian policemen. More than 2,000 inmates were put to work felling trees and sawing lumber. Hard labor and lack of food caused many deaths among the camp population. Those too weak to work were summarily shot. Not a single one of the prisoners who came to Jagala from Terezín survived. The commandant of the Jagala camp, Alexander Lask, an Estonian SS officer, was arrested in Canada after the war and committed suicide during an interrogation.

The 500 women working at the Jagala camp included seventy-five "selected" from the Terezín transport. In December 1942, all the women were taken to Tallin, where they were placed into the city prison and put to work clearing away the rubble and debris after Allied air raids. In December 1943, the seventy-five women were taken to the labor camp of Erida, some sixty kilometers from Narva. Young women were assigned to auxiliary services for the German army. They worked in the kitchens and kept the officers' quarters clean. The Erida camp was hastily evacuated before the Soviet army arrived and the women were transferred to an emergency camp near the harbor of Tallin, where they were again put to work clearing away debris and digging trenches. Many of them collapsed from exhaustion. The sick and those unfit to work were taken to the concentration camp of Kiviyli, where they were killed. Those who survived were taken to the Stutthof concentration camp. While none of the men from the Terezín transport survived, a comparatively high proportion—forty-five out of seventy-five—of the women "selected" from that transport remained alive. At least one of them wrote a detailed account—eighty-seven pages—about their sufferings.[37]

Deportations from Terezín to the Lublin Area and Maidanek

Beginning in March 1942 transports from Terezín were sent to ghettos and labor camps in German-occupied Poland. The ghettos and camps in the Lublin region served the Germans as labor reservoirs and as transit stations for those deported Jews scheduled for extermination.

The extermination of Jews in the Lublin region, known under the code name "Aktion Reinhard" (Operation Reinhard), was under the direction of SS Obergruppenführer Odilo Globocnik, who had been chosen for this task by Heinrich Himmler. "Aktion Reinhard" included not only the extermination of Jews in gas chambers in several parts of the Lublin region, but also the valuation and sorting of all valuables taken away from the deportees before their extermination. All jewelry and cash taken from Jews were sent to the *Wirtschaftsverwaltungshauptamt* (WVHA; Central Office of Economic Administration) in Berlin and from there to the State Bank. Globocnik's reports to Himmler include lists of valuables and foreign currency worth millions, taken from Jewish deportees. It has been established that huge sums from this source were sent to Switzerland and used for the purchase of raw materials vital to the German war effort. Globocnik, who was responsible also for the operation of the extermination camps of Chelmno, Treblinka, Belzec, Sobibor, and Maidanek, to which Jews from the Terezín ghetto were also sent for extermination, was doing his job so well that he was promoted to the rank of general and was later transferred to the Yugoslav front to direct operations against partisan fighters. He committed suicide after the war.

At the end of 1943, "Aktion Reinhard" was stopped, most of the extermination camps in "Lublinland" were liquidated,[38] and the main extermination center was transferred to Auschwitz. However, before that, transports from Terezín were still sent to other places. Thus, three transports totaling 3,001 men, women, and children were sent from Terezín to the Polish town of Izbica nad Wieprzem. The local Jewish population had been "evacuated" and the empty homes were assigned to the Jews from Terezín and Germany. The first of the three transports arrived at Izbica on March 13, 1942. The Nazis saw to it that the letters sent by inmates from Izbica to Terezín should give a rosy picture and have a calming effect on the Jews still in Terezín. Prisoners from this transport were divided into groups and put to work at construction, debris clearance, and peat digging. Eventually, 150 young men from this transport were sent to the camp at Janowice, where they were assigned to roadbuilding. Two weeks after their arrival at Izbica women with children and old people were moved to the extermination camp of Belzec.

The second transport from Terezín arrived at Izbica on March 19, 1942. About a week later, 300 men found fit for work were "selected" and also sent to Janowice. All the others—some 700 people—were sent to Belzec for extermination.

The third transport left Terezín for Izbica on April 27, 1942. On the way it stopped at Lublin, where 400 men between the ages of sixteen and forty-five were "selected" and taken off the train. The remaining 600 continued to Izbica on April 30. A few of them were put to work in the vicinity. Those unfit for work, especially women and children, were taken to Chelmno. Between October 1 and 25, 1942, all the prisoners working in the vicinity were gathered in Izbica. Anyone caught hiding was summarily shot. Altogether about

2,000 deportees were herded into trains and transported to the extermination camps of Belzec and Maidanek. Some of them managed to escape the roundup, to find a hiding place and even employment among the gentiles in the countryside. Among the three transports that went from Terezín to Izbica only eleven persons survived.

In order to facilitate the extermination of the deportees from Izbica, the commandant of the Belzec concentration camp, SS Hauptsturmführer Hans Höfle, demanded that transports directed to the Lublin region should already be sorted at the station of departure into two categories: those fit for work and those destined for *Sonderbehandlung* (special treatment). Whenever such a division was not feasible, the trains were ordered to make a stop in Lublin, where the sorting would be done. At the same time Höfle ordered the creation of an additional transit center in the village of Piaski. In order to make room for the new arrivals, he had the original Jewish population transferred to Belzec. After this evacuation Piaski was sealed off, and the incoming Jews were not permitted to have any contacts with the local non-Jewish population.

Early in April 1942, a transport of 1,000 men, women, and children from Terezín arrived at the town of Trawniky. From there the prisoners had to march fourteen kilometers to Piaski. In the Piaski ghetto they still found several dozen local Jews, along with Jews who had been deported from Germany in two transports. Those fit to work were assigned to digging canalization trenches and laying cables. Women, children, and the aged were left to vegetate and starve in the ghetto. At the end of April another 650 inmates, mainly women with children and elderly people, arrived from Terezín. From the first transport of 1,000 people, 350 younger men were "selected" at Höfle's orders in Lublin. They were sent to Maidanek, where they were put to work sorting the luggage and personal effects of those who had been sent to Maidanek earlier for extermination. After they had finished their work, they, too, went to the gas chambers.

Additional transports from Germany swelled the population of the Piaski ghetto to 7,000. Due to inhuman sanitary conditions, contagious diseases, particularly typhoid fever and dysentery, began to spread. On June 22, 1942, armed SS units drove approximately 6,000 prisoners to the Trawniky railroad station, where they were herded into waiting cattle cars. Their final destinations were Belzec and Sobibor. Only a very small number of deportees among them—including five from Terezín—succeeded in escaping and managed to survive.

Another transit ghetto for transports of Jewish deportees to the Lublin region was in the village of Rejowiece, where a transport of 1,000 inmates from Terezín arrived on April 18, 1942. Those found fit for work were immediately sent to the nearby Sawina labor camp, where most of them were assigned to agricultural work. Women, children, and the aged were left at Rejowiece. The Sawina camp was plagued by dysentery and typhoid fever; as a result, most of the inmates died. Those who stayed alive were sent back to Rejowiece about three months later. After a week at Rejowiece, they were sent, together with those who had been classed as unfit for work at the outset, to the extermination camp of Sobibor. Many of them had already died on the way there, shot by their SS escorts. Only two men in this transport from Terezín survived.

On April 25, 1942, another transport was dispatched from Terezín, this time to Warsaw. The 1,000 men, women, and children in this transport were not sent to the Warsaw ghetto but were placed into one of the Warsaw synagogues which had not yet been demolished. On arrival, one hundred men classed as fit for work were sent to the labor camp of Rembertów near Warsaw. They were assigned to roadbuilding and agricultural work. Three weeks later those who had not been put to work were gradually sent, in several groups, to the extermination camp of Treblinka. There, 300 men were "selected" for construction work within the camp. After two weeks only nine of them were still alive. The others had been killed by the bayonets of their Ukrainian guards. Women, children, and elderly people went immediately to the gas chambers. In the spring of 1944, when Soviet troops were approaching Warsaw, the inmates at Rembertów tried to escape. With very few exceptions they were killed. Only eight men survived from that Terezín transport.

Lublin was the headquarters of the SS command responsible for the enslavement and extermination of Jews deported to the Lublin region from almost all the Nazi-occupied countries. The Lublin ghetto was liquidated in November 1942, and the Jews who survived were sent to extermination camps. Those who tried to resist deportation were gunned down on the spot. In the neighborhood of the ghetto there was a concentration camp which was liquidated at the same time as the ghetto. Its inmates were transferred to Maidanek, only five kilometers away.

Originally the Maidanek camp had been set up for Soviet prisoners of war. These, however, had been gradually liquidated and, beginning in the fall of 1941, Maidanek was filled with Jews deported from Germany, Austria, Holland, and Slovakia. Before long the camp was expanded and divided into five sections, each of which could accommodate 6,000–8,000 inmates. In the spring of 1942 the first gas chambers were built and in May the killing of inmates with Zyklon B gas, which had been tried out successfully at Auschwitz, was introduced at Maidanek.

Altogether three transports—a total of 3,000 men, women, and children—were sent from Terezín to Maidanek. The first transport left Terezín on May 17, the second on June 13, 1942. Nobody from these two transports survived. The names on the luggage found after the liberation of the camp are the only proof that these unfortunates indeed arrived at Maidanek. One single witness survived the third transport, which was dispatched on June 25, 1942. After the "selection" on their arrival, 750 people were immediately sent to the gas chambers. The remaining 250 were used for a time for construction work in the camp. Ultimately, they shared the fate of their women, children, and parents. The lone exception was a watchmaker. He was sent to Auschwitz, where he was put to work repairing thousands of watches taken from Jewish victims. Eventually he was sent to do the same work at the concentration camp of Oranienburg near Berlin, where he survived the war.[39]

On July 24, 1944, SS men at Maidanek hastily began to clear the camp because Soviet troops were approaching. The SS command fled from Lublin and the SS guards in Maidanek did not have enough time to kill all their prisoners. The last 600 inmates organized themselves into a resistance movement, occupied the camp administration offices, and killed or captured the remaining SS men. Those SS men caught alive were handed over to Soviet officers. Thus the Germans were not able to destroy their gas chambers before the arrival of the Soviets. As a result, the gas chambers and the crematorium, together with hundreds of still uncremated corpses and the storeroom with boxes of Zyklon B gas, could be shown to the war correspondents who came with the Soviet troops. Among the reporters there was V. Borek, a correspondent for a

Czech-language newspaper, *Československé Listy,* which was published in Moscow during the war. In Maidanek, Borek discovered traces of Jewish families which had been deported[40] from Třeboň, České Budějovice, and Brno. He also came upon hundreds of Czech fairytale books, Slovak schoolbooks, and notebooks.

On April 28 and 30, 1942, two transports bearing a total of 2,000 inmates of Terezín were deported to the Polish town of Zamosc, about sixty kilometers from Lublin. The first of these two transports was placed into the ghetto. Two weeks later those found fit for work were "selected" and taken to the labor camp in Komarow. From there they were eventually transferred to Maidanek, where they were assigned to construction work within the camp until September 1942. Most of them were shot during a mass killing operation in November. Those who survived that operation met their death in one of the gas chambers. Women who had children with them and elderly people had been taken in trucks to the extermination camp of Chelmno as early as the middle of May. Five men from this first transport survived.

The second transport from Terezín arrived at Zamosc on May 3, 1942. The train stopped in Lublin, where all the luggage was unloaded. In Zamosc the deportees were placed into dilapidated wooden barracks near the railroad station, where Jews deported from Germany had already been living for some months. There was no water in this camp. The SS men allowed only four buckets of water for the entire transport each day. On the third day after their arrival, about 600 men and women were declared fit for work and were ordered to dig ditches and lay cables at an airport under construction. Prisoners were beaten, abused, and summarily shot for the slightest breach of camp discipline. They had to work fourteen hours each day, seven days a week. Prisoners no longer fit for work were taken in trucks to the extermination camps of Chelmno and Belzec. Before long, however, the Zamosc camp was filled up again with new transports from Germany, Austria, and Slovakia.

Early in the morning on October 17, all the inmates at Zamosc were herded into the main square of the town and lined up in columns of four. The columns, totaling 4,500 inmates, were surrounded by motorized SS units and, followed by heavy machine guns mounted on trucks, set out on foot for Izbica, a march of twenty-one kilometers. Whoever could not keep in step was shot.

Almost half of the prisoners, mainly elderly people, women, and children, perished on this death march. On October 19, the survivors were taken to a place near the Izbica railroad station where 12,000 deportees from other transports had already been assembled. All were herded by the SS men into waiting cattle cars. Families were torn apart, and those who put up resistance were shot. One train after the other arrived at Belzec. There all the prisoners were killed in the gas chambers. Nineteen men from the Terezín transport managed to escape from the death march to Izbica. They found asylum and work with Polish peasants and survived the war.

On June 12, 1942, another 1,000 prisoners were deported from Terezín to Trawniky, where a ghetto had been set up. Outside the town there was a labor camp where Jews were put to work at a plant of Többens, a German firm which supplied equipment for the Wehrmacht. Those classed as unfit for work were set apart from the others and, a few days after their arrival, were sent to the extermination camp of Belzec. At the end of October 1943 work at the Többens plant was stopped, and the Jews were assembled in the labor camp and shot there by the SS men on November 3. Nobody from this transport survived.[41]

Another transport, totaling, as in most cases, 1,000 men, women, and children, was dispatched from Terezín on July 14, 1942. At the railroad station of Minsk the SS "selected" thirty-five men as fit for work and took them, together with their families, to the labor camp at Maly Trostinec, about seventeen kilometers from Minsk. All the others were ordered to leave their luggage at the railroad station and to board waiting trucks which took them into the woods outside the town. There they were shot by SS killing squads and buried in mass graves which had been prepared for them. Only two men from this transport survived. They managed to jump from the moving train and hide in the woods.[42] Roaming through the woods they finally came upon a group of Soviet partisans who had been parachuted into the area. From them the fugitives learned that Czechoslovak army units had been formed in the Soviet Union. They were spirited into Russia, where they joined the Czechoslovak army unit under the command of General Ludvík Svoboda, participated in the Dukla campaign, and returned to Czechoslovakia as liberators in the spring of 1945.

Between August 4 and September 29, 1942, a total of 15,004 men, women, and children were sent in ten transports from Terezín to the East. The trains would stop about seventeen kilometers behind Minsk, in a completely unpopulated area, in the middle of a wide stretch of meadows. The deportees were ordered to get off the train, keep quiet, and leave all their luggage and valuables on the train. Out of each transport thirty to forty men were "selected" as physically fit for work. They were assigned as "specialists" to sort the luggage of the new arrivals. Special sealed cars were waiting to take the prisoners to the Blahovština forest, some ten kilometers east of Minsk. All the passengers were killed by exhaust gas let into the sealed trucks even before they arrived at the place where mass graves had been dug for the victims. The burial of the corpses was carried out by a special detail of inmates under the supervision of SS killing squads. Out of the 15,004 who had come from Terezín, only eight—they were among those "selected" as "specialists"—survived. One of them testified regarding the fate of the others:

> On September 8 a transport of 1,000 prisoners left Terezín for Maly Trostinec. Before Brest-Litovsk the prisoners had to get off the train and transfer into railroad cars which were open, as distinct from the closed cattle cars which had been used before. On September 12 the train pulled into a station which bore a sign reading "Minsk." After about two hours of stops and starts, the train came to a stop in an open area about fifteen kilometers behind Minsk. In front of every railroad car three SS men were waiting with machine guns. Their commander ordered us to get out of the train and to leave our luggage and coats behind. Another SS officer from a group that had been looking on added, "You won't need any luggage; you will receive uniforms at the camp. Money has no value here. You will not need watches; there is an electric watch at the camp. You will not need fountain pens because all correspondence is forbidden under pain of death. You are to hand over all these objects within ten minutes. If after that time any of the items I have mentioned is found on anyone, that person will be shot on the spot." One young woman on whom some cash was found in the body search had to undress completely in front of all the others and was killed by a bullet in the back of the neck. Forty-four men were set apart. All the others were killed in *dušegubkas* ("soul destroyers," as the special sealed cars were called) and dumped into mass graves.[43]

Each transport was treated in a similar manner. As soon as the selected "specialists" had unloaded the luggage from the train and loaded it upon trucks, about half of them were shot then and there.

The rest were taken to Malý Trostinec, where the SS command was operating a country estate of some 250 hectares that had been confiscated from its former Jewish owners and included large stables for horses and cattle. The work on the estate was done by some 400 Jewish deportees from Vienna and Terezín and about 200 Russian prisoners of war. They lived in the adjacent concentration camp to which the surviving "specialists" of the transports from Terezín were now also brought. The inmates slept in pigsties and woodsheds and had to work twelve hours a day in return for miserable food rations. The slightest breach of camp discipline was punished by shooting or hanging and the bodies of the offenders were left hanging for several days as a warning to the others. From time to time "selections" were made and inmates classed as too weak to work were gassed to death along with the sick in special sealed cars which took the bodies to the mass graves for burial.

A special section of the camp was reserved for some seventy inmates who belonged to the *Sonderkommando* (special detail). These inmates, mostly Soviet prisoners of war, were under particularly stringent guard. They dug the mass graves and buried the dead under SS supervision. At the beginning of 1943, the SS began to cover up all the traces of their crimes. The *Sonderkommando* was enlarged and placed under even stricter guard than before. Inmates were ordered to open up the mass graves, disinter the decomposing corpses, and cremate them on grills constructed especially for this purpose from railroad tracks and sleepers. In the fall of 1943 the killings in the *dušegubkas* were stopped. Those marked for extermination were taken to the extermination camp of Maidanek. In June 1944, as the Soviet army came closer, the SS gradually liquidated the camp at Maly Trostinec and finally set fire to it on June 30. About twenty-five prisoners managed to escape from the burning ruins and hide in the nearby woods, where they were liberated by the Russians on July 3, 1944. Among those saved were eight of the men who had been deported from Terezín.

Mass killing operations in the Minsk area were directed by the commander of the *Sicherheitsdienst* in Minsk, SS Obersturmbannführer Eduard Strauch, to whom the commanders of killing squads and of the *Sonderkommando* at Malý Trostinec reported. Strauch, who had been a lawyer and a high bank executive before the war, had joined the Nazi party in the late 1920s and became Heydrich's favorite expert in the annihilation of Jews. In April 1948 he was sentenced to death by the International Military Tribunal at Nuremberg, but this sentence was later commuted to life imprisonment. He died in a prison hospital in 1955.[44]

On May 17, 1942, 1,000 men, women, and children were deported from Terezín to a transit camp at Ossow, which had been set up for transports destined for the extermination camp Sobibor, north of Lublin. Nobody from this transport survived. It is assumed that they all perished in the gas chambers of Sobibor. The transport sent there from Terezín on July 28, 1942—this one, too, was composed of 1,000 men, women, and children—probably met the same fate. This assumption is substantiated by the testimony of witnesses, who, while sorting the clothes of the murdered deportees, had found in some of them identity papers of persons who had been deported from Terezín.[45]

Between October 5 and 22, 1942, five transports carrying a total of 8,000 men, women, and children left Terezín for the death camp of Treblinka. On arrival, a few dozen able-bodied men were "selected" from each transport, while the rest went straight to the gas chambers. There were thirteen gas chambers at Treblinka, but no crematorium, so the dead bodies were first buried in mass graves. Later the dead were cremated in open pits and on specially constructed grills placed over ditches. The men "selected" from the transports for work were assigned to sort, store, and prepare for shipment to Germany the personal effects of Jews who had already been exterminated. Those selectees were called *Arbeitsjuden* ("work Jews"); many of them were eventually exterminated in their turn. The number of Jews killed in Treblinka has been put at 730,000. About 1,000 railroad cars carrying the personal effects of the deportees were sent to Germany. There were also twenty-five cars loaded to capacity with sacks of hair cut from the heads of women who had been killed.

On August 2, 1943, a long-prepared inmate revolt broke out at Treblinka. Prisoners dug a tunnel from the labor camp to the SS arms store. There they overpowered the guards, picked up weapons, and then set fire to the wooden buildings in the camp and fled into the woods. One of the organizers of the rebellion was Zhelo Bloch, a former captain in the Czech army, who had been deported to Treblinka from Terezín. Bloch was killed in the fighting with the SS.

All police and SS units in the area were mobilized; they surrounded the woods in which the Jews were hiding and killed every one they found. Among those who survived this search, there were two deportees from Terezín. One of them, Richard Glazer, published several articles about his participation in the Treblinka revolt. The last article, "Die Stimmen von Treblinka" [The Voices from Treblinka], appeared in *Baseler Zeitung* (Basel) on September 2, 1978.

Franz Stangl, the commandant of Treblinka, was also the first commandant of Sobibor. His whereabouts were discovered in 1967 by Simon Wiesenthal in São Paulo and he was extradited by the Brazilian authorities to the Federal Republic of Germany. In 1970 he was tried in Düsseldorf and sentenced to life imprisonment. In an interview with Gitta Sereny, a journalist writing for the London *Daily Telegraph Magazine,* he gave the following description of his first visit to Treblinka:

... In the station was a train full of Jews, some dead, some still alive ... [It] looked as if it had been there for days ... It was Dante's *Inferno.* It was Dante come to life. When I entered the camp and got out ... on the *Sortierungsplatz* [sorting area] I stepped knee-deep into money. I didn't know which way to turn, where to go. I waded in notes, currency, precious stones, jewelry, clothes. They were everywhere, strewn all over the square. The smell was indescribable; the hundreds, no, the thousands of bodies everywhere, decomposing, putrefying. Across the square, in the woods, just a few hundred yards away on the other side of the barbed wire fence ... there were tents and open fires with groups of Ukrainian guards ...[46]

About a year after his conviction Stangl died in prison of a heart attack.

After the inmate revolt, Treblinka was leveled and the area planted with trees and bushes. After the war, the Polish government erected a monument at the site of the gas chambers.

Deportations to Auschwitz

Late in the fall of 1942, the transports to the Lublin region ceased. During the two-year period from October 26, 1942, to October 28, 1944, Jews were deported to Auschwitz, which was a whole complex of labor and concentration camps adjoining German war plants. Spread over a territory of forty square kilometers, the Auschwitz complex was strictly guarded and the area had been cleared of all its prewar Polish population. The Germans referred to the entire area as *Interessengebiet Auschwitz* (Auschwitz area of interest). The main Auschwitz camp, erected in 1940 near the Polish industrial town of Oswiecim (population 7,000), became the center of the complex, from which thirty-nine branch camps were directed.

Between 1942 and 1944 a total of 44,839 men, women, and children were sent in twenty-nine transports from Terezín to Auschwitz. Out of this number, only 2,865 survived the war. About 80 percent of the deportees were sent straight from the trains to the gas chambers located only about 400 meters from the railroad siding. Of the remaining 20 percent "selected" for labor, 94 percent perished from starvation, disease, exhaustion, or as the result of torture by guards.[47]

In the ghettos, the transit camps, and the labor camps the Nazis systematically demoralized the inmates in order to prepare them for extermination. The SS personnel assigned to carry out the "Final Solution" were put through special psychological training. "Graduates" of these courses knew how to break the spirits of the prisoners already on the train journey so that they would not be capable of resisting when they arrived in the ghetto or at the camp. The deportees traveled for several days and nights crammed into closed cattle cars in an atmosphere of ever-growing tension and despair. The sick lay in their excrement together with the bodies of those who had died during the journey, and could not even be removed from the cars. Everyone yearned for the end of the journey, to get out of the stench, to breathe fresh air, to wash, eat, drink, and grasp at a last straw of hope. Under these circumstances the mere thought of resistance seemed absurd. It is difficult, indeed almost impossible, to grasp the feelings and thoughts of those who traveled aboard these death trains. One of them described the experience as follows:

> We passed the last desk with lists of deportees and finally arrived at the railroad platform. SS Scharführer Heindl, his stick in his hand, herded us into the railroad cars. He yelled insults and administered beatings. The small freight car into which we were herded had two small openings in its sides, but even these had been boarded over. Our knapsacks and suitcases had to be left in front of the freight car. They were tossed in after us and piled up in the middle of the car. A sack of bread was also tossed in. Then the heavy doors of the freight car were closed and were locked from the outside. [But the train did not move]. It was completely dark. Gradually we

got used to the darkness which changed into gloom. Finally we were able to count how many of us there were in the car. There were sixty-eight of us, mainly old women, a few men, no children, but several sick people who had to lie down. People began to search for their suitcases. We were only four younger men in the car. At first we attempted to introduce some order. Then we distributed the knapsacks and suitcases and tried to arrange the crowded people in such a way that everyone would be able to sit down on his own suitcase or knapsack. We succeeded in this endeavor only after several hours of strenuous work. The smell in the tightly sealed car gradually became unbearable. We were locked up for seven or eight hours but we still could hear yelling outside, indicating that others were being herded into railroad cars behind us. Finally we felt the pull of the locomotive and the train slowly began to move. It traveled the short distance of the siding at Bohušovice, where it came to a brief stop, then started to move again. The first thing we did was to use our pocket knives and other available tools to pry off the boards that sealed the openings in the upper part of the car walls. At last we were able to breathe again. Meanwhile, it had grown dark outside. Everyone was very tired and gradually fell asleep. But [the quiet] did not last long. We had one single bucket in the middle of the crowded car to use as a toilet. The first person went and, of course, tripped over all the others. And then the stampede began. One after the other stumbled to the bucket. In a little while the bucket was full and we younger prisoners had the task of emptying it. This could be done only through the opening in the upper part of the car. In doing this we could not avoid getting all dirty ourselves. This terrible job had to be repeated twelve times before we arrived at our destination. We had neither water nor soap with which to wash ourselves. Nobody could sleep anymore. The older people were very agitated; some of them acted as if they had gone crazy. The train arrived at Dresden . . . [T]he train continued on its journey. The sun rose and the train kept moving all day long. Nobody ate anything, despite the fact that we had been hungry in Terezín. The bread remained untouched. Nervousness spread and we younger people had our hands full maintaining at least a little order. It grew dark again. In the upper openings we saw the glow of blast furnaces. We were passing through the industrial regions of Upper Silesia. Finally, despite the anxiety and nervousness around me, I fell asleep. Suddenly I was awakened by shouts. The brilliant light of arc lamps came in through the openings of the car. I looked out and the first thing I saw was a double fence of barbed wire. I saw insulators made of porcelain. The barbed wires were probably electrified. Nearby I saw a four-cornered tower, about fifteen meters high. I saw a group of SS men and unknown figures in striped blouses coming toward our freight cars. I did not know what to make of them. One such figure had a yellow armband on his striped blouse with the black letters "KAPO."* I wondered what that meant. All of a sudden one door of our car opened. One of the striped men jumped inside and yelled, "Quick! Quick! Everybody out! Everybody out! Leave all your things in the car!" I asked whether I could keep my canvas shoulder bag, but the only answer I got was, "Quick! Quick!" Outside, the SS men were yelling. Finally all of us, even the old and sick, were out of the car. The men were immediately separated from the women. The men and women each formed a double line and advanced toward a tall SS officer. The man in front of me was running a high fever and was shivering. One could see at once that he was sick. "Are you sick?" the SS man asked him. "Yes, I have a fever," he answered. "To the right!" the SS man shouted, accompanying his command with a slight movement of his right hand. I was next in line.

"Age?"
"Forty."
"Healthy?"
"Yes."
"To the left!"

I moved to the left side, where a small group of younger people was already waiting. Our group was taken to a sauna, where our clothes were taken away and our hair was cut. After we had washed ourselves we were given striped prisoners' garments to put on. The old and the sick, but also young women with small children, were taken to the other side. They did not know they were going to their death, to the gas chambers and the crematoria of Auschwitz-Birkenau.[48]

The first transport of 740 men, 1,020 women, and 106 children left Terezín for Auschwitz on October 28, 1942. Of the total of 1,866 persons on this transport, 350 men between the ages of fifteen and fifty were "selected" on arrival for work. All the others were taken directly from the railroad siding to the gas chambers of Birkenau. Their bodies were cremated on pyres over open ditches. Before the four large crematoria and eight gas chambers had been completed in March 1943, Jews from mass transports were exterminated in the so-called Bunkers No. 1 and No. 2. These were the official names for the first gas chambers set up in two peasant huts in the village of Brzezinka, which had been cleared of all its original population.

---

* "Trusty" or overseer at a concentration camp. *Kapos* were inmates appointed by the SS officers in charge of the camp; some *Kapos* were German non-Jews who had been imprisoned in the camp on criminal charges, but in all-Jewish camps there were Jewish *Kapos*. *Kapos* received special privileges. Some were helpful to their fellow inmates but others were hated and feared because of their cruelty.

Near the bunkers were wooden barracks, where new arrivals undressed and left their personal effects. They were then ordered to enter the gas chambers—for delousing, they were told. Crystals of Zyklon B gas were tossed into the chamber through openings in the wall. Half an hour later the bodies were removed to the open area behind the bunkers and dispatched in carts over a narrow railroad line to the open cremation ditches and grills. Each layer of corpses was covered with rags and firewood before the next layer of dead bodies was piled on top. Then gasoline was poured over the bodies so they would burn more readily. This was done under the supervision of the SS by inmates from a *Sonderkommando*. The first members of this special detail had been "selected" from among prisoners who had come from Slovakia.

The 350 men "selected" from the first Terezín transport were taken to Central Camp Auschwitz I, where twenty-five of them had been beaten to death within a week. All the others were taken to Auschwitz III (Monovice), about seven kilometers from the central camp, where they were put to work building a plant for the Buna works which belonged to the I. G. Farben concern. Only twenty-eight of these men survived the war.

Those deported from Terezín were not the first Jews from the Protectorate of Bohemia and Moravia to arrive in Auschwitz. As early as the spring of 1941 the Gestapo in Brno and Moravská Ostrava had begun sending to Auschwitz Jews who had been arrested for political reasons. They arrived singly or in small groups, became easy targets of sadist *Kapos* and SS guards, and perished soon after their arrival in Auschwitz.

On October 5, 1942, an order was issued for the transfer of all Jewish inmates from concentration camps in Germany proper to Auschwitz. The order supposedly applied to approximately 40,000 Jews who had been arrested since Hitler's ascent to power. However, at the time this order was announced, only about 1,600 of the 40,000 were still alive in the concentration camps of Buchenwald, Dachau, Sachsenhausen, Mauthausen, and Neuengamme. When they arrived in Auschwitz they were not put through the "selection" procedure, nor were they killed in gas chambers. They were classed as political prisoners and were kept apart from the others, in case they should be required for further interrogations. Among these prisoners there were also about eighty from Bohemia and Moravia.

Only eight of them who had been able to secure "specialists'" jobs—doctors, male nurses, and some craftsmen needed for the day-to-day operation of the camp—survived.

Mass transports continued and prior to February 1943 five additional transports from Terezín brought 7,001 men, women, and children to Auschwitz. Out of all these transports 687 men and 404 women were "selected" for work. However, living conditions in the camps of the Auschwitz complex were so inhuman that only ninety-six survived.

Some basic changes were made when two transports dispatched from Terezín arrived in Auschwitz on September 6 and 7, 1943. Deportees from these mass transports were not put through "selection." The 5,007 men, women, and children from both transports, including the sick and the bodies of those who had died on the way, were taken along with their luggage from the railroad siding to Birkenau. There the prisoners from Terezín were placed into thirty wooden horses' stables of the unfinished camp in Sector B-II-b. There were no roads in the camp and the inmates waded up to their knees in mud. There was no drinking water; in the public washroom there was running water only twice a day for short periods. Bad sanitary conditions gave rise to many diseases, with the result that within half a year 1,140 people from these two transports had died.[49] The camp into which these Terezín deportees were placed was known as "the Czech family camp" because, as distinct from the other camps where families were separated by the "selections," whole families were put into this camp together. The "Czech family camp" was isolated from the other seven camps in Birkenau; all contact with inmates of the other camps was forbidden. The Terezín deportees were not permitted to leave their camp. They were put to work building roads for the camp and adapting the horses' stables as living quarters for humans.

The camp commander, SS Untersturmführer Hans Schwarzhuber, appointed as *Lagerälteste* (camp elder) one Arno Boehm, not a Jew but a *Berufsverbrecher* ("professional criminal") who had been an inmate of the main camp. However, all the other functionaries in the "family camp" were Jews from the two September transports. This made life a little more bearable for the deportees from Terezín. The inmates of the "Czech family camp" were given many privileges denied the inmates of the other camps. This was done in order to quell rumors that would have caused panic among the Jews who were still in the "model ghetto" of Terezín. The inmates of the "family camp" were permitted to keep their personal belongings and to wear their own clothes. The women did not have their hair cut off, children and pregnant women received special rations of milk and butter, and they were permitted to receive food packages. Each month they were given postcards to use for writing to relatives and friends in Terezín. The SS censored the messages on these cards and made certain that the senders gave their return address as *"Arbeitslager* (Labor Camp) Birkenau near Neu-Berun, House No. . . . ." In this way the connection of Birkenau with the dreaded Auschwitz was to be concealed.

Fredy Hirsch, who had been one of the youth leaders in Terezín, received permission from Commandant Schwarzhuber to organize the education of children in the "family camp." Barracks Block No. 30 was furnished as a schoolroom, where teachers not only taught the children the usual school subjects but also had their pupils put on theater performances and concerts, which were sometimes attended by SS men and even by Schwarzhuber himself. An infirmary and dispensary were set up in two of the barracks. The camp was frequently visited by the notorious Dr. Josef Mengele, who was performing various medical experiments with twins, for which he asked the assistance of inmates who were physicians by profession.

Everything seemed to indicate that the SS command in Auschwitz was taking a special interest in the Jews deported from Terezín. SS men were strengthening this impression by spreading the rumor that Czech Jews were under the protection of the International Red Cross and that after half a year they would be released in exchange for German prisoners of war. Artisans among the inmates who could enter the "family camp" from time to time informed the deportees from Terezín about what was really happening in Birkenau. Although the "family camp" was less than a kilometer from the crematoria and flames flared from the chimneys night and day, the inmates of the "family camp" did not want to believe that the bodies of Jewish deportees were being cremated there. Even when they later found out that this was indeed the case, they kept trying to silence their fears by convincing themselves that they would be treated as "privileged characters."

Two subsequent transports of 5,007 men, women, and children

left Terezín on December 15 and 18, 1943. Like the deportees in the September transports, these, too, were placed into the "family camp," by that time already under somewhat better conditions, but unlike the inmates of the September transport, those who arrived in December were not permitted to keep any of their personal belongings. The only one among the new arrivals not sent to the "family camp" was Jakub Edelstein, the *Judenälteste* of the Terezín ghetto. When he arrived in Auschwitz he was separated from his family and imprisoned in Block No. 11 of the main camp.

In the middle of February 1944, the "family camp" received a visit from Adolf Eichmann and two officers of the *Reichssicherheitshauptamt* (RSHA) in Berlin. They inspected the camp. Eichmann expressed appreciation for Fredy Hirsch's work in the children's block and even asked him to prepare a memorandum for the International Red Cross about the education of children at the camp.

On March 2, the inmates were once again given postcards but this time they were told, in view of "delays caused by censorship," to postdate their messages as having been written on March 25, 1944. Two days later, Kateřina Singerová, an inmate working as a typist in the office of the women's camp command, overheard a telephone conversation between two SS officers about preparations for the *Sonderbehandlung* that would be accorded to the inmates of the "family camp" on the day when their six-month "quarantine period" would end. Knowing what *Sonderbehandlung* meant, she immediately informed the artisans in Camp Sector B-II-d. Two inmate plumbers then paid a visit to the "family camp" under the pretense of having to make emergency repairs there. They reported the conversation to two Jewish camp officials, Fredy Hirsch and a man named Jokl, but their warnings were not taken seriously.

On March 5, Commandant Schwarzhuber came to the "family camp" and assembled all the inmate officials. He praised them for the work they had done so far and told them he would need their help in the erection of a new "family camp" not far away, at Heydebreck, to which all those who had come from Terezín to Birkenau the previous September would be transferred within three days. He assured the inmate officials that they would be allowed to perform their functions at Heydebreck as well. The inmates would be permitted to take all their belongings with them and would receive special supplementary food rations for the journey. Schwarzhuber asked the officials to inform their fellow inmates and to start preparations for the transfer immediately.

Once again warnings were sent by the "old-timers" in the main camp, who kept urging the inmates of the "family camp" to organize resistance. There was a group of men and women determined to set fire to the straw mattresses in the wooden barracks at a prearranged time. The fire would be a signal for a revolt of the inmates and the neighboring camps and of the *Sonderkommando* in the crematoria. The artisans even smuggled ampules filled with lighter fuel into the "family camp" for this purpose.

The SS guards tightened their precautions, while Schwarzhuber, sometimes accompanied by Mengele, kept visiting the "family camp" to allay the apprehensions of the inmates by well-planned stratagems and cunning talk designed to weaken the willpower and resolution of those who were preparing the revolt. In the morning of March 7, 1944, all the inmates scheduled for transfer received clean linen. In the afternoon they were escorted to the showers at the delousing station known as the "sauna," not far from Crematoria Nos. 4 and 5. After their bath the inmates were moved to the neighboring Quarantine Camp B-II-a and placed into barracks. On the next day, toward evening, they were herded into covered trucks escorted by an unusually large number of SS men armed with machine guns. The trucks moved out of the camp onto the highway leading to the Auschwitz railroad station but then turned off into a side road which led to Crematoria Nos. 2 and 3. The inmates realized they had been tricked and clamored for resistance and revolt. *Kapos* on guard duty fell upon them and beat some of them to death. At that point Fredy Hirsch and Jokl ended their lives by taking poison. They did not want to see the massacre of women and children with which they believed the revolt would end.

During the night from March 8 to March 9, 1944, 3,797 Czech Jews were killed in the two giant gas chambers connected with Crematoria Nos. 2 and 3. Those who attempted to resist were herded with blows into the gas chambers. As they marched to their deaths, the prisoners sang the Czechoslovak national anthem and the Jewish national anthem, *Hatikvah*.[50] Some were bayoneted to death. Only seventy persons from both transports survived—mainly doctors, nurses, twins, and individuals suffering from certain infectious diseases whom Mengele excepted because he needed them for his evil experiments.

This massacre had a crushing impact on inmates throughout the Auschwitz complex. The blow was heaviest for those who had arrived from Terezín the previous December. They now lived in mortal fear that their fate would be the same once their six-month "quarantine period" ended. They prepared to offer resistance. Though they knew that resistance would be in vain, they wanted at least to die with honor. They knew that effective help could come only from outside. But did the world know what was happening at Auschwitz? Those who had come from Terezín were certain that if someone could escape and inform the free world, his eyewitness accounts would arouse world opinion and the Nazi outrages would be forced to stop.

In the morning of April 5, 1944, alarm sirens screamed over the camps of Birkenau, signaling that one of the inmates had escaped. The identity of the escapee soon became known: it was Siegfried Lederer, the *Blockälteste* (block elder) of one of the barracks in the "family camp." Lederer escaped in a SS uniform and reached Prague without difficulty. A few days later he made his way into the Terezín ghetto from which he had been deported five months earlier.[51] In Terezín he told the truth about Auschwitz to a small group of friends gathered in the loft of one of the barracks. They did not believe him. They showed him dozens of postcards dated after that night between March 8 and 9, when, according to Lederer's account, the senders had been killed. Lederer warned his friends not to report for transports. He urged them to plan resistance, to seek contacts with partisan units, and to escape from Terezín. He also contacted Rabbi Dr. Leo Baeck, a member of the *Judenrat* in Terezín. It turned out that Dr. Baeck had known for some time that Jews were being murdered in Auschwitz but he had not acted on this knowledge. "Leo Baeck followed a policy of non-revelation in view of his judgment that nothing could have been done to change the course of events. It was, in his view, advisable not to let victims know the truth and to spare them the agony and ultimate desperation that comes from knowledge that the end is near and there is absolutely no way out."[52]

Lederer returned to Terezín one more time, bringing with him two revolvers and parts for a radio receiver. Again he advised his friends on how to make contact with the partisans in the Brdy mountains. He wrote a detailed report about both the Terezín ghetto and the "family camp" in Birkenau and sent it through the Swiss consulate in Prague to the International Red Cross in Geneva.[53]

Unfortunately Lederer's warnings had no impact on developments in the Terezín ghetto. Deportations to the East continued. On May 15 and 18, 1944, two more transports left Terezín for Auschwitz with 5,003 men, women, and children. On arrival, all these, too, were placed into the Czech "family camp" at Birkenau, which the new arrivals, on the basis of information they had obtained, expected to be liquidated on June 20. They armed themselves secretly with knives, gasoline, sticks, and stones, and they resolved that when the order for transfer was given, they would set fire to the wooden barracks. The tension became even greater when postcards were once again distributed to the inmates to be used for writing to their families.

On the crucial day, June 20, two SS men from the political department of the Gestapo picked up Jakub Edelstein from his quarters in Block No. 11 of the main camp. They informed him that his interrogation was now over and that he could rejoin his family. They took him to the crematorium in Birkenau, where he met his wife, his son, and his aged mother-in-law, who had been brought there from the "family camp." And so the first *Judenälteste* of the Terezín ghetto saw his family for the first time after six months in the execution hall of the crematorium. All four were put to death by an SS killing squad.[54]

Three weeks after the execution of Jakub Edelstein, the "family camp" was indeed liquidated but Berlin had given up the idea of exterminating all its inmates. The main reason for this change in plans was Germany's deteriorating military situation. The Germans were badly in need of manpower. SS Hauptsturmführer Joseph Kramer, who had succeeded Schwarzhuber as commandant of the Birkenau camps, visited the family camp and announced that some of the inmates would be sent to work in Germany proper and that only those unfit for work would remain in the camp. The appropriate "selections" were made by Drs. Mengele and Franz Lucas in June 1944. Only men between the ages of sixteen and fifty and women between the ages of fifteen and forty were admitted to the "selection" procedure. All the others, including women who refused to be separated from their children, were gassed.[55]

The first transport from Birkenau to Germany left on July 1, 1944. It took 1,000 men from the Czech "family camp" to the concentration camp of Schwarzheide, about fifty kilometers north of Dresden. The men were put to work building highways and clearing away rubble from Allied bombings, and were assigned to a Göring plant which produced synthetic fuel. On July 8, another 528 men were taken by trucks to Blechhammer, one of the branch camps of Auschwitz, to build underground bunkers. The first women's transport from the "family camp," numbering 1,000, left Birkenau on July 4 for Hamburg, where the women were divided into three groups and sent to the concentration camps of Weddel, Eidelstedt, and Tiefstack. The women, too, were put to work on construction projects, at munitions plants, and at cleaning away rubble. On July 9, another transport, this one made up of 250 women, was sent to Christianstadt, a branch of a large concentration camp, Gross-Rosen. There the women worked at constructing roads and railroad lines, sleeping in tents even under the worst weather conditions. On July 10, a third transport of about 500 women from the "family camp" left Auschwitz for Stutthof near Danzig. There they were divided into smaller groups and sent to several smaller branch camps to do slave labor, mainly at roadbuilding and to work as farmhands. Just before the end of the "selection," about eighty boys between the ages of fourteen and sixteen were added to the women who had been found fit to work. About sixty of them were sent as apprentices to German munitions plants.

There were about 6,000 persons—men above the age of fifty, women over forty, boys under sixteen, girls under fifteen, mothers (even under the age of forty) who did not want to be separated from their children, and the sick and the weak of all ages—who did not pass the "selection." Despite Kramer's promise that those found unfit for work would be permitted to remain in the "family camp," they were all killed in the gas chambers during the night on July 10 and 12, 1944.

Most of those who were sent to work in Germany perished from exhaustion or starvation or in Allied air raids. In most places they were not permitted to take cover in air-raid shelters. During the final months of the war those still alive were moved from one camp to another. Of the 17,517 men, women, and children who had been deported from Terezín to the Czech "family camp" at Birkenau, 1,167 lived to see the end of the war.

When the liquidation of the Terezín ghetto was begun, additional transports arrived in Auschwitz. None of these transports was placed into the "family camp." That camp had been converted into one of the many regular Birkenau camps, and was now no different from any of the other camps in the Auschwitz complex. Between September 28 and October 28, 1944, eleven trains from Terezín arrived at Birkenau. These transports contained a total of 18,402 men, women, and children. About 5,500 men and women were "selected" as fit for work. Within two weeks they were sent to labor camps and munitions plants in Germany. Of these, 5,500, 1,574 survived the war; 12,902 men, women, and children from these transports went to the gas chambers.

The final transport to arrive from Terezín on October 28, 1944, included eighteen leading members of the ghetto's *Ältestenrat* (Council of Jewish Elders). All of them were taken directly to the crematorium and shot.[56]

Some of the SS men responsible for the crimes committed in Auschwitz were apprehended and sentenced after the war. Among them there were also several who had participated personally in the murder of Jews from Bohemia and Moravia. Hans Schwarzhuber was sentenced to death by the British Military Tribunal in Hamburg and executed on February 3, 1947. His successor, Joseph Kramer, who was later commandant of the Bergen-Belsen concentration camp, was sentenced to death by the British Military Tribunal in Lüneberg and executed on November 17, 1945. Rapportführer Fritz Buntrock, who had assisted both commanders and was known for his brutality toward camp inmates, was sentenced to death by the Supreme Polish National Tribunal in Krakow and executed on December 22, 1947. Dr. Mengele escaped to South America. His colleague, Dr. Franz Lucas, was tried by a West German court in Frankfurt and sentenced in 1964 to three years and three months in prison. The German jury tried to justify the minimal punishment by the argument that Lucas had freely admitted his participation in the "selection" process, had never agreed with the policy of extermination, and had shown regret for his acts.[57]

Rudolf Hoess, the founder and supreme commandant of all the camps in the Auschwitz complex, was discovered after the war hiding in the British occupation zone under the alias of Rudolf Lang. He was extradited to Poland, tried in Warsaw, and hanged on gallows put up in front of the first Auschwitz crematorium. One of the questions he answered during his trial referred to the inmates of the "Czech family camp." Asked by the Polish prosecutor why those deported from Terezín had been killed after six months in the "family camp," Hoess replied that the main task of those inmates had been to write letters to the outside world with favorable comments about life in the camp to refute the reports that the Jewish deportees were being exterminated. It was known that reports of the exterminations had leaked out and it was considered necessary to "reassure" world opinion as well as the tens of thousands of Jews in the Terezín ghetto. But after six months, the *Reichssicherheitshauptamt* (RSHA) in Berlin considered that the inmates of the family camp had finished their job and could now be exterminated.[58]

THE SLOVAK STATE[59]

INITIAL STAGES: EVACUATION

On October 6, 1938, after the Munich agreement, an autonomous Slovak government was established by Slovak politicians in Žilina. At that time (according to the census of 1930) 136,737 Jews were living in Slovakia. However, more than 40,000 of these lived in the fertile southern and southeastern regions inhabited mostly by Hungarians, which, as a result of the Vienna award of November 2, 1938, were annexed by Hungary.

Under the new circumstances, the power in Slovakia was in the hands of Andrej Hlinka's *Ludová Strana* (People's party), headed by the Catholic priest Dr. Jozef Tiso.[60] This party had already been known for its anti-Semitic tendencies during the First Czechoslovak Republic. Now, its leaders openly declared that they regarded it their duty to "solve the Jewish problem" in Slovakia in the German way.[61] By following a radically anti-Jewish policy they hoped to secure Hitler's support against Hungarian territorial aspirations which in their view posed a threat to Slovakia's future. The anti-Jewish policy of the new Slovak government was supported by the German ethnic minority in Slovakia, which had been organized politically into the *Deutsche Partei* (German party), headed by Franz Karmasin, a supporter of Nazi Germany.

The growing anti-Jewish propaganda brought new followers to the People's party, not only because anti-Semitism in Slovakia, where Jews formed 4.5 percent of the total population, had always been stronger and less inhibited than in Bohemia and Moravia, but also because many Slovaks now saw an opportunity for personal gain at the expense of the Jews. Units of the party's paramilitary arm, the *Hlinkova Garda* (Hlinka Guard), and the *Freiwillige Schutzstaffel* (FS; voluntary "defense squads" organized by the German party) marched through the streets of the Slovak capital, Bratislava, provoking rows with Jews who were then arrested and had their homes and stores looted. Jews were publicly blamed for the loss of the regions annexed by Hungary and accused of having strengthened the Hungarian elements in Slovakia. Hlinka Guard and FS units raided the homes of Jews who had been born in the "lost territories," turned the Jews out in the middle of the night, and expelled them into the territory annexed by Hungary. The Hungarian authorities refused to accept the deportees and returned them to Slovakia. In the meantime, however, Hlinka Guard and FS members had occupied the homes and stores of the Jews whom they had expelled. Such was the situation when SS Hauptsturmführer Adolf Eichmann paid his first visit to Slovakia in order to negotiate with the Slovak leadership about the "evacuation" of the Jews.[62]

On March 14, 1939, the Slovak parliament officially declared the establishment of an independent Slovak state, and the government almost immediately began to pass laws excluding Jewish citizens from all leading positions in the economy of the new state, from the state civil service, and from the army. The government also ordered the registration of all Jewish property for the purpose of eventual confiscation. At the Salzburg Conference of July 28, 1940, the Slovak leaders agreed to introduce in Slovakia a National Socialist regime, an obligation that resulted in the promulgation of even stricter anti-Jewish regulations. After Tiso's election as president of the new state, Dr. Vojtech Tuka became Prime Minister and Minister of Foreign Affairs, and Alexander (Šaňo) Mach, the commander of the Hlinka Guard, Minister for Internal Affairs.

In September 1940, the new government launched a wide anti-

Jewish campaign with instructions to all motion picture theaters to show the German anti-Semitic film *Jud Süss*. At that time Bratislava officially welcomed Eichmann's colleague SS *Hauptsturmführer* Dieter Wisliceny, who had come to act as the government's adviser for Jewish affairs.[63] Members of Wisliceny's staff were attached to Slovak ministries and other official agencies charged with the enforcement of the "solution of the Jewish problem" in Slovakia. One of them took over the training of functionaries of the People's party; another SS officer, Viktor Nageler, organized the units of the Hlinka Guard along the lines of SS units. These units were charged by the Ministry for Internal Affairs with the enforcement of the anti-Jewish program.[64]

In the initial phase of "solving" the Jewish problem, the Slovak government permitted the emigration of affluent Jews who had surrendered all their property to the state. Jews without any means were also permitted to leave. Some set out for Palestine on boats sailing on the Danube to the Black Sea. These transports were mostly organized and financed by Jewish organizations in other countries. By the end of 1941 7,116 Jews had left the Slovak state, 2,727 of them for Palestine.[65] Hundreds of young Jews crossed the borders illegally into Poland and Hungary; many of them eventually contacted and joined the Czechoslovak armed units that were formed abroad. According to the census of December 15, 1940, the Slovak state, excluding the territories lost to Hungary, had a total population of 2,653,654, of which 88,951 were Jews. The total value of property owned by Jews was estimated at more than 4 billion Slovak crowns, which at the time represented a value of some 135 million dollars.

Law No. 45 of September 16, 1940, created the *Ústredný Hospodársky Úrad* (ÚHU; Central Economic Office), which was charged with the task of organizing the "solution of the Jewish problem" in Slovakia. The head of this newly formed agency, Augustin Morávek, was sent to Germany to study Nazi methods for the "solution." After Morávek's return, ÚHU began to issue orders depriving Jews of their basic civil rights. Their freedom of movement was limited, they were forbidden to have contacts with non-Jews, and their property gradually was confiscated. By the end of 1941, more than 10,000 Jewish businesses had been liquidated and nearly 2,000 larger ones transferred to Aryan ownership.[66] Those who gained the most from this Aryanization were the leaders of the new Slovak puppet regime, their families, and their friends. President Tiso, for instance, secured one of the country's largest Jewish enterprises for his sister. The property of the Jews of Banovce was transferred to his own parish.[67]

ÚHU also directed the psychological preparation of the Slovak populace for the "evacuation" of the Jews. Morávek's annual report of ÚHU for 1941 ended with the declaration: "The Jewish problem in Slovakia will be solved when the last Jew has left the frontiers of the state."[68]

The law of September 30, 1940, created the *Ústredna Židov* (ÚŽ; Jewish Office) in Bratislava, which was subordinate to ÚHU. The new organization was to represent Jews vis-à-vis the Slovak authorities and guarantee that relevant government orders would be duly carried out.[69] By the end of September 1940 the activities of all Jewish organizations in Slovakia had ceased, their offices had been closed, and their assets confiscated. The emigration files of the Palestine Office were taken over by the *Ústredna Židov*.

September 1941 saw the introduction of a "Jewish Code" condensing all the limitations applying to Jews in the Slovak state into 270 paragraphs.[70] German diplomatic correspondence described this code as "much more severe than the Nuremberg Laws" and the Slovak press boasted that the Slovak Jewish Code should serve as an example for other European states to follow.[71]

The code stipulated that Jews had to fulfill quotas of forced labor. For this purpose the Ministry for Internal Affairs set up labor camps for Jews at Vyhne, Sered, and Nováky, and Jewish labor centers at Jihlava, Nitra, Žilina, Svätý Júr, and Zohor.

In the fall of 1941, 10,000 of the 15,000 Jews still living in Bratislava were forced to leave their homes and were evacuated, equipped only with bare personal necessities, to the eastern Slovak district of Sariš-Zemplín and to labor camps there. By that time ever-growing numbers of Jews found it impossible to earn a living and became dependent on support from the *Ústredna Židov*. However, the funds of the *Ústredna Židov* were rapidly exhausted and the Slovak government was looking for ways of ridding itself of the many Jews who had been reduced to destitution. For this purpose the Ministry for Internal Affairs created another organ, the so-called "Department 14," which was to search for hidden Jewish property and to make plans for the evacuation of the Jews from Slovakia. Dr. Anton Vašek, who was appointed head of the new department, was known for his cruelty in dealing with Jews and was often referred to as the "King of the Jews." [72]

That fall, too, Slovak leaders, including President Tiso and Prime Minister Tuka, were invited to Hitler's headquarters. There, in conference with Heinrich Himmler, they learned for the first time about the Nazi plan for the evacuation of all the Jews of Europe to the territories which Germany had gained by the defeat of Poland. When asked by Foreign Minister Joachim von Ribbentrop whether the Slovak government intended to repatriate Slovak citizens of the "Jewish race" who were then living in Germany, the Slovak representatives agreed that such Slovak Jews should be deported from Germany directly to the East, under the condition that their assets would be transferred to the Slovak state.

At the beginning of 1942, the German Ministry of Labor requested 20,000 Slovak workers to be sent to munitions plants in Germany. Instead of Slovaks, the Slovak government offered to send 20,000 young, able-bodied Slovak Jews. Berlin agreed and, in February 1942, Tuka signed an agreement with the German ambassador in Bratislava concerning the deportation of 20,000 unmarried Jewish men and women between the ages of sixteen and thirty-five to be used for forced labor in the Reich.[73] Eichmann, who stepped in at this stage, asked the Slovak government to pay 500 Reichsmarks for every Jew to be deported under this agreement, to cover the cost of training and living arrangements.[74] He also insisted that these Jews must be deprived of their Slovak citizenship. After somewhat protracted negotiations, the Slovaks agreed to Eichmann's terms under the condition that none of these Jews would be sent back to Slovakia and that Germany would not claim any of the assets they would leave behind in the Slovak state. We know from the correspondence of the Slovak diplomat Joseph A. Mikus that the Slovak government paid to Germany, in advance, a total of 100 million Slovak crowns for the deportation of 20,000 Jews.[75] It is known, too, that Tuka and Mach were pressing Eichmann to facilitate also the deportation of relatives of the deported men and women "because it would not be Christian to separate families."[76]

DEPORTATIONS FROM THE SLOVAK STATE

The organization of deportations was in the hands of Vašek's Department 14 which was assisted by the Slovak Hlinka Guard and the German party's FS units. As early as March 1942, young Jewish men and women were assembled in Bratislava, Poprad, Žilina, Sered, and Nováky under the pretext that they would be given employment at labor centers. In these "concentration centers" Jews were beaten up by Hlinka Guardists who brutally herded them into cattle cars for deportation. The train which left Poprad on March 26, 1942, carrying 999 Jewish girls was the first mass transport of Jews from Slovakia to arrive in Auschwitz. Four days later 1,000 young women were sent to Auschwitz, this time from Bratislava. Kateřina Singerová, one of the few who survived, recalled:

In March I was called to Bratislava. We were told we would be going to Poland in order to prepare homes there also for members of our families and that everyone would be working at his own occupation. Guardists drove us into the cattle cars of a train escorted by armed guards. The next day we arrived at Auschwitz, where we were taken off the train and, with SS men shouting and their dogs barking, we were taken to the camp not far from the station. There they took away all our belongings, including clothes and underwear, and put us into dirty uniforms, full of lice, which had been left behind by Soviet prisoners of war who had perished. They also took our good leather shoes and gave us wooden shoes which cut through our skin at every step. The most horrible impression on us was the fact that they cut our hair and shaved our bodies. We were put to work at building barracks and roads and at canalization and swamp clearance. We had no shovels, no pickaxes, no wheelbarrows. We had to load the muddy earth by hand onto primitive stretchers or carry it from place to place in the folds of army shirts and jackets. The barracks were not heated during the winter, there still was no kitchen in the camp, and the food, turnip soup brought in by cars, arrived cold. Hungry, exhausted women had to work even in the rain and snow. They fell like flies and many, in despair, were seeking escape at the high tension wire of the fence . . .

In May members of our families began to arrive in Auschwitz. Immediately on arrival, they were "selected" by SS men near the train for "light" and "heavy" work. "Light" work meant a quick death in the gas chambers, "heavy" work meant a hopeless life and a cruel death in the camp. In Slovakia the families had been promised that they would be reunited with their sons, daughters, brothers, and sisters, but most of these were no longer alive.[77]

THE ANNIHILATION OF CZECHOSLOVAK JEWRY 309

During March and April 1942, more than 17,000 young Jews, men and women, were deported from Slovakia to Auschwitz and Lublin. They were put to work under the most difficult and subhuman conditions at building the Auschwitz-Birkenau camp, as well as the camps of Belzec, Treblinka, and Maidanek. Within three to six months an overwhelming majority had died of exhaustion, starvation, or sickness, or else they had been beaten to death. Among the women only those who, thanks to their professional qualifications, were employed as translators and typists at the SS camp headquarters or as nurses in the inmate hospital had a chance to survive. Of the men only those could survive who had the good fortune of being assigned to artisans' details, in storerooms, tailors' and shoemakers' workshops, or as assistants to doctors in the camp hospitals.

It was from among the Slovak Jewish inmates that the camp administration organized the first *Sonderkommando*, which had a crew of 300. This *Sonderkommando* was assigned to the task of digging mass graves at Birkenau for thousands of dead Jewish inmates and Soviet prisoners of war whose bodies were rapidly decomposing. This was before the procedure was changed and the dead were no longer buried but cremated. The young Slovak Jews looked for ways to avoid this horrible assignment. In their despair, they planned a mass escape. However, their plans were discovered. During roll call one evening at the end of November 1942 they were encircled by armed SS men and taken from the Birkenau camp to Auschwitz I, where they all were shot. An account of their fate was given by Arnošt Rosin, the only one of the 300 to survive.[78]

At the insistence of Tuka and Mach, Eichmann agreed to arrange transports of entire families, with promises of reunions with relatives who had already been deported. As a result, in May and June 1942 over 10,000 men, women, and children were taken in eleven transports to the Lublin area where they were distributed in the overcrowded ghettos and transit camps. There they worked or vegetated until they were finally shot by SS killing squads or gassed at Belzec, Sobibor, or Treblinka.[79]

On May 15, 1942, after more than 40,000 Slovak Jews had already been deported, Law No. 68/1942 on the "evacuation of Jews" from the Slovak state was promulgated. By that time reports about the fate of the deportees had already begun to spread and the Jews were desperately trying to avoid deportation to the East.[80] Some 7,000 escaped to Hungary, others secured false or forged baptismal certificates or spent enormous amounts of money for certificates attesting to their vital importance for the economy of the state.[81]

Reports about the fate of the deported Jews also reached certain dignitaries of the Roman Catholic Church. At the end of July 1942, the papal nuncio informed President Tiso that Jews deported to the Lublin region were being exterminated. To pacify the Vatican, Prime Minister Tuka asked Dieter Wisliceny to permit an official Slovak commission to visit the places where the deported Jews were supposed to have been "resettled." Wisliceny discussed this request with Eichmann, who replied that such a visit was not possible because most of the deportees were already dead.[82] Only after Tuka had contacted Himmler directly with the threat that he, Tuka, would stop the deportations, was a commission, including Wisliceny, permitted prearranged visits to certain specified places at the end of the summer of 1942. One of the places chosen for a visit was the little town of Konskawola in the Lublin region, where about 1,000 Polish Jews who had been "evacuated" to the extermination camp of Sobibor had been hurriedly replaced by 1,025 Slovak Jews from the family transports and a ghetto had been hastily organized, complete with an *Ältestenrat* (Council of Jewish Elders) chosen from among the new arrivals.[83] The commission was accompanied by Fritz Fiala, correspondent of the Bratislava German-language newspaper, *Grenzbote,* whose reportage, which was entitled, "Jews in New Settlements" and included pictures and interviews with women deportees, was given wide publicity.[84] The commission even visited Auschwitz. Kateřina Singerova describes this visit as follows:

> Early in the fall it became known that a commission would visit the camp. The rags of our striped prisoners' uniforms were replaced by dresses. We were even given underwear and white handkerchiefs to cover our cropped hair. Girls who were working in the offices of the SS camp administration were chosen to act as our spokesmen. They were told how to behave and threatened that even one wrong answer would mean not only the loss of a relatively comfortable job but also severe punishment. The officers told them: "You will say you are working at your professions, according to your qualifications. You are doing fine. You were permitted to

keep everything you had brought here with you, that you can write letters freely and receive food parcels . . ."

When the commission arrived, we lined up in rows of five behind the emptied barracks. Only selected women, especially groomed for the occasion, were permitted to approach members of the commission standing at a distance of about fifteen meters from us. They were also photographed. Women who tried to raise their hands or to step out of line were taken away by women guards and beaten up. Later, when new transports arrived, some of the women told us that they had read about us in Slovak newspapers and had even seen pictures of some of us . . .[85]

According to a report of the Slovak ministry of transport, dated January 14, 1943,[86] fifty-seven transports totaling 57,752 Jewish men, women, and children had been deported from Slovakia by the end of 1942. Of these, 39,006 had been deported to the Lublin region and 18,746 to Auschwitz. According to the statistics of the repatriation authorities, only 348 of these returned to Czechoslovakia after the war.

The last Slovak transport of 1942 arrived at Auschwitz on October 21. Of 1,000 men, women, and children, 121 men and 181 women were "selected" for work. The rest were sent straight to their deaths.[87] At that time four large gas chambers and crematoria were still in the process of construction and the deportees were exterminated in the small crematorium of Auschwitz I. Filip Müller, who was working in the crematorium (he had been deported to Auschwitz from Sered nad Váhom), survived and recalled, among other things:

The guards drove some 700 exhausted men, women, and children straight from the train to the crematorium courtyard. They were met by SS men who suddenly began to swing their cudgels and to shout at the half-dead people, ordering them to undress quickly. Frightened, not understanding why they should have to undress in the open courtyard, the Jewish deportees hesitated. However, the SS men did not give them even a moment's respite. Their shouts of *"Los! Los! Ausziehen! Schneller machen!"* (Hurry! Hurry! Undress! Make it snappy!) became louder and were accompanied by an even more threatening swinging of sticks. Fear and helplessness were in the eyes of the people. Some slowly began to undress, trying to communicate with others. When the SS men noticed this, they rushed into the crowd and their cudgel blows rained upon the heads of the Jews. In the chaos that ensued, women cried and ran about helplessly, seeking protection from their men. Dazed and bewildered, the frightened men, unable to orient themselves, could not even think of resisting. The unexpected brutality of the SS men broke the passive resistance of the shocked people, who now quickly tore the clothes and underwear from their bodies. When all had undressed, the SS men herded the naked men, women, and children into the crematorium building and jammed them into the gas chamber, which they then sealed hermetically. Two of the SS men, wearing gas masks, climbed the steep platform and scattered crystals of Zyklon B through special openings leading to the ceiling of the gas chamber. The cries for help, mixed with laments and choking coughs, which could be heard even through the doors, stopped after about ten minutes. Then there was only the terrifying stillness of innocent victims who had been murdered in an unspeakably torturous fashion.[88]

Cessation and Resumption of Deportations

The *Nebenregierung* (literally, "the other government"), known also as the "Working Group," created by the leadership of the *Ústredna Židov*,[89] felt that its main task was to bring the deportations to a stop. The "Working Group" was able to make contact with Jewish deportees in the camps and ghettos of Poland. With the help of the "Working Group," about fifty Slovak Jews who had escaped from the camps were brought back to Slovakia and from there sent to comparative safety in Hungary. Through secret channels, the "Working Group" conveyed news of the tragic developments in the camps to Jewish organizations in Hungary, Switzerland, Turkey, and Palestine. In one of the reports, sent by Gisi Fleischmann, perhaps the most outstanding member of the "Working Group," we read:

Undoubtedly the news is entirely true, as the refugees (those that escaped) come from different places and report the same or similar things. The indiscriminate extermination of men, women, and children in large numbers is an everyday occurrence, and this extermination is carried out systematically by a few people. Mountains of corpses are lying in the graves which they (the victims) themselves have dug and the earth covering them sometimes continues to move, which indicates that some of the corpses were actually buried alive. Thousands of children have been collected from the camps and ghettos and mowed down by machine guns. People, regardless of sex, have to undress completely before being shot, and are often chased and hunted . . . before . . . the death blow.[90]

The report continues in the form of a coded letter:

> Unfortunately, we are receiving less and less news from there. It is as if people buried under debris, one after the other, cease to show signs of life.[91]

In Istanbul, these reports were received by Chaim Barlasz, the representative of the Jewish Agency for Palestine. Barlasz showed them to the papal nuncio, Monsignor Angelo Roncalli (who was to become Pope John XXIII), asking him to intervene in Rome and suggesting that the Vatican put pressure on the Slovak government to stop the deportations.[92] The intervention from the Vatican and the concentrated efforts of the "Working Group," which culminated in the establishment of close ties with certain members of the Slovak government and in an outright bribing of Dieter Wisliceny,[93] brought the deportations of Jews from the Slovak state to a stop at the end of October 1942. There were to be no more deportations from Slovakia for two whole years.[94]

Even the attempts of Šaňo Mach, the Minister for Internal Affairs, to resume the deportations in the spring of 1943 did not succeed. For in the meantime, thanks to the initiative of the "Working Group," the production of furniture, textiles, footwear, toys, and some chemical goods in Jewish labor centers had reached such a volume that it had become an important factor in the Slovak economy. In 1943 the value of this production was 40 million Slovak crowns and 3,000 men and women whose brains and hands had been responsible for this achievement were safe from deportation. That was why Mach met with vehement opposition from a number of influential ministers and government officials who argued that it would be more useful to utilize the remaining Jews for the Slovak economy than to deport them.[95]

However, at the end of September 1944, the transports were resumed. This was done to punish the Jews because Jews had participated in the Slovak uprising that broke out on August 29, 1944. It was a well-known fact that able-bodied young Jewish men had run away from the labor camps at Šered, Vyhne, and Nováky, joined Slovak patriots, and fought side by side with them against the Germans. Unfortunately, it soon became clear, too, that the uprising had been premature and inadequately prepared so that even at this last stage of the war the German army found it an easy thing to occupy Slovakia and to quell the revolt. The Slovak freedom fighters had to retreat into the mountains and 18,937 of them were captured by the Germans. This figure included 4,653 Jews. Of the latter, 2,257 were shot by the Germans on the spot; the rest were taken to Sered for deportation to the East.[96]

On September 21, 1944, Heinrich Himmler himself came to Bratislava and ordered the deportation of all Jews from Slovakia. The enforcement of this order was entrusted to SS Sturmbannführer Alois Brunner, who was notorious for his ruthlessness and cruelty.[97] Brunner ordered all remaining Jews to assemble in the Sered camp of which he was the commandant. Hlinka Guard and FS units hunted mercilessly for Jews all over Slovakia. Nobody was spared. Neither baptismal certificates nor presidential exemptions were of any avail now. Brunner ordered the leaders of the *Ústredna Židov* to evacuate all Jews from Bratislava to Sered within two weeks. When this order was not carried out within the given time limit, FS and Hlinka Guard units surrounded all Jewish homes in Bratislava on September 28, 1944. Over 1,800 Jews caught in this roundup were locked into cellars, where they were tortured; many were killed. Brunner also ordered the liquidation of the *Ústredna Židov* and sent its entire leadership to Sered for deportation to the East.

On September 30, 1944, a deportation train with 1,000 persons aboard left Sered for Auschwitz. This time, however, there was no "selection" on arrival; all the deportees were taken from the station straight to the gas chambers. Six more transports followed but of those 6,936 deportees from Slovakia none were sent to the gas chambers. At Himmler's order the killing by gas in Auschwitz had been stopped on November 2, 1944, and the dismantling of all gas chambers and crematoria begun. The deportees were gradually moved to concentration camps in Germany, where a relatively large number managed to survive.

The last transport of Slovak Jews to Auschwitz left Sered on October 17, 1944. Among the passengers were the last two surviving members of the "Working Group," Rabbi Michael Ber Weissmandl and Gisi Fleischmann. Rabbi Weissmandl jumped off the moving train and survived the war.[98] Gisi Fleischmann was taken directly to the crematorium and shot at Brunner's order.[99]

In November 1944, three more transports totaling 2,732 men, women, and children were sent from Sered to the concentration camp of Sachsenhausen and Ravensbrück in Germany. The last of all the transports to leave Sered was sent to Terezín. It contained 1,638 Slovak Jews and arrived in Terezín on April 7, 1945.[100] After that there still remained in Slovakia about 5,000 Jews who were either living with false Aryan papers or were hidden in bunkers and other hiding places.[101]

A total of 70,058 men, women, and children were deported in sixty-eight transports[102] from a Slovak state headed by a Catholic priest for no other reason except that they were Jews. Of this number less than 4,000 survived the war. Ninety-four percent of the Jews deported from Slovakia perished. The government of the Slovak state, and those who allowed themselves to be ruled by it without protesting against its actions, must accept their share of responsibility for the sufferings and death of these victims.

CZECHOSLOVAK TERRITORIES ANNEXED BY HUNGARY

In 1939 there were about 42,000 Jews in the areas of Slovakia that were ceded to Hungary under the Vienna award of November 2, 1938. More than 102,000 Jews were living in Subcarpathian Ruthenia. In 1941 the Hungarian government headed by László Bardossy declared some 10,000 Subcarpathian Jews, who held either Polish or Russian citizenship, as stateless, and in August of that year these Jews were deported to Soviet- and German-occupied territory in the Kamenec-Podolsk area. A month later all of them were shot by German execution squads under the command of SS Gruppenführer Friedrich Jeckeln.[103]

For the approximately 800,000 Jews who lived in the territory of "Greater Hungary" during World War II, official anti-Jewish restrictions remained largely limited to their elimination from important business positions, from public life, and from the army. The most drastic regulations were those recruiting younger Jewish men into Hungarian forced labor camps and auxiliary formations of the Hungarian army. Hungary remained firm in opposing pressures from Germany to adopt Nazi methods for "the solution of the Jewish problem."

As Germany's military situation began to deteriorate, the chances of survival for Jews still living in Hungary improved. The Hungarian government headed by Nicholas Kállay, seeking contacts with the Western Allies, used as one of its channels the *Vaadat Ezra VeHatzalah* (Jewish Committee for Help and Rescue) in Budapest, which was in touch with influential Jewish organizations in Geneva and Istanbul.

Hitler himself had to intervene to put an end to this relatively happy state of affairs. In the middle of March 1944, he invited the Hungarian regent Admiral Nicholas Horthy to Klessheim Castle and presented him with an ultimatum: Kállay must be replaced and representatives of the German police and the SS must be authorized to enforce the measures which had to be taken against Jews in Hungary. If Hungary failed to comply with these requests, Horthy was told, it would become necessary for the German army to occupy Hungary. Horthy yielded to Hitler's threats. The newly appointed prime minister, Döme Sztójay, took into his cabinet representatives of the Hungarian Fascist Arrow Cross party, and the new Minister for Internal Affairs, Andor Jarosz, set up a special "Commissariat on Jewish Affairs" headed by László Baky, State Secretary in charge of the Hungarian police, and László Endre, State Secretary in charge of Jewish affairs. Lieutenant Colonel László Ferenczy, a notorious anti-Semite, was appointed liaison officer among the new commissariat, the gendarmerie, and the German police.

Meanwhile, Adolf Eichmann arrived in Budapest with his staff and 150 members of an SS commando. He and his Hungarian negotiating partners in the Ministry for Internal Affairs agreed to create a ghetto in every larger town and to order all Jews to wear the yellow Star of David. On March 31, 1944, Eichmann had his first talk with members of the newly appointed Central Council of Hungarian Jews in Budapest. He assured them that the Jews in Hungary would not be in danger as long as they did not cooperate with the Communists and with other resistance groups.

On April 7 Minister for Internal Affairs Jarosz ordered mass arrests of "Communist and Galician" Jews in the provinces. Roundups were conducted also in Užhorod, Mukačevo, and Košice, with the aim of concentrating thousands of Jews at assembly points for deportation for forced labor in Germany. To this end, the Commissariat on Jewish Affairs had at its disposal 5,000 Hungarian gendarmes and 150 SS men. The whole campaign was directed by Lieutenant Colonel Ferenczy, who reported directly to Eichmann. Brutal gendarmes drove 10,000–15,000 Jews at a time to heavily guarded brick factories in Košice, Užhorod, Mukačevo, and Marmaros-Sziget and kept them there for days and weeks on end without the most basic sanitary installations. Eichmann's method of maneuvering the Jews into a hopeless situation so that the local population and public administration should come to view them as a burden worked once again. On May 5, 1944, when the number of Jews crammed into uninhabitable dwellings had reached about 200,000, Endre and Baky asked Eichmann to have these Jews "evacuated" to Germany as quickly as possible. At a "transport conference" in Vienna held under Eichmann's chairmanship, representatives of the German and Hungarian Ministries of Transport agreed to arrange for the number of trains necessary for a daily load of 12,000 Jews to be evacuated from Hungary.[104]

Meanwhile, some hurried preparations for the immediate future had been going on in Birkenau. The ovens and chimneys of the four crematoria were badly in need of repair. A three-kilometer sideline was built which led from the railroad station of Auschwitz directly to the crematoria. The three-track addition, which had been completed at the end of April 1944, created sufficient space between the two camps to permit the unloading and "selection" of the new arrivals in the immediate vicinity of the "death factories." The number of inmates in the *Sonderkommando* charged with the task of cremating the corpses of those killed in the gas chambers was increased and SS men assisting at the "selection" were overheard remarking jokingly that they would soon be feasting on "good Hungarian salami."

While these activities were going on, two young Jewish prisoners, Walter Rosenberg (Rudolf Vrba), nineteen years old, and Alfred Wetzler, twenty-six years old, who had been deported from Slovakia to Birkenau in the spring of 1942, escaped from Birkenau. They were well acquainted with the machinery and operation of the extermination camp, because they had been in a position to observe its development from the early stages. After a difficult and danger-fraught journey Rosenberg and Wetzler arrived in Slovakia on April 21 and were given first aid and a hiding place by the family of a Jewish doctor in Žilina. At Liptovský Svätý Mikuláš they were contacted by a member of the "Working Group," Oskar Krasňanský, who wrote down what he learned from them about Auschwitz in a record of thirty pages, to which he appended a map of the extermination installations and the urgent recommendation that the Allies should bomb these installations and the railroad tracks leading to them. At the end of April Dr. Rudolf (Rezsö) Kasztner, chairman of the *Vaadat Ezra VeHatzalah* in Budapest, took this detailed eyewitness report to Budapest.[105] One copy was sent to Switzerland and, with the assistance of the American embassy in Berne, reached Washington. There the report was passed on from one American government agency to another. Only on November 8, 1944, was it finally sent by the director of the U.S. War Refugee Board, John W. Pehle, to the U.S. Department of War with an urgent request that the extermination machinery be destroyed by an air attack.[106]

On May 27, 1944, two other Jewish prisoners, Arnošt Rozin and Czeslaw Mordovic, succeeded in escaping from Birkenau. On June 8, 1944, they met Rosenberg and Wetzler in Liptovský Svätý Mikuláš and reported to Oskar Krasňanský about the continuous stream of transports bringing tens of thousands of Jews from Hungary to Auschwitz, where more than 80 percent were sent from the trains straight to the gas chambers. The Vatican, informed about these reports by Dr. Giuseppe Burzio, the papal nuncio in Bratislava, sent a special delegate to Bratislava to verify the unbelievable news. At Burzio's request, Krasňanský brought the escapees to the Svätý Júr monastery, where the papal legate had a secret talk with them that lasted five hours. He promised to do everything in his power to stop the deportations of Jews from Hungary.[107]

In the meantime, however, the assembling of Jews for further deportation continued under Eichmann's supervision and was carried out with unspeakable cruelty by Hungarian gendarmes. In the mass camp at Mukačevo, where 25,000 Jews were concentrated at one time, a typhoid epidemic erupted. Similar conditions prevailed at the centers in Chust and Košice. Since the centers were all fenced in and heavily guarded, escape was unthinkable. Hundreds of men and women, presuming that they were being taken to their deaths, refused to enter the deportation trains. They threw themselves upon the tracks and refused to budge. Hungarian gendarmes shot all of them while the others looked on.[108]

Beginning on May 15, 1944, four trains left Hungary for Auschwitz each day with the precision of the devil's own clockwork. Each train consisted of forty-five cattle cars, with eighty to ninety men, women, and children jammed into each car. The trains crossed the Slovak border near Prešov and continued on sidelines through the Carpathian woods to Auschwitz. During a period of forty-six days more than 400,000 Jews were deported from Hungary to Birkenau. Among them were 42,000 from concentration centers in former Czechoslovak territory occupied by Hungary, and 90,000 from Subcarpathian Ruthenia. The following statistical table gives the numbers of those deported from each center between May 15 and July 9, 1944:

From former Czechoslovak territories		From Subcarpathian Ruthenia	
Bardějov	3,000	Mukačevo	26,000
Levice	4,000	Užhorod	14,000
Komárno	8,000	Berehovo	10,000
Nové Zámky	7,000	Sevljuš	8,000
Dunajská Streda	8,000	Chust	10,000
Košice	12,000	Tiačevo	10,000
		Marmaros Siget	12,000
Total	42,000	Total	90,000

Of the 42,000 Jews deported from former Czechoslovak territory occupied by Hungary, 3,500 returned to Slovakia after the war. Since Subcarpathian Ruthenia was annexed by the Soviet Union in 1945, there are no data available about the number of Jews who survived deportation from that area. About 5,000 Subcarpathian Jews opted for Czechoslovak citizenship and settled mostly in the frontier regions of Bohemia which formerly had been inhabited by the Sudeten Germans.[109]

Not until July 1944 did reports brought by the Slovak Jews who had escaped from Auschwitz first appear in the Swiss and British press. On July 7 Foreign Secretary Anthony Eden and Brendan Bracken spoke in the House of Commons about the "extermination of 700,000 Hungarian Jews." On July 9, following the intervention of the Catholic Church and a sternly worded note from the U.S. Department of State to Horthy, the Hungarian government ceased all deportations to Auschwitz. Thus more than 300,000 Jews then still in Hungary were saved from death in the gas chambers.[110] But the 42,000 Jews from the former Czechoslovak regions occupied by Hungary were not among those fortunate ones, and for 90,000 out of the 102,000 Jews who had once lived in Subcarpathian Ruthenia it was also too late.

APPENDIX

DEPORTATIONS FROM THE TEREZÍN GHETTO TO GERMAN-OCCUPIED TERRITORIES IN EASTERN EUROPE

Destination	Date	Number of Deportees	Number of Survivors	%
Baltic States:				
Latvia — Riga	January 1, 1942	1,000	102	
Latvia — Riga	January 15, 1942	1,000	15	
Estonia — Raasiki	September 1, 1942	1,000	45	
Total		3,000	162	5.4%
Poland—Lublin district:				
Izbica	March 13, 1942	1,001	6	
Izbica	March 17, 1942	1,000	3	
Izbica	April 27, 1942	1,000	1	
Piaski	April 1, 1942	1,000	4	
Piaski	April 23, 1942	1,000	1	
Rejowiece	April 18, 1942	1,000	2	
Lublin-Maidanek	May 17, 1942	1,000	0	
Lublin-Maidanek	May 25, 1942	1,000	1	
Lublin-Maidanek	June 13, 1942	1,000	0	
Trawniki	June 12, 1942	1,000	0	
Zamosc	April 28, 1942	1,000	5	
Zamosc	April 30, 1942	1,000	19	
Sobibor	May 17, 1942	1,000	0	
Sobibor	July 28, 1942	1,000	0	
Treblinka	October 5, 1942	1,000	0	
Treblinka	October 8, 1942	1,000	2	
Treblinka	October 15, 1942	1,998	0	
Treblinka	October 19, 1942	1,984	0	
Treblinka	October 22, 1942	2,018	—	
Total		22,001	44	0.2%
Warsaw	April 25, 1942	1,000	8	0.8%

APPENDIX

Destination	Date	Number of Deportees	Number of Survivors	%
Baltic States:				
Latvia — Riga	January 1, 1942	1,000	102	
Latvia — Riga	January 15, 1942	1,000	15	
Estonia — Raasiki	September 1, 1942	1,000	45	
Total		3,000	162	5.4%
Belorussia:				
Minsk	July 7, 1942	1,000	2	
Maly Trostinec	August 4, 1942	1,000	2	
Maly Trostinec	August 20, 1942	1,000	0	
Maly Trostinec	August 25, 1942	1,000	1	
Maly Trostinec	September 8, 1942	1,000	4	
Maly Trostinec	September 19, 1942	2,000	0	
Maly Trostinec	September 21, 1942	2,020	0	
Maly Trostinec	September 22, 1942	1,000	1	
Maly Trostinec	September 23, 1942	1,980	0	
Maly Trostinec	September 26, 1942	2,004	0	
Maly Trostinec	September 29, 1942	2,000	0	
Total		16,004	10	.63%

APPENDIX

DEPORTATIONS FROM THE TEREZÍN GHETTO TO AUSCHWITZ

Date	Number of Deportees	Number of Survivors	%
October 26, 1942	1,866	28	
January 20, 1943	2,000	2	
January 23, 1943	2,000	3	
January 26, 1943	1,000	39	
January 29, 1943	1,000	23	
February 1, 1943	1,001	29	
September 6, 1943	2,479	28	
September 6, 1943	2,528	10	
October 5, 1943	53	0	
December 15, 1943	2,504	279	
December 18, 1943	2,503	449	
May 15, 1944	2,503	120	
May 16, 1944	2,500	8	
May 18, 1944	2,500	273	
September 28, 1944	2,499	382	
September 29, 1944	1,500	79	
October 1, 1944	1,500	306	
October 4, 1944	1,500	128	
October 6, 1944	1,550	78	
October 9, 1944	1,600	23	
October 12, 1944	1,500	78	
October 16, 1944	1,500	117	
October 19, 1944	1,500	53	
October 23, 1944	1,715	186	
October 28, 1944	2,038	144	
Total	44,839	2,865	6.4%

NOTES

1. See Livia Rothkirchen, "The Jews of Bohemia and Moravia: 1939-1945," John G. Lexa, "Anti-Jewish Laws and Regulations in the Protectorate," in the present volume, pp. 3-74 and 75-103, respectively.
2. See Ladislav Lipscher, "The Jews of Slovakia: 1939-1945," in the present volume, pp. 222-3.
3. H. G. Adler, *Theresienstadt* (Tübingen: 1955), pp. 13, 37, 63.
4. Arthur D. Morse, *While Six Million Died: A Chronicle of American Apathy* (New York: 1967), pp. 30, 60, 203.
5. YVA (Yad Vashem Archives), Jerusalem, Document DN 30-1.
6. Idem.
7. Adler, *Theresienstadt,* p. 17.
8. YVA, Group 0-59-65. Testimony of Mordechai (Marek) Neuer.
9. YVA, Testimony of Max Gruenbaum.
10. YVA, Group 0-59, 1, 63, 84. Testimonies of A. Alter, Mordechai (Marek) Neuer, and V. Ueberreich.
11. See also Erich Kulka, "Jews in the Czechoslovak Armed Forces During World War II," in the present volume, pp. 340, 389-98.
12. E.g., Hitler's address to the Reichstag on January 30, 1939.
13. IMT (International Military Tribunal), Document PS-710.
14. A photocopy of the complete document is in the files of the YVA, Jerusalem.
15. Karel Lagus and Josef Polák, *Město za mřížemi* [City Behind Bars] (Prague: 1964), p. 65.
16. See Appendix.
17. YVA, Protocol 033-1. Testimony of Dr. Alice Eckstein.
18. Isaiah Trunk, *Judenrat: Jewish Councils in Eastern Europe under Nazi Occupation* (New York: 1972), pp. 284-85.
19. YVA, Protocol 033-1.
20. Ota Kraus and Erich Kulka, *The Death Factory* (Oxford: 1966), p. 190; H. Langbein, *Menschen in Auschwitz* [People in Auschwitz] (Vienna: 1972), pp. 141, 220.
21. E.g., testimony of A. Kalfus, YVA, 03-1650.
22. František Kafka, *Krutá léta* [Cruel Years] (Prague: 1963).
23. See Zdenek Lederer, "Terezín," in the present volume, pp. 104-64.
24. D. Dombrowska, "Wysiedleni Żydzi zachodnoeurope jscy v getcie lódzkim" [West European Jews Exiled to the Ghetto of Lodz], *Biuletyn Zydowskiego Instytutu Historicznego* [Bulletin of Jewish Historical Institute] (Warsaw: 1968), pp. 131-33.

25. IMT, Document PS-3921. Daluege was sentenced to death and executed in Prague on October 20, 1946.
26. Gerald Reitlinger, *Die Endlösung: Hitler's Versuch der Ausrottung der Juden Europas 1939-1945* (Berlin: 1956), pp. 244-45. This book was originally published in English in New York in 1953 and again in a second, augmented edition in 1961 under the title *The Final Solution: The Attempt to Exterminate the Jews of Europe 1939-1945*. However, the author used the German version, which contains material not included in the English original.
27. Lederer, "Terezín," in the present volume, pp. 104-64.
28. These camps were run by the SS.
29. Lagus and Polák, *Město za mřížemi*, p. 311.
30. IMT, Prozess XI, Document H6-2586: "Das Wannseeprotokoll." English translation from *A Holocaust Reader*, ed. Lucy S. Dawidowicz (New York: 1976), p. 78.
31. Ota Kraus and Erich Kulka, *Massenmord und Profit* [Mass Murder and Profit] (Berlin: 1963), pp. 61-117.
32. Reitlinger, *Die Endlösung*, pp. 103, 245.
33. O. Kaplanas, *Das Fort 9 klagt an* [Fort 9 Accuses] (Vilnius: 1976).
34. YVA, 93-2015, Testimony of E. Nobel. 03-2595, Testimony of Martinowski.
35. Reitlinger, *Die Endlösung*, pp. 244-45.
36. YVA, E-7-3. Testimony of S. Gerstein.
37. YVA, 033-6. Testimony of Irma Petrášková.
38. Ota Kraus and Erich Kulka, *Noc a mlha* [Night and Fog] (Prague: 1958), pp. 118ff.
39. Zdenek Lederer, *Ghetto Theresienstadt* (London: 1953), p. 215.
40. Kraus and Kulka, *Noc a mlha*, pp. 85f.
41. Trunk, *Judenrat*, p. 418.
42. Lagus and Polák, *Město za mřížemi*, p. 312.
43. Ibid., p. 313.
44. Reitlinger, *Die Endlösung*, p. 592.
45. Kraus and Kulka, *Noc a mlha*, p. 76.
46. Gitta Sereny, *Into That Darkness: From Mercy Killing to Mass Murder* (New York: 1974), p. 157. The original version was quoted in the London *Daily Telegraph Magazine*, October 8, 1971.
47. For statistical details on the transports see Appendix, p. 322.
48. Lagus and Polák, *Město za mřížemi*, pp. 293-95.
49. Kraus and Kulka, *The Death Factory*, pp. 172-74.
50. Filip Müller, *Auschwitz Inferno. The Testimony of a Sonderkommando* (London: 1979), pp. 110ff.

51. Lederer escaped together with one of the guards of the "family camp," a Rumanian-German SS man named Viktor Pestek, who had fallen in love with Renée Neumann, a Jewish girl in the "family camp," and who sought a hiding place for himself, Renée, and her mother. See Erich Kulka, "Five Escapes from Auschwitz," in *They Fought Back,* ed. Yuri Suhl (New York: 1975), p. 201. The entire story was published in a historical novel by Erich Kulka, *Útěk z tábora smrti* [Flight from a Death Camp] (Prague: 1966).
52. Trunk, *Judenrat,* p. xxxi.
53. Two months after the dispatch of Lederer's report, an International Red Cross commission visited the ghetto in Terezín. The commission had plans to visit also a "labor camp in Upper Silesia," probably Birkenau. However, the commission was satisfied with the staged "model ghetto" in Terezín and canceled its planned visit to the labor camp. See *Oral History Division,* Hebrew University, Jerusalem, catalog no. 3, p. 114; also Zdenek Lederer, "Terezín," pp. 142–143 in the present volume, and Otto D. Kulka, *Ghetto in an Annihilation Camp* (Jerusalem, Yad Vashem Almanac [in print]).
54. Kraus and Kulka, *The Death Factory,* p. 176.
55. *Soudcové Žalobci Obhájci* [Judges, Plaintiffs, Advocate] (Prague, 1966); Bernd Naumann, *Auschwitz* (New York: 1966), pp. 154 f., 398–99; Kraus and Kulka, *The Death Factory,* pp. 177–80.
56. In addition to the transports to Auschwitz, ninety prisoners were sent in several groups to the concentration camp of Bergen-Belsen. None of them survived. See Lagus and Polák, *Město za mřížemi,* p. 325.
57. B. Naumann, *Auschwitz Prozess* [The Auschwitz Trial] (Frankfurt on the Main: 1965), p. 534; an English translation was published in 1966.
58. Kraus and Kulka, *The Death Factory,* p. 180.
59. For a more detailed study on the Holocaust era in Slovakia, see Ladislav Lipscher, "The Jews of Slovakia: 1939–1945," in the present volume, pp. 165–261.
60. This party was founded in 1918 by Hlinka, a Catholic priest with strong rightist, anti-Masaryk, and anti-Beneš views who ardently championed a separate Slovak state. After his death during the Munich crisis in September 1938 Hlinka was succeeded as head of the party by Tiso, the future president of the Slovak puppet state. In July 1945 Tiso was sentenced to death by the National Court of Justice in Bratislava and executed.
61. Conversations between Marshal Hermann Göring and the Slovak ministers Ferdinand Durčanský and Alexander (Šaňo) Mach, IMT, vol. III, pp. 148–49.

62. Livia Rothkirchen, *The Destruction of Slovak Jewry* (Jerusalem, 1961); Oskar Neumann, *Im Schatten des Todes* (Tel Aviv: 1956).
63. Wisliceny was sentenced to death by the National Court of Justice in Bratislava and executed in 1946.
64. Edict published in the official gazette, *Úradné noviny*, Bratislava, 12/6/1941. See also F. Steiner, ed., *Tragédia slovenských Židov* [The Tragedy of Slovak Jewry] (Bratislava: 1949) and Erich Kulka, *Tusa Končia stopy SS* . . . [Here End the Footprints of the SS] (Bratislava: 1965), p. 3.
65. Emil F. Knieža, "The Resistance of the Slovak Jews," in *They Fought Back,* ed. Yuri Suhl, pp. 176–81.
66. Anton Vašek, *Die Endlösung der Judenfrage in der Slowakei* (Bratislava: 1942), p. 42.
67. Rothkirchen, *The Destruction of Slovak Jewry,* p. xv.
68. After the war Morávek succeeded in fleeing the country and could be sentenced only *in absentia.*
69. For details, see Lipscher, "The Jews of Slovakia: 1939–1945," in the present volume, pp. 175, 185–186.
70. Idem. See also F. Steiner, ed., *Tragédia slovenských Židov* [The Tragedy of Slovak Jewry], pp. 42 f.
71. German diplomatic correspondence between Wuester and Weizsäcker. *The Trials of the War Criminals before the Nuremberg Tribunal,* NMT, Trial XIII NG-4409, p. 230.
72. Rothkirchen, *The Destruction of Slovak Jewry,* p. xvii.
73. NMT, Trial XII, NG-2586, p. 246.
74. IMT, Vol. XXXVIII, RF-1216, pp. 745–46.
75. IMT, Vol. IV, p. 359.
76. YVA, M-5/33-9.
77. Kraus and Kulka, *Továrna na smrt* [Czech original of *The Death Factory*] (Prague: 1946), p. 188.
78. Institute of Contemporary Jewry, Hebrew University, Jerusalem. Oral History Division, catalog no. 3, 1970, p. 120. Rosin escaped from Birkenau to Žilina, Slovakia, on May 27, 1944, together with Czeslaw Mordowic. The report of these two men, which reached the War Refugee Board in Washington, D.C., was classified as the first eyewitness testimony on the extermination of Jews from Hungary in Auschwitz. See Kraus and Kulka, *Noc a mlha* [Night and Fog], pp. 344–56 (Second ed., 1966).
79. Reitlinger, *Die Endlösung,* pp. 440–42.
80. Report by Rabbi Dr. Armin Frieder, microfilm, YVA, M-5-46/1. Rabbi Frieder's papers were rescued and edited by his brother Eman-

uel and sent in manuscript form for publication to Yad Vashem in 1982.
81. See also Lipscher, "The Jews of Slovakia: 1939-1945," in the present volume, pp. 198-200.
82. Reitlinger, *Die Endlösung,* p. 443.
83. Trunk, *Judenrat,* p. 326.
84. *Slovenská Politika,* Bratislava, 11/7/1942. See reproduction in F. Steiner, ed., *Tragédia slovenských Židov,* p. 116.
85. Kraus and Kulka, *Tovární na smrt,* p. 189.
86. Photocopy of the report in YVA, M-5/18/14. However, the findings of the National Court of Justice in the criminal case against Dr. Anton Vašek give the official figure as 57,837. (See Lipscher, pp. 000-000 in this present volume.)
87. *Zeszyty Oswiecimske,* Oswiecim, 1958, No. 3, p. 111.
88. Oral History Division, catalog no. 3, 1970, p. 119. Müller, *Auschwitz Inferno,* pp. 11ff.
89. See Lipscher, in the present volume, pp. 205-207; Neumann, *Im Schatten des Todes,* pp. 39-45 and 113-20.
90. Oskar Neumann, *Gisi Fleischmann: The Story of a Heroic Woman* (Tel Aviv: 1970), p. 28.
91. Idem, p. 29.
92. Rothkirchen, *The Destruction of Slovak Jewry,* p. xxxii.
93. See Lipscher, in the present volume, pp. 222-223.
94. Neumann, *Gisi Fleischmann,* p. 23.
95. YVA, M-5/2/8. ÚŽ session of January 1944.
96. J. Lettrich, *History of Modern Slovakia* (London: 1956), p. 308. See also Lipscher, in the present volume, pp. 229-233.
97. After the war, Brunner was sentenced to death and executed in Vienna in May 1946.
98. Ben Hecht, *Perfidy* (New York: 1961), p. 264.
99. Neumann, *Gisi Fleischmann,* p. 35.
100. Lederer, *Theresienstadt,* p. 170.
101. Rothkirchen, *The Destruction of Slovak Jewry,* p. xlvii
102. This figure does not include those deported in trucks and is therefore not quite exact. In 1981-82 some groups of Slovaks in the United States and Canada started a campaign for the canonization of Tiso. See "Jozef Tiso, Executed War Criminal, To Be Proclaimed a Martyr," in Newsletter no. 19/1982, published by the Public Committee of Auschwitz Survivors, Jerusalem.
103. Reitlinger, *Die Endlösung,* p. 468.

104. Martin Gilbert, *Auschwitz and the Allies* (London: 1981), pp. 181 f., 207 ff.
105. Oral History Division, catalog no. 3, p. 117, testimony of Oscar Krasňansky; Hecht, *Perfidy,* p. 59.
106. Rudolf Vrba and Alan Bestic, *I Cannot Forgive* (London: 1963; New York: 1965); Erich Kulka, "Auschwitz Condoned," *Wiener Library Bulletin* (London: 1969), no. 14.
107. Kulka, "Five Escapes From Auschwitz," in *They Fought Back,* p. 196. See also Kraus and Kulka, *Noc a mlha* [Night and Fog], pp. 350 ff.
108. Hecht, *Perfidy,* pp. 136-37.
109. The figures in this table are taken from Randolph L. Braham, *The Destruction of Hungarian Jewry* (New York: 1963), pp. 968-69. There are certain discrepancies between these figures and data given by the "Documentation Action" of the Jewish Religious Congregation in Bratislava. The latter, compiled in 1948, was probably based on incomplete information. See also Gilbert, *Auschwitz and the Allies,* pp. 225 f., 269-72, 300.
110. Reitlinger, *Die Endlösung,* pp. 490-92. The reasons why so many Jews could be exterminated and why help came too late are exposed in Walter Laqueur, *The Terrible Secret* (London: 1980).

II. Resistance

JEWS IN THE CZECHOSLOVAK ARMED FORCES ABROAD DURING WORLD WAR II*

by Erich Kulka

INTRODUCTION

The overwhelming majority of Czechoslovakia's Jewish population perished in the Holocaust.[1] The memory of these innocent, defenseless victims is dishonored when they are compared to flocks of sheep driven without protest to the slaughter. Not enough emphasis has been placed on the courageous stand and the heroic conduct of those Jews from Czechoslovakia who, having escaped the gas chambers by fleeing from their country, fought for the restoration of Czechoslovakia's independence as members of Czechoslovak army units formed in Allied countries during World War II.

Representatives of the present regime in Czechoslovakia have declared over and over again that the battles fought by the Czechoslovak units in World War II were a cornerstone of modern Czechoslovak history, that they had washed away the shame of capitulation and occupation and revived the Hussite tradition of the Czech fighting spirit. However, the participation of Jews in these battles is largely passed over in silence. Czechoslovak historiography, unable to conceal the Jewish contribution entirely, limits itself to a few scanty remarks on the subject. It is the purpose of this study to show the significant role played by Jewish volunteers from Czechoslovakia in the defeat of Nazi Germany.

---

* This article is the result of research conducted for the Institute of Contemporary Jewry at the Hebrew University, Jerusalem.

CZECH AND SLOVAK LEGIONS IN POLAND
(1939-40)

After the capitulation in Munich in the fall of 1938, and again after the Nazi occupation of Bohemia and Moravia in March 1939, thousands of Czechoslovak citizens left the country. Most numerous among the emigrants were those most acutely endangered: the Jews. Many crossed the border illegally into Poland, from where they hoped to find a way to one of the free countries. Refugees, Jewish and gentile, who ran afoul of Polish guards were either imprisoned or sent back into Czechoslovakia. Some were even handed over to the Germans. In many instances, however, the Poles telephoned the Czecho-Slovak consulate in Krakow to ask whether the consulate was ready to assume the care of the refugees. The standard answer of the consular staff—holdovers from the old regime, not new appointees of the German Protectorate—was that the refugees should be sent to Krakow, "with the exception of Jews." [2]

One Jewish woman who was stopped at the Polish border later recalled:

> When, after three days of interrogation, the Gestapo saw that I was not a spy but only a Jewess, I was turned over to the [Czecho-Polish] frontier guard at Petřvald. The guard beckoned to me and said: "Poland is that way. Don't come back!" He let his dog loose at me and chased me into the woods. It was getting dark, it started to rain and I had nowhere to hide. Wet through and through, I was caught by a Polish frontier patrol. They put me in prison and interrogated me at the station. In the morning they wrote out a report and when I signed that I would return to the Protectorate, they let me go. I started in the direction of the border, but I lost my way. Dead tired, I spent the night in a cemetery. In the morning I stopped a passing truck and the driver took me to the [headquarters of the] Jewish community at Bielsko. There I was registered, given instructions how to behave and handed a train ticket to Katowice, where I was to report at the Jewish community [headquarters]. I did so and was sent to a center for refugees from Czechoslovakia, where I was assigned a place to sleep and supplied with the most necessary things. I filled in the questionnaires for a British visa and waited three months for a transport. In the meantime, on September 1, 1939, the war broke out. German planes bombarded Katowice and the whole group from the refugee center fled in the wake of the retreating Polish army. We were a group of 300 Jewish refugees and we had difficulties in getting transportation even for the sick and the children.

When we arrived at the little [Polish] town of Sarna, the Poles put us on a train and transported us to the Soviet border.[3]

Until May 1939 most of those who fled from Czechoslovakia to Poland were Jews, Social Democrats, or Communists. After that, a growing number of soldiers from the demobilized Czechoslovak army crossed the border, either individually or in organized groups, intending to join a "Czechoslovak legion," which, according to exaggerated rumors spread in the Protectorate, was in the process of formation in Poland. For instance, the underground newsletter *V boj* [The Struggle] carried a report that "the first Czech legion has been organized in Poland and 8,000 men are armed and ready for battle."[4] News of this kind encouraged also many Czechoslovak Jewish intellectuals to flee to Poland. One such individual recalled after the war:

> I was studying in Prague. When the city was occupied by the Germans, I decided to leave for Poland with a group of friends. We received the news that General Lev Prchala had crossed the border with his troops and was organizing [Czechoslovak] armed resistance [in Poland]. At the end of March 1939, our group, mostly students who had been expelled from the universities because of their Jewish origin, went to the Ostrava region. From there we succeeded in crossing the border at an unguarded spot to Bielsko [Poland]. At the headquarters of the Bielsko Jewish community we were given railroad tickets to Krakow and instructions to contact the Jewish community there. In Krakow, we were told that other groups of young men had arrived before us and were waiting for their British visas. When we said that we wanted to join the Czechoslovak armed units of General Prchala, nobody seemed to have heard about such units, and we were directed to the Czechoslovak consulate.[5] There we spoke with an official, Dr. Taraba. We were unable to get any information from him about Prchala or any other Czechoslovak army unit. When we asked whether we could enlist in the [French] Foreign Legion, Taraba told us that Jews were not accepted there. So we returned to the Jewish community [headquarters] and registered like all the others waiting for British visas.[6]

Jewish refugees received help from their coreligionists and from Jewish organizations in Poland. But the non-Jews, who expected a friendly reception from their brother Slavs, were disappointed to find that they could get help neither from the Poles nor from organizations of fellow Czechs who had settled in Poland long before the

German invasion of Czechoslovakia. The non-Jewish refugees had no choice but to turn to Jewish charity organizations, which were now helping all refugees from Czechoslovakia, regardless of nationality or religion.[7] With the growing influx of refugees, the needs soon exceeded the capacities of the Jewish organizations. This led to constant tensions. The troubles started in Katowice and reached their peak in Krakow, where the refugees were categorized into three main groups: political, military, and economic. The last one was numerically the strongest because it included those persecuted for racial reasons: i.e., the Jews.[8]

The first Czechoslovak army group was created in Krakow at the end of April 1939, with the consent of the Czechoslovak consul Znojemský. The group was formed by about forty officers of lower rank, who elected a Lieutenant Kaleta as their commander. By the middle of May the number of volunteers had reached 100 and was still growing. Another account describes the reception accorded to a Jewish volunteer who attempted to join this military group:

> The consular official showed an interest in me—up to the moment when the question of my religion was raised. I said that I had no religion. The official then wanted to know the religion of my parents. When I told him that my parents were Jewish, he said that [my case] would be decided at a later date and with that, put an abrupt end to the interview.[9]

Initially, members of the military group lived in private accommodations. It took prolonged negotiations before the Polish military administration allocated them an empty camp in the village of Malé Bronowice, near Krakow. One of the first inhabitants of that camp describes it as follows:

> The camp had a capacity for about 600 people, but it eventually housed 3,000 Czechoslovak volunteers who were gradually allotted quarters there. The [volunteers] had neither uniforms nor weapons. The sentries had wooden clubs instead of rifles, and in the middle of August the group received ten rifles, without any ammunition, for a thousand men. Not even the camp commander wore a uniform.[10]

In deciding from case to case whether to accept a Jewish volunteer, the military group agreed that a Jewish volunteer could be accepted if he could prove that he had attended Czech schools and gave his nationality as Czech, Slovak, or Ruthenian.[11] Jews who reported their nationality as German, Hungarian, or Jewish were rejected. However, these criteria were not enforced in the case of Jewish physicians who had served as officers in the Czechoslovak army. They were needed because there were very few doctors among the non-Jewish volunteers.[12]

In June 1939 a Czech lieutenant colonel, Ludvík Svoboda, arrived in Poland as a stowaway on a coal train. He made contact with the group and, as the highest-ranking officer on hand, was named its commander.

At the beginning of August 1939, the Polish port of Gdynia on the Gulf of Danzig was closed. This brought the refugees to despair. The Jewish committees met in an attempt to relieve the catastrophic situation. There were about 300 young men in the "economic" refugee category. The committee requested one of its members, Dr. Michael Jellinek, to negotiate with the Czechoslovak consulate. Although the consulate office was closed when he arrived there, Jellinek was admitted when he presented a certificate showing that he was an officer of the Czechoslovak gendarmerie. By a stroke of good fortune, the official who received him turned out to be an old friend, Dr. Oldřich Maláč, an intelligence officer with whom Jellinek had worked during the mobilization at police headquarters at Moravská Ostrava in 1938. When Jellinek asked him why the consulate kept rejecting Jewish volunteers, Maláč took out a document from his safe, showed it to Jellinek, and told him: "This is an agreement between (the Czechoslovak) Ambassador Slávik and (the Polish) Foreign Minister [Lieutenant Colonel Josef] Beck. It permits the creation in Poland of a [military] unit which will be incorporated into the French Foreign Legion. For that purpose, the military camp at Bronowice was temporarily put at the disposal of the Czechoslovaks. The agreement was secret so that the Germans should not know about it. It was agreed that the soldiers should not be permitted to move about freely outside the camp, and also that there should be no Jews in the camp." Jellinek retorted that to his knowledge there were, in fact, several Jewish volunteers in the group. However, Maláč answered that these were only a few specialists, mainly doctors, whose services were badly needed. When Jellinek asked what, then, should become of the 300 young, able-bodied

Jewish refugees, Maláč suggested that Jellinek initiate direct negotiations with Commander Svoboda. He immediately telephoned to make an appointment for Jellinek.

At Svoboda's office in the barracks of Malé Bronowice, Jellinek requested that he be accepted into the group. He showed the commander his personal documents. Jellinek recorded the conversation as follows:

> Svoboda studied my documents thoroughly and then said, "On the basis of these papers we will gladly accept you. We need people like you." I answered, "There is only one catch. I am a Jew by religion and by nationality and I intend to state this also on my application form." Svoboda: "Must you do that? Is it so important?"
>
> Jellinek: "It is, because I am not alone. There are about 300 others like myself."
>
> Svoboda was silent for a while. Then he started trying to talk me out of it. Finally he took me for a walk in a nearby woods so that nobody should overhear our conversation. He was very polite and tried very diplomatically to find a way out. We talked for about two hours. Then I asked Svoboda a straightforward question, "Please tell me, sir, who are you? You know from my documents who I am, but who are you? Are you a Czechoslovak officer loyal to the constitution of Czechoslovakia, or are you a paid mercenary of Colonel Beck?"
>
> Svoboda was taken aback and his face turned red. "How do you know about that?" he asked.
>
> "Your question proves that not only I, but you, too, know about that agreement," I answered. "And how do I know it? Well, you could have seen from my papers that I am an intelligence officer. So it is my duty to know about that sort of thing."
>
> Svoboda walked on in silence for some time. Finally he said in a conciliatory tone, "All right, bring me your Jews."
>
> Two days later our group was ready. We met near the Jewish mensa [students' dining hall] in Krakow, and from there we marched to the barracks at Malé Bronowice. Nobody thought of secrecy any longer. War was obviously imminent, and additional volunteers were joining us all the time. Some of them had heard only now for the first time of the existence of a Czechoslovak army group.[13]

At the end of August 1939, most of the troops were transferred to the new Czechoslovak military camp at Lesźna near Baranowice.[14] Only a small group was left in Bronowice with the task of liquidating the camp and absorbing new refugees who were joining in the last moment.

On September 3, 1939, after the war with Germany had broken out, the then president of Poland, Ignacy Moscicki, issued a decree creating a "Czech and Slovak Legion in Poland" under Polish command.[15] This legion, composed of the troops in Malé Bronowice and Lesyná, was to be augmented by Czechs and Slovaks who had settled in Poland [prior to the fall of Czechoslovakia]. The Polish Marshal Rydz Szmigly appointed General Lev Prchala commander of the Legion. The staff of the Legion arrived at Lesyná on September 7, together with equipment received from the Polish army: four heavy and nine light machine guns, 5,400 cartridges, 500 gas masks, and 100 field shovels.[16] Very soon quarrels broke out among the men in the Legion. In some groups there was talk that there were too many Jews among the soldiers. Two written reports should serve as ample illustrations of the atmosphere which prevailed in the Legion. Max Kriegel, a second lieutenant in the medical corps, was to recall:

> There were about 200 Jewish officers and men in the Legion. Captain Novák from the Czechoslovak consulate also came to Lesyná. He found it hard to take that Jews should be able to join the Legion in spite of his opposition. He made the Jews feel this at every turn.[17]

Karel Fanta gives additional details:

> The day after his arrival at Lesyná, Captain Cyril Novák called out the names of some soldiers and formed [them into] a separate 'Jewish platoon.' He assembled us frequently and asked us whether we were not afraid, whether we really wanted to fight. He wanted to know what schools we had attended. He tested us to see whether we spoke Czech correctly, and some of us had to sing the Czechoslovak national anthem for him. He told us that whoever failed to act like a real Czech would be sent back to the Protectorate.[18] Svoboda regarded expressions of anti-Semitism as a delicate matter and tried to hush up all complaints.[19]

In the afternoon of September 11, there was an air raid alarm. The men were ordered into a train armed with anti-aircraft guns. At the Hluboczek Wielki railroad station German planes bombed the train and destroyed the station. The anti-aircraft commander ordered the formation of a 'defense ring' and put Cadet Officer Gruenbaum from Jeseníky in command. As a new wave of German bombers approached, Gruenbaum ordered the men to open fire. The gunners, frightened by the low-flying planes, fled to take cover. But Gruenbaum, ignoring the danger, ran from the commander's post to the nearest machine gun and began to fire at the attacking planes. He was hit in the stomach by shrapnel and had to be operated on then and there without anaesthesia.[20] He kept encouraging the surgeons, repeating again and again, 'All I regret is that I did not shoot down at least one of them.' After Gruenbaum had died of his wounds, one of the doctors, Dr. Taraba, said, 'Some Jew tried to act the hero and died of his own stupidity.'[21] But when Gruenbaum was buried at the Jewish cemetery of Tarnopol, the deputy commander of the Legion said in his speech at the graveside, 'I will not tolerate any incitement against Jewish members of the Legion. This one of our men who fought and fell as the first soldier of our legion was a Jew.'[22]

Poland was in a state of utter chaos. For some time the officers of the Legion were isolated from the world outside. When it became clear at last that the Russians and the Germans had signed an agreement to divide Poland between themselves, Colonel Svoboda, acting on orders from General Prchala and Ambassador Slávik, decided to lead the Legion to the Rumanian border. He sent ahead a group of officers to negotiate for permission to enter Rumania.[23] Meanwhile, however, the marching troops of the Legion had run afoul of advancing Soviet army units. The diary of Lieutenant Michael Jellinek contains the following entry for September 20, 1939: "During the march from Horodyszce the horses sank deep into the mud and our battalion was left without vehicles. At last we came to the village of Rakov. Darkness. Shooting. *'Ruky verch'* (Hands up). We are taken prisoner by the Russians."[24] Soviet soldiers disarmed the Czechoslovaks and their commander and took them to the border village of Husiatyn.[25]

The remainder of the Legion, about 200 men, were divided on the march from the camp of Bronowice. The smaller part found refuge with Czechs who had settled around Kvasilov, in the Volhynian region. The larger group, about 120 men, led by Captain Divoký, crossed the border into Rumania and was sent from there by the military attaché, Lieutenant Colonel Heliodor Pika, via Beirut to Palestine. This group formed the nucleus of the Czechoslovak battalion that was stationed in the Middle East.[26]

The troops captured by the Russians were taken in trucks to dilapidated barracks in Kamenec Podolsk, about fifteen kilometers from the Rumanian border. In this new environment anti-Semitic provocations occurred even more frequently than before. Lieutenant Jellinek reported the incidents. As a result of Jellinek's complaint, Svoboda assembled all the Jews and declared that he would take steps against Dr. Taraba, who had been responsible for spreading most of the anti-Semitism. He further promised not to tolerate any discrimination against, or persecution of, Jews in the Legion and asked to be informed about every incident of anti-Semitism.[27] The order of the day for the Second Company included a prohibition against any talk or action liable to lead to ethnic or racial intolerance.[28]

The fact that the Soviet Union felt bound by its agreement with Germany made the situation of the captured Czechoslovak Legion troops very precarious. It is to the credit of the Czechoslovak government-in-exile that, after difficult diplomatic negotiations, and mainly in exchange for highly valuable military intelligence, it succeeded in obtaining Soviet permission for the gradual transfer of the POWs to the Czechoslovak army unit which, in the meantime, had been formed in France. In the spring of 1940, about 160 of the interned volunteers were transported to France. Second Lieutenant Josef Gold, who was in the last transport, recorded:

> There were about sixty of us, mostly Jews. We had Turkish transit visas. Before we arrived at Istanbul, France had been occupied by the Germans. The Turkish authorities did not want to let us land, but the captain of the Soviet boat on which we had traveled refused to take us back. [Colonel] Svoboda, who was in command of the transport, negotiated with the Turkish authorities. In the end we were permitted to disembark in Istanbul. Svoboda returned to the Soviet Union. Two months later we continued on our way to Haifa.[29]

After the fall of France, the transports were temporarily stopped, but they were resumed two months later from Suzdal in northeastern Russia, where the troops of the Legion had been transferred in the meantime.[30] Lieutenant Jellinek, who had left for Palestine in one of the transports from Suzdal, writes:

> In August 1940, sixty men of the Legion left via Moscow and Kiev for Odessa. After two days in Odessa, we were taken aboard a Soviet boat to the Turkish [Mediterranean] port of Mersin. The Polish warship *Warszawa* was already waiting there and at the beginning of October, it brought us, together with Polish soldiers, to the port of Haifa.[31]

Altogether some 700 Czechoslovak soldiers were sent to the Middle East. Of these, about 200 were Jews. The transports from the Soviet Union continued until April 1941, when the Czechoslovak military mission headed by Lieutenant Colonel Heliodor Pika arrived in Moscow. The reports transmitted by the Czechoslovak Intelligence Service to its Soviet counterpart indicated that the Germans were making preparations for an attack on the Soviet Union. As a result, the last transport of Legion members was canceled. Second Lieutenant Kriegel, who had been scheduled to leave with the last transport, recorded: "Everything was ready for our departure for Palestine when, two days before the fixed date, an order came from Moscow saying that we were to remain in Russia to form the nucleus of a new Czechoslovak military unit."[32]

Of the original 900 officers and men who had come there with the Legion from Poland, only twenty-seven officers and sixty-six noncommissioned officers and men remained in the Soviet Union. After a special training course at the Oránky camp, they were transferred to the First Czechoslovak Infantry Battalion in the city of Buzuluk, 180 kilometers southeast of Kujbyshev.[33]

CZECHOSLOVAK REFUGEES IN SOVIET LABOR CAMPS

Thousands of Jewish refugees caught in Poland at the time of the German invasion fled to the part of the country that was occupied by Soviet troops under the Ribbentrop-Molotov Pact. Most of the refugees, mainly with the help of Jewish organizations, managed to find shelter and work in Lwow and the surrounding area. The Russians were recruiting labor units in Lwow, but very few of the refugees volunteered. In the spring of 1940, the Russians started to round up Polish intellectuals and "capitalists." It was rumored that these Poles would be transported to Siberia. Before long, the Soviet hunt was directed also against Jewish refugees.

From dozens of written accounts we have been able to reconstruct the fate of those who, having escaped from the German wolf, fell into the paws of the Russian bear. Malvina Lanzer, who, with her husband and three sons, was among the first Jewish refugees from Czechoslovakia to be caught in Lwow, stated:

At four o'clock in the morning we were awakened by the Soviet militia. Our official residence permits were entirely ignored, and we were driven out of our apartment. We were able to take only the most necessary things with us. A horse-drawn wagon that had been waiting in front of the house took us to the railroad station, where we were herded into a cattle car in a long deportation train. The train stopped only at large stations, where we received rations of bread and dried fish. After a terrible journey of twelve days we got out of the train, together with thousands of other refugees, at an unknown station, where, again, horse-drawn wagons were waiting for us. But this time we could place only our luggage on the wagons. We marched through one day and one night. Finally, we arrived at a camp in a deep Siberian forest. The camp was divided into sections by barbed wire fences and guarded by sentries stationed on watchtowers. The guard allotted one small room in one of the barracks for all five of us. My husband and the two older sons went to work in the woods. If they filled their daily quota of work, they received 800 grams of bread per day. Many of the people in this camp died of hunger, exhaustion, and accidents at work.[34]

Malvina Lanzer's eyewitness account was supplemented by that of her youngest son, Kurt:

In our sector, which was reserved for families, there were about 1,200 prisoners. They worked mostly in groups of fifteen under the supervision of armed guards and a foreman who checked the daily production quotas. Whoever did not fill his quota or did not report for work, such as women taking care of children, received only the basic daily ration of 300 grams of bread. At the end of 1941, we learned that a Czechoslovak army had been formed in the Soviet Union. Father went to the camp commander and registered all of us as volunteers.[35]

Similar testimonies were given by Czechoslovak Jewish refugees who found shelter among Czechs living in Volhynia, by those who fled from the newly established Slovak puppet state, and by those who tried to escape the cruel guards and "Arrow Cross" Fascists of Hungary.

The Jewish refugees included a rather high percentage of Communists. From the testimony of one of them, David František Elefant, we learn, among other things, that:

The party organs scrutinized our group of political refugees and differentiated among those who were considered politically reliable and those who were regarded as "problematic." Those found "reliable" were permitted to live in Soviet territory in comparative freedom. After the outbreak of war between Germany and the Soviet Union [in June 1941] they were among the first to join the Czechoslovak army, where they were soon assigned to responsible jobs. On the other hand, those who were not regarded as "reliable" were unexpectedly surrounded by the militia one day and deported to labor camps.[36]

The refugees from the Nazi concentration camp at Nisko formed a special category. In the fall of 1939, the Nazis had sent about 2,500 young Jewish men to Nisko to build the camp. Nisko is situated west of the river San, which, in 1939, formed the demarcation line between the German and Soviet sectors of Poland. Jewish deportees in Nisko took the opportunity to cross the river, singly and in groups, to the Russian side. One of the first to escape from Nisko was Arthur Alter, a reserve officer from Moravská Ostrava. He recalled:

I had been working in Nisko for about a month when I decided, along with a group of about thirty friends, to escape to the Russians. At the end of November, we waded without difficulty to the other bank of the river San. We were almost immediately stopped by a Soviet patrol and escorted to the refugee center at Lwow. From there, we came to Stanislawov. There were many Jews who gave us work. One night in May, Soviet policemen broke into the night shelter where we were staying together, checked our identity papers, and declared that all Jewish refugees were hostile to the Soviet state. They took us to the station, squeezed us into railroad cars, and deported us to Siberia. As far as I know, about 600 Jews succeeded in escaping from Nisko. About half of these joined Svoboda's army via Soviet labor camps.[37]

In the Soviet Union thousands of Jews from Czechoslovakia who had escaped Nazi persecution and concentration camps now found themselves experiencing the horrors of another totalitarian regime. Dozens of testimonies and written depositions from survivors of Stalin's labor camps read like chapters from Solzhenitsyn's *Gulag Archipelago*. In fact, they revealed the terrible secrets of the Siberian camps even before Solzhenitsyn did. Thus, Dr. Marek (Mordechai) Neuer, who was working as a prison doctor in the camps of the Kandalaksa region, recorded that on some days as many as 200 inmates died in camps as a result of hunger and exhaustion. The doctor signed the death certificates but was not permitted to state the causes of death. These were given in each case by the political officer who had to be present at the signing of the death certificates and who also collected them so that none of the documents remained in the hospital. Even the camp doctor could not find out where the bodies were taken for burial.[38]

The exact number of Jewish refugees from Czechoslovakia deported to Soviet labor camps is unknown. Many survivors estimate it to be over 4,000. At least 1,500 of them perished during the period from the Ribbentrop-Molotov Pact to the outbreak of war between the Soviet Union and Nazi Germany.[39] Many who survived eventually joined the Czechoslovak army unit formed in the Soviet Union.

THE CZECHOSLOVAK ARMY IN FRANCE

Following the Munich capitulation of September 1938 and the occupation of the rest of Czechoslovakia on March 15, 1939, thousands of Czechs sought refuge in France and Great Britain. The French government did not show much understanding for the problems of refugees. The French authorities issued residence permits only at the recommendation of Czechoslovak diplomatic representatives. During the period from Munich until the German occupation of Czechoslovakia, the Czechoslovak ambassador in Paris, Dr. Štefan Osuský, considered himself the representative of Czechoslovakia in her post-Munich frontiers only. As a result, Czechoslovak consulates in France refused to certify the Czechoslovak citizenship of refugees from territories ceded to Germany under the Munich agreement. The refugees turned for help to the *Sdružení uprchlíků z Československa* (Committee of Refugees from Czechoslovakia, officially recognized in France under the name of *Comité des Refugiés de Tchécoslovaquie*), which had been created in October 1938 on the initiative of Dr. Stephen Barber, a member of the Czechoslovak Committee of the World Jewish Congress. Barber (who represented the Jewish party of Czechoslovakia) and other spokesmen of the committee—Leopold Goldschmidt (who represented the German Social Democratic party), Willy Koehler, and Ladislav Schulz (two former members of the Czechoslovak parliament representing the German section of the Communist party of Czechoslovakia and the Hungarian section of the Czechoslovak Social Democratic party, respectively) gained access to the powerful police commissioner of Paris. As a result, Paris police headquarters issued to the refugees identity cards which enabled them to reside in Paris. Most of the Czechoslovak refugees in France, of course, were Jews. However, only a few of them had belonged to political parties in Czechoslovakia. Most of them were regarded not as political refugees but as refugees who had left Czechoslovakia for racial and economic reasons. In March 1939, growing tensions among the various groups of Czechoslovak refugees in France led to the creation of the *Association des Juifs de Tchécoslovaquie en France* (*Svaz Židů z Československa ve Francii,* or Association of Jews from Czechoslovakia in France). The executive of this organization consisted of Dr. Rudolf Braun (representing the Zionists), Dr. Wilhelm Freund (German Social Democrats), Kamil Kleiner (Czech-Jewish movement), Bedřich Sborowitz (Jewish party), and Dr. Stephen Barber (secretary general). When Barber joined the Czechoslovak army in March 1940, he was succeeded by P. Donath, who performed his duties until the day the Germans entered Paris. The headquarters of the Association at 55, rue du Faubourg, Montmartre, Paris 9e, soon became a place to which hundreds of refugees, and later on also Jewish soldiers, turned for help.[40]

After the proclamation of the Slovak puppet state and the German occupation of the rest of Czechoslovakia, the attitude of the Czechoslovak embassy in Paris and of the Czechoslovak consulates in France toward the refugees improved. It must be remembered that the staffs of the embassy and consulates were appointees of the old Republic and not of the new German overlords. They now registered the refugees as potential volunteers for a Czechoslovak army in exile.

On September 2, 1939, the day after the German invasion of Poland, the French mobilized. On that day, too, Ambassador Štefan Osuský asked the French government for permission to organize a Czechoslovak armed force on French territory.[41]

However, Major Bartík, of the Czechoslovak military intelligence, had gone from London to Warsaw as early as May 9, 1939, to inform the French embassy there that as many as 4,000 Czechoslovak volunteers might join the French Foreign Legion. At the same time, he brought the news of an agreement with the French that, if war broke out, Czechoslovak refugees who enlisted in the Foreign

Legion would be released to serve in a Czechoslovak army. The French military authorities had reserved for these an army camp at Agde between Narbonne and Béziers in the south of France. (As already mentioned, Jewish refugees from Czechoslovakia in Poland were not then mobilized along with other Czechoslovak refugees there.)[42]

By August 1939, 1,212 Czechoslovak volunteers had been transported in small boats from the Polish port of Gdynia to France. According to one of the volunteers, Miroslav Šigut, they were divided into two groups when they arrived at Lille. The first group, men who had served in the Czechoslovak air force, was taken directly to Paris. "Members of the second group, in which there were also several Jews, signed a declaration of intention to join the Foreign Legion. They were sent via Marseille and Oran [Algeria] to the military camp of Sidi Bel Abbes, where we went through a period of very rigorous training."[43]

But there were also other ways which led to the Foreign Legion. After the fall of Poland, for instance, individuals and entire groups fled through Slovakia and Hungary to Belgrade, Yugoslavia, where they were received by Czechoslovak organizations which had contacts with the French embassy in Belgrade. Second Lieutenant Otto O. Spira from Moravská Ostrava was in one of these groups. He records:

> There were thirty-five of us, mostly Jews. At the French embassy we were given a choice: either we would volunteer for the Foreign Legion or else they would send us back to the Protectorate. Via Beirut, Marseille, and Oran, we reached the training camp of Sidi Bel Abbes. The conditions there were difficult, and the treatment of the soldiers inconsiderate. Our commanders were French and German officers who had already been serving in the Legion for years.[44]

In the middle of September 1939, Czechoslovak volunteers from all the camps of the Foreign Legion were assembled and sent via Oran and Marseille to the Czechoslovak military camp at Agde, where they arrived on September 26. This group, which consisted of about 600 officers and men, became the nucleus for the Czechoslovak army that was organized in France. Another 600 volunteers, mostly Jewish refugees from Paris and other cities, arrived at Agde on October 11. The vast majority of this transport were enlisted men; a few were reserve officers. Many of them had never gone through the mandatory period of service in the Czechoslovak army, and for reasons of age, physical condition, and insufficient knowledge of the Czech language, they were confronted with difficulties unknown to those who had the experience of two years in the army. Five days after the arrival of this contingent, the First Czechoslovak Infantry Regiment was created.

For reasons of their own, the British and the French initially refused to recognize a provisional Czechoslovak government. After prolonged negotiations, it was agreed that the *Československý národní výbor* (Czechoslovak National Council), which then had its seat in Paris, would be recognized *de jure* as a government. The council, which had eight members, was headed by former President Dr. Eduard Beneš.[45] One of the first acts of the council in Paris, on November 11, 1939, was to issue mobilization orders. The Czechoslovak military mission in the town of Agde, which was charged with carrying out the order, prepared an organizational framework for three infantry regiments and one reserve depot.

Even before the outbreak of war in September 1939, the Czechoslovak consul general in Jerusalem, Josef M. Kadlec, who had refused to give up his position to the Nazis, announced a preliminary draft of Czechoslovak citizens into the Czechoslovak army. At that time approximately 1,200 Czechoslovak Jews who had fled to Palestine had registered with the Czechoslovak consulate as potential volunteers. About half of them were ready to begin military service immediately. At that point, numerous problems of identification arose. About one-third of the registered volunteers had come to Palestine as "illegal" immigrants, and many of them had destroyed their identity papers to avoid being deported by the British mandatory authorities.* In a letter to Beneš dated November 30, 1939, Kadlec mentioned the case of eight Jewish refugees in Palestine, who, when faced with deportation to Germany, had chosen to commit suicide instead.[46] After the outbreak of World War II, about

---

* For an explanation why many Czechoslovak Jewish refugees who had settled in Palestine chose to retain Czechoslovak citizenship even though they had no intention of ever returning to Czechoslovakia, or were regarded as Czechoslovak citizens because they could not obtain Palestine citizenship under the British mandatory law, see Avigdor Dagan, "The Czechoslovak Government-in-Exile and the Jews," in the present volume, pp. 475-476. [Ed.]

300 Jewish volunteers who had come to Palestine from Czechoslovakia were concentrated in the British military camp at Sarafand, southwest of Ramleh. On November 12, they left for Marseille. Their arrival at the Czechoslovak military camp at Agde set off demonstrations of anti-Semitism fomented by certain Czech career officers who suddenly realized that the Jews now constituted virtually half of their total unit.[47] Consul Kadlec, who felt he had to justify his decision to send this group of Jewish volunteers to France, wrote that those were "exclusively Jews who were ready to shed their blood and to sacrifice their lives fighting Hitler." General Sergej Ingr, then the chief of staff for the Czechoslovak army in exile and later to be Minister of National Defense in the government-in-exile, was of a different opinion; he requested Kadlec not to include any substantial numbers of Jews in the next group of volunteers to be shipped to France, and went so far as to describe the Jews as "undesirable elements."[48] As a result, out of 150 registered volunteers in the next transport from Palestine, only thirty-eight were sent to France. Those who were rejected joined the British army.

New volunteers were still arriving from Czechoslovakia (from the Nazi-occupied "Protectorate" and to a lesser extent also from the Slovak puppet state), despite the fact that by then any attempt to escape from that country meant risking one's life. The stories of these escapes, a number of which have been recorded in taped interviews and personal memoirs, are evidence of the courage and determination of men who decided to leave their families, friends, and property and embark upon an odyssey that for most of them did not end until five or six years later. These stories give a vivid picture of the behavior of Jews and also of gentiles who in many instances risked their lives and those of their families to assist the volunteers along their escape route. Of course, not all the contacts proved equally helpful. In many cases, the gentile contacts did not carry out their promises to help, and some even handed the Jews over to the authorities. But on the whole, the manner in which, between 1938 and 1941, several thousand Czechoslovak Jews managed to join the armed forces in France, England, the Middle East, and the Soviet Union constitutes a heroic chapter in world history. It refutes the allegation that the Jews overwhelmingly went to their deaths without making any significant efforts to resist their fate.

One such escape is described by Reserve Lieutenant Dr. Mirek Kerner, who at the time of the Munich surrender in September 1938 was serving with his artillery regiment near Znojmo, not far from the border of Nazi-occupied Austria:

> I returned to my job with the Ministry of Railways in Olomouc, but was dismissed in February 1939 because of my Jewish origin. I became a member of a resistance group of reserve officers in the Kyjov region. When we found ourselves in danger of being arrested by the Gestapo, my friend Adam and I decided to escape to France. We planned to travel via Nitra; this was the escape route used by officers fleeing from Czechoslovakia. In Nitra, we and three other officers were taken in by the Protestant pastor. As he guided us to the Hungarian border, the pastor learned that the men who had been helping him smuggle his protégés across the border into Hungary had been caught and arrested. We returned to Nitra. I had also been recommended to the owner of a café in Nitra, a Mr. Freund, who was running a Jewish 'underground railroad.' That same night Freund took us to Sered, and from there we were taken by local Jews into Hungary. There, at a secret address, I met the Czechoslovak consul,* who furnished us with the necessary travel documents. With the help of a Jewish friend, we succeeded in reaching Belgrade, from where we were sent by the French consulate via Saloniki, Beirut, and Alexandria to Marseille. At the beginning of January 1940, we reached our destiny, Agde, where we joined the Czechoslovak army that was then in the process of formation.[49]

At approximately the same time another Jewish officer, Second Lieutenant Karel Plaček from Kyjov (he eventually settled in Tel Aviv, where he took the name David Porath) arrived at Agde with another group and by another route; as a trained and experienced officer of the quartermaster corps in the Czechoslovak army, he supervised the reception of new arrivals at the Agde camp and their outfitting before their departure for the front lines.[50]

The publication of the mobilization order for the Czechoslovak army in France brought a continuous flow of new volunteers from all over the country: Slovaks, mostly miners and farmers, who had settled in France long before the Munich surrender. They felt, in fact, more French than Czechoslovak, but the mobilization was carried out consistently, and many Czechoslovak citizens were brought

---

* Like Consul Kadlec in Jerusalem, this official, too, had refused to make way for a Nazi successor. [Ed.]

to Agde, often by force, by Czechoslovak officials in France when they showed reluctance to report for induction on their own.

The attitude of these "old-timers" contrasted sharply with that of the refugees, including the Jews, who were determined to join the fight against Nazi Germany. Other "old-timers," however, shared the feelings of the refugees. Among the volunteers there were many men from the Czechoslovak colony in Paris, founded by members of the Czech Legion from World War I, who had found wives and livelihoods in France and had decided to remain there. These were mostly businessmen, artisans, and many professional people, but there were also a great number of students. Not all of these would-be volunteers were accepted for service in the Czechoslovak army because many of them were found physically unfit for military service.[51]

By December 1939, there were 4,000 officers and enlisted men in the Agde camp. Of these, 800 were Jews. Their life in the army was not easy. Those who tried to analyze the reasons for the anti-Jewish feeling that prevailed came to the following conclusions: Many of the young Czechoslovak career officers at the camp had been educated at the military academy of Hranice, an institution noted for the extreme nationalism of some of its leading instructors. Most of these officers did not speak any foreign language. This made it even more difficult for them to adapt themselves to life as exiles in France, and they envied the Jews for their ability to communicate in several languages, to make contacts, and to gain advantages through their greater adaptability. However, Jewish refugees who had been living abroad for many years or who came from territories lost under the Munich agreement did not speak Czech well and therefore preferred to speak German, Hungarian, or Yiddish among themselves. Many patriotic Czechs regarded this as a provocation. Also, the Czech officers resented the fact that many of the Jewish refugees had been able to leave Czechoslovakia together with their wives, so that their unhappiness at being refugees in an alien land was mitigated by the moral support they received from the presence of their families in their vicinity, or at least somewhere else in France, while most of the Czech non-Jews had been compelled to leave their families in Czechoslovakia. The officers compensated for their feelings of inferiority and frustration by humiliating the Jews at every opportunity and tormenting them during the daily drill. Many of the

Jews had a university education, but in the army they were ordinary enlisted men. Nevertheless, the Jewish volunteers were determined to fight against Nazi Germany; they remained loyal to the Czechoslovak government-in-exile and performed their duties to the best of their ability.

As the problems of the Jews in the Czechoslovak army mounted, the need was felt for a spokesman who would be able to represent the interests of the Jewish refugee soldiers, and particularly to see to it that the religious needs of the men were met. It was agreed that these functions required the services of a Jewish chaplain. The man coopted for this purpose with the aid of the *Association des Juifs de Tchécoslovaquie en France* was Alex Kraus, who hailed from Buština in Subcarpathian Ruthenia. Kraus had not been a rabbi in his native Slovakia but a teacher at a business college. However, he spoke not only Czech and Slovak but also Hungarian, German, and Yiddish, and, most important, was familiar with the mentality of Jews from various regions of Czechoslovakia. He was given a certificate of ordination by the French *Grand Rabbin* (Chief Rabbi) Isaiah Schwarz and shortly before Passover 1940 received a commission as a second lieutenant in the chaplaincy corps. He became a well-liked, vigorous and generally recognized spokesman of the Jewish soldiers. His appointment helped lift the morale of the Jews in the Czechoslovak army in France, as had the well-organized Hanukkah celebration that had been arranged for the Jewish soldiers in Agde the previous December.[52]

In January 1940, some 500 Czechoslovak members of the International Brigade that had fought on the Communist side during the Spanish civil war arrived at Agde from the refugee camp at Gurs in the south of France. Among them were several dozens of Jews. Some of these *Španěláci* ("Little Spaniards"), as they were called, protested against manifestations of anti-Semitism and the denigration of Jewish soldiers. However, their influence in this respect was very limited because they were known to have established contacts with the Communists and were therefore under the close scrutiny of the French and Czechoslovak military security authorities, who handed over such suspected traitors to the French police.[53]

Groups of volunteers continued to arrive at Agde between February and May 1940, up to the very day the troops were sent from there to the front. A group of about 120 volunteers, led by Lieutenant Richard Pollak, arrived from England. This group, which had completed its basic military training in England,[54] was composed mainly of German Social Democrats from the Sudeten territory and of Jews. The last group, which consisted of 125 volunteers led by Captain J. Lízálek, came from Beirut and included forty Jewish reserve officers and enlisted men.[55]

By May 1940, the Czechoslovak forces in France, totaling about 10,000 officers and men, had formed the First Czechoslovak Division under the command of General Rudolf Viest, a former inspector general of the Slovak army who was also a member of the Czechoslovak National Council in Paris. (He was succeeded in the following month by General B. Miroslav [Neumann].) By the end of May, two complete Czechoslovak infantry regiments were prepared for battle. The other units were not yet ready for front-line action. In addition, hundreds of Czechoslovak citizens served with the French air force, many of them with great distinction. But only a small number of Jews were able to join the air force, although many had submitted applications.[56]

AFTER THE FALL OF FRANCE

On June 6, 1940, after France's military situation had become critical, the French supreme command ordered the transfer of both Czechoslovak infantry regiments from Agde to the front line. By June 11 and 12 these troops had arrived in an area between Montigny-sur-Aube and Atricourt, about 200 kilometers southeast of Paris.

The two regiments together numbered 5,200 men. The second regiment, which consisted of 2,593 men, was incorporated into the 239th French Division and on June 10 was sent to defend the crossing of the river Marne between l'Ourcq and La Ferté-sous-Jouarre. Initially, the Germans were unable to cross the sector defended by the Czechoslovaks. But then, on orders from the commander of the 239th Division, the Czechoslovak regiment retreated and, after a march of 100 kilometers to Vilbert-Rozay, it was transferred by train to Gien, where it defended the Loire area until June 18. Exhausted and weakened by casualties, the regiment covered the retreat of the crumbling French army. The tired and hungry Czechoslovak troops fought their way through from Souesmes to the St.

Georges region, and from there via Nontron-Narbonne to the Mediterranean port of Sète in the south of France. There, boats were waiting to evacuate them. The Loire front collapsed completely. Throngs of civilians frantically fleeing for their lives mingled with the soldiers, each trying to reach one of the boats on his own because all thoughts of an organized retreat had to be abandoned. This is how some of the men of the second regiment described the situation in their testimonies.[57]

The first regiment was incorporated into the 23rd French Division. Thus, the two Czechoslovak units were separated from each other. The troops led by Colonel Kratochvíl took up defensive positions near the Grand Morin river, in the region of Boissy, Coulommiers, and Mouraux. In the evening of June 13, they encountered German advance units, but no fighting developed because the French commander ordered the Czechoslovak troops to abandon their positions and to cover the retreat of French units. The Germans, who in the meantime had occupied Paris, were quickly advancing to the south. At daybreak on June 15 the Czechoslovak regiment reached Montreaux and started crossing the Seine. However, the French had destroyed the bridges while the First Battalion of the Czechoslovak unit was still holding up the enemy on the northern bank. This placed the Czechoslovaks into a critical situation from which they could extricate themselves only by swimming across the Seine and leaving all their equipment behind to the Germans. Hundreds of refugees were killed on the northern bank by German bombardments.[58] In the panic caused by the bombardment, many Czechoslovak soldiers mingled with fleeing French columns and lost contact with their own units.[59]

Early in the morning of June 16, the remnants of the first infantry regiment reached Gien, about 100 kilometers south of Paris. Two battalions of the regiment, reinforced by a battery of French artillery, were ordered to defend the bridge across the Loire. They managed to hold the bridge for two days, causing heavy losses to the enemy. This armed encounter came to the Germans as a surprise, for they had no longer expected to meet resistance. But on June 18, the Czechoslovak unit was ordered to retreat in the direction of Argent and St. Montaine. The situation was already recognized as hopeless. The regular front collapsed. The enemy kept advancing on both wings of the Czechoslovak formation without meeting any resistance, and there was the danger that the Czechoslovak soldiers might be trapped and captured by the Germans.[60]

This actually happened in a few cases. On June 19, for instance, Second Lieutenant Klein and three noncommissioned officers were captured by German tank crews. They were taken to a POW camp, where they found twenty other Czechoslovak soldiers. Klein succeeded in concealing his Jewish origin. In October 1940, he escaped from a prison camp in Avlon to Unoccupied France. From there, he ultimately managed to reach the Czechoslovak army unit in Palestine.[61] But only a few were as fortunate as Klein. Many others—their exact number is unknown—perished. The high command of the Wehrmacht issued an order that any Czechs captured while fighting on the side of the Allies would be executed. Those identified as Jews were handed over to the Gestapo for execution.

On June 19, with the approval of the French high command, the Czechoslovak fighting units set out via Chateauroux, Agen, Toulouse, and Carcassonne to their original training base at Agde. The day before, Marshal Henri Pétain had declared the capitulation of France.

The Czechoslovak political and military representatives had no illusions about what would happen once France had surrendered to Germany. It was clear to them that the Germans would ask for the extradition and internment of all Czechoslovak soldiers. Immediate action was of the essence. The plan was for the Czechoslovak forces to make their way to the south coast for evacuation to Britain by way of the Mediterranean Sea. The formations had to be kept intact as much as possible, because it seemed certain that after the fall of France, Germany would invade Britain and the Czech troops could then play an important role in defending the last bastion of democracy in Europe.

General Sergej Ingr, the chief of staff for the Czech troops, succeeded in persuading the French high command that it was in France's own interest to have the Czechoslovak troops out of the country before the Germans moved in. Consequently, Colson, the French Minister of War, issued an order that the boats *Formigni* and *Bernadotte,* lying at anchor in the port of Sète, were to be turned over immediately to Czechoslovak troops for their evacuation to North Africa. However, before the actual embarkation could begin, the armistice was signed, and it contained a clause forbidding French vessels to leave the ports at which they happened to be at the time.[62]

The British government promised Dr. Eduard Beneš every possible assistance in the evacuation of the Czechoslovak units. Four British and three Egyptian ships were immediately sent to Marseille, Port Vendres, Sète, and other French ports with orders to evacuate the Czechoslovaks. But the chaotic conditions prevailing in France made it difficult to reorganize the dispersed units and to ensure that everybody arrived at the embarkation points in time. The number of dead and wounded was estimated at 300, but more than 1,000 men were missing. Out of the 5,200 infantrymen who actually took part in the fighting, only about 1,600 reached Sète. Most of those who arrived in time for evacuation belonged to formations which had not been sent to the front.

The British kept their promise to Beneš: their ships arrived as planned and the main embarkation took place at Sète between June 17 and 27, 1940. In addition to the soldiers, there were in Sète also several hundred Czechoslovak civilians who had fled to France from other Nazi-occupied countries. Many of them were Jews. They desperately tried to get on the boats with their families. However, the division command decided that the wives and children of Czechoslovak military officers and men should be the only civilians included in the evacuation. At the same time, the commanding officers of individual units were authorized to exclude from evacuation any persons whom they considered "politically unreliable and persons who . . . because of their behavior and personal qualities, do not deserve to remain in our ranks." This order was, of course, badly abused by career officers who saw it as an opportunity to settle personal accounts with the Jews and to vent their anti-Semitic feelings. Many Jewish soldiers and their relatives were refused access to the boats. There were heartrending scenes at the port of Sète. Desperate people tried to jump aboard the boats as the landing bridge was raised. They fell into the sea and were drowned. Among the Jewish civilians who were turned away was Dr. Ludwig Levy, the aged chief rabbi of Moravia. He was left to die in occupied

France while his only daughter was serving as a nurse with the Czech Red Cross in London during the worst months of the *blitz*.[63]

The last boat left Sète on June 27, 1940, five days after the signing of the armistice between France and Germany. Most of those who had missed the boat fled from Agde to Marseille, where Czechoslovak consular officials loyal to Beneš and his provisional government helped smuggle them onto boats about to sail for Yugoslavia, Africa, and the Middle East. Of the Czechoslovak airmen in France, 932 were brought by sea to England; only twenty-eight of them remained in France.

Many non-Jews, however, refused to be evacuated, particularly Czechs and Slovaks who had been living in France for many years and who had been inducted into the Czechslovak army against their will. There were also many who believed unfounded rumors that the Czechoslovak army had been disbanded; as a result, they simply did not report back to Agde but returned to their families and jobs in their French home towns. Some of the Jews, under the impression that there would be no Czechoslovak army for them to join, left France for Portugal and other countries; a few hundred stayed on in France with their families. Some of them joined the French *maquis* underground units. We know of at least one Jewish underground fighter from Czechoslovakia, E. Friedmann, who lost his life in action near Montpelier.[64]

Of the 10,000 members of the Czechoslovak armed forces in France, only about 4,000 officers and men arrived in Sète in time to be evacuated. Five hundred civilians were evacuated along with the soldiers.[65]

The total number of Jews evacuated from France during the period immediately preceding and following the French surrender to Germany has been estimated at between 800 and 1,000.[66]

The sea voyage from Sète to Gibraltar and from there to the British ports of Liverpool, Southampton, and Plymouth lasted almost two weeks. Conditions on the boats varied from fair to very poor. The main problem was overcrowding. Also, of course, the ships had to proceed without escort through an area in which German U-boats were hunting for Allied merchant vessels. As for the Jewish evacuees, they were harassed by demonstrations of anti-Semitism from their gentile fellow passengers even during the time they spent at sea.

A CZECHOSLOVAK ARMY UNIT IN THE MIDDLE EAST

Refugees from Czechoslovakia who escaped to Yugoslavia were received by a Czechoslovak military mission headed by General Andrej Gak. From there, with the help of the French embassy, they were sent on to Beirut, where they waited in a French internment "depot" for boats to take them to France. The last group scheduled to leave Beirut received the news about the fall of France just before embarkation. There was reason to fear that after the signing of the armistice, the Vichy French government would intern these Czechoslovak refugees in Syria and perhaps eventually extradite them to the Germans. Intelligence Staff Captain Siman, who was responsible for the men once they had been passed by a special mixed Czechoslovak-French commission, managed to inform Consul General Kadlec in Jerusalem about the presence of these refugees in the Middle East.[67]

While Czechoslovak troops evacuated from France were sailing for England, Kadlec was already negotiating with the British military authorities in Palestine about asylum for the Czechoslovak soldiers then stationed in Syria. On June 29, 1940, 206 Czechoslovaks crossed the border from Syria into Palestine. In Palestine they were taken over by the British and were allotted temporary quarters in the village of Az Sumeiriya, near the old Roman aqueduct north of Haifa. The British general, Brunskill, with whom Kadlec was negotiating, suggested that the men be incorporated either into British labor battalions or into the Polish division which had also just arrived in Palestine with 6,000 fully armed and trained men. Kadlec refused, and, having in the meantime established contact with Beneš in London, presented on July 5 a memorandum to the high commissioner for Palestine, Sir Harold MacMichael. In this memorandum, he informed the high commissioner that he, Kadlec, had been authorized to organize a Czechoslovak military unit in the Middle East which would fight side by side with Great Britain against the common enemy. At the same time, he asked that the 250 Czechoslovak officers and men in the camp of Az Sumeiriya (a few small groups of latecomers had been added to the original 206) be recognized as a Czechoslovak military unit within the framework of the British army, with the right to be augmented by further Czechoslovak volunteers. On July 13, the British agreed to permit the formation of a Czechoslovak unit which would be materially assisted by the British military administration.[67]

The issue of recruiting Jewish volunteers gave rise to various problems. When soldiers had been needed for service in France, the British authorities had supported the recruitment of Jewish volunteers in Palestine. But now their attitude had changed, because they did not want to antagonize the Arabs. In the course of further negotiations, the high commissioner agreed to receive into the group fifty additional Jews who had been living in Palestine as bona fide immigrants for some time and forty-five who had entered Palestine illegally and had been interned by the British. Consul General Kadlec and Colonel Koreš, the officer in command of the unit, had to declare in writing they were taking upon themselves the responsibility to see to it that the acceptance of so many Jewish soldiers would not harm the unit and to promise that the ratio between Jews and non-Jews in the unit would not be changed.[68]

The volunteers formed a provisional field company composed of four regular platoons and one platoon for special tasks. This special platoon was made up entirely of supernumerary officers up to the rank of captain.[69] This was supposed to solve the problem of surplus officers for whom there were no enlisted men to command, but in fact it led to dangerous tensions. The officers resented what they considered their degradation. They wanted to command enlisted men, not live together in a platoon where they themselves were treated much like ordinary soldiers. Some of the prewar immigrants from Czechoslovakia supported the disgruntled officers and blamed Kadlec for the situation. It was believed that of the approximately 8,000 Czechoslovak Jews who had settled in Palestine, about 1,800 were then ready to join the Czechoslovak armed forces immediately. The campaign against Kadlec stopped only after he got in touch with Moshe Shertok (later Sharett), the head of the political department of the Jewish Agency, and the latter had declared that the Czechoslovak unit's recruitment of Czechoslovak Jews living in Palestine ran counter to the policy of the Jewish Agency (which was involved in a struggle to gain British approval for the formation of a Jewish army to fight against the Germans under its own flag).[70]

The status of the Czechoslovak unit in Palestine and the morale of its members were both considerably bolstered by the declaration of Foreign Secretary Anthony Eden, which was read in the British House of Commons on July 23, 1940, recognizing the Czechoslovak provisional government that had its seat in London and was headed by President Beneš. On July 28, the Czechoslovak unit in Palestine was inducted by Consul General Kadlec in the camp in Gedera.[71]

Most of the Jewish volunteers who came to the Gedera camp knew English. As a result they were assigned duties involving contact with the British, duties which the Czech supernumerary officers coveted but could not have performed because they did not speak English. The jealousy on the part of the frustrated officers again led to incidents of anti-Semitism, to chicanery, threats, and even physical attacks on Jewish soldiers. This state of affairs could not be kept secret, and before long it was reported in the press. Unable to get help from the commanders of the Czechoslovak unit, the Jewish soldiers finally decided to present their complaints to the British general in command at Sarafand. Consul General Kadlec was informed of the situation and made aware of the possible consequences. He asked authorization from London to put an end to this state of affairs, which was endangering the good name of the Czechoslovak army.[72] Meanwhile, General Andrej Gak, having been appointed chief of the Czechoslovak military mission in the Middle East, arrived in Haifa from Belgrade. He immediately visited the unit at Gedera to view the situation and to observe the mood of the troops at first hand. He attempted to settle complaints and arbitrate quarrels and began negotiations to reorganize the unit. The British high command informed the British military authorities in Palestine that Gak had been authorized, in cooperation with the British military administration, to organize the Czechoslovaks in Palestine into army units which would be an integral part of the Czechoslovak army in the United Kingdom.[73] Gak informed High Commissioner MacMichael that eventually the Czechoslovak unit would be supplemented also by members of the Czech and Slovak legions organized in Poland who were then still interned in the Soviet Union.

In September 1940, the first transport of Czechoslovaks from the Soviet Union arrived in Haifa via the Turkish port of Mersin. That same month a group of twenty-five Czechoslovak air force men was sent from Gedera to England; officers, engineers, and specialists in various fields were also transported to England to work in the British war industry. Among them were a number of Jewish reserve officers.

THE CZECHOSLOVAK INFANTRY BATTALION 11-EAST

On October 28, 1940, Czechoslovak Independence Day, the officers and men of the Czechoslovak unit, fully uniformed and armed, staged a parade in Tel Aviv. Among the dignitaries on the reviewing stand were High Commissioner MacMichael; General Neame, the supreme military commander for Palestine and Transjordan; Moshe Shertok (Sharett), representing the Jewish Agency for Palestine; the Chief Rabbi of Tel Aviv; and delegations representing various Polish and British military units. An order of the day was published, announcing the formation of a Czechoslovak military group in the Middle East composed of the Czechoslovak Infantry Battalion 11-East, and the Czechoslovak Training Center-East. The battalion was commanded by Lieutenant Colonel Karel Klapálek, the training center by Colonel Koreš, who was also commanding officer of the Gedera camp.[74]

Many Czechoslovak Jews who had made their way "illegally" into Palestine after the fall of France now joined the Czechoslovak army. One of the first "illegal" transports to leave Prague for Palestine had been the "Black Rose" (named after the Prague Cafe Černá Růže, where the organizers of the transport had their headquarters). This transport had set out with some 700 young men and women via Znojmo for Vienna, from where it sailed down the Danube on the S.S. *Frostula*. The boat left Vienna for a Rumanian port on September 3, 1939, the very day that the war had broken out. When they heard that the war had begun, Czechoslovak reserve officers among the passengers (at the initiative of Second Lieutenant Artur Hanák-Fleischmann) immediately formed a group of about 150 volunteers. After their arrival in Haifa, they contacted Consul General Kadlec, who put them in touch with the British command in Sarafand.[75]

Another group of about 300 men, women, and children succeeded in embarking on the barge *Spyroula,* but that boat was stranded in the Danube delta because the passengers could not present valid visas for Palestine. They contacted the writer Dr. František Langer, who had been commander of the Czechoslovak army medical corps before the Nazi occupation and a close disciple of Tomáš G. Masaryk. Langer informed Jan Masaryk, the future foreign minister in the London-based Czechoslovak government-in-exile. Thanks to Masaryk's intervention in London, the refugees were able to continue on their journey.[76]

About 500 Jewish men, women, and children sailed aboard a barely seaworthy riverboat on the Danube as far as the Aegean Sea, where the vessel foundered on a small uninhabited island near Crete. After five days they were picked up by a British torpedo boat and taken to an internment camp in Alexandria, Egypt. Five months later, some of the men were released to join the battalion under the command of Lieutenant Colonel Klapálek.[77]

Of the many thousands of Jews who were registered at the Nazi *Zentralstelle für jüdische Auswanderung* (Central Office for Jewish Emigration) in Prague, about 700 men, women, and children were permitted to emigrate to Palestine after paying huge sums of money. They left Prague and Brno for Vienna in September 1940. From Vienna they set sail, along with a group of Austrian Jews, aboard the S.S. *Melk.* At the initiative of two reserve officers in the Czechoslovak army, E. Gregr-Gruenhut and A. Braun, these refugees, too, formed a military unit, which consisted of sixty volunteers. In the Rumanian port of Tulcea the passengers were transferred to a small cargo boat, the S.S. *Milos.* By the time the *Milos* reached Cyprus, the military unit aboard numbered 104 reserve officers and men. In Limassol, the British commander of the harbor promised to inform the concerned British and Czechoslovak authorities in Palestine that the refugees aboard the *Milos* were determined to join the Czechoslovak armed forces.

As the *Milos* approached Haifa harbor, she received orders from the British not to permit anyone to disembark. The large steamship *Patria,* with about 1,300 Jewish refugees from Germany and Austria aboard, was anchored offshore. Passengers from the *Milos* were forced to transfer to the *Patria,* which was to carry all the refugees to the island of Mauritius. The *Patria* was waiting for the arrival of another boat, the S.S. *Atlantic,* which was bringing additional "illegal immigrants." A Czechoslovak intelligence officer, Major Petr, who meanwhile had received the news from Limassol, came to the *Patria* on a patrol boat, welcomed the volunteers, and made a detailed list of their names. He advised Lieutenant Gregr-Gruenhut, who had been named commander of the group, and Second Lieutenant Jindřich Hora, its secretary, not to accept additional volunteers because the quota for Jews in the Czechoslovak armed forces was filled for the time being. He tried to secure from the British the immediate release of the volunteers, but without success. Eventually, however, it was agreed that the volunteers would be taken off the boat at one of the ports on the way to Mauritius and returned from there to the Czechoslovak army unit in Palestine.

The *Atlantic* arrived in Haifa harbor on November 25, 1940, and the transfer of passengers to the *Patria* began almost immediately. However, there was an explosion; the *Patria* keeled over and quickly began to sink. Within twenty minutes, most of the ship was flooded. Among the 280 who perished in the panic that followed were fourteen members of the Czechoslovak military unit. They were buried at the cemetery in Bat Galim. The 1,700 survivors were taken to the British "clearing camp" in Atlit and were released after a nine months' quarantine.[78]

Members of the military unit who had come from the S.S. *Milos* were given three separate barracks in the Atlit camp so that they were able to continue their military training. An officer of the Czechoslovak battalion, Lieutenant Pavel Steiner, visited them regularly. On August 27, 1941, the volunteers were taken to the Kayat beach camp, near Haifa, to report to a Czechoslovak recruiting commission. Those above the age of forty-five were rejected; the remaining eighty-five officers and men were sent to the Czechoslovak battalion.

At the initiative of Kováč, an engineer and reserve officer in the Czechoslovak air force, a group of ninety-two volunteers was organized, composed of internees who had been taken from Palestine to Mauritius. Kováč addressed a petition to the Czechoslovak government-in-exile in London, asking that the group of volunteers be accepted into the Czechoslovak armed forces. In March 1942, he received a positive reply, and, in June, the volunteers left Mauritius. Kováč and six other officers went to London; the rest, to Czechoslovak army units in the Middle East.[79]

At the end of 1940, the Czechoslovak unit was transferred from the comfortable camp at Gedera to a field camp near Jericho, where they received training in desert warfare and became acclimatized to desert conditions. After two and a half months, they were transferred via Suez to Egypt, and on February 25, 1941, they camped at Sidi Bashir, about twenty kilometers east of Alexandria. "The anti-Semites," the commander, Lieutenant Colonel Klapálek, was to write in his memoirs, "sometimes . . . painted abusive graffiti on the tent that served as a mess hall. It was found that some officers were responsible for inciting others to acts of bigotry. We, of course, put an end to that."[80] Klapálek's statement is borne out also by the testimony of Second Lieutenant Michael Jellinek, who at the time demanded that an anti-Semitic poster be removed and complained about the anti-Semitic behavior of several young Czech officers.[81]

On March 18, 1941, the Czechoslovak unit was moved away to the other side of Alexandria and encamped at Agamiyin, where its main task was to guard camps for German and Italian prisoners of war. At the time the unit numbered about 400 men. However, between March and May 1941, 680 officers and men from the Czech Legion who had been interned in the Soviet Union arrived in the Middle East in eleven transports. Before coming to Agamiyin they had to pass through a strict scrutiny in the British camp at Kayat beach. Some of the Communists and left-wing elements—they were generally called "star men" (after the Red Star)—were interned or imprisoned on the basis of reports written by right-wing officers with whom they had come into conflict while on Soviet territory. Several Jewish soldiers who sought the "star men's" protection against chicanery by extreme nationalist officers were also placed under arrest.

Perhaps the most serious incident occurred in Suzdal in October 1940, during an officers' training course for members of the Czech Legion. Cadet Officer Erik Kürti was abused and brutally beaten by anti-Semites. At first neither the company commander nor the officer in command of the training course reacted to Kürti's complaints. Only after twenty-five officer candidates had asked, in protest, to be struck from the list of participants in the training course did the officer in command expel those responsible for the incident.[82]

The provocateurs from Suzdal now continued their anti-Jewish activities also in Agamiyin. Their first victim was Second Lieutenant Jellinek, whom the officers of the Legion blamed for having enlisted too many Jews and Zionists in the Czechoslovak military unit in Bronowice and Lesznâ; he was also accused of having supported the Communists during his internment in the Soviet Union and of having slandered the British. The confrontation took place in the officers' mess, where officers of the former Legion spoke about Jewish soldiers in desultory, humiliating terms. When Jellinek protested against these anti-Semitic remarks, one of the officers provoked him into a row; in the scuffle which ensued, the anti-Semite fell and hurt his hand. Jellinek was called to the officers' court of honor, found guilty, stripped of his rank, and dismissed from active service. He appealed to the Czechoslovak government-in-exile in London but the appeal was never given a proper hearing. Only after the Soviet Union had entered the war on the side of the Allies was he notified that he had been acquitted on the charge of supporting the Communists. Jellinek joined his family in Herzlia and eventually became a member of *Haganah*, the underground defense force of Palestine's Jewish community.[83]

Another anti-Semitic incident occurred in Agamiyin on May 12, 1941. Several drunken soldiers from the group that had come from internment in Russia broke into the tent of the auxiliary company at the training center and insulted the Jews in the company. Instances of anti-Semitic violence became so frequent that Lieutenant Colonel Klapálek had to intervene and publicly condemn the "Nazi-like behavior spreading within the unit." He was, however, apparently afraid of punishing these excesses in an appropriate way. Even a non-Jewish intelligence officer, Lieutenant L. Dvořák, reported that "the excesses . . . would have deserved a stricter punishment because expressions of racial hatred not only contradict the principles on which our state was created but also indicate that some individuals approve of the ideology which this war is supposed to wipe out."[84]

In the spring of 1941, General Erwin Rommel's armies forced the British troops under General Sir Archibald Wavell to retreat. It became vital that the Allies hold Tobruk, because the fall of Tobruk would have meant the loss of Egypt. In this critical situation, the Czechoslovak Infantry Battalion 11-East was ordered to defend the airport at Degheile. A few days after the Czechoslovak unit took up its positions, its commander, Lieutenant Colonel Klapálek, was informed by the British that German paratroopers had been dropped in the area. Klapálek and his staff prepared a new defense plan, which, in fact, delayed Rommel's preparations for a decisive attack and gave the British valuable time to take up new positions.

The news of the German attack on the Soviet Union changed the situation overnight. On the next day, June 23, 1941, the battalion received notice to be ready for transfer. Soon the unit was on the move again. It returned to Egypt and continued from there in trains and trucks through Palestine over 1,000 kilometers to Rosh Pinah, in the north of Palestine. The British plan was to annihilate the Vichy French troops in Syria as quickly as possible and to prevent the Germans from gaining access to the Mosul oil fields, no matter what the cost.

The battalion encamped near Banias, at the foot of Mount Hermon. The first company, which was entrusted with the task of controlling the highway from Mardjayoun (Lebanon) to Metulla in the Upper Galilee, soon found itself engaged in battle. The artillery of a French Foreign Legion unit bombarded the Czechoslovak positions and hit the munitions magazine of the infantry. The first victim on the Czechoslovak side was a Jewish soldier, Jiří Haas from Brno. His body was taken to Palestine and buried at Kibbutz Dan. Another Jewish soldier, Karel Weiner, was captured by Vichy French troops.[85]

Thanks to the professional skill of the chief medical officer, Captain Leopold Fürth, the Czechoslovaks gained the confidence of the Syrian Druzes, whose sheik had been a patient of Dr. Fürth. The Druzes showed their gratitude by acting as reliable guides in the difficult mountain terrain and bringing news about the movements of the Vichy French. This was a great help in the pursuit of the enemy. Five days before the French capitulated, the Czechoslovak unit occupied the last enemy stronghold in Mardjayoun.[86] The Eleventh Battalion now had its headquarters at Aleppo, but its troops were dispersed on guard duty throughout Syria. At the end of August 1941, eighty-five Jewish officers and men who had survived the sinking of the S.S. *Patria* joined the battalion.[87]

DEFENDERS OF TOBRUK

In October 1941, the Czechoslovak Infantry Battalion 11-East was given a new assignment. It was transferred to the largest transit camp in Palestine, Es Zib, and on October 16 it continued from there via Suez to Alexandria. Finally, on October 21, 634 Czechoslovak officers and men boarded two torpedo boats which took them safely through mine fields to the harbor of Tobruk. The Czechoslovak unit was ordered to prevent the enemy from penetrating to the highway which linked the Libyan cities of Derna, Tobruk, and Bardia. Perhaps the greatest responsibility placed upon the unit was a mission assigned by Lieutenant Colonel Klapálek to a special group of twenty-four men armed mainly with heavy machine guns. The commander of this group was Lieutenant Gregr-Gruenhut, who had survived the sinking of the S.S. *Patria*. [88] This mission was successful and gave valuable support to the attack by Polish forces on Italian positions.

Tobruk was under constant German and Italian bombardment. The first Czechoslovak soldier among the defenders of Tobruk fell on October 30, 1941. He was Leo Gutfreund, a Jewish volunteer from Jemnice. He had offered to relieve an exhausted friend under full enemy fire. Badly wounded, he died in the arms of his brother, who was an officer in the battalion. [89] In November, a Jewish officer, Lieutenant Klein, was wounded in action. On December 5, two more Jewish soldiers, Jiří Spitz and Rudolf Kohn, were killed when a German submarine sank a Red Cross ship evacuating wounded men from Tobruk to Alexandria. [90] Nevertheless, the anti-Semites from the former Czech Legion continued to provoke their Jewish comrades in arms. They kept abusing them and refused to serve under Jewish officers. Lieutenant Colonel Klapálek tried to fight this reprehensible anti-Semitism with gentle reprimands. [91]

On November 18, 1941, the British started their long-awaited major offensive from the Libyan-Egyptian border in the direction of Tobruk. The Czechoslovak battalion was ordered to attack during the night between December 9 and 10. Among those cited for conspicuous bravery in action in this attack were Lieutenants Klein and Pavel Stein. [92]

The Czechoslovak battalion remained at Tobruk until April 7, 1942. It was then relieved by South African units and transferred from Fort Capuzzo, via the El Ameyria camp in Egypt and Suez, to Palestine. There it was sent to more comfortable quarters at a camp in Bat Galim near Haifa.

Of the more than 600 Czechoslovak defenders of Tobruk, about 45 percent were Jews. Among the eighteen Czechoslovak graves at the military cemetery in Tobruk six are those of Jews: Jiří Haas, Leo Gutfreund, K. Kaufmann, Jiří Spitz, Rudolf Kohn, and Karel Weiner.[93]

THE CZECHOSLOVAK 200TH LIGHT ANTI-AIRCRAFT REGIMENT

Within a month of its return to Palestine, the Eleventh Infantry Battalion was reorganized into the 200th Light Anti-Aircraft Artillery Regiment, and in May 1942, the unit began training with anti-aircraft guns. However, there were two obstacles which had to be overcome: a lack of guns for training and a lack of manpower. The British supplied the guns; the men were supplied from among Czechoslovak Jews who had settled in Palestine. The British-imposed quota of Jewish volunteers for the Czechoslovak army was lifted. With the consent of British authorities, a mobilization of Czechoslovak citizens was proclaimed in all British possessions. To make the call more attractive, the Czechoslovak government-in-exile issued a decree declaring all confiscations and forced transfers of property from Czechoslovak citizens during the German occupation as null and void. It was stressed that this decree was applicable, however, only to those who had fulfilled their duty as citizens by serving in the Czechoslovak army abroad. Volunteers arrived from Egypt, Teheran, India, and as far away as Shanghai. These groups always included some Jews. Within two months the number of volunteers from among Czechoslovak Jews in Palestine had reached 600. In June 1942, a transport of eighty Jewish volunteers arrived at the training center at Sidi Bishr from Mauritius, where they had been interned as "illegal" would-be immigrants to Palestine.[94] By August 1 the regiment had 1,271 officers and men, and the percentage of Jews in the regiment had risen to sixty.

Meanwhile, the situation of the Allies in Africa had become critical. Rommel had started a new offensive and Tobruk fell to the Axis forces on June 21, 1942. Rommel captured 25,000 British soldiers.

The British were forced to take a last stand at El Alamein. They were in danger of losing the military port of Alexandria, which would have meant the loss of all of Egypt.[95]

In this situation, the importance of the Czechoslovak troops increased. On June 15, 1942, General Sergěj Ingr, the chief of staff, who in the meantime had become Minister of National Defense in the Czechoslovak government-in-exile, had visited Haifa to inspect the Czechoslovak army in the Middle East. Earlier in the war Ingr had made no secret of his view that Jewish soldiers were "an element not too suitable for fighting" and that he was not much interested in these "undesirable elements."[96] But two years of fighting had helped change his attitude. He now showed an unusual interest in the Jewish soldiers and their problems. One of the results of this new interest was an order to appoint a special chaplain for the Jews serving in the Czechoslovak army in the Middle East. With the help of Rabbi Dr. Samuel Arje from Smíchov, near Prague, a suitable candidate was found in Dr. Hanuš Rezek (Rebenwurzel) from Strážnice, who, after a short period of training at the Jerusalem rabbinate, was appointed to officer rank and took up his duties with the Czechoslovak army. He did not see his functions as limited to religious work but took an interest also in the personal problems of his coreligionists and intervened fearlessly against all expressions of anti-Semitism, wherever they occurred.[97]

New recruits were transferred from Bat Galim first to Es Zib near Nahariya and later to the training center in Sidi Bishr. By July 1942, there were 324 men at this training center; more than half of them were Jews. In September the unit was moved again, this time to the environs of Haifa.[98]

The regiment was composed of three battalions, 500, 501, and 502. On July 17 Battalion 500, equipped with fifteen anti-aircraft guns, took over the defense of the port of Haifa, which, after the partial evacuation of Alexandria, became for a time the most important supply port for the Egyptian front. By the end of the month, Battalion 501 had been entrusted with the defense of Beirut. Meanwhile, Battalion 502 was completing its training. An urgent appeal sent from London at that time spoke of the vital need for reinforcements in the Czechoslovak air force. Of 300 volunteers under the age of thirty, the recruiting commission chose 171, who left the Middle East for England during the second half of October 1942.[99]

At the end of September 1942, General Bernard L. Montgomery took over the command of the British Eighth Army and began a well-prepared decisive attack at El Alamein. This time Rommel's *Afrika Korps* was crushed and by May 1943 the Germans had been forced to give up all hopes of conquering Africa.[100] The battlefront was moving away from Palestine and air raids on Haifa were becoming rarer. In the fall the 200th Regiment was transferred once again, this time to the Judean desert. There, at a camp near Jericho, anti-Semitism erupted once again. This time it was caused by a new element. Among the *Afrika Korps* soldiers who had been captured by the Allies there were many who hailed from the Sudeten territory. Some of them now claimed that they were in fact not ethnic Germans but Czechs, and in August 1942, after their claim had been accepted by Czechoslovak intelligence officers, thirty of these men were inducted into the Czechoslovak army. Klapálek, now a full colonel, applied strict disciplinary measures which put an end to overt anti-Semitism, at least temporarily.[101] However, among those accepted into the Czechoslovak army there were also sixty members of the Communist party of Palestine; this enabled anti-Semitism to survive under the disguise of "anti-Communism."

Just before the end of 1942, some Czechoslovak troops were sent to the Libyan desert. The rest were led aboard trains in Jerusalem and sent via Alexandria to Tobruk. Battalions 500 and 501 took over the anti-aircraft defense of Tobruk, Battalion 502 the defense of the airports of El Adem and Bu Amud. The latter battalion was almost entirely Jewish and was generally known as the "Shalom (Peace) Battalion." Its highest-ranking officer was Staff Captain Felix Süsskind-Sládek, who was later transferred to the Czechoslovak army in the Soviet Union.[102]

With the retreat of the Axis armies, Tobruk lost its importance as a base of operations. The Czechoslovak troops were not sufficiently employed and were uncertain about their future. They were ready to fight, and many wanted to join Lieutenant Colonel Ludvík Svoboda's army in the Soviet Union. At the same time, the First Battalion was training at Buzuluk, getting ready to fight; however, it was short of manpower.

For some time, this situation remained unchanged. Then, in March 1943, some troops were selected for training at the officers' school in Haifa. Of the thirty-one candidates chosen, twenty-six were Jews. The course ended in June, and in July all the graduates left for England. On April 23 the regiment was visited by General Andrej Gak, the head of the Czechoslovak military mission in the Middle East. The official reason for Gak's visit was the unveiling of a memorial to the fallen soldiers erected by their comrades with their own funds at the Tobruk cemetery. Colonel Klapálek used the opportunity to express the desire of his men for transfer to the front. Gak did not reply, because it had been agreed beforehand that the regiment was to be transferred to England. This agreement became known only through an order issued by the British commander on June 12, 1943. On July 5, 1943, officers and men of the Czechoslovak army in the Middle East gathered at the military port of Tewfik, south of the Suez Canal, to board the British ship *Mauretania*. After a long, exhausting journey around the Cape of Good Hope, the *Mauretania* reached Liverpool on August 11. The troops were taken to the Wivenhoe camp, near Colchester. On August 18, President Beneš visited the camp and awarded the War Cross to the entire unit. On August 26 the Czechoslovak 200th Light Anti-Aircraft Regiment was disbanded and incorporated into the Czechoslovak army in England.[103]

Even before the regiment had embarked for transfer to Britain, General Gak had informed the officers that the Czechoslovak army in England was suffering from a surplus of officers and that as a consequence not all of them would be assigned to officers' duties. He therefore candidly advised the supernumeraries in the regiment not to join the transport for England but to find a place in the war effort in the Middle East instead. As a result, some of the officers joined the Free French forces of General Charles de Gaulle. Some of the physicians were taken into the British army, and ten officers were sent to the Soviet Union. Gak tried to find employment for twenty others in the Middle Eastern war industry. Lieutenant Fantl, a member of this group, testifies:

> The negotiations concerning our employment in war industry dragged on for months. In the end the idea was given up, and it was decided that we should be transferred in January 1944 to Klapálek's troops in England. Just at that time, President Beneš was passing through Cairo on his way back to London from negotiations in Moscow. When he learned from the chief of the military mission that supernumerary officers were about to be sent to

England, Beneš ordered them sent immediately to the Soviet Union, where there was a shortage of officers. Arrangements for Soviet visas took four months, so the group did not leave for Moscow until May 5, 1944. Among the seventeen officers in the group were seven Jews (B. Bass, Engineer Gregr, František Fantl, Dr. J. Fantl, J. Hein, J. Herz, and J. Stein).[104]

After the departure of the Czechoslovak troops from the Middle East for England, about 300 military personnel remained behind in Palestine. They were to create and maintain a Czechoslovak administrative staff in Jerusalem, with the purpose of recruiting able-bodied Czechoslovak citizens in Palestine for the Czechoslovak army units in Britain and the Soviet Union. Colonel P. Kumpošt, who was appointed head of the new organization, took over some of the officers who had served in the now-disbanded Czechoslovak military mission in the Middle East. General Gak, the chief of the mission, became a liaison officer on the staff of General Dwight D. Eisenhower.

About 100 of those serving in the 200th Czechoslovak Light Anti-Aircraft Regiment—the supernumerary officers and many Czech Jews—did not join the transport to England. Some of the Jews who chose to stay behind explained that they did not want to experience any more anti-Semitism.

Available statistical data give the total number of men who served in the Czechoslovak military units in the Middle East as 2,489. Of those, 49.48 percent were Jews. The historian Toman Brod believes that this is not an accurate figure because not all soldiers of Jewish origin professed the Jewish religion. This is borne out by the testimony of Lieutenant Jindřich Hora: "In addition to those who declared themselves as Jews, there were also many Jews who had been baptized or indifferent to Judaism, and [even] some who claimed to profess no religion. I estimate that according to their origin, the participation of Jews in the Middle East must have been at least 60 percent of all the officers and men."

Others arrive at similar estimates. The correctness of these estimates seems to be borne out by the statistical table of Czechoslovak military personnel (See p. 437); this data is broken down according to country or national origin. The results show that 62 percent of the total number of men in the army were Jews.[105]

TENSIONS IN CHOLMONDELEY PARK

After the fall of France in June 1940, Hitler was master over all of Europe, except for the Soviet Union, which, however, had been neutralized by the Ribbentrop-Molotov non-aggression pact. The Germans were preparing to deal a fatal blow to Great Britain. The British reacted by dismissing the soft and undecided Neville Chamberlain and replacing his weak government with one headed by the great, indomitable leader Winston Churchill. The bombardment of British cities by the *Luftwaffe* and the epic battle of Britain that followed lasted from August to October 1940 and ended in a British victory. The *Luftwaffe* suffered heavy losses, and the Germans had to shelve their plans for an all-out invasion of England.

Several hundred Czechoslovak airmen participated in the Battle of Britain.[106] The fall of France and the appointment of Churchill as prime minister created a favorable climate for the aims of Czechoslovak resistance in Allied lands. Britain was in dire need of allies, and the arrival of 4,000 Czechoslovak soldiers and airmen was most welcome. Naturally, it also helped strengthen the position of President Beneš; the British government was now ready to recognize the Czechoslovak provisional government and its advisory organ, the State Council.[107]

After the atmosphere of defeatism and chaos that had prevailed in France ever since the outbreak of the war and that had left its effect on the Czechoslovak troops there, England represented a dramatic change. The British were friendly toward men in uniform, whether British or of Allied nations. Soldiers found it easy to get rides from motorists. In each village the local branch of the WVS (Women's Voluntary Service) ran a canteen for the soldiers. Many men were invited to private homes.* Despite the grim military situation, both the press and the population displayed an air of quiet optimism. All this could not fail to have a gradual impact on the mood and behavior of the Czechoslovak servicemen who had just arrived from the Continent. Other elements, too, accounted for ba-

---

* The soldiers were aided, in some instances, also by the Self-Aid Association of Jews from Bohemia, Moravia, and Slovakia in England, which had its headquarters in London and of which Karl Baum and Dr. Viktor Fischl (Avigdor Dagan) were joint secretaries.

sic changes in the attitude of the men. The regime of Ambassador Osuský was a thing of the past. Whereas in France, the distance between the camp in Agde and Czechoslovak headquarters in Paris had seemed prohibitive, President Beneš, Jan Masaryk, and several of their colleagues who enjoyed the confidence of the vast majority of the Czechoslovak soldiers were now within easy reach in London. The result was that the Czechoslovak servicemen felt more free in England to voice their grievances and to seek redress for them than they had in France.

The Czechoslovak troops that had been evacuated to England from France were housed in a tent camp at Cholmondeley Park near Chester. There, the general atmosphere was tense. Soldiers were rebelling against the arrogant, insulting behavior of some of their officers and commanders. The army administration was reluctant to deal with the soldiers' complaints. As a result, the situation quickly deteriorated.[108]

This state of affairs was particularly unpleasant for the Jewish soldiers. The anti-Semites among the officers continued to insult and humiliate the Jewish men in England as they had in France, and the position of the Jews in the Czechoslovak army became intolerable. It was generally agreed that something would have to be done, but there was no agreement on how to proceed. Some wanted to make their point in a legal manner, within the framework of Czechoslovak army discipline. Others, influenced by extreme leftist elements, simply wanted to solve the problem by quitting the Czechoslovak army. When all those who refused to obey orders from their superiors were asked to step forward, about 500 men stepped out of their formations. They were denounced as mutineers, surrounded by guards, and taken to a separate part of the camp, where they proceeded to elect their own commanders and spokesmen.[109]

The situation became even tenser when one of the officers—a Lieutenant Šumandl—began to shout at Jewish soldiers standing in line for their rations and called them "stinking Jews." Chaplain Alex Kraus and Corporal Rudolf Braun protested. A sharp exchange of words ensued, in which Chaplain Kraus was accused of treason and placed under arrest. Kraus immediately requested an interview with his commanding officer. Once it was proven that he had never made the statements attributed to him that "with the fall of France, the authority of the Czechoslovak army command no longer existed," he was promptly released. However, the two officers who had made the false accusation and were known for their anti-Semitic attitudes got away with a mere reprimand from their commanding officer.[110] This provocation was the culmination of anti-Semitism within the ranks and helped shake the morale of the Jewish soldiers considerably. As a result, growing numbers of Jews sought release from the Czechoslovak army.

In this crisis, a committee composed mainly of those who had defended the interests of the Czechoslovak Jewish refugees in France was created and its members (Private Stephen Barber, Corporal Rudolf Braun, Major Brichta, Second Lieutenant Artur Hanák-Fleischmann, Lieutenant Mirek Kerner, and Second Lieutenant Alex Kraus) issued an appeal urging Jewish soldiers to remember that they represented their coreligionists who were still in occupied Czechoslovakia as well as the entire Jewish people engaged in a life-and-death struggle against the Nazis. The committee therefore felt that the proper place for a Jewish soldier from Czechoslovakia was in the Czechoslovak army, where he would have an opportunity to fight against Nazism. The appeal also stressed that the Jews of Czechoslovakia identified themselves fully with the struggle of President Beneš and his government for the restoration of a free, democratic Czechoslovakia in a free Europe.

On July 23, after unsatisfactory negotiations with representatives of the army command, members of the committee left for London to discuss further steps with representatives of the *Ústřední rada národních Židů Československa* (Central Council of "National" Jews from Czechoslovakia).[111] They also told Prof. Selig Brodetsky, a member of the executive of the Jewish Agency for Palestine, about their situation. The chairman of the National Council, Dr. Leo Zelmanovits, tried to persuade the delegates that they had no alternative but to remain in the army and continue the fight against anti-Semitic excesses from within the ranks. He pointed out that an exodus of Jews from the Czechoslovak army would create an unfavorable impression among the Czech public in the occupied homeland. Finally, Dr. Zelmanovits reminded the delegation that the numerically strong and disciplined Jewish participation in the armed forces had been decisive in President Beneš' nomination of a Jewish representative to the State Council.[112] The delegation also met with the Minister of National Defense, General Sergej Ingr, but that meeting proved unsuccessful and the committee therefore decided to request an audience with President Beneš.

On July 26, Dr. Beneš, uneasy because of the developments in the army, decided to visit Cholmondeley Park together with several members of his government. On that occasion the group of 500 protesting "rebels" issued a declaration stating, among other things, that: "The Czechoslovak army in France is chauvinistic. Soldiers speaking German or Hungarian or their mother tongue are to be punished, and an 'Aryan clause' is operative with regard to the [acceptance of Jews as] airmen. . . . There is no place in our ranks for supporters of Nazi theories about racism and anti-Semitism." The protesting soldiers paraded past Beneš as a special unit led by their oldest officer, Second Lieutenant Schwarz.

In an address delivered after the parade, President Beneš urged all to behave in a tolerant manner toward each other and made it clear that he would not tolerate anti-Semitism in the army. Afterwards, he received a delegation of eight Jewish soldiers, including Corporal Rudolf Braun, Lieutenant Artur Hanák-Fleischmann, and Chaplain (Second Lieutenant) Alex Kraus. These men handed a written memorandum to the President, asking that the military command speak out clearly against anti-Semitism and investigate all justified complaints of anti-Semitism.[113] The President listened attentively to the presentation, then pointed out that in the army, matters relating to complaints about violations of the law had to be dealt with through the appropriate channels. In the case of the complaints of the Jews, it was decided that their spokesmen would be given a formal hearing before the assembled commanding officers of all units, including the chief of staff and the head of the secret service.

This hearing was held at Cholmondeley Park shortly after President Beneš's visit. The Jewish delegation consisted of Major Brichta (the highest-ranking Jewish officer in the camp), Lieutenant Artur Hanák-Fleischmann, Chaplain (Second Lieutenant) Alex Kraus, Corporal Rudolph Braun, and Private Stephen Barber. The Jewish spokesmen made it quite clear that the Jews were willing to carry out their duties in every respect but that they would insist that their rights and freedoms and their full equality before the law would be scrupulously respected by all concerned. Those guilty of violating these principles, they declared, should be relieved from positions of command and assigned to other duties.

On the day following Beneš's visit to the camp, an order of the high command was read to all assembled troops announcing the discharge of all the "mutineers" from the Czechoslovak army, effective immediately. On July 28, 1940, 539 men were handed over to the British authorities and transferred from Cholmondeley Park to the British internment camp at Oswestry, about forty kilometers southwest of Chester. Most of those discharged were Communists and former members of the International Brigade from the Spanish civil war, who regarded the Czechoslovak army as "imperialistic." However, about 150 Jewish soldiers voluntarily left along with those discharged because they refused to tolerate the anti-Semitism any longer.[114] The discharged troops did not have to stay in the internment camp for long. In September 1940, many of them applied to join the British Military Auxiliary Pioneer Corps; 460 of them were accepted and were employed at military construction projects. The rest were released from military service.[115]

The exodus of one-seventh of all men from the Czechoslovak army led to a stormy session of the State Council. Minister of National Defense Ingr and other representatives of the military establishment were severely criticized for not having relieved irresponsible officers of their posts and for not even having attempted to investigate complaints of anti-Semitism. Members of the State Council were worried about the unfavorable reaction of the British press and British public opinion.[116]

This meeting, and the formal complaint from the Jewish spokesmen at Cholmondeley Park, did not fail to have an effect. Colonel Janouch, who had been the commanding officer of the First Infantry Regiment in France, and other lesser offenders were removed from their posts.

The Jewish soldiers found support mainly in Minister V. Majer, a Social Democrat, and the chief education officer, Lieutenant Colonel Z. Bechyně. Chaplain Kraus, as the respected spokesman for the Jewish soldiers, was able to intervene in a dignified manner and often obtained positive results. Perhaps the main reason for the persistence of anti-Semitic incidents was the fact that the older officers, though anxious to stop the excesses of their younger colleagues, were reluctant to employ stern measures because they had been educated in the democratic traditions of Tomáš G. Masaryk.

THE INDEPENDENT CZECHOSLOVAK BRIGADE

Following the discharge of the "mutineers" from the army, the First Czechoslovak Infantry Division, which initially had been formed in France, was reorganized into the *Československá samostatná brigáda* (Independent Czechoslovak Brigade) under the command of General B. Miroslav (Neumann). It is estimated that about 30 percent of the soldiers in this brigade were Jews.

The reorganization created some new problems. Of the 3,276 men serving in the Brigade at the time—this number included also those working at the Czechoslovak ministry of national defense in London—about 700 were officers. But there were only 300 officer assignments available. What was to be done about the remaining 400 officers? Obviously, the tendency was to give priority to career officers; reserve officers would be commissioned only in accordance with certain criteria. A high proportion of the reserve officers were Jews, and because only a minority of them received commissions, this led to new tensions between the fortunate officers who were appointed to the command staff and the rest, who, despite their rank, were, in fact, put on a par with ordinary soldiers. The protests which followed culminated in a petition sent on November 1, 1940, to President Beneš. About 150 officers threatened to leave the ranks and join another Allied army unless their situation were resolved. Beneš passed the complaint to his military bureau. The brigade command reacted by declaring that those who would not remove their signatures from the petition would be regarded as mutineers, with all the attendant consequences. About sixty officers thereupon dissociated themselves from the petition. Of the rest, twenty-nine were handed over to military courts and sixty-three were discharged from active service as "physically unfit." The remaining unassigned officers were placed into special units where they served as ordinary soldiers, receiving an enlisted man's pay of six shillings and sixpence a day. Most of those accorded this treatment were Jewish reserve officers. In a debate about this problem, Professor V. Klecanda, a member of the State Council, said: "It is cruelly unjust to state that these officers, many of whom left Czechoslovakia in order to fight against Hitler's Germany, have refused to serve in the Czechoslovak army and thus brand them publicly as mutineers."[117]

In the fall of 1941, the Independent Czechoslovak Brigade was transferred from Cholmondeley Park to Leamington Spa and environs, about thirty kilometers southeast of Birmingham. Leaflets protesting against the intolerable situation were distributed at the camp. At the same time, anti-Semitic tendencies began to appear in Czechoslovak publications in Britain. Both *Čechoslovák,* the official organ of the government-in-exile, and the army's daily news bulletin *Naše vojsko* raised the question of whether the Jews regarded Czechoslovakia as their fatherland or whether they were a rootless element that could not be settled permanently anywhere.[118] The author of an article entitled "Two Worlds" in *Čechoslovák* of January 30, 1942, coined a new word, *emigrantština* ("emigrants' disease") to define the undesirable attitudes which were attributed to the Jews. He claimed that his objections were not against Jews as a people but only against this "emigrants' disease." He stressed that among "real Czechs and Slovaks there is no real anti-Semitism." Stephen Barber replied that all this was only an excuse to hide the author's own anti-Semitism.[119] Mirek Kerner, A. Steiner, A. Lederer, Rudolf Braun, and others defended the Jews in the Czechoslovak army not only in the Czech newspapers but also in the British press.[120]

After the Soviet Union entered the war against Germany, there was a slight change for the better. Thus, when eighty-five men of the Second Battalion sent a petition to President Beneš protesting the appointment of Captain L. Kubín, who was known for his anti-Communist and anti-Semitic views, as adjutant to the battalion commander, the Ministry of National Defense was forced to rescind the appointment.[121] The changed situation also helped increase the number of volunteers. It must be borne in mind that the conditions prevailing in the Czechoslovak army were generally known, and that as a result many refugees chose to work in agriculture, the war industry, or civilian anti-aircraft defense rather than join the army. Many young officers displayed openly hostility toward those who, coming from the Sudeten region, spoke German better than Czech, and toward progressive Jewish intellectuals, whom they called *Židobolševici* ("Jew Bolsheviks").[122] This, too, changed following the

Soviet Union's entry into the war. Before the end of 1941, the brigade had been enlarged by 433 new volunteers, most of them Jews. Ludvík Kain, who, before joining the brigade, had worked with a group of colleagues on an English farm, testified:

> We were joining the Czechoslovak army under very difficult conditions. We resigned ourselves to the fact that, notwithstanding our university education, we had no hope of ever being admitted into the school for officers or NCOs. And, in fact, they never sent any of us there. Even though many of us had been decorated with military crosses and medals for courage and merit, we remained ordinary soldiers until the end of the war. Jews were not promoted to higher rank, and Jewish soldiers and officers were never sent to special training courses.[123]

These people had joined the brigade even though they were aware of the prevailing conditions. Yet, they could not remain silent all the time. It was difficult for them to believe it was mere coincidence that Jewish members of the brigade were never sent to the courses for paratroopers and others organized by the British army. Sergeants Berger, Ehrlich, Schwarz, and their spokesman, Second Lieutenant Artur Hanák-Fleischmann, therefore decided to act. Hanák-Fleischmann was platoon commander in the Second Infantry Battalion, a formation of 1,200 men, one-third of whom were Jews. He informed Battalion Commander Lieutenant Colonel Vladimír Přikryl that Jewish members of the battalion were being kept from attending courses for paratroopers. Přikryl explained to Hanák-Fleischmann that this was not due to anti-Semitism but solely to the fact that the courses were meant to train soldiers for sabotage work within Czechoslovak territory, and it was felt that Jewish soldiers would be far more endangered than others if they were to be used for such assignments. Despite that statement, Hanák-Fleischmann recorded,

> About a week later I was ordered to put my name down, together with Sergeant Ehrlich, for the next paratroopers' training course, and other Jews followed later. At that time, we first began to receive news about the deportation of Jews from the Protectorate and their extermination at concentration camps. We tried to persuade our superiors—and we also spoke about this with representatives of the Zionist organization—that we should be dropped near concentration camps and ghettos to perform acts of sabotage.

A commando unit of Jewish paratroopers was in fact formed, but despite great efforts, we did not succeed in getting ourselves sent into action.[124]

Chaplain Kraus negotiated with Professor Selig Brodetsky of the Jewish Agency in London about the uses to which Hanák-Fleischmann's group could be put, the idea being that paratroopers should be dropped over Slovakia and Subcarpathian Ruthenia in order to warn the Jews there and to help organize resistance. However, this plan, too, was never carried out. The British War Office and other British authorities pointed out that it would be inexpedient to send planes to "very distant" targets and that also, in principle, they were opposed to "separate actions" relating to specific groups. The sole objective to be kept in mind at all times was to expedite the defeat of Nazi Germany and her partners.[125]

The change caused by the outbreak of war between the Soviet Union and Germany brought back the "mutineers"[126] who had left the Czechoslovak army in July 1940 and who were then serving in the British Military Auxiliary Pioneer Corps. Despite opposition from the Czechoslovak Ministry of National Defense and the brigade command, President Beneš declared, on December 24, 1941, an amnesty for "Czechoslovak citizens who had refused to serve in the army or had been dismissed." By the end of February 1942, practically all those who had left Cholmondeley Park had rejoined the brigade in Leamington, where they continued their training until April 1942, when they were transferred and entrusted with the defense of the small area between Seaton and Sidmouth on the southern coast of England. In August, they were assigned the same task for the area between Great Yarmouth and Southwold on the east coast. In March 1943, while Czechoslovak troops in the Soviet Union were participating in heavy fighting around Kharkov, Czechoslovak soldiers in England were merely guarding yet another small area between Felixstowe and Walton-on-Naze on the east coast.[127]

Thanks to the efforts of Chaplain Kraus, the Jews in the brigade were kept busy with an intensive, well-organized program of Jewish religious and social activities. Services were held on the holidays, and whenever the chaplain visited a unit. If there was a need for getting together a *minyan* (prayer quorum) for a special purpose, there was no difficulty in finding the required ten men. Jews in hospitals received visits from the chaplain. Over the years, a spirit of cohesion and brotherly understanding developed among the Orthodox, the Liberals, and the non-practicing Jews. Somehow, many of the sharp differences that might have existed between them before the war mellowed under the impact of their mutual concerns, such as the fate of the loved ones they had left behind in Czechoslovakia.

Lieutenant Kraus served as the brigade's chaplain until the beginning of September 1943, when the Czechoslovak military unit from the Middle East was transferred to England and was incorporated into the Independent Czechoslovak Brigade. Dr. Hanuš Rezek (Rebenwurzel), chaplain of the Middle East Unit, then became the chaplain of the unified formation, while Chaplain Kraus was transferred to the Czechoslovak air force.[128]

THE INDEPENDENT CZECHOSLOVAK ARMORED BRIGADE

On September 1, 1943, the merger of Colonel Klapálek's Middle East regiment and the Independent Czechoslovak Brigade in England resulted in a new formation, the *Československá samostatná obrněná brigáda* (Independent Czechoslovak Armored Brigade), which was placed under the command of General Alois Liška. The new formation (including the reserve formation) had a complement of 4,370 (365 officers, 3,681 enlisted men, and 324 other military personnel at the depot in Southend on Sea). According to statements from its members, approximately one-half the men were Jews.[129] In the medical corps, the Jews were in the absolute majority. The medical corps in the Ministry of National Defense was headed by Colonel (later General) Dr. František Langer. The commander of the ambulance corps, V. Janča, was not Jewish, but among his medical officers were L. Blitz, K. Frankl, G. Gratzinger, H. Kirchenberger, E. Kohn, S. Mueller, O. Schlesinger, H. Tauber, K. Varadi, and others. In the spring of 1944 many of the physicians were transferred to the Soviet Union. H. Tauber then became chief medical officer of the Independent Czechoslovak Armored Brigade. His deputy was A. Schwarz.[130]

In some respects the political situation in the Armored Brigade was different from what it had been in the original Independent Czechoslovak Brigade; in others, it was the same. About 150 active officers were gradually transferred to Czechoslovak formations in the Soviet Union; they were replaced by reserve officers who were sympathetic to the needs of the enlisted men. Developments on the Russian front and Beneš's agreement with Moscow opened the way for more overt left-wing and Communist activities within the army. There were numerous Jews among the Communists in the Armored Brigade. However, the increase in the number of Jewish soldiers once again strengthened the anti-Jewish mood fomented by reactionary officers and Fascists among the troops. Non-Jewish Communists sided with the Jewish soldiers, who in turn became sympathetic toward Communism because they believed that Communism would lead to the elimination of anti-Semitism. This again was the beginning of a vicious circle that gave the anti-Semites new excuses for even cruder excesses.[131]

On August 30, 1944, seven weeks after D-Day, 4,259 officers and men of the Armored Brigade embarked at Portsmouth and within a week had crossed the English Channel to Courselles and Arromanches in Normandy.[132] From there, they were transferred to Falaise. The decision to keep the Czechoslovak troops in the rear for the time being was another cause for dissatisfaction among the troops, who were anxious to be sent to the front. During the period of waiting, the Jewish soldiers celebrated the High Holidays with Chaplain Rezek (Rebenwurzel) conducting services in the field.[133]

The Allied push into northern France and Belgium had been swift, and supplies of food, fuel, and ammunition had to be moved as quickly as possible from the Normandy beachheads to keep up with the advancing Allied forces. One of the first assignments given to the Czechoslovak Armored Brigade was to provide convoys of trucks that traveled from Omaha Beach to Brussels with the urgently needed supplies. Among the drivers of the vehicles were many Jews who, on their return to the base camp, brought news about the situation of the Jews in Belgium. Hundreds of Jewish children had been hidden by Catholic families; most of the parents of these youngsters had been deported. With the liberation of Belgium by the Allies, the Catholic families were anxious to hand over the children to what was left of the Jewish community. Immediate help was needed to set up a children's home for the young survivors. In his diaries, Chaplain Rezek (Rebenwurzel) recalls how the Jews in the Brigade organized a fund-raising drive for this purpose. They collected a total of about 250,000 Belgian francs (including contributions from quite a number of gentiles), a substantial sum that helped the Relief Committee in Belgium to inaugurate the home.

On October 5, the Brigade moved to the coast near Calais and relieved Canadian and British formations besieging Dunkirk, where the Germans had concentrated 13,000 men under the command of Vice-Admiral Frisius. This area is crisscrossed by numerous channels, which the Germans used to inundate the entire front. The German positions were also otherwise well fortified so that accessible approaches had to be found. During these operations, and in the course of German surprise forays, the brigade lost five of its men between October 8 and 10. Two of the dead, Corporal O. Gabriel and Private K. Spira, were Jews.[134]

The brigade's first large-scale attack took place on October 28, 1944, when it was decided to celebrate Czechoslovak Independence Day with a military victory. The aim was to surprise and overpower the enemy's forward resistance points. The battle was a success. An entire German battalion was annihilated; 150 Germans were killed and 356 captured. On the Czechoslovak side, thirty-two were killed. According to the testimony of an assistant to Dr. K. Frankl, who was in charge of the field hospital, most of those killed and wounded were Jewish soldiers.[135]

The second battle in which the Czechoslovak troops participated, and which took place on November 5, 1944, had a very different outcome. Since the Germans had reinforced their positions after the losses of the previous battle, it was decided to repeat the attack, this time on the eastern part of the enemy's defense perimeter, and penetrate his defenses there. The operation was to be supported by a British anti-aircraft brigade and also by British Typhoons. The Czechoslovak troops advanced behind forty-three tanks of the Armored Brigade, but the advance was stopped and the entire action beaten off by an unexpectedly strong German cannonade. Most of the tanks were trapped in mine fields, and without the tanks the infantry had no chance. It was forced to retreat under constant enemy gunfire and suffered heavy casualties. The official statistics do not give casualty figures for individual battles, but unofficial figures given by those who were present at the field hospital speak of 105 killed and about 300 wounded.[136] Among the casualties was a Jewish soldier, Private Rudolf Jellinek. He had volunteered to participate in the attack in order to obtain priority for a furlough to visit his sister, who had survived the war in hiding in Brussels and had sent him word that she was anxious to see him. It was a heartbreaking task to bring her the news of what had happened to her brother.

After this defeat, it was decided to encircle the Germans and pin them down. The Germans tried several times to penetrate the tight circle around Dunkirk, but were forced each time to retreat to their positions. The last battle took place between April 10 and 16, 1945. The Germans organized simultaneous sallies in three directions, succeeded in surprising the Armored Brigade, and occupied several of its strongholds. However, Czechoslovak reinforcements quickly entered the breach, forcing the enemy to retreat with heavy losses. Unofficially, the losses of the Czechoslovaks were estimated at about 50 dead and 100 wounded and missing. The official data put Czechoslovak losses during the siege of Dunkirk at 167 killed, 461 wounded, and 40 missing.[137] The official statistics do not specify how many of the casualties were Jews, but unofficial testimonies estimate that they comprised at least half the total.[138] The lists of those buried in the cemeteries near Dunkirk include thirty-eight Jewish names.* Many others are mentioned in numerous testimonies of those who took part in the siege.

The siege of Dunkirk ended officially on May 10, 1945, when Vice-Admiral Frisius capitulated to the troops of General Liška. However, two events that occurred even before seem to be more eloquent symbols of the German defeat. One was the fact that Jewish soldiers of the Czechoslovak Independent Armored Brigade were able to celebrate a Passover *seder* in the former German officers' club at De Panne, on the French-Belgian border. One of the participants, Walter Überreich-Urban, recalls:

> About 150 officers and men of our unit were present. An American unit nearby sent a delegation led by their chaplain. Never in my life will I forget

---

* Graves of Czechoslovak soldiers can be found in the cemeteries of Boubourg (France), Adinkerque (Belgium), and Cassel (Germany). There are also other cemeteries in villages in that area where soldiers of the Czechoslovak Brigade are buried. In August 1959, a number of Czechoslovak war dead were transferred to the (newly created) Czechoslovak National Cemetery at La Targette near Arras. This cemetery includes a few tombstones marked with a Star of David, but there are many other graves obviously those of Jewish soldiers but not identified as such.

that evening. In the casino, where, only a short time before, German officers and Nazis who wanted to exterminate us had been drinking, we Jews now sat; we, persecuted and humiliated Jews, freely celebrating our great, traditional Passover night.[139]

The other event preceding the official end of the siege was General Montgomery's decision, at the request of the Czechoslovak military authorities, to transfer a symbolic unit of 140 men from Dunkirk to the operational sector on Czechoslovak territory. One anti-aircraft battery, reinforced by an additional unit of motorized infantry, left Dunkirk on April 23, 1945, and advanced toward the western frontiers of Czechoslovakia. Again, we have a record from one of the participants, the Jewish soldier W. Gutwillig-Galat:

> We joined a formation of the Third American Army of General [George S.] Patton. On May 1, we entered Czechoslovak territory near Cheb. On May 7 we liberated Plzeň [Pilsen]. American officers stopped our further advance at Rokycany. They refused to let us continue in our advance because, as they said, there had been an agreement between the Great Powers that this area was to be liberated by Soviet troops. We reached Prague only on May 28, in time for the festive big parade of the Czechoslovak units which had been fighting in the West.[140]

JEWS IN THE CZECHOSLOVAK AND BRITISH AIR FORCES

Before World War II, the airmen in the Czech army were part of an elite corps. A Jew could join the Czech air force only in exceptional cases, because, even then, Jews were kept out of the officer corps. One of the few exceptions was Reserve Officer John Federmann, who served from 1941 as navigator with the 311th Squadron, together with the pilot Rudolph Körper of Plzeň. Navigator J. Korda (Kohn) described the situation prevailing at that time: "The Czech wing of the RAF was run by Czech career officers. There was a great reluctance to allow any Jewish personnel to fly. The spirit in the highest echelons of the air force was highly anti-Semitic, and if someone wanted to fly, he had to conceal the fact that he was Jewish. Some changed their names and identified themselves as having no religious affiliation."[141]

The excuse used for justifying the practical existence of an "Aryan paragraph" in the Czechoslovak air force during World

War II was the alleged apprehension that in case a Jewish airman was shot down over enemy territory, the Germans would not treat him as a prisoner of war, as they would treat Czechs or Slovaks, but would shoot him on the spot. The consequences of this attitude were cited by Josef Valo, a member of the State Council. He told the story of volunteer Richard Frankl, a Jewish refugee from Czechoslovakia, who had come to England all the way from Argentina to join the Czechoslovak army.

> At the Czechoslovak House in London he met a group of civilians and soldiers and began to talk to them. At first the conversation was quite friendly. But when he expressed his wish to join the air force, they told him he had better not apply because he was a Jew. When he protested, he got a slap in the face and when he tried to defend himself, he was knocked down and beaten so badly that he had to go to a hospital for medical treatment.[142]

From the testimony of Josef Margolius we know the experiences of those who eventually were accepted by the air force: "During the war, I suffered every day because of my Jewish origin. First they kept calling us stinking Jews and gave us only ground duties at the airports. Then they let us load the cannons and mockingly called us, 'Sokol' [after the prewar athletic organization in Czechoslovakia]. I was a sergeant and, in my despair . . . I asked to be transferred to Svoboda's army. But I was disillusioned there as well."[143]

There was a change in the situation only after the Czechoslovak air force had suffered serious losses. At the end of 1942 there were 1,340 Czechoslovak airmen in Britain. Of these, 299 were officers on active duty. In the course of the air battles, many lost their lives, and quite a number were missing, wounded, or captured. Those who had passed the prescribed number of flight hours were transferred to non-combatant duties.[144] There was one reservoir for replacing the losses: namely, the Jews.[145] Among the young Jewish refugees there was a group of about 300 youths, mostly the sons of Jews from the Sudetenland who had remained in the Protectorate and perished in German concentration camps.[146] They had been brought to England in August 1939 in special children's transports with the assistance of British relief organizations. At the time they came to England they were between fourteen and seventeen years old; by the beginning of 1943, they were either approaching or had already reached military age. To replenish the decimated ranks of the air force, Czechoslovak military authorities now decided to tap this reservoir. But they still did not permit any of the Jewish recruits to become pilots. The following was the experience of at least two from this group. Frank Schön from Moravská Ostrava came to England as a boy of fifteen. At eighteen, he joined the Czechoslovak armed forces and served in the ground staff of the air force. Unable to stand the anti-Semitism of his superiors, he requested his commanding officer to transfer him to the Royal Air Force. After all, he pointed out, he would be fighting the common enemy there, too. The commanding officer shouted at him: "It is your sacred duty to fight fascism in the Czechoslovak army. We cannot forbid you to serve with the British because we are practically prisoners here. But when we come home, we will settle our accounts with each of your kind." Schön completed training as a gunner and navigator in the RAF, and remained in England after the war.[147]

Another case is that of eighteen-year-old Josef Rudinger, who interrupted his studies in London and volunteered in 1942 with a group of friends for the Czechoslovak air force. Although he and his friends had received top marks from the British officers who had tested them and recommended that they be accepted for training as pilots and navigators, the Czechoslovak officers decided otherwise. Instead of Rudinger, "they selected for training a semi-illiterate individual who came from Argentina just because he had been a member of the Sokol organization there." Jewish soldiers were trained at an air force base under the command of Colonel Duda, a notorious anti-Semite.[148]

The Czechoslovak air force in England consisted of three fighter wings (nos. 310, 312, and 313) and one bomber wing (no. 311). Each wing had twenty-four to thirty planes. In 1943, the 311th Wing was transferred from the Bomber Command to the Coastal Command, a transfer which involved much higher demands on navigators. Jewish soldiers proved to be best qualified for this task. Out of fifteen who graduated from the radar school, nine were Jews. They were sent for operational training to the Bahamas, where the crews for operational flights of the 311th Wing were grouped together. There was hardly any crew without Jews. In one bomber, for instance, three out of a crew of eight were Jews. The navigator was J. Schück, the radio operator was Josef Rudinger, and the gunner H. Pollak. In another bomber the navigator was J. Dezider, the radio operator P. Wechsberg, and the gunner A. Pollak.[149] J. Korda (Kohn), who became a navigator and crew captain in 1943, recalled: "I had two Jewish men in my crew. One was called Hoch; the name of the other was Kudla. I think his original name was Kellner, and he came from Brno. Both men were bombardiers and gunners. In other crews, about 30 percent were Jews."[150] The changeover from Wellington to Liberator bombers demanded the addition of a mechanic to the crew of each plane. Again, among the ground service staff, Jewish mechanics were found to be so reliable that after a special training course many of them were added to the flying personnel.

In May 1944, after the Czechoslovak air force had suffered further losses, intensive recruitment was carried out among young soldiers, including many Jews. One of those Jews who was accepted, H. Brecher, recalls: "During training in the air force barracks, we numbered about 40 percent Jews. We passed courses as radio operators and gunners for the Liberator type bombers."[151] Korda (Kohn), who was wounded in the head on one of his many bombing missions, recorded: "At that time, there were about 150 men in the flying personnel of the 311th Bomber Wing; about 40 percent of these were Jews." He adds:

> The RAF also used many Jewish civilian boys who spoke a perfect German and who would fly aboard British bombers as part of the crew. They spoke through radio communications to the German air fighters, in German, and misled them by giving them wrong information so that they would not attack the RAF planes. Many of these Jewish boys, who had no status in the RAF, were killed or captured by the Germans. Those who were taken prisoner [by the Germans] did not survive.[152]

There were many more Jews in the bomber wing, in both the flying and ground personnel, than in the fighter squadrons. However, in order to make up for its losses, the Czechoslovak air force was compelled to open its fighter units to Jews, and, in the end, especially in the 310th and 312th Wings, there was a high percentage of Jews. K. Schick, who came to England with a group of Jewish refugee volunteers from Shanghai, recalls two Jewish fighter pilots, "Epstein from Prague and Schnitzer from Brno, both of whom survived." Schick was appointed by the RAF as squadron adjutant to the 313th Czechoslovak Wing and thus held one of the most important ground assignments, but he remained the only Jew in his unit. He also states in his deposition:

> Some of the officers resigned themselves to the influx of Jews into the air force and behaved very decently toward their Jewish comrades in arms. Others, however, could not swallow it and made no secret of their anti-Semitic feelings. One of them, Colonel Schiffner, publicly declared that he hated Jews. I know he was reprimanded for it by General Janoušek, but it did not help. At the beginning, there were enough pilots and professional air force officers, but there were not enough young people to take over after them, and there was also a shortage of ground personnel. Without Jews they could hardly have mustered more than one squadron. The number of Jews in ground personnel can be estimated at several hundred.[153]

Probably the most decorated Jewish member of the Czechoslovak air force was Josef Rudinger, who, at the end of 1943, was awarded the Czechoslovak War Cross as a crew member of a bomber that had sunk a German submarine. He was then an officer candidate. By the end of the war, he had risen to captain and held two War Crosses and three medals for merit.

But even Rudinger's distinguished war record is far overshadowed by that of Lieutenant Otto Smik, one of the aces of the Czechoslovak air force, whose Jewish origin was unknown during the war and was revealed only many years later in the testimony of Miroslav Šigut, who was an officer and bomber pilot in the Czechoslovak air force:

> Otto Smik was the first Czechoslovak to be sent for special training to Canada, where I met him in 1942. We became friends, and Smik confided everything to me. He was born in 1922 near Tbilisi, Georgia [USSR]. His father served in the Austro-Hungarian army during World War I and was taken prisoner by the Russians. After the war, he married a Russian Jewess, and they settled in Georgia. When the Czechoslovak government established diplomatic relations with the Soviet Union in 1935, Czechoslovaks living in Russia were permitted to return to Czechoslovakia. Smik's parents then settled in Bratislava. In 1939, Otto Smik escaped from Slovakia and joined first the Czechoslovak army in France and later the Czechoslovak air force in England. Smik was exceptionally capable, so he advanced rapidly and became a squadron leader. He also flew with our squadron. In 1943 he

was shot down over Holland but within two months he had made his way back from the German front to England. He was decorated and became leader of the 127th British Squadron, a great distinction for a Czechoslovak. In November 1944, he was again shot down over Holland; his body was found many years later in a canal near the Dutch town of Zwolle." Otto Smik received five Czechoslovak War Crosses, the Czechoslovak Medal for Courage, and the British Distinguished Flying Cross. Šigut ends his testimony with the words: "Much was written about Otto Smik in Czechoslovakia, but his real story, particularly the fact that he was born a Jew, was known only to a very few of his friends."[154]

The *Svaz letců svobodného* Československa (Free Czechoslovak Air Force Association) in England dedicated a bronze plaque to the memory of members of the Czechoslovak air force killed during the war. It is now on display at the Czechoslovak National House (74 West End Lane, London N.W. 6) and bears 511 names of "those who gave their lives for freedom." Over fifty of the surnames on the plaque are Jewish.[155]

THE FIRST CZECHOSLOVAK INFANTRY BATTALION IN THE SOVIET UNION

On June 21, 1941, Hitler ordered the invasion of the Soviet Union. Less than a month later, Jan Masaryk, the Minister of Foreign Affairs in the Czechoslovak government-in-exile, signed an agreement with the Soviet ambassador in London, Ivan Maisky, under which the Soviets recognized the existence of the Czechoslovak Republic within its pre-Munich borders and approved the creation of Czechoslovak military units from Czechoslovak citizens living in Soviet territory.[156]

However, it was not until December 8, 1941, that the Soviet-Czechoslovak mixed military commission first heard that the Soviets sanctioned the formation of an independent Czechoslovak infantry battalion as soon as possible. The main reservoir of manpower for this battalion were the Czechoslovak refugees interned in Soviet labor camps, who were given amnesty only after protracted negotiations, because the NKVD persistently refused to release Czechoslovak citizens suspected of espionage. On January 10, 1942, the Soviet general Panfilov was able to inform the chief of the Czechoslovak Military Mission, Lieutenant Colonel Heliodor Pika, that the NKVD had given orders to free all the Czechoslovak refugees who had been interned or imprisoned.[157] Immediately thereafter, the military mission launched a vigorous recruitment drive. It was decided to station the unit in the town of Buzuluk, which, after the advance of German armies, had become the temporary seat of the Czechoslovak embassy. The commander of the battalion, Lieutenant Colonel Ludvík Svoboda, was operating from the embassy. He chose as his adjutant a Jew, Cadet Officer Pavel Steiner-Skalický, and sent him to Buzuluk to prepare quarters for the new unit. Four other Jewish volunteers—Samet, M. Stemmer, Belak, and Artur Alter—were assigned to assist Steiner in this task. Svoboda himself arrived at Buzuluk on December 28, 1941, and soon thereafter, the first volunteers were recruited. In his book *Z Buzuluku do Prahy* (From Buzuluk to Prague), Ludvík Svoboda lists the names of the first thirty volunteers "who escaped the Gestapo by the skin of their teeth." He does not mention that twenty of those whom he names were Jews.[158]

The first woman volunteer, Nurse Malvína Friedmann of Berehovo (Beregszász), Subcarpathian Ruthenia, came to Buzuluk in January 1942. She, too, was Jewish. Svoboda was not certain whether, according to regulations, women could join the Czechoslovak army; before inducting Nurse Friedmann, he sought instructions from the government-in-exile in London. However, Nurse Friedmann insisted that the recruitment appeal which had brought her to Buzuluk had said nothing about women not being accepted, and she informed Svoboda that she had no intention of leaving. Many volunteers who had come from Soviet internment and prison camps were sick, so that the need for a nurse was becoming increasingly urgent. Eventually, Svoboda had to give in; he even helped Malvína Friedmann with a recommendation that she organize a special Czechoslovak department at the local hospital of Buzuluk. Before long this department was filled to capacity because the volunteers arriving from labor camps were in bad shape; about 70 percent of them had to be hospitalized immediately.[159]

Czechoslovak historiography divides the volunteers who came to Buzuluk into the following categories: political refugees, veterans of the International Brigade from the Spanish civil war, Communists, progressive intellectuals, Czechoslovaks who had emigrated to the Soviet Union before the war, and *utečenci* (refugees) from Czechoslovakia. Though the last-named category was the most numerous, it is mentioned only in passing by Communist historians. However, there exist hundreds of documents and personal testimonies which prove the important role played by this group. The present study is based mainly on these testimonies.

Thus, for instance, the statement of David Elefant, who arrived in Buzuluk in January 1942 with six other Jewish Communists:

> Svoboda was very much surprised by our healthy appearance, because we looked so different from the Jewish volunteers who had been coming from the camps. There were about 100 volunteers, mainly Communists; about 70 percent of them were Jews who arrived in Buzuluk before the end of January 1942 from various parts of the Soviet Union. A far bigger stream of volunteers was coming from Soviet labor camps. Most of them were Jews. Never before have we seen people in such a pitiful state, and for most of us Communists it was a depressing experience. None of us had ever been in any of these camps, and even if we had heard of them, it was difficult for us to imagine under what inhuman conditions these refugees had been forced to live. The state of these people engendered a lot of anti-Soviet feeling. Svoboda at that time did not try to stop the anti-Soviet remarks of his men because he felt as they did.[160]

Or, to quote the Social Democratic member of the Czechoslovak parliament, Dr. Vilém Bernard, who came to Buzuluk at the end of February 1942:

> Three categories of volunteers could be found there. One group consisted of less than 100 men who were left of the original Czechoslovak legion that had been organized in Poland. [We know from the testimony of Kurt Fanta, one of this group, that of 88 people, 20 were Jews—nine of them officers—who, again, are not mentioned in Svoboda's book.] These were setting the tone because the command was in their hands. Another group consisted of a few political refugees who had survived the critical period in relative freedom. Among them were refugees who had been persecuted for racial reasons. The people in the third group made the worst impression on us. These were the Jewish refugees from the camps. They outnumbered the other two groups by far. I remember many young people dying of typhoid fever immediately after their arrival. The number of those who had to be sent to the hospital, often in a hopeless state, was terribly high. Typhoid fever claimed many victims, but doctors—and all the doctors in Buzuluk at that time were Jewish—succeeded in overcoming the epidemic in a relatively short time.[161]

In some of the Soviet labor camps the commanders refused to release the Czechoslovak prisoners who had gained amnesty and even tried to conceal the recruitment appeal from them. In such cases the Czechoslovak embassy intervened with the Soviet authorities. Vilém Bernard, who handled these matters at the embassy, where his party comrade Zdeněk Fierlinger served as minister, recorded:

> Usually we would send notes to the Soviet Ministry of Foreign Affairs, asking them to intervene. In most cases they complied with our wishes, but the replies were delayed. Sometimes they took half a year to come; sometimes we received no answer at all. In most cases, we were informed that the man in question had either already died at the camp or was on his way to Buzuluk. In cases of death, we received death certificates which usually gave a weak heart or "sclerosis" as the cause of death. As the age of most of the dead was around twenty and the places where they died were notorious camps, we had a pretty clear picture of the truth. My superior, the minister Zdeněk Fierlinger, had to sign, or at least add a paragraph, to the notes, but he disliked doing it, because he disliked anything that was reminiscent of the negative side of Soviet life.[162]

It was impossible to obtain information about the number of Czechoslovak prisoners or about the places where they were held. Neither the Soviet authorities nor the leaders of the Communist party of Czechoslovakia in Moscow, who had such lists available, were willing to cooperate. However, the Czechoslovak military mission was interested in every able-bodied Czechoslovak who was a potential soldier. Lieutenant Colonel Pika therefore tried to obtain detailed information from the volunteers who came to Buzuluk. On the basis of their testimony, he was able to prepare a detailed map of the labor camps and to obtain some idea of the number of Czechoslovak citizens held at each of them. He then intervened for their release whenever he could.[163]

Among those who now arrived at Buzuluk there were also some volunteers who had been fighting in the ranks of the Soviet army. One of them was Corporal Teodor Fiš, who later became a colonel on the general staff in Prague. A political refugee, he had volunteered in Lwow at the end of 1939 and fought in the Red army near Voroshilovgrad. After an order had been issued that Czechoslovaks should be sent to fight in their own army, he came to Buzuluk. In his testimony we read: "There were fifteen of us, and we reached the Battalion on February 11, my birthday. I was Number 315 and they recognized my rank of corporal. When Lieutenant Kudlič, a member of the recruiting commission, learned from the questionnaire that I was of Jewish origin and a Communist to boot, he warned me: 'We shall not permit any politics here and certainly not Communists. If you do not behave yourself, you will come to a bad end.' " Fiš later became the leader of the Communist party cell in his unit and thus also a member of the executive committee of the party organization within the Czechoslovak army in the Soviet Union. He was therefore well informed. He adds: "Gradually, a whole group of refugees whom they had refused to accept in the military unit in Krakow came together in Buzuluk. I estimate the number of those who were living at liberty in the Soviet Union at about 200. About 80 percent of them were Jewish refugees."[164] Like others questioned, he, too, recorded:

> The most numerous group were so-called 'economic refugees' who were concentrated in Lwow. These refugees had not wanted to answer Soviet labor recruitment appeals. In later roundups they had been deported by the Soviet authorities to labor camps as undesirable aliens. They were now arriving [in Buzuluk] emaciated, with frozen limbs, typhoid fever, and dysentery. They saw the army as their only hope for survival. They therefore undertook the journey regardless of their health. Many succumbed to the hardships of the journey.

Karel Hahn, who had escaped from the Nazi camp at Nisko only to be sent to a Soviet camp, reached Buzuluk in April 1942: "I was given the registration number 556, which represented the total number of men in the battalion at the time. Of these, about 400 were Jews. Later, when the number reached 800, the number of Jewish volunteers was about 600."[165]

The Lanzer family mentioned earlier in this study was separated after their release from the Panino camp. The father and two older sons were sent to Buzuluk; the mother and the youngest son made their way to Uzbekistan, where they worked at a *kolkhoz* (collective farm). Half a year later they were permitted to reunite. In the meantime, however, the father had died and one of the sons had to have several frozen toes amputated. The youngest son, who was now fourteen, volunteered in September 1942 and was accepted at a military school, where there were at least two more Jewish cadets, the fifteen-year-old sons of the volunteers Frešl and Rosenbaum.[166] Kurt Lanzer, who left Czechoslovakia in 1948, fought in the Israeli War of Independence and eventually settled in Haifa, says:

> Among the soldiers gathered in Buzuluk, Jewish volunteers in my estimate formed a majority: 80 percent. In our free time we were continuously exposed to propaganda intended to convince us that we should be grateful to the Soviet Union until our dying day. The Beneš government was never even mentioned; it was as if it did not exist. Among the soldiers there were also many Orthodox Jews. They had a separate hall where they could hold their religious services. Jewish soldiers who wanted to observe the holidays were exempt from drill on those days. They were free. On the whole, religious observance was not suppressed in the battalion in Buzuluk.[167]

In March 1942, military training was initiated under the direction of Captain Lomský and under the supervision of Soviet instructors. The training had to proceed without weapons; there were rumors that the Russians did not trust the Czechoslovak unit and therefore did not wish to supply it with the necessary weapons. This state of affairs did not add to the morale of the troops. In April, schools for officers and NCOs were opened, and later other special courses were begun. Svoboda's principle of selecting future commanders according to proven military skills rather than according to school graduation certificates worked against Jewish intellectuals, many of whom had received draft deferments because of their university studies and therefore had not attained officer rank. They were not selected for training at officers' schools and Captain Lomský, who made no attempt to conceal his anti-Semitic feelings, put them through every possible hardship during their military training.[168]

Simultaneously with the organization of the battalion, an independent reserve company was formed that included mostly older men and women who were physically unfit for combat duty. They were assigned all kinds of auxiliary duties according to their abilities.

Malvína Friedmann, who through her initiative and perseverance had made it possible for women to join the army, was followed by other female volunteers, including women who had been interned in Soviet camps. Some of them were Communists or otherwise politically active; others were wives of officers or of active Communists. Altogether there were twenty-four women in the battalion; nineteen of them were Jewish. All of them had to go through basic training. After that, eighteen women passed a nursing course and were assigned as *sanitářky* (medical orderlies) to individual companies. Several women were trained as radio operators, a few worked in the education department, and one (Dr. Božena Hermann) was assigned to the judge advocate's division.

Most of the statistical tables prepared by the Czechoslovak military mission give no data on Jewish soldiers. One of the few official documents to deal in part with this subject can be found in the army publication *Směr Praha* (Direction Prague). There, the 606 Czechoslovak soldiers who were registered in Buzuluk as of May 1, 1942, are divided according to nationality as follows: 110 Czechs, 21 Slovaks, 19 Subcarpathian Ruthenians, 124 Czech residents in the Soviet Union, 43 Czech residents in Poland, 3 Hungarians, and 286 Jews.[169] But even if the 286 Jewish soldiers, who represented 47 percent of all the troops, exceeded all the other ethnic groups, this figure does not do justice to reality by far. According to the estimate of all informed participants, the number of Jewish volunteers at Buzuluk was between 70 and 80 percent of the total. We have a testimony from two volunteers, the Taussingers, that explains the discrepancy between the official figures and the unofficial estimates, which are much higher. "During the recruiting at Buzuluk, Czech officers tended to register Jewish nationality only in the cases of those Czechoslovak Jews who spoke Yiddish and who insisted that their nationality be put down as Jewish. The majority of Jewish volunteers, though they made no attempt to conceal their Jewish origin, registered their nationality according to the language they ordinarily spoke."[170] So it came about that a large percentage of Jewish soldiers were registered as Czechs or Slovaks. It must also be remembered that there were among the Jewish soldiers many Communists who preferred not to have their nationality registered as Jewish. This explains the disparity between the statistical tables and the actual number of Jews who served in the army.

Jewish volunteers showed loyalty both to the command of their battalion and to the Soviet authorities. They were grateful that they had been released from the labor camps and given a chance to fight against Nazi Germany. At the same time, they found it impossible to forget the nightmare of their experience in the Soviet camps, and the subject appeared again and again as an anti-Soviet argument.[171] Those among the Jewish volunteers who were Communists and were therefore permitted to live in freedom without having to go through the traumatic experience of the Soviet camps pressed their non-Communist coreligionists not to mention these things in public. Where this did not help, the *politruks* (Communist party liaison officials who supervised ideological education in the army) intervened, and the NKVD apparatus found good reason for sending "troublemakers" back to forced labor. One of those punished was the Prague lawyer Dr. František Polák who after the war published two books about his experiences in Gulag camps.[172]

Even more tragic was the fate of Dr. Karel Goliath, a Jewish volunteer in Buzuluk, formerly an attorney in Moravská Ostrava, who was interned in various labor camps until September 1955, when he was released after years of intervention by such personages as General Svoboda, Zdeněk Nejedlý (a member of the Czechoslovak government immediately following the war), and the writer Ivan Olbracht. Goliath's efforts to prove his innocence were frustrated by a decision of the regional prosecutor of Moravská Ostrava on August 4, 1961, declaring Goliath as not responsible for his conduct and recommending that he be placed into the custody of a psychiatric institution for "preventive care." Since then Dr. Goliath has been living at the *Útulek sociálního zabezpečení* (health care facility) in Moravská Ostrava.[173]

Klement Gottwald, the head of the Czechoslovak Communist party delegation in Moscow, was well informed about the views of the troops in Buzuluk. On May 26, 1942, he came to Buzuluk with a delegation from his party and with a Social Democratic member of the Czech parliament, Bohumil Laušman, to address the 700 officers and men of the battalion in the hall of the Buzuluk motion picture theater. He warned the troops that expressions of anti-Soviet or anti-Communist feelings would not be tolerated on Soviet soil. To those unable or unwilling to forget their experiences in the Soviet camps he said: "Think what would have happened to you if you had fallen into Hitler's clutches. . . . It is high time for you to forget about personal recriminations for alleged wrongs and to realize that the Soviet people have suffered a thousand times more than all of you together." Gottwald also had consultations with his party comrades in the battalion. He informed them that Comrade Bedřich Reicin[174] had been named head of the party organization in the army[175] and would maintain contact with Moscow. During his visit Gottwald also promised Svoboda to intervene with the Soviet authorities on behalf of refugees from Subcarpathian Ruthenia (which was then occupied by Hungary) interned in Soviet labor camps. The Soviets, however, claimed that these people could not be released under the amnesty applicable to Czechs and Slovaks because they were regarded not as Czechoslovaks but as citizens of Hungary. Among these people there were also Jews.[176]

Shortly after Gottwald, Zdeněk Fierlinger, the Czechoslovak minister to the Soviet Union, also visited the battalion at Buzuluk. He met with Svoboda and spoke separately with each of the commanding officers. The results of these talks soon became known. Svoboda switched from talk about Masaryk and Beneš to extravagant praise for Soviet ways. He also indicated that the battalion would soon have to join the fighting on the front lines.[177]

The Communist party organization began to take part officially in the affairs of the battalion. Of seven members of the executive committee, Reicin, the chairman, and five others, Dr. F. Engel, Teodor Fiš, E. Frešl, H. Kopold, and H. Petránek-Ackermann, were Jews.[178] Each company had an education officer assigned to the task of influencing the unit's views along pro-Soviet lines.

The government-in-exile in London was informed about the situation by the chief of the military mission, Colonel Pika. In July 1942, Beneš sent the Minister of National Defense, General Ingr, to Buzuluk. Ingr spoke to Svoboda and the battalion's commanding officers and addressed the troops. Svoboda later summed up the situation: "We did not obey Ingr but Gottwald."[179] An eloquent expression of Svoboda's feelings was his letter to Stalin of August 28, 1942, in which, basing his request on what he claimed was the will and consensus of Czechoslovak officers and men, he urgently requested permission to join with the Czechoslovak battalion in the battle against the common enemy and to fight at the front alongside the Red Army.[180] In September he received a positive reply, and in October the first Soviet weapons arrived for the Czechoslovaks.

Svoboda received a strong reprimand from London: "We regard it as highly out of place that you should turn directly to representatives of the Soviet Union."[181] Ingr objected to the battalion's entry into actual combat because he believed that the unit was not sufficiently trained and was badly armed and short of experienced officers and commanders. President Beneš was afraid that if this numerically weak battalion went into independent action on the battlefield it would be decimated. But all these apprehensions and objections were ignored and the government-in-exile did not dare to take any further steps. The soldiers could not be told that their commander was risking their lives on Gottwald's orders only because his party, in order to strengthen its influence, had to show its allegiance to the Soviet Union through military action.[182]

THE BATTLE OF SOKOLOVO
(MARCH 1943)

As soon as the training of the Czechoslovak Infantry Battalion was completed, 979 soldiers were selected and sent to the front on January 30, 1943. The rest of the battalion remained at Buzuluk and was reinforced by additional refugees released from Soviet camps. The unit that came to the battlefront consisted of 26 officers, 10 sergeants, 237 other non-commissioned officers, 668 enlisted men, and 38 women soldiers.[183] According to the estimates of veterans, more than 70 percent of the men and women were Jews.[184] The government-in-exile in London viewed the high percentage of Jews as a "precarious state of affairs."[185]

On March 1, after an exhausting march of 400 kilometers, the battalion reached the ruins of Kharkov, from where the Russians had expelled the Germans only a short time earlier. Teodor Fiš, who was then a corporal, vividly recorded how this unit, which had been installed in some old school buildings, was suddenly awakened by an alarm in the middle of the night and had to start marching south again in $-30°$ Centigrade weather because the Germans, having regrouped, were preparing to recapture Kharkov as a revenge for their defeat at Stalingrad.[186] Soviet forces defending the city had been so greatly weakened that the Czechoslovak unit, though itself weary and spent, was one of the fittest formations on the Kharkov front. The Soviet general Kozlov, explaining the situation to Svoboda and his staff, marked on the map an area around the Russian villages of Timčenkov, Sokolovo, Mirogorod, and Arťuchovka on the banks of the river Mža. The battalion was ordered to occupy defense positions along the river and not to let a single German tank get through to Kharkov.[187] The battalion reached the frozen river on the evening of March 3, 1943, and the staff prepared a plan of action which was approved by the Soviet command.

The most important part of the plan was the defense of the village of Sokolovo, which was entrusted to Lieutenant Jaroš, the commander of the First Infantry Company. This company was reinforced by several other platoons, bringing the total strength to 360 men, mostly Jews. Malvína Friedmann, the Tobiáš sisters, and two other nurses were assigned to this company.[188] The formation was to be supported by a Soviet artillery regiment which had only four guns left intact. The left wing of the defense was formed by the second company, with the support of four Soviet tanks, in the vicinity of Artuchovka, while the third company, around Mirogorod, was supposed to cover the right wing.

The work on the defensive positions was completed in the morning of March 8. The day before, the first German tanks had penetrated to Pervomajskaja. By that time the Soviet regiment, which was supposed to delay a German attack on the Czechoslovak positions, had only ninety-five men left and had been forced to retreat. It became clear that the Czechoslovaks were practically on their own. At noon, fourteen German tanks appeared, heading toward the positions set up by the Czechoslovaks in the northwest part of Sokolovo.[189] The defenders hit three of the tanks that were mired in the terrain. German soldiers jumped out and ran for cover in the nearby woods, and the rest of the German tanks quickly turned back. Heartened by this initial success, the Czechoslovak soldiers left their bunkers and cheered.[190] This lack of caution proved to be their undoing. A part of the crews had remained in the damaged German tanks; now they knew the positions of the Czechoslovak army. The anti-tank defenses and the first line of machine-gun nests were put out of action and, in the chaos that ensued, those who were not killed attempted to flee to positions in the second line of defense. Meanwhile, the German tanks, which, it turned out, had only pretended to retreat, fanned out in various directions; five of them attacked the right and six the northwest end of Sokolovo. Two hours later, about sixty more German tanks, coming from the direction of Gontar, penetrated the center of Sokolovo.[191] The German tanks concentrated their firing power on the machine-gun platoon that had been added to the infantry company under the command of Lieutenant Jaroš. The machine-gun platoon consisted of thirty men. Half of them (including the brothers Walter and Norbert Lanzer, Jakob Hans, Vojtěch Gláz, Ignac Spiegel, Arnošt Steiner, Silbiger, and others) were Jews. The first direct hit killed one of the Lanzer brothers and seven others. Hynek Strompf had this to say about the second machine-gun platoon:

> Our platoon commander was killed right at the start of the battle. The command was taken over by Lieutenant Albert Elovič, from Berehovo [Beregszász]. He was an experienced machine gunner and he performed his task very well, but after an hour's battle, both of our machine gun platoons had been put out of action. Of eight heavy machine guns, only one was left intact, and of fifty men, only twenty-six remained. All the others had been either killed or seriously wounded. Our casualties were so heavy because we had been sent out to fight tanks without adequate weapons. Behind our positions there were two Russian artillery pieces in firing positions, but they were put out of action by direct hits right at the start of the battle.[192]

At five o'clock in the afternoon, Svoboda spoke for the last time over the field telephone with Lieutenant Jaroš, who reported that the situation was becoming desperate since the enemy was already very close to the church tower from which Jaroš was directing the battle. Svoboda ordered Jaroš not to retreat under any circumstances and told him his plan. The third company and another machine-gun platoon was to attack the enemy from the rear. However, the first Russian tank that was to bring help to the defenders broke the ice in the river and was put out of action. It now became clear that the river Mža had in fact become a tank trap which performed the task of the defenders, namely, not to let the Germans cross to the other bank. Nevertheless, the battle of Sokolovo continued. The church tower sustained a direct hit. Lieutenant Jaroš and his observer, Hugo Redisch, joined the defenders in front of the church and were both killed.

Nurses were treating wounded soldiers under fire. Malvína Friedmann carried eleven wounded men from the battlefield. Those nurses not assigned to the field platoons were concentrated in the group of medics led by Second Lieutenant Max Kriegel, who was in direct contact with command headquarters and was in a good position to observe the action. He recorded:

An inadequately armed infantry company, composed mostly of Jews, was sent to an advance position across the river Mža. When the commander, Svoboda, announced from his position of command that the Germans had prepared about seventy tanks for an attack, the Russians brought into play one *katyusha* (a firing weapon with many barrels). It shot one round at the German positions and then retreated because it had run out of ammunition. Soviet artillery was also put out of action. During the attack on Sokolovo, our gunners put seven German tanks out of action. When Lieutenant Ignac Spiegel, a veteran of the Spanish civil war, saw the hopelessness of the situation, he threw himself, with a belt full of hand grenades, under a German tank, which ran over him and exploded. Lieutenant J. Frank, who commanded two mine-throwers, kept firing desperately against the Germans. In the end, he was killed by German machine gun fire.[193]

The battle of Sokolovo ended on the evening of March 8. The Germans occupied the burned-out village and dug themselves in near the river. The next day, Colonel Svoboda received an order to counterattack. Corporal Vojtěch Gláz, who the day before had fought with the machine-gun platoon in Sokolovo, was now assigned to the attacking unit. He testified: "The Germans allowed us to come within firing range and then attacked, inflicting heavy casualties upon the second company because the soldiers on the ice had no place to take cover."[194] Another Jewish participant in the action, Lance Corporal Moshe Hofmann, recorded: "In the evening, seriously wounded comrades from the first company were crawling over the frozen river, and we had been trying to save them under enemy fire. It was a horrible night; nevertheless, we had to keep fighting until the following night, unprepared and exhausted, and then counterattack. My friend Private Spiegel from Mukačevo was among those who fell. The second company numbered 150 men; more than one-third of them were Jews."[195]

The counterattack ended in disaster. The firing across the frozen river continued for hours. Again, we can read in the deposition of Max Kriegel: "We suffered great losses and did not recapture Sokolovo. Perhaps we were saved from a massacre only because German intelligence was so bad that they were unaware of our desperate situation."[196] Second Lieutenant A. Alter testifies in a similar vein: "In the course of three days, 500 soldiers, mostly Jews, were killed or seriously wounded. Colonel Svoboda used us on that occasion as strategic guinea pigs in the fight against the Germans."[197]

On the evening of March 12, the Germans made one more attempt to cross the Mža river. However, they were stopped by concentrated fire from the other bank, and nine of their tanks got stuck in the broken ice. Abandoning the idea of crossing the river, they penetrated the Soviet front in other places and occupied Kharkov, thus cutting the supply lines to the Czechoslovak positions. German bombers also destroyed the transports supplying food and carrying wounded. These transports were the responsibility of the supply squad commanded by Lieutenant Maximilian Holzer. The situation deteriorated even more when a sudden thaw made it impossible to use sleds, the most important means of winter transportation.[198]

In the evening of March 13, the decimated battalion received its marching orders. With Kharkov encircled, there was the danger that the rest of the Czechoslovak unit might fall into the hands of the Germans. The soldiers therefore retreated, taking with them only the barest minimum of equipment in order to be able to move faster. The only other possible retreat was through a narrow corridor defended by Soviet armored troops. The only remaining bridge over the river Donec was destroyed by the Russians as soon as the last soldier of the Czechoslovak battalion had crossed.[199] On March 17, the battalion reached Nový Burluk, where, for the first time, it was out of danger. It arrived at its final destination, Veseloje, on March 31, 1943. However, many soldiers who were too weak and spent to keep up with the rest joined the others only days later.

Of course the Czechoslovak Communist party delegation in Moscow, together with Zdeněk Fierlinger and Colonel Svoboda, exerted every effort to turn the military debacle of Sokolovo into a political victory. Impressed by the courage and devotion of the Czechoslovak troops, the Soviets decided to show their first fighting ally in the best possible light. Nikita Khrushchev, then a member of the Supreme Defense Council of the USSR, and General Vatutin flew to Veseloje to congratulate the decorated heroes personally.[200] Film shots of the military parade and of the decorated Czechoslovaks were shown in Soviet motion picture theaters and published in the Soviet press together with the decree of the Supreme Soviet awarding decorations to eighty-seven Czechoslovak officers and men. It was not mentioned that thirty-three of these soldiers were Jews.[201] Mikhail Ivanovich Kalinin, chairman of the presidium of the Supreme Soviet, decorated Svoboda with the Order of Lenin. The underground Communist paper in Prague, *Rudé Právo*, wrote: "How proud and enthusiastic every Czech must be when he reads about the courageous conduct of our brothers at the front!"[201] Indeed, Czechoslovak soldiers serving in the Middle East were requesting transfers to Svoboda's formations. Czechoslovak soldiers in England sent a resolution to the government-in-exile demanding: "We want to be sent to the front. We want to fight as courageously and bravely as our compatriots in the Soviet Union."[203] To counteract the popular echo of Beneš's broadcast from London, the German Reich Protector, Hans Frank, brought to Prague five Czechoslovak soldiers who had been captured at Sokolovo. What these captives said was thoroughly exploited by German propaganda; it was published also in book form with a comment about organizing a "Jewish-Czech unit" (*žido-česká jednotka*) in the Soviet Union.[204]

The importance of the battle of Sokolovo was particularly stressed by Klement Gottwald, who declared: "The battle of Sokolovo made up for the capitulation of the Czechoslovak army in 1938, when soldiers despaired and began to doubt that we, the twentieth-century Czechs, were worthy of our Hussite forebears. Our field unit proved that these fears were unfounded and that our nation showed itself once again to be worthy of the fighting tradition of Jan Žižka [hero of the Hussite wars]."

The historic role of the Jews and their importance in the war has never been officially recognized in Czechoslovakia.[205] The most that has ever been said officially about the participation of the Jews was in one of Svoboda's speeches, in which he conceded that "citizens of Jewish nationality behaved just as bravely as members of other nationality groups."[206] He said that much in a speech to his soldiers after the battle of Sokolovo. He added in an interview that, as the commander of the unit, he realized that "Jewish soldiers saved not only the honor of the Czechoslovak army, but also the honor and career of its commander."[207]

THE FIRST INDEPENDENT CZECHOSLOVAK BRIGADE IN THE SOVIET UNION

When the Soviets finally extended their amnesty to refugees from Subcarpathian Ruthenia, they released many more prisoners from the labor camps. As a result, a new wave of volunteers arrived in Buzuluk, and at the beginning of 1943, it was decided to form from them a reserve regiment under the command of Lieutenant Dočkal. The training of the new recruits was largely in the hands of Jewish instructors from the original reserve company, under the command of Staff Captain Altmann. Among the Jewish instructors of the four companies into which the reserve regiment was divided were, among others, Lieutenant Gustav Meier and Sergeants Max Sandel and Alfred Hlaváč. The medical staff was trained by Second Lieutenant Dr. Walter Winter.

At the meeting of the Czechoslovak-Soviet mixed military commission in Moscow on April 29, 1943, it was decided to form the First Independent Czechoslovak Brigade in the Soviet Union. The seat of this brigade was to be Novochopersk, and Colonel Jan Kratochvíl was appointed its commander.[208]

After five weeks of rest during which many of the wounded returned from hospitals in Veseloje, 670 officers and men of the First Battalion left for Novochopersk, a small district town with a population of 8,000 on the railroad line between Kujbyshev and Kharkov. They arrived on May 9.[209] The next day they were joined by 1,410 Ukrainians from the reserve regiment in Buzuluk. There were about fifty Jewish soldiers among them.[210] Another transport of 300 soldiers arrived in June; it was composed of Czechoslovak citizens from Czechoslovak territories occupied by Hungary who had been freed from Soviet labor camps; about 100 of these men were Jews.[211] The group was under the command of Lieutenant Gustav Meier. On July 6, some 200 Slovak officers and men released from a Soviet POW camp were welcomed at the railroad station of Novochopersk. These were soldiers of the Slovak "Motorized Division" who at first had fought side by side with the Germans but had gone over to the Russian side in May 1943.[212] Their arrival set off increased anti-Semitism in the brigade.

Before long, the commander of the brigade, Colonel Kratochvíl, who tried to carry out Ingr's ideas, found himself in conflict with Colonel Svoboda, who by this time was completely under the spell of Klement Gottwald. At Gottwald's insistence, the government-in-exile in London transferred Kratochvíl to the military mission in Kujbyshev, while Svoboda was entrusted with the organization and command of the brigade. Thus, Ingr's efforts to bring the brigade's command under the influence of the Beneš government were frustrated.[213]

Svoboda took over the command of the brigade on July 12, 1943. The brigade at that time numbered 2,574 men, 2,240 of whom were fit for combat duty. The number of Jews at this point was estimated at one-fifth of the total.[214] During the second half of July, another 200 men released from Soviet camps volunteered for the brigade. Half of them were Jews. Cadet Officer Vojtěch Gláz, one of those who received the new recruits on their arrival, recorded: "I was surprised how many of my coreligionists I found among the new arrivals. In the group that came in August there were about 200 Jews from units of the Hungarian labor service who had been taken prisoner by the Russians. From time to time there were Jews even in the groups of Ukrainians coming from Buzuluk."[215] These soldiers established contacts with Jewish families in Novochopersk. On Sabbaths the local synagogue was filled with Czechoslovak soldiers, and during the High Holidays there was not enough room for all those who came to the services.[216]

The percentage of Jews in the brigade was not as high as it was in the First Battalion. However, Jews held important positions in the lower officer ranks. Those who had proven their bravery at Sokolovo were promoted. Of about 200 graduates of the school for non-commissioned officers, half were Jews. But even among those who came from Soviet prison camps there were many who advanced quickly in the ranks. Thus, for instance, Reserve Second Lieutenant Alexander Mermelstein-Mašek, after completing artillery training and an officers' course, was assigned to the staff of the commander of an artillery company.[217] Sergeant Arnošt Boehm was appointed commander of the company's vehicles; Lieutenant Rosenzweig commanded a communications unit and Sergeant Brunn was squad leader in a cavalry intelligence platoon;[218] etc. Women soldiers had proved their mettle at Sokolovo and were now pillars of the medical service headed by Lieutenant Dr. F. Engel.

Svoboda began to organize the brigade according to instructions from the representatives of the Czechoslovak Communist party in Moscow, who were eager to send the new formation to the front as quickly as possible. The brigade was to be built on the Soviet model. It was to be composed of three infantry battalions, one tank battalion, one artillery regiment, and one anti-aircraft unit. Sixty men were sent to tank training centers and, after passing the course, twenty Jewish graduates were promoted to subaltern rank. Due to the shortage of officers, Cadet Officer Richard Fischl was appointed chief of staff to the commander of the tank battalion. The shortage of officers was a serious problem. Out of ninety-two graduates from the officers' course at Novochopersk, seventy-four took part in the battle of Sokolovo; of these, fifty-seven were Jews. The best graduates, Fiš, Schoengut, Gross, Frank, and others, had to wait for months for their official commissions while filling in at officers' assignments. Jews found it even more difficult to attain reserve officer rank. Thus, Erich Mautner, who had been a second lieutenant in the reserves before the war, had to start out as a private and fight his way through to the rank he had held in the prewar Czechoslovak army.[219] An effort was made to relieve the shortage of officers by transferring some higher ranks from the Czechoslovak formations in the Middle East and in England, but their arrival was delayed by endless inspections from Soviet authorities and by the stalling tactics of the Communist party cell in the brigade. There were 175 card-carrying Communists in the brigade. About half of them were Jews.[220] As already mentioned, the party organization in the Czechoslovak army was headed by Gottwald's confidant Corporal Bedřich Reicin, who, acting as an extension of the Moscow leadership of the Czechoslovak Communist party, exerted a crucial influence on the commander of the brigade.[221]

The training period was drawn out and the departure of the men for the front was delayed. There were not enough men in the formation. This obstacle was overcome only at the end of September, when a transport of more than 900 men from the Krasnogorsk "reeducation" camp for prisoners of war arrived at Novochopersk. Among the men there were also about 400 Jews from Hungarian labor service units.[222] One of them, Mikuláš Hecht, recalls: "We arrived at Novochopersk three days before our departure for the front. Some of us had no military training at all, and we were lucky that there were many Jewish non-commissioned officers in the brigade who took care of us and trained us on the way to the front and in the trenches in the use of our weapons . . . I was assigned to a mine-throwing company of 130 men commanded by Lieutenant Bedřich. About 80 percent of the men in the unit were Jews and we often had sharp exchanges with the Ukrainians, who kept provoking us with their anti-Semitic remarks."[223]

The transport of 3,517 members of the brigade to the front began on September 30, 1943. Well-informed participants estimate the number of Jewish officers and men at 1,200.[224] On the day of the brigade's departure, the minister of national defense appointed thirteen new lieutenants, of whom ten were Jews.[225] Most of them were assigned as commanders of infantry and machine-gun companies destined to bear the brunt of future fighting.[226] Novochopersk was 950 kilometers from the war region around Kiev. The nine trains carrying the Czechoslovak troops were strafed by German bombers. One transport was forced to stop at the railroad station of Jachnovščina, where the tracks were blocked by a train carrying oil that had been set on fire. The Germans spotted the Czechoslovak transport and bombed the train; two of the cars sustained direct hits. All but six of the men in the second artillery battery were killed. Lieutenant Dr. Armin Scheer, assisted by Jewish nurses, operated on some of the wounded in an improvised emergency room at a nearby *sovchoz* (state-owned Soviet farm). In the little garden of the railroad station 108 men were buried in a mass grave.[227]

The river Dnepr was 150 kilometers from Priluky, the last stop, where the troops left the train and continued in long marches, crossing the river on a Soviet pontoon.[228] Between October 18 and 23, they reached the wooded terrain assigned to them, about twenty kilometers from Priorki, on the outskirts of Kiev. Early in the morning of November 3, 1943, the Russians began their offensive on Kiev. The Czechoslovak brigade advanced behind Soviet tanks in a strip two kilometers wide. Their task was to fight their way through to the center of the city. The Soviet offensive on Kiev has been described in detail in many publications, but our aim here is to record at least in part the role of Jewish soldiers in the Czechoslovak brigade during this operation.[229] The advance platoon commanded by Corporal Laco Presser gave cover to a platoon of Soviet soldiers threatened by the Germans and succeeded in holding the position until Soviet reinforcements could launch a counterattack against the Germans. Corporal Vilém Kahan and Private Richter showed conspicuous bravery during this operation.[230] The task of neutralizing German resistance in the zone of attack was assigned to the First Company. The key role here was played by a platoon led by Sergeant Fleischmann. Corporal Nathan Koenig described the fighting of the second infantry company as follows: "Our commander, Lieutenant Arpád Hofman, fell in the first encounter with the Germans. Our company, which distinguished itself in the battle, was decimated. Among those killed in battle were forty Jewish soldiers."[231]

The attacking force was led by Sergeant Arnošt Steiner; it managed to destroy one German bunker after the other. So did the machine-gun platoon commanded by Lieutenant Reichl,[232] which destroyed other points of resistance and fought its way through to the outskirts of Kiev. In the battle for Syreč, one of the suburbs, Private Josef Mueller, a Jew, distinguished himself by his bravery. Corporal Steinberg repaired the phone connection under heavy enemy fire, and, after establishing contact with the commander's observation point, secured an effective direction of fire.[233] Artilleryman Rosenberg was decorated for bravery in battle. Private Kestenbaum rescued two wounded men from an exposed area. After giving them first aid, Kestenbaum returned to his platoon and continued to advance against the enemy with his anti-tank rifle.[234] The commander of his platoon, Second Lieutenant Stramberger, was badly wounded in one leg. Despite great pain he continued to give orders and to direct the fire. Finally he was taken to a field hospital, where his leg had to be amputated.[235] During the street fighting in Kiev, the medical corpsman Andrej Gross showed great courage and devotion to duty. Though himself wounded, he continued to rescue wounded comrades. With their anti-aircraft battery, Lieutenant Meier and his deputy, Sergeant Rabiner, secured the advance of infantry units and were among the first to reach the center of Kiev. Among those who fought inside the city and lost their lives was the commander of a mine-throwing platoon, Corporal Alfred Elsner.[236]

The official figures of the casualties suffered by the Czechoslovaks during the battle of Kiev are thirty killed, four missing, and eighty wounded. An entry in the war journal for November 2, just before the battle started, shows a loss of 216 men compared with the number of those who had left Novochopersk. This discrepancy was never officially explained.[237]

On November 6, 1943, the day Kiev was liberated, the presidium of the Supreme Soviet awarded the Order of Suvorov to the Czechoslovak Brigade. The Soviets decorated 139 members of the brigade (including all the Jewish commanders of fighting units), and 294 members of the brigade received the Czechoslovak War Cross.[238] Antonin Sochor and Richard Tesařík, the commanding officers of the tank company and of the automatic rifle unit, respectively, both of them gentiles, received the highest award—the title of Hero of the Soviet Union.* Lieutenant Sochor recommended Sergeant Arnošt Steiner for the same honor but his recommendation was not passed on to the Soviet authorities, despite the fact that the commander of the brigade, Colonel Svoboda, had spoken of Steiner in most admiring terms: "I have seen many things in two wars, but rarely exploits similar to those of Steiner. Arnošt Steiner, tough, short, with sharply-cut features and quick dark eyes, a fighter and commander with courage, was everywhere. He always appeared and disappeared at the right time. He directed the firing calmly, with concentration and energy, pointed out spots of enemy resistance and kept explaining the situation even under the heaviest fire like a schoolteacher in front of a blackboard."[239] So much for Svoboda. But Arnošt Steiner, though he was a Communist and professed Czech nationality, was of Jewish origin, and so the very idea of awarding him the title of Hero of the Soviet Union could not possibly be suggested to the Soviet authorities. The brigade command decided it was not desirable that the contribution of the Jews to the Czechoslovak brigade should be recorded in the history of Czechoslovakia.[240]

After the capture of Kiev, the brigade was sent to Vasilkovo for a rest. However, this respite was soon interrupted by an order to pursue the Germans, who were now grouping tanks in the area around Zhitomir and were preparing a counterattack. The minethrowers' company, the first Czechoslovak unit to make contact with the enemy, suffered heavy casualties near Čerňachov.[241] The Soviet offensive, which began on December 24, 1943, forced the Germans to retreat, and the Czechoslovak brigade now prepared to attack the German positions near Bílá Cerkev.[242]

---

* The same award was given to Unit Commander Josef Buršík, who was arrested on charges of treason following the Communist take-over in 1948. He is presently living in London. All references to Buršík's award have been deleted from official Czechoslovak records.

At that time, Colonel Svoboda left for Moscow to be present at President Beneš's negotiations with the Soviets. The brigade was placed temporarily under the command of Lieutenant Colonel Vladimír Přikryl, who had arrived from England only a short time earlier.[243] In the midst of preparations for the battle near Bílá Cerkev, another group of fourteen officers arrived from England. This group was headed by Colonel Krátký, who took over command of the tank battalion. Among the officers in this group there were three Jewish lieutenants: Otta Heller, Arnošt Lederer, and Mirek Kerner.[244]

The battle for Bílá Cerkev began with an attack on the village of Ruda. The village was captured by the Czechoslovak brigade, flanked on either side by Soviet formations, but the fighting was fierce and the casualties suffered by the brigade were twice as heavy as those suffered in the battle of Kiev. However, the way had been prepared for an attack on Bílá Cerkev.[245]

It was at this stage of the fighting that the Czechoslovak delegation returned from Moscow with a decision to form a Czechoslovak airborne brigade in Jefremov. Lieutenant Colonel Přikryl was appointed its commander. His staff included several experienced Jewish officers and instructors. The brigade was to be formed from more than 2,000 men from the Slovak Motorized Division who had defected from the German side.[246] The reserve unit from Buzuluk was also transferred to Jefremov.

The Germans stubbornly defended their positions around Bílá Cerkev and the Czechoslovak brigade suffered heavy losses, particularly while crossing the river Ros. Among those killed during this operation was Sergeant Brunn, the commander of a cavalry platoon of sixty men.[247] At the beginning of January 1944, Bílá Cerkev was finally captured, and the weakened and exhausted brigade was sent to the village of Truški for a brief rest. There the troops received congratulatory messages from both Soviet and Czechoslovak authorities for the role which the brigade had played in the Bílá Cerkev action. A number of officers and men were promoted. Among them were the following graduates of the officers' school—Mikuláš Hecht, A. Felter, J. Rosenthal, J. Buchwalder, and J. Halm.[248]

After a brief respite at Truški, the brigade was moved in night marches through rain and mud to the Něnadycha-Buděnivka region, about sixty kilometers south of Bílá Cerkev. But before the brigade could take up new defensive positions, the Germans pierced the Soviet defense system and were threatening the Russian rear. After repeated attempts, the companies commanded by Lieutenants Kvapil and Reichl succeeded in gaining a foothold at the eastern end of the village of Ostrožany and in hand-to-hand fighting forced the enemy to retreat to the western part of the village. Among those who distinguished himself in this action was Corporal Hugo Koval.[249]

In the next stage of the fighting the Czechoslovak troops were pushed back across the river, with their positions exposed to ceaseless German attack. Gunner Mikuláš Ezrovič recalls: "On the third day of the fighting the left flank of our defense was attacked simultaneously by seven German Tiger tanks and fifteen of their planes. The tanks were heading directly for our positions. Some of the men wavered, but the women jumped out of the trenches first and ran to the guns. We shot hundreds of rounds of ammunition in direct shelling. One of our guns sustained a direct hit. A Ukrainian boy from another gun crew was killed. But the women who manned the guns did not waver for a moment. Jewish and Ukrainian women held off three German attacks. The presidium of the Supreme Soviet decorated all eight women gunners, among them Greta Goldmann and Věra Hecht."[250]

The fighting was part of a Soviet encircling operation, in which fourteen German divisions were annihilated. When the Russians had closed the ring near Zvěnigorodka, they called upon the Germans to capitulate, but the Germans opened machine-gun fire on the Russian negotiators.[251] On February 9, 1944, the Soviet army therefore decided to strike a final blow. Units of the Czechoslovak brigade were assigned to cover certain German positions. Teodor Fiš recalls: "The situation on the Upper Tikič was particularly dramatic. It was changing all the time. Sometimes it was we who were encircled; sometimes it was the Germans. Many of the operations were directed from commanding positions by Jewish officers and in the field by Jewish subalterns acting as company, platoon, and unit commanders. Particularly Captain Biheller, the commander of the artillery unit, his chief of staff, Second Lieutenant Mermelstein, and the commander of the tank squad, Second Lieutenant Gross, who was killed in the operation, distinguished themselves."[252]

In this final phase of the fighting the brigade was already far too weakened to be fit for further independent fighting action. At the beginning of March 1944, the brigade was therefore taken from the front and transferred by train to the small Volhynian town of Rovno for reorganization. In September 1943, the 3,517 men of the brigade left Novochopersk for the front. After less than six months, their number had fallen to 1,839. This should give a sufficiently clear picture of the casualties suffered by the brigade. Participants estimate that about 300 Jewish officers and men were among those killed or seriously wounded.[253] On March 23, 1944, the Supreme Soviet decided to decorate 126 members of the Czechoslovak brigade for bravery shown during these war actions. Among those awarded Soviet orders and medals were twenty-five Jews: twelve officers, twelve NCOs, and one private.[254]

THE INDEPENDENT CZECHOSLOVAK ARMY CORPS

After its return from the front, the decimated Czechoslovak brigade was placed in several towns of the Volhynian region, where there was a Czech ethnic minority of 45,000. These descendants of emigrants who had come from Bohemia and Moravia to the Ukraine in the nineteenth century were still bound by sentimental ties to their old homeland; as a result, the call to join the Czechoslovak army was answered within four weeks by more than 12,000 volunteers, men and women.[255]

This growing influx of new manpower made it possible to begin with the planned reorganization of the brigade, which, as of March 26, 1944, had 5,325 members.[256] New commanding officers and additional instructors were needed. On April 1, 1944, a course was started to which fifty-six experienced subalterns, including twenty Jews, were assigned.[257] The sudden influx of new recruits affected also the position of the Jews in the brigade. Their percentage in the total decreased considerably, but at the same time their importance increased. However, even the ablest, bravest, and politically most reliable among them found their Jewish origin an obstacle. In the qualification lists kept by the higher officers, various marks and notes were often found next to the names of Jewish officers, usually the letter Ž for *Žid* (Jew).[258] On the other hand, there was such a shortage of available cadres that even those higher-ranking commanding officers who made no secret of their aversion to Jews had no choice but to appoint them to responsible positions. So, for instance, in the mine-throwing company, where 80 percent of the men were Volhynian Czechs, the commander was Captain Biheller, whose staff was headed by Lieutenant A. Mermelstein. Second Lieutenants Steinberg, Fischl, and Schoengut were commanders of artillery batteries. Sergeant Bielefeld commanded the telecommunications company, and Second Lieutenant P. Wechsberg was in charge of transportation.[259] The staff of the artillery commander included two Jewish officers. The growing number of troops also required the services of additional doctors. The head of the medical corps, Lieutenant Dr. F. Engel, issued an order that all brigade members who had taken at least four semesters of medicine be transferred from other units to the medical corps. Thus the medical corpsmen Vojtěch Gláz, Michael Lebovič, Josef Rosenthal, and others worked as army doctors. The training of dozens of women volunteers from Volhynia as nurses was organized and directed by Corporal Nurse Malvína Friedmann, who by then had married a man by the name of Fanta.[260]

On April 9 and 10, 1944, the brigade was moved farther to the west, on the Ozděniž-Kombrovo-Antonuvka line. Some of the formations, commanded mostly by Jewish officers, had already inflicted casualties on the Germans during their training period.[261] The brigade advanced toward the Czechoslovak frontier. At the beginning of May 1944, it was transferred to the area around Černovice (Cernauti) in Bukovina, where work was begun on the formation of the First Independent Czechoslovak Army Corps, in accordance with the discussions that had been held during Beneš's consultations in Moscow. In order to secure control also over this part of the army, the London government-in-exile appointed General Jan Kratochvíl as commander of the corps.[262] However, this decision did not meet with the approval of the Moscow leadership of the Communist party of Czechoslovakia, which wanted to see its own man, General Svoboda, in command of the corps.

The corps, now counting more than 16,000 members (including 600 women), was composed of three infantry brigades, one airborne brigade, one tank brigade, one artillery regiment, one air force regiment, and other special units. The command set up headquarters at Sadagora and the various formations were stationed at Sniatyn, Proskurov, Černovice, Kamenec Podolsk, and Lužany. In all these places the soldiers underwent intensive training until the end of August 1944.[263]

While the troops were being prepared for battle, a tragic miscarriage of justice occurred at Sadagora. Lieutenant Maximilian Holzer, who had been imprisoned for thirteen months on charges of having failed to secure the necessary supplies for the units fighting in Sokolovo, was brought before a Czechoslovak court-martial on June 20, 1944. The trial took three days, and delegations of observers were brought in cars to Sadagora from all the distant units. Propaganda depicting Holzer as a cowardly Jew was circulated among the troops. Second Lieutenant Isidor Šnek, who attended the trial as an observer, recorded his impressions as follows:

> Holzer defended himself, but he was not given a chance to speak coherently; the chairman of the court martial kept stopping him. From the facts presented by the accused, from testimonies of witnesses, and from the obdurate attacks of the prosecutor, it was obvious that Holzer had not really been to blame for the collapse of the supply system during the battle of Sokolovo, and the whole proceedings made the impression that this was to be a specially motivated show trial with the outcome decided in advance.[264]

Holzer was sentenced to death and was to be shot by a firing squad. The chairman of the court-martial, Winterstein, considered the death penalty as too harsh and unjust, but he was outvoted by the four other judges. Holzer appealed against the sentence. At the same time, he availed himself of the opportunity given him under the law to volunteer for a penal company which participated in dangerous front-line operations. Holzer lost his life in the first such operation. According to the recorded opinion of a member of the corps, the engineer Šimon Šachta, Holzer did not fall in battle. The commander of the penal company, the notorious Ukrainian bandit Bojko, allegedly had been ordered not to permit Holzer to return alive.[265] After the war it turned out that Holzer's guilt had never been properly established. This is borne out also by the testimony of another member of the corps, Michael Štěpánek-Stemmer, who later became a press officer at the Ministry of National Defense in Prague: "In a press conference on the occasion of the twentieth anniversary of the battle of Sokolovo, General Svoboda (the colonel had been promoted to the rank of general in December 1943 by President Beneš in Moscow) declared that Holzer's case was a tragic misunderstanding such as could occur in the excitement and tension of battle."[266] (However, the fact remains that it was Svoboda who with his own hand tore the officer's insignia from Holzer's uniform, had him arrested, and also acted as the most important witness for the prosecution during the trial.)

In addition to the Volhynian Czechs, there were among the new recruits Jewish volunteers, people from territories occupied by the Hungarians who had been drafted into Hungarian forced labor units and sent to the battle areas to dig trenches and clear mine fields. Some of them had escaped to the Russian side of the border; others, captured in the fighting, had been brought to the Soviet Union as prisoners of war. After careful screening and thorough training, they were assigned to duties in the Independent Czechoslovak Army Corps. Corporal Jakob Friedmann, who was in one of these groups, recorded: "After our training in Sadagora, our group of thirty Jews was assigned to the communications company. Commander Kurt Fanta saw that we were in miserable shape and was considerate to us. He took us to his bunker every evening and trained us most patiently."[267]

At the beginning of June 1944, a group of sixteen Czechoslovak officers arrived in Černovice from England. Seven of them were Jews. Artillery Lieutenant Jindřich Fantl was assigned to the third brigade. He recorded: "There was a catastrophic shortage of officers, the exact opposite of the situation in the Czechoslovak formations in the Middle East. There, in a platoon of twenty-five men, half had a university education. Here we had illiterates. The brigade commander appointed me chief of staff for an artillery regiment because the Ukrainian commander could not handle the job."[268]

Most of the Jewish volunteers came from the Rumanian part of Bukovina. When the Russians occupied Černovice, they found in the area about 17,000 Jews who had survived Rumanian and German persecution.[269] Many of them had some ties to Czechoslovakia. Many of the older ones had been born in the Czech Historic Lands during the period of the Habsburg monarchy and still could speak some Czech. Quite a number of the younger ones had gone to Czechoslovakia to study after the introduction of the *numerus clausus* (Jewish quota) at Rumania's institutions of higher learning. There were also several hundred Jews who had escaped to Bukovina from Slovakia and Subcarpathian Ruthenia in order to avoid being drafted into Hungarian labor units.[270] After the Red Army had liberated Bukovina, the Soviets launched their own mobilization drive for forced labor units. In the testimony of Second Lieutenant Pavel Dobrý and his wife, Eva, we read: "Every night Soviet soldiers would encircle another part of the city and search the houses. They turned the people out of their houses and took them straight to trucks to be sent away to work at Donbas and elsewhere. Intervention did not help; not even when it was proved that these people were Jewish victims of persecution."[271] Some of the Jews in the area were sent to Soviet labor camps in Siberia. In order to save their daughters from being drafted into forced labor, fathers looked for single Jewish soldiers in the Czechoslovak units to marry them; this was one way of saving the girls from deportation or worse. About seventy such marriages took place with the approval of the corps command.[272]

A group of about fifteen Czechoslovak Jewish officers, most of them from England, tried to help those endangered Jews who had ties with Czechoslovakia; they advised those who wanted to join the corps on how to act before the recruiting and inspection commissions. Members of the commissions, particularly the physicians who examined the recruits, were given the facts of the situation, and the Soviet liaison officer was cooperative. On induction into the corps, each recruit automatically became a Czechoslovak citizen; Czechoslovak citizenship was conferred also upon the members of his immediate family to remove them from Soviet or Rumanian jurisdiction.[273] Trucks waiting in front of the recruiting centers carried the families of the recruits to the safety of the Czechoslovak army camp. Altogether some 200 Jewish families were saved in this way, and the corps gained about 600 soldiers. They proved their mettle especially in the battle of the Dukla Pass in the fall of 1944; most of them lost their lives in this operation.[274] Among the recruits there were also quite a few doctors who had studied in Czechoslovakia and were now able to render effective help in the medical corps. About fifty young Jewish women volunteers were engaged in medical duties and in communications and code work; some of them were even placed into combat units. Unfortunately, the efforts of the fifteen Jewish officers on behalf of their fellow Jews in Bukovina were discovered about three weeks later. As a result, the recruiting commissions were reorganized, recruitment procedures became stricter, and the initiators of the action to help the Jews in Bukovina, including Lieutenant Artur Hanák-Fleischmann, were transferred to the airborne brigade and sent to the front.[275]

The Jews who had seen fighting action since Buzuluk belonged to the most reliable cadres. According to a confidential report on the organization of the tank brigade's commanding staff, ten out of thirty officers were Jews. The Jewish lieutenants, Teodor Fiš, J. Hein, J. Reiner, E. Rosenzweig, and others were particularly useful in training new recruits and organizing new units.[276]

Early in June 1944, a delegation headed by Zdeněk Fierlinger and Communist party representatives Klement Gottwald and Zdeněk Nejedlý visited Černovice. Once again, Gottwald addressed the troops. He also met with the party cell committee and gave new instructions for the intensification of "educational activities." In his speech to the troops he promised that in a free Czechoslovakia the principles of democracy would be guaranteed.[277]

At the time, when preparations for departure for the front lines were already in full swing, about 100 Czechoslovak officers from England arrived at Sadagora; of these, forty were Jews. Though they were not adequately prepared for combat duty, most of them were assigned to fighting units which departed for the Carpathian mountains.

According to statements from well-informed veterans of the corps, there were in the period from July to September 1944 some 1,600 to 1,800 Jewish officers and men in the various units of the corps. Exact figures could be found in the Czechoslovak state archives, but at this writing the relevant material has not been made available to interested researchers.[278] The data which are accessible are often misleading and give only a part of the picture. Thus, for instance, the work of the Czechslovak military historian Colonel Miroslav Šáda states that as of September 1, 1944, the corps had a total complement of 16,451. The breakdown of this figure into nationality groups does not include numerical statistics for members of the Jewish national entity in the corps. Jews are mentioned only in terms of percentages among the other nationality groups: 53 percent Czechs, 19 percent Slovaks, 22 percent Ukrainians, 3.5 percent Jews, and 2.5 percent others. On the basis of a total of 16,451 members in the corps, this would mean that the corps had only 575 Jews. But in fact, the 3.5 percent includes only those who reported Yiddish as their mother tongue and who insisted on having their nationality registered as Jewish. It does not include soldiers of Jewish faith or Jewish origin who were registered as members of other nationality groups according to their everyday language. Šáda's work completely ignores the 600 Rumanian Jews recruited at Černovice and the hundreds of Jewish volunteers from Soviet POW camps who sacrificed their lives in such great number during the Dukla operation.[279]

According to the original plan, the corps was to advance with the Soviet armies in two directions: from the north through Poland to Krakow and Moravská Ostrava and from the south through Hungary to Užhorod, Bratislava, and Brno. The government-in-exile in London demanded effective Soviet help for the Slovak uprising (August–October 1944). This was promised under the condition that the decisive role would be taken by the Czechoslovak army corps. As one of the veterans put it, "It was expected that two rebel Slovak divisions, under the guise of guarding the Slovak state from a Bolshevik invasion, would stand ready at the entrance to the Dukla Pass and that the units of the corps would then enter Slovakia in full glory." That was the arrangement. However, the Slovak generals did not keep it, and 26,000 of their soldiers allowed themselves to be disarmed by the Germans without offering the slightest resistance. This changed the military situation entirely. Units sent to the area around Sombor, in order to cross the Užok pass into Subcarpathian Ruthenia, were now ordered to march to Krosno, about 100 kilometers away. "We entered Krosno," one of the participants recalls (and the testimonies of other veterans confirm his recollections), "because we were assured by our commanders that the Germans had already run away. But while our company was marching through the main street of Krosno, the Germans opened machine gun fire on us from high vantage points all around the town. We had many dead and wounded and escaped encirclement only by dispersing into fields nearby."[280] The Czechoslovak units that entered the town were massacred. But even the formations that were still intact and advancing around Krosno toward the villages of Machnowka and Wrocanka found themselves under fire and suffered enormous casualties.

Nurse Terezie Elefant, who was working in the improvised field hospital, recalled: "Car after car brought the wounded to the main square of the small town of Odrzykon, north of Krosno. We did not even have enough time to put up hospital tents; new wounded were being brought in all the time and nothing had been prepared for them—no drugs, no bandages, not even food. There were about 500 wounded lying on the ground, just on some hay."[281] Other veterans estimate the number of dead and wounded at about 1,200. Among them were about 300 Jewish soldiers, mainly from the Third Brigade, which suffered the heaviest casualties.[282]

The blame for the catastrophe was placed mainly on the corps commander, General Jan Kratochvíl. It was claimed that he did not have reliable intelligence reports of his own but had relied fully on the data about the enemy's strength and positions which had been fed to him by the Russians.[283] At any rate, the Soviet high command and Gottwald took advantage of this opportunity to get rid of Kratochvíl. Marshal Ivan Štěpanovič Koněv, who was to participate in the capture of Berlin and to become supreme commander of the Warsaw Pact nations in 1955, personally removed Kratochvíl from the command of the corps and replaced him with the man whom the Communists had wanted to have at that post in the first place: General Ludvík Svoboda.[284] At the same time, Colonel Střelka was relieved as commander of the Third Brigade and Colonel Satorie was appointed in his place.

General Svoboda, as the new commander of the Czechoslovak army corps, informed the Soviet command that the Germans had amassed 2,000 infantrymen and sixty tanks at his sector of the front. In view of the numerical superiority of the enemy troops and the losses suffered by the corps, he called for a change in the fighting strategy of the Czechoslovak formations. However, the commander of the 38th Soviet Army insisted that the corps carry out the original orders despite the fact that the attacking power of the corps had been reduced to 600 bayonets. The First Infantry Brigade attacked, was repulsed, and suffered heavy losses. Nevertheless Marshal Koněv ordered Svoboda to renew the attack that very afternoon.[285]

While the fighting for the town of Dukla went on, a group of officers from England arrived from Sadagora. Among the new arrivals were two generals, Karel Klapálek and Josef Sázavský. The former took over the command of the Third Brigade while the latter became commander of the First Brigade. Most of the officers were sent directly to the units fighting at the front; some of them, including Captain Heller from Kolin, fell on the same day. The officers were shocked by this state of affairs, for which they had not been prepared. The units they were supposed to command were so decimated and spent that the soldiers were hardly able to carry out their orders.[286]

The presence of General Klapálek was a great asset. As a lieutenant colonel, he had been in command of the Czechoslovak troops in the Middle East, where many Jewish soldiers had been fighting under him. The commander of the communication company, Lieutenant Kurt Fanta, said of him: "Klapálek was an outstanding commander and knew how to stand up for his men. We followed him blindly. His relations with the Jewish soldiers were the best possible."[287] The commander of the rear of Klapálek's third brigade was Lieutenant Mirek Kerner, who went with Klapálek through the whole Dukla campaign.[288]

Lieutenant Arnošt Steiner distinguished himself particularly in the action aimed at removing the last and most difficult obstacle on the way to the Czechoslovak frontier. He outfoxed the Germans and led his company so that they attacked the Germans from the rear and annihilated them.[289] However, Steiner was not the only Jewish commander to excel in the fighting. Second Lieutenant Laco Presser, for instance, led his men in fierce hand-to-hand fighting, in which a whole German unit was finished off by bayonets. All the weapons of this German unit were taken by Presser's men. Second Lieutenant Gross directed the fire of his mine-throwers' battery so ably that 400 German soldiers and their commanders were put out of action. The infantry company under the command of Lieutenant Reichl suffered heavy casualties; of 120 men, only eighteen were able to remain in action. Nevertheless, Reichl and his decimated unit managed to hold the sector assigned to him for several days.[290] Jewish physicians, too, gave ample proof of their courage; for instance, the battalion doctor Marek Neuer carried wounded down from the hills under heavy enemy fire.[291] Second Lieutenant Gláz, a medical corpsman who substituted for the chief physician of the tank battalion, volunteered to take charge of first aid at the front. "Just look at that! Here's a Jew actually asking to be transferred to the front line!" Colonel Janko exclaimed in astonishment. At Janko's recommendation, Gláz was later awarded the Czechoslovak War Cross.[292]

However, many lost their lives through the fault of their superiors. Platoon commander Corporal Feierwerger, for instance, stated:

> One Saturday afternoon we received an order to be ready. I reported that the terrain in front of us was open and unguarded and that the Germans were lying in wait in the hills around us. I explained that without artillery support it would be impossible to penetrate and that to attack [under these circumstances] would be clear suicide. But my commander replied: "A soldier does not think of what is or what is not possible. He carries out his orders. That's all." The Germans allowed us to come nearer and then began to mow us down by well-aimed fire. After half of the platoon members had been killed, we were ordered to retreat, but the Germans kept firing even while we tried to save our wounded. We retreated to trenches and waited for a katyusha battery to destroy the woods from which the Germans were firing. Then we repulsed the weakened enemy without suffering any further losses. Although both the Soviet and our own commanders knew of the situation beforehand, they drove us on as if they were herding us to the slaughter. We had the impression that they wanted to get rid of us before they reached Czechoslovakia. It looked that way at least to us Jewish soldiers. These hazardous tactics, which caused unnecessary casualties, continued, and before we had crossed the border most of our men were dead.[293]

Similar conclusions may be found in the testimonies of Lieutenants Fanta, Šachta, and Kriegel and in that of Nurse Corporal Malvína Fanta-Friedmann.[294]

In spite of the fact that unit commanders had complained again and again that their troops had reached the limits of exhaustion, the Soviet command kept ordering them to continue their attacks. The commander of the first brigade, Lieutenant Colonel Novák, claimed—after his brigade had lost 60 percent of its men—that his formation had been decimated to such an extent that he had been unable to carry out the order for a new attack. The Soviet liaison officer, an NKVD man, accused Novák of refusing to obey orders. Novák was immediately relieved of his command and brought before a Czechoslovak court-martial.[295] No case could be made against him for trying to preserve the lives of soldiers.[296] But President Beneš's sharp protest that "the casualties at Dukla were terrible" was rejected by General Svoboda. And when the president did not substantially change his mind even after he had visited the Dukla battlefield, Svoboda asked the director of the president's office, Jaromír Smutný, to tell Beneš: "During the battles at Dukla things looked bad. But things were much more horrible in the [Nazi] concentration camps. Our units in the Soviet Union lost about 4,000 men. But more than 300,000 of our people perished in the concentration camps. Ask the president who is responsible for those sacrifices."[297]

At five o'clock in the morning of October 6, 1944, the first advance patrols penetrated into Czechoslovak territory. Three hours later, General Sázavský crossed the borders of the state and raised the Czechoslovak flag at the milestone marking the frontier on the Dukla Pass. But not much later his car struck a mine and he was killed only sixteen days after he had arrived from England to assume command of the Third Brigade.

There are dozens of testimonies from survivors of the campaign which would be worth quoting but which have been left out due to limitations of space. There is, for instance, the case of Mordechai Gruen, who participated in every battle after Sokolovo and was wounded at Dukla for the sixth time. After a period of convalescence in Lwow he returned to his fighting unit and on October 28, 1944, he was decorated and promoted to the rank of lieutenant. Or the story of Otakar Huppert, the commander of an anti-tank platoon, who was wounded at Dukla for the second time. As he was about to be transported to a hospital together with another wounded man, his friend A. Sonnenschein, a Russian soldier came to the train and started to shout anti-Semitic insults: "If I find a Jew here, I'll throw him out of the train. Those stinkers are sitting in the rear to avoid fighting." Despite his wounds, Huppert hobbled up to him and told him: "Well, here you have one Jew." A Soviet officer who happened to be present reprimanded the man and saved the situation.[298] But perhaps the most appropriate ending for this chapter is a fragment from the testimony of Lieutenant Alexander Mašek-Mermelstein, chief of staff of the mine-throwers' unit, who was wounded in the fighting near Krosno. After recovering at a hospital in Kiev, he returned to the corps and later participated in the last battle for the Dukla Pass. In his deposition, he recorded that his bed in the hospital had been next to that of a badly wounded Soviet captain, David Azarov. Azarov told Mermelstein: "You will live to see the creation of a Jewish state and you yourself will go to live there."[299]

Lieutenant Albert Elovič, one of the most decorated members of the Czechoslovak army, who was wounded twice in the Dukla campaign and promoted to the rank of captain for his military exploits, regards the battle for Dukla as a tragic example of wrong strategy planning. "The logical thing would have been to wait for the Soviet army to enter Slovakia from the south. The Germans would have seen that they were in danger of being encircled and would have retreated. We could have waited another month and Dukla would have fallen into our hands without any casualties." The case of Elovič would deserve to be treated in more detail than the scope of this study permits. However, at least a few facts must be cited here. In the battle of Sokolovo, Elovič commanded a company of machine gunners. Out of 107 men in the company only seven survived. Elovič, though wounded, continued firing from his machine-gun nest until Soviet troops arrived. No less than 118 German dead were counted near his machine-gun nest. Elovič was awarded the Order of the Red Star, the Czechoslovak War Cross, and the Medal for Valor. In his opinion, the battle of Sokolovo was a catastrophic defeat caused by lack of weapons and by the inexperience of the officer corps. Later Elovič was chosen by the Soviet command to act as liaison officer between the Soviet and the Czechoslovak army staffs. He participated in the battles of Kiev, Bílá Čerkev, and all the subsequent battles of the campaign. After Dukla, the Czechoslovak government-in-exile in London appointed him liaison officer to the government's delegation to the liberated territories, which had set up headquarters in Chust, Subcarpathian Ruthenia. In this capacity, Elovič tried to recruit and train fighters in the operations area in Subcarpathian Ruthenia. However, he ran afoul of Soviet agents who had been sent there to organize a popular movement against the Czechoslovak government and to agitate for the annexation of Subcarpathian Ruthenia by the Soviet Union. Accused by a Slovak Communist agitator that he was obstructing these Soviet activities, Elovič was arrested by order of the Soviet general Mechlis and was made commander of a penal company. After ten days of fighting near Bardějov he was again seriously wounded. After he recovered he came to Košice, where, in the meantime, the Beneš government had established its seat, and was sent to Constanza to head the Czechoslovak liaison mission to the UNRRA (United Nations Relief and Rehabilitation Administration). In the original edition of General Svoboda's book, which is no longer in print, several pages were devoted to Elovič's heroic war record. But his name was expunged from subsequent editions because he left Czechoslovakia after the Communist coup of February 1948.

The quotations which follow seem a fitting conclusion for this study.

The first is from the book *Tři roky druhé světové války* (Three Years of World War II) by President Beneš, which was published in London in 1943: "No war can be won without an army. A nation must constantly fight for its freedom, also militarily. That is why we must have an army here. That is why it is important for us from the very beginning to form a military body, however small. That is why we have welcomed with so much joy every one of our soldiers who came from home or from somewhere in exile to volunteer for our ranks." [300]

The second is from a speech by Arnošt (Ernst) Frischer, a member of the State Council in London, who became chairman of the Council of Jewish Religious Congregations in Czechoslovakia after the war. In an address delivered at the solemn first meeting of the reconstituted Council of Jewish Religious Congregations, Frischer declared: "The participation of Jewish soldiers in the Czechoslovak army abroad was great and decisive on all fronts. In terms of numbers, it surpassed the Czech 'national Aryan element' in whose name Czechoslovakia collaborators had persecuted those of their Jewish fellow citizens who had been unable to escape the Nazis in time." [301]

Our final quotation comes from an editorial by the noted publicist Ferdinand Peroutka.[302] Entitled "What, Again?" it was written in December 1945 as a comment to what had happened in Slovakia, where, especially in Snina and Topolčany, the return of Jewish survivors from Nazi concentration camps was met with anti-Semitic disturbances and even pogroms. Slovak intelligence found excuses for the crudest demonstrations of anti-Semitism. The Jews, it was alleged, had not participated in sufficient numbers in the Slovak uprising. In reply to this allegation Peroutka wrote: "It is known that at the time (of the Slovak uprising) Slovakia was almost completely 'cleaned' of Jews with the zealous aid of Slovak [Hlinka] 'guardists.' [These Jews went through] their most difficult time at the gates to the gas chambers and in the death transports. From where, then, should Jewish legions suddenly have materialized in Slovakia?

Those who would have been most able to fight perished in the gas chambers or somewhere near a barbed wire fence in the freezing cold, and perhaps the last thing they felt was Slovak hands pushing them on this road. Nevertheless, there are about 1,000 Jewish graves in the Dukla pass. That was where those Jews who were able to fight met their end. Out of 100,000 Slovak Jews, 80,000 perished. Do we have to add anything more unpleasant to that? If we were to discuss Jewish participation in the fighting, we would have to talk not only of one particular area but of the entire army abroad, and that might be a dangerous piece of research with possible inconvenient results. What should we say if we were to find out, as well we may, that at some point half the troops in our Western army were Jewish? Or that more than half the units in our glorious First Regiment in Russia consisted of Jews? If one day the Jews should get their wish to have their percentile participation in the fighting ascertained, they will certainly have no reason to be ashamed. If it would promote domestic tranquility and vindicate justice, these figures should be made available. And if anyone should ask what purpose these facts would serve, the answer is: These facts should serve the cause of truth."

No additional quotations are needed. Despite repeated requests from research institutes and individual historians, the archival material, figures, and data about Jewish participation in the Czechoslovak armed forces abroad have not been made available to date. In 1969, the Institute for the History of Contemporary Jewry at the Hebrew University in Jerusalem included in its research program a project entitled "Participation of Czechoslovak Jews in the War Against Nazi Germany." In the framework of this project, several hundred Jewish veterans of Czechoslovak military actions during World War II were approached and testimonies, recollections, and depositions were gathered from individuals who are now dispersed all over the world.[303] These testimonies constitute the foundations for this study. The truth they reveal is clear and irrefutable.

With regard to the participation of Jews in "Svoboda's Army" there are no exact figures available. According to a report published after the war by Chaplain Hanuš Rezek (Rebenwurzel),* the num-

---

* After the war Rezek (Rebenwurzel) returned to Prague, where he served as a rabbi until his death in an airplane crash in 1947.

ber of Jews who participated in the entire campaign was 2,300 men and women. According to this report, 640 Jewish officers and men lost their lives in the fighting and about 800 were seriously wounded. Other veterans estimate that the number of Jewish casualties was higher.[304] What can be stated with more accuracy is the fact that of the total of 288 Soviet decorations awarded to members of the Czechoslovak Army Corps, fifty-six went to Jews. This means that Jewish officers and men received 20 percent of all the decorations awarded. Even more eloquent is the fact that 35 percent of the Jewish participants were deemed worthy of receiving Soviet orders and medals.[305]

In prewar Czechoslovakia, Jewish citizens constituted 2.46 percent of the total population. At the time of World War II, the average participation of Jews in formations of the Czechoslovak armed forces abroad was 50 percent and sometimes higher. This means that their military participation was more than twenty times what would be expected according to their demographic ratio.[306]

The Jews of Czechoslovakia have nothing of which to be ashamed and much of which to be proud.[307]

APPENDIX 1

MEN KILLED WHILE SERVING WITH CZECHOSLOVAK ARMY UNITS BASED IN FRANCE, GREAT BRITAIN AND THE MIDDLE EAST

A complete list of Jewish officers and men who died in action while serving in Czechoslovak armed forces during World War II has not been made available to date. The following list of those whose dates of death and places of burial are known is based on information supplied by the late Jan Lom, past chairman of the Czechoslovak branch of the British Legion, Dr. Stephen Barber, the municipality of Bourbourg, France, and from various other sources. This list includes only soldiers who died while serving with Czechoslovak units based in France, Great Britain, and the Middle East.

Name and Rank	Date of Death	Cemetery
Sgt. R. Alt	1/18/1941	Liverpool Jewish Cemetery
Lance Cpl. Max Apfelbaum	12/12/1944	Bourbourg (France)
Cadet Officer Otto Auffärber	10/4/1944	Jerusalem Military Cemetery
Capt. Gejza Viktor Barany	3/12/1943	Ramleh Military Cemetery (Israel)
Sgt. H. Beck	3/13/1944	
Cadet Officer Vilém Bergler	11/5/1944	Adinkerque (Belgium)
Sgt. J. Bleier	5/17/1943	Harrogate Cemetery
Pvt. Bedřich Blumenthal	4/15/1945	Longueness (St. Omer, France)
Pvt. Pavel Bodansky	4/15/1945	Bourbourg (France)
Pvt. G. Bruck	5/22/1945	Chartham Cemetery
Pilot Officer Bunzl	10/18/1942	
Pvt. Ludvík Davidovič	11/5/1944	Adinkerque (Belgium)
Pvt. Leopold Diamant	10/22/1944	Cassel Municipal Cemetery (Germany)
Pvt. Josef Doppler	10/15/1944	Adinkerque (Belgium)
Corporal B. Dubský	11/15/1940	Hampstead Cemetery
Pvt. Alfred Ebel	10/29/1944	Pas de Calais (France)
Pvt. J. Ehrmann	5/13/1944	Northampton Cemetery
Pvt. Samuel Eisenberg	6/12/1940	St. Martin sur Ocre Loiret (France)

Name and Rank	Date of Death	Cemetery
Cadet Officer Ladislav Elbert	11/5/1944	Adinkerque (Belgium)
Lt. Arnošt Elbogen	8/11/1944	New Eastern Cemetery, Amsterdam (Holland)
First Sgt. I. K. Englaender	1/1/1945	Tain Cemetery
Lt. K. Faden	9/7/1942	Birmingham Jewish Cemetery
First Sgt. F. Fanta	4/26/1944	Chichester Cemetery
Sgt. Herbert Federman	1943	Rhodes
Pvt. Ota Fried	11/5/1944	Adinkerque (Belgium)
Pilot Officer O. Friedlaender	9/29/1942	
Pvt. Alexander Friedmann	8/18/1943	Ramleh Military Cemetery (Israel)
Pvt. L. Gerstmann	3/23/1944	Northampton Cemetery
Cadet Officer Imrich Glasel	12/5/1944	Cassel Municipal Cemetery (Germany)
Pvt. Hugo Glasner	2/9/1945	Bourbourg (France)
Cadet Officer Jan Gottlob	11/8/1940	Ramleh Military Cemetery (Israel)
Pvt. Andrej Gruenbaum	10/28/1944	Cassel Military Cemetery (Germany)
Pvt. K. Gruenwald	10/10/1941	Birmingham Jewish Cemetery
Pvt. J. Guensburg	4/3/1943	Ramsay Cemetery
Lance Cpl. Leo Gutfreund	10/30/1941	Tobruk Military Cemetery (Cyrenaica)
Sgt. V. Güttner	10/28/1944	Cassel Municipal Cemetery (Germany)
Lance Cpl. Jiří Haas	7/6/1941	Ramleh Military Cemetery (Israel)
Lt. Stefan Hacker	11/5/1944	Cassel Municipal Cemetery (Germany)
Cadet Officer Max Hahn	10/27/1944	Bourbourg (France)
Cpl. Abraham Hanzel	12/20/1944	Cassel Municipal Cemetery (Germany)
Pvt. Ota Hauser	1/15/1945	Cassel Municipal Cemetery (Germany)
Sgt. F. A. Heller	11/18/1943	

Name and Rank	Date of Death	Cemetery
Cpl. J. Herčík	6/2/1944	Galashiels Army Cemetery (Scotland)
Pvt. František Hersch	6/18/1940	Fleury les Aubrais (France)
Pvt. Salomon Herskovits	12/12/1944	Bourbourg (France)
Cpl. W. Hirsch	7/25/1940	Whitchurch Cemetery
Pvt. Rudolf Jellinek	11/5/1944	Pas de Calais
Cpl. Arthur Karpe	1/22/1945	Adinkerque (Belgium)
Staff Sgt. K. Katz	10/3/1944	
Lance Cpl. Leopold Katz	10/13/1944	Cassel Municipal Cemetery (Germany)
Flight Officer V. Kauders	1/10/1945	St. André d'Auray (France)
Pvt. Karel Kaufmann	12/3/1941	Tobruk Military Cemetery (Cyrenaica)
Pvt. Josef Klein	4/15/1945	Bourbourg (France)
Pvt. Maximilian Klein	6/19/1940	St. André d'Auray (France)
Pvt. Bedrich Kohn	11/4/1944	Adinkerque (Belgium)
Pvt. Rudolf Kohn	12/5/1941	Tobruk Military Cemetery (Cyrenaica)
Staff Sgt. Imrich Kormanovič	3/3/1942	Creil, Oise (France)
Lance Cpl. Armin Korngut	1/22/1945	Bourbourg (France)
Lance Cpl. Ladislav Lackovič	12/20/1944	Adinkerque (Belgium)
Lt. W. Landsman	6/15/1945	
Pvt. Jindřich Langer	10/29/1944	Pas de Calais (France)
Pilot Officer J. Leskauer	1/16/1941	
Cadet Officer Rudolf Lifčic	4/17/1941	Jonkerbos Military Cemetery (Holland)
Pvt. Alois Loebl	10/18/1944	Bourbourg (France)
Pvt. B. Loewenwirth	3/9/1941	Birmingham Jewish Cemetery
Pvt. L. Loewy	7/29/1944	Edinburgh Piershill Cemetery
Pvt. Izak Lorber	10/28/1944	Cassel Municipal Cemetery (Germany)
Cadet Officer Max Mann	10/17/1944	Bourbourg (France)
Cadet Officer Jiří Mautner	10/28/1944	Adinkerque (Belgium)

Name and Rank	Date of Death	Cemetery
Cpl. Jakob Marvan-Mermelstein	10/28/1944	Adinkerque (Belgium)
Cadet Officer J. J. E. Mueller-Mirovsky	1/24/1945	London East Ham Jewish Cemetery
Pvt. Kurt Neurad	6/16/1940	Fleury (France)
Pvt. Z. Novosad	11/14/1941	Stratford-on-Avon Cemetery
Cadet Officer Jiří Oberlaender	4/6/1945	Pas de Calais (France)
Pvt. Alexander Paták	1/4/1945	Cassel Municipal Cemetery (Germany)
Pvt. E. B. Pick	3/3/1945	London East Ham Jewish Cemetery
Pvt. Josef Ples	1/9/1945	Cassel Municipal Cemetery (Germany)
Lance Cpl. František Polák	10/23/1944	Pas de Calais (France)
Lt. Josef Politzer	4/11/1942	Bergen-op-Zoom Military Cemetery (Holland)
Pvt. V. Příbram	2/9/1944	London East Ham Jewish Cemetery
Pvt. Heinz Propper	11/5/1944	Adinkerque (Belgium)
Maj. Evžen Reichenthal	6/12/1945	Ramleh Military Cemetery (Israel)
Pvt. Alexander Rosenfeld	12/10/1944	Cassel Municipal Cemetery (Germany)
Pvt. David Rothenberg	11/5/1944	Adinkerque (Belgium)
Sgt. J. Rubin	8/29/1943	
Pvt. Imrich Schoenfeld	4/15/1945	Bourbourg (France)
Pvt. Evžen Schwarcz	11/5/1944	Adinkerque (Belgium)
Pvt. M. Schwarz	1/24/1944	Rainham Jewish Cemetery
Pvt. Y. Schwarz	11/28/1941	London East Ham Jewish Cemetery
Squadron Leader Otto Smik	11/28/1944	Ghent (Belgium)
Cadet Officer Jiří Spitz	12/5/1941	Tobruk Military Cemetery (Cyrenaica)
Pvt. B. K. Stein	5/7/1944	Northampton Cemetery
Pvt. Kurt Steiner	9/16/1944	Bayeux Military Cemetery (France)

Name and Rank	Date of Death	Cemetery
Sgt. Julius Stierheim	4/15/1945	Bourbourg (France)
Pvt. T. Tandler	8/11/1941	Nottingham South Cemetery
Pvt. Michal Ullor-Ulm	2/5/1940	Agde (France)
Cpl. A. Umlauf	8/26/1940	Chester Cemetery
Pvt. H. Waldstein	2/22/1945	Birmingham Jewish Cemetery
Cpl. Herbert Weil	11/5/1944	Adinkerque (Belgium)
Capt. Robert Weil-Mechura	2/28/1941	Ramleh Military Cemetery (Israel)
Pvt. F. Wilhelm	1/26/1941	Birmingham Jewish Cemetery

APPENDIX 2

Of the 106 Czechoslovak soldiers killed in the battle of Sokolovo, the following 36 were Jews:

Pvt. Desider Bass	Pvt. Norbert Lanzer
Pvt. Walter Blasenstein	Pvt. Walter Lanzer
Pvt. Arnošt Bleiweiss	Pvt. Alfred Nasch
Pvt. Michal Bodner	Pvt. Jan Oberster
Sgt. Arnošt Brodavka	Pvt. Kurt Pressburg
Pvt. Arpád Czinner	Lance Cpl. Hugo Redisch
Pvt. Vilém Feldcer	Pvt. Alex Salamon
Pvt. Kurt Finkelstein	Pvt. Herman Schwarz
Cpl. Viktor Fisch	Lance Cpl. Ignac Spiegel
Pvt. Samuel Fruchter	Pvt. Kurt Steir
Pvt. Josef Fuhrman	Pvt. Max Tauber
Cpl. Eduard Goldberger	Pvt. Egon Traub
Pvt. Kurt Gross	Pvt. Leo Wechsberg
Pvt. Josef Grossman	Pvt. Ervín Weinberger
Pvt. Kurt Kafka	Lance Cpl. Bohumil Weisman
Pvt. Julius Kahan	Pvt. M. Weiss
Cpl. Max Katner	Cpl. Max Wimmer
Pvt. Izák Kessler	Sgt. Kurt Wolf

Note: The above list does not include some 18 Jewish men who died of wounds in transit from the battle area or in hospitals.

APPENDIX 3

The following additional names of Jewish soldiers killed in action at Sokolovo or in the surrounding area are listed on pp. 25 and 26 of *Dějiny židovstva ostravského* [History of the Jews of (Moravská) Ostrava] published by Izidor Zehngut, president of the city's Jewish Religious Congregation, in 1952:

Karel Egger, age 34	Kurt Steuer, age 26
Erich Huterer, age 23	Arnošt Sudmak, age 30
Albert Kornhauser, age 45	Samuel Truchter, age 29
Egon Presser, age 25	Erich Unger, age 38
Bedrich Schaff, age 35	Vítězslav Witmann, age 30
Josef Schlachet, age 25	

APPENDIX 4

CZECHOSLOVAK JEWISH RECIPIENTS OF SOVIET MILITARY MEDALS AND DECORATIONS*

Order of the Red Flag
Sgt. Arnošt Brodavka
Pfc. Hugo Redisch
Sgt. Bedřich Reicin
Pvt. Ignác Spiegel
Pvt. Josef Švéd
Sgt. Kurt Wolf

Order of the Patriotic War, 2d Class
Lt. František Engel
Lt. Jiří Frank
Pvt. Mikuláš Hans
Pvt. Hermann Kalchmann
Pvt. Jan Scheimann

Order of the Red Star
Sgt. Vojtěch Eckstein
Lt. Albert Elovič
Sgt. Erik Frešl
Sgt. Malvína Friedmannova
Pvt. Peter Györi
Pvt. Bernard Menachovský
Pvt. Hermann Schwarz

Medal For Valor
Pvt. Sára Ackermannová
Pfc. Greta Goldmannová
Pvt. Bedřich Scharf
Cpl. Bedřich Steiner
Sgt. Max Weber
Pvt. Bohumil Weissmann

Medal For Merit in Action
Cpl. Kurt Markovič

Other Decorations
Lt. Alfred Benedikt
Cpl. Gerneman Berkovič
Sgt. Kurt Brun
Pvt. Petr Brun
Lt. Karel Buechler
Sgt. Chaim Cuckiermann
Lt. František Engel
Lt. Ladislav Fischman
Sgt. Berthold Goldzweig
Lt. Jaromír Hecht
Pfc. Věra Hechtová
Pfc. Salomon Klausner
Lt. Bedřich Kopold
Staff Capt. Ervín Líbal
Lt. Gustav Meier
Sgt. Bernard Menachovský
Sgt. Bedřich Rabiner
Sgt. Pravomil Reich
Sgt. Robert Reich
Lt. Bedřich Reicin
Lt. Vladislav Reichl
Lt. Armin Scheer
Pvt. Ladislav Steiner
Lt. Bedřich Stepper
Sgt. Vilém Ueberreich

---

* A complete list of Jewish recipients of Czechoslovak military decorations during World War II is not available to date.

NOTES

1. See Gerald Reitlinger, *Die Endlösung: Hitler's Versuch der Ausrottung der Juden Europas 1939-1945* (Berlin: 1956), pp. 562–63.
2. Rudolf Kopecký, *Československý odboj v Polsku v roce 1939* [Czechoslovak Resistance in Poland in the Year 1939] (Rotterdam: 1958).
3. Yad Vashem Archives (YVA), Jerusalem: Collection of testimonies and documents on the participation of Czechoslovak Jews in the war against Nazi Germany. Record group 0-59-19. Testimony of Malvína Fanta-Friedmann.
4. *Archiv ústavu dějin Komunistické strany Československa* [AÚD KSČ; Archives of the Institute for the History of the Communist party of Czechoslovakia], Prague. Underground pamphlet dated May 4, 1939. Also Toman Brod and Eduard Čejka, *Na západní frontě* [On the Western Front] (Prague: 1963), p. 34.
5. YVA 0-59-18. Testimony of Kurt Fanta.
6. Ibid.
7. Kopecký, *Československý odboj*.
8. Bedřich Reicin and J. Mareš, *Věrni zůstaneme, sborník reportáží a dokumentů* [We Shall Remain Faithful: A Collection of Reportages and Documents] (Moscow: 1943).
9. YVA 0-59-51 Moshe Landa.
10. YVA Michael Stemmer 03/3030.
11. Kopecký, *Československý odboj*, p. 38.
12. Of the seven doctors at Bronowice, six were Jews: Blitz, Kodíček (Kohn), Liebkind, Mahler, Silbiger, and Schoen. Dr. Taraba was the only non-Jew.
13. YVA 0-59-39 Michael Jellinek.
14. Brod and Čejka, *Na západní frontě*, p. 59.
15. Václav Vuk, *Proti přesile* [In the Face of Overwhelming Force] (London: 1942), p. 170.
16. Brod and Čejka, *Na západní frontě*, p. 61.
17. YVA 0-59-40 Max Kriegel.
18. YVA 0-59-18 Karel Fanta.
19. YVA 0-59-39 Michael Jellinek.
20. Brod and Čejka, *Na západní frontě*, p. 63.
21. YVA 0-59-39 Michael Jellinek; also Protocol YVA 03/2868.
22. YVA 0-59-18 Kurt Fanta.
23. Kopecký, *Československý odboj*, p. 84.
24. YVA 0-59-39 Michael Jellinek.
25. YVA 0-59-29 J. Gold.
26. Brod and Čejka, *Na západní frontě*, p. 27.
27. YVA 0-59-39 Michael Jellinek.

28. *Historie a vojenství* [History and the Act of Warfare], vol. 1956, no. 1, p. 8.
29. YVA 0-59-29 J. Gold.
30. *Směr Praha* [Direction Prague]. Memories of members of the First Independent Army Corps in the Soviet Union (Prague: 1955), p. 22.
31. YVA Protocol 03/2868 Michael Jellinek.
32. YVA 0-59-48 M. Kriegel.
33. *Směr Praha,* p. 171.
34. YVA 0-59-81 Malvina Lanzer.
35. YVA 0-59-52 Kurt Lanzer.
36. YVA 0-59-9 Elisheva Hermann-Cohen.
37. YVA 0-59-1 A. Alter. See also Livia Rothkirchen, "The Jews of Bohemia and Moravia: 1939-1945," in the present volume, pp. 24-26.
38. YVA 0-59-63 Marek (Mordechai) Neuer.
39. Czechoslovak historiography and war literature does not even mention the imprisonment of Jewish refugees from Czechoslovakia in Soviet labor camps. The only exception is Věra Tichá's *Po boku mužů* [Side by Side With the Men] (Prague: 1966), which contains unusually candid and well-documented reports about life in Soviet camps.
40. According to documents in possession of Dr. Stephen Barber, copies at YVA. Bulletin of *Association des Juifs de Tchéchoslovaquie en France,* Paris, March 1940.
41. Vuk, *Proti přesile,* p. 55.
42. YVA 0-59-18 Kurt Fanta.
43. YVA 0-59-76 Miroslav Šigut.
44. YVA 0-59-79 Otto O. Spira.
45. Vuk, *Proti přesile,* p. 179.
46. AÚD KSČ F 40, cat. no. 5/15.
47. Brod and Čejka, *Na západní frontě,* pp. 84-88.
48. Toman Brod, *Tobrucké krysy* [The Rats of Tobruk] (Prague: 1967), pp. 27-28.
49. YVA Testimony of Dr. Mirek Kerner.
50. Testimony of Karel Placěk (David Porath), Yad Vashem Archives.
51. YVA 0-59-55 A. Lustig and others.
52. YVA Testimony of Stephen Barber, Bulletin of *Association des Juifs* . . . , March 1940.
53. Brod and Čejka, *Na západní frontě,* p. 556.
54. YVA. Testimony of Richard Pollak.
55. YVA. Testimony of J. Lízálek.
56. Vuk, *Proti přesile,* p. 57.
57. YVA 0-59-79 Otto O. Spira.
58. *Czechoslovakia Fights for Freedom* (London: 1941).

59. Brod and Čejka, *Na západní frontě*, pp. 121-22.
60. Brod and Čejka, *Na západní frontě*, p. 123.
61. Letter from a liaison officer in Haifa, dated December 29, 1940.
62. Vuk, *Proti přesile*, p. 128, 132.
63. Brod and Čejka, *Na západní frontě*, pp. 144, 551.
64. YVA 0-59-50 Alex Kraus; testimony of Dr. Stephen Barber.
65. Brod and Čejka, *Na západní frontě*, p. 145.
66. YVA 0-59-2 F. Beer; 0-59-79 O. Spira; 0-59-50 A. Kraus; also testimonies by Dr. Stephen Barber and Karel Plaček (David Porath).
67. YVA Manuscript of Josef M. Kadlec (Altmann collection), p. 1.
68. Brod, *Tobrucké krysy*, p. 37.
69. YVA. Manuscript of Josef M. Kadlec, p. 18.
70. YVA. Manuscript of Josef M. Kadlec, pp. 19-20; see also Avigdor Dagan, "The Czechoslovak Government-in-Exile and the Jews," in the present volume, pp. 475-481.
71. Karel Klapálek, *Ozvěny bojů* [Echoes of Fighting] (Prague: 1966), p. 29.
72. Ibid., pp. 29-30.
73. Brod, *Tobrucké krysy*, p. 40.
74. Ibid., p. 44; Klapálek, *Ozvěny bojů*, pp. 33, 36.
75. YVA 0-59-33 A. Hanák-Fleischmann.
76. Brod, *Tobrucké krysy*, p. 48.
77. Klapálek, *Ozvěny bojů*, p. 71.
78. The disaster was caused by explosives which had been smuggled into the boat by members of the *Irgun Z'vai Leumi*, the underground group associated with the Revisionist party, forerunner of Menahem Begin's Herut party. The *Irgun* believed that under international maritime law the British could not deport survivors of a shipwreck. It was not expected that the ship would sink so quickly and that the explosion would claim so many lives. Brod, *Tobrucké krysy*, pp. 48-50; Klapálek, *Ozvěny bojů*, pp. 69-71; YVA 0-59-37 Jindřich Hora; also testimony of E. Enoch.
79. Klapálek, *Ozvěny bojů*, p. 70. *Věstník ŽNO* [Bulletin of the Jewish Religious Community], Prague, no. 14/1946, p. 132. Also testimony of E. Enoch mentioning among the officers Finger, Hirsch, Nettl, and Lájoš. (YVA, 2/25/75).
80. Klapálek, *Ozvěny bojů*, p. 46.
81. YVA 03/2868 Michael Jellinek.
82. Brod, *Tobrucké krysy*, p. 64. Testimony of O. Hornung, pp. 16-17.
83. YVA 03/2686 Michael Jellinek.
84. Brod, *Tobrucké krysy*, pp. 184-85. War diary of the Czechoslovak Infantry Regiment, entry for May 15, 1941.

85. Leopold Firt, *Od Eufratu až po Benghazi* [From the Euphrates to Benghazi] (Prague: 1948), p. 112; Brod, *Tobrucké krysy,* p. 88. Firt is the Czech spelling of Fürth.
86. Firt, *Od Eufratu* . . . , p. 118; Klapálek, *Ozvěny bojů,* p. 66.
87. Klapálek, *Ozvěny bojů,* p. 69; YVA 0-59-37 Jindřich Hora.
88. Klapálek, *Ozvěny bojů,* p. 81.
89. Ibid., p. 98; Brod, *Tobrucké krysy,* p. 112.
90. YVA 0-59-37 Jindřich Hora; Klapálek, *Ozvěny bojů,* p. 44.
91. Brod, *Tobrucké krysy,* pp. 182–83.
92. Firt, *Od Eufratu* . . . , p. 162.
93. Brod, *Tobrucké krysy,* pp. 153, 155.
94. See Aaron Zwergbaum, "From Internment in Bratislava and Detention in Mauritius to Freedom," *The Jews of Czechoslovakia,* vol. II, pp. 599–654.
95. Firt, *Od Eufratu* . . . , p. 209.
96. Brod, *Tobrucké krysy,* p. 29.
97. YVA 0-59-20 J. Fantl; YVA 0-59-66 Hanuš Rezek (Rebenwurzel).
98. YVA 0-59-20 J. Fantl; also Brod, *Tobrucké krysy,* pp. 166–68.
99. Brod, *Tobrucké krysy,* p. 171; Klapálek, *Ozvěny bojů,* p. 127.
100. Klapálek, *Ozvěny bojů,* p. 130.
101. Brod, *Tobrucké krysy,* pp. 170, 172; YVA 0-59-20 J. Fantl.
102. Brod, *Tobrucké krysy,* pp. 1720, 172; YVA 0-59-20 J. Fantl.
103. YVA. Testimony of H. Tauber.
104. Brod, *Tobrucké krysy,* p. 145; Klapálek, *Ozvěny bojů,* p. 147; YVA 0-59-20 J. Fantl.
105. YVA 0-59-37 Jindřich Hora; Brod, *Tobrucké krysy,* pp. 183, 224–25. The statistics quoted in these sources yield the following information about Jewish participation in the Czechoslovak army in the Middle East:

Area from which volunteers came to join the army	Jewish participation	
	Percent	Number
Balkans	30	171
Soviet Union	25	115
Palestine	100	1,113
Other areas/Mauritius (80) Shanghai (50) Other (20)	43	150
Of 2,489 volunteers who joined in the Middle East, 1,549 (i.e., 62 percent) were Jews.	62	1,549

106. *Čechoslovák v Orientě*, no. 5, December 31, 1940, YVA.
107. Brod and Čejka, *Na západní frontě*, pp. 164–65.
108. YVA. Testimony of J. Lízálek.
109. YVA 0-59-51 M. Landa; also Brod and Čejka, *Na západní frontě*, p. 172.
110. YVA 0-59-50 Alex Kraus; also YVA, testimony of Rudolf Braun.
111. YVA, Collection of documents of Dr. Stephen Barber.
112. YVA 0-59-50 Alex Kraus. See also Avigdor Dagan, "The Czechoslovak Government-in-Exile and the Jews," in the present volume, pp. 454–64.
113. YVA Testimony of Dr. Mirek Kerner.
114. YVA 0-59-51 M. Landa; also Brod and Čejka, *Na západní frontě*, p. 173.
115. Czechoslovak citizens in Great Britain during World War II enjoyed the legal status of refugees and were protected by British law. This protection made it possible for Czechoslovaks to leave the army prior to 1942. After that date citizens of Allied countries were subject to draft into the armed forces of their governments.
116. *Archiv Národního Shromáždění* [Archives of the National Assembly, ANS], I, February 2, 1941, p. 9.
117. ANS I, Defense Committee meeting, February 5, 1941, p. 12.
118. YVA 0-59-2 F. Beer.
119. YVA Collection of documents of Dr. Stephen Barber.
120. YVA 0-59-50 Alex Kraus; also testimony of Dr. Mirek Kerner.
121. Brod and Čejka, *Na západní frontě*, p. 271.
122. YVA 0-59-40 Ludvík Kain.
123. YVA 0-59-40 Ludvík Kain; YVA 0-59-2 F. Beer; YVA 0-59-34 L. Harris.
124. YVA 0-59-31 H. Hájek; YVA 0-59-33 Artur Hanák-Fleischmann.
125. YVA 0-59-50 Alex Kraus.
126. See Notes 110–13.
127. Brod and Čejka, *Na západní frontě*, p. 377. Also testimonies of Walter Überreich-Urban YVA 0-59-85 and Hanuš Rezek (Rebenwurzel) YVA 0-59-66.
128. YVA 0-59-50 Alex Kraus.
129. YVA 0-59-2 F. Beer; also testimonies of Stephen Barber and Karel Plaček (David Porath).
130. YVA Testimony of H. Tauber. The army medical corps was headed by General František Langer and directed by him from the Ministry of National Defense of the Czechoslovak government-in-exile in London. The civilian medical services of the Czechoslovak Red Cross

were headed by a Jewish doctor, Oto Klinger, who also was President Beneš's personal physician.
131. YVA. Testimony of B. Bernes.
132. Brod and Čejka, *Na západní frontě*, pp. 472-73.
133. YVA 0-59-85 Walter Überreich-Urban; YVA 0-59-66 Hanuš Rezek (Rebenwurzel).
134. Brod and Čejka, *Na západní frontě*, pp. 479-82.
135. YVA. Testimony of H. Tauber.
136. YVA 0-59-85 Vilém Überreich-Urban; also testimony of H. Tauber.
137. Brod and Čejka, *Na západní frontě*, pp. 489-90, 503.
138. YVA Collection of documents of Stephen Barber.
139. YVA 0-59-85 Walter Überreich-Urban.
140. YVA 0-59-27 W. Gutwillig-Galat.
141. YVA 0-59-46 J. Korda (Kohn).
142. B. Laštovička, *V. Londýně za války* [In London During the War] (Prague: 1961), p. 286. Also ANS I Plenary session of the State Council, January 23, 1943.
143. YVA Testimony of Josef Margolius.
144. Brod and Čejka, *Na západní frontě*, pp. 396-97.
145. YVA 0-59-40 Ludvík Kain; YVA 0-59-46 J. Korda (Kohn); YVA 0-59-68 Josef Rudinger.
146. YVA 0-59-7 H. Brecher; YVA 0-59-65 František Pollak.
147. YVA 0-59-5 F. Bobek.
148. YVA 0-59-68 Josef Rudinger.
149. Ibid.
150. YVA 0-59-46 J. Korda (Kohn).
151. YVA 0-59-7 H. Brecher.
152. YVA 0-59-46 J. Korda (Kohn).
153. YVA 0-59-72 K. Schick.
154. Brod and Čejka, *Na západní frontě*, pp. 407, 437, 444-45; Eduard Čejka, *Zlomená křídla* [Broken Wings] (Prague: 1968), pp. 163-97; YVA 0-59-76 Miroslav Šigut. Šigut mentions in his testimony the names of other Jewish airmen: Epstein, Sicher, Schück, Horšic, Weiss, Freimann, Poláček, Vránský, Bock, Braun, Kauders, and A. Pollak. Of those who survived, a Jew who stood out for valor in the Czechoslovak air force in Europe was Navigator (later Wing Commander) Dr. Jan Gellner, of Brno, who now resides in Caledon East, Ontario, Canada and teaches at York University. He was decorated with a High Canadian order (information from *Kanadské Listy*, Toronto, June 15, 1983).
155. According to information from former members of the Czechoslovak air force, the following among the fallen airmen whose names appear

on the bronze tablet at the Czechoslovak National House (74 West End Lane, London N.W. 6) were of Jewish origin: F. Bonisch, O. Bureš, F. Binder, J. Bittner, H. Beck, S. Bauer, T. Bleier, I. Englaender, A. Elbogen, E. Fechtner, P. Friedlaender, A. Fuchs, F. Fuchs, V. Goth, J. Hornung, V. Hanzl, Z. Heller, V. Kauders, K. Katz, O. Kestler, T. Leslauer, J. Landsmann, R. Lifschitz, O. Mandler, A. Meyer, E. Politzer, T. Politzer, D. Politzer, B. Pohner, O. Smik, J. Stránský, T. Schwarz, O. Schamberger, T. Zeitler, V. Zeimert, Z. Eichelman, K. Weiss. A complete list is not obtainable. One former member of the Czechoslovak air force, Flight Officer J. Korda (Kohn), estimates that at least twenty more, who had Czechified their German-sounding surnames to facilitate their acceptance into the air force, should be added here. YVA list of names of Czechoslovak airmen killed in the war. *Bulletin issued by Association of Czechoslovak Airmen in England* (Appendix I).
156. *Information Bulletin of the Czechoslovak Consulate General in Jerusalem,* July 19, 1941, YVA.
157. AVHU (Archive of the Institute of Military History, Prague), The Czechoslovak Military Mission in the Soviet Union, No. 226/taj. 42.
158. Ludvík Svoboda, *Z Buzuluku do Prahy* [From Buzuluk to Prague] (Prague: 1963), pp. 61–62; also YVA 03/3030 Michael Stemmer.
159. YVA 0-59-19 Malvína Fanta-Friedmann.
160. YVA 0-59-15 David Elefant.
161. YVA 0-59-4 Vilém Bernard.
162. YVA 0-59-4 Vilém Bernard.
163. Ibid. Pika was sentenced to death during the Slánský trial of 1951 and executed. The maps of Soviet labor camps were presented by the prosecution as proof of Pika's espionage activities against the Soviet Union.
164. YVA 0-59-22 Teodor Fiš.
165. YVA 0-59-30 Karel Hahn.
166. YVA 0-59-81 Malvína Strebinger-Lanzer.
167. YVA 0-59-52 Kurt Lanzer.
168. YVA 0-59-16 Terezie Elefant.
169. *Směr Praha,* p. 484.
170. YVA 0-59-84 A. Taussinger.
171. YVA 0-59-4 Vilém Bernard.
172. František Polák, *Jak žili a umírali sovětští otroci* [Life and Death of Soviet Slaves] (New York: 1960); František Polák, *Cestou ze sovětského koncentráku* [On the Way From a Soviet Concentration Camp] (New York: 1959).

173. Photocopies of documents relevant to Dr. Goliath's case are in the Kulka collection of the Yad Vashem Archives in Jerusalem.
174. YVA 0-59-22 Teodor Fiš. Reicin, son of a cantor in Plzeň (Pilsen), joined the Communist party in 1926 as a boy of fifteen and soon worked his way up to the position of head of the youth education department. By the 1930s, he already was an intimate of party chairman Klement Gottwald. During World War II, Gottwald made him his chief observer of political developments in the Czechoslovak army in the Soviet Union. After the war Reicin was given the rank of general and appointed chief of Czechoslovak military intelligence and deputy minister of national defense. Despite his devotion to the Communist cause and his alienation from his Jewish background, Reicin became a victim of the anti-Jewish campaign which culminated in the Slánský trial. He was arrested and accused of Zionism, Trotzkyism, espionage, and high treason. Together with Slánský he was sentenced to death and executed in Prague in November 1952. See *Proces s vedením protístátného sprisahaneckého centra na čele s Rudolfom Slánským* [Trial of the Anti-State Conspiracy Headed by Rudolf Slansky] (Prague: 1953), pp. 483, 575, 580 ff.; see also Meyer, Weinryb, Sylvain, Duschinsky, *The Jews in the Soviet Satellites* (New York: 1953), pp. 164, 168, 177-78.
175. YVA 0-59-22 Teodor Fiš.
176. Svoboda, *Z Buzuluku do Prahy,* pp. 79, 89, AVHU letter, May 31, 1942.
177. YVA 0-59-48 Max Kriegel.
178. YVA 0-59-22 Teodor Fiš.
179. Svoboda, *Z Buzuluku do Prahy,* p. 84. YVA 0-59-22 Teodor Fiš.
180. Ludvík Svoboda, *Výběr z projevů a článků* [Selection of Speeches and Articles] (Prague: 1972), pp. 24-25.
181. AVHU, Prague, No. 786, September 15, 1942; Tichá, *Po boku mužů,* p. 36.
182. Peter Gosztony, "Die tschechoslowakische Armee in der Sowjetunion 1941-1944," *Politische Studien* (Munich: 1962), p. 572 ff.
183. Svoboda, *Z Buzuluku do Prahy,* p. 86.
184. The testimonies of about seventy participants (YVA Record Group 0-59) give the percentage of participation as having been between seventy and eighty. The Bulletin of the Council of Jewish Religious Communities in Prague, *Věstník Rady ŽNO,* in several articles published between 1945 and 1951, gives the percentage as seventy-five.
185. Brod, *Tobrucké krysy,* pp. 25-31.
186. YVA 0-59-20 Teodor Fiš.

187. *Za svobodu Československa* [For the Freedom of Czechoslovakia] (Prague: 1959), p. 142.
188. Tichá, *Po boku mužů*, p. 183.
189. *Za svobodu* . . . , p. 146.
190. Svoboda, *Z Buzuluku do Prahy*, p. 118.
191. *Za svobodu* . . . , pp. 146–47.
192. YVA 0-59-82 Hynek Strompf.
193. YVA 0-59-48 Max Kriegel.
194. YVA 0-59-28 D. (Vojtěch) Gláz.
195. YVA 0-59-36 Moshe Hofmann.
196. YVA 0-59-48 Max Kriegel.
197. YVA 0-59-1 A. Alter.
198. Svoboda, *Z Buzuluku do Prahy*, p. 158.
199. Teodor Fiš: *Mein Kommandeur, General Svoboda* [My Commander, General Svoboda] (Vienna: 1969), p. 49.
200. Ibid., pp. 53–55.
201. Bedřich Reicin and J. Mareš, *Sokolovo* [Collection of Reportages and Documents] (Prague: 1948), pp. 275–78.
202. *Za svobodu* . . . , p. 191.
203. Ibid., p. 161.
204. Reicin and Mareš, *Sokolovo*, pp. 181–82.
205. YVA 0-59-30 Karel Hahn.
206. *Pravda*, Moscow, April 8, 1943.
207. YVA 0-59-18 K. Fanta.
208. *Za svobodu* . . . , pp. 226–27.
209. The 670 officers and men remained from the original 979 members of the regiment. This means that 309 men lost their lives.
210. YVA 0-59-58 Gustav Meier.
211. Ibid.
212. Svoboda, *Z Buzuluku do Prahy*, pp. 164–66; Fiš, *Mein Kommandeur* . . . , p. 62.
213. *Za svobodu* . . . , p. 231.
214. YVA 0-59-82 Hynek Strompf; YVA 0-59-18 K. Fanta.
215. YVA 0-59-28 D. (Vojtěch) Gláz.
216. YVA 0-59-27 Alex Mašek-Mermelstein.
217. Ibid.
218. *Za svobodu* . . . , p. 271.
219. YVA 03-3030 Michael Stemmer.
220. Tichá, *Po boku mužů*, p. 79; also YVA 0-59-18 K. Fanta.
221. YVA 0-59-18, 19 K. Fanta, Malvína Fanta-Friedman.
222. YVA 0-59-35 Mikuláš Hecht; YVA 0-59-54 M. Lavi; YVA 0-59-48 Max Kriegel.

223. YVA 0-59-35 Mikuláš Hecht.
224. *Za svobodu* . . . , p. 296.
225. Ibid., p. 294.
226. YVA 03/3030 Michael Stemmer.
227. *Za svobodu* . . . , p. 205; Tichá, *Po boku mužů,* p. 84.
228. Svoboda, *Z Buzuluku do Prahy,* pp. 180-84; *Směr Praha,* p. 486; YVA 0-59-35 Mikuláš Hecht.
229. *Za svobodu* . . . , pp. 342-43.
230. Ibid.
231. Ibid.; YVA 03/1882 N. Koenig.
232. Svoboda, *Z Buzuluku do Prahy,* p. 197.
233. *Za svobodu* . . . , p. 353; also YVA 0-59-61 Josef Mueller.
234. Svoboda, *Z Buzuluku do Prahy,* p. 195; also YVA 0-59-47 B. Kowartovski.
235. Svoboda, *Z Buzuluku do Prahy,* p. 201; *Za svobodu* . . . , pp. 353-54.
236. Fiš, *Mein Kommandeur* . . . , p. 71; Svoboda, *Z Buzuluku,* p. 205; also YVA 0-59-58 Gustav Meier.
237. 3,517 left for the front. The war diary entry for November 2, 1943, gives the number as 3,301. The discrepancy of 296 most probably shows the total losses during this period.
238. Fiš, *Mein Kommandeur* . . . , p. 71; *Za svobodu* . . . , pp. 361, 365, 367; also YVA 03/3030 Stemmer.
239. Svoboda, *Z Buzuluku do Prahy,* p. 201.
240. *Věstník Rady ŽNO,* Prague, no. 15/1947, p. 217; *Za svobodu* . . . , pp. 375, 380; also YVA 0-59-71 S. Šachta.
241. YVA 0-59-35 Mikuláš Hecht.
242. *Směr Praha,* p. 487; *Za svobodu* . . . , p. 391.
243. Fiš, *Mein Kommandeur* . . . , p. 74.
244. Kerner was transferred to Jefremov and appointed commander of the school for supply officers. In his unpublished treatise, "Jewish Soldiers in the Czechoslovak Army in Exile Within the Soviet Armed Forces," he recalls that at the time of his arrival in the Soviet Union, "compared with the Czechoslovak units in Great Britain," overt, anti-Semitism had been "non-existent." But later, when units of Tiso's Slovak army crossed over to the Soviet side and were sent to Jefremov to form the backbone for the Second Parachutists' Brigade, these Slovak units caused the first overt anti-Semitic incidents. They tried to prevent Jewish soldiers from becoming parachutists, although many Jewish officers, men, and even women, were members of the brigade and were eager to participate in the training. The Slovaks resented the idea that Jews should be among the first liberating troops to be dropped over Czechoslovak territory.

245. *Za svobodu...*, p. 420; YVA 0-59-9 E. Cohen-Hermann; YVA 0-59-61 Josef Mueller. War diaries give the casualties in the battle as 214 dead, wounded and missing. Veterans claim that at least 300 were killed or seriously wounded.
246. Vladimír Přikryl, *Pokračujte v horách* [Continue In the Mountain], (Prague: 1947), p. 34. The parachutists' brigade was formed mostly with Slovaks who had gone over to the Allied side. Jewish officers and instructors attached to this formation encountered flagrant anti-Semitism. At least one case was brought before the Czechoslovak court-martial at Sadagora. A Slovak lieutenant, Dezider Miškej, who publicly threatened to hang fifty Jews once he was back in Slovakia, was sentenced to one month in prison. The sentence was published in the army paper *Naše Vojsko v SSSR* [Our Army in the USSR], no. 209/ 1944, YVA.
247. B. Kopold, *Přes Bílou Čerkev na západ* [Through Bílá Cerkev to the West] (Moscow: 1944), pp. 37-39; also YVA 0-59-84 Vilém Überreich-Urban.
248. *Za svobodu...*, p. 425, 433.
249. Ibid., p. 438.
250. Tichá, *Po boku mužů*, pp. 106-108.
251. *Za svobodu...*, p. 443; also YVA 0-59-22 Theodor Fiš.
252. YVA 0-59-22 Teodor Fiš.
253. *Za svobodu...*, pp. 447, 453; also YVA 0-59-18 K. Fanta; YVA 0-59-22 Teodor Fiš; YVA 0-59-57 Alex Mašek-Mermelstein; YVA 0-59-71 S. Šachta.
254. The names of recipients of decorations were published in *Československé Listy,* Moscow, November 6, 1944, p. 5.
255. YVA 0-59-57 Alex Mašek-Mermelstein.
256. *Za svobodu...*, p. 454.
257. YVA 0-59-57 Alex Mašek-Mermelstein.
258. YVA 03/3030 Michael Stemmer.
259. YVA 0-59-57 Alex Mašek-Mermelstein.
260. YVA 0-59-19 Malvína Fanta-Friedmann.
261. *Za svobodu...*, p. 458.
262. YVA 0-59-22 Teodor Fiš; YVA 0-59-57 Alex Mašek-Mermelstein; YVA 0-59-58 Gustav Meier; also Fiš, *Mein Kommandeur...*, p. 89, and *Směr Praha,* p. 409.
263. *Směr Praha,* p. 490.
264. YVA 0-59-78 I. Šnek; Erich Kulka, *Židé v Československé Svobodové Armádě* [The Jews in Svoboda's Army] (Toronto: 1979), pp. 254-58.
265. YVA 0-59-71 S. Šachta.
266. YVA 03/3030 Michael Stemmer; also testimony of Mirek Kerner. On account of testimony submitted by F. Vernon-Vohryzek, attorney at

the court-martial, the Court of Appeals in London subsequently commuted Holzer's death sentence to ten years' imprisonment. YVA F. Vernon-Vohryzek, February 1979.
267. YVA 0-59-25 J. Friedmann.
268. YVA 0-59-20 H. Fantl.
269. Hugo Gold, *Die Geschichte der Juden in der Bukowina* [History of the Jews in Bukovina] (Tel Aviv: Part I-1958; Part II-1962).
270. YVA 0-59-71 S. Šachta; YVA 0-59-33 Artur Hanák-Fleischmann.
271. YVA 0-59-11 Pavel and Eva Dobrý-Gutmann.
272. YVA 0-59-20 H. Fantl; YVA 0-59-26 M. Friedner.
273. YVA 0-59-71 S. Šachta; YVA 03/3030 Michael Stemmer.
274. YVA 0-59-33 Artur Hanák-Fleischmann.
275. Tichá, *Po boku mužů,* p. 120; also YVA 03/3030 Michael Stemmer.
276. Svoboda, *Z Buzuluku do Prahy,* p. 264.
277. YVA 0-59-33 Artur Hanák-Fleischmann, YVA 0-59-30 K. Hahn, YVA 0-59-22 Teodor Fiš.
278. YVA 03/3030 Michael Stemmer, who at the time had access to the archives of the Institute for Military History in Prague, testified that Colonel Šáda, while writing his work, had not been permitted to use material concerning Jewish participation in the Czechoslovak war effort. The request of the Institute for the History of Contemporary Jewry at the Hebrew University in Jerusalem for permission to use material containing relevant data about Jewish participation was never answered.
279. Miroslav Šáda, "*Vznik I. československého armádního sboru* [The Genesis of the First Czechoslovak Army Corps]," published in *Historie a vojenstvi* [History and Military Art] (Prague: 1956), no. 4, p. 549.
280. YVA 0-59-35 Mikuláš Hecht.
281. Tichá, *Po boku mužů,* pp. 143, 150, 153; also YVA 0-59-16 Terezie Elefant.
282. Tichá, *Po boku mužů,* pp. 150-154, 156; also YVA 0-59-71 S. Šachta.
283. Svoboda, *Z Buzuluku do Prahy,* pp. 288-90.
284. Ibid., p. 304. Also Tichá, *Po boku mužů,* p. 159.
285. Fiš, *Mein Kommandeur* . . . , p. 101.
286. YVA 0-59-20 H. Fantl.
287. YVA 0-59-18 K. Fanta; YVA 0-59-78 I. Šnek.
288. Testimony of Mirek Kerner, YVA. In his previously quoted work Kerner also recalls: "The corps was supposed to be used in the liberation of Subcarpathian Ruthenia, an operation which many of its members who hailed from that easternmost part of prewar Czechoslovakia were eagerly anticipating. When later the orders of the corps were changed and the corps crossed the Carpathian mountains directly into Slovakia, some Jewish soldiers tried to visit their home-

towns in Subcarpathian Ruthenia. They encountered strong hostility from the local Ukrainian authorities and the Soviet army command ... It then became clear to the Jewish corps members formerly hailing from this part of Czechoslovakia that they had lost their homeland for good."

289. Svoboda, *Z Buzuluku do Prahy,* pp. 299-300, 308; Tichá, *Po boku mužů,* p. 158.
290. *Naše Vojsko v SSSR* [Our Army in the USSR], November 3, 1944; Svoboda, *Z Buzuluku do Prahy,* p. 319; YVA 0-59-18 K. Fanta.
291. *Naše Vojsko v SSSR,* ibid.
292. YVA 0-59-28 D. Gláz.
293. YVA 0-59-21 A. Feierwerger.
294. YVA 0-59-19 Malvína Fanta-Friedmann; YVA 0-59-18 K. Fanta; also Tichá, *Po boku mužů,* p. 156.
295. Testimony of Mirek Kerner, who defended Lieutenant Colonel Novák. Although Novák was found not guilty, he was expelled from the Soviet Union and transferred to England.
296. Fiš, *Mein Kommandeur* . . . , pp. 101-102.
297. Svoboda, *Z Buzuluku do Prahy,* pp. 344-45.
298. YVA 0-59-38 Otakar Huppert.
299. YVA 0-59-57 Alexander Mašek-Mermelstein. Following the Communist take-over in 1948, Mermelstein was arrested in Czechoslovakia. He now resides with his family in Natanya, Israel.
300. Edouard Beneš, *Tři roky druhé světové války* [Three Years of World War II] (London: 1943), p. 120.
301. *Věstník Rady ŽNO,* Prague.
302. Ferdinand Peroutka, *"Tak tedy zase?* [What, Again?]," *Svobodné Noviny,* Brno, December 2, 1945.
303. Collection of Testimonies and Documents, Yad Vashem Archives, Jerusalem, 1976.
304. YVA 03/2640 M. Gruen; YVA 0-59-20 H. Fantl.
305. A complete list of decorations received by officers and men of the Czechoslovak Armored Corps was published in *Československé Listy,* Moscow, February 2, 1945, p. 6.
306. Erich Kulka, *Hayehudim betsvah Svoboda bebrit Hamoatsot* [Jews in Svoboda's Army in the Soviet Union] (Tel Aviv: 1977). A Czech version of this book was published in Toronto in 1979 under the title *Židé v československé Svobodově armádě.*
307. It should be mentioned that the Czechoslovak Jews abroad volunteered to become members of the armed forces though they also had the choice of working in auxiliary military services or in the defense industry.

BIBLIOGRAPHY

Směr Praha [Direction Prague]. Memoirs of members of the First Independent Army Corps in the Soviet Union. Prague: 1955.

U děla na Středním východé. Kronika československého 200. lehkého protiletadlového pluko—Východního [At the Guns in the Middle East: A Chronicle of the Czechoslovak 200th Light Anti-aircraft Battalion—East]. London: 1944.

Za svobodu Československa [For the Freedom of Czechoslovakia]. Prague: 1959.

The Jews in the Soviet Satellites. New York: 1953. Section on Czechoslovakia by Peter Meyer, pp. 40-191.

Beneš, Eduard, *Šest let exilu a druhé světové války* [Six Years of Exile and World War II]. Prague: 1946.

———, *Tři roky druhé světové války* [Three Years of World War II]. London: 1943.

Brod, Toman, *Tobrucké krysy* [The Rats of Tobruk]. Prague: 1967.

Brod, Toman and Čejka, Eduard, *Na západní frontě* [On the Western Front]. Prague: 1963.

Čejka, Eduard, *Zlomena křídla* [Broken Wings]. Prague: 1968.

Firt, Leopold, *Od Eufratu az po Benghazi* [From the Euphrates to Benghazi]. Prague: 1948.

Fiš, Teodor, *Mein Kommandeur General Svoboda* [My Commander, General Svoboda]. Vienna: 1969.

Gosztony, Peter, "Die tschechoslowakische Armee in der Sovietunion 1941-1944," *Politische Studien.* Munich: 1962.

Klapálek, K., *Ozvěny bojů* [Echoes of Fighting]. Prague: 1966.

Kopecký, Rudolf, *Československý odboj v Polsku v r. 1939* [Czechoslovak Resistance in Poland in the Year 1939]. Rotterdam: 1958.

Křen, Jan, *V emigraci* [In Emigration]. Prague: 1969.

B. Laštovička, *V Londýně za války* [In London During the War]. Prague: 1961.

Polák, František, *Jak žili a umírali sovětští otroci* [Life and Death of Soviet Slaves]. New York: 1960.

———, *Cestou ze sovětského koncentráku* [On the Way From a Soviet Concentration Camp]. New York: 1959.

Přikryl, Vladimir, *Pokračujte v horách* [Continue in the Mountains]. Prague: 1947.

Reicin, Bedřich and Mareš, J., *Věrni zůstaneme sborník reportáží a dokumentů* [We Shall Remain Faithful: A Collection of Reportages and Documents]. Moscow: 1943.

———, *Sokolovo* (Collection of Reportages and Documents). Prague: 1948.

Reitlinger, Gerald, *Die Endlösung: Hitler's Versuch der Ausrottung der Juden Europas 1939-1945.* Berlin: 1956.

Svoboda, Ludvík, *Z Buzuluku do Prahy* [From Buzuluk to Prague]. Prague: 1963.

———, *Cestami života* [On the Paths of Life]. Prague: 1971.

———, *Výběr z projevů a článků* [Selection of Speeches and Articles]. Prague: 1972.

Tichá, Věra, *Po boku mužů* [Side By Side With the Men]. Prague: 1966.

Vuk, Václav, *Proti přesile* [In the Face of Overwhelming Force]. London: 1942.

THE CZECHOSLOVAK GOVERNMENT-IN-EXILE AND THE JEWS

By Avigdor Dagan

The high percentage of Jews among the emigrants from Czechoslovakia after Munich and after the subsequent "Ides of March" occupation in 1939 certainly requires no special explanation. The Nazi record left no room for doubt that the Jews in Czechoslovakia would be the first in the occupied nation to find themselves in deadly peril. As a consequence, the pure instinct of self-preservation made Jews in Czechoslovakia more acutely motivated than other Czechoslovaks to seek refuge abroad. The fact that most of the refugees from Czechoslovakia were Jews was to cause some embarrassment and many problems to the Czechoslovak government-in-exile that was established in London under the leadership of Eduard Beneš, who had been president of the Czechoslovak Republic from 1935 to 1938.

ANTI-SEMITISM IN THE CZECHOSLOVAK ARMED FORCES AND WITHIN THE GOVERNMENT-IN-EXILE

Indeed, Beneš encountered the "Jewish problem" even before his government-in-exile was accorded official recognition by Great Britain.* The very first attempts at organizing Czechoslovak participation in the armed anti-Nazi resistance abroad even before the outbreak of World War II brought the question what to do about the

---

* A Czechoslovak provisional government was recognized by Great Britain on July 21, 1940; the government-in-exile, on July 21, 1941.

Jews. The Czechoslovak ambassador in Warsaw, Juraj Slávik, who later became a member of the Beneš government-in-exile in London, signed an agreement with Poland's Foreign Minister, Lieutenant Colonel Josef Beck, a notorious anti-Semite, regarding the creation in Poland of a Czechoslovak military unit that would be incorporated into the French Foreign Legion. This agreement discriminated against Jewish volunteers. When Slávik signed the agreement, he certainly did so with the knowledge of Štefan Osuský, the Czechoslovak ambassador in Paris. There is no documentary evidence indicating whether or not he had the approval of Dr. Beneš. However, there can be no doubt that Beneš must have been aware even in Paris, where he had set up a *Národní výbor* (National Council) in November 1939, of certain anti-Semitic incidents and tendencies, mainly among younger members of the officer corps in the military camp at Agde in the south of France, which had been turned over by the French to the Czechoslovak army-in-exile.

These anti-Jewish trends in the Czechoslovak anti-Nazi resistance are described in some detail in another study included in this volume,[1] as is the further development of this chronic evil, which was never fully overcome in Czechoslovak army units formed in the Allied countries during World War II. The problem of anti-Semitism brought Beneš face to face with a political dilemma that became even more acute when the Czechoslovak government-in-exile set up its bureaucratic apparatus and gradually formulated its postwar political aims. This dilemma had many aspects, of which the following are only a few:

1. The armed forces were the most important political instrument of the Czechoslovak government-in-exile. Their numerical strength was of the utmost importance and there was no way of concealing the fact that they included a high percentage of Jews. On the other hand, it was not in the best interest of the government-in-exile to publicize this, because it was feared that the German propaganda machine might present the Czechoslovak armed forces abroad as a "Jewish army" (as it was indeed to do) and that this image might alienate the Czechoslovak populace at home from the government-in-exile in London. As a consequence, the fact that that Jews constituted fifty percent, and at times even more, of the Czechoslovak army abroad was never mentioned and was not officially acknowledged even after the war. On the other hand, since hatred of the

Jews was a basic part of the enemy's ideology, Beneš's government-in-exile found it difficult to admit that the ranks of those who were supposed to fight this evil were themselves not entirely immune to its poison.[2]

Attempts were made to minimize the presence of anti-Semitism in the Czechoslovak armed forces abroad. Sir R. H. Bruce Lockhart, the British representative to the Czechoslovak provisional government, stated in his report addressed to Viscount Halifax as Britain's Foreign Secretary on December 17, 1940:

> ... From my talks with [President Beneš and M. Jan Masaryk] I deduce that there is very little truth in Mr. Namier's[3] assertion that the Czechs are developing anti-Semitic tendencies. In the army there was some months ago some discrimination against Jews, partly, I think, because the Jewish refugees from Czechoslovakia were the first to escape and some of them, at least, succeeded in transferring certain sums of money to this country. But M. Zelmanovič[4] himself admitted that conditions for Jews in the army had improved very much, and President Beneš himself has taken strong measures to check any anti-Semitic sentiments among the Czechoslovak officers. When he paid his first visit to the Czechoslovak camp, he selected a Jew as his officer of the day. Of the first four Czechoslovak pilots whom he decorated with the Czechoslovak Military Cross, two were Jews. The Czechs, in fact, have the best reputation of all Continental nations for their treatment of the Jews, and they are not likely to fall from their high standards in times like these. Moreover, President Beneš is very sensitive to world opinion and knows the power of international Jewry. M. Jan Masaryk has assumed his father's role as the chief opponent of anti-Semitism, and he is the idol of the American Jews ... [5]

Obviously this minimizing effort was successful. Later, the existence of anti-Semitism among Czechoslovak army officers was flatly denied. Thus, in a conversation at his London residence with two representatives of the London section of the World Jewish Congress, Dr. Noah Barou and Sydney S. Silverman, M.P., on April 17, 1941, Beneš assured his visitors explicitly "that there was no anti-Semitism either in the Czech army or press."[6]

2. With the official recognition of the Czechoslovak government-in-exile in London and the establishment of its official wartime organs, it became clear that it would be virtually impossible to staff the government's offices without using the members of the Czechoslovak Jewish refugee intelligentsia who were available in England.

The Ministry of Foreign Affairs, for instance, particularly its information service, would have been unthinkable without certain able journalists who were Jews (though some of these had been baptized). This was true also for most of the other positions that required regular contact with British authorities, if for no other reason but that only very few non-Jews among the Czechoslovak emigrés had a working knowledge of English. As a consequence, Jews who were needed for these essential civilian assignments were exempted from military service; this again led to jealousy and a further increase of anti-Semitism in the armed forces.[7]

3. It must be remembered that Beneš had to consider not only the right-wing elements in the Czechoslovak officer corps but also the differences of opinion which prevailed within the government-in-exile itself. Alongside an outspoken philo-Semite such as Jan Masaryk there were others, such as General Sergěj Ingr, the chief of staff, who became Minister of National Defense in the government-in-exile and who, at least at a certain stage of the war, frankly declared that he regarded the Jews in Czechoslovak army units as "undesirable elements." This should help to explain why Beneš's policies toward the Jews so often resembled balancing acts.

4. Yet another important facet of the dilemma was presented by the policies of the prewar Czechoslovak Republic toward national minority groups in Czechoslovakia. The democratic republic founded by Tomáš G. Masaryk probably granted its national minorities more rights than did any other state. But it was precisely this liberal policy that made possible the emergence and survival of the Nazi movement of Konrad Henlein in the Sudetenland and thus eventually also the tragedy of Munich. Thus, when the government-in-exile set about to formulate its postwar plans for Czechoslovakia, one of its first decisions was that there could be no return to the old policies toward minorities. "The absurd state of affairs . . . cannot be renewed,"[8] Beneš wrote in January 1942. Discussing possible solutions of minority problems throughout the postwar world, he set down three general guidelines:

a) The creation of states that would be nationally as homogeneous as possible;
b) Population transfers on the largest possible scale to help effect such homogeneity;

c) The protection of minorities in the future should consist primarily in the defense of human democratic rights and not of national rights.

According to Sir R. H. Bruce Lockhart,[9] Beneš had used the formula "a state which will be as homogeneous as possible" as early as the fall of 1940, only a few months after the fall of France and the removal of the *Národní výbor* (National Council), the predecessor of the government-in-exile, from Paris to London.

Naturally, this change in attitude toward national minorities in general was bound to have implications also for the envisioned place of the Jewish minority in postwar Czechoslovakia.[10] In fact, as we shall see, it affected relations between the government-in-exile and the Jews even while the war was going on. Beneš persistently refused to acknowledge that there was any difference between the Jews and other minorities. "[A] minority is [a] minority," was his answer to Dr. Leo Zelmanovits when the latter tried to make him aware of the differences.[11] When Dr. Noah Barou and Sydney Silverman, M.P., in their interview with Beneš on April 17, 1941, attempted to discuss the position of the Jewish minority in postwar Czechoslovakia, Beneš firmly replied that "as a matter of principle, all the minority questions would have to be settled simultaneously on the principle of minority representation."[12]

5. The plans for postwar Czechoslovakia early showed a tendency to envision basic changes in the country's social structure. The Soviet Union's entry into the war on the side of the Allies in June 1941, the creation of a Czechoslovak army in the Soviet Union, the upgrading of the political importance of the Czechoslovak Communist party leadership in Moscow headed by Klement Gottwald, and Moscow's order to activate the Communist group among Czechoslovak emigrés in Britain, a group which was comparatively strong in numbers, forced Beneš and his government to reassess their plans for Czechoslovakia's future. The government-in-exile was influenced also by reports which it was receiving regularly from Prague about the views of the underground leaders at home and which it presumed reflected the attitude of wide circles among the Czech and Slovak population at home.

As early as January 1942 Beneš wrote of a "planned economy," of "a new and audacious social policy," the "development of a more thoroughgoing economic and social democracy," and "notable equalizations." He also reminded his readers that "Fascism and Nazism were social revolutions as well as nationalistic excesses."[13] Translated from the abstract language of political theory into the plain idiom of economic reality, all this indicated a consensus of opinion that, after the war, larger industrial enterprises in Czechoslovakia should be nationalized. It so happened that many of these concerns had been owned by Jewish families before the war. It soon became clear that Jewish owners of smaller enterprises, too, would have difficulties in "de-Aryanization" proceedings after the war.[14]

6. Finally, there was a whole complex of questions regarding the attitude of the government-in-exile toward Zionism and the Jewish homeland in Palestine. Here Beneš tried to continue the pro-Zionist policy of President Tomáš G. Masaryk. He did so quite intelligently but, as in so many other things, without the human warmth of his great predecessor. It was fortunate for both Beneš and the Jews that he was able to leave the direct contacts between the government-in-exile and the world Zionist leadership in the hands of his Minister of Foreign Affairs, Jan Masaryk.[15]

JEWISH REPRESENTATION IN THE STÁTNÍ RADA (STATE COUNCIL)

Though issues of direct concern to Czechoslovak Jews certainly did not occupy top priority in the long-range postwar plans for Czechoslovakia, they frequently cropped up in the routine work of the government-in-exile and of President Beneš himself. A good example of how intensively Beneš sometimes had to deal with matters of explicit Jewish interest is the struggle for Jewish representation in the *Státní rada* (State Council), which was to serve as a quasi-parliamentary advisory body to Beneš and the government-in-exile.

Under pressure from many quarters, Beneš felt that the appointment of such an advisory body was not only necessary but also desirable from the point of view of democracy. However, as soon as concrete negotiations about the actual composition of the Council were started, it became obvious that he had opened a Pandora's box. New claimants to representation turned up all the time. The Czechoslovak emigrés in Britain were certainly not representative of the entire population of Czechoslovakia. As Beneš himself told Barou and Silverman on April 17, 1941, "of about 9,000 Czechoslovak citizens at present in England, only 1,500 were Czechs (or Slovaks), the remainder being Germans or Jews."[16] It was just as unfeasible to make up the State Council from former members of the Czechoslovak parliament who were living as emigrés in England "because it had been discovered that of the forty former deputies now in this country, ten were Czechs, eleven Germans, and about sixteen German or Czech Communists." Also, "there had been thirty-six political parties in Czechoslovakia" and Beneš was unwilling to replicate such a fragmented constellation.[17]

In her well-documented study on the attitude of the Czechoslovak government-in-exile toward the Jews and the Jewish homeland in Palestine, Dr. Livia Rothkirchen drew a clear picture of the struggle of the Jews for representation in the *Státní rada*.[18] Only a very few details might be added. When the question of Jews being represented as a national minority in the *Státní rada* was raised, it was found that the Czechoslovak Jewish refugees in Britain were split into three groupings: Zionists, non-Zionist Orthodox, and assimilationists. The assimilationist *Svaz Čechu-židů* (Union of Czecho-Jews) had been temporarily resurrected in London solely for the purpose of protesting against the appointment of a special Jewish representative in the *Státní rada*. Whether this was a spontaneous action of a group of Czech Jews advocating assimilation, or whether, as was widely assumed by the Czechoslovak Jewish refugees at the time, it was an intervention orchestrated by circles close to Beneš (who may have been interested in using such a group as a tactical weapon in his negotiations with the Zionists) could, of course, never be established.[19] As for the non-Zionist Orthodox Jews, the story was different. The *Federace ortodoxních židů z Československa* (Federation of Orthodox Jews from Czechoslovakia),[20] which was affiliated with and supported by the World Agudas Israel organization, was deeply involved in welfare and relief activities financed by the Refugee Trust Fund maintained by the Czechoslovak government-in-exile. In fact, welfare work was the primary interest of the non-Zionist Orthodox among the Czechoslovak Jewish refugees in Britain. Their sole political aim was the establishment of a "Jewish desk" in the Ministry for Internal Affairs similar to the desks already set up by the government-in-exile for Catholic and Protestant affairs. They had no desire for special representation in the *Státní rada*.

The only organized Czechoslovak Jewish group with clear-cut political claims and objectives included the Zionists of all shades, who were united in the *Ústřední rada národních židů Československa* (Central Council of National Jews from Czechoslovakia).[21] This group insisted on special representation in the *Státní rada*. It made its claim known at a very early stage and in a very articulate manner. The chairman of the Central Council, Dr. Leo Zelmanovits, who had been secretary general of the Jewish party in Czechoslovakia before the fall of the Masaryk republic, had taken up contact with President Beneš as early as December 1939, offering him the full cooperation of "national Jews." During a visit (with Rabbi Dr. Hugo Stránský) at Beneš's London residence on December 4, 1939, he inquired about the creation of an advisory body to the *Národní výbor*, which then still had its seat in Paris. Beneš replied that there was an intention to form such a body but that "first the National Council [i.e., the *Národní výbor*] has to be transformed into a government. Only then shall we begin to form an advisory body. It stands to reason that you (the Jews) should have your place and be represented in this advisory body."[22]

When the formation of the *Státní rada* entered its final stage, Zelmanovits became very active. However, he did not at first achieve the results for which he had hoped.

There were several reasons for Zelmanovits's initial failure:

1. As we have seen, Beneš had made up his mind at an early date that there would have to be basic changes in Czechoslovakia's minority policy. In his view, the problem of the Jewish national minority was part of a larger complex of minority problems, and he felt that he could not appoint a representative of the Jewish minority to the *Státní rada* without first solving the problem of representation for the anti-Nazi German minority.[23]

2. Zelmanovits's argument of "continuity"—i.e., that Czechoslovak citizens of Jewish nationality had had their own elected representatives in the Czechoslovak parliament in Prague before the fall of the republic and were therefore entitled to this privilege also in the *Státní rada*, the parliament-in-exile—failed to move Beneš. He parried that "he could hardly form it [the *Státní rada*] on the basis of political parties, as there had been thirty-six political parties in Czechoslovakia."[24]

3. Beneš found even Zionist (as distinct from Jewish party) representation unacceptable because, as he explained to Bruce Lockhart, "if he agrees to Zionist representation in the Council, he will be faced with similar demands for representation from other small groups."[25]

4. As already mentioned, Beneš could—and did—argue that there was disunity on this subject even among the Jews. While the majority of the Central Council of National Jews from Czechoslovakia favored Zelmanovits as the representative of the Jewish national minority in the *Státní rada,* Jewish members of the Czechoslovak armed forces asked for the appointment of one from their own ranks, Dr. Rudolf Braun, a lawyer from Prague, who, like Zelmanovits, had been active in the Jewish party.

5. Beneš had a personal dislike for Zelmanovits. This dislike was based partly on personal prejudice and partly on the president's aversion to some of the political methods used by Zelmanovits, which Beneš regarded as undue pressure. At least since 1935, Beneš had harbored serious doubts about the efficacy of the World Jewish Congress, a Zionist-oriented organization. Nahum Goldmann, a founder and eventually president of the World Jewish Congress, himself recalls in his autobiography how, only a few days after the promulgation of the Nuremberg Laws, Beneš, who was then Czechoslovakia's Minister of Foreign Affairs, had asked him to visit him at his hotel in Geneva,

where for two hours he [Beneš] reproachfully demanded to know why the Jews did not react on a grand scale, why my friends and I did not immediately call an international Jewish congress and declare all-out war on the National-Socialist regime. He assured me that he and many other non-Jewish statesmen would give us their full support. "Don't you understand," he shouted, "that by reacting with nothing but halfhearted gestures, by failing to arouse world public opinion and take vigorous action against the Germans, the Jews are endangering their future and their human rights all over the world? If you go on like this, Hitler's example will be contagious and encourage all the anti-Semites throughout the world."[26]

"I have never felt so uncomfortable and ashamed as I did during those two hours," Goldmann adds. "I knew Beneš was right." From that time on, Beneš did not take seriously any threats of Jewish wrath, which, in his view, proved toothless at a time most critical for the Jews themselves.

In November 1940 Beneš decided that the *Státní rada* should have forty members but that, for the time being, he would appoint only thirty-two. The remaining eight seats would be left vacant to accommodate any political maneuvering that might be needed in the future. It was not then Beneš's intention to appoint a member of the *Státní rada* to represent the Jews. In his diary (November 25, 1940), Jaromír Smutný, President Beneš's *chef de cabinet,* records in Beneš's own words what the latter had decided to "propose" to the Zionists, whom he had invited for a final meeting. Instead of naming a Jewish representative to the *Státní rada,* the president had decided to create a kind of special advisory body on Jewish affairs, a triumvirate of "trustees" composed of one Zionist, one [non-Zionist] Orthodox, and one [assimilationist] Czecho-Jew. "If they refuse [this proposal]," the president told Smutný, "I shall tell them later that the representative of the Zionists will be Dr. [Angelo] Goldstein. When Zelmanovits, whom the Jews do not want, hears about this, he will quickly be in favor of 'trustees.' "[27]

Another remark Beneš made on that occasion to his *chef de cabinet* was typical of his lack of objectivity with regard to Zelmanovits. "I liked it," he said, "that as a man of convictions, he [Goldstein] went to Palestine, while Zelmanovits fled to London." (Goldstein [1889–1947], who had represented the Jewish party in the Czechoslovak parliament from 1931 to 1939, had settled in Palestine in 1939 and opened a law office in Tel Aviv.)

The final meeting with the Zionists, for which Beneš was then preparing himself, did not exactly follow the scenario he had envisaged. Zelmanovits rejected the suggested triumvirate of "trustees" but, contrary to Beneš's expectations, he did not change his mind when Beneš mentioned the possibility of appointing Dr. Goldstein. Probably to the president's surprise, he agreed with the choice, pointing out only that, to the best of his knowledge, Dr. Goldstein would not be able to arrive in London from Palestine in time for the opening session of the *Státní rada,* which was to take place on December 11, 1940. He proposed that, pending Dr. Goldstein's arrival, he, Zelmanovits, should be temporarily appointed to deputize for Goldstein. The president refused, pointing out that if he should decide to appoint Goldstein, he would appoint him *ad personam,* not as a Zionist. It would therefore be out of the question that someone else should act as his stand-in. Zelmanovits interpreted this rejection as a declaration of war.

On the eve of the opening session of the *Státní rada*, the Central Council of National Jews from Czechoslovakia [28] published a declaration, dated December 10, 1940, protesting against Beneš's failure to appoint a representative of the Jewish minority to the *Státní rada*. Issued in the form of a press release, this declaration was sent not only to Beneš and to the government-in-exile but was also distributed among Jewish organizations and was given as wide publicity as possible. After pointing out that, according to the census of 1930, the last to be taken in the pre-Munich Czechoslovak Republic, fifty-three percent of the Czechoslovak citizens of the Jewish faith had declared themselves Czechoslovak citizens of Jewish nationality; that, for the twenty years of the existence of a democratic Czechoslovak Republic, this national minority had made important contributions to the welfare and prosperity of the state; and that after Munich and the subsequent German occupation of Czechoslovakia, national Jews had placed themselves at the disposal of the forces working toward the restoration of a free, democratic Czechoslovakia, the declaration went on to state:

> The representatives of the Jewish minority in Czechoslovakia regarded it as obvious that in continuation of the good tradition in the Czechoslovak Republic, the national Jews would be represented in the body which is to replace the Czechoslovak Parliament in exile.
>
> We deeply regret having to express our disappointment that until now this has not happened, and as a result the Czechoslovak State Council is meeting without having representatives of this part of the population among it.

However, the declaration (worded in a rather uncertain English) left the door open for future talks. It ended with the words: "With unshakeable belief in the ideals of the late President Liberator T. G. Masaryk, we still await that our just claim will be acceded to in the very near future." [29]

Simultaneously with the release of this declaration, Zelmanovits, now on the warpath, mobilized allies from the World Jewish Congress, the Board of Deputies of British Jews, and influential personalities from the headquarters of the World Zionist Organization and from the Jewish Agency in London. On December 16, 1940, he even visited Sir R. H. Bruce Lockhart, who reported the conversation the very next day in his communication addressed to the Foreign Secretary.[30] Before writing his report, Bruce Lockhart, as the British representative to the Czechoslovak provisional government, discussed the matter with Beneš and Jan Masaryk, "as it would be most unfortunate if a Zionist problem were to be added to the other difficulties of the Provisional Czechoslovak Government." Perhaps Bruce Lockhart was influenced by these conversations, or perhaps he himself was somewhat biased; at any rate, in the very first sentence of his report, he described Zelmanovits as "the self-styled leader of the Czechoslovak National Jews," and further on he notes that "President Beneš is also irritated by M. Zelmanovits, who had no political standing in the former Republic," though in fact Zelmanovits was the former secretary general of Czechoslovakia's Jewish party. "He is said to be a mischief-maker," Bruce Lockhart's report continued, "who has developed political ambitions in exile, and Dr. Beneš dislikes his blackmail methods and, above all, his approach to the British Jews."

Bruce Lockhart proceeded to explain what he meant by "blackmail methods." He reported that Zelmanovits's visit to Beneš had been preceded by one from Professor Lewis B. Namier ("I have considerable respect for Mr. Namier's erudition, but his scholarly and other virtues are impaired by the violence of his Zionist sentiments"), who told Bruce Lockhart much the same story as Zelmanovits and "ended it with the unpleasant statement that 'Beneš must remember that Zionist representation in the State Council is not an internal Czechoslovak problem but a matter of interest to all Zionists throughout the world.'" Bruce Lockhart did not omit to report also the personal advice he, Bruce Lockhart, had offered to the president: "President Beneš had agreed to receive Mr. Namier next week. The two men are old friends, and I have reminded the President that during the last war Mr. Namier wrote *The Case for Bohemia.* A little judicious flattery may perhaps soften the harshness of Mr. Namier's Zionism."[31]

No record could be traced about Namier's conversation with Beneš, but if it took place at all, it does not seem to have moved things one way or the other. More than three months later, on March 28, 1941, the president agreed to receive Dr. Zelmanovits once more; however, the results of the meeting were meager. In his notes written immediately after his conversation with Beneš, Zelmanovits summarized the interview as follows: "President Beneš himself would like a solution for the time being, which would be acceptable to both sides, without thereby creating any prejudice, and at the same time the question of participation on the State Council would be left open until there was general agreement." Zelmanovits also recorded that the president had promised to make a concrete proposal of a temporary solution "in a very short time."[32] However, weeks went by and no proposal from the president was forthcoming.

Zelmanovits, who may, perhaps, be criticized in some respects but certainly deserves recognition for his perseverance, apparently did not see any other way of reaching results except by asking friendly Jewish organizations to renew their intervention. It was only a few weeks later, on April 17, 1941, that Beneš received at his home the two representatives of the London section of the World Jewish Congress, who were soon followed by a delegation from the Board of Deputies of British Jews.

The response was not immediate but the efforts of Zelmanovits and his supporters were not entirely wasted. On the one hand, Beneš was anxious that his government-in-exile should not create the impression of being dominated by Jews. However, he was a realist and, while he did not overestimate the political clout of Jewish organizations, he did not want to project the image of an anti-Semite. Involving himself in an open dispute on a Jewish issue that he did not even consider of special importance, he felt, might be damaging to his world image and might even jeopardize more important goals.

At this stage Beneš was helped to resolve his dilemma by the events of history. On June 22, 1941, Hitler tore up the Ribbentrop-Molotov pact. The massive German attack on the Soviet Union helped change the attitude of Czechoslovak Communists who until then had persistently labeled the Allied struggle against Nazi Germany as an "imperialist war." Beneš now filled six of the eight vacant *Státní rada* seats with Communists; one of his appointees was Karl Kreibich, a German who had been a Communist deputy in the Czechoslovak parliament from the Sudeten region. Beneš felt this would be an opportune moment also to solve the problem of Jewish representation on the *Státní rada* and thus put an end to what he considered a tiresome matter and also avoid unpleasant repercussions.

Beneš had, in fact, been weighing an exigency plan for some time. We know from the entry in the diary of his *chef de cabinet,* Jaromír Smutný,[33] that as early as November 25, 1940, the president had been considering Dr. Angelo Goldstein as the best choice in case he could not avoid appointing a Jewish representative. "The Jews," he said to Smutný at the time (he meant the non-Zionists who might have opposed the appointment of an individual who had once represented the Jewish party in the Czechoslovak parliament), "will not be able to object because Goldstein is a Jew, and I shall appoint him as such, not as a Zionist." The president knew that there had been a conflict between Goldstein and the Czechoslovak consul general in Jerusalem, Josef M. Kadlec. Goldstein and the Zionist leadership were opposed to the consul's attempt to enlist Czechoslovak Jewish refugees in Palestine in Czechoslovak army units, because the Jewish Agency was then negotiating with the British for the creation of a separate Jewish military unit to fight against the Germans alongside the Allied forces. However, Beneš did not regard this conflict as a serious obstacle to Goldstein's appointment. "I shall approach Kadlec and ask him to make it up with Goldstein. When he hears that he [Goldstein] is likely to be appointed, he will be ready [to do] anything."[34] In December 1940 Beneš confirmed his intention to Bruce Lockhart, who wrote in his report to the foreign secretary:

> The President is prepared to nominate Dr. Goldstein, who is a prominent Zionist, as a member of the Council, not, however, as a representative of Zionism, but as a prominent former deputy of the Czechoslovak Parliament. The only drawback to this solution of the problem is the fact that Dr. Goldstein is in Palestine and cannot hope to arrive in this country for several weeks.[35]

However, it seems that later Beneš had either decided to temporize, or else the opposition inside the Czechoslovak "establishment" in Britain or in the Middle East to Goldstein's appointment had been more formidable than he had expected. For on April 17, 1941, he told Dr. Noah Barou and Sydney S. Silverman of the World Jewish Congress "that he had thought of nominating Dr. Angelo

Goldstein but that he had encountered considerable opposition from Jewish circles when they learned of this intention. Then, too, some trouble had arisen between the representative of the Czech [armed] forces in Palestine and Dr. Goldstein over the question of mobilization of Czech nationals. . . . Dr. Goldstein could not be on the State Council and at the same time pursue a policy not in accordance with such representation."

The truth is that Dr. Goldstein on his part was not really interested in moving from Tel Aviv to wartime London. Also, it seems that some Czechoslovak Zionists criticized him for having left behind in Prague those who had regarded him as their leader. This may have been a factor in his desire to remain outside the glare of publicity, which, he feared, he would not be able to avoid if he were appointed to the *Státní rada*. Another consideration may have been that Dr. Chaim Kugel,[36] the other former representative of the Jewish party in the Prague parliament, who had also emigrated to Palestine, had already relinquished his Czechoslovak citizenship and had become a naturalized citizen of what was then the British mandate of Palestine. In any event, while no one can state with certainty what Goldstein's response would have been had he actually been named to the *Státní rada*, we do know—and this fact is confirmed by private conversations and correspondence between Dr. Goldstein and some of his friends—that he seemed rather disinclined to accept.

As month after month went by without an indication that his persistent efforts would end in success and it became clear to him that he himself had hardly any chance of being appointed to the *Státní rada*, Dr. Zelmanovits came up with a final suggestion. All that time he had been in correspondence with his close friend Arnošt (Ernst) Frischer,[37] who, like Goldstein, had settled in Tel Aviv. As chairman of the Jewish party in Czechoslovakia from 1935 to 1939, Frischer had, in fact, been Zelmanovits's political chief, and he had been cooperating more closely with him than with anyone else. Zelmanovits now suggested to Frischer that he, Frischer, become a candidate for the *Státní rada* instead of Goldstein. After a somewhat protracted exchange of letters between London and Tel Aviv, Frischer agreed. But it was not until the fall of 1941 that the Central Council of National Jews from Czechoslovakia approached President Beneš to propose Arnošt Frischer as the representative of the Jewish nationality group in the *Státní rada*. On November 18, 1941, almost two years after Zelmanovits had first begun his efforts for Jewish representation in the *Státní rada*, Beneš appointed Frischer as a member of that body but not as a representative of the Jewish party, nor even explicitly as a representative of the Jewish national minority. Officially, Frischer's appointment was *ad personam*. Frischer arrived in London at the end of November and soon thereafter assumed his duties as a member of the Czechoslovak parliament-in-exile. He proved a hard-working and very conscientious representative.

THE GOVERNMENT-IN-EXILE AND THE HOLOCAUST

In June 1942, Samuel M. Zygelboim, who represented the Bundists* in the *Rada Narodowa* (National Council) of the Polish government-in-exile in London, passed on to the British press the first report that the Germans were using gas chambers for the liquidation of Jews in the concentration camps of Poland and that 700,000 Jews had already been killed in this manner. The report also spoke of pogroms organized by the Germans in the Lublin area where, according to Zygelboim's source, many Jews from Czechoslovakia had been concentrated.[38]

This report coincided with the news about the annihilation of the Czech village of Lidice as a reprisal for the assassination of Reinhard Heydrich. President Beneš received a cable of sympathy signed by the leaders of the World Jewish Congress, to which he replied: "Confident that tide will turn and that just and stern retribution will be meted out to the guilty."[39] The destruction of Lidice and the massacre of its population may have increased the awareness of both Czechoslovaks and Jews that they were struggling against a common enemy.

At about the same time, the government-in-exile was receiving information about deportations of Jews from Slovakia. It was decided to approach the Vatican and ask the Church to use its influence with the Catholic rulers of the Slovak state. On July 6, 1942, an

---

* The Bund was a Socialist, anti-Zionist Jewish workers' movement centered primarily in Eastern Europe.

official Czechoslovak delegation[40] visited the Catholic Bishop of London, Meyers, and handed him an *aide-mémoire* to be passed to his superior, Cardinal Hinsley, Archbishop of Westminster, with the request that Hinsley intervene through Rome. The *aide-mémoire* noted that, according to official reports of the Slovak Press Bureau, at least 48,000 Slovak Jews had already been deported. It described the conditions under which the deportees were compelled to live and which were "grossly at variance with the principles of Christian ethics" and "an outrage upon humanity":

> The Government of the Czechoslovak Republic, with its temporary headquarters in London, therefore begs Your Eminence to bring the above facts to the notice of the Holy See and to suggest that representations should be made to the authorities at present in charge of Slovakia, with the request that all further deportations of the Jewish inhabitants from Slovakia to Poland should be discontinued, and that those who have already been deported should be enabled to live under tolerable conditions.[41]

(It is interesting to note that one of the members of the delegation that called on Bishop Meyers was Dr. Juraj Slávik, the former Czechoslovak ambassador to Poland, now a member of the government-in-exile, who had signed the agreement with Foreign Minister Josef Beck mentioned at the outset of this article).

Bishop Meyers promised immediate energetic action and, not much later, the Vatican representative in Bratislava was indeed instructed by Rome to intervene with the Slovak authorities,[42] through his intervention could hardly be regarded as successful.

In August and September 1942, the office of the World Jewish Congress in Geneva received the incredible details of the German plan for the extermination of European Jewry. The Congress saw to it that the information reached the governments of the free nations, including the governments-in-exile with temporary headquarters in London.[43]

The Czechoslovak government-in-exile, or, more accurately, President Beneš, was then regarded in London (not entirely without justification) as having the most reliable information about developments in Germany and German-occupied Europe. The Beneš government-in-exile was therefore the first to be approached by the Jewish leadership. On September 29, Dr. Noah Barou and Alexander L. Easterman of the London section of the World Jewish Congress visited Beneš to discuss reports received about the planned mass extermination of the Jews.

According to the cable sent by Barou and Easterman after the meeting to the Executive of the World Jewish Congress in New York,[44] Beneš was surprised by the report. He undertook to put "his machinery" in motion and to investigate the matter "thoroughly." He seemed to be somewhat skeptical about the authenticity of the report, for the cable states that he strongly advised against giving publicity to the report "until [it was] fully investigated [and its] authenticity [was] reasonably established." He feared that the report might be Nazi propaganda planted to "provoke reaction giving them excuse [to] extend outrages."

For more than a month Barou and Easterman heard nothing from Beneš. On November 6, 1942, Easterman wrote to Beneš, reminding him of his promise to make "enquiries regarding the information contained in the report," and asking whether the "result of [the] enquiries" had "enabled [him] to form any definitive conclusions upon the authenticity of the report."[45] The president's reply, which is better quoted here in full, was dated November 11, 1942, one day after the president had received a visit in the same matter from Arnošt Frischer, the Jewish member of the *Státní rada.*

Dear Mr. Easterman,
I was just about to inform you of the results of my enquiries, when I received your letter of November 6th.
As I told already Mr. Frischer when he came to see me yesterday, I obtained two replies to my enquiries and both were rather in a negative sense. According to my reports there seem to be no positive indications that the Germans should be preparing a plan for a wholesale extermination of all the Jews. From the reports which I have at present in hand, it would appear that such a plan does not exist and I therefore cannot give you any confirmation of the information which you received in this matter.
This, of course, does not mean to say that the Germans are not going perhaps to proceed against the Jews with ever growing brutality. In fact, the more they see that they themselves are lost, the more will their fury and their terror increase—against the Jews as well as against the other subjugated peoples. But this has, in my opinion, nothing to do with any special plan such as you mentioned when you and your delegation came to see me. And my doubts regarding the existence of any such plan are further

strengthened by the fact that, although innumerable Jews are being terribly persecuted and practically starved, there are others, however small their number may be, who still remain in their original places and even are almost unhindered.

I shall continue, however, to follow the matter and I shall let you know any further information which I might obtain in the matter.

Yours sincerely,
(s) E. BENEŠ[46]

In retrospect, of course, Beneš's letter reflects, to say the least, a lamentable lack of insight. Many other great statesmen of that time shared with President Beneš the inability to believe the unbelievable, but few went on record in the regrettable way that he did in his letter to Easterman. Yet, though the views expressed in this letter can hardly be defended, it is only fair to say a few words about the difficult circumstances under which Beneš was working at the time. For several months during the second half of 1942, the Czechoslovak government-in-exile had been virtually cut off from all radio contact with the resistance movement at home because the Germans had succeeded in discovering and destroying all the underground transmitters. Thus, the flow of information between Prague and London during that particular period was very thin. The reports that arrived that year from occupied Czechoslovakia, as far as could be ascertained, did not show any signs of serious concern on the part of the Czechoslovak populace for the fate of Czechoslovak Jewry, and certainly even less for the fate of the Jews in general. Indeed, some of the reports from Czechoslovakia that reached London contained expressions of hope that, after the war, Jewish influence in all spheres would be limited to a minimum. Finally, it can hardly be denied that among those responsible for the gathering of information from German-occupied Europe there were elements interested in keeping certain intelligence from the president and in a position to do so. Whatever led Beneš in the end to write to Easterman as he did, it certainly was not lack of sympathy or goodwill on the part of the Czechoslovak government-in-exile. As a matter of fact, the minister of foreign affairs, Jan Masaryk, perhaps did more than others in the public outcry that followed soon, even before any of the Allied governments had confirmed the report received by the World Jewish Congress. On October 29, 1942, thirteen days before

Beneš had sent his letter, a mass protest meeting was held at the Albert Hall in London, with Masaryk one of the principal speakers, along with Dr. William Temple, Archbishop of Canterbury; Lord Robert Cecil of Chelwood (a main architect of the Covenant of the League of Nations and then president of the League of Nations Union), and General Wladyslaw Sikorski, head of the Polish government-in-exile. Masaryk's speech received the loudest applause of all. Perhaps the following paragraph from his address should be quoted here:

> In my country the Jews were equal citizens with us all. We had no troubles. And when Czechoslovakia again takes its rightful place in the heart of Europe, our Jewish brethren will be welcome and I count on their cooperation in building up what Hitler has destroyed. My love, my prayers, my understanding go out to the Jews today and every day. We owe them a frightful debt.[47]

There is no record of any further communication from President Beneš to the World Jewish Congress in the matter of the report from Geneva, but no further comment was necessary, because only ten days after the unfortunate letter from Beneš, the U.S. Department of State invited Rabbi Stephen S. Wise, a founder of the World Jewish Congress and then president of the American Jewish Congress, to Washington in order to inform him that the sad, shocking truth of the report could now be officially confirmed. This confirmation was announced by the Jewish Agency in Jerusalem on November 22.

Now that the reports of the Nazi plan and its implementation had been verified beyond the shadow of a doubt, the Czechoslovak *Státní rada* held a special session on December 15, 1942, at which the deputy chairman, Jožka David, read a declaration condemning all those responsible for the barbarism against the Jews. The declaration ended with the following words:

> We know that the most effective medicine against this German plague is a quick victory. However, we have to do already today what can be done. It is necessary that the Allied governments already today should make a clear declaration on behalf of all decent people in the world. A common protest has to be made and a declaration of common responsibility of all those who take part in whatever way in the realization of the plans of the German

devils. It is necessary also to attempt relief actions wherever possible. Every child that can be torn from the claws of the murderers must be saved. Just as it would have been an eternal shame for our nation had we in any way participated in the work of the German hellhounds, whatever we do to help our suffering Jewish fellow citizens will forever serve our honor.[48]

On the next day, December 16, 1942, Foreign Secretary Anthony Eden, on behalf of all the Allied governments, read in the House of Commons a similar condemnation of the Nazi atrocities against the Jews. On the same day British Zionist women organized a protest meeting in London's Wigmore Hall to which President Beneš's wife sent a strongly worded message.[49] That evening, Dr. Hubert Ripka, the Beneš government's deputy foreign minister in charge of information,[50] broadcast to the people of Czechoslovakia a warning that "the massacres of the Jews are only a dress rehearsal for the massacres of other enslaved nations."[51]

It is true that these declarations did not go beyond words, but then it seems that no one would have been capable of doing much more at the time. In December 1942 Moshe Shertok (later Sharett), who was then the head of the Jewish Agency's political department, was visiting London from Jerusalem and saw Jan Masaryk, with whom he had been on friendly terms for many years. The main—and difficult—subject of their talk was the planned establishment of special Jewish armed units to fight alongside the Allied forces and the possibility of transferring Jewish members of Czechoslovak armed forces to these units. In the course of the conversation Masaryk and Shertok also discussed the desperate situation of European Jewry. Shertok was able to paint additional black shadows on the somber picture already known. Yet, when Masaryk asked what concrete contribution the Czechoslovak government-in-exile might make to alleviate the plight of the Jews in Nazi Europe, Shertok could not give him a clear reply. Nevertheless, certain things, though of course they appeared tragically paltry when measured against the immense extent of the catastrophe, were done. For instance, the representatives of the Czechoslovak government-in-exile in Geneva, Stockholm, and Lisbon were instructed to assist in the rescue of individuals and small groups wherever feasible. They were also allotted funds for this work as well as for sending food parcels through the Red Cross to Terezín and to Jewish deportees in Poland.[52] It can be said that, however limited the results of these efforts, the Czechoslovak government-in-exile certainly did not do less than other Allied governments of that time.

The efforts also continued later. In March 1943 a report reached London that the Germans were ready to allow 3,000 Jews from Slovakia to emigrate to Palestine. Czechoslovak authorities in London passed the news on to Fritz Lichtenstern (later Peretz Leshem), the head of the *HeHalutz* office in London, and to Berl Locker, the London-based member of the Jewish Agency Executive. The difficulties, as described by Locker, were that at the time the only Palestine immigration certificates available were for children, that there were no transportation facilities from Slovakia to Rumania, from where Jewish refugees still could make their way to Palestine, and that the Turkish authorities were refusing to issue transit visas to Jews on their way to Palestine. Nevertheless, the Jewish Agency sent Salomon Adler-Rudel to Stockholm to cooperate with Vladimír Kučera, the representative of the Czechoslovak government-in-exile there, and Jan Masaryk contacted the British to discuss the possibility of making 3,000 additional certificates available for these special cases.[53]

Another Czechoslovak rescue initiative resulted from a meeting between Alexander Easterman, who was then the political secretary of the London section of the World Jewish Congress, and Dr. Hubert Ripka, on March 18, 1943. Easterman came prepared with concrete suggestions for help to the remaining European Jews, both during the war and immediately after the liberation. Impressed by Easterman's exposé, Ripka approached the foreign ministers of all the Allied governments-in-exile based in London. At Ripka's suggestion a jointly signed cable was sent to Foreign Secretary Anthony Eden, who was then in Washington, asking him to raise the problem of assistance to the Jews in his talks with American authorities. The British Foreign Office had, in fact, proposed joint consultations with the Americans on this subject as early as January 1943, but the cable from the Allied foreign ministers may well have been the factor that led to the convening of the Anglo-American Conference on Refugees, which met in Bermuda in April 1943. The Czechoslovak initiators could hardly be blamed for the complete failure of the conference, which, after prolonged negotiations, did not succeed in saving a single Jew.

Only after this failure did the Americans create a special body, the War Refugee Board, to aid the Jews who still survived in Nazi Europe. One of the concrete decisions taken by the United States was that whenever U.S. forces liberated a German concentration camp, the Americans would see to it that the inmates would be moved without delay to an area well behind the Allied battle lines. This was intended to avoid a recurrence of the tragedy that befell the survivors of a camp in Yugoslavia which had been liberated by Soviet and partisan forces, only to be recaptured by the Germans while the inmates were still there.

Hubert Ripka was informed of these and other developments by Nahum Goldmann, the president of the World Jewish Congress, at a dinner given by Goldmann in London on February 28, 1944.[54] This was the first meeting between Goldmann and the Czechoslovak Deputy Foreign Minister, but Ripka immediately won Goldmann's trust. Goldmann confided to Ripka that while the British were not likely to create anything similar to the U.S. War Refugee Board, the World Jewish Congress was negotiating with the Polish government-in-exile for the establishment of such an organization. He also told Ripka that a major conference of world Jewry was planned for May 1944 in the United States, in which even representatives of Soviet Jewry might participate. He asked Ripka that it be made possible for Arnošt Frischer, the Jewish member of the Czechoslovak *Státní rada,* to attend also. Finally, Dr. Goldmann took the opportunity to express to Ripka the gratitude of world Jewry for the many pronouncements by leading Czechoslovak statesmen condemning anti-Semitism and for all the efforts which the Czechoslovak government-in-exile had been making to help Jews. "We do not thank you too often," he said, "because it became quite natural for world Jewry to see in Czechoslovakia one of those few countries where Jews can always expect to be treated decently and with justice. In [the case of] Poland we have to be happy [with] every positive step. With you we take it for granted. But that does not make our gratitude any less deeply felt."[55]

Among the many condemnations of anti-Semitism from Czechoslovak leaders to which Goldmann referred, perhaps at least one more deserves to be quoted here. On September 29, 1943, the Jewish New Year, Jan Masaryk said in a broadcast from London to Czechoslovakia:

Jews in their rich history have suffered much, but none of their sufferings was as horrible, unbearable, and massive as the present ones. The fate of the Jews could teach our generation what anti-Semitism can lead to. . . . It all started with anti-Semitism and ended with war. . . . It is true that every nation can be judged by its behavior toward the Jews. We have behaved decently. . . . Anti-Semitism is barbarism and shame, which will forever remain a mark of disgrace [upon] the Germans. . . . For us it must serve as a reminder that anti-Semitism is only the first step toward pan-Germanism. With the second step they would drive the knife into our backs. The Jews today are suffering even more than anyone else. In the Polish ghettos things are even worse than in Dachau and Oranienburg. I beg you to help them wherever you can.[56]

THE GOVERNMENT-IN-EXILE AND JEWISH NATIONAL MINORITY RIGHTS

Although the appointment of Arnošt Frischer to the *Státní rada* was explicitly characterized as *ad personam*, those national Jews from Czechoslovakia who had not settled in Palestine or relinquished their Czechoslovak citizenship and had no further interest in legal ties with the "old country" felt that they now had in the government-in-exile a representative of their own who would safeguard their interests as a national minority group. However, it should have been clear to them from the beginning that the Jews in Czechoslovakia could not expect a restoration of their political rights as a national minority after the war. The most they could hope for was the enactment of legal guarantees to protect their rights as a religious minority.

It must be remembered that from the very outset the national minority rights of the Jews in Czechoslovakia had not been based on a solid consensus of opinion. When, immediately after World War I, the constitution of the Czechoslovak Republic was under discussion, the recognition of the Jews as a separate national minority group under the law of the land was opposed even by certain Jewish circles.[57] One of the firmest opponents of legislation establishing national minority rights for the Jews in Czechoslovakia had been Dr. Alfred Meissner, an assimilated Jew and a Social Democratic member of the Czechoslovak parliament, who had acted as reporter for the parliamentary constitutional committee. (Meissner was to serve as Minister of Justice in 1920 and again from 1929 to 1934.)

It was only due to the insistence of President Tomáš G. Masaryk that a compromise solution was worked out. The constitution adopted by the Czechoslovak Republic on February 29, 1920, did not define the concept of a "nationality group," nor did it enumerate the nationality groups or national minorities to be recognized by the state. However, it was explicitly made clear in the *Důvodová zpráva,* the official explanatory report adopted along with the constitution, that these omissions had been made on purpose so that any Czechoslovak citizen who so desired could declare himself a member of the Jewish nationality group and do so freely in population censuses, national elections, and any other acts where his conscience required it. But even if the constitution of 1920 had been more explicit in defining the national minority rights of the Jews, it is highly questionable whether such provisions could have been relevant to the conditions that could be expected to follow World War II.

We know from the diary of Jaromír Smutný that as early as 1940 President Beneš expressed doubts about the future of national minority rights in postwar Czechoslovakia: "We do not know what will eventuate in connection with the minorities after the war. Maybe they will be completely removed."[58] In March 1941 Beneš candidly told Dr. Leo Zelmanovits that while he recognized the principle of "continuity" in matters of foreign policy, he did not feel bound by that principle in matters of domestic policy, including national minority rights.[59] The president's attitude became clear beyond any doubt early in 1944, when Beneš already had spoken quite openly to his biographer Compton Mackenzie[60] about moving the German population out of Czechoslovakia after the war. In fact, according to Mackenzie, Beneš had already obtained the approval of Churchill, Stalin, and Roosevelt for such a step in 1943.[61]

After such a proposed solution of the German minority problem (and there was no reason to believe that the Hungarian minority would have fared much differently) it would hardly have been realistic to expect that the Jews in postwar Czechoslovakia could have retained their prewar national minority rights unchanged. At this point we might mention an incident which Beneš related to Dr.

Noah Barou and Sydney Silverman when they visited him on April 17, 1941. It seems that during the Peace Conference at Versailles, the American delegation had attempted to insert clauses for the protection of Jewish minorities in the treaties with the "succession states." The representatives of Poland (Ignace Jan Paderewski) and Rumania (Ion Bratianu) were ready to accept such clauses, but Beneš, who was then the foreign minister of the new Czechoslovak Republic, refused to sign. "He explained to President Wilson that it would be an insult to his country if he signed such a clause and said that it would only provoke anti-Semitism. He then asked President Wilson whether he [Wilson] would sign a similar clause for the United States. President Wilson had laughed and the matter had been dropped."[62]

It should be clear that beyond equality before the law, security from discrimination, and their rights as a religious minority, anything the Jews of Czechoslovakia obtained under the constitution of 1920 was due to the personal attitude and influence of Tomáš G. Masaryk. At the same time, it must be said to the credit of Masaryk's successor, Eduard Beneš, that he loyally continued the policies introduced by Masaryk and never attempted to change them. Beneš also upheld Masaryk's pro-Zionist policy. However, confronted by a new situation, when the shock of the German occupation had led him to reassess the entire complex of national minority problems, it seemed to him that the problem of the Jewish minority required a new approach as well.

In dealing with the question of Jewish national minority rights in postwar Czechoslovakia, Beneš now sought to turn his pro-Zionist attitude to his advantage. According to Dr. Zelmanovits, Beneš had already stated early in 1941 that "the granting of minority rights will not need to be taken into account as far as the Jews are concerned. . . . After the establishment of a Jewish state [in Palestine] it will be up to the Jews in the countries where they live to decide whether they are for Palestine or for assimilation [in the national sense of the term] to the people of the country where they live."[63]

Two years later, on May 21, 1943, in a conversation in Washington with Nahum Goldmann and Stephen S. Wise, Beneš expressed "serious doubts concerning the wisdom of demanding simultaneously a Jewish state and minority rights in the countries where Jews live."[64] Beneš's statement came as something of a shock to the leaders of the World Jewish Congress, who, as Goldmann put it, regarded this view as "difficult to identify with the liberal ideas that he [Beneš] had always upheld." When Goldmann explained that all the Jews wanted was "recognition of the fact that there is a Jewish people in the world, that the Jewish citizens of the various states have the right to remain members of the Jewish people, that they may continue to instruct their children in the Hebrew language and in Jewish values, to display a deep interest in Palestine and in the Jewish fate everywhere, to cultivate their heritage and cultural ties," and when he concluded that this was really all that the World Jewish Congress meant when it spoke of minority rights, Beneš retorted, "Whoever told you that I oppose such legitimate demands misunderstood me."[65]

In fact, there had been no basic change in Beneš's personal ideas and attitudes, but he was faced with a radically changed situation to which, realist that he was, he had to adapt all his political decisions, including those concerning national minorities. Not even he could have guessed then how irrelevant the restoration of Jewish national minority rights would become in view of the almost vanishing Jewish remnant that returned to Czechoslovakia after the war.

THE GOVERNMENT-IN-EXILE AND THE ZIONIST LEADERSHIP

The change in their approach to national minority rights did not imply a change in the pro-Zionist views held by the leaders of the Czechoslovak government-in-exile. Nevertheless, during the early months of World War II there was a sudden clash of interests that threatened to develop into a serious crisis in relations between the Czechoslovak government-in-exile and the Zionist leadership.

Of those Jews who had come to Palestine from Czechoslovakia, there were, at the time World War II broke out, over 6,000 who had not formally relinquished their Czechoslovak citizenship. The overwhelming majority of the immigrants from Czechoslovakia regarded Palestine as their new, or, perhaps more accurately put, their old-new motherland, where they expected to remain for good. However, under the British mandatory law in force at the time, a Jewish immigrant could opt for Palestine citizenship only two years after his legal immigration into the country. "Illegal" immigrants—individuals who had entered Palestine and remained in there without the official immigration certificate issued by the British authorities—did not have this option at all. But even many Czechoslovak Jews who had entered Palestine as legal immigrants were in no hurry to give up their old citizenship not out of any wish to return to Czechoslovakia after the war but because of the widespread, though unfounded, assumption that restitution for everything they had been forced to leave behind in the "old country" would be easier, or perhaps at all possible, to obtain only if they remained citizens of Czechoslovakia.

However, as far as the Czechoslovak government-in-exile was concerned, retention of Czechoslovak citizenship, no matter how motivated, meant that such individuals had retained not only the rights but also the obligations of Czechoslovak citizens. Thus, on April 4, 1940, the Czechoslovak consulate general in Jerusalem published a general mobilization proclamation for Czechoslovak citizens residing in Palestine.[66] This call was not only unwelcome to many Jews from Czechoslovakia who regarded Palestine, not Czechoslovakia, as their permanent home but it met with opposition also from the political leadership of the Jewish Agency for Palestine. A similar call to arms had already been issued in October 1939 and had been answered by some 1,200 Jewish volunteers.[67] But while that early call had been merely in the nature of an appeal for volunteers, the proclamation issued in April 1940 read more like a compulsory draft notice. It stipulated expressly that the notice was applicable to all males between the ages of eighteen and fifty "irrespective of whether they [had ever] served in the Czechoslovak army or not." It seems that the idea behind this notice was not necessarily immediate induction but merely to have those eligible for army service register with recruiting commissions so that the Czechoslovak authorities might know how many males from Palestine would be available for service when needed. The information bulletin issued by the consulate general stated: "Conscription will be on the basis of voluntary enlistment, but it is obligatory for all Czechoslovak citizens to present themselves before the recruiting commissions, and failure to comply [with this notice] will be judged according to the laws of [postwar independent] Czechoslovakia."[68] The proclamation was even more explicit on this point. It included a statement to the effect that those who failed to obey this order would be regarded as deserters.

The Czechoslovak authorities in exile—represented, in this case, by Consul General Josef M. Kadlec in Jerusalem—were acting with the knowledge and approval of the British mandatory authorities in Palestine and were well within their rights. However, it was equally clear that, mostly because of their need to mobilize the largest possible number of men in the shortest possible time, the Czechoslovak authorities in Palestine did not show the slightest understanding for the fact that the situation of Czechoslovak Jews in Palestine was, in most cases, quite different from that of Czechoslovak emigrés in any other country.

The mobilization notice came as a shock to the leaders of the Czechoslovak Zionists who had settled in Palestine. Consul General Kadlec complained about their campaign against the notice. The clash was not kept out of the press,[69] a fact that added to Kadlec's annoyance. The possibility that Czechoslovak Jews who had settled in Palestine might be drafted into the Czechoslovak army set off consternation among the Zionist leadership not only for obvious reasons but also because, as already indicated earlier, the Jewish Agency was conducting negotiations with the British government for the formation of an all-Jewish military force to fight under the Allied command as a "Jewish brigade." As it was, the negotiations proved to be long and arduous; the British government did not authorize the formation of the Jewish Brigade Group until four years later, on August 17, 1944. Clearly, the acceptance of the Czechoslovak mobilization order by Czechoslovak Jews in Palestine would have seriously weakened the Jewish Agency's position in the struggle for the Jewish military unit. That is why the Zionist leadership found it imperative to fight against the mobilization order issued by Consul General Kadlec.

In this situation the personal friendship between Foreign Minister Jan Masaryk and Leo Herrmann, the Czech-born secretary general of *Keren HaYesod,* one of the major financial institutions of the World Zionist Organization, proved an important asset.[70] Herrmann initially suggested a compromise, namely, "to form the Czechoslovak Jews into a unit to be trained in Palestine, for the present as part of the Czechoslovak army."[71] This was, of course, hardly a realistic solution. It would have meant actually dividing the Czechoslovak armed forces in the Middle East into two distinct parts, the larger Jewish and the smaller non-Jewish, a fact which certainly would have been eagerly exploited by enemy propaganda and which, in addition, would probably have led to an increase of tension and anti-Semitism.

Another way had to be found. On April 10, 1940, six days after the issuance of the mobilization notice, Moshe Shertok (Sharett), head of the Jewish Agency's political department in Jerusalem, visited Consul General Kadlec in Jerusalem. On that occasion Kadlec assured him that while "every Czechoslovak citizen was bound to appear before the Examination Committee . . . , only those who would volunteer their services would actually be enlisted for service with the Czechoslovak Units in France."[72] On the same day, Lewis B. Namier, representing the London Executive of the Jewish Agency, was sent to Masaryk to explain to him "that the position of the Jews who had gone back to the Jewish National Home [i.e., Palestine] was radically different from that of Jews resident in other countries" and to ask "whether some instructions could be given to M. Kadlec not to press in the matter of calling them up."[73]

Masaryk promised to act. However, the fast-moving events of the war, including the fall of France and the evacuation of Czechoslovak troops from that country, made communications between Jerusalem and London difficult. As a result, Masaryk's intervention did not come until the end of July 1940, in the form of a letter from Masaryk to Leo Herrmann. To this letter Masaryk had attached a personal letter addressed to Kadlec, which he asked Herrmann to hand to the consul general.[74] In this letter Masaryk requested Kadlec in the future to discuss all matters involving Jewish interests with Herrmann and "not to take any steps affecting Jewish status or interests of Czechoslovak Jews in Palestine without prior consultations" with him.

Herrmann handed Masaryk's letter to Kadlec on July 31, 1940. The consul general "promised to act accordingly," yet his promise was not carried out to the last dot and so, on November 10, 1940, Herrmann had to visit Kadlec again to remind him of Masaryk's letter and, in particular, of the fact that "Mr. Masaryk explicitly stressed that he definitely recognizes in principle that Jews who migrate to Palestine in order to settle there are not to be prevented from doing so—even if they still hold Czech passports and are formally considered to be Czech nationals—so that they may fulfill their obligations as Jews and Zionists without their loyalty to their country of origin being doubted." Now, Herrmann continued, he had learned of a number of cases of Jews from Czechoslovakia in Palestine who at the time had not registered for the Czechoslovak army and were now having difficulties in getting their Czechoslovak passports renewed. Kadlec assured him that this was probably due only to some misunderstanding, because "obviously every Czech in Palestine, whether or not he had reported when registration for the Czech army had been announced, could have his [Czechoslovak] passport renewed and would be treated like any other Czech national."[75]

In the same report Leo Herrmann mentions that Masaryk had discussed also with Beneš the attitude of Jewish immigrants toward Palestine and the problem of their undoubted loyalty to their country of origin. We know from Jaromír Smutný's diary that, though Beneš knew Kadlec was opposed to the appointment of Angelo Goldstein to the *Státní rada,* this did not influence Beneš's decision to name Goldstein. "That is understandable," Beneš is reported to have remarked concerning Kadlec's attitude, "for Goldstein was not too pleased when Kadlec took the recruits away from him. [In the end Kadlec] failed and that is what Goldstein really wanted."[76]

Of course, it was difficult for Kadlec to accept the idea that Herrmann, because of his personal friendship with Foreign Minister Masaryk, should be able virtually to overrule the Jerusalem consulate in matters concerning Jewish immigrants from Czechoslovakia. Kadlec found some allies among the military. Thus strengthened, he was able to exercise certain counterpressures. Though the tug-of-war was quiet on the whole, it continued for quite a long time. In fact, the problem was finally resolved only in June 1942, when General Sergěj Ingr, Minister of National Defense in the Czechoslovak government-in-exile, visited the Czechoslovak units in the Middle East. On June 19, he met with Moshe Shertok and Leo Herrmann.[77] Although, at least in the beginning of the war, Ingr had not been known for a particularly positive attitude toward Jewish participation in the Czechoslovak resistance (at one point, as we have already indicated, he characterized the Jews in the Czechoslovak army as an "unreliable and undesirable element"),[78] the conversation between the minister of national defense and the two Zionist officials was conducted in a very friendly spirit. Ingr even expressed admiration for the constructive work done by the Jews in Palestine. Shertok stressed that "the Jewish Agency was anxious that Czechoslovak Jews should be allowed to manifest their allegiance to Palestine and the Jewish National Home—whether they had already acquired Palestinian citizenship or not—by not being forced to join the Czechoslovak army." General Ingr assured the Jewish Agency representatives that "no compulsion was being exercised."[79]

Reporting to the London Executive of the Jewish Agency a few days later, Herrmann noted to this point:

> The . . . Proclamation did not threaten direct compulsion, a point expressly confirmed by Lieut. General Ingr. . . . The wording of the call to enlist in the Czechoslovak Army had it that "every Czechoslovak national would be certain to respond to the call so that already now the representative authorities abroad and later on the military as well as the civic authorities at home, when Czechoslovakia would be free again, should be able to treat him as a citizen of legal standing."
>
> Owing to the complex nature of the conditions under which many Jews had come to Palestine in recent years, this warning was bound to produce considerable effect. For a large number of them had come as refugees, often leaving their families and belongings behind. As refugees they are debarred from acquiring Palestine nationality. Even the people who intend to remain permanently in Palestine are handicapped in making plans for the future owing to the uncertainty of their national status, that is to say of the risk they run of losing their Czechoslovak citizenship and passport here and now without any certainty of being able to acquire Palestine nationality. . . .
>
> In spite of the attitude taken up by *Hitachdut Olei Czechoslovakia* [the organization of Jewish immigrants from Czechoslovakia in Palestine and later in Israel] . . . a relatively large number of Czechoslovak Jews, estimated at about 1,500, answered the call to register, including a fair proportion of officers of the reserve. . . .
>
> Though the Czechoslovak authorities exercised no compulsion, their propaganda was of a pretty comprehensive nature; hence the Jews who did not or could not acquire Palestine nationality and in preference to joining the Czechoslovak forces joined, or intend to join, the British forces, ran the danger of being regarded as deserters from the Czechoslovak point of view.[80]

These were some of the arguments used by representatives of the Jewish Agency in the conversation with General Ingr. In the discussion that followed, Herrmann summed up the stand of *Hitachdut Olei Czechoslovakia* (with which the Jewish Agency identified) as follows:

> All Jews who have come to this country with the intention of making it their and their children's home should join the British Army, whilst those Jews who had come for a temporary stay and intended eventually to return to Czechoslovakia belonged into the Czechoslovak Army. Naturally this did not apply to people who intended returning to Czechoslovakia solely for the purpose of taking out their relatives, or attend[ing] to business matters. But should they wish to remain [in Czechoslovakia] permanently, the Czechoslovak Government, people and Army had an absolutely legitimate claim on them. . . . Naturally, Jewish nationals could also join the Czechoslovak Army (and, in fact, many professing Jewish nationality had joined the Czechoslovak Army in England), but the principle (outlined above) should be recognized as the guiding one, always allowing for border[line] cases to be judged on their [individual] merits.[81]

General Ingr "readily accepted the above presentation" and from that point on the principle agreed upon became the basis for solving all problems connected with the drafting of Czechoslovak Jewish immigrants in Palestine into the Czechoslovak armed forces. The principle was set forth in writing in a "Memorandum on the Status of the Jews from Czechoslovakia who have come to Palestine,"[82] which was handed to Ingr on that occasion on behalf of *the Hitachdut Olei Czechoslovakia.*[83]

THE GOVERNMENT-IN-EXILE AND THE JEWISH HOMELAND

The pro-Zionist tendency among the leaders of the Czechoslovak government-in-exile can be traced from the beginning of World War II to its very end. At least Beneš and Jan Masaryk persevered in the same line also after their return to Prague following the war. Some believe that this was merely a continuation of the direction set by Tomáš G. Masaryk. Some skeptics, however, claim that the Czechoslovaks found Zionism, with its aim of settling Jews in Palestine, the Jewish National Home, a welcome help in solving their troublesome minority problem.

Beneš was convinced that a Jewish state would be established after the war. He said so as early as March 1944,[84] and again to Dr.

Noah Barou and Sydney S. Silverman of the World Jewish Congress a month later, when he explicitly promised that "he and his government would do their best to facilitate finding a reasonable settlement of the Jewish question after the war."[85] In fact, there is an even earlier statement to this effect in a letter written by Deputy Foreign Minister Hubert Ripka to Chaim Weizmann on the occasion of the Annual Conference of the Zionist Federation in London on October 20, 1940. It was also Ripka who, at a reception given by the World Jewish Congress on May 29, 1942, in honor of Arnošt Frischer, declared in a toast that after the war the Jewish problem must not be left in the hands of individual states but "must be solved on a world scale and in a world forum."[86]

Many statements, speeches, and declarations of Jewish interest were made by members of the Czechoslovak government-in-exile. All these statements are pro-Jewish. Many of them are frankly pro-Zionist. At least a few of them should be quoted in this study. For instance, when the Zionist Federation in London arranged a mass rally on October 30, 1942, to mark the twenty-fifth anniversary of the Balfour Declaration, both President Beneš and Foreign Minister Jan Masaryk sent written messages to Chaim Weizmann. (Both messages are quoted in their original English text.) In his message, Beneš said:

The Balfour Declaration, the twenty-fifth anniversary of which you are celebrating in these days, found us Czechoslovaks also in the middle of a struggle for independent state life. This contributed certainly also to the fact that we Czechoslovaks have always been following with sympathies the Zionist efforts for the creation of a Jewish National Home in Palestine. My great predecessor and teacher T. G. Masaryk recalls in his Memoirs, how deeply impressed he was in November 1917 by the manifestation of 150,000 Jews in Kijev who gathered in front of the British Consulate in order to express their thanks for the Balfour Declaration. He also recalls the conference of small nations, which under Masaryk's chairmanship took place in Philadelphia in October 1918. The memorable declaration about the common aims of small nations was then signed also by a representative of the Zionists.

I am mentioning these reminiscences from World War I to remind you of the vivid connections that had existed from the very beginning between our and your struggle for liberation. In the quarter of a century since the Balfour Declaration, the Jews in Palestine have done a great deal. I believe they will be able to continue this work in their National Home with an even greater success after this war. Its nearing end binds us with the [additional] tie of [a] common[ly shared] victory.[87]

Jan Masaryk's message was, as usual, more emotional:

> Twenty-five years ago, the Balfour Declaration gave the Jewish people hope for the future. None of us could have even dreamt then what was in store for them. My Government and myself want to assure you of our deep sympathy and understanding. I personally shall never rest till human dignity is returned to those sons and daughters of Israel who will escape alive out of the Teutonic Beelzebub's clutches. Palestine is almost the only star in the stormy sky of present-day iniquity. I hope and pray that the United Nations will succeed in destroying Hitler before his devilish plan of annihilation is realized. There is not a minute to be lost. There are too many graves already.[88]

An even higher degree of mutual understanding than that shown in these and similar public declarations is reflected in conversations of Beneš and Jan Masaryk with leading Jewish personalities of the time. The close friendship between Masaryk and Chaim Weizmann is well known but several extant documents show how openly world Jewish leaders discussed some of their most confidential political moves also with President Beneš. Beneš's belief in a Jewish state—and in his conversations he consistently spoke of a Jewish "state," not merely of a "Jewish National Home" in Palestine[89]—was so strong that Jewish leaders did not hesitate to involve him in important missions.

Thus, a letter from Rabbi Stephen S. Wise to President Beneš, written on November 12, 1943, contains the following passage that reflects the relationship between the two men:

> May I . . . remind you of the interview which you granted to Dr. Goldmann and myself in Washington, when we discussed the attitude of Soviet Russia to[ward] our affairs? At your request we submitted to you a short memorandum on the subject which, I hope, is still in your possession.
> Since then I have had the pleasure of a talk with [Soviet ambassador Ivan] Maisky during his last visit to this country, and found him favorably disposed towards the idea of a Jewish Commonwealth in Palestine.
> I think that an inquiry from you might perhaps elicit more clearly the attitude of the Soviet Government, and indicate whether they would be willing to support our claim before the Council of the United Nations.[90]

In his autobiography Nahum Goldmann cites another case in point:

> When President Beneš . . . went to Moscow in March 1945, he had promised Weizmann and me to raise the Palestine question with Stalin. Upon his return he told us that he had indeed spoken briefly about Palestine with Stalin, who had said that he knew serious wrong had been done to the Jewish people in recent years and he would do everything he could do to make up for it. Beneš was to assure his Jewish friends that they need not worry about the position of the Soviet Union.[91]

At the time, of course, this message from Stalin was received as news of great significance.

POSTWAR CZECHOSLOVAKIA

But notwithstanding all these manifestations of personal and political friendship, postwar realities in Czechoslovakia, notably the rather unexpected strength of the Communist party immediately after the war, made it difficult for Beneš and his new Czechoslovak government to fulfill all the expectations of the Jews. In December 1945 Alexander L. Easterman visited Prague on behalf of the World Jewish Congress. In his conversations with President Beneš and Prime Minister Zdeněk Fierlinger, who during the war years had represented the Czechoslovak government-in-exile in Moscow, Easterman discussed problems outlined in the report of the executive officers to the National Conference of the World Jewish Congress (British section), which took place in London on May 12, 1946:

Bohemia and Moravia
It is to be deeply regretted that in the liberated democratic state of Czechoslovakia the position of Jews has become difficult and uncertain. . . . The long years of Nazi occupation and the persistent inculcation of Nazi doctrines has left an aftermath of which anti-Semitism is a principal factor. . . . Jews have lost their national minority status; they must be either Czechs or Slovaks. . . . Little has been done to restore their possessions to them or to compensate them, despite the proclaimed policy of the Government for restitution to the victims of Nazi persecution and the enactments published to give effect to it. . . . Jews who were technically of German nationality . . . [though] victims of Nazi persecution, are still deemed liable,

as Germans, to expatriation and confiscation of their property. Having been discriminated against by the Germans, these Jews are now being discriminated against by Czechoslovakia.

Slovakia
In Slovakia, the Jewish situation is one causing the gravest anxiety. Anti-Semitism is virulent as before the war. . . . The autonomous Government contains a large proportion, many of them in leading positions, of avowed anti-Semites who served the Fascist Government under the Nazi regime. They have obstructed and failed to carry out the decrees for restitution of Jewish and other property confiscated and stolen during the war; many of the Government officials are themselves the benefactors of this confiscation and spoliation. . . .

Subcarpathian Ruthenia
Under the . . . Treaty by which this territory was ceded by Czechoslovakia to the Soviet Union, the Jews were refused the right to opt for Czech or Slovak nationality. Before the Treaty was entered into, about 6,000 Subcarpathian Jews emigrated to Bohemia and Moravia and applied for Czechoslovak citizenship.[92] This . . . has not yet been granted to them and they are under threat of forced repatriation. . . .

In his report to the London conference on his conversations with Beneš and Fierlinger, Easterman stated:

Both gave assurances that discriminatory measures would not be taken against the Jews . . . but [that] Jews would be accorded full equality and freedom and that restitution of their stolen and confiscated property would be carried out.[93]

And he adds:

There can be no question of the goodwill and good intentions of the Président and Government of Czechoslovakia, but it must be stated with regret that these assurances have not, as yet, been put into practical effect.[94]

But despite the fact that the situation described above caused a certain tension and made for increased Jewish emigration from postwar Czechoslovakia, particularly to Palestine, the basic pro-Zionist attitude of the Czechoslovak government had not changed. In October 1945, when the *Keren HaYesod* celebrated its twenty-fifth anniversary,[95] Jan Masaryk sent the following handwritten message:

For 25 years the KH has been working and achieving remarkable results. Today, when the war is over—as far as the field of battle is concerned—the war which the Jewish people are waging in order to save the remaining small minority of the supermartyrs is far from finished. I have often said and repeat it today that as long as the Jewish problem is not solved, as long as there remains any race discrimination anywhere, we have no right to call ourselves civilised human beings. . . .

The people of Israel paid an unspeakably terrible price for the stupidity of all who made a pogrom or a ghetto a shocking reality. Let us try to repay our obligation—we cannot repay it all—but let us do all we can. It is our duty.[96]

Probably the last declaration of this kind from Czechoslovakia was made by President Beneš himself, almost exactly half a year before the Communist takeover in February 1948. On August 12, 1947, a Conference of European Zionist Federations took place in Karlovy Vary (Carlsbad), at which the Palestine Jewish Agency Executive was represented by Moshe Shertok (Sharett), Eliyahu Dobkin, Joseph Sprinzak, Moshe Sneh, S. Z. Shragai, Rabbi Judah L. Fishman (Maimon), and Nahum Goldmann. Beneš's special message to this conference was read at the opening session. The president reiterated his previous statements about the necessity for a comprehensive solution of the Jewish problem after the war:

It will, first of all, be necessary to put a radical and permanent end to racism and anti-Semitism. At the same time your aspirations for an independent homeland should be fulfilled. I regard the creation of a Jewish state in Palestine as the only just and possible solution of the world Jewish problem. I promise that whenever and wherever an opportunity offers itself, I shall help promote this solution.[97]

In retrospect, it is interesting to read the message sent to that same conference by the minister of information, Václav Kopecký, a Communist. Kopecký, who was not known for philo-Semitism, declares his "sympathies with your enormous efforts to make this piece of land, which was once the land of your fathers, your common home again." He then proceeds to explain his sympathy with Zionist aims:

The fact alone that you are trying to change the instrument of imperialism of one of the four Great Powers into an economically and politically independent state throws a light on the difficulties of your position and your struggle.⁹⁸

But while he finds it necessary to state that there may, of course, be different views about Zionism, Kopecký stresses in his message that

in one thing all freedom-loving and progressively-thinking people all over the world are united: in the feelings with which they are following your struggle and in the conviction that this fight is just and morally justified. For my own nation I can assure you that a people that twice in its history was near extinction and regained freedom only by using all of its last strength and by sacrificing the blood of its best sons, [such a] nation is not indifferent to the efforts of another nation that is not asking for anything but a base for its free and dignified human existence.⁹⁹

The text of Kopecký's message helps us understand why, despite all their ideological reservations about Zionism, even the Communists in Czechoslovakia, when they first came to power, followed a "pro-Zionist" line.¹⁰⁰

NOTES

1. See Erich Kulka, "Jews in the Czechoslovak Armed Forces Abroad During World War II" in the present volume, pp. 337-422.
2. On anti-Semitism in the Czechoslovak army during that period, see, e.g., Toman Brod and Eduard Čejka, *Na západní frontě* [On the Western Front] (Prague: 1965), pp. 389-90.
3. Sir Lewis B(ernstein) Namier (1888-1960), a historian and official of the Jewish Agency, was born in Poland, settling in England in 1907. He was professor of modern history at the University of Manchester from 1931 to 1953. A staff member of the British Foreign Office from 1915 to 1920, he later became political secretary (1929-31) and eventually political advisor (1938-45) of the Jewish Agency. He first met Beneš while serving as advisor to the British delegation at the Versailles Peace Conference on matters concerning the Habsburg empire. The meeting between Namier and Bruce Lockhart to which the latter refers here was arranged by Frank Roberts, who was then in charge of the Central European desk of the Foreign Office. After the meeting, Bruce Lockhart reported to Roberts that Namier, "the prominent

Zionist," had told him that "the Czechs had become anti-Semites," giving instances of discrimination against Jews. Bruce Lockhart commented: "These [reports] are probably true. But the real burden of his grievance was Dr. Beneš's refusal to give a special seat in the new State Council [*Státní rada*] to a representative of the Czechoslovak Zionists." Bruce Lockhart's report to Roberts is dated December 17, 1940. (Public Records Office, London, FO C 9969.)
4. Dr. Leo Zelmanovits (1907–1969), former secretary general of the Jewish party in Czechoslovakia.
5. For a full text of Bruce Lockhart's report, see Livia Rothkirchen, "The Czechoslovak Government-in-Exile: Jewish and Palestinian Aspects in the Light of Documents," in *Yad Vashem Studies on the European Jewish Catastrophe and Resistance,* vol. 9 (Jerusalem: 1973), pp. 184–86.
6. Memorandum on the conversation in World Jewish Congress Archives, London.
7. In the course of his conversation with Dr. Barou and Silverman, Beneš cited the fact "that there were many Jews in the Czech 'civil service' " as proof that there was no anti-Semitism in the Czechoslovak government-in-exile. However, except for the president's personal physician, Dr. Oto Klinger, there were virtually no Jews in the president's office or in his closest entourage.
8. Eduard Beneš, "The Organization of Postwar Europe," *Foreign Affairs,* New York, January 1942.
9. Report by Sir R. H. Bruce Lockhart to Foreign Secretary Viscount Halifax, October 7, 1940 (Foreign Office Archives 371/24289).
10. See Aharon Moshe Rabinowicz, "The Jewish Minority," in *The Jews of Czechoslovakia,* vol. 1 (Philadelphia: The Jewish Publication Society of America, 1968), pp. 155–265.
11. Leo Zelmanovits, "Record of My Visit to President Beneš on March 28, 1941" (Central Zionist Archives, Jerusalem, A 280).
12. Memorandum in World Jewish Congress Archives, London. Also in Rothkirchen, "The Czechoslovak Government-in-Exile," *Yad Vashem Studies . . .,* vol. 9, pp. 190–96.
13. Eduard Beneš, "The Organization of Postwar Europe," Foreign Affairs, pp. 16–17. See also Compton Mackenzie, *Dr. Beneš* (London: 1946), p. 282, giving the president's views on this subject as expressed in conversations during the spring of 1944.
14. For actual developments in Czechoslovakia immediately after the war, see Kurt Wehle, "The Jews in Bohemia and Moravia: 1945–1948," in the present volume, pp. 499–530, and Yeshayahu Jeli-

nek, "The Jews in Slovakia: 1945-1949," in the present volume, pp. 531-50.
15. See Viktor Fischl [Avigdor Dagan], *Hovory s Janem Masarykem* [Conversations with Jan Masaryk] (Tel Aviv: 1952), pp. 60-66; (Munich: 1973), pp. 87-96.
16. World Jewish Congress Archives, London.
17. Ibid.
18. Rothkirchen, "The Czechoslovak Government-in-Exile," *Yad Vashem Studies* . . ., vol. 9, pp. 157-99.
19. The group of those advocating assimilation was headed not, as inaccurately stated in some sources, by the writer Josef Kodíček but his brother Milan, a businessman.
20. The most active figure in this group was Rabbi Meir Raphael Springer, a young rabbi from Boskovice, Moravia, who eventually settled in London, where he was (1982) honorary general secretary of the Jewish Rescue and Relief Committee of the Agudas Israel World Organization.
21. Members of the Political Committee of the Central Council, headed by Dr. Leo Zelmanovits, were Dr. Otto Arje, Dr. Stephan Barber, Karl Baum, Josef Boehm, Dr. Viktor Fischl [Avigdor Dagan], Dr. Arthur Heller, Rudolf Jokl, Vítězslav Kessler, and Rabbi Dr. Hugo Stránský.
22. Memorandum by Dr. Leo Zelmanovits on his and Rabbi Stránský's visit at Beneš's residence in Putney, London, on December 4, 1939. (Central Zionist Archives, Jerusalem, Z 4/20.376). See also Rothkirchen, "The Czechoslovak Government-in-Exile," *Yad Vashem Studies* . . ., vol 9, p. 161.
23. Diary of Jaromír Smutný, the president's *chef de cabinet,* entry for November 25, 1940, in *Dokumenty z historie československé politiky 1939-1943* [Documents from the History of Czechoslovak Politics 1939-1943] (Prague: 1966).
24. Conversation with Dr. Noah Barou and Sydney S. Silverman, M.P. Memorandum in World Jewish Congress Archives, London.
25. Bruce Lockhart's report addressed to Viscount Halifax as Foreign Secretary, December 17, 1940 (Public Record Office, London, FO 371). Reprinted in Rothkirchen, "The Czechoslovak Government-in-Exile," *Yad Vashem Studies* . . ., vol. 9, pp. 184-86.
26. Nahum Goldmann, trans. Helen Sebba, *The Autobiography of Nahum Goldmann: Sixty Years of Jewish Life* (New York: 1969).
27. Diary of Jaromír Smutný, entry for November 25, 1940. In the same entry, Smutný remarks, "The President's tactics with the Jews are masterly."

Smutný's diary contains other items not uninteresting from the Jewish point of view. Thus, the entry for December 9, 1940:

> [Minister of Social Welfare Ján] Bečko phoned to ask whether I knew [the former president of the Jewish Religious Congregation of Prague,] Dr. [Emil] Kafka. He would like him to work as secretary to Minister Nečas. I told him that I found this strange. He is an old gentleman, again a Jew, but otherwise I regard him as very serious.

In another entry (June 8, 1941) Smutný writes about his conversation with Jaroslav Stránský, who later became Beneš's Minister of Justice:

> This is the whole problem of his life. Ever since his childhood he carried in himself an inferiority complex because of his Jewish origin. He felt it in a particularly bitter way when in January 1939 the [Law] Faculty received a communication from Kapras [himself a professor of law, who, after Munich, became Minister of Education] that Stránský should stop his lectures. He avoided this by taking leave of his colleagues in writing but [imagine] what he must have felt when he had to leave the university because of his origin. . . . I must admit I felt sorry for Stránský.

28. The name used by the organization on that occasion was "National Council of Jews from Czechoslovakia."
29. The full text of the declaration is reprinted in Rothkirchen, "The Czechoslovak Government-in-Exile," *Yad Vashem Studies* . . ., vol. 9, pp. 186–87.
30. Bruce Lockhart to Viscount Halifax, December 17, 1940.
31. See note 3 above.
32. Zelmanovits, "Record of My Visit to President Beneš." See also Rothkirchen, "The Czechoslovak Government-in-Exile," *Yad Vashem Studies* . . ., vol. 9, pp. 188–89.
33. Diary of Jaromír Smutný, entry for November 25, 1940.
34. Ibid.
35. Bruce Lockhart to Viscount Halifax, December 17, 1940.
36. Dr. Chaim Kugel (1897–1956), a pioneering Hebrew educator, founder and director of the Hebrew Gymnasium at Mukačevo, Subcarpathian Ruthenia, had represented the Jewish party in the Czechoslovak parliament from 1935 to 1939. Settling in Palestine in 1939, he was active in the labor movement there and became the first mayor of the city of Holon, a position he held from 1950 to 1956. For Kugel's activities in prewar Czechoslovakia, see volumes I and II of *The Jews of Czechoslovakia* (Philadelphia: 1968 and 1971).
37. Arnošt (Ernst) Frischer (1887–1954), a civil engineer, returned to Czechoslovakia after the war and became the first president of the reestablished Council of Jewish Religious Congregations in Czecho-

slovakia. See also Wehle, "The Jews in Bohemia and Moravia: 1945-1948," in the present volume, p. 501ff. For Frischer's activities in prewar Czechoslovakia, see volume II of *The Jews of Czechoslovakia*.
38. *The Daily Telegraph,* London, June 25, 1942.
39. Cable from President Beneš to Rabbi Stephen S. Wise and Dr. Nahum Goldmann, June 26, 1942 (Copy in author's files).
40. The delegation was composed of M. Slavík, former Czechoslovakia ambassador to Belgium, who had good connections in the Catholic Church, Arnošt Frischer, and Dr. Viktor Fischl [Avigdor Dagan].
41. Copy in author's files.
42. See Ladislav Lipscher, "The Jews of Slovakia: 1939-1945," in the present volume, pp. 217-218.
43. Translation (from the German) of a report on the situation in Eastern Europe, dated August 15, 1942. The report was received from the Geneva office of the World Jewish Congress on September 14, 1942. (Copy in author's files.)
44. This cable, dated September 30, 1942, was addressed to Maurice Perlzweig and Dr. Stephen S. Wise. (World Jewish Congress Archives, London).
45. World Jewish Congress Archives, London.
46. World Jewish Congress Archives, London.
47. The full text of Masaryk's address is in the author's files.
48. The full text of David's declaration is in the author's files.
49. The full text of Mme. Beneš's message is in the author's files.
50. Dr. Hubert Ripka (1895-1958) was political editor of the leading Czech liberal daily, *Lidové Noviny,* before the war. Returning to Czechoslovakia after the war, he served as minister of foreign trade in the postwar government from 1945 to 1948, when he resigned and settled in England.
51. Quoted from Viktor Fischl [Avigdor Dagan], "The Jewish Suffering[s] and the Conscience of the World," *Spirit of Czechoslovakia,* London, January 1943.
52. Reports from Arnošt Frischer to the Jewish Agency in London, dated December 18, 1942, and June 17, 1943. (Central Zionist Archives, Jerusalem).
53. This information is from notes taken by the author in London at the time. He attended most of the meetings at which these matters were discussed.
54. Among the others present at the dinner were Alexander L. Easterman, Arnošt Frischer, and Dr. Viktor Fischl [Avigdor Dagan].
55. From copy of a report about the dinner, in the author's files.

56. Jan Masaryk, *Volá Londýn* [London Calling] (London: 1945), p. 202.
57. See Angelo Goldstein, "Právní podklady židovské politiky v Československu" [The Legal Basis of Jewish Politics in Czechoslovakia], in *Czechoslovak Jewry—Past and Future* (New York, 1943).
58. Diary of Jaromír Smutný, entry for November 25, 1940.
59. Zelmanovits, "Record of My Visit to President Beneš."
60. Mackenzie, *Dr. Beneš*, p. 293.
61. Ibid. However, see also John Wolfgang Brügel, *Tschechen und Deutsche* [Czechs and Germans] (Munich: 1974), pp. 169–95, which casts doubt on the accuracy of Beneš's statement as noted by Mackenzie.
62. Beneš repeated this story in greater detail to his biographer Edward B. Hitchcock. See Hitchcock, *Beneš, the Man and Statesman* (London: 1940), pp. 187–91.
63. Letter to Dr. Arieh Tartakower, World Jewish Congress, dated March 8, 1941. (Central Zionist Archives, Jerusalem, A 280/28). In reply to this report, Dr. Tartakower drafted a letter to President Beneš, which was sent on April 9, 1941, on behalf of the American Jewish Congress and the World Jewish Congress and was signed by Stephen S. Wise, Nahum Goldmann, and Maurice Perlzweig. The following excerpts summarize the principal points of the letter:

> We were informed by our friends that this strange decision [not to include a Jewish representative in the *Státní rada*] . . . made by you was motivated by your conviction that the Jewish problem should be solved by establishing a Jewish commonwealth in Palestine. All nationalistic Jews should concentrate themselves in this commonwealth and all Jews in other countries must be assimilated. There is no place, according to this theory, for national minority rights for the Jewish people. Such rights are to be reserved only for minorities which have their own states in adjacent countries.
>
> May we, with all due respect, emphasize that we regard this conception as a grave danger for the Jewish people, against which we feel it our duty to raise our warning voice . . . Without directing our views against any group of the population, since we recognize the right of every national minority to its own free life, may we point out that the Jewish national minorities were always the most loyal citizens of their respective states, since their claims for national minority rights, not being based on any territorial claims, could always be brought into perfect harmony with the interests of the state. It is therefore hardly to be understood why this most loyal national minority should be deprived of its rights.
>
> Since in a statement published by you in your capacity as the President of Czechoslovakia on June 21, 1940, the Munich treaty was declared null and void and it was emphasized that the present Czech Government is the direct successor of the Czech government as it was before Munich it is clear that the prescriptions of the Constitution, and among them also the prescriptions safeguarding the national minority rights of the Jewish population, must be strictly observed; your plan of depriving the Czechoslovakian Jews of

their minority rights is without doubt in contradiction to this fundamental principle.

We would like to take this opportunity of answering two other arguments which may be cited against our claims: namely, that there are many Jews in Czechoslovakia who are not interested in having national minority rights since they feel that they are Czech by nationality, and that there is no unity among the Jews themselves on the fundamental questions of the Jewish policy in Czechoslovakia. Both arguments have in reality nothing to do with the principle of Jewish minority rights. It is true that the percentage of Jews claiming their Jewish nationality is smaller in Czechoslovakia than in the countries of Eastern Europe, where the overwhelming majority of all Jews consider themselves Jews by nationality and are closely connected with all Jewish interests. But even so more than a half of the Jewish population of Czechoslovakia (186,642 out of 356,830), according to the census of 1930, declared themselves Jews by nationality; and according to a private scientific study of the year 1938, 58 percent of all Czech Jews belonged to the Jewish nationality. It is therefore more than just that the national minority rights be granted to this majority of Czech Jews. As to the lack of unity among the Jews themselves, we do not think that this can be an obstacle in granting them minority rights. We would not suggest, and we never have, that these rights be forced on the entire Jewish population. Jews who wish to become assimilated with the Czech population are free to do so. The existing differences of opinion among the Jewish orthodoxy and other groups of the Jewish population in Czechoslovakia have nothing to do with our claims for national minority rights, since these claims are also shared by the orthodox groups, although from another point of view, namely the religious.

We feel it our duty to point out, in the last sentences of our memorandum, the great danger inherent in your plan to the Jewish population not only of Czechoslovakia, but of the other European countries as well. The Jewish minority rights were recognized in a more or less liberal manner by almost all the countries of Eastern and Central Europe, where the attitude toward the Jewish population is not always so friendly. By depriving the Jewish population in your country of its national minority rights on the grounds given by you, you will certainly endanger not only its national minority rights but even its civic position and the possibilities for its future development. There might be some countries, not so eager to assimilate their Jewish citizens, which might accept the slogan of enforcing their emigration from the respective countries on the basis of the principles formulated by you. Such great harm might thus be inflicted on the interests of the Jewish population, the extent and intensity of which can scarcely be overestimated.

May we express the hope that the points made in this memorandum will convince you of the utmost undesirability of depriving the Czech Jews of their minority rights, and that the policy of justice and loyalty to all free citizens will be continued by the Free Czech Government under your splendid leadership. (*World Jewish Congress Archives, Jerusalem*).

64. Letter from Dr. Arye Léon Kubowitzki, head of the Rescue Department of the World Jewish Congress in New York from 1943 to 1945, to Arnošt Frischer, dated May 24, 1943. (Central Zionist Archives–Z 4/15047). Kubowitzki was to serve as secretary general of the Congress from 1945 to 1948. Settling in Israel in 1948, he Hebraized his

surname to Kubovy and held a number of diplomatic posts, including that of minister to Czechoslovakia and Poland, a position he held from 1951 to 1952, when he was accused by the Czechs of complicity in a "Zionist conspiracy."
65. Ibid.
66. For full text of this proclamation, see Rothkirchen, "The Czechoslovak Government-in-Exile," *Yad Vashem Studies* . . ., vol. 9, photographic facsimile facing p. 168.
67. See Josef M. Kadlec, *Svatá Země v československém odboji* [The Holy Land in the Czechoslovak Resistance] (Prague: 1947), pp. 51 f. See also Kulka, "Jews in the Czechoslovak Armed Forces," in the present volume, pp. 346–47, 366.
68. *Informační Bulletin čs. zahraniční akce,* Jerusalem, April 4, 1940.
69. See, for instance, *Palestine Post,* April 4, 1940.
70. Leo Herrmann (1888–1951), a leading Zionist in Prague before World War I, served as secretary of the World Zionist Organization from 1913 to 1920, when he was appointed secretary general of *Keren HaYesod,* a position he held, first in London and then in Jerusalem, until his death.
71. This suggestion was passed on to Jan Masaryk by Lewis B. Namier less than a week after the mobilization order was issued.
72. Letter from Moshe Shertok [Sharett] to Consul General Josef M. Kadlec, dated April 19, 1940. (Central Zionist Archives, Jerusalem). Printed also in Rothkirchen, "The Czechoslovak Government-in-Exile," *Yad Vashem Studies* . . ., vol. 9, pp. 178–79.
73. Letter from Lewis B. Namier to Jan Masaryk, dated April 10, 1940. (Central Zionist Archives, Jerusalem). Printed also in Rothkirchen, "The Czechoslovak Government-in-Exile," *Yad Vashem Studies* . . ., vol. 9, p. 177.
74. Report from Leo Herrmann to Moshe Shertok [Sharett], dated August 2, 1940. (Central Zionist Archives, Jerusalem).
75. Report from Leo Herrmann to Moshe Shertok [Sharett], dated November 11, 1940. (Central Zionist Archives, Jerusalem). Printed also in Rothkirchen, "The Czechoslovak Government-in-Exile," *Yad Vashem Studies* . . ., vol. 9, pp. 180–82. The word "Czech" in the quoted report is to be construed as synonymous with "Czechoslovak."
76. Diary of Jaromír Smutný, entry for November 25, 1940, two weeks after Herrmann's report. Printed in Rothkirchen, "The Czechoslovak Government-in-Exile," *Yad Vashem Studies* . . ., vol. 9, pp. 182–83.
77. The others present at the meeting were Consul General Kadlec, General Andrej Gak (commander-in-chief of the Czechoslovak forces in the Middle East), and the military attaché Lieutenant-Colonel J. Kalla.

78. See Kulka, "Jews in the Czechoslovak Armed Forces," in the present volume, p. 347.
79. Minutes dated June 19, 1942, probably dictated by Leo Herrmann. (Central Zionist Archives, Jerusalem).
80. Letter from Leo Herrmann to the London Executive of the Jewish Agency for Palestine, dated June 28, 1942. (Central Zionist Archives Z 4/14766).
81. Ibid.
82. Central Zionist Archives, Jerusalem, S 25/6585.
83. Immigrants from Czechoslovakia were not the only Jewish newcomers in Palestine to face this problem. The Central Zionist Archives (10389/1) contain correspondence on the same problem affecting Dutch Jews in Palestine.
84. Letter from Dr. Leo Zelmanovits to Dr. Arieh Tartakower, dated March 8, 1941. (Central Zionist Archives A 280/28). See note 63.
85. World Jewish Congress Archives, London.
86. From notes in the author's files.
87. The full text of Beneš's message is in the author's files.
88. The full text of Masaryk's message is in the author's files.
89. The president's interest in active cooperation can be traced also in Dr. Arye Léon Kubowitzki's report to Arnošt Frischer on Beneš's meeting with Nahum Goldmann and Stephen S. Wise (see note 64), where we read: "In connection with the Jewish postwar demands, he [Beneš] asked to be informed of our program, as he would regret it if he would have to defend a viewpoint opposed to our own."
90. Central Zionist Archives, Jerusalem, Z 4/15047.
91. Goldmann, *Autobiography of Nahum Goldmann,* p. 243.
92. Actually, the number was closer to 5,000.
93. The report was published in London in July 1946. (Central Zionist Archives, Jerusalem).
94. Ibid.
95. *Keren HaYesod* was, in fact, founded in July 1920 but because of wartime conditions the celebration was not held until the fall.
96. The handwritten letter, dated October 1945 and reproduced here in facsimile, is in the Central Zionist Archives in Jerusalem.
97. See *Věstník Židovské náboženské obce v Praze* (Bulletin of the Jewish Religious Congregation in Prague), September 1, 1947.
98. Ibid.
99. Ibid.
100. For the practical assistance given to Palestine's Jewish community in its struggle for independent Jewish statehood, see Ehud Avriel, "Prague and Jerusalem: The Era of Friendship," in the present volume, pp. 551-566.

III. The Aftermath

THE JEWS IN BOHEMIA AND MORAVIA: 1945–1948*

By Kurt Wehle

Czechoslovakia, as reborn in 1945, was in many respects a different country from the one we had known before the tragic events of 1938–1939. One of the major changes, which had a profound impact on the living conditions of the Jewish survivors of the Holocaust, was the fact that after the war the eastern and western parts of the country developed along two sharply divergent lines. This survey, which deals with the immediate post-1945 history of the Jews in the Historic Lands, must of necessity begin with a review of organized Jewish life in Bohemia and Moravia during the period of the Nazi occupation.

Following the collapse of the Czechoslovak Republic in 1939, the *Židovská Náboženská Obec* (*Israelitische Kultusgemeinde*), i.e., the Jewish Religious Congregation of Prague, was gradually transformed from a purely religious and congregational body into an administrative agency with relatively broad powers and quasi-governmental functions.[1] It was, above all, given jurisdiction over the

---

* This study is based on a lecture delivered at a public meeting of the Joseph Popper Lodge of B'nai B'rith in New York City on November 10, 1951. The facts, evaluations, and judgments reported and expressed herein are based on my own personal experience as secretary general of the *Rada* (Council of Jewish Religious Congregations in Bohemia and Moravia) from 1945 to 1948, and, except where otherwise indicated, represent my personal recollections. In reformulating this lecture for publication, I received valuable advice and suggestions from Dr. J. W. Brügel, to whom I wish to express my gratitude. I would also like to thank Professor Yeshayahu Jelinek for his help in supplying the documentation data for most of the notes.

entire network of Jewish Religious Congregations within the Protectorate of Bohemia and Moravia; the other congregations in the Protectorate—to the extent that they had not been liquidated—became mere branch organizations of the Jewish Religious Congregation in Prague. In addition, the Jewish Religious Congregation in Prague was given jurisdiction over individuals who had no ties, religious or otherwise, with the Jewish community but who, under the Nuremburg racial laws, were classified as Jews.

On the face of it, the very idea that any Jewish communal institution should have been granted such broad authority under the Nazi regime would seem hard to believe. However, it can be better understood when viewed in terms of the nature of Hitler's war against the Jews. Hitler's plan was, in fact, to force the Jews to assist in their own destruction, to help organize their own annihilation. This explains why the Nazis entrusted new administrative functions to the Jewish Religious Congregation and, incidentally, also why they conferred quasi-autonomy upon the inmates of the ghettos and concentration camps. However, the Nazis did not reckon with the courage, the intelligence, the resoluteness, the moral strength and sense of responsibility of their victims. These were the weapons employed also by the leaders of Czechoslovak Jewry in its struggle for survival during the Nazi occupation.

The Jewish Religious Congregation of Prague, which later became officially known as the *Ältestenrat der Juden* or *Židovská Rada Starších* (Council of Jewish Elders), functioned until the Prague uprising on May 5, 1945, when heavy fighting in the city's Josefov district, where the Council had its headquarters, made it impossible for the Council to continue its work. The functions of the Council of Jewish Elders were then still quite extensive, but the overwhelming majority of the people whom the Council had been intended to serve were gone. By the end of the war, the total Jewish population of the Protectorate of Bohemia and Moravia outside Terezín had shrunk to less than 3,000. Of these, about 800 individuals were Jews by religious affiliation; another 2,000 persons were classified by the Nazis as Jews in accordance with the racial doctrine set forth in the Nuremberg laws.

In view of the general chaos that prevailed in Prague in May 1945 it was hardly surprising that the Jewish Town Hall, which had served as the headquarters of the Council, had been closed down.

Even before the final collapse of the Nazi regime on May 9, 1945, several members of the Council of Jewish Elders, in an effort to salvage what remained of the community's assets, broke away from the Council and organized a *Národní Výbor k likvidaci Židovské Rady Starších* (National Committee for the Liquidation of the Council of Jewish Elders). Precisely what these men intended to do with the Jewish assets thus rescued is not clear; however, it is known that even at this early date some of them at least planned to turn over the assets of the Jewish community to the postwar Czechoslovak Republic.

This was the situation when the first Jewish survivors returned from the death camps. There was no functioning official Jewish body in Prague, or anywhere else in the country, for that matter. During the second week of May 1945 Dr. František Friedmann, the last chairman of the Council of Jewish Elders, announced that he was prepared to reconstitute the Jewish Religious Congregation of Prague. (By that time, Friedmann was already seriously ill; he died soon afterwards.) The revival of the Jewish Religious Congregation was carried out late in May 1945 after the return of Arnošt (Ernst) Frischer to Prague from London, where he had represented the Jewish party in the *Státní rada,* the Czechoslovak State Council. Frischer enlisted the cooperation of several other Jewish leaders who had returned to Czechoslovakia from the concentration camps. Thus, Prague once again had an organized and recognized Jewish Religious Congregation and the Jewish returnees had a center to which they could turn for help and guidance.

For the sake of clarity, it should be pointed out that the National Committee for the Liquidation of the Council of Jewish Elders, soon to be renamed *Národní správa židovské Rady Starších* (National Administration of the Council of Jewish Elders), continued to exist side by side with the reconstituted Jewish Religious Congregation. For months, too, the National Administration of the Council of Jewish Elders was run by the same group of individuals that were in charge of two other agencies, the *Národní správa majetkových podstat Vystěhovaleckého fondu a Majetkového úřadu* (National Administration of the Assets of the Fund for Jewish Emigration) and the state-supervised Property Office, both of which superintended the management of Jewish assets that had not been claimed by their rightful owners or by the latters' heirs.

The Jewish community was faced with problems that seemed to defy solution. The main obstacle lay in the fact that all the assets and files of the various prewar Jewish Religious Congregations were now in the hands of the two National Administrations. It is impossible to describe the emotions that filled the hearts of those who, for the first time since they had left their homes, entered the rooms that had seen so much of the history of Czech Jewry, and sat in the seats of the martyrs who had fallen victim to the Nazi terror. But there was no time for sentimentality. Sick, tired, and shattered though they were, and grief-stricken over the loss of their loved ones, the men who had placed themselves at the service of the cause had but one aim: to rebuild the Jewish community.

The first task they set for themselves was the civic and economic rehabilitation of the remnants of Czech Jewry. The immediate aim was the abolition of all discriminatory measures against Jews as individuals and as members of a religious group, and, above all, the elimination of the consequences of that discrimination—insofar as this was humanly possible. Top priority was given to the care of the returnees, the liquidation of the Terezín ghetto and the recovery of the Jewish assets there, the reinstitution of religious services, the restoration of Jewish communal assets to the respective Jewish Religious Congregations, the initiation of restitution proceedings, and, of course, the rebuilding of Jewish communal life in general. To begin with, there was the problem of deciding who, for the purposes of Jewish communal activities and institutions, was to be regarded as a Jew. Before 1939, naturally, only those who professed the Jewish religion were regarded as members of the Jewish Religious Congregations. But after the German occupation of Bohemia and Moravia on March 15, 1939, the definition of "Jew" had been extended by law to include also persons of Jewish origin who were not practicing Jews and individuals who, because they had a Jewish parent or grandparent, had been classed as *Mischlinge* ("half-castes") under the Nuremberg laws. As already indicated, the Nazis forced the Jewish Religious Congregation to take charge of these persons also. Under the conditions that prevailed immediately after the war, when all surviving victims of racial discrimination, regardless of their personal Jewish identity, were in dire need of help, the newly reconstituted Jewish Religious Congregation felt that it could not limit its services to persons who regarded themselves as members of the Jewish faith. During the years of German rule, the Jewish Religious Congregation had set up a special department, known as "Department B" (from *Bez vyznání* or "religiously unaffiliated") to handle the affairs of individuals who were Jews by "race" only. Thus, the persons under the jurisdiction of this department came to be designated officially as "B-Jews" (or "non-Mosaic Jews"), while Jews who professed the Jewish faith were officially referred to as "A-Jews" (or "Mosaic Jews"). Now that the Germans had gone, it was decided to treat the so-called "B-Jews" as Jews in that the official Jewish organs would fight for the civil, political, and personal rehabilitation of these individuals as it did for that of all other Jews left in the country.

What were the motivations that led to this decision? The main consideration was an ethical one: the pressures from without, to which they all had been subjected during the war years, had created a bond between the "A-Jews" and the "B-Jews" which did not break even after the pressures had been removed. The impact of the experiences they had gone through together had been too strong and too deep. Incidentally, contrary to all expectations, instances of defection from the Jewish fold in Czechoslovakia were very rare after the liberation. On the contrary, many of those who had never considered themselves as Jews until Hitler had stamped them as such joined or rejoined the Jewish community after the war.

There were also political considerations. It was important to forestall the possibility that the "B-Jews" might form an organization of their own, pursue their own policies on questions of rehabilitation, and, from sheer necessity, come under the influence of one of the postwar Czech political parties. Still another factor was the belief that the voice of the organized Jewish community would carry far greater appeal with the authorities and with public opinion if it could state that it represented all the victims of racial persecution. Subsequent developments proved this estimation to have been right.

In Slovakia the arrangements were somewhat different. There, following liberation, a dividing line had been drawn between the strictly "Jewish" functions of the Jewish religious community, on the one hand, and the activities connected with rehabilitation, on the other. The former functions were taken over by the *Ústredný Sväz židovských náboženských obcí na Slovensku* (Central Union of Jewish Religious Congregations in Slovakia), hereafter referred to as the *Ústredný Sväz*, while the latter were carried on by a new organization founded expressly for this purpose, the *Sdruženie fašistickým režimom rasove prenásledovaných* (Organization of Victims of Racial Persecution at the Hands of the Fascist Regime), popularly known as SRP. But in actual fact, the division between the two functions was on the surface only, for the business of both organizations was conducted by the same two men: Rabbi Dr. Armin Frieder and Dr. Albert (Vojtěch) Winterstein.[2]

In Prague the "B-Jews" as a group were not represented in the agencies of the Jewish community and later also not in the *Rada Židovských náboženských obcí v Čechách a na Moravě* (Council of Jewish Religious Congregations in Bohemia and Moravia), hereafter referred to as *Rada*. But in Bratislava, the capital of Slovakia, they were represented as a separate group in the SRP.

Obviously, the arrangement whereby the Prague Jewish Religious Congregation was to deal also with the problems of the "B-Jews" was not intended to be more than temporary. Nevertheless, it continued, by and large, until March 1948. After that time, all work on behalf of Jewish rehabilitation came to an end, so that the question was no longer relevant. There is a certain wry humor in the fact that the writer Egon Erwin Kisch, an ardent Communist who had left the Jewish fold long before, should have been named honorary chairman of the *Rada* shortly after the Communist takeover in February 1948.[3]

During the period immediately after liberation, the Jewish population of Czechoslovakia was composed of the following elements: a small group of Jews (almost all of them living with non-Jewish spouses) who had escaped deportation; returnees from the concentration camps or from exile abroad; veterans of the Czechoslovak army-in-exile; and Jews who had fled from Subcarpathian Ruthenia following the annexation of that province by the Soviet Union in June 1945.

Compared with the prewar picture, there were two significant changes: first, an increase—caused by the arrival of relatively large numbers of refugees from Subcarpathian Ruthenia—in the percentage of strictly Orthodox Jews; and second, a change in the age composition of the community.

Once again, as before the war, there were the two main ideological groupings: the Zionists and the adherents of the assimilationist

"Czech-Jewish" movement. (The German assimilationist Jews in Czechoslovakia had never formed an organized group of their own.) Of the two, the Zionists were the stronger both in actual numbers and in terms of activity. The war had brought about a basic change in the relationship between the two movements, which had been bitter opponents for decades before the Nazi occupation. The collaboration of Zionist and "Czech-Jewish" leaders in Prague and in the Terezín ghetto during the war years had created an atmosphere of solidarity between the two groups. Although there had been no change in the fundamental ideology of either group, it can be said that their differences had become less acrimonious, so that it was possible for the Zionists and the assimilationists to find a common platform when it came to vital problems affecting the whole community. One should not dismiss the possibility that the political attitude of the "Czech-Jews" had been influenced also by the conduct of a part of the Czech gentile population during and immediately following the period of Nazi occupation.

The Zionists reconstituted their organizations, with the center of their activities shifting east to Slovakia. The first postwar convention of Czechoslovak Zionists was held in the summer of 1946 in Luhačovice, a well-known spa in Moravia.[4] The "Czech-Jews," by contrast, allowed many months to pass before deciding to revive their organization.[5] The most striking demonstration of the change in the attitude of the "Czech-Jews" was that they not only did not oppose the efforts of the *Rada* on behalf of Czechoslovak Jews of German nationality but in fact vigorously stood up for their rights.

No reliable detailed information is available on the political affiliation of the Jews in postwar Czechoslovakia. Many Jews were members of the Social Democratic party and there was a relatively large contingent of Jewish Communists. Some Jews were affiliated with the Czechoslovak Socialists, a party somewhat to the right of the Social Democrats. But except in the case of the Communist party, political affiliations played a negligible role in post-1945 Czechoslovak Jewish life. Some of the Jewish Communists were ideologically close to the Czech-Jewish movement, while others had no Jewish interests at all and participated in Jewish life only to the extent dictated by the party line or on explicit instructions from the party leadership. It should be noted that the Communist party was eager to have observers and representatives in the Jewish Religious Congregation and the *Rada*. It must be said, however, that during the first few months after the war even these individuals followed the dictates of their conscience rather than those of political ideology; some of them were instrumental in establishing contacts with Communists in power which proved helpful to the Jewish community.

Most of the Jews who had migrated to Bohemia, Moravia, and Slovakia from Subcarpathian Ruthenia were Zionists and joined the various Zionist groups in the cities and towns where they settled. Those who belonged to the ultra-Orthodox, non-Zionist *Agudath Israel* tended to give their support on political matters to the assimilationist "Czech-Jewish" movement. It may be of interest to note here that, under the electoral agreement made for the first postwar elections to the Jewish Religious Congregation in Prague, the representatives of *Agudath Israel* were included in the number of candidates apportioned to the "Czech-Jewish" movement.

Individuals who left Soviet Subcarpathian Ruthenia to settle in Czechoslovakia were assigned a special civil status. They were officially known as "optants" because they had "opted" for Czechoslovak citizenship when the choice between Soviet and Czechoslovak citizenship was put to them under a Soviet-Czechoslovak agreement signed on June 29, 1945. However, this agreement and the Czechoslovak provisions for its implementation contained ambiguities which were exploited by the Russians, on the one hand, and by Communist officials in the Czechoslovak Ministry for Internal Affairs, on the other, to deny the rights of Czechoslovak citizenship to thousands of immigrants who happened to be Jews. Under the explicit terms of the agreement only members of the Czech and Slovak nationality groups were accorded the right to opt for Czechoslovak citizenship. As a result, Jewish citizens of Czechoslovakia who had declared themselves members of the Jewish nationality group in the 1930 census, the last to be held before the war, were not permitted to exercise this right of option.[6] This provision affected almost all the Jewish newcomers from Subcarpathian Ruthenia, for at the time of the 1930 census almost all the Czechoslovak Jewish citizens in that province had taken advantage of their right to declare themselves members of the Jewish nationality group if they so desired. As a result, almost 12,000 postwar Jewish refugees from Subcarpathian Ruthenia were now regarded not as citizens of Czechoslovakia[7] but (in view of the annexation by the Soviets of their home province) as citizens of the Soviet Union and were therefore faced with deportation, or, as it was put euphemistically, with "repatriation," to Subcarpathian Ruthenia. However, in many instances, tragedy could be averted thanks to the intervention of the *Rada* and the *Ústredný Sväz,* as well as an organization that had been formed by the "optants" themselves to protect their interests.

I personally know of only one incident in which a truckload of Jewish "optants" was actually taken to the Slovak-Soviet border to be turned over to Soviet border guards. However, the Soviet border guards refused to accept the deportees; they explained that they did not want any Jews. This was the truth. The Soviets did not want these Jews back; they only wanted the return of the non-Jewish Ukrainians and White Russians who had fled from Subcarpathian Ruthenia. But the Czechs and Slovaks did not want these Jewish refugees either. Fortunately, however, a large proportion of the refugees had found employment in Czechoslovakia as factory workers or farmhands so that the Czechoslovak Ministry of Labor supported intervention to permit them to remain in Czechoslovakia proper.

Before their status was finally settled, Jewish "optants" in many localities were rounded up for deportation. At one point, the situation of the "optants" seemed so precarious that within a period of only a few weeks some 6,000 of them fled illegally into the American occupation zone of Germany. Eventually, however, new nationality criteria were established, and by the beginning of 1948 only a few hundred Jews were left in Czechoslovakia without definite citizenship status.

In this aspect (like in many others) of the struggle for Jewish civil and political rights in Czechoslovakia, the Jewish representatives were greatly aided by Foreign Minister Jan Masaryk.

The upheaval brought about by the war and the Holocaust resulted in a downward shift in the social structure of Czechoslovak Jewry. Only a few Jews in postwar Czechoslovakia were independent businessmen and entrepreneurs. Most of the Jews were white-collar employees, and a larger proportion than before the war were employed in the civil service. There also had been a realignment in the occupational structure. As already indicated, most of the Jews who had fled into Czechoslovakia proper from Subcarpathian Ruthenia were employed as factory workers, farmhands, and craftsmen. However, it must also be noted that a relatively large number of those Jewish citizens of Czechoslovakia who had not declared themselves members of the German nationality group at the time of the 1930 census were now hired by the government as administrators of businesses and factories which had been confiscated from their original Jewish owners by the Nazis and were therefore now retained by the Czechoslovak authorities as "enemy property."

With what hopes and expectations did Jews return to Czechoslovakia from the army-in-exile, the concentration camps, and the countries that had given them refuge during the war years? It goes without saying that many of them cherished hopes of finding members of their families alive in Czechoslovakia. But what concerns us most today is the yearning of the returnees to live again as equals among equals. In this regard, however, the returnees met with more disillusionment than they might reasonably have expected, and the reconstituted Jewish communal agencies had to devote much of their effort to the struggle for full civil and political rights and for unconditional equality.

We cannot disregard the influence of German anti-Jewish policies in Bohemia and Moravia and that of Fascist rule in Slovakia on the non-Jewish populace. For years the gentiles had been pitted by their Nazi overlords against the Jews and all things Jewish. Moreover, thousands of gentiles had benefited from the confiscation of Jewish property and from the elimination of the Jews from Czechoslovak life.

True, there were many Czechs who, themselves happy that war and foreign rule had come to an end at last, welcomed their returning Jewish friends with open arms and with a genuine desire to help them in their readjustment. But could all this compensate for the thousands of Czechs and Slovaks whom recent history had taught nothing and who remained cold and indifferent to the returning Jews?[8]

It was not surprising that those Czechs and Slovaks who had hated the Jews before the war should have remained anti-Semites. But it came as something of a shock to find that many gentiles whose attitude had been "neutral" before the war had now become out-and-out Jew-baiters. Anti-Semitism in Czechoslovakia had the same religious, economic, and partly also racial motivations as it did anywhere else. But in Bohemia and Moravia the most frequently claimed motive was that of nationality: the Jews who lived there were hated because they were regarded as Germans! There was no change in this attitude after the war, and since the hatred for all things German was fierce and directed at everything German, it extended also to those Jewish citizens of Czechoslovakia who had declared themselves members of the German nationality group in the 1930 census. During the first few months following the war, it happened that Jews who had just taken off the yellow badge with the Star of David which had been imposed upon them by the Nazis were forced by Czechs to put on a new badge of shame—a white armband with the letter "N" for *Němec* ("German"). They were in danger of being deported to Germany. Jews who had held professorships at universities in Czechoslovakia before the war and had listed the German language as their mother tongue were now denied the pensions to which they were entitled as Czechoslovak citizens under Czechoslovak law.

Many Czechs, and even more Slovaks, found it difficult to readjust, and to put back under lock and key, as it were, those hatreds which they had been able to express with complete freedom during the Nazi era. It must be understood, too, that anti-Semitism was given additional fuel by yet another emotional factor: the resentment felt by gentiles who had acquired Jewish property during the period of Nazi occupation and were now looking for arguments against restoring it to its rightful owners or their heirs. These resentments must be taken into account if one is to understand the mood of the gentile populace in postwar Czechoslovakia.

What went on in the minds of the youngsters who desecrated Jewish cemeteries after the war?[9] What were the thoughts of the revenue officer who in 1946, a year after the end of Nazi rule, still addressed his tax payment notices, Nazi-fashion, to Bedřich *Israel* Kohn or Emma *Sarah* Kohn, or of the court clerk who still addressed his summonses to Mr. Such-and-Such, Israelite? What are we to make of the anti-Jewish excesses in Topolčany, Snina, Nové Zámky, Galanta, and Bratislava, and of the anti-Jewish demonstrations in Varnsdorf?

From the very outset, the postwar Jewish leadership fought against Czech and Slovak anti-Semitism by all available means and received understanding from the authorities. It would certainly be wrong to create the impression that the Czechoslovak government approved of the anti-Semitic outrages that were committed in Czechoslovakia after the war. As a matter of fact, President Beneš, Jan Masaryk, and other Czech leaders were outspoken in their condemnation of anti-Semitism. Yet, the government, particularly officialdom on the lower administrative levels, was either unwilling or unable to take strong action against it. The efforts of Jewish spokesmen met with some success, but there were months on end during which the Jews had good reason to feel bitter and frustrated. During that period one Jewish newspaperman put the following rhetorical question to the non-Jewish public: "In view of the fact that only so few Jews have survived [the Nazi Holocaust], might the Czechs and Slovaks not find it possible to forgive us for having been remiss in our duty to die during the Nazi occupation?"

To understand the situation more fully, it is important for the student of that period to obtain an insight into the feelings of those who led the fight for right and justice on behalf of the Jews of Czechoslovakia at the time. Perhaps the following excerpt from the address which I delivered at the public convocation of Slovak Jewry held in Bratislava on March 16, 1946, in the presence of Slovak officials, may be of help in this respect:

... It happens only rarely that a person finds the strength and readiness to reflect, on his own, on the meaning of life, on his purely human obligations ... This is what we have to consider when, on the one hand, we think of our sufferings and our losses, of the anguish which seizes us daily as we think of our children, our spouses, our parents, our brothers who perished in the Nazi extermination camps, and when, on the other hand, we realize the coolness which surrounds us, the little understanding we encounter, and the immense difficulties which hamper our efforts to rebuild our lives. This realization guides us in our work and proceedings. It has to guide us, even if—as a consequence—we are forced to suppress our reluctance and our dislike for stressing over and over again our distress, our grief, and the persecution and injustice we had to endure. We ask ourselves: Do our fellow citizens really have no knowledge of the extent and totality of the Fascist and Nazi persecution of the Jews? ... Is it not enough to realize that hardly ten percent of Czechoslovak Jewry survived the horrors of persecution? We know the answer to our question: It is the indolence of the human heart against which we have to fight; it forces us to point again and again to our human and civic rights and to the horrors and privations which we have survived only by accident and as if by a miracle ...[10]

Things came to a point where Jewish representatives felt called upon to appeal to Czech anti-Fascist circles to put a stop to the outrages, not for the sake of the Jews but for the sake of their own morality. Only then did the anti-Fascists—or, let us say, the decent folk—sit up and take notice. Accordingly, protest demonstrations against anti-Semitism were organized. In one such demonstration, held in April 1947, Jan Masaryk, speaking, as he always did, from the very depths of his heart, took note of the large number of Jews in the audience. Gentiles were not so well represented.

In October 1945 there were in Bohemia and Moravia about 10,000 "A-Jews" and 5,000 "B-Jews"; in Slovakia there were 20,000 of the former and 8,000 of the latter. About 90 percent of prewar Czechoslovak Jewry had been lost in the war. When news gradually came of what some other nations under the Nazi hell, such as the people of Bulgaria, had done for their Jews during the war, and how the Catholic Church of France had saved thousands of Jewish children, one began to ask how it came about that in terms of the percentage murdered, the losses of Czechoslovak Jewry during the war had been second only to those of the Jewries of Poland and Lithuania.

The study of the behavior of the Czech and Slovak populace during the war years must be left to historians of a future era. But it must be said that during the immediate postwar period, the Jews voiced no complaints—at least not regarding the wartime conduct of the Czech and Slovak populace—and that no polemics were carried on regarding this subject. However, several Czech leaders (non-Jews) felt obliged to raise the question on their own. Thus, Dr. Václav Vacek, lord mayor of Prague, a Communist, wrote an article for the first issue of *Věstník Židovské obce náboženské v Praze,* the news bulletin of the Jewish Religious Congregation of Prague, in which he declared that the Czech people had kept faith with the Jews during the war and that the blame for all the trouble which had befallen the Jews rested squarely upon the shoulders of the German Fascists.[11] Václav Kopecký, the Minister of Information, insisted that Germans had not succeeded in their efforts to induce the Czechs to participate in the German racist outrages. Nothing is known about Vacek's own conduct. However, with respect to Kopecký it is important to point to an anti-Semitic outburst of his in Teplice[12] in 1947, in which he referred to the Jews from Subcarpathian Ruthenia as "those bearded Solomons" and "this Jewish scum" who "cannot be put on a par with Czech freedom fighters."

A mood completely different from Vacek's and Kopecký's words is reflected in the resolution adopted by the *Synoda Českobratrské Cirkve Evangelické* (Supreme Organ of the Czech Brethren's Protestant Church), on December 6, 1945:

> The Synod hereby expresses its profound sorrow over the terrible sufferings which befell the Jews during Nazi rule and extends its sympathy to the surviving innocent martyrs. The Synod admits that not even our Church had sufficient courage or [moral] strength to offer resistance to the fury which the foes of Christ poured out upon the Jews . . .[13]

However, this document did not express the dominant mood of the Czech populace. As a result, the social estrangement between the "Aryans" and the "non-Aryans," which of necessity had set in during the era of the Nazi Protectorate, persisted long after the war and never disappeared entirely. Most of the Jews associated chiefly with one another and kept close to the organized Jewish community. It was therefore not surprising that the Jews who remained in the country were eager to rebuild Jewish life and to form a strong Jewish community, and that they supported the agencies of organized Czechoslovak Jewry with a zeal and enthusiasm which no one could have imagined prior to the war.

As already indicated, the chief instruments in the struggle for Jewish recovery and rehabilitation in the western parts of Czechoslovakia were the Jewish Religious Congregation of Prague and the *Rada*. The Slovak counterparts of these agencies were the *Ústredný Sväz* and *Sdruženie fašistickým režimom rasove prenásledovaných* (SRP), the Central Union of Jewish Religious Congregations and the Organization of Victims of Racial Persecution, respectively. For purposes of mutual consultation and maximum effectiveness in promoting the common aims of all these organizations, a coordinating committee[14] was set up to serve as the nucleus for a future representative body that was to speak for all of Czechoslovak Jewry.

In Prague the ceremonies marking the birth of the *Rada* in the fall of 1945 represented the first Jewish public demonstration in Czechoslovakia since the war. Greetings and good wishes were received on this occasion from individuals and organizations near and far, including the Jewish community of Moscow. By that time there were fifty-nine Jewish Religious Congregations in Bohemia and Moravia and 105 in Slovakia.

In its formal aspects, the *Rada* was the successor of the prewar *Nejvyšší Rada* (Supreme Council of Federations of Jewish Religious Congregations of Bohemia, Moravia, and Silesia),[15] but in fact it was intended as a political organization rather than as a strictly religious body.

It may be of interest to recall the following incident in connection with the *Rada*. The supreme organ of the Jewish community was supposed to have a written constitution which would have become effective upon its publication in the official gazette. For years before the war the *Nejvyšší Rada* had been in the process of drafting a constitution, but the Nazis took over Czechoslovakia before the draft document could be adopted. One day late in 1944, a crate sent by the Council of Jewish Elders in Prague arrived at the Schwarzheide concentration camp, where I was an inmate.[16] The crate was filled with loaves of bread for the inmates. When the crate was opened and the bread was unwrapped, it was discovered that the loaves had been wrapped into pages from the draft constitution of the *Nejvyšší Rada* and related documents. By reading through these papers, I learned a great deal about the problems involved in the drafting of that constitution and about the heated debates that had taken place on the subject. Little did I know then that only a year later I myself would be assigned the task of drafting a new constitution for the reconstituted central Jewish representative body of Bohemia, Moravia, and Silesia. Unfortunately, the postwar draft constitution was to share the fate of its predecessor; the former disappeared during the Nazi era and the latter during Communist rule.

In any event, the postwar *Rada* operated until 1948 on the basis of provisional by-laws that had been approved by the Ministry of Education and gave the *Rada* all the powers it required.[17]

Regular religious services were resumed immediately after the war in Prague, Bratislava, and a number of other places. Of the rabbis who had been active in Bohemia before the war, only the chief rabbi, Dr. Aladar Deutsch, and Rabbi Dr. Richard Feder, who had been a well-known teacher and preacher in the town of Kolín, had returned. Dr. Hanuš Rezek (Rebenwurzel), who had served as chaplain for Jewish soldiers in the Czechoslovak army-in-exile, also returned to Prague, where he served for a time as acting chief rabbi. Dr. Deutsch was succeeded by Dr. Gustav Sicher, who returned to Czechoslovakia from what was then Palestine to assume the chief rabbinate.

Problems relating to *shehitah* (slaughter of kosher meat) were solved with dispatch and to the satisfaction of all concerned; the number of kosher restaurants and public soup kitchens during that period was proportionally greater than before the war. The demand for these kosher food services came mainly from the new members of the community and, to a great extent, from the hundreds of Jewish transients, refugees from Poland and Rumania, who found temporary asylum in Bohemia and Slovakia.

In this context one achievement must be mentioned which did credit not only to Czechoslovak Jewry, the Zionist organization, *B'riha*,* and the American Jewish Joint Distribution Committee (JDC), but also to the Czechoslovak authorities and the United Nations Relief and Rehabilitation Administration (UNRRA). It is connected with the mass exodus of Jews from Poland during the postwar era when the Polish government was unable to put a stop to pogroms and other anti-Jewish outrages that were daily occurrences throughout the country. The refugees from Poland poured into Bohemia and Moravia in a state of incredible misery. In this emergency the Czechoslovak government once again practiced those principles of humanity which the people of Czechoslovakia had demonstrated so often before in their history. The refugees who entered Czechoslovakia in organized groups (e.g., *B'riha* transports) were given temporary shelter at reception camps set up for this purpose in the border towns of Náchod and Broumov. The camps were administered by Czechoslovak officials but their day-to-day operations were conducted by the above-named Jewish organizations. The money came primarily from the Czechoslovak government (which allocated UNRRA funds for the camps) and in part from the JDC. There was a reception camp also in the town of Aš through which many hundreds of refugees passed on their way into the American occupation zone of Germany.[18]

---

* The underground Zionist organization which between 1945 and 1948 aided and conducted the mass migration of Jews from Eastern Europe to Palestine.

In addition to the organized migration, totaling about 150,000 refugees, there was a steady unorganized stream of refugees from Poland, Rumania, and Hungary whom the Jewish Religious Congregation of Prague placed into reception camps and hotels. From time to time crises occurred when hundreds of refugees were faced with the threat of deportation, but in each instance deportation was averted. Indeed, when it came to dealing with the Jewish refugees from Poland, it may be said that the Czechoslovak government was in league with the Jews against the Polish authorities.[19]

As already mentioned, steps were taken almost immediately after the end of the war to meet the religious needs of the surviving Jews. Cultural work was also started. The first issue of the *Věstník Zidovské obce náboženské v Praze* appeared in September 1945. *Věstník* soon became an influential organ with many functions; notably, it served as the mouthpiece of the *Rada* and the Jewish community at large and proved an excellent weapon in the fight for Jewish rights. Later on, the Jews in Slovakia, too, began to publish a newspaper, the *Tribúna*. Jewish cultural activity in Prague consisted primarily of the restoration of the Jewish Museum and its exhibits.[20] The museum, in cooperation with the *Rada,* published two books, one dealing with the old ghetto of Prague, the other with the city's ancient Jewish cemetery. The *Rada* also began work on the publication of a book about the Terezín ghetto and cooperated with its author, Zdeněk Lederer, but the Communist takeover put a stop to this project.[21] The publications department of the museum started research projects which were carried out particularly by Dr. Otto Muneles. Muneles and Dr. Berthold Jeiteles (the latter moved to New York in 1949) were the sole survivors of Prague's prewar group of modern Talmudic scholars.

Experts were asked to prepare plans for the preservation of historical sites in Terezín and for the artistic landscaping of the Terezín cemetery.

The restoration of Jewish cemeteries was a major concern of Czechoslovak Jewry. In Bohemia and Moravia alone there were hundreds of Jewish burial grounds, many of which had national landmark status. In many instances the return of such cemeteries to the Jewish community involved considerable effort and sometimes even litigation, particularly in the case of Jewish cemeteries that had been taken over by municipalities during the German occupation and converted into parks. It was extremely difficult to decide the fate of those cemeteries and synagogues that could no longer serve their original purpose; in many cases political realities had to be taken into account at the expense of piety and Jewish religious law.

Outside the major cities it was practically impossible to provide Jewish education for children and adolescents. There was almost no Jewish religious instruction in the rural areas. However, as much attention as possible was given to the other needs of Jewish youth. Homes for children and teenagers were set up, as were convalescent homes and *hakhsharot,* where young men and women were taught the occupational skills needed for a life of pioneering in Palestine. In Prague, day camps were organized for the children of transient refugees.

What was done to provide material assistance for the Jews in postwar Czechoslovakia? It must be stressed that, immediately following liberation, the Czechoslovak government launched an emergency aid program to benefit all repatriates, regardless of religion. The repatriates were given cash, clothing, linen, and shoes, as well as free medical and hospital care. Later, laws were passed awarding indemnification to war widows, orphans, and invalids. But while this help may have met the needs of the average gentile repatriate, it was not sufficient for the Jewish survivors. Ninety percent of the non-Jewish repatriates had families and property waiting for them on their return and were able to resume work in the occupations they had pursued before the war. The average gentile returnee was therefore able to complete his personal and economic readjustment in a matter of only a few weeks. The Jewish returnees, by contrast, had lost their families and their possessions. As a consequence, they were in need of additional help, which had to be supplied by the Jewish community.[22] That this help could be given to them is due to the splendid work of the JDC.[23] The JDC began operations in Bratislava at the beginning of April 1945 and, a few days after liberation, also in Prague. It continued its activities in Czechoslovakia until 1950. Political assistance was received notably from the World Jewish Congress (WJC),[24] of which the *Rada* and *Ústredný Sväz* had both become affiliates. A cordial relationship was also established with the Czechoslovak Jewish Representative Committee in the United States, which had been organized during the war and was affiliated with the WJC in New York. Close relations were maintained with the Central British Fund (CBF—a fund-raising body that had been established to help refugees from Nazi oppression settle in England and other countries), the American Jewish Committee, the ORT, and the OSE.[25] All these organizations provided the Jews of Czechoslovakia with material assistance. The WJC sent food and clothing, and for some time helped maintain a children's home in Prague. The CBF made available a loan for the restoration of the Jewish Home for the Aged in Prague and provided scholarships for students. ORT conducted programs of vocational retraining, particularly in the border areas of Bohemia; OSE, in cooperation with the JDC, maintained a sanitorium in the Tatra mountains.

The social services rendered to the Jewish returnees by Jewish organizations included financial support, gifts of clothing, linen, consumer articles and food, counseling, and medical treatment, care in the Jewish hospital, and, where necessary, admission to Jewish homes for the aged, to children's homes, or to young people's hostels. After the war, three Jewish homes for the aged—in Prague, Poděbrady and Brno—were set up. Funds for these social services came from the JDC, the *Rada,* the *Ústredný Sväz* and the Czechoslovak government. A total of 900,000 Czech crowns from UNRRA funds was allocated for the rebuilding of the Jewish home for the aged in Prague; the *Rada* also received money from the Czechoslovak government to help support certain categories of Jewish repatriates.

Almost all the money which the *Rada* contributed to cover its social services, as well as the funds which were used for administrative expenses, came from the Jewish assets that had remained in the Terezín ghetto at the end of the war. Immediately following the liberation, all Jewish property and assets left in Terezín after the departure of the Germans, as well as the funds in the bank accounts of the *Jüdische Selbstverwaltung Theresienstadt* (Autonomous Jewish Administration in Terezín), which amounted to 400 million Czech crowns, were placed under the jurisdiction of the Czechoslovak Ministry of Social Welfare as a quasi-national administration. However, the ministry official who was placed in charge of these Jewish assets did not accept the idea that they should be treated as Jewish property or that the Jews should have any right to control or to claim them for themselves. Like most Czechoslovak bureaucrats, this official, too, regarded the ghetto assets as abandoned German property that had become the property of the Czechoslovak nation as "spoils of war." The Soviet occupation authorities, incidentally, also held that the ghetto assets were "spoils of war" and as a result whole wagonloads of the most valuable items of ghetto property were shipped off to the Soviet Union.

However, with the help of the then Minister of Labor and Social Welfare, Dr. Jozef Soltész, and his closest associates, this state of affairs was changed. In January 1946 the government issued an order essentially awarding these assets to the organizations representing victims of racial persecution. The day-to-day decisions arising from that order were entrusted to a ministerial committee. One central commission and several special commissions were then set up, in which most of the members were Jewish and without whose approval the ministry was not authorized to take any action. As a result, a total of sixty million Czechoslovak crowns was turned over to the *Rada*. Textile goods, machinery, tools, etc., in the value of millions of crowns were distributed among individual victims of racial persecution and among various Jewish institutions.

Thousands of books were transferred to the Jewish Museum in Prague; most of these were eventually sent to the Hebrew University in Jerusalem. Several million Terezín "ghetto crowns" (scrips) were stored in the museum building; plans to turn these scrips into cash with the help of the major Jewish organizations were never realized. In this connection, it should be pointed out that allocations from the Terezín assets to individuals were supposed to be subtracted from indemnification claims made by the recipients. But the import of this ruling was merely academic, for, with the exception of advance payments of up to 50,000 crowns in cash, Czechoslovakia to date has not granted any indemnification payments to victims of Nazi persecution.

Dr. Soltész and Foreign Minister Jan Masaryk were the only members of the government who took a genuine and warmly sympathetic interest in Jewish problems, were actively concerned with providing relief for victims of Nazi persecution, and proved to be devoted, helpful friends.[26] It was thanks to Soltész that the *Rada* was accepted as a partner in all negotiations regarding the rehabilitation of victims of Nazi persecution. However, the results fell short of expectations. Despite strenuous efforts and protracted negotiations, the *Rada* did not succeed with one of its basic demands, namely the assignment of heirless Jewish property for the rehabilitation of victims of racial persecution. The *Rada* had in mind a procedure which was basically the one subsequently implemented in the Federal Republic of Germany by the establishment of the Jewish Restitution Successor Organization (JRSO). The proposal was for the creation of a government agency to receive and administer funds confiscated by the Nazis and not claimed by their rightful owners, with the understanding that if these funds remained unclaimed for a certain period of time they would be turned over to the *Rada* to be used for rehabilitation purposes. Instead, the Czechoslovak government decided to set up within the prime minister's office a kind of watchdog agency to superintend the management of the funds involved. Although the *Rada* was represented in that agency, its goals were boycotted from the very outset by the so-called *Fond národní obnovy* (National Rehabilitation Fund), a government organ which pursued diametrically opposed economic aims.

How, then, was the restitution problem handled in Czechoslovakia? The guiding principles in this respect were a declaration issued by the Allied governments in 1943, a decree enacted by President Beneš in 1945, and the Restitution Law of 1946.[27] In general, the Restitution Law provided a relatively sound basis for an equitable solution of the restitution problem. The *Rada* had an opportunity to exert some influence on this legislation, but here, too, as in so many other instances where Jewish representatives had helped in the drafting of legislation, they encountered difficulties and unpleasant surprises. Thus, in the case of the Restitution Law, representatives of the Slovak right-wing parties had proposed—literally at the last moment—an amendment which, had it been accepted, would have all but killed restitution in Czechoslovakia. When it learned of the proposed amendment, the *Rada* waged a veritable *blitzkrieg* on the prime minister's office and the Ministry of Justice, and in the end obtained an acceptable formulation of the law. While the *Rada* did not succeed in effecting a positive solution of the problems relating to heirless assets, it did, at least, manage to prevent the enactment of unfavorable legislation and to put through a law whereby the final disposition of these assets was to be held in abeyance until the passage of subsequent, more definitive regulations. The efforts in this regard continued practically without a stop until the Communist takeover in 1948. One decisive setback came in the summer of 1947 with the enactment of the Currency Liquidation Fund Law[28] under which these heirless assets, along with the Terezín estate, were to be taken over by the Czechoslovak state. In other words, Jewish assets were to be confiscated all over again. The counteroffensive that the *Rada* then unleashed on both the legislative and executive fronts was unprecedented. The adoption of the crucial provision in this law had been brought about in an underhanded manner, and though the Jews had the sympathy even of some rightwing members of parliament and of the Union of Former Political Prisoners, the law was passed. The only remaining hope lay in presidential intervention. As a matter of fact, President Beneš was convinced of the justice of the Jewish case. But when the government gave him a formal declaration to the effect that nothing would be done with the heirless property to violate Czechoslovakia's international obligations, he decided to let the bill become law. Although the government's declaration to President Beneš was basically different from the assurances that had been given to representatives of the *Rada*—and to Alexander L. Easterman of the World Jewish Congress,[29] who had come to their assistance—it might have been used successfully, if the Communist takeover had not put an end to all endeavors in this respect.

Jan Masaryk was outraged at the passage of the law, but he did not have sufficient influence in the cabinet to change the situation. The *Rada*'s defeat on this issue gave good reason to wonder whether the democratic administration of law and justice would be able to survive in Czechoslovakia.

Efforts to obtain restitution for individuals, on the other hand, brought positive results, particularly in the case of houses. Restitution involving other kinds of property was obtained only with great difficulty and was, in part, obstructed by the gradual nationalization of private property. Difficulties were encountered particularly in restitution cases involving landed property. Those most adversely affected were Jewish citizens of Czechoslovakia who had declared themselves members of the German or Hungarian nationality group in the census of 1930. The somewhat unfortunate formulation of the criteria determining nationality group status and the rigid rules governing exceptions to these regulations were exploited by the opponents of restitution—from supreme court justices down to petty

"Aryanizers"—for the invalidation of restitution claims. The issues of *Věstník* from this period[30] are filled with reports of continuous protests and debates on the subject. The aim of the Jewish leadership was to obtain recognition for the principle that any Czechoslovak Jew—regardless of whether he had belonged to Category A or Category B—who had suffered racial persecution during the Nazi occupation had a right to restitution irrespective of the nationality he had reported on the 1930 census sheet. It seemed natural that the loyalty of all such Jewish citizens to the Czechoslovak state was to be taken for granted, and that the burden of producing proof to the contrary devolved on the state.

During the year following the liberation of Czechoslovakia the concepts of nationality had become so badly garbled and subject to so much misinterpretation that the parties in disputes involving such cases often found themselves talking at cross-purposes. It was not until September 1946[31] that a measure of clarity was introduced into the issue through an order from the Ministry for Internal Affairs, which proved helpful in problems of restitution and nationality status.[32]

The manner in which the Czechoslovak bureaucracy dealt with restitution claims was clearly indicative of trends which gradually came to pervade the entire structure of the Czechoslovak state. Since most of the assets of Czechoslovak Jews had been confiscated by the Nazis, who had been the enemies of Czechoslovakia, it was understandable that initially the Czechoslovak state should have taken them over as "enemy assets." But this should have been done only with the understanding that eventually these assets should be returned to their rightful owners or their heirs. However, here, too, the bureaucracy followed the path of least resistance. In cases of business concerns subject to nationalization by virtue of their size the answer was, of course, simple. But in other cases, the opponents of restitution had to find ways of preventing the restoration of the property to its lawful owners. As a rule, the *Rada* in such problems could not count on help from the political organizations on either the right or the left, but what little assistance was received came from the former rather than from the latter. Those directly responsible for most of the difficulties were in the secretariat of the Communist party and in the Central Federation of Trade Unions, which was headed by a Communist, Antonín Zápotocký.

The opponents of restitution based their arguments on their interpretation of the "public interest" and on their alleged apprehension that the change might disrupt the smooth operation of the concerns in question. The Jewish representatives, on the other hand, claimed that it was in the "public interest" that existing legislation (including the restitution laws adopted by the Czechoslovak government) should be carried out in full. The decline in respect for the law demonstrated in these cases was a portent of the end of democracy in Czechoslovakia.

Concerns involved in restitution proceedings were paralyzed by strikes, demonstrations, and workers' riots organized by the Central Federation of Trade Unions, culminating in the strike at the Beer textile factory in Varnsdorf.[33] There the Communist party and the Central Federation of Trade Unions fomented a general strike in the entire district to prevent the implementation of a court decision temporarily restoring the factory, which had been confiscated by the Nazis, to its rightful owner, a Jew by the name of Beer. The nationalization laws were not applicable to this factory. The agitation resulted in anti-Semitic demonstrations and in the end Beer was taken into "protective custody." His attorney, a gentile, was attacked by the mob as a traitor and had to flee for his life.

At this point it was generally felt that things had gone too far. The non-Communist parties recognized the dangers inherent in the situation. They understood that, contrary to Communist allegations, the Jewish leadership was not fighting for the "capitalist" interests of a big industrialist but for the preservation of law and order. But when representatives of the *Rada* called on Zápotocký, he told them in no uncertain terms[34] that no matter what befell, he would prevent the return of larger business and manufacturing concerns to their Jewish owners.[35]

For some time *Rada* representatives had vainly sought to obtain an interview with Prime Minister Klement Gottwald. Only after his private secretary was told that if the prime minister would persist in his refusal to receive them the *Rada* would be forced to address its grievances to him through the press did Gottwald agree to meet with the delegation. The first thing he said to the *Rada* representatives during that conference was that he would not permit himself to be blackmailed by threats to use the foreign press against him. It was explained to him that he had misunderstood the statement; the

Rada had never intended to attack him through the *foreign* press. The rest of the interview was conducted in a calm and objective manner. Gottwald ordered the investigation of a number of problems. The most significant result of the visit, however, was that Gottwald rejected the demand of the Central Federation of Trade Unions for the cessation of all restitution proceedings involving business or manufacturing concerns temporarily under government administration.[36]

In order to prevent further excesses such as those in Varnsdorf, Gottwald ordered the appointment of mixed commissions on a fifty-fifty basis which were to invite the *Rada* to participate in all hearings involving victims of racial persecution. However, in the very first case to be examined by such a commission, Gottwald's directive was simply ignored. When the case was negotiated at the Ministry of Industry, the *Rada* was not admitted; the explanation given was that no other "church groups" had been asked to participate. Nonetheless, the *Rada* solved this problem by having the Jewish petitioner confer power of attorney on an individual who was a member of the *Rada*. Actually, this was the only instance in which the *Rada* was denied official status.

At this point it should be recalled that, as early as January 1946, the *Rada* had prevailed upon the government to set up a special department for Jewish affairs in the Prime Minister's Office. In accordance with the wishes of President Beneš, this department was to coordinate all governmental measures relating to the rehabilitation of victims of Nazi persecution, to examine all draft legislation pertinent to this problem, and to channel the *Rada*'s grievances and petitions to the proper authorities.[37]

Although this department did some good work, it lacked sufficient authority to fulfill the high hopes which the Jewish community had placed in it. Also, notwithstanding Jewish protests and without consulting President Beneš, Premier Gottwald simply abolished it long before it could have completed its task. This is only another practical example of the confusion that characterized the attitude of the Czechoslovak authorities toward the Jews and their problems at the time. They said they considered it undesirable to maintain a special "department for Jewish affairs," because they claimed that this was a form of discrimination against the Jews who, now that the Nazis were gone, had automatically become equal citizens of the reconstituted Czechoslovak Republic—which of course was not the case.

In this context, mention should be made of a memorable audience of Czechoslovak Jews with President Beneš that took place on March 20, 1947. The delegation that called on the president consisted of representatives from the Czech Historic Lands and from Slovakia. The head of the Slovak deputation, Dr. Vojtěch (Albert) Winterstein, informed Beneš of the intolerable conditions under which the Jews in Slovakia were living. The president took copious notes and was obviously upset. He said that he was not surprised about this deplorable state of affairs but that he was virtually powerless to do anything about it. Indeed, he pointed out, the central government had been unable to make any headway even in some vital problems in Slovakia that affected the welfare of the entire state. Arnošt (Ernst) Frischer, the head of the delegation from Bohemia and Moravia, then gave the president a report on the "vital problems" of the Jewish population there, telling him, among other things, about the Varnsdorf incident and Zápotocký's reaction to the Jewish protest. The president's answer reflected the full tragedy of the situation and Beneš's own feeling of impotence in the face of imminent national and personal tragedy. In a casual tone of voice, he said: "Yes, gentlemen, as far as our colleague Zápotocký is concerned, the revolution is not yet over."

This survey would be incomplete if it did not dwell at least briefly on the attitude of Czechoslovak Jewry toward the developments that were taking place in Palestine after the war. All of Czechoslovak Jewry followed with keen interest the events that led up to the establishment of the state of Israel. Accordingly, both the *Ústredný Sväz* and the *Rada* took a stand on every question relating to the Jewish state in the making, and *Rada* representatives testified before the Anglo-American Committee of Inquiry on Palestine[38] that visited Prague in order to hear their views on the subject of the Jewish homeland. After the adoption of the United Nations resolution calling for the establishment of a Jewish state in Palestine, the *Rada* conveyed the thanks of Czechoslovak Jewry to the Czechoslovak government, particularly to President Beneš and Foreign Minister Jan Masaryk, for the support which Czechoslovakia had given to the partition resolution at the United Nations. The adoption of this resolution on November 29, 1947, was hailed by joyous impromptu demonstrations among Jews in Prague and throughout Czechoslovakia. The *Rada* and *Ústredný Sväz* arranged mass rallies in Prague, Brno, Bratislava, and other Czechoslovak cities. At the Prague gathering, which was held in Smetana Hall, a message of heartfelt congratulations from President Beneš was read.[39] This was probably the only event following the end of World War II that brought genuine elation to Czechoslovak Jewry.

It must be clear from this study that almost from the time of liberation in May 1945 many portents of Czechoslovakia's "Communization" made themselves felt also in the Jewish sector of the population. But in February 1948 events began to be precipitated, culminating in the establishment of a Communist regime in Czechoslovakia. As a result of the Communist takeover, the *Rada* was forced to discontinue all its activities in the field of rehabilitation and as early as March 1948 it waived all Jewish claims to the funds from the Terezín assets. The American Jewish Joint Distribution Committee (JDC) continued some of its work in Czechoslovakia until 1950, when it was ordered to stop all its activities there. On its departure the JDC left behind substantial funds to cover for some time the cost of the social services rendered by the *Rada* and the *Ústredný Sväz*. A detailed report on this period would exceed the framework of this article.[40]

On the whole, it may be said that notwithstanding all the difficulties of the postwar transition period, Czechoslovak Jewry early in 1948 had been well on the way toward rebuilding its communities and resuming—if not in quantity, then at least in quality—its role on the world Jewish scene that had always been quite remarkable. But then the events of February 1948 brought these encouraging developments to an abrupt end.

NOTES

1. *Úkoly Židovské náboženské obce v Praze* [The Tasks of the Jewish Religious Congregation in Prague], *Věstník židovské obce náboženské v Praze* (Bulletin of the Jewish Religious Congregation of Prague), 8, no. 2, p. 28; January 1946, p. 2.

2. See also Yeshayahu Jelinek, "The Jews in Slovakia: 1945-1948," in the present volume, pp. 533-34.
3. "Složení nového výboru a představenstva RŽNO" [Composition of the New Executive and Board of the Council of Jewish Religious Congregations], *Věstník*, 10, no. 14, April 2, 1948, p. 54; "Egon Ervín Kisch," *Věstník*, 10, no. 15, April 9, 1948. Kisch did not enjoy his new office for long; he died in March 1948.
4. "Sionistický sjezd v Luhačovicích" [The Zionist Convention at Luhačovice], *Věstník*, 8, no. 8, August 1, 1946, p. 70.
5. "Stanovisko," *Věstník*, 8, no. 9, November 5, 1946; "K valné hromadě Svazu Čechů-židů 18. ledna 1948 v Praze" [On the General Assembly of the Czech-Jewish Federation], *Věstník*, 10, no. 3, January 16, 1948, p. 27; "Zdařilá valná hromada Svazu Čechů-židů" [Successful General Assembly of the Czech-Jewish Federation], *Věstník*, 10, no. 4, January 23, 1948, pp. 35, 36; "K valné hromadě Svazu Čechů-židů" [On the General Assembly of the Czech-Jewish Federation], *Věstník*, 10, no. 5, January 30, 1948, pp. 46-48.
6. "Právní postavení židů ze Zakarpatské Ukrajiny" [The Legal Position of Jews from Subcarpathian Ruthenia], *Věstník*, 7, no. 11, September 1, 1946, p. 100.
7. Stefan Engel, "Ratio legis," *Věstník*, 8, no. 3, March 30, 1946, pp. 18-19; Kurt Wehle, "První kroky do svobody," [First Steps to Freedom], *Věstník*, 8, nos. 4-5, May 5, 1946, pp. 30-33; Wehle, "Státní občanství" [Citizenship], *Věstník*, 8, no. 1, January 25, 1946, p. 7.
8. Just a few personal impressions to illustrate this point: Certainly it was heartwarming on my return to have my little shoemaker from before the war serve me coffee and bread, resole my one pair of shoes free of charge and then slip me a 100-crown note as a parting gift. To be sure, I felt touched and comforted when a gentile friend came and returned to me a suit which I had given him as a gift before my deportation. But on the other hand, imagine my feelings when, waiting in a long line outside the Housing Department, I heard a woman say, "Just look at all those Jews! There must have been some leaks in those gas chambers. It looks as if more Jews got back than there were here to start with."
9. "Pustošení židovských hřbitovů" [The Vandalization of Jewish Cemeteries], *Věstník*, 9, no. 21, October 28, 1947, p. 309; "Ministerstvo vnitra a ministerstvo informací proti hanobení židovských hřbitovů" [The Ministry for Internal Affairs and the Ministry of Information Against the Desecration of Jewish Cemeteries], *Věstník*, 10, no. 10, March 5, 1948, p. 113.

10. Kurt Wehle: "Slovo k židům na Slovensku" [A Word to the Jews in Slovakia], *Věstník,* 8, no. 3, May 30, 1946, pp. 17-18.
11. *Věstník,* 7, no. 1, September 1, 1945.
12. *Věstník,* 9, no. 7, April 1, 1947, p. 91.
13. *Věstník,* 8, no. 1, January 25, 1946, p. 4
14. "Dohoda o zřízení koordinačního výboru" [Agreement on the Creation of a Coordinating Committee], *Věstník,* 9, no. 9, May 1, 1947, p. 126.
15. See Volume I, pp. 308 ff.
16. From July 1, 1944, to April 18, 1945.
17. "Z historie ústavy židovské náboženske společnosti" [From the History of the Constitution of the Jewish Religious Community], *Věstník,* 9, no. 22, October 6, 1947; "Ústava židovské náboženské společnosti [The Constitution of the Jewish Religious Community], *Věstník,* 10, no. 4, January 23, 1948, p. 40.
18. Files of Dr. Albert (Vojtěch) Winterstein (AW), minutes of the regular meeting of the SRP, April 11, 1946. Cf. also Yehuda Bauer, *Flight and Rescue: Brichah* (New York: 1970).
19. One incident gave rise to much resentment against the officials who were to blame for it. A small transport of about twenty-five refugees from Poland was seized by the Czechoslovak authorities in Náchod on the grounds that they had violated some regulations, and the unfortunate refugees were about to be deported back to Poland. However, the *Rada* managed to convince the Ministry for Internal Affairs that if these refugees would be returned to Poland they would be subject to severe punishment, perhaps even the death penalty. The ministry thereupon informed the *Rada* that everything was in order, which meant that, after a token period of imprisonment, the refugees would be moved westward by way of Bratislava. Half an hour later, however, word was received from Náchod that the refugees had already been sent back across the Polish border and had been turned over to Polish frontier guards. This happened only a few hours before Yom Kippur. Difficult as it was to accept, the fact was that the *Rada* had been deliberately deceived by an official of the Ministry for Internal Affairs. The official in question was subsequently ordered by the ministry to make an apology to the *Rada,* but the *Rada* was never able to find out what became of the hapless refugees.
20. Kamil Kleiner, "Židovské museum v Praze" [The Jewish Museum in Prague], *Věstník,* 8, no. 7, p. 54. See Hana Volavková, "The Jewish Museum of Prague," in the present volume, pp. 577-80.
21. Lederer's book was published in London (1953) in a revised English edition under the title *Ghetto Theresienstadt.* For his article "Terezín," see in the present volume pp. 104-64.

22. Central Zionist Archives (CZA), Jerusalem, File S26/1390, Chaim Barlasz, Report on Emigration and Rescue in European Countries, Jerusalem, June 25, 1946.
23. Adolf Beneš, "American Joint Distribution Committee," *Věstník,* 8, no. 8, August 1, 1946, pp. 65–66.
24. Morris Pearlman, "A Visit to Czechoslovakia," *The Jewish Chronicle* (London), November 22 and 29, 1946.
25. The ORT is an international Jewish organization set up for the vocational rehabilitation and reorientation of Jewish refugees; OSE operates in the areas of preventive medicine, medical education, public health, and child care. Both organizations were originally created in aid of Russian Jews. Their names are abbreviations from the Russian. ORT stands for *Obshczestvo Rasprostranenya Truda* (Sredi Evreyev), and OSE (or OZE) for *Obshczestvo Zdravookhranenya Evreyev.*
26. Soltész's attitude toward the problems of Jewish war survivors can best be seen from the following incident. One evening I received a telephone call at my home from his secretary, asking me to come to Soltész's office the next morning. A conference of representatives of all competent ministries had been called to meet at the prime minister's office that day to discuss the administration and disposition of assets confiscated by the Nazis during the occupation period. When Soltész learned that the *Rada* had not been invited to the conference, he decided to have me attend as one of the experts representing his own ministry. In this way I had a chance to present the views of the Jewish community, which Soltész shared. While the *Rada* was not officially represented at the conference, all those present—about 100 highly placed officials—understood that I was, in fact, speaking for the *Rada.*
27. Law No. 128 of May 16, 1946, Collection of Laws and Ordinances of the Czechoslovak Republic.
28. AW, File IV/3 Circular Letter of the Council of Jewish Religious Congregations in Bohemia and Moravia, No. Uo/489, Prague, June 17, 1947: *Připomínky k vládnímu návrhu zákona o likvidačním fondu měnovém* (Tisk UNS c. 619); Letter, USŽNO and SRP to the Presidium of the Czechoslovak government, No. Uo/551, July 16, 1947.
29. AW, Letter of Alexander L. Easterman to Dr. Albert (Vojtěch) Winterstein, July 22, 1947; letters of Dr. Winterstein to the World Jewish Congress in New York and London, August 6, 1947.
30. Fr. Fuchs, "Víra v 5. květen" [Faith in the Fifth of May], *Věstník,* 8, nos. 4–5, p. 28; Kurt Wehle, "První kroky do svobody" [First Steps to Freedom], *Věstník,* 8, nos. 4–5, May 5, 1946, pp. 30–33; "K novému výnosu" [On the New Decree], *Věstník,* 8, no. 2, October 1, 1946, p. 99; "Jak se provádí restituce žid. majetku" [How the Restitution of Jewish

Property is Being Carried Out], *Věstník,* March 5, 1947; "Staŕy stesk nad novou vyhláškou" [An Old Lament Over the New Decree], *Věstník,* 9, no. 7, pp. 93–94.
31. "Konečně jasno" [Clarity at Last], *Věstník,* 8, no. 10, September 10, 1946, p. 87. "Aby pravda zvítězila" [That Truth May Prevail], *Věstník,* 8, no. 11, October 1, 1946, pp. 1–2.
32. In connection with this ministerial decree many tragicomic incidents, resulting from the confusion that prevailed among the authorities, might be cited. For instance, many Jewish cemeteries were confiscated by the Czechoslovak government as "enemy property" because the individuals buried in that particular cemetery had spoken only German during their lifetimes! Highly placed officials felt called upon to apologize whenever they used the terms "Jews" and "Jewish" with reference to Jews and Jewish problems. It seems they feared one would think they were using these designations as terms of abuse. But their disgust at the pejorative connotation of the name led to absurdities since they did not consider that, after all, the Jews and Jewish problems were still very much alive and that there was no alternative but to refer to them by their proper name. The ministerial decree of 1946 carried these apprehensions to extremes by using the phrase "individuals of so-called Jewish origin" in quotation marks to designate people of Jewish origin, and the words "so-called Jews" to designate Jews. The limit of absurdity was the sentence, "Nazism struck its first blow against the so-called 'Jews.' "
33. "K událostem ve Varnsdorfu" [On the Events at Varnsdorf], *Věstník,* 9, no. 6, pp. 69–74.
34. I was a member of the *Rada* delegation that visited Zápotocký. "Your people had us workers shot, and now, once again, you are defending them against our workers," he said. "You'll never learn your lesson." He made allusions to long-past (and in this case absolutely irrelevant) management-labor incidents and oversimplified the problem by equating the Jews with the big industrialists. The representatives of the *Rada* did not ignore this affront but gave him an appropriate reply. In the end he shouted hysterically that it was outrageous that he should be held up as an anti-Semite when, in fact, he respected the Jews, and so forth. I then told him that in his next radio address he should tell his entire people that he detested anti-Semitism, that he supported complete restitution, and that he would invoke stringent penalties upon functionaries of the Central Federation of Trade Unions found guilty of anti-Jewish excesses. The conference ended without the official niceties customary on such occasions.

35. "Varnsdorfský případ" [The Varnsdorf Case], *Věstník*, 9, no. 7, April 1, 1947, pp. 88–89; "K projevu ministra informací Václava Kopeckého v Teplicích-Šanově" [On the Statement by Minister of Information Václav Kopecký at Teplice-Šanov], *Věstník*, 9, no. 7, April 1, 1947, p. 91.
36. AW, Minutes of the meeting of the expanded committee of the SRP, March 26, 1947; "Predstavitelia čsl. Židovstva u pana prezidenta a u členov vlády" [Representatives of Czechoslovak Jewry Call On the President and Members of the Government]. *Spolkové Zlaté USC* (Bratislava), April 1, 1947, p. 1. Cf. AW, File II/7, letter from ÚSŽNO and SRP to Klement Gottwald, No. 1210/47, May 15, 1947.
37. AW, File IV/3, Letter from *Rada* and ÚSŽNO to the Czechoslovak government, No. Uo/551, July 16, 1947.
38. "The Anglo-American Committee of Inquiry on Palestine," *Věstník*, 8, no. 3, March 30, 1946, p. 21. AW, File IV/3, "Memorandum ÚSŽNO podané 2/14/1946 Anglo-americké vyšetřovací komisii po schválení Dr. Clementisom," Minutes of the meeting of the expanded committee of the SRP, February 20, 1946.
39. "President Dr. Eduard Beneš zapsán do 'Zlaté knihy' " [President Dr. Eduard Beneš inscribed in the Golden Book (of the Jewish National Fund)], *Věstník*, 10, no. 3, January 16, 1948, p. 25.
40. "Provolání" [Proclamation], *Věstník*, 10, no. 10, March 5, 1948, p. 109; "Czech Leaders Deposed. Action Committee's Drastic Steps," *The Jewish Chronicle* (London), March 19, 1948; "Akční výbor RŽNO se představil" [RŽNO Actions Committee Is Introduced], *Věstník*, 10, no. 11, March 12, 1948, pp. 117–19; "Zapis o mimořádné schůzi výboru Rady ŽNO, konané dne 10. března 1948" [Minutes of the Extraordinary Meeting of the RŽNO Executive Committee on March 10, 1948], *Věstník*, 10, no. 12, March 19, 1948, p. 134. Cf. AW, File IV/3, Letter from Ústredný Sväz Cionistický (USC; Central Zionist Union) to the Central Action Committee of the National Front, April 5, 1948.

THE JEWS IN SLOVAKIA: 1945-1949

by Yeshayahu Jelinek

After the war had ended, the last of the German soldiers had left the territory of Slovakia, and the concentration camps had been emptied of their surviving inmates, the true extent of Slovak Jewry's disaster came to light. According to the official census, there had been 136,737 Jews in Slovakia in 1930.[1] A census taken in 1938 counted 85,045 individuals of the Mosaic faith.[2] This last figure did not, of course, include Jews in Slovak territory annexed by Hungary on November 2, 1938, where there were about 40,000 Jews.[3] In June 1946 a total of 28,000 Jews, survivors of the Holocaust and returnees from abroad, were living in Slovakia.[4]

The purpose of this study is to survey the situation of the remnants of Slovak Jewry during the period beginning with the termination of hostilities in the spring of 1945 and ending with the mass emigration of Jews from Slovakia in 1949. It should be emphasized at the outset that at the time of this writing very little basic research—historical, demographic or psychological—has been done on this traumatic era in the history of Slovak Jewry. Also, much still remains unsaid about such subjects as the contribution of Slovak Jewry to *B'riha*, the "illegal immigration" of Holocaust survivors to Palestine between the end of the war and the establishment of the state of Israel, and the part of Slovak Jews in Israel's War of Independence. Although there is considerable primary material at our disposal,[5] much data remain inaccessible.

No definitive study exists on the attitude of the Czechoslovak leaders in London and Moscow during the war years, or of the various Slovak underground organizations, toward the Jews and their future status in the postwar republic. There is at present only one work that touches upon the attitude of the Czechoslovak government-in-exile in London. Livia Rothkirchen states that Dr. Eduard Beneš and his associates did not anticipate granting minority rights in Czechoslovakia after the war to any group, including the Jews.[6] It seems that occasionally the underground Slovak Communist party voiced indirect objections to the persecution and particularly the deportation of Jews in Slovakia.[7] But the few extant documents regarding the attitude of the non-Communist Slovak underground would indicate that it was colored by a certain amount of distrust and lack of sympathy for the Jews.[8]

As early as August 17, 1941, the Czechoslovak government-in-exile issued a proclamation invalidating all racial legislation and on January 5, 1943, it was a cosigner of a proclamation to the same effect by seventeen Allied governments in London.[9] The political leaders of the Slovak anti-Fascist uprising (August–October 1944) issued a decree annulling the laws of the state of Slovakia, which naturally included the anti-Jewish legislation enacted by the German puppet state.[10] One gains the impression, however, that the Slovak anti-Fascist leadership was somewhat hesitant about restoring all the rights to the Jews, particularly in the economic sphere. In a letter to the author dated May 5, 1973, Dr. Martin Kvetko, a former leader of the Slovak Democratic party, stated that "the Slovak National Council had no particular Jewish policy either during the uprising or thereafter."[11]

The survivors of the Holocaust in Slovakia faced a variety of problems, social, economic, administrative, and political. Jewish survivors returned to their former homes from the woods and other hiding places, from concentration camps and countries of exile, from partisan units, from Allied armies, and from Czechoslovak military units which had fought on the Western and Eastern fronts. Many of the smaller prewar Jewish communities had disappeared because most of their members had perished and the remnants tended to gather in the larger towns and cities, mainly for reasons of personal safety and higher standards of living.[12] Considerable efforts were made to rehabilitate the returnees both physically and psychologically. Local and international organizations, Jewish and non-Jewish, gave their help. During the initial period following the war, the population was kind to the Jews who had returned. Many non-Jews who had "sequestered" Jewish property during the war returned it to their rightful owners. However, this situation changed once the populace discovered that the local authorities did not particularly like the Jews and that the central government of the postwar Czechoslovak Republic was either too busy or too indifferent to devote particular attention to the Jews and their problems. Before long, there was a growing trend toward open anti-Semitism on the part of the Slovak populace.

The decision of the postwar Czechoslovak government regarding the settlement of Czechoslovakia's national minority problems had repercussions also for the status of the Jews. While they were still in exile, Czechoslovak statesmen had resolved to expel the German and Hungarian ethnic minorities from Czechoslovakia after the war and to turn the republic into an ethnic state consisting of Czechs and Slovaks. Only the Ukrainian minority in Eastern Slovakia was permitted—probably due to pressures from the neighboring Soviet Union—to develop a national life of its own.[13] The request of the Slovak Jews for representation as a national entity in the Slovak National Council in Bratislava and in the Provisional Legislative Assembly in Prague was turned down.[14] The Jewish national entity which had been recognized as a separate minority group in the prewar republic had lost its official status.[15] Thus, Jews of German and Hungarian nationality were regarded as Germans and Magyars and it was only after long and arduous negotiations with the Jewish organizations that the government decided to let them remain in Czechoslovakia instead of expelling them as they had other members of the German and Hungarian ethnic minorities.[16]

The Jewish community in postwar Slovakia was led by three central organizations: (1) The Organization of Victims of Racial Persecution at the hands of the Fascist Regime (*Sdrúženie fašistickým rezimom rasove prenasledovaných*), popularly known as the SRP; (2) The Central Union of Jewish Religious Congregations in Slovakia (*Ústredný sväz židovských náboženských obcí na Slovensku*), known as ÚSŽNO; and (3) The Central Zionist Union (*Ústredný Sväz Cionistický*), known as the ÚSC.

The leadership in all three organizations was almost identical. Outstanding among the leaders were Rabbi Armin Frieder (who, after his death in 1946, was replaced in the ÚSŽNO by his brother, Emanuel), Dr. Oskar Neumann (who, after his emigration to Israel in 1946, was replaced in the ÚSC by Oskar Krasniansky), and Dr. Vojtěch (Albert) Winterstein, who acted as secretary-general of the SRP until the end of 1948 and represented Slovak Jewry in the World Jewish Congress.

Both the SRP and the ÚSŽNO were founded in June 1945. The objective of the SRP was to protect and promote the interests of the victims of racial persecution "without regard to their religion and nationality."[17] The long delay in the granting of official status to the SRP (as well as to the ÚSC, which was founded in July 1945) reflected the reluctance of the Czechoslovak authorities to see different categories of victims of racial persecution represented in one single organization.[18] The creation of the ÚSŽNO, on the other hand, met with little official opposition and the authorities willingly approved Rabbi Frieder's plan to unify the various Jewish religious organizations then existing in Slovakia. However, the Central Board of the Autonomous Orthodox Jewish Religious Congregations objected to the unification. The struggle between the strictly Orthodox community and the non-Orthodox Jews dated back to 1869 and had continued ever since. Bitterness increased when Zionism grew stronger in Slovakia and clashed with the followers of the ultra-Orthodox, non-Zionist Agudath Israel. During and after the Holocaust Slovak Orthodox Jewry suffered considerable attrition because of the Nazi horrors, the secularization of the survivors, and subsequent mass emigration. There had been a change in the power structure among the various segments of Slovak Jewry, and the strength of the Zionists increased. Moreover, the Commissioner for Education and Public Enlightenment in Slovakia, a Communist, supported Rabbi Frieder's initiative for unification. On September 15, 1945, the commissioner issued an order for the merger of the Central Board of Autonomous Orthodox Jewish Religious Congregations and the "Jeschurun" Federation of Jewish Religious Congregations into the single ÚSŽNO under the leadership of Rabbi Frieder. Although the final merger was preceded by a long struggle, it eventually materialized in January 1947.[19]

Not all the Jews in Slovakia joined the postwar Jewish religious congregations. Some had become secularized. Others preferred to conceal their Jewish identity and merge into the general population. A considerable number entered the Communist party, which then enjoyed high prestige because of its part in the struggle against

Fascism. Also, several thousands of Jews had converted to Christianity during the war in the hope of saving their lives. Not all of these people returned to Judaism after the war, but the SRP represented their interests also as victims of Nazi persecution.

In addition to the officially sanctioned communal bodies, the Zionists and non-Zionists in Slovakia created a great variety of organizations, youth movements, and clubs. Strengthened ties were developed with Jewish bodies abroad, particularly with the World Jewish Congress (WJC), the American Jewish Joint Distribution Committee (JDC), and the Jewish Agency for Palestine.

ÚSŽNO made contact with its sister organization in Prague, the Council of Jewish Religious Congregations in Bohemia and Moravia. Relations between these two organizations were not always the best; the two entities were divided by cultural, sociological, and historical differences as well as differences in mentality and temperament. While the Czech organization felt that the religious congregations should be centered in Prague, the nation's capital, the Slovak Jews, claiming greater numbers and deeper piety, wanted the center to be in Bratislava, the capital of Slovakia. Thus, despite repeated attempts, the Czech and Slovak Jews were not able to merge into one single communal organization until the Communists forced them to do so in 1949. In the meantime, however, a coordinating committee effected cooperation between the two organizations whenever an emergency called for concerted action.[20]

The main burden of defending Jewish interests and the struggle to obtain equal rights for Jews in both theory and practice was assumed by the SRP. The SRP insisted that it would not be enough to abolish the anti-Jewish legislation enacted during the Nazi era. New laws would have to be passed to counteract the evil of anti-Semitism and to aid the victims, particularly by giving them material assistance.[21] The struggle for the return of Jewish property to its rightful owners was long and bitter. Jewish stores, shops, homes, and land had been "Aryanized"—a euphemism for robbery under cover of law. The Fascist Slovak regime had canceled all kinds of occupational and professional licenses held by Jews, thus in effect depriving Jews of their livelihoods. The victims now asked for a renewal of their licenses. They searched for the securities, valuables, savings, and movable property which had been taken from them during the war. The Slovak puppet state had forced Jews to pay a variety of taxes; these payments were still on deposit in closed accounts in the country's banks. There also was the question what to do with the property left behind by Jews who had perished. The SRP argued that nobody should be allowed to profit from the actions of the Fascist regime and from the property of its victims, dead or alive.[22] Indeed, Presidential Order No. 5/1945, one of the first laws to be enacted in liberated Czechoslovakia, proclaimed the abolition of "Aryanization" and the restitution of "Aryanized" property to its Jewish owners. However, this presidential order became a casualty in the Slovak fight for self-determination. The Slovak political parties did not recognize legislation enacted by the president of the Czechoslovak Republic. Local politicians wanted to ensure the authority of their own institutions over the territory of Slovakia and to prevent Prague from returning to the dominant position it held before the war. They therefore did not accord recognition to laws not passed by their own institutions, the Slovak National Council and its executive branch, the Board of Commissioners. This was the first, but not the last, instance in which restitution had to suffer because of the dispute between Prague and Bratislava.[23]

The central government of Czechoslovakia took a more liberal stand on problems involving Jews than did the regional government of Slovakia. There are several reasons for this phenomenon. Anti-Semitism was less open and virulent among the Czechs than among the Slovaks. The great geographic distance between Prague and Slovakia made the statesmen in the capital less susceptible to pressure from the Slovak war profiteers and Aryanizers. Also, the central government was aware of the possible international reaction to maltreatment of the Jews. Anti-Fascism, a sense of justice, and, in some cases, a bad conscience induced various Czech personalities to accord fair treatment to Jews.[24] Thus the actions of the Prague parliament, the central government, and various Czech individuals often forced Bratislava to retreat.

It would be unjust to ignore the fact that some Slovak politicians, Communist and non-Communist, were men of genuine goodwill, friendly toward the Jews. However, the political climate in Slovakia did not always permit these individuals to reveal and demonstrate their sympathies. The Slovak National Council was Slovakia's supreme legislative institution; the executive power lay with the Board of Commissioners. These two bodies represented an accommodation between Slovak particularism on the one hand and the centralism emanating from Prague on the other. In the contest between these two trends, the Slovaks were on the retreat.[25] Nevertheless, they were powerful enough to advance, or to freeze, certain social and political processes, and restitution became a bone of contention between the political parties. The local authorities in charge of implementing the laws and orders relating to restitution were not particularly eager to act. The Provisional Legislative Assembly (the first postwar Czechoslovak parliament) passed a restitution law as early as May 16, 1946, but the enactment of this law did not solve the practical problems involved.[26] Jewish leaders described the law as "fair but not generous."[27] Slovak authorities, on the other hand, boycotted even this moderate law, or at least they hamstrung it with red tape and with various excuses for failing to implement it. The Office of the Commissioner of Justice, which was in charge of applying and enforcing the law, was particularly resourceful in its circumvention.[28] This attitude was abetted by inaction on the part of the courts. Jewish stores and other business enterprises were not returned to their legal owners but turned over to a *národný správca,* a "national manager."[29] In a few rare instances the management of the concern was entrusted to its original owner, but the official transfer of the enterprise to its rightful owner entailed immense difficulties.

The issue of restitution of landed property was a chapter by itself. The Slovak state had confiscated all land owned by Jews. The Jews in the southern regions of Slovakia which had been occupied by Hungary following the so-called "Vienna Award" of November 2, 1938, also lost their landed property. Although the ordeal of the Jews in Hungary was different from that of Slovak Jewry, the results were the same: most of the Jews in both regions were exterminated and those who survived were left virtually destitute. Now, after the war, the survivors of the Holocaust asked that their landed property, which had been parceled out during the war under the pretext of "agrarian reform," be returned to them. However, the authorities could not accept the idea that property once assigned to a peasant under agrarian reform should be returned to its original owner. Moreover, the postwar Czechoslovak Republic instituted agrarian reforms of its own, which, combined with the "Slovakization" of lands carried out by the Slovak authorities, affected mostly properties owned by Hungarians and Germans—a designation which at that time applied to many Jews. As a result, fields which somehow had been returned to their Jewish owners (minus acreage taken off under the "agrarian reform" regulations) were confiscated once again, this time under the pretext that their owners were not ethnic Czechs or Slovaks but "Magyars."[30] Since the restitution law of May 16, 1946, also stipulated the return of landed property, Slovak Democratic members of the Czechoslovak parliament (followed by the Communists) proposed an amendment to the law specifying that fields of thirteen hectares or less should not be returned to their original owners. Jewish landowners affected by this amendment were to be paid a token indemnity from an unspecified source.[31]

The World Jewish Congress intervened against the expropriation of heirless Jewish property by the Czechoslovak Republic. This intervention was initiated not only for the sake of the Czechoslovak Jewish communities, which requested the property for their own sick and needy, but also to prevent the establishment of a precedent for the rest of liberated Europe.[32]

As already pointed out, the problems faced by the Jews in Slovakia were not legislative and administrative only but also very much of a social nature. In the course of time the Jews encountered great hostility from a considerable part of the Slovak gentile population.[33] In fact, the negative response of the Slovak public to restitution induced the authorities to slow down restitution proceedings and occasionally even to stop them altogether. Indeed, anti-Semitism in Slovakia at times reached almost wartime proportions. During the war anti-Jewish riots and pogroms had been set off by official Fascist organizations; now they occurred spontaneously. Among the numerous pogroms and outrages, those in Prešov (in the summer of 1945),[34] in Topolčany (in the fall of 1945),[35] and in Bratislava (in the summer of 1946[36] and again in the summer of 1948)[37] should be mentioned. During the winter of 1945 bands of the Ukrainian Bendera nationalists murdered Jews in the villages of Ulič and Kalbasy in Eastern Slovakia and also attacked Jews elsewhere. The villagers looted the property of their victims and expelled the two Jewish girls who survived the massacre.[38] The police and the courts showed enormous leniency toward the offenders.[39] Naturally, these anti-

Jewish outbreaks in Slovakia, which ranked with those of postwar Poland, caught the attention of the world press.[40]

Anti-Semitism was no novelty in Slovakia, and the Fascists still left in the country did their best to promote it. Particularly those Fascists who had Aryanized Jewish property and now fomented riots to obstruct its return to its rightful owners found allies in many of the "national managers" who had been appointed by the government to oversee Jewish property taken from the Germans, Hungarians, and Aryanizers. Many of these individuals, appointed because they had fought the Nazis as soldiers or guerrillas, hoped to become legal owners of the property entrusted to them; they regarded it as only just compensation for their participation in the war. Consequently, in some instances the "national managers" actually joined the Aryanizers in instigating anti-Jewish riots. As later investigations proved, the main initiator of these demonstrations was the clerical-Fascist underground of the Slovak People's party, which aimed at obstructing democratic trends in Slovakia and exploited anti-Semitism to this end. The demonstrators coined slogans demanding an independent Slovakia and opposing Communism and the new Czechoslovak central regime.[41] The fact that policemen and soldiers participated in the anti-Jewish demonstrations and riots revealed the full extent of the plight in which the Jews found themselves.[42] In view of the passivity or indifference of the police and security agencies, Jews found it necessary to develop rudimentary self-defense measures.[43]

The authorities were well aware of the spread of anti-Semitism, but they took only minimal action to suppress it. In Slovakia a sharp power struggle was taking place between the Communists and the democratic parties. Though some of its members had a Fascist background, the Communist party to the public mind represented the anti-Fascist resistance. As a result, a large number of Jews initially sympathized with the Communists.[44] The backbone and leadership of the Democratic party, too, was composed of anti-Nazis. But since the Democratic party constituted the only alternative to the Communists, it attracted many unsavory elements tainted by a Fascist past and so it became the representative of Slovak nationalism.[45] In their competition for popularity, neither the Communists nor the Democrats were eager to be stigmatized as "philo-Semites."

Instead, the two parties strove to outdo each other in placing obstacles in the path of restitution. Though leaders of both parties repeatedly assured the Jews of their goodwill, the behavior of the officials representing them in the various government agencies offered a different picture.[46]

The Communist party was opposed to restitution also on ideological grounds. The Communists claimed that the Jews in the past had not always acted in the best interests of the Slovak people. The Communists wanted to deprive the Aryanizers and the war profiteers of their ill-gotten gains but they insisted that property once owned by wealthy Jews should not be returned to its original owners but should be turned over to the state as a first stage in the socialization of the Slovak economy.[47]

Leading figures in the Democratic party were also averse to restitution; they saw it as "interference in the sanctity of the private property and an infringement upon the principle of the lawful order." In their view, the Jewish property had been given away in accordance with an existing legal order, that of the Slovak state. Hence the responsibility for "Aryanization" lay with those who had enacted the laws and the Democrats did not see why those who had merely received the property should now be made to suffer for it.[48]

As for the Slovak public, its members said that the Jews were extortioners because they wanted to get their property back.[49] One ironic element in the anti-Jewish campaign was the accusation that Jews did not participate in the anti-Nazi resistance![50]

The authorities and the public accused Jews of having engaged in activities "hostile" to the nation. They pointed, above all, to the fact that many Jews spoke Hungarian or German rather than Slovak. Loud German and Hungarian speech of indolent individuals in streets and public places provided the Jew-baiters with excuses. The older generation of Jews was accustomed to these languages; indeed, some of them did not even know the Slovak language. In an effort to remove this irritant factor in the relations between the Jews and the Slovak nationalists, Jewish organizations opened courses in the Slovak language.[51]

But there were even more serious factors that stirred up anti-Semitism in postwar Slovakia. Slovakia was short of food and of manufactured goods. Among those who exploited this situation for personal gain there were also a few Jews. Some of them had been forced into these sordid activities because other means of making a livelihood were closed to them. Others were merely part of the great army of profiteers which flooded postwar Europe and exploited the general misery. The gentile population envied the Jews who could appeal to the aid and charity of their brethren. When Jews received gift parcels from the JDC and UNRRA, the general population resented it, particularly when some of these parcels found their way into the black market. Exaggerations about "Jewish speculation" further exacerbated the hatred, and consequently Jewish speculators were punished more severely than their gentile counterparts. The authorities even used the allegations of Jewish black marketeering as an excuse for their efforts to impede the legal process of restitution.[52]

When articles criticizing the treatment of Jews in Slovakia appeared in the world press, local and state authorities asked spokesmen for Slovak Jewry to deny the allegations. The authorities were angered particularly by articles in the Hungarian press, especially since they served as a weapon in the Hungarian campaign against Czechoslovakia. The Jewish leaders were reluctant to deny the reports in the world press, but felt obligated to stand with the Czechoslovak government against neighboring Hungary in an eventual peace conference.[53]

The Slovak authorities took steps to punish those who had collaborated with the Nazis during the war. Among those sentenced were several well-known active anti-Semites. Generally, however, the prosecution of local Fascists left much to be desired and, in fact, the trials often served only to arouse the public against the Jews.[54]

Yet, there were instances in which Slovaks showed sympathy for the Jewish people and understanding for their problems. The great exodus of East European Jewry, particularly Polish Jewry, passed through Slovakia. Local authorities not only turned a blind eye to the activities of *B'riha* but even gave active assistance to the underground Zionist organization in bringing Jewish refugees to what was then Palestine. Local *B'riha* workers received legal, material, and moral support even from Communist officials until 1949, when rigid Stalinism clamped down on Czechoslovakia.[55]

When the state of Israel came into existence, the Slovaks participated in the military assistance which Czechoslovakia sent to the new state. Of course it should be remembered that in those early days Slovakia's powerful neighbor, the USSR, was a supporter of the state of Israel. As for the Jews of Slovakia, they were galvanized by the rise of the Jewish state; they collected millions of crowns for Haganah and the Jewish National Fund. Even during the early days of the Communist regime, Jewish youth joined the Israeli armed forces and their elders followed them to the old-new country[56] while it was still possible for them to leave Czechoslovakia.

The first four postwar years discussed in this study saw a resurgence of Jewish life in Slovakia. The reconstituted congregations restored the synagogues that had been destroyed, cleaned the cemeteries that had been desecrated, built new *mikvaot* (ritual baths), and erected memorials to the victims of the Holocaust. *Yeshivot* were active in Bratislava and Košice. Jewish pupils at the public schools received religious instruction after school hours. During the months immediately following the liberation kosher restaurants and soup kitchens supplied food to the needy. The Jewish hospital in Bratislava reopened.[57] Several Jewish cooperatives were active in Bratislava, Galanta, Rimavská Sobota, and other places. When it became clear that the Slovak press was waging a campaign against the Jews and that no newspaper came out in their defense, the Jews established a weekly, *Tribúna*, in June 1947.[58]

The General Zionists, WIZO, *Mapai, HaShomer HaTzair, D'ror, Mizrachi, HaOved,* and the Revisionists were all united under the Central Zionist Union (ÚSC). The Maccabi sports movement resumed activities. So did the ultra-Orthodox, non-Zionist Agudath Israel. Among the worldwide Jewish philanthropic organizations active in Slovakia during the early postwar years were WJC, OSE, JDC, the Jewish National Fund, *Keren HaYesod,* and the Palestine Office. A so-called "Documentary Action" gathered evidence on the Holocaust and transferred the material to the Yad Vashem Memorial Authority in Jerusalem. The Zionist movement devoted much attention to the surviving youth. *HaShomer HaTzair, B'nei Akiba, Gordonia, Maccabi HaTzair, D'ror,* and *B'rit Trumpeldor* divided the youngsters among themselves, organized summer and winter camps for them, and prepared them for emigration to Palestine. In Palestine young Czechoslovak Jews established several kibbutzim of their own or joined existing kibbutzim.

There was a steady emigration of Jews from Slovakia after the war. Embittered survivors of the Holocaust saw the country as a huge graveyard and were anxious to leave it. The Communist takeover in 1948 persuaded many others who had been reluctant to leave that Slovakia was no longer a safe place for Jews.

During the early postwar years the Czechoslovak authorities encouraged the emigration of Jews. They were interested not only in getting rid of Jews, but also in clearing the country of minorities in general. This was the reason why the Communists supported Jewish emigration to Israel until 1949.[59] However, the authorities expected the Jews to leave quickly. Raphael Friedl, the representative of the Jewish Agency for Palestine in Prague, was told in no uncertain terms that the authorities would not countenance a gradual emigration extending over a period of years.[60] At the Zionist conference of January 1949 in Piestany, the last to be held in Czechoslovakia, the Israeli envoy, Ehud Avriel, stated that 20,000 Jews would be permitted to emigrate.[61] This meant, for all practical purposes, all the Jews of Czechoslovakia who were interested in going to Israel. The Czechoslovak authorities made it clear that those who decided to remain in Czechoslovakia would be expected to assimilate without reservations.

After the Communists had consolidated their position of power, the Jewish institutions were reorganized and Zionists gradually eased out from them. In the fall of 1948 the security agencies arrested several prominent Jews for alleged financial machinations.[62] Gradually all Jewish institutions except for the religious congregations were prohibited or else they disappeared because of lack of members. Under pressure of the government, the Central Union of Jewish Religious Congregations in Slovakia (ÚSŽNO) was amalgamated with the Council of Jewish Religious Congregations in Prague and placed under the supervision of the Communist party. Before long, organized Jewish life in Slovakia ceased to exist. Only rudimentary forms of Jewish religious life continued in Slovakia after 1949.

NOTES

1. Livia Rothkirchen, "Slovakia 1918-1938," in *The Jews of Czechoslovakia,* vol. I (Philadelphia: 1968), p. 102.

2. *Územie a obyvateľstvo Slovenskej republiky a prehľad obcí a okresov odstupených Nemecku, Maďarsku a Poľsku* [Country and Population of the Slovak Republic; a Survey of Settlements and Counties Ceded to Germany, Hungary, and Poland] (Bratislava: 1939), p. 11.
3. Jörg K. Hoensch, *Der ungarische Revisionismus und die Zerschlagung der Tschechoslowakei* [Hungarian Revisionism and the Breakup of Czechoslovakia] (Tübingen: 1967), p. 188.
4. ÚSC report to the Congress of Czechoslovak Zionists at Luhacovice, Moravia, July 4–7, 1946, *Židia na Slovensku dnes,* CZA, File S5/1943. See also Kurt Wehle, "The Jews of Bohemia and Moravia, 1945–1948," in the present volume, pp. 499–530.
5. See bibliography at the end of this study.
6. Livia Rothkirchen, "The Czechoslovak Government-in-Exile: Jewish, and Palestinian Aspects in the Light of the Documents," *Yad Vashem Studies,* Vol. 9 (Jerusalem: 1973), pp. 161, 162. See also Avigdor Dagan, "The Czechoslovak Government-in-Exile and the Jews," in the present volume, pp. 449–95.
7. Ladislav Lipscher, "Jewish Participation in the Anti-Fascist War of Defense in Slovakia in the Second World War" (in Hebrew), *Yalkuth Moreshet,* 14, (April 1972), pp. 121–26.
8. Vilém Prečan, *Slovenské Národné Povstanie, Dokumenty* [The Slovak National Uprising, Documents] (Bratislava, 1965), Document Nos. 6 (p. 67), 19 (p. 89), 93 (p. 229). Cf. Dr. Jozef Lettrich, Statement: *Židia a československý domácí odboj na Slovensku,* Washington, D.C., December 29, 1964, and an interview with Yeshayahu Jelinek, Washington, D.C., December 1964.
9. *Věstník židovské obce náboženské v Praze* [News Bulletin of the Jewish Religious Congregation of Prague], June 3, 1946. Cf. Jan Masaryk, *Volá Londýn,* [London Calling] (London: 1945), pp. 202–203.
10. Decree No. 1/1944, Law Gazette of the Slovak National Council.
11. See CZA, File S/26, 1081, Letter of Leo Herrmann to the Political Department of the Jewish Agency for Palestine, November 19, 1944.
12. The information on the number of new congregations varies. Avigdor Dagan, in "Jews of Czechoslovakia after the Second World War" (in Hebrew), *Yahadut Chechoslovakia* (Tel Aviv: 1969), p. 193, questions the figure given in one of the sources. The Paris Yiddish-language newspaper *Unzer Welt* (February 5, 1948) claims that there were over one hundred congregations. *Die aussäen unter Tränen, mit Jubel werden sie ernten* [Those That Sow Amidst Tears Shall Reap in Joy] (Psalm 126)]. (Prague: 1959), p. 125, speaks of a total of forty-two congregations.

13. *Prehľad dejín KSČ na Slovensku* (Bratislava: 1971), p. 343. Cf. Marta Vartiková, ed., *Komunistická strana Slovenska, Dokumenty konferencií a plen 1944-1948* (Bratislava: 1971), pp. 210, 645. Five Ukrainians were coopted to the Slovak National Council. See *Slovenská Národná Rada, 1943-1949* [The Slovak National Council, 1943-1949] (Bratislava Vojtěch (Albert); 1949), p. 66.
14. See Archives of Vojtěch (Albert) Winterstein (AW), Protocols, Sessions of the Executive Board, SRP, August 10 and September 14, 1945.
15. For Jewish nationality, see Aharon Moshe Rabinowicz, "The Jewish Minority," in *The Jews of Czechoslovakia,* vol. I, pp. 155-266. For renunciation of Jewish nationality status, see AW, File IV/3, Memorandum to the Office of the Commissioner for Internal Affairs, October 29, 1945; Protocol, Session of the Advisory Committee, ÚSŽNO, August 19, 1945; draft of a letter to President Beneš, November 1945; circular letter sent by the Office of the Commissioner for Internal Affairs, November 5, 1946; *The Jewish Chronicle* (London), November 29, 1946.
16. AW, File IV/3, SRP, Circular Letter No. 11, October 9, 1946. It should be pointed out, however, that the authorities occasionally seized upon various pretexts to expel additional Jews. See also Kurt Wehle, "The Jews in Bohemia and Moravia, 1945-1948," in the present volume, pp. 499-530.
17. *Zprávy ÚSC,* July 5, 1945; *Tribúna,* October 8, 1948.
18. AW, File IV/1, Report of Dr. Vojtěch (Albert) Winterstein about his discussion with Deputy Premier Viliam Široký, December 14, 1945. Široký said: "Minister Viktory would not like to permit this, for the good of the Jews themselves, in order to prevent their isolation," Cf. CZA, File S5/761, ÚSC to Jewish Agency for Palestine, January 29, 1946; S5/761, Rafi (Raphael) Friedl, Prague, to Jewish Agency for Palestine, November 12, 1947.
19. AW, Letter No. 21.670/1940-5/Prez., The Commissioner for Education and Public Enlightenment to the Central Board of the Autonomous Orthodox Jewish Religious Congregations and to the "Jeschurun" Federation of Jewish Religious Congregations, September 15, 1945. Cf. Circular Letter No. 1, ÚSŽNO, July 1, 1946, and January 6, 1947; Protocol, The Festive Session of the new Presidium of ÚSŽNO, February 4, 1947. Cf. Aron Grünhut, *Katastrophenzeit des Slowakischen Judentum* [The Era of Catastrophe for Slovak Jewry] (Tel Aviv: 1972), pp. 129-32.
20. AW, File IV/1, Report of Dr. Winterstein about his visits to Prague and London, August 1945; CZA, File S5/761, Memorandum, Meeting of Czech and Slovak leaders, October 10, 1945; AW, Protocols, Session

of the Advisory Board of ÚSŽNO, July 28, September 19, October 7, and November 11, 1946; letter of Dr. Winterstein to WJC, London, April 21, 1947, and to WJC, New York, August 6, 1947; AF, Protocol, Session of the Board, ÚSŽNO, No. 15, July 22, 1948.

21. See ÚSŽNO and SRP memoranda to the authorities, AF, July 7, 1945; AW, File II/4, August 7, 1945; File II/5, December 6, 1945; File IV/3, March 13 and September 11, 1946, et al.

22. See examples AW, File II/4, Memorandum of Dr. Winterstein to the Commissioner for Trade and Industry, August 7, 1945; SRP, Circular Letter No. 44, December 15, 1947.

23. Jaroslav Barto, *Riešenie vzt'ahu Čechov a Slovákov 1944–1948* (Bratislava: 1968), p. 37; AW, File IV/2, Report on the meeting with Dr. Jozef Lettrich, chairman of the Slovak National Council, October 13, 1946.

24. *Věstník,* August 1, 1945; AW, Report about the meeting with President Beneš, December 14, 1945 (See also article by Kurt Wehle in the present volume); Protocol, Session of the Extended Committee, SRP, January 16, 1947; CZA, File St/761, "Palcor," to Jewish Agency for Palestine, August 23, 1946; etc.

25. Eugen Steiner, *The Slovak Dilemma* (Cambridge: 1973), p. 75–92.

26. No. 128/1946, Collection of Laws and Ordinances of the Czechoslovak Republic.

27. CZA, File S5/1643, Report to the Congress of Czechoslovak Zionists, July 4–7, 1946. Cf. AW, Protocol, Session of the Extended Committee, SRP, May 20, 1946.

28. AW, File II/7, Letter No. 37.214/1946-6, Office of the Commissioner of Justice to the Presidium of the Board of Commissioners, September 21, 1946; letter from Council of Jewish Religious Congregations, Prague, to ÚSŽNO, October 22, 1946; letter from SRP to the Office of the Commissioner of Justice, October 10, 1946, etc.

29. Both the title and the functions of the office suggested the idea that the enterprises under such management had been taken from an enemy and should therefore be kept on behalf of the nation. After the war, all Aryanized enterprises in Slovakia were put under "national management."

30. AW, File IV/3, Letter from Dr. Winterstein to the Presidium of the Slovak National Council, January 8, 1946; letter from SRP and ÚSŽNO to the Commissioner for Internal Affairs, July 15, 1946; Circular Letter from SRP No. 11, October 9, 1946; *Tribúna,* February 20, 1948, etc.

31. AW, File II/7, Publications of Parliament, no. 753, July 7, 1947, Proposal of Deputy Dr. Martin Kvetko and colleagues; Publications of

Parliament, no. 856, October 27, 1947, Proposal of Deputy Dr. Michal Falt'an and colleagues, *Tribúna,* November 21, 1947.
32. AW, Letter from Alexander L. Easterman to Dr. Winterstein, July 22, 1947; *The Jewish Chronicle* (London), August 28, 1947.
33. Of the numerous descriptions of this state of affairs, see particularly the perceptive article "Das Überbleibsel des Judentums in der Slowakei" [The Remnant of Slovak Jewry], in *Maccabi* no. 20, (Basel).
34. Vartiková, *Komunistická strana Slovenska,* p. 192.
35. *Věstník,* September 24 and October 3, 1945; *The Jewish Chronicle* (London), October 12, 1945.
36. CZA, File S26/1639, "Translation of Report Prepared by SRP Re: Outrages Committed During the Meeting of the Partisans Held at Bratislava from August 1–5, 1946."
37. AW, File IV/3, SRP and ÚSŽNO: Memorandum, August 24, 1948; "Chairman of the Communist Party of Slovakia, Viliam Široký, at the Session of the Party's Central Committee," *Tribúna,* October 10, 1948.
38. CZA, File S6/4561, Protocol with the Survivors of the Murder, December 10, 1945; AW, File, letter from SRP to the Secretariat of the Central Committee of CPCZS, January 4, 1946.
39. E.g., the case of Jozef Čepiga of Bardejov, Eastern Slovakia, who attacked and insulted Jews for almost three years and was never punished. AW, Protocols, Session of the Extended Committee, SRP, January 27, October 1, and November 12, 1947; letter from SRP to the Office of the Commissioner for Internal Affairs, April 15, 1947; *Tribúna,* October 24, 1947.
40. *The Jewish Chronicle* (London), August 17, 1945; June 7 and August 9, 1946; June 20, 1947; and August 27, 1948; *New York Post,* October 2, 1945; *New York Times,* April 10, 1947.
41. Barto, *Riešenie vzťahu Čechov a Slovákov,* p. 112 ff.; AW, File IV/1, Anti-government and anti-Jewish leaflet, Summer 1948; *Tribúna,* January 16, 1948.
42. *Věstník,* September 24, 1945; AW, Protocol, Session of the Extended Committee, SRP, August 22, 1946; Protocol, Extraordinary Session of the Extended Committee, SRP, August 23, 1948.
43. AW, Protocol, Session of the Extended Committee, SRP, August 22, 1946; Extraordinary Session of the Extended Committee, SRP, August 23, 1948.
44. Yehuda Bauer, *Flight and Rescue: Brichah* (New York: 1970), p. 181; CZA, File S5/752, letter from Rafi (Raphael) Friedl, Prague, to Dr. Leo Lauterbach, Jerusalem, April 16, 1947; letter from O. Krasniansky to Jewish Agency for Palestine, May 5, 1947.

45. Joseph A. Mikuš, *Slovakia* (Milwaukee: 1963), pp. 164–67; Konštantin Čulen, *Vznik a zánik Demokratickéj strany na Slovensku* (Middletown, Pa.: 1950), pp. 45–50; Cf. Josef Lettrich, *History of Modern Slovakia* (New York: 1955), p. 239; Lubomir Lipták, *Slovensko v 20. storočí* (Bratislava: 1968), pp. 267–71.
46. AW, File II/7, SRP and ÚSŽNO: A Proposal for a Speedy and Easy Implementation of Restitution Law No. 128/1946 in Slovakia, July 19, 1946. Cf. n. 20.
47. Vartiková, *Komunistická strana Slovenska*, p. 97; Barto, *Riešenie vzťahu Čechov a Slovákov*, p. 37; AW, Protocol, Session of the Extended Committee, SRP, February 26, 1947; File II/7, letter from SRP and ÚSŽNO to Premier Klement Gottwald, May 15, 1947.
48. See interpretation of the expression "public good" in the Restitution Law by Kornel Filo, Commissioner for Supply and Provisions, AW, File II/7, Letter No. 142.329/1946-I/2, Filo to the Chairman of the Board of Commissioners, August 30, 1946.
49. AW, Protocol, Session of the Extended Committee, SRP, May 20, 1946; *Tribúna*, September 19, 1947, "Jewish Vengefulness, Extortionism, and Other 'Specialties,'" p. 3; September 12, 1947, Peter Bludny, "They Demand Modesty," p. 20.
50. Dr. Albert (Vojtěch) Winterstein, "In Accord with the Interests of the Members of Resistance," in *Tribúna*, July 11, 1947; Circular Letter ÚSŽNO, No. 19811/47: The Documentation Action, December 2, 1947. The articles of Msgr. Jur Koza Matejov in *Katolícke Noviny* (Bratislava), YVA, File No. M-5/42-I. For Jewish participation in the resistance, see Yeshayahu Jelinek, "The Role of the Jews in Slovakian Resistance," *Jahrbücher für Geschichte Osteuropas, Neue Folge*, XV, 3 (1967), pp. 415–22; Emil F. Knieza, "The Resistance of Slovak Jews," in Yuri Suhl, ed., *They Fought Back* (New York: 1967), pp. 176–81, and n. 4.
51. AW, Protocols, Session of the Extended Committee, SRP, September 30, 1946, and October 1, 1947; SRP, Circular Letter No. 39: Letter of the Presidium of the Office of Settlement for Slovakia, July 14, 1947; File IV/3, letter from SRP to the President of the Slovak National Council, August 27, 1947; SRP, Circular Letter No. 41: "SRP Branch in Nové Zamky in Combat Against the Use of the Magyar Language," October 11, 1947.
52. AW, File IV/3, letter from SRP and ÚSŽNO to the Office of the Commissioner for Internal Affairs, December 16, 1946, and February 5, 1947; Protocols, Session of the Extended Committee, SRP, December 19, 1946, and February 5, 1947; SRP, Circular Letter No. 18: "The

Fight Against the Black Market and Anti-Jewish Propaganda," December 23, 1946; *Tribúna,* December 19, 1947.
53. See examples in AW, File IV/1, Correspondence with the Czechoslovak Ministry for Foreign Affairs and Consultations in the Executive Committees of SRP and ÚSŽNO, March, April, and May 1946.
54. *The Jewish Chronicle* (London), August 9, 1946: "Slovak Commissar Hanged," April 11 and May 2, 1947; *Hatzofeh* (Jerusalem), December 24, 1947.
55. AW, File IV/1, Dr. Winterstein's report to the European Congress, WJC, August 1945; Protocol, Session of the Extended Committee, SRP, June 6, 1946; CZA, File S26/1390, Report by Haim Barlasz: Emigration and Rescue in the European Countries (December 1945–April 1946), June 25, 1946; a personal account of Emanuel Frieder to the author, May 1973, cf. AF, Office of Commissioner for Internal Affairs, ordering that assistance be given to ÚSŽNO, March 12, 1949, and Protocol, Session of the Executive Committee, ÚSŽNO, August 16, 1949.
56. AW, Protocol, Session of the Extended Committee, SRP, March 30 and May 4, 1948; CZA, File S6/1637, letter from Palestine Office, Prague, to Jewish Agency for Palestine, Jerusalem, August 5, 1948.
57. *Die aussäen unter Tränen . . .* pp. 122–209; Avigdor Dagan, "Jews of Czechoslovakia," in *Yahadut Chechoslovakia,* pp. 138–40, 192–98; Emil F. Knieza, "The Return of the Expelled," in Mordechay Ben-Zeev (Mori Farkas), ed., *The Book of Michalovce* (1969), p. 92.
58. AW, Protocol, Session of the Extended Committee, SRP, September 23, 1946, January 27 and 29, April 30, and May 28, 1947.
59. *The Jewish Chronicle* (London), March 5, 1948; CZA, File S5/3673, letter from L. Rosenthal, Bratislava, to Jewish Agency for Palestine, March 18, 1948; *Tribúna,* March 19, 1948.
60. CZA, File S5/725, letter from R. Friedl to Jewish Agency for Palestine, July 15, 1947. Cf. S5/752, letter from R. Friedl to Jewish Agency for Palestine, May 5, 1947; S5/725, R. Friedl to Jewish Agency for Palestine, November 12, 1947.
61. *The Jewish Chronicle* (London), January 21, 1949. Cf. *Haderech* (February 1949), pp. 5, 13.
62. AW, File IV/3, letter from ÚSC to the Central Action Committee of the National Front, April 5, 1948; *Tribúna,* October 8, 1948, CZA, File S5/752, letter from Dr. P. Marz, Jerusalem, to Jewish Agency for Palestine, November 9, 1948; AF, Protocols, Session No. 19 of February 25, 1949, and No. 20 of May 11, 1949, of the Board of ÚSŽNO; *The Jewish Chronicle* (London), February 25 and March 11, 1949.

BIBLIOGRAPHY

The study is based on following sources:

A. Documents
   a) Central Zionist Archives (CZA), Collections S5, S6, S26.
   b) Yad Vashem Archives (YVA), Steiner Collection, Files M5/39, 40 and 42.
   c) Private archives of the late Dr. Albert (Vojtěch) Winterstein (AW). This is the most important deposit, although a great part of it was unfortunately lost. The author appreciates the kindness of Dr. Ladislav Winterstein, Haifa, Israel, who permitted him to inspect this collection.
   d) Private archives of Mr. Emanuel Frieder, Natanya, Israel. The author appreciates the kindness of Mr. Frieder, who permitted him to inspect his papers.
B. Press
   a) *The Jewish Chronicle* (London)
   b) *Tribúna* (Bratislava)
   c) *Věstník židovské obce náboženské v Praze* (Prague)
   d) *Zprávy Ústredného Sväzu Cionistického na Slovensku* (Bratislava)
   e) *Haderech* (Bratislava)
C. Miscellaneous primary and secondary sources

PRAGUE AND JERUSALEM: THE ERA OF FRIENDSHIP

By Ehud Avriel*

Under Presidents Tomáš G. Masaryk and Eduard Beneš the Czechoslovak Republic had been consistently friendly toward the aspirations of Zionism. The national liberation movements of the Jews and of the peoples of Czechoslovakia had emerged almost simultaneously. The leaders of both movements shared a very similar background. Theodor Herzl, the founder of modern political Zionism, was much at home in the atmosphere that inspired the Czech and Slovak independence movements. The realization of the Zionist dream in kibbutz and moshav, in workshops and on farms, at schools and universities, and the renaissance of authentic Hebrew culture and the Hebrew language continued to attract the interest of Czechoslovakia's leaders even after the establishment of the Czechoslovak Republic, when Zionism was still on its way toward actual Jewish statehood. The heroic self-defense of the Jews in Palestine, necessitated by Arab aggression and British intransigence, received constant moral support and encouragement from the leaders of the Czechoslovak Republic between the two world wars.

---

* Ehud Avriel, a key figure in the procurement of Czechoslovak aid for the Jewish state in the making, and subsequently Israel's first minister in Prague, died on August 27, 1980. It was felt that certain references in Mr. Avriel's manuscript were in need of clarification and amplification. It was therefore decided to add to the manuscript excerpts from Mr. Avriel's own book, *Open the Gates: The Dramatic Personal Story of "Illegal" Immigration to Israel* (New York: Atheneum Publishers, 1975), in which he goes into considerable detail on Czechoslovak aid in Israel's struggle for independence. (A Hebrew version of this book appeared in Israel in 1976 under the title *Pit'hu Shearim*.) The excerpts quoted from *Open the Gates* are printed in italics. [Ed.]

During the era of the Nazi terror, common suffering forged strong bonds of mutual sympathy. The leaders of the Czechoslovak resistance in London kept in constant touch with the London representatives of the Jewish Agency for Palestine. Both were less than full-fledged governments, but both were totally committed to a struggle on two fronts: the war against Hitler, which meant to support the Allied cause, reinforce the battle lines, and in general to do whatever was necessary to hasten an Allied victory, and the battle on the home front, which entailed saving as many lives as possible, redressing whatever evils could be redressed, and strengthening the victims of persecution in their determination to survive until the ultimate victory of justice and right.

After the Holocaust, the Zionist organization, the various Zionist youth movements, and the *HeHalutz* pioneering organization were quickly revived in liberated Czechoslovakia and, assisted by a benevolent government, they all prepared with renewed strength to help those remnants of Czechoslovak Jewry who wished to settle in Palestine. The friendly relationship between the Zionist movement and the Czechoslovak authorities culminated during the winter of 1947–48, when Czechoslovakia became, in fact, an active partner in the crucial operations that resulted in the emergence of the independent state of Israel.

Hoping to force a solution of the "Palestine problem" through chaos, the British abdicated the responsibilities they had assumed under the Mandate. Eventually, the United Nations Special Commission on Palestine (UNSCOP),[1] on which Czechoslovakia was represented, proposed a partition of Palestine, with the complete termination of foreign rule and the establishment of two independent states—one Jewish and one Arab—in what was formerly the British Mandate of Palestine.

As early as 1946, David Ben Gurion, as chairman of the Jewish Agency for Palestine, had assumed full responsibility for the defense of Palestine's Jewish community. He examined the well-concealed arsenals of the underground Jewish defense forces and found them utterly inadequate. When the United Nations partition plan was first discussed, Ben Gurion foresaw two possible developments, both leading to the same end. In the fall of 1947, he told his colleagues on the Jewish Agency Executive that if the United Nations were to approve the partition, the Arab states would certainly do everything in their power to thwart the establishment of a Jewish state. If, on the other hand, the United Nations would not accept the partition plan, the Arab extremists would regard it as a proof of weakness and as an invitation to annihilate the Jews of Palestine. In either case, war was inevitable, and the Jews of Palestine would have to be prepared.

The tension surrounding Palestine at the time aroused the interest of greedy arms merchants. With the decision at the United Nations drawing closer, Ben Gurion resolved to step up the acquisition of needed weapons and to turn the carefully planned top-secret operation, already begun clandestinely, into a rush job of the highest urgency. During that period representatives of the Jewish Agency, and even private Jewish individuals, were besieged with offers of arms and military equipment, guns, naval vessels, and fighter aircraft. Most of these proposals turned out to be figments of greedy imagination evoked by the approaching showdown in the Middle East. When they were checked for authenticity, they were discovered to be either unrealistic or based on nonexistent "merchandise."

In the meantime, of course, the Arab states did not remain idle. Even while the Jewish Agency was making its first contacts with Czechoslovak authorities and arms manufacturers for badly needed weapons, the Syrian ministry of defense dispatched one Captain Abdul Aziz Kerine to Prague with orders to purchase in Czechoslovakia 10,000 rifles, as well as 1,000 light and 200 heavy machine guns. The Syrian captain's task was much easier than that of the Jewish representative from Palestine, for he represented a sovereign state and there was no question of Syria's right to acquire military equipment for her army, even if that army was preparing a war of aggression in defiance of the United Nations. And so Captain Kerine received the supplies he had been sent to obtain.

However, his luck did not last. A sudden storm in the Adriatic forced the Italian boat carrying the Syrian cargo to take shelter in a tiny cove on the Italian coast. There, the boat was detained to give Italian authorities time to inspect its cargo, for suspicion had been cast upon the true purpose of the weapons from Czechoslovakia. Could they have been intended not for Syria but for would-be initiators of civil strife in Italy on the eve of that country's first postwar election? Eventually, the boat was permitted to continue on its journey, but it was sunk by the Haganah, the Jewish defense force in Palestine.* When the weapons from Czechoslovakia finally reached the Middle East, they did not go to the side for which they had been intended but became the first arms to equip the soldiers of the newly established State of Israel.

The same Swissair plane that brought the Syrian captain to Prague carried yet another prospective purchaser of Czechoslovak weapons. This was Ben Gurion's personal envoy,** and his destination was the famous Zbrojovka munitions plant in Brno, which had opened its doors to the representatives of the fledgling army that was fighting for the independence of the Jewish state.

* * *

During the period immediately following World War II, the Czechoslovak government, having just reestablished its authority in its liberated homeland, showed understanding for the problems and the struggle of the Jewish underground liberation movement in Palestine. It also demonstrated willingness to help the Jews rebuild their lives in the Jewish homeland.

The collapse of the Nazi regime had ended Hitler's plans for the annihilation of European Jewry. However, most of the survivors of the Holocaust were unable to return to their former homes. Their families had been murdered, entire Jewish communities had been wiped out and the gentile populations, with only few exceptions, had been indifferent to the "Final Solution." An ever-growing stream of desperate survivors was gathering on the borders of Czechoslovakia, clamoring for passage toward the coasts of Western Europe and Yugoslavia, where they hoped to set sail for Palestine, the place they instinctively felt held their only hope for a new life.

As early as mid-October 1945 Foreign Minister Jan Masaryk provided the *B'riha*[2] branch of the Haganah with nine complete trains to transport Jewish survivors of the Holocaust from the Polish bor-

---

* One version of how this happened is given in Leonard Slater, *The Pledge* (New York: Simon & Schuster, 1970), p. 240: A Haganah sabotage team fixed a mine to the hull of the boat and sank her. The Arabs managed to salvage the arms and to place them aboard another ship. However, that ship in turn was boarded and seized at sea by the crew of a Haganah "fishing boat" and the weapons were transferred to two Israeli corvettes. [Ed.]

** This was Mr. Avriel, who in his original manuscript chose to use the modest anonymity of the third person throughout when writing about himself. [Ed.]

der to Austria and to the American occupation zone in Germany. From these, the refugees moved on to seaports from which they hoped to sail for Palestine. The Czechoslovak government imposed only one condition; namely, that the trains bypass Prague, where the watchful British had set up a center of operations against the "illegal" movement of Jewish refugees to Palestine. The humanitarian attitude of the Beneš government had an immediate effect also on the policy of neighboring Poland. For a time, the Polish government abolished all restrictions on Jewish emigration and, before long, despite strong British pressures, a daily exodus of 2,500 to 3,000 Jewish refugees from Poland, Russia, Rumania, Hungary, and other countries passed across the Czechoslovak borders.

In July 1946 the Czechoslovak government headed by Klement Gottwald, a Communist, but with Jan Masaryk still as Minister of Foreign Affairs, decided to give the *B'riha* organization official legitimacy as a rescue agency for Holocaust survivors and to initiate close cooperation between this branch of Haganah and the Czechoslovak Ministry of Social Welfare. This momentous decision made the migration of the survivors from the East to the displaced persons' camps in the West somewhat more humane than hitherto. Czechoslovakia's example set new standards in the occupation zones of West Germany. If Czechoslovakia, which was then still in a state of semi-starvation, was ready to share her meager provisions with the refugees, the well-fed armies of the Western Allies could not refuse to supply rations to the newly arriving survivors.

As the volume of *B'riha*'s rescue activities increased, the Haganah outpost in Prague grew in importance. It was only natural that the Haganah should post in the capital of friendly Czechoslovakia also a representative of *Rekhesh,* the Haganah's arms acquisition unit. The choice fell on Dr. Otto Felix, who had been one of the first Czech Zionists to settle in Palestine and had Hebraized his name to Uriel Doron.[3] Doron had been living in Tel Aviv as a rather successful businessman for many years when the Haganah asked him to undertake the mission to Prague. In Czechoslovakia he was warmly received by many old friends from before the war who now held key positions in government, industry, and banking. It was from Doron that Ben Gurion received the first indication that Czechoslovakia might be ready to sell arms to the Haganah.

Ben Gurion acted swiftly. I was ordered to leave Jerusalem for

Paris and Prague just before the United Nations voted in favor of the Palestine partition plan. In Paris, by lucky coincidence, I met Robert Adam, who before the war had represented the Zbrojovka arms concern of Brno in his native Rumania and who had lived briefly in Palestine.

> *[Adam] put his briefcase on the low table between us and took out two catalogues of armaments produced by the famous Czech [Zbrojovka] arms factory at Brno. Without any preliminaries, Robert Adam pointed out to me the rifles and machine guns he thought we would need. And in the self-assured tone of an expert, he quoted prices and delivery dates that sounded like hard facts and not the sweet and expensive tales I had heard before.*[4]

Adam and I arrived in Prague together on November 29, 1947, just as the adoption of the United Nations resolution to establish a Jewish state in Palestine was being celebrated in the streets of Jerusalem.

> *The representative of the Czech armsworks was at the [Prague] airport to meet us. So was my friend Felix [Uriel] Doron, the Haganah man in Prague. . . .*
> *Less than an hour after we had entered the offices of the Zbrojovka, Brno . . . we had concluded the deal. Adam was at home in these offices, and the younger of the two Czech directors had been at school with [Uriel] Doron, who was born in Prague . . .*[5]

One of the major obstacles that had to be overcome before the deal could be implemented was that an arms purchase of this magnitude could be made only by a sovereign government. Since the Haganah did not represent a sovereign state (the state of Israel was proclaimed only six months later) it had to obtain official credentials from some foreign nation. My Palestine Jewish underground colleagues in Paris and I had obtained blank stationery from the Paris embassy of a country the name of which still cannot be revealed.

* * *

> *Doron and I rushed to the Czech Foreign Office with a letter of introduction to Jan Masaryk [who] was visibly delighted that his country could help us and pleased that we were able to overcome "technical difficulties." He was certain that his communist deputy, Vlado Clementis, would likewise favor assisting our war effort. "For me, it is enough that you defend yourself against your enemies.*

But Clementis will he happy to know that by fighting for your life you undermine British imperialism in the Middle East."[6]

On December 1, 1947, two days after the adoption of the United Nations resolution, the first arms deal was concluded between Czechoslovakia and the future Jewish state.

Sympathy for the Zionist cause and for the plight of the survivors of Hitler's terror played an important role in the Czechoslovak policy of support and assistance to the Jews of Palestine during that crucial period in Jewish history. But there were other eminently important factors that cannot be overlooked. Together with most of the other governments of Western and Central Europe, the Beneš government in Czechoslovakia was greatly attracted by the possibilities of the American Marshall Plan. Between the end of World War II and the Communist takeover, Prague regarded itself as a natural partner of those nations who agreed with the American approach to the reconstruction of postwar Europe. In fact, during the summer of 1947, this attitude—which initially was shared even by the Communist Premier Gottwald—brought Czechoslovakia dangerously close to a confrontation with the Soviet Union. When Moscow prevented Prague from joining the Marshall Plan, it meant the isolation of Czechoslovakia from her traditional and natural economic ties with the West. To her utter consternation, Czechoslovakia found herself suddenly cut off not only from economic but also from social and political links she had regarded as vital for the survival of democracy. Her normal trade channels were rapidly drying up, and her coffers were emptying at an alarming rate. There were also other European governments that were badly in need of hard currency. They had at their disposal German (and Allied) surplus weaponry left from the war, and they, too, felt a certain degree of responsibility toward the Jewish people. Yet the government of Czechoslovakia was the only one ready and willing to sell arms to the Jews of Palestine not clandestinely but openly as a government and to facilitate the transaction in every possible way; it even kept the prices low, though the situation would have made it quite tempting to follow the opposite course.

The Communist takeover in February 1948 and the death of Jan Masaryk two weeks later caused apprehension among the representatives of the future Jewish state in Prague. However, to their great satisfaction, they found a most benevolent and cooperative party in Vladimír Clementis, Masaryk's successor as foreign minister. Arrangements for aid to the Jewish state-to-be had to be kept secret because of constant interference from suspicious British (and American) agents who were eager to discover the extent of Czechoslovakia's involvement in the Middle East conflict. The routing of Israel's purchases to destinations outside the Middle East area was helpful in that it made it easier for Israel's Czech friends to withstand British and American pressures, particularly after the United Nations had enacted an arms embargo against all countries engaged in war. During this period the close relations between Clementis and his Communist counterparts in the adjacent "people's republics" facilitated even further the transit of refugees through Czechoslovakia on their way to Israel and helped in negotiations with Rumania and Yugoslavia concerning the transportation of arms bought by Israel in Czechoslovakia. Without going into details at this time, it should be mentioned here that the successful capture of the Czechoslovak weapons bought by Syria and their redirection to the Haganah arsenals would not have been possible without Czechoslovak and Yugoslav help. The arms purchased by the Haganah from Czechoslovakia immediately upon the outbreak of hostilities following the United Nations partition arrived safely at the port of Tel Aviv via Yugoslavia on a small steamship, the SS *Nora*,[7] at a time when they were most desperately needed, in April 1948, at the start of *Operation Nahshon*. This was the operation that opened the road to Jerusalem and kept Jerusalem in Israeli hands.

* * *

When Czechoslovakia first decided to sell arms to the Jews in Palestine and to support their war effort, she did so as if an independent Jewish state had already come into existence. The dealings between the Czechoslovak authorities and the representatives of the Haganah were as between two sovereign governments, and many problems that had beset the Haganah's arms acquisition program in earlier days disappeared. Haganah representatives were able to choose their weapons from catalogs rather than do it surreptitiously. As larger quantities of arms became available, the Haganah could afford to be less conservative in their use. Also, in most cases the prices for the armaments went down. However, two problems remained for as long as Palestine was under British control: the shipment and unloading of the weapons.

While no foreign power, however sympathetic, was able to help solve this problem, the government of Czechoslovakia, in a sensational move, made delivery of the arms to Palestine substantially easier. In response to urgent pleas from Ben Gurion to send the arms bought in Czechoslovakia by air if it could not be done expeditiously by sea, I approached the Czechoslovak government for permission to bring foreign planes to a secluded airfield, load them with arms and fly them to their destination. The Czechoslovak authorities agreed. The military airfield of Žatec, some seventy-five kilometers west of Prague, was put at the disposal of the Haganah. The field was given the code name "Etzion base" in honor of Kibbutz K'far Etzion, in the Judea mountains between Jerusalem and Hebron, which had fallen to the Jordanian army. A senior Haganah officer, Yehuda Brieger (who later Hebraized his surname to Ben Chorin), was appointed commander of what became an exclusive Haganah base, out of bounds even to most Czechoslovak personnel. In a matter of days, the first American DC-4s arrived, along with American pilots who had volunteered for service in the Haganah.

The "Etzion base" made it possible to speed up arms and ammunition deliveries. Urgently needed rifles, machine guns, antitank mortars, and other military equipment could now be sent from Czechoslovakia to Israel by air. Also, there was a safe place for storing some of the aircraft the Haganah had bought as surplus from the United States military authorities in Europe. The planes all needed a thorough overhaul before they could be used either for arms transports or for bombing missions by the fledgling Israel air force, and they had to be re-equipped with weapons because the Americans had stripped them of all arms before selling them.

In April 1948, a month before the proclamation of the state of Israel, the Czechoslovak government sold to the Haganah an initial consignment of German-made Messerschmitt aircraft. The range of these World War II planes was much too short for direct flights from the "Etzion base" to Israel, and their bodies were too large to be placed within any of the heavier American aircraft that were at "Etzion" for repairs. However, technical personnel of the Czech plant responsible for the sale of the planes helped dismantle the

Messerschmitts so that the parts could be transported to Israel in American planes. Everyone at "Etzion" (both the Israelis in Prague and their Czech friends knew what was going on) celebrated this event as a victory of sheer willpower over seemingly impossible technical odds. That was how Israel's air force was founded with Czechoslovak help.

The well-known Israeli poet Chaim Guri, who was then in Budapest on behalf of the Palmah (the commando units of the Haganah) to reorganize the Zionist youth movement in Hungary, came to Prague to work out a plan for the training of parachutists for the future Israeli air force. Again, it was with the help of Czechoslovak experts that a top secret two-month training course was organized. Guri was given the rank of captain, and all the participants in the course wore Czechoslovak army uniforms. The trainees were Haganah members who had been stationed in other European countries and had been ordered to Czechoslovakia to take the parachutists' course. They immediately went into rigorous training in such skills as commando combat, techniques of survival behind enemy lines, and the use of explosives. This training program was shrouded in secrecy, first and foremost for fear of detection by the British, but also because of the possibility that even in the Czechoslovak general staff there might have been individuals who would not have regarded a close partnership between the Czechoslovak army and the Haganah as compatible with the Communist orientation of the new Czechoslovak regime.

Two groups of Israeli airmen came to the "Etzion base" in quick succession. The first was composed of seasoned pilots who had served with the British Royal Air Force and who needed just relatively brief retraining on the German Messerschmitts they had previously known only indirectly, as dangerous adversaries. This group included such men as Ezer Weizman and Motti Hod, who later became Israel's Minister of Defense and commander of the Israeli air force, respectively. In the second group, as already indicated, there were young American Jewish pilots and mechanics who had come as volunteers to assist the Israeli recruits at the "Etzion base," which by then (the summer of 1948) had become a vital element in Israel's war effort. These Americans moved about the little town of Žatec, sporting their showy T-shirts, quite conspicuous in the drab surroundings of postwar Czechoslovakia. They were startled to learn that they would have to "lie low"—not because of the Czechs, who patiently bore with the Israelis and gave them their full support, but because of the roving eye of American intelligence.

One of the men in this group was Sam Pomerantz, a veteran of the U.S. air force. A serious, soft-spoken man, he had left a secure job in the United States to join the Haganah team in Czechoslovakia. When the Czechoslovak government sold Israel a number of Spitfire IX planes, Pomerantz took it upon himself to devise a way of ferrying them from the "Etzion base" at Žatec to Israel. With the help of friendly Czechoslovak technicians, he experimented with the installation of additional fuel tanks under the wings of this small, versatile fighter plane. After an unprecedented flight from eastern Czechoslovakia, with only one refueling stop in then-friendly Yugoslavia, the squadron of Spitfires reached Israel. There was only one casualty: Sam Pomerantz, who was killed when the Spitfire he piloted crashed into a mountain after taking off from the Yugoslav airfield at Titograd.

Soon after this spectacular incident, the "Etzion base" at Žatec was closed. Beset by constant pressures from Great Britain and the United States, and by opposition from within the Czechoslovak Communist party, the Czechoslovak government decreed that Haganah operations at the Žatec airfield had to end. However, they continued for a time on a reduced scale before ceasing altogether at the end of 1948.

* * *

When the independence of the state of Israel was proclaimed on May 14, 1948, many governments were quick to recognize the new nation. The Soviet Union and the United States headed the list. Czechoslovakia was among the nations that extended unqualified recognition, both *de facto* and *de jure;* indeed, she was the first to propose the immediate establishment of full diplomatic relations with the Jewish state. Within forty-eight hours after the proclamation of Israel's independence, heads of diplomatic missions on both sides had been appointed.[8]

Czechoslovak assistance to the young Jewish state covered the most unexpected fields. For instance, Czechoslovakia became Israel's mentor in the art of formal diplomacy. The hastily concocted letters of credence for Israel's first minister plenipotentiary to Prague proved totally inadequate. Since the time for their presentation to the president of Czechoslovakia had already been set, the Protocol Office at Hradčany Palace proposed that an empty envelope, rather than the unsuitable document, be presented at the ceremony, and that the real thing should be substituted once the new Israeli Ministry of Foreign Affairs had approved a more professionally worded text based on Czechoslovak diplomatic routine. With only slight modifications, this text has been the standard form used by Israel ever since at diplomatic ceremonies of this kind the world over.

Several members of the Haganah's *Rekhesh* team now joined the staff of the Israeli legation in Prague. The fact that most of these individuals were of Czech origin, spoke Czech, and intimately knew the country in which they now represented Israel proved helpful and important.[9] Josefovská 7, the clandestine address of Haganah headquarters in Prague, emerged from the underground at last.

Israel's first commercial agreement with a foreign country was signed with Czechoslovakia. The experience acquired by the Israeli team in these negotiations served the country well in future commercial diplomacy. A framework for cultural cooperation between Czechoslovakia and Israel was also worked out, mainly with the assistance of such Czech-born Israelis as Zeev Shek (who later was to serve as Israel's ambassador to Austria and Italy), Yosef Millo (Pacovský, who was to become founder and director of the Kameri [Chamber] Theater of Tel Aviv), and Ruth Klinger.

After the establishment of the state of Israel, the Czechoslovak authorities showed great understanding in helping Jews incapable of adjusting to the Communist regime to emigrate to the Jewish Homeland.[10] As its additional contribution to the strengthening of the new state, the government of Czechoslovakia even permitted the formation of a brigade (popularly known as the "Gottwald Brigade") to serve as soldiers and pioneers in Israel.[11]

It remains to be stressed that initially, representatives of the state of Israel were able to maintain close contacts quite openly with leaders of the Jewish community and the revived Zionist organization of Czechoslovakia. Dr. Gustav Sicher, the chief rabbi of Prague, was a frequent guest at the Israeli legation. It was due to encouragement from Foreign Minister Masaryk that Irma Polák, a WIZO (Women's International Zionist Organization) leader in prewar Czechoslovakia, came to organize a generous outpouring of contributions for Israel from Jewish communities all over the country. With the permission of Czechoslovakia's National Bank, substantial funds were placed at the disposal of the Israeli government to cover part of the hard currency payments for some of Israel's purchases in Czechoslovakia other than military hardware.

* * *

Many theories have been advanced to explain why Czechoslovakia continued her cooperation with Israel during the period immediately following the Communist accession to power in February 1948. One widely prevailing view is that Czechoslovakia's initial pro-Zionist policy was orchestrated by the Soviet Union, which was bent on filling the power vacuum created in the Middle East by Britain's departure from the area. The Soviets, it is claimed, shrewdly calculated that by funneling military aid through one of their satellites to the young state of Israel, which was then fighting for its very survival, they would reap the eternal gratitude of Jews in Israel and of Zionists throughout the world. Others point out that—notwithstanding ideological reservations—the Socialist Zionist movement, as represented by the Labor Zionist parties, held out much greater promise to Soviet political strategy than the backward Arab regimes controlled by feudal kings and effendis.[12]

In fact, however, we have no definite evidence that the Soviet Union approved Czechoslovakia's continued assistance to Israel after February 1948. The beginning had been made not by a Soviet satellite government in Prague but by a Czechoslovak government that still had been able to make its own decisions and had made them in accordance with the traditional Czechoslovak friendship for Zionism. That decision had been taken in an atmosphere of almost worldwide support for the establishment of a Jewish state in Palestine. And even after she had become a "people's democracy," Czechoslovakia remained faithful, at least for a short time, to the principles on which she originally had based her decision to support Zionism and Israel.

At the time of Israel's birth and during the period immediately preceding and following this development, the friendship between the peoples of Czechoslovakia and Israel was certainly founded on much more than what La Rochefoucauld describes as a "reciprocal conciliation of interests." The fact that such relations could exist between these two countries in the past would justify at least some hope for the future.

NOTES

1. Formed in April 1947, UNSCOP consisted of eleven member states of the United Nations. Czechoslovakia was represented by Karel Lysický.
2. The organization charged with the task of conducting Holocaust survivors from Eastern Europe to the West. See also Kurt Wehle, "The Jews in Bohemia and Moravia: 1945–1948," in the present volume, p. 514.
3. Doron later became a high official in Israel's Ministry of Foreign Affairs and served as economic counselor at the Israeli embassy in Rome. He died in 1964.
4. Ehud Avriel, *Open the Gates: The Dramatic Personal Story of "Illegal" Immigration to Israel* (New York: Atheneum Publishers, 1975), p. 333.
5. Avriel, *Open the Gates,* p. 334.
6. Avriel, *Open the Gates,* pp. 335–36.
7. For a detailed account of the journey of the SS *Nora* see Avriel, *Open the Gates,* pp. 343–45, 347, 350–52.
8. Avriel's Czechoslovak counterpart as the first Czechoslovak minister to Israel was a Jew, Dr. Eduard Goldstücker, who in his youth, before joining the Communist party, had been a member of *HaShomer Ha-Tzair* in Slovakia. In 1950, at the time of the Slánský trial, he was recalled from Israel, arrested and sentenced to a long prison term. Rehabilitated in the late 1960s, he became professor of German literature and dean of the faculty of philosophy at the Charles University in Prague. A well-known expert on Franz Kafka, he is now living in England.
9. The deputy head of the legation was Dr. Uriel Doron. The first secretary and chief political officer was Rafael Ben Shalom (Friedel), who had been an outstanding member of the Jewish underground in Slovakia during the Nazi era. The press counselor was Dr. Uri Naor (Hans Lichtwitz), who formerly had edited (with Felix Weltsch) the Prague Zionist weekly *Selbstwehr* and later became Israel's ambassador to Chile. The commercial attaché was Shimon Ohrenstein, who was to be one of the defendants in the Slánský trial in Prague (November 1952), in which Rudolf Slánský, a former secretary-general of the Communist party and vice-premier of Slovakia, along with thirteen other high party and state officials, was charged with "Trotskyite-Titoist-Zionist" activities.
10. During the first two years following the establishment of Israel, about 19,000 Czechoslovak Jews, representing about half of all the Jewish survivors in Czechoslovakia, settled in the Jewish state. See Oskar Neumann, "Czechoslovak Jews in Israel," in *Encyclopedia of Zionism*

and Israel, ed. Raphael Patai (New York: Herzl Press/McGraw-Hill, 1971), p. 234.

11. The idea of the brigade was first suggested by the Association of Jewish Participants in the Czechoslovak Resistance Campaign (*Sdružení židovských účastníků československého odboje*), which was headed by Staff Captain Šimon Šachta, a former officer of Ludvík Svoboda's army and, from 1945, a member of the Czechoslovak general staff. It was Šachta who, on June 25, 1948, signed an agreement for the formation of the brigade with Ehud Avriel, the Israeli minister in Prague. (A copy of the agreement is in the Yad Vashem Archives, Jerusalem, YVA-0-59.) The brigade was subsequently referred to as the "Gottwald Brigade" because it had been created with the explicit approval of Premier Gottwald.

About 1,500 men, many of them former members of Czechoslovak army units that had fought abroad alongside Allied forces, volunteered. They were processed at the military academy at Hranice. Those found fit for service were sent to a training camp at Střelná near Olomouc (Moravia), which had been equipped by the Czechoslovak Ministry of Defense. The training program was directed by the brigade's commander, Colonel Antonín Sochor, who had been awarded the title of "Hero of the Soviet Union" during the war.

In September 1948, 1,280 men who had passed the training course were transferred, along with some 700 members of their immediate families, to Mikulov, from where they were sent to Israel in four transports. The first of these transports left Czechoslovakia at the end of September 1948; the last, early in February 1949. The officers in charge of the transports were appointed by the Communist party with special instructions to see that the brigade should remain a separate entity and should not take part in the actual fighting. Although some of the volunteers from Czechoslovakia participated in battle in the Negev, the brigade as such was never used for combat duty, partly because the transports arrived rather late, but primarily because the Israeli general staff was unwilling to be restricted in any way regarding the use of troops under its command.

The overwhelming majority of the men who came to Israel with the Gottwald Brigade decided to settle in Israel. Among the few who returned to Czechoslovakia were three of the four transport commanders. These men were arrested as "Zionist agents" during the anti-Semitic purge trials held in Czechoslovakia during the early 1950s and were sentenced to long prison terms. They were released and rehabilitated during the 1960s. (See testimonies of members of the brigade, Yad Vashem Archives, YVA-0-59.)

12. Eugen Löbl, who had been Czechoslovakia's Deputy Minister of Foreign Trade until his arrest as one of the principal defendants in the Slánský trial, recalls in his book on the trial (*Svedectvo o procese* [Testimony on the Trial], Bratislava: 1968) that he was approached in 1948 by the head of the export department of the Zbrojovka munitions plant in Brno, who informed him that the Egyptian government was interested in purchasing from Zbrojovka an entire munitions plant to be set up in Egypt. The Egyptians were willing to pay a high price, in hard currency. The Ministry of National Defense approved the export. "I asked [Vladimír] Clementis about the attitude of the Ministry of Foreign Affairs," Löbl writes. "Clementis answered that [the Soviet chief delegate to the United Nations] Andrei Vyshinsky, would be passing through Prague within the next few days on his way to Moscow and he [Clementis] would meet with him at the airport and ask about the stand of the Soviet government. After his talk with Vyshinsky, Clementis informed me that Vyshinsky had not even wanted to hear about such a transaction, and that therefore the Ministry of Foreign Affairs could not give its approval to the export."

THE JEWISH MUSEUM OF PRAGUE

By Hana Volavková

HISTORICAL ROOTS

The present and by now world-famous State Jewish Museum of Prague, the lasting monument to a once-great Jewry, was created in response to tragic circumstances that are only too well known. However, its foundations had already been laid at the beginning of the century, in 1906, when the first Jewish Museum of Prague was founded by Dr. Salomon Hugo Lieben.[1]

Jews have lived in Bohemia and Moravia for over a thousand years, and many local Jewish religious congregations strove over the centuries to safeguard historic relics. Thus, the Jewish Religious Congregation of Mladá Boleslav preserved priceless ceremonial objects in one of its halls. There were also several outstanding individuals who contributed to the preservation of Jewish cultural treasures and historical documents.[2] However, a Jewish museum in the formal sense of the term was not established in the Czech lands until the pioneer work of S. H. Lieben.

The immediate impetus for the creation of the original Jewish Museum of Prague was the threat to Jewish relics and art treasures posed in 1906 by the impending demolition of three synagogues in the Prague ghetto (the *Neuschul,* the *Zigeunerschul,** and the Great Court Synagogue) for reasons of urban reconstruction.[3] That year Lieben, with his principal coworker, August Stein,[4] founded the "Association for the Foundation and Maintenance of the Jewish

---

* The Zigeunerschul was named for its builder, a Jew by the name of Salkind Zigeuner.

Museum in Prague." A. Hahn was elected chairman of the organization. The group quickly proceeded to acquire items of historic and artistic value from old synagogues and Jewish town halls all over the Historic Lands, enlisting the cooperation of provincial Jewish religious congregations and private collectors. The first public exhibition was held in 1909, and in April 1912 the museum was opened to the public at its permanent quarters, a building owned by the *Chevra Kadisha* (Jewish Burial Brotherhood) in the old ghetto of Prague.

The museum continued to grow during the era of the first Czechoslovak Republic, benefiting from the wave of interest in Jewish culture which developed in Czechoslovakia between 1920 and 1930. The Jewish museum of Mikulov (Nikolsburg), Moravia, founded in the 1920s, made an important contribution to the Prague Museum in the form of a collection that included the ceramic jugs used by the *Chevra Kadisha* as well as other ceremonial objects. In 1928 a new Jewish museum was founded in Prešov, Slovakia. By 1938 the Jewish museums of Czechoslovakia (including the museum in Prague) housed a total of approximately 13,000 inventory items.

THE HOLOCAUST ERA

Origins of the Central Jewish Museum

Following the German occupation of Czechoslovakia and the establishment of the Protectorate of Bohemia and Moravia, Jewish museology entered upon a new—and truly absurd—phase. By the spring of 1942, as transports to the death camps became routine and whole towns and villages lost their Jewish populations, as religious congregations were decimated and synagogues closed, Jewish leaders desperately sought means of preserving precious archives, art objects, and other cultural treasures left unattended throughout the country.

Ironically, it was the Germans, who, through their systematic program of "centralization" and "concentration," unwittingly helped provide a solution for this problem. On June 17, 1942, the Protectorate government ordered the transfer of all materials of Jewish cultural and historical interest such as libraries, archives, and ceremonial objects from the provinces to the headquarters of the

Jewish Religious Congregation of Prague.[5] Jewish officials hoped that Jewish ceremonial objects, relics, and treasures in transit would merge unobtrusively with other general mailings and transfers and thus reach Prague safely. Since shipping firms and movers had shown reluctance to handle Jewish property without direct orders from the *Zentralstelle für Jüdische Auswanderung* (Central Office for Jewish Emigration), it was essential to obtain the cooperation of German authorities if Jewish relics were to be saved from loss and destruction by moving them all to one place in Prague.

At the time, the so-called Provincial Department of the Prague Jewish Religious Congregation, known also as "Section Seven," was headed by Dr. Karel Stein. At Stein's suggestion, the Jewish Religious Congregation invited several experts to work out a plan for the creation of a central Jewish museum where cultural objects from the entire Protectorate could be kept and safeguarded. Foremost among these planners was Dr. Josef Polák, an eminent museologist, who had helped found the Jewish museum in Košice, Slovakia. Under Dr. Polák's direction, a comprehensive plan for a central museum in Prague was drafted and submitted to the *Zentralstelle*.

The plan proposed that "the innumerable priceless Jewish historical and artistic relics and monuments which had been scattered all over the country should be gathered together [in one place] and classified." The Germans approved the plan. After all, the idea of a centralized depository for Jewish "culture" probably did not seem to them much different from depositories for other confiscated Jewish property—from furniture to musical instruments, from iceboxes to bathtubs—that had been gathered in Prague for storage and eventual shipment to Germany. Thus, the short-term aims of the Jewish leaders and of the Germans coincided: both sides, each for entirely different reasons, were interested in gathering Jewish cultural treasures in Prague. The Jewish leaders hoped that someday all these objects would be returned to their rightful owners, while the Germans, acting through the *Zentralstelle*, consented to the plan in the firm conviction that the Reich would be victorious and that these collections of precious objects would remain as the only relics of the "extinct Jewish race."

On July 30, 1942, the *Zentralstelle* was informed that the premises of the original Jewish Museum of Prague would not have sufficient space to house all the expected material.[6] A building at 2430 Jáchymova Street, which had once housed a Jewish school, was chosen to accommodate the new acquisitions.

Shortly after the Jewish religious congregations in Bohemia and Moravia had been notified of the new arrangement, a spate of Jewish cultural treasures began to stream into Prague. Tablets of the Ten Commandments came down from the eastern walls of provincial synagogues; Torah scrolls and *parokhet* (Ark curtains) were stripped from the holy Arks. Menorahs were taken off their stands, and holy books were removed from bookcases. All the ceremonial objects thus collected, including some 2,500 Torah scrolls, were sent to Prague, where they were sorted, catalogued and given file numbers. Photographs of Jewish cemeteries, synagogues, and relics of buildings of Jewish interest reached the comparative safety of what was now known as the Central Jewish Museum in Prague.[7] The treasures of the 156 Jewish religious congregations that were gathered in Prague were a reflection of the life and spirit of Bohemian and Moravian Jewry. The largest single category was that of books and precious manuscripts. The second largest was archival material. The most valuable objects were religious textiles, particularly *parokhet,* dating from 1592 to 1938, and approximately 6,000 pieces of ceremonial silver.

On August 3, 1942, systematic work was begun at the Central Jewish Museum in Prague to classify and arrange the assembled objects into permanent exhibits that would illustrate the Jewish life and culture of the past. The exhibits were to be installed in a group of buildings near the old Jewish cemetery; among these buildings were the High Synagogue, the *Altneuschul* (known in Czechoslovakia as Staro Nová Synagoga),* the Klaus Synagogue, and the Pinkas Synagogue.

The staff of the museum consisted of thirty persons, approximately one-third of whom were trained museologists, archivists, and other experts. Among the key officials of the museum, in addition to

---

* According to some authorities, the name refers to a decree providing that the new (*neu*) synagogue had to be built on the same site as the old (*alt*) one. Tradition, however, has it that the name derives from the Hebrew *al t'nai* ("on condition that"). According to this legend the original builders of the synagogue used stones from the ruins of the Temple in Jerusalem in the foundations for the Prague edifice under the condition that when the Messiah came the synagogue would be dismantled and the stones returned to Zion. [Ed.]

Dr. Polák, were Dr. Tobias Jacobovits, a former librarian who had been active with the Jewish Religious Congregation of Prague since the 1920s, the historian and educator Dr. Anton Engel, and the well-known theatrical artist František Zelenka. Superintending these officials on behalf of the *Zentralamt für die Regelung der Judenfrage in Böhmen und Mähren* (Central Office for the Settlement of the Jewish Problem in Bohemia and Moravia, successor of the *Zentralstelle*) was SS Obersturmbannführer Karl Rahm, who eventually was to become the commandant of the Terezín ghetto. Rahm, an Austrian, had started out in life as a locksmith in Vienna.

The records of the museum's planning board give a vivid picture of the work done at the museum between 1942 and 1944.[8] The operational expenses of the museum (about 200,000 crowns per month) were borne entirely by the dwindling Jewish community.

The agenda of the meeting of the museum board on October 5, 1942, included plans for an exhibit of Jewish books and manuscripts at Prague's High Synagogue, which had been built in 1568.[9] The minutes of the board contain a report by František Zelenka that the architectural work on the museum was entering its final stage and that the High Synagogue was being restored at a cost of 208,162 crowns. Over half of this amount was spent for display cases. According to the above record, the transfer of books to the High Synagogue for the exhibition was to begin on Friday, November 20, 1942. That evening *Obersturmbannführer* Rahm was informed that the exhibition would open the following Monday, November 23.

Although it had been organized in great haste, the exhibition had on display a fine series of Hebrew manuscripts and books from the recently acquired collections. This was a source of some comfort, since the original library of the Jewish Religious Congregation in Prague had already been confiscated by the Gestapo before 1942.[10]

There were seventy-four samples from various Hebrew print shops and also an assortment of newly collected manuscripts prepared by Dr. Jacobovits, who had helped install a similar exhibit in Prague in 1927 and now compiled a guide book for the exhibition at the Central Museum.[11]

Although vested with considerable power, the *Zentralstelle*, which supervised the museum, was subject to the control of the authorities in Berlin. Therefore, when the *Zentralstelle* received an announcement on December 15, 1942, to expect an official visit from the Reich, the *Zentralstelle* feared that this might be a disciplinary action for having approved the establishment of the Central Jewish Museum in Prague. But it turned out that the visiting German officials only wished to inspect the exhibit of books at the High Synagogue, to see the *Altneuschul,* and to visit the old Jewish cemetery. The inspection tour went smoothly and without untoward incident. Thus, the museum's annual report for 1942 sounded an optimistic note at a time when over two-thirds of the Jewish population of the Protectorate were in the process of being deported to their deaths.

In November 1942 Obersturmbannführer Rahm approved the plans for an exhibit conceived by Dr. Polák and Zelenka for the Klaus Synagogue:[12] a pageant of "Jewish Life from the Cradle to the Grave." In creating this exhibit, Polák and Zelenka managed to confront the Nazis—whose ideology justified mass murder—with the Fifth Commandment, "Thou shalt not kill." Under the circumstances, this in itself was a courageous undertaking. No attempt was made to draw parallels between the religion, customs, and traditions of Judaism and those of other creeds or national entities, or to explain to the visitors the meaning of the Jewish holidays or the evolution of Jewish traditions.

The exhibit began in an anteroom with small almsboxes and the caption, "a gift made in secret pacifies anger" (Proverbs 21:14). The first cubicle was dedicated to rituals associated with birth and was conceived in a merry, folkloric style. The second, devoted to marriage, featured white Torah Ark curtains and shone with a pure radiance. The cubicle devoted to burial was decorated with black curtains that created a somber mood. The decor conjured up a dramatic effect. The symbolic elements of Jewish life as well as the gay mood of the Jewish festivals were entirely missing from the exhibit. After all, it was hardly possible, for instance, to present the Sabbath as a day of light, rest, and peace when the Nazis had made the Jewish Sabbath a day of slave labor no different from any other and when a summons to a death transport was as likely to be delivered on the Sabbath as at any other time. Thus, each exhibit conveyed its own silent message with an eloquence that transcended the items on display.

On April 6, 1943, the German officials were given a guided tour of the exhibits by Salomon Krämer and Herbert Langer, the newly installed leaders of the *Ältestenrat* (Council of Jewish Elders). On the whole, the Germans had no criticism to make of the exhibits, except for the section devoted to the Torah and the dietary laws. They insisted on having certain crude supplements added to this section, but these debasing elements failed to mar the overall effect of the exhibit.

The Museum of the Prague Ghetto

In the fall of 1942 the planning board of the Central Jewish Museum turned its attention to the old Jewish Museum of Prague founded by Dr. Lieben, which was still housed in the building originally owned by the *Chevra Kadisha* and which, as distinct from the Central Jewish Museum, had come to be known among museologists as the "Prague Museum" or the "Old Museum." Over the next two years, several meetings of the board were devoted to discussions of how best to use the facilities and resources of the "Old Museum." Eventually it was decided to convert the "Old Museum" into a museum of the Prague ghetto.

In the entrance hall maps, models, and photographs were put on display showing the development of the Jewish community of Prague over an uninterrupted course of a thousand years. The adjoining room was dedicated to the memory of Prague synagogues, which once had been the centers of Jewish life in the ghetto. There were the treasures of the Maisel Synagogue: the Maisel ensign, a banner which in the olden days had been borne in processions of Jewish trade guilds; the beautiful Ark curtain; a Torah mantle with an inscription embroidered in tiny pearls—two outstanding examples of Prague textile art from the Renaissance period.

The treasures of the Pinkas Synagogue were represented by precious silver utensils dating from the eighteenth and nineteenth centuries. These objects had been created in Prague and donated by the goldsmith Zappert. Also among the exhibits were two rare specimens of Renaissance garments, the cloak and banner of the Marrano and pseudo-Messiah Solomon Molcho, which had been preserved at the Pinkas Synagogue.

A small room next to the staircase was dedicated to the memory of Prague's most outstanding rabbis. There were books written by the legendary Rabbi Judah Löw ben Bezalel and printed during the

Renaissance, certificates awarded to the renowned Rabbi David Oppenheim (d. 1736) and signed by Charles VI, Holy Roman emperor and king of Hungary, and also a portrait of the learned rabbi and historian Salomon Judah Rapaport, painted by the Czech artist Antonín Machek.

The staircase leading to this room was lined with portraits by Jewish artists, illustrating the costumes and occupations of Prague Jewry. A guidebook for this exhibit was compiled by Hana Volavková.

Though they were valuable and interesting, these exhibits were not enough to fill the building. The full potential of this somber building was not really utilized until 1961, when it held the first exhibit in Czechoslovakia to commemorate the events of World War II, and again in 1970, when it housed an exhibit entitled "Culture in Terezín," based on an article by Norbert Frýd. Another exhibit and the unveiling of a memorial plaque at the museum paid tribute to Dr. Josef Polák, who had worked for the museum until the day of his arrest.

RECONSTRUCTION OF THE ALTNEUSCHUL

Of the edifices under the jurisdiction of the Central Jewish Museum, the *Altneuschul* was the most important. Built around the year 1268 in early Gothic style, it is today the oldest extant Jewish house of worship in Europe.[13]

The first item on the agenda of the planning board was the restoration and reconstruction of the *Altneuschul* and its adaptation for museological purposes. However, though plans for this project had been discussed as early as October 5, 1942, and Zelenka had promptly proceeded with the preliminary surveys, the actual reconstruction had not been completed by the end of 1944, as is evident from complaints of procrastination voiced by Dr. Jacobovits at a meeting in the fall of that year.

Among the reasons for the delay in carrying out the reconstruction of the synagogue were clashes among the key staff members of the Central Jewish Museum regarding basic approaches and policies. For example, Dr. Jacobovits believed that no object actually belonging to the *Altneuschul* should be removed from the building while Dr. Polák and Zelenka argued that valuable *parokhet* should not be kept in the synagogue because the building was too damp. In essence, it was the clash of a traditionalist religious viewpoint against the expert opinions of professional museologists.

Another difference of opinion involved the ultimate fate of the objects collected from provincial congregations and deposited with the museum. Dr. Jacobovits, who was optimistic about the future, regarded the museum merely as a place where valuable objects might be stored for temporary safekeeping in Prague until they could be returned to their original owners, the Jewish religious congregations in the provinces.

An interesting exhibit was planned for the women's section of the synagogue. On the basis of a monograph by Zdenka Münzer, which explored certain similarities between Christian architecture of the early Gothic[14] period and architectural features of the *Altneuschul,* Dr. Polák prepared a photographic exhibit on this subject. However, this material had to be curtailed on the orders of Obersturmbannführer Rahm, who objected to the crosses on some of the slides since architectural elements indicating a former coexistence between Jews and Christians were unacceptable to the Nazis.

THE PINKAS SYNAGOGUE

The Pinkas Synagogue, located near the old Jewish cemetery of Prague, was completed in 1535. It was built in the Renaissance style, with a number of Gothic features. The family of Aharon Meshullam Horowitz, builder of the synagogue, had been entrusted with the safeguarding of the cloak and banner of Solomon Molcho, the false Messiah who had been executed in 1532 by order of the Emperor Charles V.

The planning board of the Central Jewish Museum first turned its attention to the Pinkas Synagogue at its meeting of April 8, 1943, when a restoration of this structure was discussed. Dr. Karel Stein presided at the meeting. The planning board was composed of Dr. Jacobovits, Dr. Polák, František Zelenka and others; H. Richter, an engineer, was invited to participate in the restoration work. Since the synagogue had been previously converted into a storage depot for objects collected from various Jewish institutions throughout the country, it was decided that the first order of business was to clear the interior so that preliminary surveys could be conducted by Zelenka.

At the board meeting of May 3, 1943, plans for an exhibit in the Pinkas Synagogue were submitted. Upon the recommendation of Dr. Jacobovits, it was decided to present the historical development of Czech and Moravian Jews, utilizing all the material that was available. Dr. Josef Polák proposed the title "Ghetto Exhibit" for this project and suggested that a chronological, evolutionary approach be stressed.

According to preliminary sketches, the ground floor of the synagogue was to be devoted largely to an exhibit covering historical developments from the earliest times until the nineteenth century, with the galleries devoted to a portrayal of Jewish street scenes. The first and second floors of the synagogue were to house exhibits on Jewish schools and the life of Jewish scholars.

However, in late 1943, with the tide of the war turning in the Allies' favor, the Germans lost interest in the Jewish museum project and decided not to engage in the reconstruction work of the Pinkas Synagogue. As a result, the exhibits were never completed. But after the war the synagogue was to become a unique memorial to the Jewish victims of the Holocaust.

COURAGE AND MARTYRDOM

The courage of the staff members of the Central Jewish Museum and their determination to produce something of value even under the most adverse conditions were more poignant and eloquent than any of the museum's physical exhibits could have been. The Holocaust took its toll also from among the men who devoted themselves to the work of the museum. Dr. Josef Polák, who belonged to an underground resistance group, was caught by the Gestapo in August 1944 and did not long survive his arrest. The Prague ghetto exhibit was the last work of this dedicated museologist in the course of a highly fruitful career. Dr. Tobias Jacobovits was deported in a transport which left Prague on October 27, 1944. This was one of the smallest transports ever to leave Prague for the extermination camps, with eighteen people aboard.[15]

Of the team that worked so industriously on the reconstruction of the Pinkas Synagogue, the first to go to his death was H. Richter, who was deported early in June 1943. František Zelenka, with a summons to a deportation transport already in his pocket, still attended a meeting of the planning board on June 21, 1943. A week later he turned his work over to his successor, Dr. Leo Mayer, and on July 8 he left Prague in a transport together with over 400 employees of the Prague *Ältestenrat*.

Dr. Karel Stein presided at the planning board's meeting of July 12, and took part in the discussions regarding the reconstruction of the Pinkas Synagogue. After the meeting he took leave of his coworkers and friends and on the following day was deported along with over 800* employees of the *Ältestenrat*. On September 7, 1943, Dr. Leo Mayer, too, said farewell to his friends on the museum staff and left Prague in a transport four days later. The great majority of the lesser known but equally dedicated men and women who had worked for the Central Jewish Museum of Prague suffered a similar fate.

THE POSTWAR YEARS

THE STATE JEWISH MUSEUM

In the decades that have passed since World War II the Jewish Museum of Prague has become closely linked with Czechoslovak museology in general. Thanks to the support of the Czechoslovak government, new exploration and restoration work has been carried on by the staff of the museum.

Restoration work on the Pinkas Synagogue was finally begun in 1950. Preliminary explorations yielded remnants of Romanesque tiles, which covered much older layers of the floor beneath. Fragments of considerable value were discovered buried under an enormous mound inside the building; this find enabled the experts to make a reconstruction of an old Renaissance porch, which turned out to have been the work of Benedict Rejt, master builder of the Hradčany Palace during the sixteenth century. Removal of the mound that had covered the fragments revealed also remnants of

---

* A position, no matter how lowly, on the staff of the *Ältestenrat* was a much-coveted prize since such employment initially seemed an "insurance," as it were, against deportation.

the old *almemor* (reading desk). These remnants were now topped by a fine Rococo trellis from the old Zigeunerschul.

In the early 1950s a bold plan was conceived to erect in the Pinkas Synagogue a memorial to the Jews of Bohemia and Moravia who had perished in the Holocaust. The memorial was envisioned as simple but imposing, consisting only of the names of the victims inscribed upon a wall, side by side, line by line. In 1953 and 1954, a selection of final designs submitted by artists was evaluated by a committee of experts headed by Professor Josef Kaplický.

The actual work on the memorial was begun in 1955 and completed in 1959. The inscriptions, and their location and spacing, were designed by the late artist Jiří John, and the work was executed in collaboration with another artist, Václav Bostík. Both John and Bostík were outstanding calligraphers and the final result was a perfectly balanced, simple, yet moving work of art: 77,297 names inscribed on the walls of the synagogue in black letters upon a cool, white background.

Through an irony of fate, this memorial was destined to last only a few years. During the 1960s the walls were severely damaged by subterranean water from the Moldau (Vltava) river and it is questionable whether the memorial can or will ever be restored.[16] However, it has already served a purpose as a witness to the inhumanity of our times and as a tribute to the 77,297 Czech Jewish martyrs of Nazism who will never be forgotten.

Among the exceptionally interesting features of the present-day Jewish Museum of Prague is its collection of silver and gold ceremonial objects and its collection of ceremonial textiles.

The collection of silver ceremonial objects, consisting of about 6,000 items, comes mostly from the period between the eighteenth and twentieth centuries, with a small number of older pieces. There are also numerous Torah breastplates and alms plates; most of these are made of silver with an admixture of copper.

The treasure of Jewish textiles consists mostly of objects sent to Prague from provincial synagogues during World War II: this is a collection unique in the world. Many of the items are of outstanding artistic quality and historic significance.[17] The sheer size of the collection in itself is striking: the museum has in its safekeeping about 2,000 Ark curtains, 1,000 draperies, 4,800 Torah mantles, and 3,000

Torah covers, *wimpels* (Torah binders),* cushions, and other ritual objects.[18]

The files and archives of the museum hold large quantities of documents and photographs of Jewish life before and after the Nazi era; these offer very important source material for scholarly research. For example, there is in the archives a whole series of documentary photographs taken by SS men themselves, recording the atrocities committed at Auschwitz.

To supplement the material gathered during the war, the Jewish Museum of Prague has been proceeding with great zeal in its search for Jewish relics and art objects from nearby areas.[19] Judaica deposited temporarily by the Jews in various provincial castles during the Nazi occupation have been moved to Prague along with many abandoned materials retrieved from the Terezín ghetto and have become the subject of an extensive program of research. Since 1948 the Jewish Museum has been able to ensure better conditions for research, and the shift from community management to direct administrative supervision by the Czechoslovak government has been a step in the right direction.

The wealth of the Jewish Museum of Prague lies not only in its artistic and historical treasures but also in its compound of buildings and monuments that are a part of the city's famous old Jewish quarter.

In 1950 the Jewish Museum of Prague was taken over by the Czechoslovak state and its name changed to the State Jewish Museum. This act brought indisputable advantages to the institution, not only in richer funding but also in that the museum thus became the official center of collection and research work for the entire Czechoslovak Republic. Consequently, the State Jewish Museum in Prague became able to carry on as a scientific institution with a considerable publishing capacity of its own, and was in a position to enlarge its staff with trained professional workers.

Thus, the State Jewish Museum in Prague finds itself in a new historic phase. It is hoped that the developments of the last

---

* The *wimpels,* often elaborately embroidered, are wrapped around the Torah scrolls to hold them together. In certain parts of Germany the swaddling bands of babies were donated to the synagogue for this purpose.

few years are only a prelude to a period of renewed vigor and significance.

NOTES

1. Salomon Hugo Lieben, *Das jüdische Museum in Prag* [The Jewish Museum in Prague] (Prague: 1925). For additional material on Dr. Lieben, see also *The Jews of Czechoslovakia*, vols. I and II.
2. One such outstanding figure was Rabbi David Oppenheim, a scholar and inveterate collector of books. This rabbi was constantly on the move, and his collections traveled with him. In 1695, while he lived in Mikulov (Nikolsburg), Moravia, he had a Torah curtain made, which he took with him to Prague and subsequently to Hamburg. By the time he died in 1736 he had amassed a valuable collection of prints, Jewish songs, and some 700 books which were deposited in Hamburg. These books were purchased by Oxford University in 1929 and placed into the Bodleian Library. The valuable Torah Ark curtain is now in the State Jewish Museum in Prague.
3. Not until the middle of the nineteenth century were the boundaries of the Jewish quarter razed. Between 1893 and 1917 the Prague ghetto was gradually demolished as obsolete and unsanitary. Thus, only a few monuments have survived: the world-famous *Altneuschul;* the Old Jewish cemetery (more precious now than ever, since the Nazis destroyed nearly all the ancient Jewish cemeteries in Europe); the Pinkas Synagogue; the High Synagogue, with a hall interior that is unique both in size and furnishings; the Klaus Synagogue, with elaborate Baroque stucco work foreshadowing transition to Rococo; and the Old Synagogue, built after the middle of the nineteenth century by Ignac Ullman and distinguished by its rich furnishings.
4. Dr. Augustin Stein (1854-1935) was the son of a provincial Czech rabbi. As an outstanding student, he was appointed tutor to the family of the prominent Czech statesman František Ladislav Rieger. Thoroughly familiar with Bohemian Jewish towns and their history, Stein published a variety of studies, including an article in *Ottovy Čechy* [Otto's Bohemia] and a number of thorough studies on the legal character of the newly established religious congregations. He was among the original founders of the Jewish Museum of Prague.
5. Hana Volavková, *The Story of the Jewish Museum in Prague* (Prague: 1966), Czech edition, pp. 60-62.

6. A document dated July 30, 1942, informed the *Zentralstelle* that the building which housed the Jewish Museum of Prague was inadequate. For the first time, also, this document proposed that an inventory of items be taken as soon as possible. By that time the Jewish Museum already contained various objects gathered from provincial communities, such as a carved cradle from Heřmanův Městec and a hand-painted circumcision chair from Udlice. Rare Torah Ark curtains from Prague were on display in massive cases and walls were adorned with portraits of rabbis and etchings of Jewish religious processions from the past.
7. For a list of monuments, see Hana Volavková, *The Story of the Jewish Museum in Prague* (Prague: 1966), Czech edition, pp. 47-8, 117. For a classification of Jewish cemeteries, see Jan Heřman, "Jewish Cemeteries in Bohemia," published in *Památková péče,* 27/4, 1967, pp. 96-106. Also, Heřman, "Jewish Cemeteries in Moravia," published in *Památková péče,* no. 3, 1968, pp. 81-87. For a list of Jewish religious congregations and objects preserved, see Hana Volavková, *The Story of the Jewish Museum in Prague.*
8. According to the report of October 5, 1942, six committees had been at work. These committees achieved the remarkable job of completing 7,832 inventory cards within two months.
9. See Olga Herbenová, "Vysoká Synagoga," in *Židovská ročenka na r. 5722* [Jewish Yearbook, 5722], 1961-1962, p. 45.
10. The library of the Jewish Religious Congregation was returned to the museum after World War II. It now forms the nucleus of the greatest collection of Judaica in Central Europe. It includes a collection of Hebrew manuscripts and incunabulae, as well as ancient Hebrew prints from Prague, the oldest dating from 1512. The Jewish Religious Congregation had built up its famous library from the literary legacies of several Jewish scholars and opened it to the public in 1874. The core of the collection was thirty-three manuscripts given to the library by the late Rabbi Salomon Juda Rapaport of Prague. (See Tobias Jacobovits, *Entstehungsgeschichte der Bibliothek der israelitischen Kultusgemeinde in Prag* [The Beginnings of the Library of the Jewish Religious Congregation of Prague] (Prague: 1927). Among the outstanding medieval monuments is the Maimonides Manuscript, which was completed on November 4, 1444. It was written by Menachem bar Isaac, who copied it for Rabbi Moshe bar Jacob. (See V. Sadek, "Aus der Handschriftensammlung des staatlichen jüdischen Museums in Prag" [From the Manuscript Collection of the State Jewish Museum in Prague], in *Judaica Bohemiae* v/2 VIII (Prague: 1969), p. 144; (Prague: 1972) p. 16.

11. The guide is reprinted in Hana Volavková, *The Story of the Jewish Museum in Prague,* Czech edition, pp. 143-49.
12. See Volavková, *The Story of the Jewish Museum in Prague,* illustrations 6F, 98, 138.
13. For a discussion of the historical and cultural significance of the building, see Zdenka Münzer, "The Old-New Synagogue in Prague: Its Architectural History" in *The Jews of Czechoslovakia,* Vol. II, pp. 520-46.
14. Ibid.
15. In his novel *Mendelssohn je na střeše* [Mendelssohn is on the Roof] (Prague: 1961), the novelist Jiří Weil, a one-time employee of the Central Jewish Museum, described the fate of Dr. Jacobovits and his grim journey in a sealed railroad car.
16. Since the late 1960s the memorial at the Pinkas Synagogue has been closed and long-range reconstruction work has proceeded at an extremely slow pace.

    Editorial Note: In 1978 Lewis Weiner, president of the Society for the History of Czechoslovak Jewry, visited Prague and met with Dr. Miroslav Jaroš, who was then the director of the State Jewish Museum. Also present at this meeting were Dr. Vladimír Sadek and Dr. Bedřich Nosek, the non-Jewish Hebraists who serve as curators of the museum. Dr. Jaroš informed him that repair work on the Pinkas Synagogue was well under way. The foundations and floor of the building had been secured and waterproofed, and the *mikvah* (ritual bath), which had been discovered during the restoration, had been insulated from the rest of the building. When Mr. Weiner stressed the importance of restoring the names of the deportees, which had been obliterated from the walls of the original structure, Dr. Jaroš replied that when the restoration of the synagogue was completed, the names of the martyrs would be reinscribed.
17. Like other ancient Jewish textiles, Torah Ark curtains from the *Altneuschul* carried inscriptions showing the date of their origin. In reading those inscriptions, experts have differed in their interpretations. For his work *Nápisy pražských peroches z let 1548-1808* (Inscriptions on the Prague Parokhet, 1548-1808), published in 1931, Dr. Polák gathered information from works translated by Rabbi Dr. Emanuel Enten and Rabbi Wiesenberger in Košice. Experts working with the Jewish Museum during the war based their studies on translations by Dr. Jacobovits (see Hana Volavková, *The Synagogue Treasures,* 1948) and by Olga Herbenová ("Synagogen-Vorhänge des 17. Jahrhunderts aus Böhmen und Mähren" [Seventeenth-Century Synagogue Curtains from Bohemia and Moravia] in *Waffen und Kostümkunde,* Jhrg. 1968. Zeitschrift der Gesellschaft für historische Waffen und Kostümkunde,

Bd. der Gesamtfolge, p. 107. The translations differ considerably. For instance, the inscription on the oldest Torah curtain in the possession of the *Altneuschul,* which was completed in 1592, was interpreted by Dr. Jacobovits as "the gift of Solomon Perlsticker, son of Abraham the martyr, and his wife Golda. The curtain was completed in 1592 by Solomon's son Pinchas and his wife Gautel." But Dr. Otto Muneles corrected the wording to read that "the curtain was donated by Solomon Perlsticker and embroidered by Solomon Golda." Data on migration, combined with formal analysis, resulted in the classification of the material into three groups: Bohemian, Austrian (Viennese), and Moravian. The inscription on the curtains often included the names of the embroiderers. Among the Prague embroiderers thus signed were not only Solomon Golda, but also a Mrs. Reichel, who signed the curtain donated by Löb Tausk to the *Altneuschul* in 1697. Juda Löb was a prominent Moravian embroiderer; several of his curtains are also deposited in the museum in Prague.

18. See Hana Volavková, *The Synagogue Treasures of Bohemia and Moravia* (Prague: 1949). Also: Olga Herbenová, *Synagogen-Vorhänge des 17. Jahrhunderts . . . ,* 1968. Also: "The Processing of Swaddling-bands in Relation to Folklore Art," lecture by Jana Doležalová, 1970. The museum's textile department was, from the very beginning, carefully installed and maintained. The depository was improved several times and in the 1950s was permanently installed in the Old Synagogue in Dušní Ulice, Prague. The depository was opened to the public in 1960.
19. In 1961, the State Jewish Museum in Prague could at last systematically arrange the archives of the Jewish religious communities on the basis of provenance. See Jan Heřman, "Jewish Community Archives from Bohemia and Moravia," *Judaica Bohemica,* 1971, VII/I and VII/II.

THE STORY OF THE CZECH SCROLLS

by Joseph C. Pick

Early in February 1964, in the nineteenth year after the last German troops had surrendered in Prague, there arrived in London 1,564 Torah scrolls representing hundreds of Jewish communities in Bohemia and Moravia that had been wiped out in the Holocaust. For over twenty years, the scrolls had lain unused and unattended in a Prague synagogue that had been converted into a warehouse. Then they traveled across Europe to England in five sealed railroad cars, the largest shipment of Torah scrolls known in Jewish history. From the London railroad station they were reverently transferred to their temporary home, the Westminster Synagogue in London. From there, over the years that have passed since, they have been sent out to Jewish communities in Great Britain and twenty other countries of the Western world, including West Germany, to be cherished as memorials to a tragic past but at the same time to be read and studied by a new generation of Jews, the guarantors of Jewish survival and rebirth.

The Torah scrolls from Czechoslovakia were part of a huge collection of Jewish ceremonial objects that the Germans had confiscated and desecrated but saved for a permanent exhibit of "relics of the extinct Jewish race," which they planned to set up following the victory of the Thousand-Year Reich.* Working under the sharp eyes of the German taskmasters, Jews in Prague were compelled to sort, classify, and catalog these treasures, and to arrange the scrolls

---

* See Hana Volavková, "The Jewish Museum of Prague," in the present volume, pp. 568–570.

in the old synagogue of Michle (a suburb of Prague) in stacks reaching from the floor to the ceiling. For the Jews thus employed, it was a short reprieve; when their task was completed, most of them were deported and eventually perished in the death camps. However, one would like to believe that as the Torah scrolls and the other sacred objects, including some of great value and antiquity, passed beneath their hands, these martyrs took comfort in the hope that ultimately Hitler would fall and that the ceremonial objects, in some cases hundreds of years old, would be returned to the restored Jewish communities.

When World War II ended, the Torah scrolls still lay in the Michle Synagogue, deteriorating from disuse, dampness, and lack of care. Eventually, the Michle Synagogue and the scrolls were taken over by the State Jewish Museum in Prague, and thus came under the control of Artia, the official agents of the Czechoslovak government in charge of "cultural properties." But there was nothing that Artia or the staff of the museum could do to preserve the Torah scrolls. In order to keep parchment scrolls from perishing, they must be unrolled from time to time. This was patently impossible to do with over 1,500 scrolls housed in desperately cramped quarters. And so the scrolls seemed condemned to slow decay until 1963, when Artia officials approached Eric Estorick, a well-known London art dealer, on one of his visits to Prague and asked him what might be done about the scrolls in the Michle Synagogue. Was there, in the West, any individual or organization interested in acquiring a very large number of Torah scrolls from Czech Jewish communities that had perished in the war? Estorick's response was positive and practical. To begin with, he said, an expert would have to make an on-the-spot inspection of the scrolls to determine their condition, more specifically, to see which of them were still ritually fit for use at synagogue services. He knew of such an expert in London: Chimen Abramsky, a historian and acknowledged authority on Hebraica and Judaica. Arrangements were made for Abramsky to go to Prague. His preliminary examination of about 250 scrolls left the scholar deeply shaken. On his return to London he reported that many of the scrolls were quite old, some dating from the early eighteenth century, others from the nineteenth. Some of the scrolls had no protective covering. Others were swathed in tattered prayer shawls. He found two scrolls wrapped in a woman's garment. Another was tied with a small belt from a child's coat. One scroll was spattered with human blood. From one of the scrolls a scrap of paper fell out, apparently left there by a *sofer* (scribe) who had examined the scroll in 1940 to see whether it was in need of repairs. "Please, God, help us in these troubled times," the note read. "It was quite incredible to see this," Abramsky said in London. "I burst into tears."[1]

While Abramsky was still in Prague, Estorick discussed the problem of the Czech scrolls with one of his clients, Ralph C. Yablon, a well-to-do, public-spirited member of London's Westminster Synagogue. Yablon in turn contacted his rabbi, Harold F. Reinhart, who had been contemplating the idea of setting up a Holocaust memorial museum in his synagogue. Perhaps, the rabbi said, some of the Czech Torah scrolls could be brought to London as a nucleus for such an exhibit. Yablon's answer was to acquire all the 1,564 scrolls from Czechoslovakia for the equivalent of $30,000, and in December 1963 the Westminster Synagogue became the official trustee for the entire collection until such time as it could be distributed elsewhere. In addition to purchasing the scrolls for the Westminster Synagogue, Yablon supplied the funds for their packing and their transportation from Prague to London.

Meanwhile, the Westminster Synagogue had organized a Memorial Scrolls Committee, of which Frank R. Waley became chairman and Mrs. G. R. (Ruth) Shaffer, honorary secretary. When the scrolls, covered with transparent polyethylene plastic, began to arrive at the synagogue on February 5, 1964, their quarters were ready to receive them. Three rooms had been set aside for the scrolls on the second floor of Kent House, the synagogue annex. Special racks had been constructed, and each scroll—or scroll fragment—was numbered and placed into a compartment marked with the corresponding number. This process of sorting and registration alone consumed several months. The day-to-day care of the scrolls became a community-wide project, involving not only Rabbi Reinhart, his wife, and Mrs. Shaffer, but also representatives of other segments of London Jewry, including Chief Rabbi Israel (later Sir Israel) Brodie; Dr. Solomon Gaon, the *haham* (chief rabbi) of the Sephardic community; Rabbi Pinhas Toledano, minister of the Wembley Sephardic congregation; and Richard D. Barnett, a prominent member of London's Spanish and Portuguese Synagogue and "keeper" in the Department of Western Asiatic Antiquities in the British Museum.

By the summer of 1964 the Memorial Scrolls Committee could begin the second step in the rehabiliation of the scrolls. With the cooperation of Dr. Gaon and others, scribes were engaged to subject each scroll to careful scrutiny from beginning to end and to record their findings for each scroll—its history, place and date of origin, distinguishing features and, most important, the condition of the rollers, the parchment, and the writing. On the basis of their condition, the scrolls were classified into five categories, from "best," i.e., fit for use at synagogue services without, or virtually without, refurbishment, to "unusable." The last category included scrolls that were bloodstained, charred, or damaged by water, and scrolls that had been torn through more than three lines of writing or where the Name of God had been erased or torn. All scrolls beyond salvage were earmarked for display as Holocaust memorials in England and elsewhere. One such scroll was lent to Westminster Abbey in 1966 as part of a special Judaica exhibit arranged by the Council of Christians and Jews to honor the Abbey's nine hundredth anniversary. (Afterwards, this scroll was installed permanently in the library of the Council of Christians and Jews in London.) Others have gone to such institutions as Leeds University, the University of York and York Cathedral in England, and to Brandeis University, Northwestern University, and the University of Rochester, New York, in the United States.

Scrolls graded in between "best" and "unusable" required various minor and major repairs before they could be used for reading at synagogue services. It soon became clear that temporary, part-time scribes would not be sufficient for this work. A full-time scribe would be required, but the Westminster Synagogue had difficulty in finding a competent individual willing to devote all his time to examining and repairing the Czech scrolls. In May 1967 such a person turned up unexpectedly at the very doorstep of Kent House. He was David Brand, newly arrived from Jerusalem, who told Mrs. Shaffer that he had been traveling to many parts of the world repairing scrolls in synagogues and wondered whether the Westminster Synagogue happened to have any scrolls in need of repair. "I shall never forget the look of astonishment and awe on his face when he saw those three rooms stacked to the ceiling with *sifre Torah* (Torah scrolls)," Mrs. Shaffer recalled.[2] Initially, Mr. Brand worked for the Westminster Synagogue on a temporary basis only, but after his wife and family came over from Israel to join him in London, he agreed to give all his time to the Torah scrolls from Czechoslovakia.

The accessories of the scrolls also received careful attention. Cabinet makers were found who could repair wooden rollers so skillfully that the new parts seemed virtually indistinguishable from the originals. Some of the *wimpels* (strips of linen or other materials used to hold the scroll together) were of historic interest because they bore, in embroidery, the name of the donor who had commissioned the writing of the scroll, and the date and occasion on which the scroll had been presented to its original synagogue. Wherever necessary, these *wimpels* were carefully washed, cleaned, and pressed by Mrs. Reinhart.

From the time of their arrival in London, the scrolls—and their eventual availability to synagogues and other Jewish institutions in the Western world—received widespread publicity in the Jewish and non-Jewish press. Hundreds of visitors flocked to Kent House to view them. To one awe-stricken Czech Christian, they looked at first glance like "hundreds of corpses in transparent shrouds." Later, becoming calmer, he described them as "a mountain of dead books, spiritual bodies, so to speak, and yet a mountain glowing with the life of revelation, law, promise."[3] Some Holocaust survivors and former refugees from Central Europe broke down and wept at the sight of the scrolls.

Before long, the Memorial Scrolls Committee was deluged with requests from synagogues, Jewish organizations, and private individuals all over the Western world for a Torah scroll from Czechoslovakia. The committee established a procedure for dealing with these requests that is followed to this day. Each application must be submitted in writing to the committee for consideration. Priority is given to small congregations, homes for the aged, hospitals, and children's camps. Scrolls are never offered for sale; they are only given on "permanent loan." If the congregation or institution ceases to exist, its scroll must be returned to the Westminster Synagogue. In order to help cover expenses, the recipients are asked to make a contribution. In 1981, this was £300. In some instances, the amount is paid in installments. For deserving cases, it may be waived altogether, but such losses are more than offset by congregations sending contributions far in excess of the amount set by the committee.

Each scroll sent away bears a small brass plaque attached to its rollers with the inscription "Westminster Synagogue," the date 5725, i.e., 1964, "Czech Memorial Scroll," and the scroll's number. The scroll is accompanied by a certificate stating that it is one of the 1,564 scrolls from the Jewish ceremonial treasures confiscated by the Nazis, and giving in Hebrew and English the name of the town from which it came. Frequently the Memorial Scrolls Committee receives letters from rabbis or Hebrew school students, requesting a history of the Czech community from which "their" scroll came. In the United States, representatives of the Society for the History of Czechoslovak Jews have participated in dedication exercises for the scrolls at various synagogues and supplied historical information on the Jewish communities where the scrolls had originated. For this purpose the society formed a special committee under the chairmanship of the author of this article.

As of 1981 (the date of the most recent report issued by the Memorial Scrolls Committee), a total of 1,297 scrolls had been catalogued. Of these, a total of 692 had been sent to various synagogues and other Jewish institutions in England and other countries as follows:

Argentina	1	Israel	61
Australia	16	Italy	2
Belgium	3	New Zealand	5
Brazil	1	Panama	1
Canada	11	Puerto Rico	1
Channel Islands	1	Rhodesia	2
Federal Rep. of Germany	5	South Africa	7
France	7	Spain	1
Great Britain	90	Switzerland	5
Holland	4	U.S.A.	466
Ireland	1	Virgin Islands	1

Total: 692

Each of these Torah scrolls has a history of its own. Among the Czech *sifre Torah* brought to the United States there were several very old scrolls. On June 9, 1973, the Rego Park Jewish Center of Queens, New York, installed into its Ark a scroll that originally had belonged to the synagogue of the town of Hostomice, Bohemia. This scroll had been written in the year 1700. Rabbi Z. David Levy of Temple B'nai Or in Morristown, New Jersey, found that the scroll received by his congregation had come from the Malvazinka Synagogue in Prague and was approximately 200 years old. A scroll from the historic *Altneuschul* was given a new home at the Marathon Jewish Community Center in Little Neck, Long Island. Congregation Beth Israel in Fayetteville, North Carolina, has a *sefer Torah* from Loštice, Moravia, which dates from the eighteenth century.

The Philip M. Klutznick Exhibition Hall at B'nai B'rith headquarters in Washington, D.C., houses a Torah scroll from the synagogue of Slavkov u Brna, better known as Austerlitz. Written at the end of the eighteenth century, this scroll survived the famous battle in which, on December 2, 1805, Napoleon won the most brilliant military victory of his career.

The Hebrew Congregation of St. Thomas, Virgin Islands, dates from the late eighteenth century. The scroll it received had served at the synagogue of Budyně nad Ohře, Bohemia, having been installed there about 1780.

Some of the Czech scrolls reinforced a link between Czech Jewry and the history of the Jews in the United States. In the summer of 1978, Temple Beth Emunah of Brockton, Massachusetts received a *sefer Torah* from the town of Rokycany, Bohemia, the hometown of Adolph Kraus of Chicago, Illinois. Kraus had left Rokycany in 1865 at the age of fifteen to settle in Chicago, where he had a distinguished career as a lawyer and civic leader. American Jewry remembers him as the international president of B'nai B'rith (1906–1925) and a founder of the Anti-Defamation League.

One Czech scroll is now in the White House. Of great antiquity, it comes from Uherské Hradiště, one of the six royal cities of medieval Moravia, where Jews appear to have lived as far back as 1342. The scroll was given to President Jimmy Carter on November 2, 1977, after he had addressed a meeting called by the World Jewish Congress in Washington, D.C. The scroll was presented to him by Nahum Goldmann, the retiring president of the Congress, who expressed the hope that Carter would install it in the Executive Mansion "as a constant reminder of our prayers for justice and peace." Carter replied, "I accept it for all those who share a common religious heritage and a common commitment to the future ... I will observe it daily in the White House as I go about my duties and it will be a constant reminder to me of the spirit of human rights, decency, and love that is exemplified by those of you represented here tonight."[4]

Several of the scrolls brought to the United States held poignant personal memories for members of the Society for the History of Czechoslovak Jewry. A scroll sent to Atlanta, Georgia, turned out to be from Mladá Boleslav, the home town of the author of this article. Its *wimpel* is embroidered with the name of the woman who commissioned the writing of this *sefer Torah* in the year 1881, Rivka Eisenschimmel. The Eisenschimmels were close friends of the author's family, and this was the scroll from which the author read his *bar mitzvah* portion almost eighty years ago.

Rabbi Dr. Hugo Stransky served his people for nearly half a century, first in Czechoslovakia, then in London, New Zealand, Australia, and finally at Congregation Beth Hillel of Washington Heights in New York City. Now he was about to retire. One of the last official functions he attended was the rededication of Torah Scroll No. 66, two hundred years old, at Temple Israel of Staten Island, New York. Sharing the pulpit with the Temple's spiritual leader, Rabbi Milton Rosenfeld, Dr. Stransky looked more closely at the scroll. Tears came to his eyes. It was the *sefer Torah* he had used in his first congregation, the synagogue of Náchod, from 1930 to 1936.

"In what condition is it?" he whispered to his colleague, his voice choked with emotion as he peered intently at the scroll before him. "Ah!" he observed, "a bit faded, but it can be read."

And so Rabbi Stransky's long career of service to his fellow Jews on three continents came to a close in America within sight of the Torah scroll he had held in his arms on his first Sabbath as a "rabbi, teacher, and preacher in Israel" in a Bohemian Jewish community that is no more.

Rabbi Stransky looked down upon the congregation gathered in the sanctuary of Temple Israel to receive the old Torah scroll from Czechoslovakia. Like the scroll, some of the men and women seated before him were remnants of ancient, vibrant communities that had fallen to the Nazi terror. Now both the people and the Torah scroll were in a new land where Jews were free to nurture the heritage of their fathers and to pass it on to their children.

APPENDIX

CONGREGATIONS AND INSTITUTIONS HOLDING CZECHOSLOVAK TORAH SCROLLS ON A PERMANENT LOAN BASIS (1981)

Editors' Note: This list is taken from the report issued by the Memorial Scrolls Committee, Westminster Synagogue, London, in 1981. In the original list the congregations and institutions are set down in alphabetical order by name. In order to show the geographical distribution of the scrolls, the editors have rearranged the list according to the countries, cities, and towns in which the institutions holding the scrolls are located.

UNITED STATES OF AMERICA

ALABAMA
   Mobile: Springhill Avenue Temple

ARIZONA
   Arizona State University
   Phoenix: Beth Am Temple
             Beth El Congregation
             Congregation Haverim
             Jewish Committee on Scouting
             Temple Beth Israel
             Temple Chaim
   Scottsdale: Temple Solel
   Sun City: Congregation Beth Shalom
   Tempe: Hillel Foundation
          Temple Emanuel
   Tucson: Congregation Chaverim

CALIFORNIA
   Apple Valley: Congregation Bamidbar Shel Maala
   Berkeley: Temple Beth-El
   Beverly Hills: Temple Emanuel
   Brae: Temple Beth Tikvah
   Brandeis: Brandeis-Bardin Institute
   Burlington: Peninsula Temple Shalom
   Canoga Park: Temple Soleal of Canoga Park
   Carlsbad: Temple Solel
   Concord: Congregation Beth Am
   Downey: Congregation Ner Tamid
   Encino: California Institute for Men

CALIFORNIA, cont.
　Eureka: Temple Beth-El
　Fresno: Temple Beth Israel
　Fullerton: Temple Beth Tikvah
　Hollywood: Temple Israel of Hollywood
　Huntington Beach: Temple Hillel Synagogue
　Livermore: Congregation Beth Emek
　Los Angeles: Hebrew Union College
　　　　　　　Leo Baeck Temple
　　　　　　　Metropolitan Community
　　　　　　　Nots Hebrew Congregation
　　　　　　　Simon Wiesenthal Center for Holocaust Studies
　　　　　　　Sinai Temple
　　　　　　　Synagogue for the Performing Arts
　　　　　　　Temple Isaiah
　　　　　　　UCLA Hillel Extension
　　　　　　　University Synagogue
　　　　　　　Valley Beth Israel Congregation
　　　　　　　Van Nuys B'nai B'rith Lodge
　　　　　　　Vista Del Mar Child Care Service
　Mission Viejo: Temple Eilat
　Newport Beach: Harbor Area Reform Temple
　　　　　　　Temple Bat Yam
　North Hollywood: Temple Beth Hillel
　Northridge: Temple Ahavat Sholom
　Palo Alto: B'nai B'rith Hillel Foundation, Stanford University
　　　　　Congregation Kol Emeth
　Sacramento: Congregation B'nai Israel
　　　　　　Sacramento Jewish Fellowship
　　　　　　United Synagogue of America
　Salinas: Temple Beth-El
　San Diego: Temple Adath Shalom
　　　　　　Tifereth Israel Synagogue
　San Francisco: Congregation Beth Shalom
　　　　　　　Congregation Kol Shofar
　　　　　　　Congregation Sha'ar Zahav
　　　　　　　Swig Camp
　San Mateo: Peninsula Sinai Congregation
　San Pedro: Temple Beth-El
　Santa Barbara: Congregation Beth Ami
　　　　　　　Congregation B'nai B'rith
　Santa Maria: Temple Beth El

CALIFORNIA, cont.
  Santa Rosa: Santa Rosa Reform Congregation
  Saugus: Temple Beth Am
  Seal Beach: Congregation Shalom of Leisure World
  Sepulveda: Temple Beth Torah
  Stanton: Temple Negev of Orange County
  Studio City: Congregation Beth Ohr
  Sumter: Congregation Sinai
  Tarzana: Temple Judea
  Thousand Oaks: Reform Temple of Conejo Valley
  Walnut Creek: Congregation B'nai Shalom
  Woodland Hills: Makor Ohr Shalom Congregation
     Temple Emet

COLORADO
  Aspen: Aspen Jewish Center
  Denver: Temple Sinai

CONNECTICUT
  Bridgeport: Congregation B'nai Israel
  Cos Cob: Greenwich Reform Synagogue
  Fairfield: Congregation Beth El
  Greenwich: Chavurat Deev-Ray Torah
  Hartford: Farmington Valley Jewish Congregation
  Madison: Temple Beth Tikvah
  Milford: Temple B'nai Shalom
  New Haven: Temple Emanuel Reform Jewish Congregation
  New Milford: Temple Sholom
  Ridgefield: Temple Shearith Israel
  Stamford: Community of Jewish Life
     Congregation Agudath Shalom
  West Hartford: Emanuel Synagogue
  Westport: Congregation for Humanistic Judaism
     Temple Israel

DISTRICT OF COLUMBIA (Washington, D.C.)
  B'nai B'rith Philip M. Klutznick Exhibit Hall
  Congregation B'nai Israel
  Congregation B'nai Israel Men's Club
  M. C. T. Mishpocheh
  Southwest Hebrew Congregation
  Temple Sinai
  Washington Hebrew Congregation
  The White House

FLORIDA
  Boca Raton: Boca Raton Hebrew Congregation
  Boynton Beach: Congregation Beth Kodesh
  Coral Springs: Coral Springs Hebrew Congregation
  Dania: Temple Beth Emet
  Delray Beach: Reform Hebrew Congregation
              Temple Emeth of the Delray Hebrew Congregation
  Deltona: Temple Shalom
  Hollywood: Temple Sinai of North Dade
  Miami: Bet Breira
          Temple Israel of Greater Miami
  Naples: Jewish Community Center
  North Miami Beach: Beth Torah Congregation
  Orlando: Congregation of Liberal Judaism
GEORGIA
  Atlanta: Ahavat Achim Synagogue
            Congregation Shearith Israel
            Temple Sinai
  Augusta: Congregation Children of Israel
  Savannah: Congregation Mickve Israel
ILLINOIS
  Buffalo Grove: Congregation Beth Judea
                Temple Chaim Reform Congregation
  Champaign: Sinai Temple
  Chicago: Bess Merens Pavilion
            Beth Am, The People's Synagogue
            B'nai Jacob Congregation of West Rogers Park
            Chicago Federation of the Union of American Hebrew
               Congregations
            Congregation Bene Shalom of the Deaf
            Emanuel Congregation
            Forest Hospital
            McHenry County Jewish Congregation
            Ner Tamid Congregation
            Northwestern University
            Temple Beth-El
            Temple Sholom
  Glencoe: North Shore Congregation Israel
  Highland Park: Congregation B'nai Torah
                 North Suburban Synagogue Beth El
  Northbrook: Congregation B'nai Shalom

ILLINOIS, cont.
Northfield: Conservative Congregation of the North Shore
Olympia Fields: Temple Anshe Sholom
Park Forest: Congregation Beth Sholom
Peoria: Congregation Anshe Emeth
Skokie: Skokie Central Traditional Congregation
Temple Judea
Wilmette: Beth Hillel Congregation
Sager Solomon Schechter Day School
Winnetka: Temple Jeremiah

INDIANA
Gary: Temple Israel
Lafayette: Temple Israel
Richmond: Congregation Beth Boruk

IOWA
Ames: Ames Jewish Congregation

KANSAS
Topeka: Temple Beth Sholom
Wichita: Temple Emanu-El

LOUISIANA
Baton Rouge: Liberal Synagogue
Temple B'nai Israel
Lafayette: Congregation Rodeph Sholom
Congregation Sholom
New Orleans: Temple Sinai
Touro Synagogue

MARYLAND
Annapolis: Congregation Kol Ami
Baltimore: Chizuk Amuno Congregation
Levindale Hebrew Geriatric Center and Hospital
Bethesda: Bethesda Jewish Congregation
Bowie: Jewish Community Center of Belair
Temple Solel of Bowie
Chevy Chase: Temple Shalom
Greenbelt: Jewish Community Center
Kensington: Temple Emanuel
Oxon Hill: Beth Chayim Congregation
Potomac: Congregation Har Shalom
Rockville: Jewish Day School of Greater Washington
Temple Beth Ami

MARYLAND, cont.
  Silver Spring: Congregation Har Tzion
  Shaare Tefila Congregation
  Temple Israel

MASSACHUSETTS
  Boston: Temple Israel
  Brockton: Temple Beth Emunah
  Brookline: Temple Sinai
  Chelmsford: Congregation Shalom
  Chestnut Hill: Temple Emeth
  Temple Mishkan Tefila
  Framingham Center: Temple Beth Am
  Hyannis: Cape Cod Synagogue
  Lexington: Temple Isaiah
  Lowell: Temple Emanuel
  Malden: Temple Tiferet Israel
  Marblehead: Temple Emanuel
  New Bedford: Temple Sinai of New Bedford, Massachusetts
  Newton Center: Temple Beth Avodah
  Temple Emanuel
  North Dartmouth: Temple Sinai
  Randolph: Temple Beth Am
  Sharon: Temple Israel
  Springfield: Springfield Jewish Home for the Aged
  Sudbury: Congregation Beth El
  Congregation B'nai Torah
  Waltham: Brandeis University
  Wayland: Temple Shir Tikvah
  Wellesley Hills: Temple Beth Elohim
  Worcester: Congregation Beth Israel
  Temple Emanuel

MICHIGAN
  Ann Arbor: Temple Beth Emeth
  Bloomfield Hills: The New Temple
  Brighton: Congregation Solel
  Detroit: Temple Beth-El
  Temple Israel
  East Lansing: Congregation Kehillat Israel
  Grand Rapids: Temple Emanuel
  Kalamazoo: Temple B'nai Israel
  Traverse City: Congregation Beth El

MINNESOTA
   Minneapolis: Temple Israel
   St. Paul: Mount Zion Temple

MISSISSIPPI
   Brookhaven: Temple B'nai Sholom

MISSOURI
   Columbia: B'nai B'rith Hillel Foundation
   Kansas City: Congregation B'nai Jehuda
                   New Reform Temple
   Richmond Heights: B'rith Sholom Kneseth Israel Congregation
   St. Louis: Congregation B'nai Amoona
                 Congregation Kol Am
                 Congregation Shaare Emeth
                 Temple Israel
                 United Hebrew Congregation
   University City: Kol Katan Congregation
                       Shaare Zedek Synagogue

NEVADA
   Las Vegas: Liberal Jewish Center
                 Temple Ner Tamid

NEW HAMPSHIRE
   Manchester: Temple Adath Yeshurun

NEW JERSEY
   Bayonne: Temple Beth Am
   Bloomfield: Temple Menorah
   Chatham: Chatham Jewish Center
   Cherry Hill: Temple Emanuel
   Clifton: Reform Temple of East Brunswick
   Closter: Temple Beth-El of Northern Valley
   East Orange: Temple Sharey Tefilo
   Elizabeth: Temple Beth El
   Englishtown: Temple Shaari Emeth
   Fair Lawn: Ahavat Achim Orthodox Congregation
                 Fair Lawn Jewish Center
                 Reform Temple
                 Temple Beth Shalom
   Flemington: Congregation Bet Tikva of Raritan Township
   Fords: Temple Emanu-El
   Hackettstown: Temple Shearith Israel
   Haddon Heights: Temple Beth Sholom
   Highland Lakes: Temple Sholom

NEW JERSEY, cont.
- *Leonia:* Congregation Sons of Israel
- *Livingston:* Temple B'nai Abraham
  Temple Emanu-El
- *Marlton:* Congregation M'kor Shalom
- *Matawan:* Temple Beth Am
  Temple Shalom
- *Metuchen:* Temple Neve Shalom
- *Morristown:* Temple B'nai Or
- *New Brunswick:* Anshe Emeth Memorial Temple
- *Ocean:* Temple Beth Torah
- *Parlin:* Sayreville Jewish Center
- *Parsippany:* Temple Beth Am
- *Passaic:* Beth Shalom Reform Temple
- *Plainfield:* Temple Sholom
- *Pompton Lakes:* Congregation Beth Shalom
- *Rosedale:* Congregation Rodef Shalom
- *Somerset:* Temple Beth-El
- *Somerville:* Temple Beth-El
- *Springfield:* Temple Sharey Shalom
- *Succasunna:* Temple Shalom, Roxbury Reform Temple
- *Teaneck:* Congregation Beth Am
  Temple Emeth Brotherhood
- *Tenafly:* Temple Sinai of Bergen County
- *Trenton:* Congregation Children of Israel
- *Vineland:* Beth Israel Congregation
- *Waldwick:* Reform Temple of Northwestern Bergen County
- *Warren:* Mountain Jewish Community Center
- *Washington Township:* Temple Beth Or
- *West Orange:* Congregation Ahawas Achim B'nai Jacob and David
- *Woodbury:* Beth Israel Congregation

NEW MEXICO
- *Rio Rancho:* Rio Rancho Jewish Center
- *Santa Fe:* Temple Beth Shalom

NEW YORK
- *Albany:* B'nai Shalom, The New Reform Congregation
  Congregation Shomray Torah
- *Buffalo:* Temple Beth Zion
- *Catskill:* Temple Israel
- *Cortland:* Temple B'rith Sholom
- *Ellenville:* Temple Rodeph Sholom
- *Geneva:* Temple Beth-El

NEW YORK METROPOLITAN AREA:
  Marathon: Marathon Jewish Community Center
  Manhattan: Central Synagogue
        Central Synagogue Community House
        Chapel of the National Federation of Temple Sisterhoods
        Congregation B'nai Jeshurun
        Congregation Emanu-El
        Congregation Habonim
        Congregation Mount Sinai Anshe Emes
        East End Temple
        Hebrew Union College-Jewish Institute of Religion
        Kutz Camp Institute, Union of American Hebrew Congregations
        New York Federation of Reform Synagogues
        New York University Law School
        Park Avenue Synagogue
        Progressive Synagogue
        Temple Beth Or of the Deaf
  Brooklyn: Beth El Jewish Center
        Shore Parkway Jewish Center
        Temple Sholom of Flatbush
  Bronx: Conservative Synagogue Adath Israel of Riverdale
        Temple Beth-El (Co-Op City)
  Queens: Garden Jewish Center of Flushing
        Hollis Hills Jewish Center
        Jewish Center of Kew Garden Hills
        Junction Boulevard Jewish Center, Lefrak City
        Rego Park Jewish Center
        Temple Beth Am of Rochdale Village, Jamaica
        Temple Isaiah
  Long Island (Nassau and Suffolk Counties):
    Baldwin: South Baldwin Jewish Center
    Bellmore: Bellmore Jewish Center Men's Club
        East Bay Reform Temple
        Temple Beth-El Men's Club
    Bethpage: Bethpage Jewish Community Center
    Central Islip: Central Islip Jewish Center
    Cold Spring Harbor: Kehillath Shalom
    Commack: Commack Jewish Center
    Deer Park: Suffolk Jewish Center
    Dix Hills: Dix Hills Jewish Center

NEW YORK METROPOLITAN AREA, cont.
   East Meadow: Temple Emanuel
   East Northport: East Northport Jewish Center
   East Setauket: Temple Isaiah
   Farmingdale: Farmingdale Jewish Center
   Great Neck: New Reform Temple
             Temple Beth-El of Great Neck
             Temple Emanuel
             Temple Israel of Great Neck
             Temple Israel of Great Neck, Youth House
   Huntington: Temple Beth-El
   Islip Terrace: B'nai Israel Reform Temple
   Jericho: Jericho Jewish Center
          Solomon Schechter Day School
   Laurelton: Temple Beth-El of Laurelton
   Lawrence: The Brandeis School
           Hillel School
   Levittown: Israel Community Center
   Little Neck: Marathon Jewish Center
   Lynbrook: Temple Emanuel
   Manhasset: Temple Judea
   Massapequa: Congregation Beth El
           Temple Sinai
   Merrick: Merrick Jewish Center
         Reform Jewish Congregation
         Temple Israel of South Merrick
   New Hyde Park: New Hyde Park Jewish Center
   Oceanside: Oceanside Jewish Center
   Patchogue: Temple Beth El of Patchogue
   Plainview: Manetto Hill Jewish Center
   Port Jefferson: North Shore Jewish Center
   Port Washington: Community Synagogue
               Port Jewish Center
   Roslyn: Shelter Rock Jewish Center Men's Club
   Roslyn Heights: Temple Sinai
   Seaford: Seaford Jewish Center
   Smithtown: Temple Beth Sholom of Smithtown
   Suffolk County: Temple Beth Torah
   Syosset: Midway Jewish Center
        North Shore Synagogue
   Wantagh: The Suburban Temple
   West Hempstead: Jewish Community Center
   Woodmere: Young Israel of Woodmere

New York Metropolitan Area, cont.
 Staten Island: Arden Heights Jewish Center
    Temple Israel
 Westchester County:
  Bedford: Congregation Shaarey Tefilla
  Brewster: Temple Beth Elohim
  Briarcliff Manor: Congregation Sons of Israel
  Chappaqua: Temple Beth-El
  Croton-on-Hudson: Temple Israel of Northern Westchester
  Hartsdale: Woodlands Community Temple
  Hastings-on-Hudson: Temple Beth Shalom
  Larchmont: Larchmont Temple
  New Rochelle: Beth El Synagogue Center
  Ossining: Congregation Dorshe Emet
  Pound Ridge: Pound Ridge Jewish Community
  Putnam Valley: Reform Temple of Putnam Valley
  Rye: Community Synagogue
  Scarsdale: Scarsdale Synagogue
    Westchester Reform Temple
  White Plains: Beth Am Shalom Synagogue
    Jewish Community Center
  Yonkers: Temple Emanuel of Westchester
  Yorktown Heights: Temple Beth Am
 Rockland County:
  Monsey: Congregation Ohaiv Yisrael
  Pearl River: Temple Beth Am
  Spring Valley: Pomona Jewish Center
    Ramat Shalom
  Suffern: Reform Temple of Suffern
  Upper Nyack: Temple Beth Torah
Rochester: Temple B'rith Kodesh
  Temple B'rith Kodesh Chapel
  Temple Sinai
  University of Rochester Chapel
Rosedale: Congregation Rodef Shalom
Saratoga Springs: Temple Sinai
Schenectady: Congregation Gates of Heaven
Syracuse: Rabbi T. S. Levy
  Young Israel of Syracuse

NORTH CAROLINA
  Asheville: Congregation Beth ha-Tephilla
  Boone: Boone Jewish Community
  Charlotte: Temple Beth Sholom
  Durham: Judea Reform Congregation
  Fayetteville: Congregation Beth Israel
  Greensboro: Beth David Congregation
      Greensboro Conservative Hebrew Congregation
  Winston-Salem: Beth Jacob Congregation

OHIO
  Akron: Temple Israel
  Cincinnati: Congregation B'nai Tzedek
      K. K. Bene Israel—Rockville Temple
      The Valley Temple
  Cleveland: The Suburban Temple
      The Temple
  Columbus: Beth Shalom Congregation
  Dayton: Temple Israel
  Toledo: The Temple

OKLAHOMA
  Tulsa: Congregation B'nai Emunah
      Rebecca and Gershon Fenster Gallery of Jewish Art
      Temple Israel

OREGON
  Portland: Congregation Beth Israel

PENNSYLVANIA
  Abington: Old York Road Temple Beth Am
  Allentown: Congregation Sons of Israel
  Coatesville: Beth Israel Congregation
  Honesdale: Congregation Beth Israel
  King of Prussia: Temple Brotherhood B'rith Achim
  Lafayette Hill: Congregation Or Ami
  Philadelphia: Congregation Ramat El
      Congregation Rodeph Shalom
      Reconstructionist Rabbinical College
      Reform Congregation Keneseth Israel
  Pittsburgh: Rodef Shalom Temple
  Spring House: Beth Or Reform Congregation
  Wallingford: Congregation Ohev Shalom

RHODE ISLAND
  Barrington: Barrington Jewish Center

SOUTH CAROLINA
  Columbia: Tree of Life Congregation
  Sumter: Congregation Sinai

TENNESSEE
  Memphis: Temple Israel

TEXAS
  Brownsville: Temple Beth El
  Dallas: Southern Methodist University Library
         Temple Emanuel
         Temple Sholom
         Tifereth Israel Congregation
  El Paso: Temple Mount Sinai
  Fort Worth: Beth El Congregation
  Houston: Congregation Beth Am
         Congregation Beth Israel
         Congregation Beth Yeshurun
         Temple Emanu-El
         University of Houston (Hillel)
  San Antonio: Temple Beth-El
  Tyler: Temple Beth El

VIRGINIA
  Alexandria: Beth El Hebrew Congregation
  Lorton: Prince William Jewish Congregation
  Norfolk: Temple Ohav Shalom
  Reston: North Virginia Hebrew Congregation
  Richmond: Congregation Beth Ahabah
         Reform Congregation
  Roanoke: Temple Emanuel
  Virginia Beach: Beth Sholom House of Eastern Virginia
  Winchester: Congregation Jewish Community Center

WASHINGTON
  Mercer Island: Temple B'nai Torah
  Seattle: Temple Beth Am

WEST VIRGINIA
  Martinsburg: Veterans Administration Center

WISCONSIN
  Beloit: Congregation in Beloit, Wisconsin
  Camp Ramah in Wisconsin
  Madison: University of Wisconsin (Hillel)

WISCONSIN, cont.
  Milwaukee: Congregation Emanu-El B'ne Jeshurun
              Congregation Sinai
  Waukesha: Temple Emanuel

ARGENTINA
  Buenos Aires: Congregation Emanuel

AUSTRALIA
  Bondi: Bondi Mizrachi Synagogue
  Brisbane: Brisbane Hebrew Congregation
              South Brisbane Hebrew Congregation
  Burwood: Mount Scopus Memorial College
  Canberra: A. C. T. Jewish Community
              Jewish Community Center
  East Brighton: Temple Beth Israel
  Gold Coast: Temple Shalom
  Kingsford Maroubra: Hebrew Congregation
  Perth: Temple David Congregation
  Stonywell: Temple Shalom
  Strathfield: Strathfield and District Hebrew Congregation
  Sydney: Bankstown War Memorial Synagogue
              North Shore Temple Emanuel
  Waterloo: Australian Union for Progressive Judaism
  Woolahra: Temple Emanuel

BELGIUM
  Antwerp: Communauté Israelite Orthodoxe Machsike Hadass
              Tachkemoni School
  Brussels: L'Union Libérale Israelite de Belgique

BRAZIL
  Salvador-Bahia: Sociada Israelita da Bahia

CANADA
  Calgary, Alberta: Shaarey Tzedec Congregation
  Dollard des Ormeaux Québec: Temple Rodeph Shalom
  Kingston, Ontario: Congregation Ir Ha-Melech
  Montreal, Québec: Shaare Hashamayim
  Ottawa, Ontario: Temple Israel
  St. Catherine, Ontario: Temple Tikvah
  Toronto, Ontario: Adath Israel Congregation
              Baycrest Centre for Geriatric Care
  Vancouver, British Columbia: Temple Sholom
  Willowdale, Ontario: Temple Har Zion
  Winnipeg, Manitoba: Temple Sholom

CHANNEL ISLANDS
Jersey: Jersey Jewish Congregation

FRANCE
Bischheim: Communauté Israèlite de Bischheim
Orsay: École Gilbert Bloch
Paris: Seminaire Israèlite de France
Union Liberale Israèlite de France
Soissy/Seine: Mouvement Juïf Libéral de France
Strasbourg: Communauté Israèlite de Strasbourg
Congregation Etz Chaim

FEDERAL REPUBLIC OF GERMANY
Frankfort on the Main: Jewish Old Age Home
Heidelberg: The chief rabbi of Baden, three Congregations in West Germany

GREAT BRITAIN
Aberdeen: Aberdeen Hebrew Congregation
Basildon: Basildon Hebrew Congregation
Bedford: Bedford Hebrew Community
Bournemouth: Bournemouth New Synagogue
Hannah Levy House
Bradford: Bradford Hebrew Congregation
The Bradford Synagogue
Brighton and Hove: Brighton and Hove Progressive Synagogue
Bristol: Bristol Liberal Jewish Group
Clifton College
Polack's House, Clifton College
Bury: Bury & District Jewish Community
Bushy Heath: Bushy & District Synagogue
Cambridge: Cambridge Jewish Residents' Association
Kings College Library
Cardiff: Cardiff New Synagogue
Cheshire: Cheshire Reform Congregation
Colchester: Colchester & District Jewish Community
Epsom: Epsom & District Synagogue
Flackwell Heath: Maidenhead Synagogue
Harrogate: Harrogate Hebrew Congregation
Harrow: Middlesex New Synagogue
Kenton: Wembley Reform Jewish Congregation
Leeds: Great Synagogue
Leeds Jewish Housing Association Ltd.

GREAT BRITAIN, cont.
        Leeds University, Department of Semitic Languages
        Sinai Synagogue
Leicester: Leicester Liberal Jewish Group
Liverpool: Liberal Jewish Congregation of Liverpool
London: Bromley & District Reform Synagogue
        Cockfosters & North Southgate District Synagogue
        Congregation Yetev Lev De Satmar
        Council of Christians and Jews
        Edgware & District Reform Synagogue
        Finchley Liberal Synagogue
        Finchley Progressive Synagogue
        Finchley Reform Synagogue
        L. H. Hammerson Memorial House
        Hampstead Reform Jewish Community
        Hendon Reform Synagogue
        Hendon Synagogue
        Hillel House
        Jewish Memorial Council
        Jewish Welfare Board
        John & Violet Rubens House
        Kehilath Chassidim Synagogue
        Levine House
        Liberal Jewish Synagogue
        The London Library
        Mesifta Talmudical College
        Mill Hill Reform Synagogue
        New London Synagogue, Beth Hamedresh
        North Finchley & Woodside Park District Synagogue
        North London Progressive Synagogue
        Northwest London Talmudical College
        Northwold Road Synagogue
        Reform Synagogues of Great Britain
        St. George's Settlement Synagogue
        Settlement Synagogue, Ilford Branch
        Southgate & District Progressive Synagogue
        South London Liberal Synagogue
        Union of Liberal and Progressive Synagogues
        West Central Liberal Jewish Synagogue
        Western Synagogue
        Western Synagogue Arthur Howitt Collection
        Westminster Central Hall
        Westminster Synagogue
        World Jewish Congress

GREAT BRITAIN, cont.
  Luton: Luton Synagogue
  Manchester: Manchester Congregation of British Jews
              Manchester Reform Youth Center
              North Manchester Reform Synagogue (Shaarei Shalom)
              Yeshurun Hebrew Congregation
  Newcastle-upon-Tyne: Gosforth & Kenton Hebrew Congregation
                        Newcastle-upon-Tyne Reform Synagogue
  Northwood: Northwood & Pinner Liberal Synagogue
              Pinner & District Liberal Jewish Congregation
  Nottingham: Nottingham Progressive Jewish Congregation
  Oxford: Oxford Jewish Congregation
  Southampton: University of Southampton, the Parkes Library
  Stanmore: Belmont & District Affiliated Synagogue
             Stanmore & Canons Park District Synagogue
             Stanmore Liberal Jewish Congregation
  Surrey: Kingston & District Progressive Jewish Congregation
           Kingston Liberal Synagogue
           Kingston, Surbiton & District Synagogue
  Tunbridge Wells: Tunbridge Wells Jewish Fellowship
  Wallingford: Carmel College
  Warwick: University of Warwick
  York: University of York

HOLLAND
  Amsterdam: Liberal Joodse Gemeente
              Verbond von Liberaal-Religieuze Joden in Nederland
  Enschede: Liberal Joodse Gemeente Twente

IRELAND
  Dublin: Dublin Jewish Progressive Congregation

ISRAEL
  Haifa: Haifa Progressive Congregation
          Leo Baeck School
  Jerusalem: Congregation Mevakshei Derekh
              Israel Movement for Progressive Judaism
              Yad Vashem
  Kfar Saba: Merkaz Vera Salomons
  Kibbutz Ketura
  Kibbutz Yahel
  Kiryat Gat: Congregation Kiryat Gat
  Netanya: Young Israel of Netanya

ISRAEL, cont.
Tel Aviv: Bet Tanach
Miscellaneous: 50 scrolls

ITALY
Bologna: Communita Israelitica
Milan: Communita Israelitica di Milano

NEW ZEALAND
Auckland: Auckland Hebrew Congregation
Hawkes Bay: Hawkes Bay Hebrew Congregation
Newton: United Synagogues of New Zealand
Wellington: Temple Sinai
Wellington Hebrew Congregation

PANAMA
Colon: Union Israelita "Agudat Ahim"

PUERTO RICO
San Juan: Reform Synagogue

RHODESIA
Bulawayo: Bulawayo Progressive Jewish Congregation
Salisbury: Salisbury Progressive Jewish Congregation

SOUTH AFRICA
Cape Town: Temple Israel Green Point
Johannesburg: The Southern African Union for Progressive Judaism
(3 scrolls)
Temple Sholom
Temple Sinai
Klerksdorp: Klerksdorp Congregation

SPAIN
Mallorca: Communidad Israelita de Palma de Mallorca

SWITZERLAND
Davos: Jewish Sanatorium Etania
Geneva: Communauté Israèlite de Genève
English-speaking Jewish Community
Lugano: Associazione Ebraica del Canton Ticino
Zurich: Liberal Jewish Synagogue

VIRGIN ISLANDS
St. Thomas: St. Thomas Synagogue

NOTES

1. *Jewish Chronicle,* London, February 7, 1964, p. 13.
2. From a lecture on the scrolls delivered by Mrs. Shaffer in November 1974, at a meeting of the Westminster Synagogue Activities Committee at Kent House. The typescript of the lecture, without further information as to day or place, was sent by Mrs. Shaffer, with a letter dated September 9, 1975, to the late Mr. Ludovit Sturc, of Larchmont, New York, then the president of the Society for the History of Czechoslovak Jewry.
3. Harold Reinhart, "Sifre Torah," reprinted from the winter 1964 issue of *Common Ground,* quarterly of the Council of Christians and Jews in London (last page, pages not numbered). Rabbi Reinhart died in August 1969.
4. Daily News Bulletin, Jewish Telegraphic Agency, November 4, 1977.

THE AUTHORS

EHUD AVRIEL (Ueberall; 1917-1980). Israeli diplomat and public servant. Born in Vienna, he settled in Palestine in 1939 and joined Kibbutz Ne'ot Mordekhai. As a member of Haganah, the defense force of Palestine's Jewish community prior to the establishment of the state of Israel, he was active in Turkey during World War II, organizing the rescue of European Jews. In 1947 he was sent to Czechoslovakia to purchase weapons for what was to become the army of the state of Israel. He served as Israel's minister to Czechoslovakia and Hungary (1948), minister to Rumania (1950), and ambassador to Ghana, Congo (Zaire), and Liberia (1957-60). From 1955 to 1957 he was a member of the Knesset, Israel's parliament, and from 1961 to 1965 deputy director general of the Foreign Ministry in charge of African affairs. From 1965 to 1968, he was ambassador to Italy. At the Zionist Congress of 1968, he was elected chairman of the Zionist Council. He is the author of *Open the Gates: The Dramatic Personal Story of "Illegal" Immigration to Israel* (New York: 1975).

AVIGDOR DAGAN (Viktor Fischl; 1912-   ). Israeli diplomat, public servant, and author. Born in Hradec Králové (Königgraetz), Bohemia, he obtained his doctorate of law and political science from the Charles University in Prague. In Czechoslovakia prior to 1939 he edited the Czech Zionist weekly *Židovské Zprávy,* and was parliamentary secretary of the Jewish party. Following the dismemberment of his country, Dr. Dagan escaped to England, where he worked closely with the Czechoslovak government-in-exile. In 1948 he settled in Israel and in 1950 joined the Israeli diplomatic corps, serving as *chargé d'affaires* in Japan and Burma, as minister in Yugoslavia and as ambassador in Poland, Norway, and Austria. Retired since 1977, he now resides in Jerusalem. A prolific writer, he is the author of *Hovory s Janem Masarykem* [Conversations with Jan Masaryk] (Tel Aviv: 1952); *Moscow and Jerusalem: Twenty Years of Relations Between Israel and the Soviet Union* (London, New York, and Toronto: 1970), four novels in Czech, Hebrew, and German, and eight books of poetry.

YESHAYAHU JELINEK (1933-   ). Historian. Born in Prievidza, Slovakia, he settled in Israel in 1949. He received his doctorate from the Hebrew University in Jerusalem and has taught history at various academic institutions in Israel and in the United States. He is the author of *The Parish Republic: Hlinka's Slovak People's Party 1939-45* (1976) and numerous studies on the history of the Jews in Eastern Europe.

ERICH KULKA (1911-   ). Historian of the Holocaust, and the Jewish resistance. Born in Vsetín, Moravia, he was an expert in the woodworking industry. Arrested by the Gestapo in 1939, he became an inmate of Dachau, Neuengamme, and Auschwitz. During the evacuation of Auschwitz in January 1945, he escaped with his twelve-year-old son and was hidden by his Czech friends from the resistance movement in the Moravian mountains. After the war, Mr. Kulka was a free-lance writer in Czechoslovakia until 1968, when he settled in Israel. He has been working closely with the Yad Vashem Heroes' and Martyrs' Authority and since 1978 has been active as a research fellow with the Institute of Contemporary Jewry at the Hebrew University in Jerusalem. His numerous words include *The Death Factory* (with Ota Kraus; English version published in London in 1966), "Five Escapes from Auschwitz," in Yuri Suhl, ed., *They Fought Back: The Story of the Jewish Resistance* (New York: 1975), and *Jews in Svoboda's Army in the Soviet Union* (in Hebrew, Tel Aviv: 1977), a Czech version *(Židí v československé Svobodově Armádě,* appeared in Toronto in 1979).

ZDENEK LEDERER (1920-1981). Author and translator. Born and educated in Prague, he was an inmate of the Terezín ghetto, of Auschwitz, and other concentration camps from 1941 until the end of World War II. After the war, he returned to Prague, where he was active as a literary and drama critic until 1947, when he settled in London. In England he worked for Radio Free Europe and the British Broadcasting Corporation. He is the author of *Ghetto Theresienstadt 1941-1945* (London: 1953).

JOHN G. LEXA (1914-1977). Jurist. Born in Ústí nad Labem (Aussig), Bohemia, Dr. Lexa settled in the United States in 1946. A lecturer on camparative constitutional law at New York University, he was co-editor of the International Seminar on Constitutional Review and secretary general of the Czechoslovak Society for Science and Art.

LADISLAV LIPSCHER (1915-   ). Historian. Born in Rajec (Žilina district), Slovakia, Dr. Lipscher was dean of the Comenius University in

Bratislava and a member of the Historical Institute of the Slovak Academy of Sciences in that city. During World War II, he was an inmate of labor camps in Čemerné, Lipt. Hrádok, and Zohor, Slovakia. Following the war, he worked with several scientific institutes, mainly in the Federal Republic of Germany. A resident of Switzerland since 1968, he is the author of several books on modern history. The study included in the present volume is an abridgment of his book, *Die Juden im slowakischen Staat 1939-1945*, which was published by R. Oldenburg Verlag (Munich and Vienna: 1980).

JOSEPH C. PICK (1891-   ). Business executive. Born in Mladá Boleslav, Bohemia, he was active in the Maccabi movement from its inception in Czechoslovakia. An executive with the Moldavia-Generali Insurance Company in Prague, he was a delegate to the International Marine and Aviation Conventions in Europe from 1927 to 1939. In 1941 he settled in the United States, where he served as consultant to the U.S. War Department and Harvard University from 1942 to 1944 and as technical advisor to the International Civil Aviation Conference in Chicago in 1944, and was active as a marine insurance broker. He now resides in Stamford, Connecticut.

LIVIA ROTHKIRCHEN (1922-   ). Historian. Born in Sevluš, Subcarpathian Ruthenia, she is a survivor of Auschwitz and Bergen-Belsen. She received her doctorate from the Charles University in Prague. In Israel since 1955, Dr. Rothkirchen has been a member of the research staff of the Yad Vashem Heroes' and Martyrs' Authority in Jerusalem since 1956 and has served as editor of *Yad Vashem Studies* since 1964. She is the author of numerous studies on the Holocaust, including *The Destruction of Slovak Jewry* (1961), and was editor (with Yisrael Gutman) of *The Catastrophe of European Jewry* (1976).

HANA (FRANKENSTEINOVÁ) VOLAVKOVÁ (1904-   ). Art historian and director emerita of the State Jewish Museum in Prague. Born in Jaroměř, Bohemia, Dr. Volavková is the author of numerous publications on Czech art and on the State Jewish Museum in Prague, including *The Synagogue Treasures of Bohemia and Moravia* (1948), *I Never Saw Another Butterfly; Children's Drawings and Poems-Terezín 1942-44* (English version, 1962), and *The Story of the Jewish Museum in Prague* (1964). Dr. Volavková resides in Prague.

KURT WEHLE (1907-   ). Born in Jablonec n.N. (Gablonz a.N.), Bohemia, he received his doctorate from the German University in Prague and practiced law in that city prior to the outbreak of World War II. A concentration camp survivor, he returned to Prague after the war, serving as secretary general of the Council of Jewish Religious Congregations in Prague from 1945 to 1948, and as chairman of the Zionist Actions Committee in Czechoslovakia and vice president of the Mapai Labor Zionist party in Czechoslovakia from 1946 to 1948. He was an attorney and assistant director of the general counsel's office of the American Jewish Joint Distribution Committee (JDC) in Paris from 1948 until 1951, when he settled in New York. He received the degree of M.B.A. from New York University in 1953. Dr. Wehle served as administrative head and director of the Czech and Austrian departments of the United Restitution Organization (URO) from 1951 to 1961. From 1956 to 1976 he worked in New York as a financial and administrative executive in the hospital field. The initiator and cofounder of the Society for the History of Czechoslovak Jews, he served as the society's first president from 1961 to 1967 and as chairman of its board from 1969 to 1974.

NAME INDEX, VOLUMES I-III*

Abraham Ben David, I:118
Abeles, Hanuš, II:210
Abeles, Joseph, III:11
Abeles, Otto, II:175
Abramsky, Chimen, III:585, 586
Acheson, Edward G., I:377
Adam, Robert, III:556
Adler, Bruno, also pseud. Roedl, Urban, I:503, 511, 520; II:587
Adler, Felix, I:552
Adler, Friedrich, I:57, 480, 482, 510, 516
Adler, Guido, I:550
Adler, Hans Günther, I:501, 558; III:67
Adler, Herbert, II:37
Adler, Hermann, I:504, 512, 520
Adler, H.G., III:65, 323
Adler, Kurt, I:542
Adler, Lazar, II:164
Adler, Norbert, I:157, 227, 229, 270, 309; II:30, 33, 35-37, 50, 178, 256, 284
Adler, Paul, I:494, 511, 517
Adler, Peter Herman, I:542
Adler-Rudel, Salomon, III:470
Ahad Ha'Am, I:19
Albrecht, Archduke, I:24
Aleš, Mikuláš, II:473, 475
Alexander, Leo, I:87
Alkalay, Abraham, I:536
Allers, Franz, I:542; II:586
Allina, Bedřich, II:202, 203
Altbach, Robert, II:37, 256
Alter, Artur, III:390, 401, 442

Altmann, A. (staff captain), III:404
Altschul, Frederick, I:393
Altschul, Oskar, I:157; II:256
Altschul, Walter, I:420
Amann, Paul, I:62, 482, 483, 511, 516
Amschelberg, Paul. *See* Amann, Paul
Ančerl, Karel, I:543, 545
Anders, Robert, II:65, 67
Andersen, Hans Christian, I:477
Andic, Vojtěch Ervin, I:435
Anninger, Otto, I:411
Anninger, Viktor, I:411
Anski, S., II:557
Arie, Otto, II:179
Arje, Minna, II:142
Arje, Samuel, I:339; II:79; III:367
Arbeles, Šimon Jakob, II:472
Arlosoroff, Chaim, II:59, 71
Arlosoroff, Sima, II:7
Armitage, Captain H.J. (commander in Mauritius camp), II:621, 622
Armstrong, Hamilton Fish, I:132
Arndt, Moritz, I:404
Arnstein, Arnold, II:178
Arnstein, Emil, II:36, 37
Arnstein, Ervin, II:57, 58, 178
Arnstein, Karl, II:215, 216
Arnstein, Otto, I:365
Aron, Moritz, I:428
Asch, Sholem, III:557
Ascher, Emil, II:211, 214
Asher, Moshe, II:97
Ascher, Zikmund, I:415
Aschermann, Eduard, II:178
Aschermann, Oskar, II:40

* *Compiled by Zdenka Münzer*

615

Ashkenazi, Eliezer, I:349
Aškenazy, Ludvík, I:451, 465
Atlas, Mosche, I:121
Auerbach, Josef, I:422, 435
Auerbach, Moshe, II:609
Auerbach-Margulies, Nancy, II:140
Augstein, Hanuš, I:373
Augstein, Ota, I:373
Augusta Victoria, Empress, I:45
Aussenberg, Adolf, III:128
Austerlitz, Mayer, I:80
Austerlitz, Theodor, I:101
Ausubel, Mathieu, I:468
Avenarius, I:454
Avriel, Ehud, III:4, 10, 14, 495, 543, 551, 564, 565
Azarov, David, III:422

Baal Shem Tov, Israel ben Eliezer, II:357
Baar, Jindřich, I:463
Bab, Julius, II:587
Bach, Johann Sebastian, I:557
Bächer, Emil, I:393
Bacher, Franz, II:248, 584
Bächer, Jiří, I:403
Bächer, Karel, I:403
Bächer, Pavel, I:370, 430
Bächer, Rudolf, I:403
Bacher, Simon, I:81
Bacher, Wilhelm, I:81
Bachrach, Jair Chaim, II:544
Bachrach, Oskar, II:65, 67
Bäck, Berci, II:105
Bäck, Herman, I:404
Badeni, Kasimir, Count, I:44, 67
Bader, Menahem, II:65
Baderle, Hanuš (Heini), II:211
Baeck, Rabbi Leo, III:39, 141, 145, 149, 299
Baier, Max, II:238
Baker, Theodore, I:547, 554
Baky, László, II:317
Balasz, Julius, II:208-210
Balfour, Arthur James, I:218
Balko, Ján, III:193, 194, 243, 244
Balló, Ede, II:498
Balzac, Honoré, I:479
Bán, Pavol, II:503
Bandler, Rudolf, I:552; III:272
Baneth, Hermann, I:346
Bánoczi, V. (journalist), I:81

Bar Jacob, Rabbi Moshe, III:581
Barber, Heinrich, II:108
Barber, Stephan S., III:11, 343, 373, 377, 435, 436, 439, 489
Bardessy, László, III:315
Bardoš, Father N. (Slovak priest), III:256
Bárkány, Eugen, I:101; II:558
Barlasz, Chaim, III:313, 528, 549
Barou, Noah, III:451, 453, 454, 462, 465, 466, 474, 482, 488, 489
Barnett, Richard D., III:586
Barry, Hugh Otter, II:629
Barta, Alexander, II:214
Bárta, Jiří (Juraj), II:208
Barth, Ernest, I:380
Barth, Gustav, I:380
Bartík, Major (Czechoslovak military intelligence), III:344
Barto, Jaroslav, III:546
Baru, Otto, II:199
Barvitius, Viktor, II:473, 478
Basch, Antonín, I:363, 395, 425
Basch, Harry, I:400
Basch, Raphael, II:370
Bass, B. (army officer), III:370
Bass, Eduard, I:465
Basso, Löb Greg, I:539
Baštýř, Mořic, II:150
Baťa, Jan, I:420
Baťa, Tomáš, I:420
Batka, Richard, I:551, 552
Bauch, Vlastislav, III:244
Baudelaire, Charles, I:479
Bauer, A. (Slovak Zionist leader), II:86, 87
Bauer, Georg, I:371, 372
Bauer, K. (student Zionist leader), II:175
Bauer, Oskar, I:387
Bauer, Rudolf, II:238
Bauer, Victor, I:534; II:175
Bauer, Yehuda, III:527, 547
Bauernfreund, Jakub, II:488, 512, 513
Baum, Karl, I:527; II:82, 93, 104; III:103, 371, 489
Baum, Leo, II:585
Baum, Oskar, I:489, 490, 511, 516, 552; II:585
Baumann, Paul, I:405
Baumgarten, Leo, II:104, 105
Bazovský, Miloš, II:505, 516

NAME INDEX

Becher, Kurt, III:235
Bechyně, Rudolf, II:248
Bechyně, Zdeněk, III:375
Beck, Alexander, II:165
Beck, Josef (banker), I:368, 417
Beck, Josef (B'nai B'rith), II:237
Beck, Lieutenant Colonel Josef (foreign minister of Poland), III:335, 450
Beck, Josef (forwarder), I:430
Beck, Josef (Société), II:236
Beck, Karl, II:237
Beck, Otto, II:79
Becking, Gustav, I:549
Bednar, Alfonz, III:248
Beer, Bedřich Salamon, II:285, 475
Beer, Béla, II:287
Beer (student Zionist leader), II:181
Beer, Julius, I:411
Beer, Kurt, III:272
Beer-Hofmann, Richard, I:489
Beethoven, Ludwig van, I:472, 553, 558
Běhal, Karel, I:368
Behr, Jan (Kurt), I:542, 552
Beinhacker, Samuel, II:210
Békeffi, Hermin, I:83
Belak, Private, III:390
Belský, Josef, I:376
Ben-Ari, Zeev. See Wagner, Wilhelm
Ben David, Abraham, I:118
Ben-Gurion, David, II:83, 89; III:552-555, 559
Ben Shalom, Rafael, III:564
Ben-Zvi, Yitzhak, II:83
Benatzky, Ralph, I:498-99, 511, 518
Benczur, Gyula, II:498
Benda, Adolf, I:428
Benedikt, Emil, I:365, 408
Benedikt, Leo, I:376
Beneš, Adolf, III:4, 528
Beneš, Bedřich, II:182
Beneš, Eduard, I:32, 98, 108, 112, 138, 149, 171-76, 224, 229-31, 244, 248-50, 261, 262, 317, 319, 324; II:243, 245, 248, 273, 274, 286, 291, 292, 299, 301, 302, 319, 396, 416, 566; III:3, 7, 29, 346, 354, 358, 369, 370-77, 379, 381, 397, 398, 403, 405, 410, 413, 414, 421, 424, 439, 449, 450, 455, 467, 468, 469, 473, 474, 475, 482, 483, 484, 485, 486, 488, 489, 490, 491, 492, 495, 519, 520, 523-25, 530, 532, 545, 546, 554, 555

Beneš, Pavel, I:407
Benešová, Hana, III:491
Benet, Mordecai, I:350; II:472
Benton, Pavel. See Berman (Benton), Pavel
Běnuška, Jozef, III:251
Beran, Philipp, I:413
Beranek, Franz, II:377
Berg, Arthur, I:415
Berger, Sergeant, III:378
Berger, Franziska, II:634
Berger, Gottlob, III:213, 234
Berger, Jakob, I:118; II: 180, 183
Berger, Martha, II:38, 40, 50
Bergl, Josef, I:6, 7
Bergler, Josef, II:471
Bergman, Albert, II:213
Bergmann, Arthur, II:40, 140, 177, 178
Bergmann, Elsa, II:141
Bergmann, Hugo, I:20, 54, 55, 60-62, 70, 170, 174, 223, 227-31, 248, 270, 471, 486, 505; II:20, 26, 30, 33, 55, 58, 61, 140, 141, 177, 251, 446
Bergmann, Leo, II:73
Bergmann, Rudolf, III:147
Bergstein, Jindřich, I:398
Berka, Arnošt, I:377, 387, 421
Berka, Otakar, II:217
Berl, Heinrich, I:551
Berl, Leo, I:416
Berman, Karel, I:548, 557
Berman (Benton), Pavel, I:382, 388
Bernard, Vilém, III:391, 392, 440
Bernstein, Siegmund, II:284
Berwald, Ludwig, III:273
Bester, Bessie, II:208
Bester, Helli, II:208
Bester, Tilli, II:208
Bestic, Alan, III:151, 248, 328
Bethman, Moritz, Baron, II:214
Bettelheim, Moses, II:367
Bettelheim, Samuel, I:7, 79; II:97, 368
Bezruč, Petr, pseud. of Vašek, Vladimír, I:45, 461, 464, 483
Biach, Adolf, I:344
Bieler, Meir, II:610, 624, 630
Biebow, Hans, III:270, 271
Biegun, Dov, II:76, 93
Bielefeld (Sergeant), III:413
Bienenfeld, A.S. (Zionist leader), II:65
Bienenstock, Max, II:63
Biezienski, Aaron, II:641

Biheller (Captain), III:411, 413
Bill, Friedrich, II:567
Bindeles, Josef, II:469, 474
Birnbaum, Herbert, II:285
Birnbaum, Nathan, I:71, 535; II:164
Birnbaum, R. (student Zionist leader), II:175
Birnbaum, Vojtěch, II:523
Bismarck, Prince Otto von, I:13
Bittermann, Max, I:362, 436; III:71
Björnson, Björnstjerne, I:78, 446
Blaho, Pavel, I:85
Blahorský, Antonín, II:634
Blatný, Fanni, II:250
Blattner, Robert, I:388
Blau, Bruno, II:584
Blau, Rabbi Moshe, II:168
Blech, Leo, I:551, 555
Bleiweiss, Harry, II:278, 283
Bleyer, Leo, II:193
Bleyer, Pinchas Ben Dov, I:537
Blitz, L. (medical officer), III:380
Bloch, Felix, III:127
Bloch, Jean Richard, I:483
Bloch, Marcel, I:406
Bloch, Rudolf, II:239
Bloch, Zhelo, III:289
Bloch-Bauer, Ferdinand, I:384
Bloch-Zavřel, Lotte, I:521
Blödy, Arpád, II:204, 205
Blüh, Irene, II:506
Blüher, Hans, II:461
Blumberg, Wolf, I:417
Blumenfeld, Kurt, I:60; II:63
Blumenthal, Hermann, I:535
Blumenthal, Siegfried, I:412
Blumgrund, Nathan, I:408
Bobasch, Leopold, I:411
Bobasch, Olga, II:40, 137, 138
Bock, Kurt, III:11
Bodensieck, Heinrich, III:61
Boehm, Arnošt, III:405
Bogdan, Elena, I:152
Böhm, Josef, I:417; III:489
Böhm, Viktor, I:417
Böhme, Horst, III:28, 30, 47
Bohnen, Michael, I:548
Bojko (Ukrainian bandit), III:414
Bolgár, Mosche, I:528
Bondi, Jonas, II:471
Bondy, Filip, I:344
Bondy, Francis, I:402

Bondy, Fritz. *See* Scarpi, N.O.
Bondy, Gottlieb (Bohumil), I:4, 5, 354; II:150
Bondy, Herbert, I:402
Bondy, Karel, I:407; II:217; III:17
Bondy, Leon, I:427
Bondy, Maximilian, I:40
Bondy, Miloš, I:407; II:212, 213
Bondy, Walter, II:476
Bonn, Hanuš, I:445, 455; II:153; III:40, 45, 147
Borek, V. (journalist), III:284
Borg, Arne, II:209
Börne, Karl Ludwig, I:473
Borochov, Dov-Ber, II:76, 77, 80, 83
Boruth, Andor, II:500
Bostík, Václav, III:578
Bourdelle, E.A. (artist), II:483
Brach, Shaul, II:355
Brach family, I:382
Bracken, Brendan, III:319
Brada, Fini, I:115; II:76, 94, 142; III:63
Brahe, Tycho, I:1; II:444
Brahms, Johannes, I:557
Brand, David, III:587, 588
Brand, Sigmund, II:40, 285
Brandeis, Adolf, I:26
Brandeis, Alexander, II:475
Brandeis, Arnold, II:199
Brandeis, Frieda, II:489
Brandeis, Jacob B., I:39, 45, 341, 352, 553
Brandeis, Louis Dembitz, I:2, 26, 164, 174; II:255
Brandeis, Richard, I:533
Brandes, Detlef, III:64, 65, 66
Brániš, J. (art historian), II:523
Braque, Georges, II:481, 487
Bratianu, Ion, III:474
Braun, Arpád, I:426; III:360
Braun, Felix, I:481
Braun, Jacob Joel, II:160, 164, 165
Braun, Mrs. Jacob Joel, II:165
Braun, Rudolf, III:344, 373, 377, 438, 457
Brauner, Hugo, II:174, 175
Braunerová, Zdenka, II:478
Brecht, Bertolt, I:490
Breisach (president of Bratislava Jewish community), II:367
Bretholz, Bertold, I:3, 6, 536

Bretholz, Wolfgang, II:586
Breuer, Isaac, II:168
Breuer, Leopold, I:343
Březina, Edita, III:49
Březina, Otakar, pseud. of Jebavý, Vaclav, I:462, 467, 482, 483
Brichta (Major), III:373
Brieger, Yehuda, III:559
Briess, Eric, I:382
Briess, Ignác, Sr., I:382
Brill, Leopold, I:416
Brock, Arnošt, I:430
Brock, Robert, I:545
Brod, Arthur, I:375
Brod, Fritta, I:495
Brod, Max, I:viii, 9, 54, 60, 71, 89, 157-59, 167, 215, 221, 223, 242, 246, 247, 260, 269, 461, 470-72, 476, 482, 486-90, 492, 500, 504-11, 520-22, 535, 552; II:26, 30, 31, 33, 52, 55, 58, 61, 139, 140, 175, 178, 180, 183, 234, 256, 257, 259, 288, 395, 444, 445, 465, 466, 482, 584, 587
Brod, Ota, I:384, 508
Brod, Toman, III:370, 434, 435, 487
Brodetsky, Selig, II:192, 276
Brodie, Chief Rabbi Sir Israel, II:12; III:586
Brody, Heinrich (Chaim), I:93, 245, 293, 311, 338, 353; II:396
Brügel, John Wolfgang, I:xix; II:243ff; III:11, 65, 492, 499
Brüll, Beda, I:526; II:193
Brune (airplane constructor), I:405
Brunn (Sergeant), III:405, 410
Brunner, Alois, III:234, 314, 327
Brunner, Felix, II:79
Brunskill (General), III:356
Buber, Martin, I:19, 476, 481, 505, 559; II:20, 59, 63, 67, 94, 177, 454
Büchler, Adolf, I:81
Büchler, Emil, II:40
Buchsbaum family, I:414
Buchwalder, J. (officers' school graduate), III:410
Budischowsky, William, I:419
Budlovsky, Max, I:368
Budzislawski, Hermann, II:586
Bukovac, Vlaho, II:48
Burckhard, Johannes (Kalenter, Ossip), II:584
Burckhardt, Carl, III:39, 235

Bureš, Prokop, II:214
Burger, Anton, III:132, 133
Burger, Emil, I:392
Burney, Charles, I:553
Burzio, Giuseppe, III:183, 318
Busch, Isidor, I:2, 23, 26
Butter, Leopold, I:344
Buzalka, Michal, III:240, 256
Byron, George Gordon, Baron, I:457

Calderon de la Barca, Pedro, I:472
Canetti, Isaac, I:419
Cantor, Ernst, I:297
Čapek, Josef, I:467; II:479, 486
Čapek, Karel, I:446-48, 467, 479, 482, 483; II:398, 463, 465
Černogurský, Pavel, III:210, 247, 250
Caro, Avigdor. *See* Kara, Avigdor
Carr, Wilbur J., III:8, 61, 62
Carter, Jimmy, President, III:590
Cassirer, Ernst, II:451
Cassirer, Fritz, II:586
Castelli, J.F., I:472
Čech, Adolf, pseud. of Taussig, Adolf, I:543, 556
Čech, Svatopluk, I:459, 460
Cecil, Lord Edgar Algernon Robert, Viscount of Chelwood, III:468
Čejka, Eduard, III:434, 436, 437, 487
Čepiga, Jozef, III:547
Čermák, Jaroslav, II:474
Černý, Bohumil, III:61, 62
Černý, Josef, I:109, 148; II:299
Černý, Václav, I:445, 453, 455
Červinka, Vincenc, I:448
Cézanne, Paul, II:514
Chadbourne, Thomas L., I:385
Chalupecký, Jindřich, I:442
Chamberlain, Neville, I:112; III:371
Chamisso, Adalbert von, I:500
Charles I, Emperor, I:17, 155
Charles IV, Emperor, I:469
Charles VI, King of France, III:574
Charmatz, Adolf, I:410
Chasanowitsch, Leon, I:218, 221, 245, 248, 254, 262
Chermesh, Haim, III:231, 232
Chitz, Arthur, I:551
Chládek, Abraham, II:521
Chmela, Leopold, III:68
Chmielnicki, Bogdan, II:356
Chopin, Frederic, I:557, 558

Christian X, King, III:135
Chrysander, Friederich, I:550
Churchill, Sir Winston, II:16; III:4, 371, 473
Chvalkovsky, Frantisek, II:5, 11, 28
Claudius, Matthias, I:503
Clemenceau, Georges, I:176, 185, 229, 250
Clementis, Vladimír, III:249, 530, 556, 557, 558, 566
Cohen-Hermann, N., III:444
Colman, Hugo, I:ix
Colson (French minister of war), III:353
Comenius (Komenský, Jan Amos), II:463
Cook, Hunt, II:629
Corot, Jean Baptiste Camille, II:478
Corwin, Pavel, II:205
Coubine (Kubin, Otokar), II:481, 486
Coulondre, Robert, III:18
Cowen, Joseph, I:223
Čulen, K., III:254
Curie, Marie, I:372
Curzon, Lord, II:27
Czech, Ludwig, II:191, 249
Czeczowiczka, Arthur, II:284

Dagan, Avigdor (Viktor Fischl), I:36, 61, 68, 101, 140, 259, 352, 444, 448, 452, 456, 526, 531, 535, 559; II:179; III:9, 10, 11, 14, 371, 436, 438, 489, 491, 544, 549
Daluege, Kurt, III:34, 35, 273
Dautwitz (scientist), I:372
David, Jakob Julius, I:57, 471, 476, 510, 513
David, Jožka, III:468, 491
Davidová, Otla, III:150
Davidowits, Julius, I:79
Davidsohn, Julius, I:79
Davis, W. Jefferson, I:432
Dawson, Dean, II:630
Degas, Hilaire Germain Edgar, II:478
DeGaulle, Charles, III:369
Demel, Ferdinand, II:584
Demetz, Peter, I:470, 482, 521
Deml, Jakub, I:462
Den, Petr, pseud. of Radimský, Ladislav, I:454-55
Derer, Ivan, I:83, 85, 104, 106, 122, 313; II:286

Deshell, Maier, III:xii
Deutsch, Aladár, I:8, 338; II:79, 137; III:48, 513, 514
Deutsch, David, I:80
Deutsch, Else, II:138
Deutsch, Emil, II:175
Deutsch, Ernst, I:489; II:211
Deutsch, Filip, I:386
Deutsch, Gustav, I:411
Deutsch, Josef, II:291
Deutschländer, Leo, II:370
Devidels, Abraham, II:471
Dezider, J. (navigator), III:387
Diamant, Paul Josef, I:124
Diamant, Samuel, I:79
Dickens, Charles, I:499
Diner, Isaac, I:77
Dix, Otto, II:505
Dobkin, Eliahu, II:71; III:71, 486
Döblin, Alfred, II:462, 464
Dobrá, Eva, III:416, 445
Dobrý, Pavel, III:416, 445
Dochanovič, Alexander, II:411
Doktor, Eduard, I:411
Doležalová, Jana, III:583
Donatello, II:483
Donath, Adolph, I:478, 511, 514
Donath, Oskar, I:6, 11, 61, 254, 350-55, 467, 531; III:62
Donath, P. (leader of Czechoslovak refugee organization in France), III:344
Donnenbaum, Berthold, II:164
Dorfsohn, S.J. *See* Harendorf, S.J.
Doron, Uriel, III:555, 556, 564
Dostoyevsky, Feodor Mikhailovich, I:440, 547
Douglas, William C., I:385
Drábek, Jaroslav, III:69
Drachmann, Eduard, II:62, 66, 67
Drázda, František, III:15
Drobný, Jan, I:102
Drucker, Leo, II:239
Dubnov, Simon Markovich, I:4, 66
Dubský, Josef, I:432
Duckwitz, George Ferdinand, III:134
Duda (Colonel), III:386
Dunant, Georges, III:38, 235, 236
Dunant, Paul, III:39, 143, 144, 145, 151
Durčanský, Ferdinand, I:113; II:578; III:325
Duschinsky, Alex, I:399; III:441

NAME INDEX

Duschinsky, Josef, II:168, 369
Dux, Hugo, II:238
Dvořák, Antonín, I:480, 482, 545, 556
Dvořák, L., Lieutenant, III:363
Dvorczak, Viktor, I:99
Dyk, Viktor, I:461, 482
Dymant, Dora, I:487

Easterman, Alexander L., III:40, 466, 470, 484, 520, 528, 547
Ebner-Eschenbach, Marie von, I:472
Eckstein, Alfred, I:426
Eckstein, Sir Frederick, I:402
Eckstein, Friedrich, I:175
Eckstein, Moshe Asher, II:97
Edelstein, Alfred, I:417; II:595
Edelstein, Jakub, II:40, 73, 75, 76, 91, 93, 94; III:12, 24, 25, 31, 38, 41, 42, 71, 106, 107, 108, 110, 118, 119, 131, 133, 135, 136, 146, 147, 297, 300
Eden, Sir Anthony, III:319, 358, 469, 470
Edison, Thomas Alva, I:402
Edwards, Pavel. *See* Eisner, Pavel
Egan, Edmund, I:127
Ehrenfeld, Caecilie, II:396
Ehrenreich, Chaim, I:528; II:376
Ehrenstein, Albert, I:491
Ehrenteil, Emanuel, I:367
Ehrlich (Sergeant), III:378
Ehrlich, Abraham, I:340
Ehrmann, Salomon, II:231
Eibenschütz, Rabbi Jonathan, II:440
Eichhorn, Simi, III:xi
Eichmann, Adolf Karl, I:116; II:576; III:23, 24, 40, 48, 106, 143, 144, 173, 189, 197, 200, 203, 206, 213, 219, 220, 222, 223, 225, 263, 265, 267, 269, 297, 304, 305, 307, 309, 310, 316, 317, 318
Eidlitz, Fritz, II:284
Einstein, Albert, I:2, 54; II:479
Eisenberg, Eugen, I:541
Eisenhower, Dwight D., III:370
Eisenschimmel family, III:591
Eisenschimmel, Jindřich, I:375
Eisenschimmel, Max, I:416
Eisenschimmel, Rivka, III:591
Eisler, Michael (leader in Jewish party), II:285
Eisner, Arnošt, II:215
Eisner, Leo, II:38, 50

Eisner, Ota, I:426
Eisner (Edwards), Pavel, I:362, 403, 468, 471, 487, 521, 523, 584; III:64
Eisner, Robert, I:428
Eisner, Rudolf, I:403
Eisner, Vlasta, II:217
Elbert, Erwin, II:181; III:147
Elbogen, Bedřich, I:384, 386, 395
Elefant, David František, III:341, 391, 440
Elefant, Terezie, III:418, 440, 445
Eliáš, Alois, III:20
Eliáš, Emil, III:29
Elisabeth, Empress, I:45, 59
Elovič, Albert, III:400, 422, 423
Elsner, Alfred, III:408
Endre, Lászlo, III:317
Engel, Alfred, I:6, 223; II:35, 54, 175, 256, 259, 265
Engel, Andrej (Bandi), II:202-04
Engel, Anton, III:571
Engel, F. (Communist leader), III:397, 405, 413
Engel, Nelly Thieberger. *See* Thieberger-Engel, Nelly
Engel, Stefan, III:526
Engelmann, Walter, I:415
Englander (Jewish National Council), II:259
Engliš, Karel, I:363
Enoch, Simon, II:40, 635
Enten, Emanuel, II:375
Eötvös, Josef, Baron, II:354
Epler, Adolf, II:402
Eppler, Georg, I:377
Eppstein, Paul, III:119, 136, 137, 139
Epstein (fighter pilot), III:387
Epstein (Evans), Alfred, I:421
Epstein (Estin), Georg, I:366
Epstein, Jacob, II:3
Epstein, Kurt, II:209, 210
Epstein, Oskar, I:270; II:55, 57, 58, 60, 62, 65-68, 177
Ernst, Heinrich Wilhelm, I:539
Estorick, Eric, III:585, 586
Evans, Alfred. *See* Epstein (Evans), Alfred
Ezrovič, Mikuláš, III:411

Fahn, Hermann, I:421
Fahn, Rudolf, I:421

Faktor, Emil, I:478, 479, 511, 514; II:587; III:43
Falk, Johannes David, I:482
Fall, Leo, I:541, 555
Fanta (Private), III:413, 421
Fanta, Berta, I:54, 70
Fanta, Karel, III:337, 434
Fanta, Kurt, III:391, 415, 420, 435, 442
Fantl, František, III:370
Fantl, G. (Zionist editor), I:526
Fantl, Jindřich H., II:238; III:11, 371, 437
Fantl, Zdeněk, II:205
Fanto, David, I:375
Färber, Meir Marcel, I:120, 325, 503, 504, 512, 520, 522, 525, 559; II:107
Farber, Ruben, I:535
Farkaš, Jonah, III:74
Farkaš, Zoltan, II:247
Fatalis, pseud. of Jeiteles, Alois Ludwig, I:356, 472, 510
Faucher, Eugene, III:8
Feder, Morris, I:420
Feder, Richard, I:344, 351, 526; II:79; III:67, 70, 73, 149, 513
Federer, Oscar, I:373; II:486
Federmann, John, III:384
Feierabend, Ladislav, III:66
Feierweger, A. (corporal), III:421
Feig, Alex, II:36, 37, 55, 60
Feig, Erna, II:141
Feigl, Bedřich, I:406; II:480-82, 487, 488
Feigl, Hugo, II:237, 487
Feilchenfeld, Max, I:427; III:26
Feilchenfeld, Otto, I:393
Fein, Norbert, II:66
Feinberg, Sidney, III:3
Feitis, Jindřich, I:427
Feiwel, Berthold, II:22, 23, 30, 94, 175
Feld, Ludo, II:508
Feldmann, Arthur, II:284
Feldmann, Gisella, II:142
Felix, Otto. *See* Doron, Uriel
Felter, A. (graduate of officers' school), III:410
Ferbstein, Karl, I:88, 94; II:37, 273
Ferda, Rabbi, Dr., III:264
Ferenczy, László, III:316
Ferrari-Kohn, Margaretta, II:216
Feuerstein, Bedřich, II:488; III:70
Feuerstein, Benzion, III:36

Feuerstein, Emil, II:239
Fiala, Fritz, III:310
Fiedler, Selig, I:539
Fierlinger, Zdeněk, II:246; III:39, 392, 397, 402, 417, 484, 485
Filkorn, Eugen, III:210, 218, 247
Fila, Emil, II:481, 484
Filo, Kornel, III:548
Finke, Fidelio, I:549
Finzi, Gustav, II:35-37, 39
Firt, Leopold, III:437
Fiš, Teodor, III:392, 397, 398, 406, 417, 440, 442, 444
Fisch, Simon, II:97
Fischel family, I:382
Fischel, Erwin, II:108
Fischel (Fischl), Karel, I:157-59, 221, 269; II:31, 256
Fischel, Otto A., II:108
Fischel, Robert, I:382
Fischer, Heinrich, I:502, 503, 511, 520
Fischer, Hynek, I:427
Fischer, Josef, III:17, 66
Fischer, Karel, I:524; II:151
Fischer, Otokar, I:442-44, 451; II:180, 465
Fischer, Raffi, III:74
Fischer, Wilhelm, II:97
Fischer von Seekamm, Egon, I:370; II:583, 585
Fischhof, Adolf Abraham, I:23, 24
Fischhof, Franz, III:66, 73
Fischl family, III:96
Fischl, Arnošt, I:387, 395
Fischl (Second Lieutenant), III:413
Fischl, Josef, I:387
Fischl, Ludwig, I:476, 510, 513
Fischl, Max, II:30, 250
Fischl, Richard, III:406
Fischl, Viktor. *See* Dagan, Avigdor
Fischmann, Arnold, I:398
Fischmann, Hanuš, I:398
Fishman (Maimon), Rabbi Judah L., III:486
Flatter, Otto, II:487
Fleischer, Max, I:480, 481, 511, 515
Fleischer, Viktor, I:471, 481, 511, 515
Fleischman (Sergeant), III:408
Fleischmann, Artur, II:503, 504
Fleischmann, Gisi, I:97, 112; II:142, 145, 169; III:37, 38, 205, 220, 234, 252, 312, 314

NAME INDEX

Fleischmann, Gustav, I:43, 51, 63, 64, 69, 74, 93, 120, 145, 150, 167, 243, 260, 267, 341, 343, 344, 345, 350, 526, 527, 529, 559; III:70
Fleischmann, Karel, II:178, 490; III:128
Fleischmann, Richard, I:421
Flesch, Josef, I:533; II:164
Foges, Josef, I:399
Fonfeder, Eliezer, II:162
Forchner, Vilém, I:368
Forgan, Ernest. *See* Freund (Forgan), Ernest
Forges, B. (Jewish leader), II:522
Francis I, Emperor, I:258; II:472, 549
Francis Joseph I, Emperor, I:45, 51, 74
Frank (Sergeant), III:406
Frank, Edgar, III:274
Frank, Hans, III:25, 403
Frank, Jacob, II:9; III:401
Frank, Karl Hermann, I:111; III:20, 35, 105, 143, 267, 273, 403
Frank, Mauritz, I:544
Frank, Rudolf, I:397
Frank-Swoboda, Lisa, I:545
Franke, Emil, I:247; II:308
Fränkel, Friedrich, II:38, 40, 50
Fränkel, Jacob, II:107, 108, 175
Frankel, Walter, II:202
Frankel, Zacharias, I:2
Frankenstein, Josef, I:236
Frankenstein, Karel, II:200
Frankl, Arthur, I:365, 392
Frankl, K. (medical officer), III:380, 382
Frankl, Ludwig August (Hochwart, Ritter von), I:23, 374, 510, 512
Frankl, Oskar, I:544, 558
Franzel, Emil, II:584, 585
Franzos, Zacharia, II:553, 554
Freiberger, Rudolf, III:147
Freilich, Max, II:86
Freilich, Samuel, II:371
Frešl, E. (Jewish volunteer), III:394, 397
Freud, Thekla, II:142
Freud, Viktor, II:75
Freund, Emil, I:366, 396
Freund (Forgan), Ernest, I:370
Freund, Ferenz, I:428
Freund, Henry, I:404
Freund, Hugo, II:230

Freund, Ida, I:54
Freund, Jiří, II:204, 205
Freund, Oswald, II:30
Freund, Otto, I:37, 365, 396, 409
Freund, Wilhelm, III:344
Frey, Josef, II:35
Frey, Julius (or Justus), pseud. of Jeiteles, Andreas (Aaron) Ludwig Josef, I:473, 510, 512
Frick, Wilhelm, III:37, 35
Frída, Emil Bohumil. *See* Vrchlický, Jaroslav
Fried, Antonín, I:400, 401
Fried, Babette, I:55, 71
Fried, Emil, II:186
Fried, Frederick, III:12
Fried, Theodor, II:238
Frieder, Rabbi Armin, I:117; II:40, 376; III:205, 209, 248, 326, 504, 533, 534
Frieder, Emanuel, III:550
Friediger, Rabbi Max, III:149, 151
Friedl, Raphael, III:543, 545, 547, 549
Friedländer, Hans, I:368
Friedman, Karel, II:215
Friedmann, E. (underground fighter), III:355
Friedmann, Elie, II:608; III:74
Friedmann, František, I:63-66, 119-21, 153, 258, 259, 261, 328, 526, 527; II:34, 175, 178, 273, 287, 288, 293, 596, 604, 605; III:12, 31, 40, 71, 73, 103, 500
Friedmann, Jakob, III:415, 445
Friedmann, Julius, I:362; III:14
Friedmann, Malvina, III:390, 394, 399, 400, 413, 421, 434, 440, 444
Friedmann, Paul, II:10
Friedmann, Philip, III:72
Friedmann, Richard Israel, III:50
Friedmann, Simon, I:340
Friedrich (Harvard University), I:401
Frischer, Arnošt (Ernst), II:273, 284, 295, 296, 300-02, 304, 308, 311, 312; III:34, 424, 463, 464, 466, 471, 472, 482, 490, 491, 493, 500, 524
Frischmann (hostage of Plzeň), III:24
Frisius (Vice-Admiral), III:38
Fritta (Taussig), Bedřich, II:198, 469, 490; III:125, 126, 127, 128, 149
Fritz, Géza, III:209

Frýd, Norbert, I:465; III:44, 45, 72, 574
Fuchs, Ernst, I:527; II:75, 91, 205
Fuchs family, III:96
Fuchs (Fox), Fred, II:209
Fuchs, Herbert, II:211
Fuchs, Hermann, II:284
Fuchs, Hugo, I:421
Fuchs, Johann Nepomuk, I:541
Fuchs, Karel, II:211
Fuchs, Miss (Fencing champion), II:214
Fuchs, Richard Robert, I:541
Fuchs, Rudolf, I:421, 483, 511, 516; II:376, 587
Führich, Josef, II:471
Fuhrman, Moritz, I:413
Funk, Samuel, II:355
Fürnberg, Louis. See Nuntius
Fürst, Bruno, II:587
Fürst, Leopold, II:199
Fürst, Sigmund Alexander, I:382; II:285
Fürst, Viliam, III:205
Fürth, Adolf, I:419
Fürth, Bernhard, I:396
Fürth, Daniel, I:396
Fürth, Emanuel, I:418
Fürth, Ernest, I:396
Fürth, Hugo, I:419
Fürth, Leopold, III:364
Fürth, Simon, I:396

Gabriel, O. (Corporal), III:382
Gádor, Herbert, II:214
Gak, Andrej, III:356, 358, 369, 494
Galat, Margit, III:69
Gandhi, Mohandas Karanichand, I:499
Gans, David, I:1, 3
Gans, Gutkind, II:544
Gansel, Willy, II:608
Ganzfried, Salomon, II:375
Gaon, Haham Salomon, III:586, 587
Gartenberg, Haim, I:537
Gaster, Haham Moses, II:15
Gauguin, Paul, II:480
Gažík, Marko, I:100
Geduldiger, Franz, I:414
Gelber, N.M., I:63, 71, 535
Gelbkopf, Max, II:190
Gellert, Grete. See Meisel-Hess, Grete
Gellert, Leo, I:393

Gellert, Oswald, I:393
Gellner, František, I:439
Gellner, Hedwig, II:141
Gellner, Jan, III:439
Gellner, Tony, II:141
George, Manfred, I:527; III:61
Gerron, Kurt, III:125, 137
Gessler, Max, I:389
Gessler, Siegfried, I:389
Gestettner, Albert, I:99
Gesling (Representative of Great Britain in Prague), I:223
Getreuer, František, II:208-10
Gewürz, Ludo, II:79
Giana, Curt, I:415
Gibian, Richard, I:434
Gieseking, Walter, I:557
Gilbert, Martin, III:328
Ginsberg, Asher. See Ahad Ha'am
Ginz, Miloš, II:201
Gladstein, Ruth Kestenberg. See Kestenberg-Gladstein, Ruth
Glaser, Adolf, I:389
Glaser, Anton, II:137
Glaser, Max. See Litumlei
Glaser, Vítězslav, I:420
Gláz, Vojtěch, III:400, 401, 413, 420, 442
Glazar, Richard, III:290
Glesinger, Egon, I:392
Glesinger, J. Ph. (timber producer & exporter), I:392
Globocznik, Odilio, III:280, 281
Glück, Guido, I:501, 511, 519
Glück, Teddy, II:209
Glück, Vajda, II:209
Glückselig, Leo, II:108
Godal, Erich, II:585
Goethe, Johann Wolfgang von, I:443, 476, 506; II:463
Gojdič, Pavel, III:256
Golan, See Goldenzeil, Menachem
Gold, Hugo, I:7, 8, 63-66, 121, 123, 325, 328, 352, 354, 355, 525, 535, 561, 562; II:104; III:445
Golda, Salomon, III:583
Goldberger, S. (president of Karlovy Vary Lodge of B'nai Brith), II:237
Goldelmann, Salomon, II:121, 124, 153, 258, 534
Goldenzeil, Menachem, II:180

NAME INDEX

Goldfaden, Abraham, I:485; II:553, 557
Goldman, Arthur, I:420
Goldmann, Greta, III:411
Goldmann, Nahum, III:457, 471, 474, 475, 484, 486, 489, 491, 492, 495, 590
Goldmark family, I:2
Goldner, Mikuláš, I:426
Goldschmidt, (Official in Federation of Jewish Congregations in Moravia), II:260
Goldschmidt, Arnošt, I:383
Goldschmidt, Lazarus, I:536
Goldschmidt, Leopold, III:343
Goldschmied, Leopold, I:527; II:35, 37
Goldstein, Angelo, I:98, 104, 107, 109, 119, 121, 136, 149, 202, 243, 258, 313, 319; II:40, 49, 178, 191, 207, 233, 235, 259, 276, 284, 288-92, 294, 296, 299, 301-313; III:458, 462, 463, 479, 492
Goldstein, David, III:252, 253
Goldstein, Leopold, I:528
Goldstein, Mosche, I:529; II:313
Goldstücker, Eduard, I:510; III:564
Goliath, Karel, III:396, 441
Goll, Yvan, I:491
Gompertz, Philipp, I:419
Gordin, Jacob, I:485; II:553, 557
Gordon, Aaron David, II:56, 59, 61, 63, 66, 67
Göring, Hermann, I:113; III:28, 29, 268, 276, 325
Görög, Wilhelm, II:285
Gosling, Sir Cecil, II:27, 180, 263
Gosztony, Peter, III:441
Gottesmann, L.L. (Revisionist leader), II:105
Gottlieb, Arnošt, II:211, 212
Gottlieb, František, I:444, 452, 464, 526; II:179
Gottlieb, Julius, II:239
Gottlieb, Leopold, I:371, 372
Gottwald, Klement, III:40, 41, 396, 397, 398, 403, 404, 406, 417, 441, 453, 523, 530, 548, 554, 555, 557, 565
Gozzi, Carlo, Count, I:499
Grab, Hedda, I:545, 557
Grab, Hermann, I:501, 511, 519
Grabe, Herman von, I:552
Gach (Student Zionist leader), II:180
Graetz, Heinrich Hirsch, I:4, 355, 485

Graf, Oskar Maria, II:587
Graf, Viktor, I:398, 433
Gratzinger, G. (medical officer), III:380
Grave, J.E. (artist), II:471
Greenberg, Leopold, II:10, 13, 15
Gregory, Karl Freiherr von, III:14, 30
Gregr, E. (Gruenhut), III:360, 361, 365, 370
Greidinger, Yizchak, II:54, 107
Greiner, Leo, I:478, 511
Grey, Sir Edward, I:163
Grillparzer, Franz, I:472, 474
Gris, Juan, II:481
Groag, Samis, I:382
Grönberg, Paul, II:35
Gropius, Alma Mahler. *See* Mahler-Gropius, Alma
Gropius, Walter, II:489
Gross, Andrej, III:406, 408, 411, 420
Gross, David, I:82, 117, 528
Gross, Hans, II:91
Grossman, Meir, II:6, 106, 107
Grossmann, Kurt R., I:xix, 115, 122, 133, 317, 322; II:583; III:61, 62
Grosz, Armand, II:486
Grosz, George, II:505
Grosz, Julius, I:528; II:104, 105
Grotte, E., II:523
Grueber, B. (German architect), II:523
Gruenbaum (Cadet Officer), III:337, 338
Gruen, Mordechai, III:422
Gruenberger, Julius, III:147
Grün, Herrmann, II:82
Grün, Nathan, I:344
Gruna, Leo, III:11
Grünbaum, Yitzhak, II:175
Grünberg, Josef, I:91; II:97
Grünberger, Hans, II:82
Grünberger, Karl, II:76, 175
Grünberger, Kurt, II:40, 94
Grünberger, Vilém, I:426
Grünfeld, Adolf, II:37, 62, 69, 73, 75, 91
Grünfeld, Alfred, II:60, 73, 284
Grünfeld, Heinrich, I:540, 552
Grünfeld, Paul. *See* Stefan, Paul
Grünfeld, Rabbi D., (Hostage of Jihlava), III:24
Grünzweig, Bedřich, III:14
Gruschka, Theodor, II:399
Grüson, (S.S. officer) III:235

Guenther, Hans, III:23, 30, 40, 45, 136, 144, 147
Günsberger, Albert, I:94
Gunther, Rolf, III:128, 142
Guri, Chaim, III:560
Gutfreund, Leo, III:365, 366
Gutfreund, Oto, II:469, 482, 483ff., 486
Guth, Karel, II:524
Guth, Otakar, III:39, 71
Gütig, Ernst, II:140
Gutmann, David, I:372
Gutman, Herbert, I:428
Gutmann, Wilhelm, I:373
Guttenstein, Heinz (Heinrich), II:40, 91
Guttmann, Mosche, II:36
Guttmann, Philip, I:381
Guttmann, Robert, II:469, 489, 490
Guttmann, Wolf, II:94
Gutwillig-Galat, W., III:384, 439

Haas, Alexander, I:394
Haas, Hugo, I:446, 452, 548; II:398
Haas, Jiři, III:364, 366
Haas, Leo, II:479, 490; III:127, 128, 149
Haas, Pavel, I:548; II:490
Haas, Theodor, I:64, 66, 68, 69; II:259, 260
Haas, Viktor, II:250
Haas, Willy, I:471, 489, 490, 511, 516, 521; II:587
Hába, Alois, I:542, 543, 546, 548
Hácha, Emil, II:273; III:3, 20, 22
Hahn, A. (Jewish Museum in Prague), III:568
Hahn, Albert, I:403
Hahn, Arnold, II:587
Hahn, Prof. Fred, III:x
Hahn, Georg, I:483
Hahn, Hella, II:205
Hahn, Karel, III:392, 440, 442
Hahn, Moritz von, I:41, 42, 67
Hahn, Otto, II:251
Hajsman family, III:96
Hála, Ján, II:505
Halevy, Abraham ben Mordechai, I:329
Halifax, Edward Frederick Lidley Lord, Earl of, III:5, 61, 63, 451, 488, 489, 490
Hálková, Elena, II:489
Haller, Herman, II:480

Halm, Alfred, I:480
Halm, J. (graduate of officers' school), III:410
Halperin, Israel, I:62, 355
Hamburg, B., I:70
Hamburger, (malt industry), I:382
Hammerschlag, Paul, I:427
Hanák, Artur (Fleischmann), III:359, 373, 374, 378, 379, 436, 438, 445
Hans, Jakob, III:400
Hantke, Arthur, I:167; II:267
Harendorf, S.J., pseud. of Dorfsohn, S.J., I:xix, 154, 528
Hargreaves, H.H., II:622
Hart, Ferdinand, II:586
Hartman, Joe, I:386
Hartmann (Jewish party), II:285
Hartmann, Karel, II:206
Hartmann, Ludo, I:473
Hartmann, Moritz, I:21-23, 25, 61, 62, 473, 510, 512; II:149
Hartmann, Paul, III:11
Hartung (Jewish singer), I:553
Hašek, Jaroslav, I:508, 511
Hatham Sofer. *See* Schreiber, Rabbi Moses *and* Sofer, Moses
Haurowitz, Regina, I:411
Haurowitz, Rudolf, I:410
Haurowitz, Siegmund, I:410
Hauschner, Auguste, I:475, 510, 513
Haushofer, Max, II:474
Havel, Rudolf, I:452, 455
Havlíček-Borovský, Karel, I:22, 61, 457, 458, 460, 524; II:150
Havránek, František, II:474
Hawthorne, Nathaniel, I:549
Hayden, Charles, I:385
Heartfield, John, II:585
Hebel, Christian Friedrich, I:474, 475
Hecht, Adolf, I:366
Hecht, Ben, III:327
Hecht, Ladislav, II:212
Hecht, Mikuláš, III:406, 410, 442, 443, 445
Hecht, Věra, III:411
Heilig, Bernhard, III:272
Heilig, Otto, II:182
Hein, J., III:370, 417
Heindl (SS Scharführer), III:291
Heine, Heinrich, I:45, 443, 448, 458, 473, 509; II:379, 463
Heine, Theodor, II:490

NAME INDEX

Heinsheimer, Alfred, I:428
Heinsheimer, Otto, I:428
Heisler, Robert, I:397
Heitler, Jindrich, I:390; II:213
Heitlinger, O., III:64
Hekš, Oskar, I:409; II:202-04
Helfert, Vladimir, I:548, 558
Helfman, M. (head of Prague Tze'ire Zion office), II:58
Heller (family), I:382
Heller (Captain), III:420
Heller, Adolf, I:544
Heller, Arthur, II:40, 82, 87, 93, 94, 489
Heller, Beda, I:422
Heller, Bernat, I:81
Heller, Carl, II:250
Heller, Erich, I:471
Heller, Fritz, I:374
Heller, Isidor, I:23, 474, 510
Heller, Josef, I:537
Heller, Ludvík, I:375
Heller, Otta, III:410
Heller, Robert, I:392; II:189
Heller, Seligman, I:57, 474, 510, 512
Heller, Wilhelm, II:285
Heller, Rabbi Yomtov Lipman, II:440
Hellman, Albrecht, I:258
Henlein, Konrad, I:111, 112; II:583; III:452
Henning, Karel, II:472
Herben, Jan, I:463
Herbenová, Olga, III:581, 583
Herder, Johann Gottfried von, I:533
Herman, Jan, III:581, 583
Hermann, Božena, III:395
Hermann, Frank, I:375
Hermann, Gustav, I:436
Hermann, Hugo, I:89, 117, 230, 525; II:35, 37, 70, 75, 177
Hermann, Ignát, II:209
Hermann, Karel, I:398
Hermann, Johann Franz von, I:3
Hermann, Ota, II:212
Hermann-Cohen, Elisheva, III:435
Herrmann, Leo, I:71, 157, 158, 174, 177, 246, 250, 251, 525; II:20, 26, 30, 36, 177, 258, 446, 596; III:12, 477, 478, 479, 480, 481, 494, 495, 544
Hersch, Julius, I:412
Hertzka, Oskar, I:427

Herz, Alice Sommer. *See* Sommer-Herz, Alice
Herz, Armin, II:205
Herz, J., III:370
Herzfeld, Alfred, I:427
Herzfeld, Arthur, I:428; II:207
Herzfelde, Wieland, II:585
Herzfelder, Emil, I:368
Herzl, Theodor, I:17, 19, 47, 59, 71, 81, 84, 271, 476, 541; II:11, 20, 22, 101, 106, 138, 186, 446; III:551
Herzog, Artur, II:40, 188, 190, 193
Herzog, Ignaz, I:387
Hesky family, III:96
Hess, Grete Meisel. *See* Meisel-Hess, Grete
Hess, Leo, III:147
Hesslein, Paul, II:40
Hevesi, Rabbi Simon, II:354
Hexner, Ervin, I:369, 437
Heydrich, Reinhard, II:33; III:17, 28, 30, 34, 35, 36, 48, 77, 92, 113, 148, 189, 264, 267, 268, 274, 275, 276, 277, 279, 288, 464
Heym, Stefan, II:587
Hickl, Leo, II:104
Hickl, Max, I:351, 356, 525, 534, 535; II:24, 77
Hieronymus, Otto, I:408
Hilar, Karel H., II:488
Hilbert, Jaroslav, I:462
Hilf, Alois, I:271, 325, 326; II:258, 260, 278
Hillel, F., I:535
Hilsner, Leopold, I:17, 67, 152, 503; III:9
Himmler, Heinrich, III:29, 69, 140, 142, 190, 234, 239, 265, 280, 307, 310, 314
Hindemith, Paul, I:547
Hinsley, Cardinal, III:465
Hirsch, Aaron, II:57
Hirsch, Arnold, II:185
Hirsch, Baron Maurice de, I:81
Hirsch, Ernst, I:394; II:251
Hirsch, Fredy, III:296, 297, 298
Hirsch, Fritz, I:394
Hirsch, Heřman, I:420
Hirsch, Isidor, I:310, 316, 339, 344
Hirsch, Markus, II:354
Hirsch, Martin, I:433
Hirsch, Morris, I:435
Hirsch, Otto, II:190, 193

Hirsch, Samson Raphael, I:52, 70
Hirsch, Stephan, I:433
Hirschbein, Perez, II:557
Hirschler, Gertrude, II:155; III:xi, xx
Hirschler, Rabbi Simon, I:93, 98, 119, 273; II:160, 161, 164
Hitler, Adolf, I:9, 106-08, 111, 113, 118, 317, 448, 495, 524; III:4, 10, 20, 34, 76, 107, 114, 140, 173, 180, 239, 242, 255, 267, 294, 303, 316, 371, 377, 396, 457, 468, 500, 552, 554
Hitschmann, Richard, I:419
Hlaváč, Alfred, III:404
Hlinka, Andrej, I:83, 108, 111, 112, 114; II:297, 304; III:28, 30, 34, 180, 303, 325
Hlošek, Jan, I:263
Hoch (Rabbi in Plzeň), III:24
Hochauser, Franz, II:105
Hochbaum, Adolf, I:403
Hochberg, Karol, III:206, 249
Hochfeld, Jindřich, I:407
Hochwart, Ritter von. *See* Frankl, Ludwig August
Hock, Simon, I:8, 26, 59, 62, 71
Hod, Motti, III:560
Hoddis, Jakob von, I:491
Hodža, Milan, I:109, 110, 122; II:302, 309, 311, 566
Hoefle, Hans, III:282
Hoess, Rudolf, III:303
Hoffman, Emmerich, I:66, 67; II:178
Hoffman, Arnošt, I:366
Hoffman, Chaim. *See* Yahil, Chaim
Hoffmann-Dvorin, F., III:248
Hoffmann, Heinrich. *See* Yahil, Chaim
Hoffmann, Kamil (Camill), I:479, 482, 511, 514; III:124
Hoffmeister, Adolf, II:488, 585
Hofman, Arpád, III:408
Hofmann, Emil, I:346
Hofmann, Lene, II:142
Hofmann, Mosche, III:401, 442
Hofmann, Richard Beer. *See* Beer-Hofmann, Richard
Hofmannsthal, Hugo von, I:479, 489
Hogarth, William, II:471
Hojda, Ferdinand, II:38, 40
Hojtasch, Heinrich, I:399
Holeček, Josef, I:463
Holitscher, Arnošt, II:250
Hollos, Eugene, II:587

Hollos, Julius, II:586
Holly, Eugen, I:154
Holzer, Maximilian, III:402, 414, 415, 445
Hönig, Bedřich, I:394, 411, 433
Hönig, Filip, I:389
Hönig, John, I:433
Hora, Jindřich, III:361, 370, 437
Horák, Karel, I:118, 119
Horb, Max, II:480-82
Horetzky, Pavel, II:609
Horn, Antal, I:82
Horn, Eduard, I:73, 81
Hornig, Salomon, II:97
Hornyanszky, Alexander, II:377
Horowitz, Aharon Meshullam, III:575
Horowitz, Lazar, II:370
Horowitz, Simon, I:82
Horthy, Istvan, I:113; III:316, 319
Horvath, Pavel, I:124, 437
Hostovský, Egon, I:xii, xviii, xix, 33, 65, 269, 333, 439, 452, 454, 455, 457, 464, 467, 482, 524, 548, 559; II:153; III:63
House, Col. Edward Mandell II, I:228
Hrušovský, František, I:120
Hrůzová, Anežka, I:67
Huber, Bohdan, II:210
Huber, Oskar, I:82
Huber, Theodor, II:210, 284
Hudec, D., III:254
Huller, Erwin, II:54
Humbarsky, Dr. (Slovak government official), III:243
Huppert, Otakar, III:442, 446
Hurban-Vajanský, Svetozár, I:78, 108, 122
Husník, Antonín, I:406
Huss, Othmar, II:284, 293, 303
Husserl, Edmund, I:58; II:445, 446
Hut, Julius, II:93
Hutter, Michael, II:180, 181
Hvass, Frank, III:151
Hynais, Vojtěch, II:477

Ibn Jacob, Ibrahim, I:1; II:348
Iltis, Rudolf, I:529; III:64
Ingr, Sergěj, III:347, 353, 367, 397, 452, 479, 481
Isaacs, Alfred, I:426
Ischaiewitsch, Mosche, II:57
Istler (artist), II:489

NAME INDEX

Istóczy, Victor, I:77
Itzhak (Isaac) of Trnava, Rabbi, I:80
Ivak, Jan, II:307

Jabotinsky, Vladimir, I:98, 154, 535; II:6, 15, 99-102, 106
Jacob, Walter, II:491
Jakobovits, Tobias, I:6, 534; III:571, 574, 575, 576, 581, 582, 583
Jacobson, Siegfried, II:586
Jacoby, Gerhard, III:66, 68, 70, 72
Jaffe, Jecheskel, II:73
Jakobson, Roman, II:521
Jaksch, Wenzel, II:584, 585; III:8
Jakub, Jiří. See Ohrenstein (Orten), Jiří
Jakuboci (Bratislava police official), II:609
Jalowetz, Heinrich, I:545
Janáček, Leoš, I:471, 482, 507, 545, 548, 551
Janko (Colonel), III:420
Janovich, Gustav, I:486, 521
Janoušek, Karel, I:432; III:388
Janowitz, Bedřich, I:428
Janowitz, Ferdinand, I:390
Janowitz, Franz, I:500, 511, 519
Janowitz, Hans, I:500, 511, 518
Janowitz, Leo, III:41, 133, 147
Jappke, Mrs. (secretary of *Selbstwehr*), II:145, 147
Jaroš, Miroslav, III:399, 400, 582
Jarosz, Andor, III:316
Jeanneret, Charles Édouard (Le Corbusier), II:489
Jebavý, Vaclav. See Březina, Otakar
Jeckelen, Friedrich, III:315
Jehlička, František, I:99
Jeiteles, Alois Ludwig. See Fatalis
Jeiteles, Andreas (Aaron) Ludwig Josef. See Frey, Julius (Justus)
Jeiteles, Berthold, III:515
Jeiteles, Itzig. See Seidlitz, Julius
Jeiteles, Jonas, II:471
Jelinek, Yehoshua, III:10, 14, 499, 526
Jellinek, Rabbi Adolf, I:535; II:40
Jellinek, Alois, II:285
Jellinek, Hugo, I:420
Jellinek, Michael, III:335, 336, 338, 362, 363, 434, 436
Jellinek, Oskar, I:498, 511, 518, 522
Jellinek, Rudolf, III:382
Jerusalem, Max, II:186

Jesenská, Milena, I:116, 486, 490; III:9
Jettel, Eugen, II:475
Ježek, Josef, III:28
Jílek, Karel, pseud. of Orten, Jiří
Jílovský, Jiří, II:475
Jiřík, F.X., II:472, 477
Jirotka, Zdeněk, III:71
Joachim, Joseph, I:539
Jodl, Alfred, III:40
Joffe, Elieser, II:63
John XXIII, Pope, III:313
John, Jiří, III:578
Jokl (Jewish camp official in "family camp"), III:297, 298
Jokl, Rudolf, II:82, 87; III:489
Jolesch, S., I:417
Josef, Ben, II:94
Joseph II, Emperor, I:14, 15, 43, 48, 49, 59, 333, 342, 469; II:367, 369, 372; III:109
Joseph, Dov, II:641
Juethner, Prof. (German National party), II:271
Juhász, Mór, I:81
Jungk, Robert, II:587
Juskovits, Moritz, II:37
Justic, Evžen, II:191, 281, 284, 288
Justitz, Alfred, II:479, 486

Kačer, Jaromír, I:405
Kadlec, Josef M., III:30, 31, 346, 347, 356, 357, 358, 360, 436, 462, 475, 477, 478, 494
Kafka (officer of Société), II:236
Kafka, Bruno, II:248
Kafka, Emil, I:89; II:36; III:39, 490
Kafka, Erik, III:147
Kafka, František, III:38, 45, 272, 323
Kafka, Franz, I:19, 34, 35, 52, 58, 65, 441, 445, 461, 468, 470, 478, 483-90, 494, 508, 510, 511, 516, 521, 522, 551; II:444, 448, 449, 465, 483, 587; III:41, 150, 564
Kafka, Hermann, I:34, 35, 484
Kafka, Josef, I:418
Kafka, Julie, I:65
Kafka, Příbram, I:389
Kagan, Rabbi Israel Meir (Chafetz Hayim), II:163
Kahan, Vilém, III:409
Kahanemann, Rabbi of Poneviezh, II:164

Kahler, Erich, I:471
Kahler, Eugen, II:476
Kahn, Franz, II:38, 40, 45, 50, 268; III:12, 50, 71
Kain, Ludvík, III:439
Kálal, Karel, I:78, 83
Kalenter, Ossip, pseud, of Burckhard, Johannes
Kaleta (Lieutenant), III:334
Kalfus, Josef, II:596; III:12
Kalina, Rudolf, I:401
Kalinin, Mikhail Ivanovich, III:402
Kalisch, Eleazar Yehiel, I:537
Kallay, Nicholas, III:316
Kallus, Elimelech, I:529
Kalmar, Gustav, I:428
Kalný, Slavo, II:213
Kaltenbrunner, Ernst, III:39, 142, 255
Kaminský, Oskar, II:199
Kamm, August, I:541
Kämpf, S.J., I:341
Kandinsky, Vasily, II:489
Kann, Jiří, II:486
Kanner, Leib, I:529
Kanter, Felix, I:353, 535
Kantor (director of Bohemian Discount Bank), III:26
Kantor, Alfred, I:387
Kantor, Max, I:365, 401
Kantor-Berg, Friedrich, *See* Torberg, Friedrich
Kaplan, Eliezer, II:58
Kaplansky, Solomon, II:84
Kaplický, Josef, III:578
Kapper, Siegfried (Vítězslav), I:22, 23, 61, 341, 439, 482, 510, 515, 524; II:149
Kapras (jurist), III:490
Kara, Abraham, I:338
Kara, Avigdor, I:338; II:440, 524, 541, 543
Karfík, Vladimír, II:470
Karlín. *See* Pollak, Richard
Karmasin, Franz, I:111, 113, 115, 254, 304
Kárný, Miroslav, III:68
Karo, Joseph, I:287
Karpe, Oskar, II:40, 76, 91, 94
Karpeles, Gustav, I:471
Karpeles, Richard, II:60
Kars, George, II:469, 475, 478, 480-82, 486, 487

Karsten, Robert, I:426
Karvaš, Imrich, III:191, 210, 247
Kašpar, Cardinal Karel, III:15
Kastein, Josef, II:181
Kastner, Erich, II:478
Kastner, Lajos, II:164
Kasztner, Rezsö, III:234, 235, 318
Kates, Michael, III:xi
Katona, Nándor (Kleinberger, Nándor), II:502
Katz, Abraham Aaron, II:160-62, 164, 165
Katz, Alfred, I:390
Katz, Arnošt, II:205
Katz (Kent), František, I:406, 433
Katz, Moshe, II:161
Katz, Otto (manufacturer), I:420
Katz, Otto. *See* Simon, André
Katz, Richard, I:502, 511, 519
Katz, Rudolf, II:572
Katz, Viktor, I:431
Katz-Forstner, Arthur, I:437
Katzburg, Menachem, II:97
Katzenelson, Abraham, II:63
Katznelson, Siegmund, I:248, 521, 525; II:20, 446
Katznelson, Yitzhak, III:4
Kauder, Gustav, II:584
Kauders, Arthur, II:269, 270, 284
Kauders, Walter (Herzl Group), II:179
Kaufman, E. (Zionist leader), II:87
Kaufman, H. (Goodrich rubber concern), I:421
Kaufman, Oskar, I:410
Kaufman, Viktor, II:75; III:17
Kaufmann, David, I:8
Kaufmann, Ferdinand, I:404
Kaufmann, J.V. (sports journalist), II:206
Kaufmann, K. (Jewish soldier buried in Tobruk), III:366
Kaufmann, Ludwig, II:94
Kaufmann, Moritz, I:549
Kaufmann, Walter, I:549
Kaufmann, Wilhelm, I:376, 377
Kayserling, Meyer, I:344
Keitel, Wilhelm, III:67
Keller & Co. (hops manufacturing concern), I:382
Keller, Rudolf, II:584
Kellner, Viktor, I:20; II:446

NAME INDEX

Kennan, George F., III:4, 22, 61, 63, 66, 68, 69
Kent, Frantisek. *See* Katz (Kent), František
Kepler, Johannes, I:1; II:444
Kerine, Abdul Aziz, III:553
Kerner, Miroslav, III:11, 348, 373, 377, 410, 420, 435, 438, 444
Kerr, Alfred, I:500
Kersten, Kurt, II:587
Kesler, Valter, II:201
Kessler, Siegfried, II:40, 77, 79, 82, 87, 93; III:489
Kestenbaum (Private), III:408
Kestenberg-Gladstein, Ruth, I:xi, xvi-xvii, 17, 21-61, 152, 167, 259, 469, 505, 524, 541, 559
Kestner, Pavel, I:413
Kettner, Marie, II:213
Keussler, Erhard von, I:547, 556
Khrushchev, Nikita, III:402
Kien, Peter, II:488, 490; III:125, 126, 127, 128
Kirchenberger, H. (medical officer), III:380
Kinský, Count, III:5
Kirpal, Irene, II:250
Kirschbaum, Josef M., III:254
Kisch, Egon Erwin, I:9, 471, 495-96, 510, 511, 517; II:445, 585; III:504, 526
Kisch, Guido, I:viii, xi, xvii, 6, 10, 11, 61-63, 71, 259, 343, 350, 352-56, 471, 527, 535, 559, 561; III:12
Kittl, Johann Friedrich, I:551
Kittl, Julius, I:535
Klang, Heinrich, III:151
Klapálek, Karel, III:359, 360, 362, 363, 364, 365, 368, 369, 380, 419, 420, 436, 437
Klapp, Erich, III:147
Klapp, Michael, I:475, 510, 513
Klatscher, Emil, I:382
Klarzimmer, Löb, I:539
Klee, Paul, II:480, 487
Klein (Lieutenant, North Africa), III:365
Klein (Second Lieutenant, French front), III:353
Klein, Dr. A. Edvard (Tibor), II:214
Klein, Edvard, I:387
Klein, Emil, II:202, 203

Klein, Herrmann, I:528
Klein, Ignaz, I:411, 520
Klein, Josef, II:354
Klein, Leopoldine, II:141, 284
Klein, Mór, II:359
Klein, Pavel, I:387
Klein, Robert, II:247
Klein, Samuel, I:94; II:376
Klein, Truda, II:213
Kleinberger, Bohdan, II:151
Kleinberger, Nandor. *See* Katona, Nándor
Kleiner, Kamil, I:400, 431, 432; III:344, 527
Kleist, Heinrich von, I:443
Klement, Rudolf, I:393
Klemeš, Jaroslav, III:65
Klemperer, Gutmann, I:352, 356
Klemperer, Otto, I:555
Klempfner, Anka, II:208
Klepetář, Harry, I:118
Klepetář, Otto, I:499, 511, 517, 518
Klička, Benjamin, I:464
Klimt, Gustav, II:479
Klinda, Ferdinand, III:247, 248
Klinger, František, II:215
Klinger, Jindřich, I:414
Klinger, Dr. Otto, III:439, 488
Klinger, Ruth, III:562
Klinger, Sigmund, I:118
Klofáč, Václav, I:158, 247; II:255
Klostermann, Karel, I:464
Klutznick, Philip M., III:590
Kmeťko, Karol, III:240
Kmetty, János, II:498
Knieža, Emil F., III:295, 326, 548, 549
Knirr, Heinrich, II:478, 480
Knobelsdorf, General von, III:265
Knoepfelmacher, Bedřich, I:344
Knöpfelmacher, Isidor, I:88; II:285
Knöpfelmacher, Julie, I:97
Kobler, Franz, I:471
Kobrin, Leo, II:557
Koch, Walter, II:243
Kodíček, Dr. (physician at Bronowice), III:434
Kodíček, Josef, I:523; II:151; III:489
Koehler, Willy, III:343
Koenen, Wilhelm, II:585
Koenig, Alma Johanna, I:471
Koenig, Nathan, III:408, 443
Koenigstein, Hugo, II:238

Koerper, Miroslav, II:236, 237
Körper, Rudolf, III:384
Kohn, Miss (fencing champion), II:214
Kohn, Albert, I:27, 63, 64, 70; II:237
Kohn, Emma Sarah, II:105; III:509
Kohn, Ervín, II:213; III:380
Kohn, Fritz, II:57
Kohn, Gustav, II:40, 55
Kohn, Hans, I:20, 25, 121, 259, 457, 471, 521, 535, 559; II:20, 26, 30, 58, 259, 446; III:62
Kohn, Dr. Jindřich, I:444, 451, 452; II:151-53
Kohn, Kamil, II:36, 65, 178
Kohn, Max, I:413
Kohn, Pavel, II:179
Kohn, Pinchas, II:160, 164
Kohn, Rudolf, I:167, 269, 270; II:30, 32, 78, 80, 81, 258; III:365, 366
Kohn, Salomon, I:55, 56, 474, 510
Kohn, Viktor, II:35
Kohner, Walter, II:40, 50, 174-76
Kohner-Bergmann, Hilda, I:479, 511, 515
Kohorn, Viktor, I:414
Kohut, Rabbi Alexander, I:533
Kokoschka, Oskar, II:503, 505
Kolár, Josef Jiří, I:458
Kolben, Emil, I:402, 405, 408
Kolin, Rabbi Shmuel HaLevi, I:350
Kolinsky (founder of Radiochema, Ltd.), I:372
Kolinský, Ota, I:415
Kolisch, Max, II:75
Kollár, Jan, II:466
Kollman, Arnošt, II:178
Kollman, Milan, II:40, 285
Kollusch. See Kalisch, Eleazar Yehiel
Komendák, Peter, III:251
Kominík, František, II:215
Kominík, Pavel, II:215
Komjády, Béla, II:210
Komlos, Soma, I:91
Kompert, Leopold, I:23, 26, 56, 61-63, 66, 356, 473, 474, 482, 510, 512
Konecsný, György, II:498
Koněv, Ivan Štěpanovič, III:419
Königsberg, S. (rabbi in Benešov), I:340, 343
Kopecký, Rudolf, III:434
Kopecký, Václav, III:xli, 486, 487, 511, 512, 530

Kopold, H. (Communist leader), III:397
Korda (Kohn), J. (navigator), III:384, 387
Koreš (Colonel), III:357, 359
Korherr, Richard, III:202
Korn, Robert, I:415
Kornblüth, Leo, II:38, 40, 50
Körner, Walter, I:392
Kornfeld, Felix, II:178
Kornfeld, Hugo, I:367
Kornfeld, Paul, I:490, 495, 511
Kornfeld, Siegmund, I:361
Korngold, Erich Wolfgang, I:476, 517, 546, 555
Kosmák, Václav, I:463, 464
Kosmas (historian), II:540
Koso, Izidor, III:189, 190, 197, 206
Kossuth, Lajos, I:82
Kosta, Vasil, I:152
Kostar, Ota, I:368
Kováč (air force engineer), III:361
Kováč, Tibor, III:205, 246
Kovács (engineer, Mauritius internee), II:635
Koval, Hugo, II:411
Koželuh, Jan, II:212
Kozlov (General, Red Army), III:398
Kozma, Tibor, I:545
Krafft, Anton, I:545
Krakauer, Emil, III:273
Král. See Weiner, Imro
Král, Václav, III:65
Král, Jiří, II:199
Kramář, Karel, I:158, 168, 247-49; II:245
Kramář, Vincent, II:487
Kramer, Joseph, III:300, 301
Kramer, Leopold, I:542
Krämer, Salo, III:47, 50, 572
Krasa, Hans, I:547, 556
Krasniansky, Oskar (Karmil), II:609; III:317, 318, 534, 547
Krátký (German theatrical agent), II:555
Krátký, Colonel, III:410
Kratochvíl, Jan, III:404, 413, 419
Kratochvíl, Karel, III:68, 351
Kratochvíl, Zdeněk, II:482
Kraus, Adolf, III:590

NAME INDEX 633

Kraus, Alex, III:350, 372, 373, 374, 375, 379, 438
Kraus, Edith, I:544, 556
Kraus, Eduard, II:235, 236
Kraus, Emanuel, II:285
Kraus, Erich, III:50
Kraus, Ferdinand, II:91
Kraus, Jiří, II:179
Kraus, Josef, I:416
Kraus, Karel, I:416
Kraus, Karl, I:471, 500, 503, 504, 510; II:465
Kraus, Leo, I:525
Kraus, Móric, I:341
Kraus, Ota, I:465; III:323, 324, 325, 326
Kraus, Otto B., I:450
Kraus, Paul, II:183
Kraus, Rudolf, II:239
Krauss, F.S. (author), I:475
Krautheimer, Richard, II:524, 525
Kreibich, Karl, III:461
Krejčí, František, II:266
Krejčí, Jaroslav, II:260
Kremenetzky, Johann, I:398
Kress, Karel, I:366
Kresta, Erich, II:179, 205
Kreuger, Ivar, I:396
Křička, Jaroslav, I:540, 543, 549, 552
Kriegel, Max, III:337, 340, 400, 401, 421, 434, 441, 442
Krieger, Jacques, II:38
Krieger, Leo, II:37
Křižík, Franz, I:402
Krofta, Kamil, II:566
Krón, Eugen, II:502, 504, 508, 512
Kroo, Sándor, I:136
Kruh, Ernst, III:74
Kubala, Otomar, III:247, 248
Kube, Wilhelm, III:274
Kubik, Jakub Birnholz, II:204
Kubín, Captain L., III:377
Kubín (Coubine), Otakar, II:481, 486
Kubowitzki, Arye Leon, III:493-94, 495
Kubovy, Arye Leon. *See* Kubowitzki, Arye Leon
Kučera, František, III:65
Kučera, Vladimír, III:470
Kudla (Kellner) (airman), III:387
Kudlič (Lieutenant), III:393
Kuffner, Karel, I:383

Kugel, Chaim, I:107, 109, 111, 121, 122, 132, 136, 144, 145, 203, 281, 319, 519; II:40, 74, 75, 93, 142, 233, 235, 284, 291, 295, 296, 301-13, 414, 416, 430-32, 436; III:463, 490
Kügler, F. (art historian), II:523
Kuh, Anton, I:519; II:587
Kuh-Kühne, Emil, I:382
Kuhn, Heinrich, II:188
Kühn, Otto, II:40
Kulka, Erich, III:3, 67, 105, 146, 252, 326, 328, 441, 444, 446, 487, 495
Kulka, Julius, II:36
Kulka, Olga, II:141
Kulka, Otto D., III:325
Kulke, Eduard, I:475, 510, 513
Kummerman, František, II:198
Kumpošt, Colonel P., III:370
Kún, Béla, I:86
Kundt, Ernst, I:111
Kupka, František, II:477, 480, 486
Kurreim,. Adolf, I:70, 535
Kürti, Erik, III:362
Kurz, Štěpán, I:557
Kussi, Milton, I:398
Kutlík, Cyril, II:376
Kvačal, Ján, II:377
Kvapil (Lieutenant), III:411
Kvapil, Jaroslav, II:258
Kvetko, Martin, III:332, 546

Lacina, Václav, I:452
Ladislaus, King, II:348
Lagus, František, II:199
Lagus, Karel, III:53
Lam, Robert, II:585
Lamač, Miroslav, II:485
Lamberg, Arnošt, I:403
Lamberger, Ernest, II:67
Lamed, Meir, I:xix
Lamm, Josef, II:55
Landa, Moshe, III:434, 438
Landau, Rabbi Ezechiel, I:60, 338, 350, 353
Landau, M.I., I:336, 341
Landau, Samuel, II:472
Landau, Simon, I:428
Landauer, Gustav, I:263, 476
Landes, Zdeněk, I:526; II:179, 181
Landesmann, Heinrich. *See* Lorm, Hieronymus

Landesmann, S. (hops manufacturing concern), I:382
Landesmann, Viktor, I:398, 427
Landman, Samuel, II:590
Landress, Sylvia, III:xi
Landsberg, Eva, II:167
Lang, David, II:503, 517
Lange, Fritz, III:276, 279
Langen, Rudolf, I:392
Langer, Felix, I:502, 511, 520
Langer, František, I:440, 441, 446, 449, 452, 482, 483; II:463, 465; III:360, 380, 438
Langer, Herbert, III:50, 572
Langer, Jiří (Georg), I:351, 449, 452, 484, 485, 553; II:153, 488
Langer, Josef, I:374; II:232
Langer, Viktor, II:211
Langmann, Philipp, I:477, 510, 514
Lann, Robert, I:370
Lansing, Robert, I:228
Lantz, Robert, II:587
Lányi, Menyhért, I:83, 121
Lanzer family, III:393
Lanzer, Kurt, III:394, 440
Lanzer, Malvina, III:340, 435
Lanzer, Norbert, III:400
Lask, Alexander, III:279
Lasus, Marck, II:40
Laub, Ferdinand, I:539
Laube, Gustav, I:371
Laufer, Josef, II:206
Laurin, Arne, pseud. of Lustig, Arnošt
Laušman, Bohumil, III:396
Lavoipierre, René, II:26
Lavry, Marc, I:508
Lebenhart, Ernst, II:37, 139, 273
Lebenhart, Filip, I:525; II:137, 180
Lebovič, Michael, III:413
Lechner, Felix, I:427
Le Corbusier. See Jeanneret, Charles Édouard
Leda. See Lederer, Eduard
Ledeč, Egon, I:543
Lederer (Zionist leader in Prague), II:87
Lederer, Arnošt, III:377, 410
Lederer, Eduard (Leda), I:35, 78, 446, 452, 524; II:151, 152; III:39
Lederer, Josef, II:237
Lederer, Richard, I:428

Lederer, Siegfried, I:477, 510, 514; III:299, 300
Lederer, Zdeněk, III:3, 147, 323, 324, 325, 515, 527
Lehman, Herbert, I:401
Lehrfeld, Hanuš, II:205
Lehrfeld, Kurt, II:205
Leiden, Gabriel, II:79
Leipen, Miss (volunteer nurse in World War I), II:138
Lelewer, Hermann, II:191, 192
Lemberger, Arnošt, III:70, 74
Lemberger, Fritz, I:421
Lenard, Dionys, III:248
Lenárt, Vilém, II:208
Lenau, Nikolaus, I:474, 478
Lengsfeld, August, I:404
Lerner, Alan Jay, I:542
Leschner, Leo, II:609
Leshem, Moshe. See Lemberger, Arnošt
Leshem, Peretz, III:470
Lessing, Gotthold Ephraim, I:509; II:463
Lessing, Theodor, II:570, 587
Lestschinsky, Jacob, II:175
Lettrich, Jozef, I:82, 120, 123, 124; III:327, 544, 546, 548
Levi, Bedřich, I:421
Levi, Sami, I:414
Levinson, Bernard, III:xii
Levy, Ludwig, III:354
Levy, Z. David, III:589
Lewisohn, Ludwig, I:494
Lewith, Otto, II:214
Lewy, L. (rabbi in Brno), II:260
Lexa, John G. III:3, 66, 323
Lhote, André, II:512
Libeňský, Václav, II:199
Libora, Max, I:414
Libra, F.A., II:486
Lichtenfeld, Salman, I:536
Lichtenstein, Alfred, I:491
Lichtenstern, Fritz, III:470
Lichtig, Herman, II:273
Lichtner, Martin, II:54, 105, 107
Lichtwitz, Hans. See Naor, Uri
Lieben, Eugen, II:258, 271
Lieben, Hugo, III:580
Lieben, Koppelman, I:59, 356; II:545
Lieben, L. (academician), II:180
Lieben, Salomon Hugo, I:6, 7, 329, 353, 356; III:567, 573

NAME INDEX 635

Lieberman, Bedřich, I:408
Liebermann, Max, I:476; II:480
Liebkind (medical officer at Bronowice), III:434
Liebstein, Karl. *See* Livneh, Eliahu K.
Liechtenstein, Franz, Prince, II:214
Liepmann, Heinz, II:587
Liliencron, Detlev von, I:468
Lilling, Adolf, II:231
Lima, Bedřich, I:377
Lindenbaum (Tirzi), Eldad, II:82
Lipscher, Ladislav, III:x, 323, 325, 326, 327, 491, 544
Lipsky, Schlome, I:112
Lipták, Lubomir, III:246, 249, 548
Lipton, M. (U.S. delegate to 13th Zionist Congress), II:61
Liška, Alois, III:380, 383
Liszt, Franz, I:554
Litumlei, pseud, of Glaser, Max, I:478, 511, 514
Livneh, Eliahu K., II:73, 207
Lízálek, J. (Captain), III:351
Lloyd George, David, I:171, 249, 263; II:13
Lobkowicz, Max, Prince, I:377
Lobosický, M. (musician), I:545
Locker, Berl, II:82; III:470
Lockhart, Sir R. H. Bruce, III:451, 453, 460, 462, 487, 488, 489, 490
Löbl, Efraim, I:415
Löbl, Eugen, III:566
Löbl, Josef, II:587
Löbl, Moritz, II:73, 75
Löbl, Otto, I:117
Löffler, Peter, I:396
Loerke, Oskar, I:500
Loewy, Alois, I:389
Loewy, Doc, II:587
Lom, Stanislav, I:462
Lomský (Captain), III:394
Longen (Pittermann), Artur, II:481, 482
Longhi, Pietro, II:471
Lorenz, Bedřich, E., I:382
Loria, Felix, II:79, 81
Lorm, Hieronymus, pseud. of Landesmann, Heinrich, I:57, 474, 475, 510, 513
Lothar, Ernst, I:471
Löw ben Bezalel, Rabbi Judah, I;1, 312, 337, 338, 342, 349, 350, 356; II:440, 450; III:573

Löw, Georg, I:541
Löw, Hans, II:103-05
Löw-Beer, Aaron, I:413
Löw-Beer, Friedrich, I:413
Löw-Beer, Jacob, I:413
Löw-Beer, Moses, I:413
Löwe, Ferdinand, I:543
Löwe, Frederick, I:542
Löwenbach, Jan, I:419, 552
Löwenherz, Josef, III:73
Löwenbach, Josef, I:552
Löwenstamm, Ernst, II:50
Löwenstein, Alfred, II:60, 285
Löwenstein, Ernst, II:399, 400
Löwenstein, Eugen, I:418
Löwenstein, Karel, I:400, 431
Löwidt family, III:96
Löwy, Erwin, I:402, 434
Löwy, Frieda, II:141
Löwy, Fritz, II:238
Löwy, Heinrich. *See* Rietsch, Heinrich
Löwy, Isak, I:486
Löwy, Josef, I:88; III:37
Löwy, Ludwig, I:402, 433
Löwy, Max, II:200
Löwy, Mizzi, II:38
Löwy, Moritz, II:137
Löwy, Paul, II:213, 239
Löwy, Robert, I:401
Löwy, Rudolph, I:401
Lubacz, Georg, II:587
Lucas, Franz, III:300
Ludin, Hans Elard, III:239, 251, 253, 255
Lueger, Karl, III:182
Lukas, Jan, III:4
Lustig, Arnošt, I:451; III:52, 435
Lustig, Emil, I:363
Lustig, Otto, I:542
Lustig, Rudolf, I:392
Lysický, Karel, III:564

Macartney, Carlile Aylmer, I:119, 124
MacDonald, James, II:568
MacDonald, Ramsay, II:83
MacMichael, Sir Harold, II:615; III:358, 359
Mach, Alexander (Šaňo), I:109, 112, 113, 117; III:174, 182, 190, 191, 192, 197, 206, 217, 256, 304, 307, 309, 313, 325
Mácha, Karel Hynek, I:445, 457

Macháček, Vincenc, II:201
Machado, Gerardo, I:385
Machar, Josef Svatopluk, I:464
Mache, Heinrich, I:371
Machek, Antonín, III:574
Mack, Julian, I:174, 228
Mackenzie, Compton, III:473
Maclay (British diplomat), III:8
Maglione, Luigi, III:183, 239
Mahé de Labourdonnais, François, II:661
Mahler (medical officer at Bronowice), III:434
Mahler, Gustav, I:2, 58, 480, 492, 508, 540, 546, 550, 552, 554-56; II:443, 465
Mahler-Gropius, Alma (Mahler-Werfel, Alma), I:492
Mahrer, Pavel, II:198
Mahtzit Ha Shekel. *See* Kolin, Rabbi Shmuel HaLevi
Maillol, Artistide, II:504
Maimonides (Moses ben Maimon), I:316
Maisel, Mordecai, II:440, 545. *See also* Meisel, Mordecai
Maisky, Ivan Mihailovič, II:572; III:389, 483
Majer, Václav, III:375
Majerová Marie, I:464
MaHaral miPrag. *See* Löw ben Bezalel, Rabbi Judah
Maláč, Oldřich, III:335
Malcolm, Sir Neill, II:568, 572; III:7
Malý, František, II:506
Malypetr, Jan, II:269
Mammer, Oskar, I:525
Mandelík, Robert, I:363, 384, 386
Mandelstamm, Max, II:186
Mandl, Bernát, I:81
Mandl, Josef, II:108, 215
Mandl, Moritz, I:411; II:79
Mandl, Richard, I:546
Mandler, Robert, III:33
Maneš, Antonin, II:472
Mánes, Josef, II:472-74
Manet, Edouard, II:478
Mangiagalli, Ricardo Pick. *See* Pick-Mangiagalli, Ricardo
Mann, Heinrich, II:363
Mann, Thomas, I:483, 500; II:463
Mannaberg, Richard, I:375

Mannheimer, Georg, I:370
Mansoor, M. (professor at University of Wisconsin), II:9
Mařatka, Josef, II:483
Marburg, Julius, I:421
Marek, Jan, III:65
Margolius, Josef, III:385
Margolius, Ota, II:223
Margulies, Emil, I:98, 120, 132, 274, 297, 325; II:34, 35, 53, 54, 57, 144, 177, 183, 273, 283-85, 288, 290, 292, 293, 296
Maria Theresa, Empress, I:534; III:108
Markl, Joseph, I:543
Markus, Vítězslav, I:524; II:272
Mark, Arnold, II:586
Marold, Luděk, II:477
Marshall, Louis, I:174, 228
Martínek, Karel, I:437
Martinů, Bohuslav, I:552
Martius (German owner of aircraft repair shop), I:406
März (Meretz), Paul, II:35, 37, 38, 40, 206, 268, 272, 278, 284, 293, 301, 306, 576; III:12
Masaryk, Jan, I:92, 264, 561; III:16, 31, 40, 41, 62, 65, 372, 389, 397, 451, 452, 454, 456, 459, 460, 467, 469, 470, 471, 478, 479, 481, 482, 483, 485, 491, 492, 494, 495, 507, 510, 511, 518, 520, 524, 544, 554, 555, 556, 557, 558, 562
Masaryk, Tomáš G., I:17, 20, 32, 37, 45, 67, 78, 86, 88, 94, 108, 111, 144, 149, 152, 158, 163-68, 175, 177, 222, 224, 229, 231, 243-45, 247, 248, 252, 254, 264, 312, 319, 324, 443, 448; II:64, 152, 180, 243, 257, 259, 263-65, 299, 352, 409, 416, 454, 463, 466, 487, 584, 588, 628; III:4, 9, 18, 454, 459, 473, 474, 481, 482, 551
Masereel, Franz, II:505
Mastný, Vojtěch, III:66
Matejov, Jur Kora, III:548
Matisse, Henri, II:481, 514
Maugham, William Somerset, I:499
Maupassant, Guy de, I:502
Mauthner, Fritz, I:57, 476, 477, 510, 513, 522
Mauthner, Viktor, II:188, 189, 193
Mauthnerová, Klára, II:188
Mautner, Erich, III:406

NAME INDEX

Mautner, Ervín, II:201
Mautner, Isaak, I:410
Mautner, Isidor, I:410
Mautner, Paul, I:396
May, Julius, I:394
Mayer, Carl, I:500
Mayer, Leo, III:577
Mayer, Sally, III:222, 234
Mayer, Samuel, II:247
Mayer, Zdeněk, I:408; II:216
Mechner, Miriam, II:142
Medek, Rudolf, I:462, 463
Medina, Sir Salomon de, II:3, 8
Mednýanszky, Lászlo, II:498
Medrický, Gejza, III:210
Mehlo, Karl, I:418
Mehring, Walter, II:479
Meier, Gustav, III:404, 442, 444
Meir Ba'al HaNes, II:379
Meisel, Mordecai, I:1. *See also* Maisel, Mordecai
Meisel-Hess, Grete, I:479, 511, 515
Meisels, Ahron Dov, I:537
Meisl, Josef, I:398
Meisler, Arnošt, I:420
Meissner, Alfred, I:152; II:246, 291; III:151, 472
Meissner, Hugo, I:69, 328
Meissner, Ludwig, II:37, 40
Melba, Nellie, I:503
Mello, Francisco Manuel de, I:185
Menachem bar Isaac, III:581
Mendele Mocher Seforim, I:486
Mendelssohn, Felix, I:553
Medelssohn, Moses, II:151
Mendl, Bedřich, I:6
Mendl, Rudolf, I:366, 396, 400, 427
Mengele, Josef, III:296, 298, 299, 300
Mengs, Raphael, II:471, 473
Menkart, Rudolf, I:418
Mere, Erwin, III:279
Meretz, Paul. *See* März, Paul
Mermelstein-Mašek, Alexander, III:405, 411, 412, 422, 442, 444
Merory, Alfred, I:404
Merten, Felix, I:366
Messinger, Jiří (Juraj), II:209
Messingerová, Elsa, II:209
Mestel, Jacob, II:553
Metternich, Clemens Wenzel Nepomuk Lothar, Prince, I:24, 473, 508
Meyer, Peter, III:74

Meyer, Stefan, I:371
Meyers (Catholic Bishop of London), III:465
Meyrink, Gustav, I:9; II:587
Michaels, Netti, II:167
Michel-Pressburger, Simon, II:379
Mičura, Martin, I:92
Mikuš, Jozef A., I:117, 124; III:307, 548
Mikus, Rudolf, III:254
Milen, Imrich Mueller. *See* Mueller-Milen, Imrich
Millo (Pacovský), Yosef, III:562
Minski, Jakob, II:40
Miroslav, B. (Neumann), III:351, 376
Mises, Ludwig von, I:406
Miškej, Dezider, III:444
Mittelhauser, Eugéne Désiré Antoine, I:92
Mochse, Ernst, III:127, 139, 140, 147
Moissi, Alexander, I:478
Molcho, Solomon, III:573, 575
Montgomery, Field Marshal Bernard L., III:368, 384
Montherlant, Henri de, I:483
Moody, J.M. (British colonial official), II:621
Moravčík, Vladimír, III:210
Morávek, Augustin, III:32, 190, 205, 208, 305, 306
Morawetz, Bohumil, I:365
Morawetz, Oskar, I:549
Morawetz, Richard, I:413, 435
Mordowic, Czeslaw, III:318, 326
Mordowicz, Betsalel, III:248
Moretsky, Lothar, I:398
Morgenstern, Jakob, II:82
Morley (diplomat), I:175
Morpurgo, Edgaro, I:367
Moscheles, Ignaz, I:539, 553
Moscicki, Ignacy, III:337
Moskowits, Moses, III:66, 68
Motzkin, Leo, I:218, 221, 245, 248, 254, 262; II:94
Mozart, Wolfgang Amadeus, I:542, 553, 557
Mrštík, Alois, I:463
Mrštík, Vilém, I:463
Mucha, Jiří, I:465
Müller, Filip, III:147, 311
Mueller, S. (medical officer), III:380
Mueller-Milen, Imrich, III:230, 231

Müller, Antonín, II:474
Müller, Eduard H., I:413
Müller, Emil, I:38
Müller, Filip, III:324
Müller, Henrik, I:101
Müller, Josef, II:285; III:408, 444
Müller, Leo, I:414
Müller, M. (editor of *Israelitisches Familienblatt*), I:528
Müller, Max, II:238
Müller, Moshe Itzhak, I:94; II:97, 98
Müller-Einigen, Hans, I:471
Munch, Edward, II:481-83, 487
Muneles, Otto, I:11, 71, 260, 356, 521, 534; III:515
Munk, Adolf, I:81
Munk, Erich, II:182, III:147
Munk, Julius, II:40
Munk, Max, II:284
Munk, Michael, I:430
Munk, Philip, II:54
Munkácsy, Mihaly, II:499, 500, 501
Münzer, Jan, II:151
Münzer, Thomas, I:499
Münzer, Zdenka, I:8, 352, 563; III:10, 575, 581
Murger, Henri, I:477
Murmelstein, Benjamin, III:39, 119, 135, 141, 142, 143, 145, 148
Musil, Mila, II:38
Mussolini, Benito, III:37
Mussy, Marie, III:142
Mužík, A.E., I:460
Muzika, František, II:488

Nageler, Viktor, III:305
Namier, Lewis M., III:451, 460, 478, 487, 494
Naor, Uri, I:242, 525, 527; II:73, 75, 76; III:564
Nath, Egon, II:239
Narzissenfeld (in HeHalutz underground), III:74
Nathan, Ludwig, II:585
Natonek, Hans, I:500, 511, 519
Naumann, Bernd, III:325
Navrátil, Josef, II:471, 473
Neame (General, British commander in the Middle East), III:359
Nebeský, Václav Bolemír, I:457, 458; II:486
Nĕcas, Jaromír, I:133; II:292, 311

Nejedlý, Zdenĕk, I:54; III:396, 417
Nĕmec, Pavel, III:230, 253
Neményi, Geza, II:214
Nemes, Albert, I:89
Nemeš, Andrej, II:488, 512, 513
Neruda, Jan, I: 458-60; II:473
Nettl, Paul, I:7, 342, 353, 480, 559, 560
Neubauer, Adolph, I:81
Neubauer, Oskar, I:408
Neuburg, Bedřich, I:419
Neuer, Marko, III:342, 420
Neuern, Robert, I:398
Neuhaus, Rabbi Leopold, III:149
Neuman, Abraham A., II:9
Neuman, Gustav, I:365
Neumann, Angelo, I:541, 542, 546, 555
Neumann, Arnošt, III:35
Neumann, Emil, I:88, 89; II:37
Neumann, Ernst, II:82
Neumann, Ervin, II:153
Neumann, Franz Josef, I:534
Neumann, Gabriel, I:366
Neumann, Hrádek, I:410
Neumann, Karl Josef, I:534
Neumann, Oskar (Jirmejahu), I:96, 101, 102, 115, 117, 118, 528; II:40, 73, 175, 273, 283, 305; III:31, 171, 185, 205, 245, 326, 327, 533
Neumann, Robert, I:477
Neumann, Samuel, II:428
Neumark, Paul, I:413
Neumarkt, Johannes von, I:469
Neurath, Konstantin von, III:29, 20, 77
Neusser, Eduard, I:372
Neuwirt, Rudolf, I:368
Neuwirth (official of Prague Jewish Religious Congregation), III:45, 71
Neuwirth, Sigmund, II:285
Nevan, Eugene, II:512-14
Nezval, Vítĕzslav, II:486
Nielsen, Carl, I:507, 551
Nietzsche, Friedrich Wilhelm, I:58, 443, 475; II:463
Noda BiYehuda. *See* Landau, Rabbi Ezechiel
Nordau, Max, I:17, 535; II:15, 186
Nosek, Bedřich, III:582
Novák, Arne, I:443, 451, 452, 455, 467
Novák, Cyril, III:337, 421
Novák, Josef, I:407
Nowak, Willi, II:481, 482, 488, 490, 513; III:127

NAME INDEX

Nuntius, pseud, of Fürnberg, Louis, I:497, 512, 517
Nussbaum, Leo, I:527

Oberländer, Max, I:414
Obernik, Grete, II:138, 141
Oesterreicher, Alois, I:404
Oesterreicher, Ignaz. *See* Rakous, Vojtěch
Ofner, Josef, I:428
Ohrenstein, Jiří. *See* Orten, Jiří
Olbracht, Ivan, I:154, 450, 464
Oliner, Isaac, I:340
Oliner, Max, II:91
Oplatek, Ervin, I:403
Oppenheim, David, I:2; II:440; III:574, 580
Orenstein (manager of leather factory), I:419
Orlik, Emil, II:476, 478, 479
Orten (Ohrenstein), Jiří (Jakub, Jiří), I;445, 452, 455; II:153; III:16, 43
Ostrovský, Řehoř, I:408
Osuský, Stefan, III:343, 450
Otten, Karl, I:494, 522

Pačenovský, Samo, II:214
Pačová, Mila, II:488
Pacovský, Otokar, II:178
Pacovský, Richard, II:188, 189, 193
Paderewski, Ignácy Jan, I:185, 229, 251; III:454
Padrta, Jiří, II:485
Pál, László, II:501
Palacký, František, I:16, 44
Palkovits, Leopold, II:309
Pam, Richard, I:393
Pam, Theodor, I:393
Pappenheim, Bertha, II:140
Pappenheim, Isidor, II:162, 164
Parisek, Eugene, I:426
Parkus, Anny, II:142
Parkus, František, III:24
Pasák, Tomáš, III:63, 64, 65
Pascheles, Jacob, I:39, 45
Pascheles, Wolf (Zeev), I:341, 533; II:472
Patton, General George S., III:384
Patz, Rabbi Norman R., III:xi
Pauco, J., III:256
Paul, Jean, I:447
Pearlman, Morris, III:528

Pečúch, Julius, III:189
Pehle, John W., III:318
Pekárek, Rudolf, I:545
Pelleg, Frank, II:239
Penížek, Josef, I:370, 523
Pereira, Emil, I:427
Pereira, Isaac, I:427
Pereira, Jacob, I:427
Pereles, Ignác Josef, II:469, 474
Peretz, Y.L., I:449, 480, 486, 533
Perlsticker, Solomon, III:583
Perlzweig, Maurice, III:491, 492
Peroutka, Ferdinand, II:315, 465; III:424, 446
Perutz, Artur, II:215
Perutz, Benedikt, I:411
Perutz, Felix, I:415
Perutz, Hans, I:411
Perutz, Hugo, I:9; II:215
Perutz, Leo, I:411, 497, 498, 518; II:587
Perutz, Paul, I:411
Perutz, Regina, I:411
Perutz, Siegmund, I:411
Pétain, Marshal Henri, III:353
Petenyi, Lea, II:167
Petr (Major, Czechoslovak intelligence officer), III:361
Petr Vok of Rožmberk, I:553
Petránek-Ackermann, H. (Communist leader), III:397
Petrželka, Vilém, I:548
Petschau, Vilda, II:204
Petschek, Eva, I:374
Petschek family, III:26
Petschek, Frank, I:437
Petschek, Friedrich, I:366
Petschek, Hans, I:366, 374
Petschek, Ignatz, I:374
Petschek, Ina-Louise, I:374
Petschek, Isidor, I:374
Petschek, Janina, I;437
Petschek, Julius, I:366, 374, 375, 393
Petschek, Martha, I:374
Petschek, Otto, I:366, 374
Petschek, Paul, I:366
Petschek, Rita, I:374
Petschek, Viktor, I:374, 433
Petschek, Walter, I:366, 375
Pfeffer, Oskar, I:383, 388
Pfefferkorn, Josef, I:414
Pfefferkorn, Richard, I:414

Pfeiffer, Josef, I:376
Picasso, Pablo, II:480, 484, 487
Piccart, J.B., II:471
Pichon, Stephan J., I:218
Pick family, III:96
Pick, Frank, I:369, 432
Pick, Hugo, II:37, 40, 175
Pick, Ignaz, II:236, 237
Pick, Jiří, I:451
Pick, Josef C., I:viii, xii, xviii, xix, 37, 65, 76, 122, 126, 153, 205, 294, 316, 359, 560; II:185 ff.; III:iv, x, xiv, 68
Pick, Karel, I:359
Pick, Oskar, I:359, 432
Pick, Otto, I:421, 482, 483, 490, 511, 516
Pick, Rudolf, I:404, 421
Pick, Vilém, I:380
Pick-Mangiagalli, Ricardo, I:541
Pik (mayor of Plzeň), III:21
Pika, Heliodor, III:338, 340, 389, 392, 440
Piloty, Karl, II:499
Pines (historian), I:486
Pinkas, Soběslav, II:473
Pinsker, Leo, I:535
Pinski, David, II:557
Piowati, Rudolf, II:208, 209
Pirner, Maximilian, II:476, 477
Pisko, Heinrich, I:413
Pittermann, Artur. *See* Longen, Artur
Plaček, Karel (Porath, David), III:348, 435, 438
Plamínková, Františka, II:147; III:20, 66
Pleschner, Max, I:524
Poche, Emanuel, II:523, 525
Podiebrad, D.J. (custodian of Prague Jewish cemetery), II:522, 541
Pol, Heinz, II:585
Poláček, Karel, I:446, 447, 452, 464, 465, 523; II:151, 465; III:16, 64, 124
Polach, Johann, II:250
Polak, Arthur, II:81
Polak, Filip, III:24
Polák, František, II:203; III:396, 440
Polák, Heřman, I:403
Polák, Irma, I:142, 526; II:40, 308; III:562
Polák, Josef, I:465; II:489, 502; III:53, 64, 569, 571, 572, 575, 576
Polanecký (airplane constructor), I:405
Polertová-Letenská, Anna, III:17
Polgar, Alfred, I:510
Politzer family, III:96
Polk, Frank, I:176
Pollak, A. (air force gunner), III:387
Pollak, Adolf, I:344; II:267
Pollak, Egon, I:542
Pollak, Ernst, I:486; II:76
Pollak, Frank, I:545
Pollak, František, III:439
Pollak, H. (air force gunner), III:387
Pollak, Heřman, I:411
Pollak, Hilda, II:476
Pollak, Josef, I:416, 527
Pollak, Leopold, II:103, 104, 472, 473
Pollak, Otto, II:182
Pollak, Richard, I:472; II:476, 477; III:351, 435
Pollak, Rudolf, II:40, 239
Pomerantz, Sam, III:561
Popper, Egon, III:147
Popper, Georg, I:366
Popper, Joseph, I:312, 313, 316; II:231, 395, 397
Popper, Viktor, I:552
Popper-Lynkeus, Josef, I:57; II:215, 445
Porath, David. *See* Plaček, Karel
Porges, Ignác Josef, II:472
Porzsolt, Aladár, II:233
Posin, Max, II:205
Pospíšil, František, II:634
Pospíšilová, Marie, III:65
Posta, Dr. (Olympic champion), II:214
Pösténýi, Štefan, III:194
Pót, Bertalan, II:501
Potochownik, Daniel, II:40
Pozděch, Augustin, III:227, 252
Pravda, František, I:463, 464
Prchala, Lev, III:333, 337, 338
Prečan, Vilém, III:544
Preisová, Gabriela, II:521, 523, 535, 538, 540, 546
Presser, Laco, III:407, 420
Přikryl, Vladimír, III:378, 410, 444
Prinz, Rabbi Joachim, II:154
Prisament, Shelomo, II:553
Prokeš, J., II:542
Propper, Josef, I:375
Prossnitz, Heinz, II:49, 50, 73
Prostějovský, Joachim, II:544
Proust, Marcel, I:441

NAME INDEX 641

Pružinský, Mikuláš, III:209
Purkyně, Karel, II:473, 474

Rabiner (Sergeant), III:408
Rabinowicz, Aharon Moshe, I:90, 120, 134, 138, 142, 145, 146, 155, 273, 280, 328, 333, 336, 505, 560; III:488, 545
Rabinowicz, Oskar K., I:20, 47, 71, 78, 94, 137, 141, 258, 269, 270, 273, 333, 471, 527; II:1, 5, 103-05, 107; III:9
Rabinowicz, Mrs. Oskar K., II:105
Rabinowitch, Shalom. *See* Sholem Aleichem
Rabinowitz, Alexander, II:105
Rachvalský, Ludvík, I:415
Rada, Vlastimil, III:16
Rademacher, Franz, III:246
Radimský, Ladislav. *See* Den, Petr
Rádl, Emanuel, II:465
Rado, Kurt, II:209
Rafael, Felix, I:400, II:207
Rahm, Karel, III:37, 45, 127, 136, 138, 139, 140, 142, 143, 150, 151, 571, 572, 575
Raimund, Ferdinand, I:474
Rákoczi, Franz, II:1, 82
Rakous, Vojtěch, pseudonym of Oesterreicher, Ignaz, I:439, 464, 465
Rapaport, Salomon Juda, I:52, 70; II:440, 472; III:574, 581
Rašín, Alois, I:362, 438; III:11
Rašín, Ladislav, III:11
Rathenau, Walter, I:402
Raudnitzki, Rudolf, II:180, 236, 237
Rauscher, George, II:508, 509
Ravasz, Viktor, III:194
Reach, Julius, I:71, 338
Reachová, Valerie, I:329
Rebenfeld family, I:418
Rechtmann, Moses, I:81
Redisch, Hugo, III:400
Redlich, Felix, I:386, 428
Redlich, Friedrich, I:413
Redlich, Harry, I:428
Redlich, Kurt, I:428
Redlich, Ludvík, I:428
Redlich, Otto, I:428
Redlich, Viktor, I:428
Reger, Max, I:478, 540, 541, 546
Reich, Mrs. (active in aviation), II:217
Reich, Adolf, I:404

Reich, Moritz, I:474, 510
Reich, Chief Rabbi S. (Vrbové), II:166
Reichel, Erža, II:217; III:583
Reichenbaum, E. (student Zionist leader), II:182
Reichental, Adolf, I:89, II:262, 263
Reicher, Ernst, II:386
Reichl (Lieutenant), III:403, 411, 420
Reichmann, Erich, II:202
Reicin, Bedřich, III:397, 406, 434, 441, 442
Reiner, Arnošt, II:210
Reiner, J., Lieutenant, III:417
Reiner, Karel, I:548, 558; II:23; III:43
Reiner, Maxim, I:295, 312
Reiner, Pavel, II:210
Reiner (Alexander), Stefan, II:515
Reiner, Vilém, I:398
Reines, Rabbi of Lida, II:95
Reinhardt, Max, I:118, 480, 493; II:478
Reinhart, Harold F., Rabbi, III:586, 588
Reininger, Hugo, I:417
Reiss, Jacob, II:40, 82, 86, 87, 94; III:411
Reiss, Max, I:397
Reiss, Rafael, III:231, 232
Reisz, Julius, I:102, 104, 107, 136, 202; II:272, 278, 280, 283, 284, 287, 289, 292, 297, 304, 312; III:251
Reizen, Abraham, I:449
Reizes, Hans, I:427
Rejt, Benedikt, III:577
Renner, Karl, II:23
Resek, Felix, II:76
Reubeni, David, I:507
Reubeni, Meir. *See* Färber, Meir Marcel
Reuchlin, Johannes, I:509
Révai, Leo, I:82
Révai, Mór, I:82
Révai, Ödön, I:82
Révai, Samuel, I:82
Reventlow, Count (Nazi leader), II:461
Řezáč, Václav, I:465
Rezek (Rebenwurzel), Hanuš, III:367, 380, 381, 425, 438, 513
Ribbentrop, Joachim von, III:173, 219, 307, 371
Richter, H. (engineer in restoration of Pinkas synagogue), III:575, 577

Rieger, František Ladislav, I:44; III:580
Riesenfeld, Bedřich, I:415
Riesenfeld, Oskar, I:415
Rietsch, Heinrich, pseud. of Löwy, Heinrich, I:550, 551
Řiháček, Petri, III:65
Řiháček, Thomas, III:65
Rilke, Rainer Maria, I:445, 468, 478, 482, 510
Rindler family, III:96
Rindskopf, Heinrich, I:419
Ring, Theodor, I:426
Ripka, Hubert, III:61, 469, 470, 471, 482, 491
Rippl-Rónai, József, II:501
Roberts, Frank, III:487, 488
Robětín, Herbert Fuchs, I:393
Robětín, Karel (Fuchs), I:393; II:212
Robinson, Armin, I:493
Robinson, Jacob I:257, 264
Roda Roda, II:587
Roedl, Urban. *See* Adler, Bruno
Röhling, August, I:17, 44, 67
Rohrer, Rudolf, M., I:536
Rokach, Ignatz, II:74, 82
Rokeah (Rokeach), Yissakhar Dov, Rabbi of Belz I:274, 308; II:358
Rokotnitz, Samuel, II:54
Rokycana, Jaroslav, I:352
Rolland, Romain, I:476, 483
Rommel, General Erwin, III:363, 364, 365
Roncalli, Angelo, Papal Nuncio (Pope John XXIII), III:313
Roosevelt, Franklin Delano, III:473
Rosenbach, Auguste, II:139
Rosenbaum (Jewish cadet), III:394
Rosenbaum, Jan. *See* Skala, Jan
Rosenbaum, Karl, II:164, 169
Rosenbaum, Michael, II:139
Rosenberg (artilleryman), III:408
Rosenberg, L. (student Zionist leader), II:175
Rosenberg, Jitzhak, I:117; II:79
Rosenberg, Shalom, I:529
Rosenberg, Walter, III:317, 318. *See also* Vrba, Rudolf
Rosenblatt, Adolf, I:398
Rosenfeld, Milton, III:591
Rosenfeld, Morris, I:533
Rosenheim, Jacob, II:164

Rosenkranz, Samuel, II:73
Rosenthal, Josef, III:410, 413
Rosenthal, Marc, III:23
Rosenzweig, E. (Lieutenant), III:417
Rosenzweig, Ladislav, I:118; III:251, 405
Rosh. *See* Reichenbaum, E.
Rosin, Arnošt, III:309
Rössner, Karl, I:406
Roth, Cecil, II:9
Roth, Chaja, III:74
Roth, Emanuel, I:392, 414, 426
Roth, Eugen, II:40
Roth, Hugo, II:465
Rothermere, Harold Sidney Harmsworth, 1st Viscount, I:99, 139
Rothkirchen, Livia, I:72, 167, 260, 273, 308, 325, 333, 560; II:577; III:10, 13, 63, 65, 67, 105, 202, 248, 323, 326, 327, 435, 455, 488, 489, 490, 543, 544
Rothschild, Albert, Baron, I:361
Rothschild family, II:26
Rothschild, Salomon, Baron, I:427
Roubitschek, Erwin, II:235, 236
Roubitschek, Sofie, II:137
Roudnicky, Rudolf, I:408
Rowohlt, Ernst, I:489
Rozsypal, Antonín, I:148; II:272
Rubens, Peter Paul, I:499
Rubinstein, Bruno, I:375
Rudel, S., Adler. *See* Adler-Rudel, Salomon
Rudinger, Josef, III:386, 387, 388, 439
Rudnay, Gyula, II:508
Rudolf II, Emperor, I:498
Rufeisen, Josef, II:35-38, 40, 46, 49, 50, 63, 256, 259, 268, 273, 302
Rumkowski, Mordechai Chaim, III:270, 271
Runciman, Lord Walter, Viscount of Doxford, III:5
Ruth, František, II:542
Rutkowski, Adam, III:248
Růžička, Max, II:235, 236
Růžička, Otokar, I: 316, 438
Rychnovský, Ernst, I:351; III:62

Sabina, Karel, I:508
Sacher-Masoch, Arthur Wolfgang, I:533
Sachs, Curt, I:549
Sachs, Leopold, I:373

NAME INDEX

Sachs, Michael, I:2, 341
Sachsel, Joseph, I:392
Šachta, Šimon, III:414, 421, 444, 445, 565
Šáda, Miroslav, III:417, 445
Sadek, Vladimír, III:581, 582
Sagan, Leontine, I:481
Sager (official in Reich Ministry of Labor), III:190
Sahl, Hans, II:587
Šalda, F.X., II:151, 481, 567; III:6, 10
Šalomon, Alexander, II:214
Salomonski, Martin, III:149
Salus, Hugo, I:461, 477, 482, 510, 514
Salzer, Imre, II:213, 285
Samek (airplane constructor), I:405
Samet (Czechoslovak army in exile), III:390
Sametz, Siegmund, I:87, 88; II:37
Samstag, Erwin, II:608
Samuel, Sir Herbert (later 1st Viscount Samuel), II:100, 261
Sandel, Max, III:404
Saphir, Dr. (leader in Jewish party), II:291
Saphir, M.G. (20th century author), I:533
Saphir, Milka, II:141
Saudek, Robert, I:480, 511, 515
Saudek, Rudolf, II:485
Sax, Hugo, III:16
Saxl, (manager of fez factory), I:418
Sázavský, Josef, III:419, 422
Sborowitz, Fritz (Bedřich), II:107, 108, 284; III:344
Sborowitz, Gustav, I:417
Sborowitz, Max, I:418
Scarpi, N.O., pseud. of Bondy, Fritz, I:501, 502, 511, 519
Schachter, Eliezer, II:87
Schachter, Raffael, I:556, 557
Schalk, Joseph, I:543
Schalková, Malvina, III:128
Schapiro, Rabbi Haim Eleazar. See Spira, Chaim Eleazar
Schenierer, Sarah, II:165, 167, 370
Scheuer, Miriam, II:143
Schick, Georg, I:542, 545; II:586
Schick, K. (Jewish volunteer in Czech forces from Shanghai), III:387, 388
Schick, Leopold, II:353
Schick, Martha, II:141

Schick, Mosche, II:359
Schidloff (tennis), II:211
Schiele, Egon, II:503
Schikaneder, Jakob, II:475
Schiller, Friedrich von, I:55
Schiller, Géjza, II:504
Schiller, Moritz, I:413
Schillinger, Samuel, II:198
Schimmerling, Hans, I:548, 549
Schindelmann, Marek, II:54
Schindler, Alexander (exporter of malt), I:382
Schindler, Ewald, II:586
Schipper, Pavel, II:205
Schkim, Otto, II:73
Schlamm, Willi, II:586
Schlesinger (student Zionist leader), I:182
Schlesinger, Gisela, II:217
Schlesinger, Max, I:378
Schlesinger, O. (medical officer), III:380
Schlesinger, Richard, I:88; II:37
Schliesser, Gora, II:91
Schliesser, Karel, III:139, 147
Schmal, Adolf, I:413
Schmeichler, Theodor, I:418
Schmerler, Siegmund, II:38, 40
Schmerling, Anton von, I:47, 68
Schmerling, Herbert, III:68
Schmitz, Siegfried, II:38, 50
Schmolka (Šmolka), Arnošt, I:398
Schmolka, František, I:417
Schmolka, Marie, I:112; II:143-45, 147, 299, 397, 567, 570, 573, 574, 583; III:6, 7, 8, 9, 19, 20, 40, 61, 62
Schmolka, Pavel, I:417, 427
Schnaase, K. (art historian), II:523
Schnabel, Arthur, I:554
Schnabel, Bertha, II:142
Schnabel, Oskar, II:203
Schnabel, Richard, I:408
Schneider, Hugo, III:271
Schnitzer (fighter pilot), III:387, 388
Schnitzler, Leopold, II:66, 67
Schoen (physician at Bronowice), III:434
Schön, Frank, III:386
Schön, Ignatz, II:54
Schön, Josef, I:35, 356, 426
Schön, Moritz, I:368
Schön, Vojtěch, III:130
Schönbaum, Emil, I:368

Schönberg, Arnold, I:542, 547, 550, 552
Schönerer, Georg Ritter von, I:18, 44, 67, 68
Schönfeld, Isák Jeiteles, II:472
Schoengut, (artillery battery commander), III: 406, 413
Schorsch, Gustav, III: 124, 125, 149
Schotky, J.M. (German topographer), II:522
Schreiber, Adolf, I:507, 551
Schreiber, Rabbi Akiba, II:161, 164, 165, 168, 368, 370, 379
Schreiber, Rabbi Moses (Hatham Sofer), I:537; II:353, 367, 374, 376. *See also* Sofer, Moses
Schreiber, Samuel, II:353
Schreiber, Rabbi Simche Bunem, II:368
Schreier (leader in Jewish party), II:210
Schreker, Franz, I:549, 556
Schubert, Franz, I:480, 552
Schück, Arnold, I:390
Schück, Ignát, I:408
Schulhof, Erwin, I:544, 546, 547
Schulhoff, Julius, I:546, 553
Schuller, Hugo, II:204, 256
Schuller, Julius, II:238
Schultz, František, II:209, 210
Schulz, Ferdinand, I:463
Schulz, Ignac, I:109; II:247
Schulz, Karel, I:370, 427
Schulz, Ladislav, III:343
Schumert, Menachem, II:641
Schünemann, Georg, I:549
Schur, Isaac, I:411
Schürer, Oskar, II:525
Schuschny, Ernst, II:79
Schütz, Otto, I:viii
Schwadron, Abraham, I:535
Schwalb, Nathan, II:609; III:50
Schwartz, Abraham Jehuda Hakohen, I:536
Schwartz, Ada, I:557
Schwartz, Emanuel, I:331
Schwartz, Jacob, II:164
Schwarz (Sergeant), III:378
Schwarz, A. (deputy chief medical officer), III:380
Schwarz, Arnošt, I:426
Schwarz, Benjamin, I:382
Schwarz, Edvard, I:365, 405, 427
Schwarz, Eugene, I:365
Schwarz, Isaiah, III:350, 374

Schwarz, Kurt, I:370
Schwarz, Willy, II:182
Schwarzbard, Ignacy, II:46, 49
Schwarzhuber, Hans, III:295, 296, 297, 298, 300
Scotus Viator. *See* Seton-Watson, Robert William
Šedivý, František, III:65
Sedloň, Jan, III:65
Segal, Arnold, I:375
Seegen, David, II:185
Seegen, Josef, I:378, 379
Seidemann, Arnold, I:398
Seidemann, Felix, II:37
Seidl, Siegfried, III:110, 132
Seidlitz, Julius, pseud. of Jeiteles, Itzig, I:473, 510, 512; II:473, 474
Seidner, Emil, I:417
Seliger, Josef, II:249
Šenšel, Ludevít, II:311
Sereny, Gitta, III:290, 324
Serenyi, Otto, I:428
Serkin, Rudolf, I:554
Seton-Watson, Robert William, I:78, 83, 118, 120, 121, 123, 124
Seydewitz, Max, II:585
Seyss-Inquart, Arthur, I:113
Sforza, Ludovico, I:498
Shabtai ben Meir Hakohen, I:350
Shaffer, Mrs. G.R. (Ruth), III:586, 587, 588
Shapira, M.W. (Deuteronomy forgery), II:9
Shapiro, Rabbi Chaim Eleazar. *See* Spira, Rabbi Chaim Eleazar
Shapiro, Rabbi Eliezer. *See* Spira, Rabbi Chaim Eleazar
Sharett, Moshe. *See* Shertok, Moshe
Shek, Zeev, III:562
Shertok, Moshe, II:637; III:357, 359, 469, 478, 479, 486, 494
Shragai, Shlomo Zalman, III:486
Sholem Aleichem, pseud. of Rabinowitch, Shalom, I:449, 489
Sicher, Gustav, I:310, 339, 344; III:514, 562
Sicher, Hanuš, II:209
Sidor, Karol, I:109, 111, 114; III:183, 210, 255
Siegwart, Hermann, I:397
Šigut, Miroslav, II:345, 439; III:388, 435

Sihoti, Malej, II:217
Silberstein, I. (silk manufacturer) I:415
Silbiger (machine-gunner), III:400
Silver, Rabbi Abba Hillel, II:639
Silverman, Sydney S., III:451, 453, 454, 462, 474, 482, 488, 489
Siman (intelligence staff captain), III:356
Simeles, Egon, II:201
Simkovič, Benjamin, III:248
Simon, André (Katz, Otto), II:586
Simon, Josef, I:428
Simpson, Sir John Hope, II:571, 575
Simpson, John R., I:385
Singer, Erica, II:211
Singer, Friedrich, III:211
Singer, Georg, I:542, 545
Singer, Ludvík (Ludwig), I:7, 88, 91, 102, 104, 117, 132, 136, 149, 157-59, 167, 170, 172, 173, 202, 221, 223, 227, 230, 231, 247, 248, 250, 251, 268, 270, 292, 311, 313, 353, 526; II:26, 30, 35, 141, 180, 256-59, 263, 270-76, 280-88, 395
Singer, Mendel, II:86
Singer, Moritz, II:40
Singer, Oscar, III:272
Singer-Berkowitz, Irma, II:141
Singerman, Bruno, I:viii
Singerová, Elsa, II:188
Singerová, Kateřina, III:297, 308, 310
Šipoš, Leo, I:91; II:262, 283, 284
Široký, Viliam, III:545
Sivák, Jozef, I:117; III:191, 209, 248
Skála (Rosenbaum), Jan, III:64
Skokan, Josef, II:200
Škroup, František, I:342, 352
Škroup, Johann Nepomuk, I:342, 352
Skutecký, Dominik, II:498, 499, 500
Skutezký, Hanuš, I:413
Slánský, Rudolf, II:251; III:441, 564
Slatinský, Arthur. See Szalatnay, Arthur
Slavíček, Antonín, II:478
Slávik, Juraj, II:286, 290; III:335, 338, 450, 465, 491
Slezák, A., III:247
Šlik, Count Kašpar, I:433
Slonitz, Hugo, I:157; II:37, 256, 396
Smagon, Albert, III:188
Smetana, Bedřich, I:508, 551, 556, 557
Smetana, Oskar, II:182
Smik, Otto, III:16, 388, 389
Šmolík, Alois, I:406
Šmolka, Arnošt. See Schmolka (Smolka), Arnošt
Smolka, Pavel. See Schmolka, Pavel
Smutný, Jaromír, III:421, 458, 462, 473, 479, 489, 490, 492, 494
Sneh, Moshe, III:486
Šnek, Isidor, III:414, 444
Snow, Edith Abercrombie, I:493
Sobota, Emil, I:254, 259, 264
Sochor, Antonín, III:409, 565
Sofer, Josef, I:350
Sofer, Rabbi Moses, I:80. See also Schreiber, Rabbi Moses
Sofer, Nahum, I:350
Sokol, Koloman, II:502
Sokol, Martin, III:192, 198, 210, 218, 219, 247
Sokol-Tůma, Karel, I:464
Sokolow, Nahum, I:98, 158, 159, 174-77, 231, 243, 250; II:15, 258
Sokolovič, Salamon, II:94
Sole, Aryeh, I:125, 167, 258, 259, 261, 274, 308, 333, 529, 560
Soltész, Josef, III:518
Solzhenitsyn, Alexander, III:342
Somlo, Alexander, I:392
Sommer, Ernst, I:499, 511, 518
Sommer-Herz, Alice, I:544, 557
Sonka, pseud. of Sonnenschein, Hugo, I:496, 511, 517
Sonnenfeld, Hugo, II:238
Sonnenfeld, Karel, II:191, 284
Sonnenfeld, Otto, II:238, 260
Sonnenfeld, Sigmund, I:81
Sonnenmark, Robert, II:40
Sonnenschein, Adolf, I:373, 374
Sonnenschein, Hugo. See Sonka
Soskin, Selig, II:106
Soukup, Antonín, II:31
Soukup, František, I:118; II:31, 257
Šourek, Karel, II:488
Sova, Antonín, I:462
Soyka, František, II:212
Soyka, Fritz, I:414
Špála, Václav, II:481, 482
Spann, A. (journalist), II:586
Spell (Spiegel), Maximilian S., III:iv
Spencer, Charles S., II:485
Spiegel, Alexander, II:36, 105
Spiegel, Emil, I:478, 510, 514

Spiegel, Ignac, III:400, 401
Spiegel, Käthe, I:7
Spiegel, Ludwig, II:248
Spiegel, Yehuda, I:154
Spinoza, Benedictus de (Baruch), I:477
Spira, Rabbi Chaim Eleazer, I:148, 274, 308, 529; II:162, 292, 297, 358, 427, 429, 553
Spira, K. (Private), III:382
Spira, Otto O., III:345, 435
Spira, Rabbi Zevi Elimelech, II:362, 379
Spiro, Emanuel, I:392
Spiro, Ignaz, I:392
Spiro, Israel Frankl, II:541
Spiro, Peter, I:392
Spišiak, Ján, III:220, 251
Spitta, Philip, I:550
Spitz, Arnošt, I:383; II:209
Spitz, Jiří, III:365, 366
Spitz, Julius, I:416
Spitz, Siegfried, II:55, 59, 60
Spitzer, Alexander, I:404
Spitzer, Heinrich, I:62
Spitzer, Karel, I:375
Spitzer, Lemel, II:162
Spitzer, Leo F., I:374
Springer, Gustav, I:418; II:164
Springer, Rabbi Meir Raphael, III:489
Springer, Siegmund, II:79
Sprinzak, Josef, II:58, 59, 63 70, 89, 486
Šrámek, Fráňa, I:483
Srdínko, Otakar, II:31, 257
Šrobár, Várro, I:85, 135, 225, 227; II:260, 264
Stalin, Josef V., III:397, 473, 484
Staněk, Josef, I:467
Stangl, Franz, III:290
Stanley, Oliver, II:632
Stapler, Herrman, II:40
Starck, Johann David, I:374
Stark, Albert, I:92
Starkenstein, Emil, I:397
Stašek, Antal, pseud. of Zeman, Antonin, I:464
Štech, V.V., II:484
Stecklmacher, Fritz, II:107, 108
Štědrý (tennis), II:211
Steed, Sir Henry Wickham, II:13
Stefan, Paul, pseud. of Grünfeld, Paul, I:511, 515, 552

Štefánek, Antonin I:85; II:281
Stein (fez manufacturer), I:418
Stein, Adolf, I:4, 351-53, 357, 427
Stein, August, I:271, 292, 309, 310, 313, 326, 341, 524, 562; II:150, 151, 153; III:580
Stein, Bohumil, II:217, 231
Stein, Erwin, I:550
Stein, František, I:405, 408; II:216
Stein, Gottlieb, I:8
Stein, Günther, I:132
Stein, Josef, I:428; III:370
Stein, Karel, II:179; III:39, 71
Stein, Karel (head of "Section Seven"), III:569, 575, 577
Stein, Mayer, I:81; II:375
Stein, Pavel, III:365
Stein, Viktor, I:307; II:233, 373
Stein, Viktor (Norgine), I:397
Steinberg (Corporal), III:408
Steinberg (2nd Lieutenant), III:413
Steiner, Arnošt, III:377, 400, 408, 409, 420
Steiner, Egon, II:238
Steiner, Ervin, III:221, 247
Steiner, Eugen, III:546
Steiner, Franz Baermann, I:501, 512, 519
Steiner, Hanna, I:525; II:40, 142, 143, 145, 147, 197, 583; III:6, 19, 20, 32, 40, 41, 42, 62
Steiner, Hugo, II:208
Steiner, Ondřej, III:205, 248
Steiner, Pavel (Pali), II:209, 210; III:361, 390
Steiner, Richard, II:175
Steiner, Siegfried, I:152; II:97, 98
Steiner-Prag, Hugo, II:476-78
Steinerova-Kende (Mr. and Mrs., canoeing champions), II:211
Steinhard, Erich, I:544, 551, 552, 558
Steinhauer, Pavel. See Strahovský, Pavel
Steinherz, Samuel, I:6, 7, 357, 527; II:174, 232, 248
Steinschneider, Georg, I:62
Steinschneider, Moritz, I:58, 352, 357; II:543
Steinschneider, Siegmund, I:24
Stemmer, Michael, III:390, 442, 443, 444
Štěpán, Václav, I:544

Štěpánek-Stemmer, Michael, III:414
Stern, Armin, II:514, 517
Stern, Arnošt, I:426
Štern, Egon, II:191, 198
Stern, Evžen, I:369
Stern, Franz, II:208
Stern, Gustav, I:369; II:151
Stern, Josef, I:381
Stern, Karel, III:4
Stern, Leopold, I:393
Stern, Ota, I:419
Stern, Rudolf, I:405
Stern, Viktor, II:251
Sternbach, Wilhelm, II:40, 285, 291, 296
Sternbach, Zeev, I:529
Sternfeld, Wilhelm, II:587
Sternschuss, Siegfried, II:235, 236
Sternthal, Isaac, I:529
Steuer, František, I:389
Stiassny, Karel, I:416
Sticker, Pepi, II:208
Stiedry, Philip, I:373, 428
Stifter, Adalbert, I:490, 503
Stillschweig, Kurt, I:249, 264
Stone, Julius, I:264
Stopford, Robert, T., III:5, 61, 62
Storch, Edmund, I:408
Stöcker, Adolf, I:36
Strahovský (Steinhauer), Pavel, II:608
Stramberger, 2nd Lieutenant, III:408
Stranský, Adolf, II:245
Stránský, Bedřich, I:375
Stŕanský, Rabbi Hugo, I:51, 330, 560; III:11, 456, 489, 541
Stránský, Jakub, II:199
Stránský, Jan, III:17
Stŕanský, Jaroslav, II:245; III:490
Stránský, Josef, I:542
Stránský, Karel, I:408
Stránský, Zikmunt, I:375
Straschnov, Hugo, I:428
Strass, František, III:127, 128, 149
Strasser, Emil, I:377
Strasser, Gregor, II:461
Strasser, Otto, II:585
Strauch, Eduard, III:288
Straucher, Benno, I:156; II:255
Strauss, Emil, II:251, 584
Strauss, Johann, I:555
Strauss, Josef, I:388
Strauss, Ludvík, I:388

Strauss, Salomon, I:426
Streicher, Julius, I:117; III:4
Stříbrný, Jiří, II:31, 257
Stricker, Richard, I:375
Stricker, Robert, I:528; II:22, 106-08, 175
Stricker, Willy, II:108
Strompf, Hynek, III:400, 442
Stroupežnický, Ladislav, I:462
Stuck, Franz von, II:480
Stummer, Karel, I:383
Sturc, Ernest, I:370; III:11
Sturc, Ludovit, I:viii; II:x; III:9, 10
Stutz, Edvard, I:365
Sudermann, Hermann, I:476
Suk, Josef, I:542, 548
Sulzer, Salomon, I:342
Šumandl (Lieutenant), III:372
Sušický, Joshua, I:53, 70, 545
Süss, Eduard, I:372
Süss, Ladislaus, II:93
Susskind, Walter, I:542, 545
Süsskind-Sladek, Felix, III:368
Süssland, Arnŏst, I:405
Švabinský, Max, II:477
Švehla, Antonín, II:31, 257, 269
Švenk, Karel, III:125, 149
Svoboda, F.X. (poet), I:460
Svoboda, Ludvík, III:286, 335, 336, 338, 368, 385, 390, 394, 400, 401, 402, 403, 404, 405, 409, 410, 413, 414, 415, 419, 421, 423, 440, 441, 442, 443, 445, 446, 565
Svozilová, Světla, II:489
Swoboda, Heinrich, I:546
Swoboda, Lisa Frank. *See* Frank-Swoboda, Lisa
Synek, František, II:207
Syrový, Jan, III:8, 28
Szalatnay (Slatinský), Arthur, II:504
Szanto, Simon, I:63
Szell, Georg, I:452; II:586
Szenes, Edmund, II:214
Szerény, Béla, I:101, 528; II:105
Szillard, Frigyes, I:88; II:37
Szmigly, Rydz, III:337
Szobel, Géza, II:509-11
Szoeni, Arthur, I:368
Sztojay, Döme, III:316

Tanzer, Ignaz, I:419
Tänzer, Ivan, II:213

Tanzer, Otto, I:419
Taraba, Dr. (physician at Bronowice), III:333, 338, 339
Tarafa, José Miguel, I:383, 384
Tartakower, Arye, II:93; III:492, 495
Tartakowskij, Boris, III:253
Taub, Siegfried, II:249
Taub, Walter, II:586
Taub, Rabbi Yitzhak (Isaak), II:358
Taube, Carlo, I:557
Tauber, Blanka, II:511, 512, 517
Tauber, Heinz, J., I:117
Tauber, H. (medical officer), III: 380
Tauber, Martha, II:142
Tauber, Moshe, I:525
Taussig, Adolf. See Čech, Adolf
Taussig, Arnošt F., II:207, 212
Taussig, Bedřich. See Fritta, Bedřich
Taussig, Edward David, I:2
Taussig, Elsa, I:508; III:65
Taussig, Friedrich, II:237; III:43
Taussig, George, II:206
Taussig, Hans. See Thomas, Hans
Taussig, Samuel, I:416
Taussing (student Zionist leader), II:180
Tedesco, Amadeus, I:553
Teichmann, Alexander, I:537
Teichner, Sandor, II:238
Teitelbaum, Rabbi Joel (Satmarer Rebbe), II:358
Teller, Prof. (speaker at Brno student Zionist celebration), II:181
Teller, Karl, II:55, 62, 69
Teller, Marcus, I:62
Teller, Max, I:23
Teller, Ota, II:217
Teltsch, Gejza, I:392
Teltscher, Richard, I:312
Teltscher, Rudolf, I:412
Temperky, Harold William Vazielle, I:230, 249, 250, 254, 264
Temple, William, Archbishop of Canterbury, III:468
Tennenwurzel, Chaim, III:221
Tesařík, Richard, III:409
Tetauer, Frank, I:465
Teweles, Heinrich, I:57, 476, 510, 513, 541, 542, 555, 556
Thein, Emil, II:35, 37
Thein, Hans, II:75

Thieberger, Friedrich, I:351, 357, 484, 490, 527; II:183, 231; III:62, 71
Thieberger, Kurt, II:38, 40
Thieberger-Engel, Nelly, I:525
Thiele, František, II:481
Thomas (Taussig), Hans, I:370
Thomas, Rudi, II:584
Thon, Zdeněk, I:451; II:153
Thorsch, Leopold, I:343
Tichá, Věra, III:435, 441, 442, 443, 444
Ticho, Nathan, I:418; II:239
Ticho, Oto, II:40, 339
Ticho, Pavel, I:418; II:239
Tiedeman, Eva, I:522
Tiegermann, Josef, II:164
Tilkovský, Bela, II:499
Tilschová, Anna Maria, I:464
Tintner, Max, II:239
Tiroler, Tibor, III:232
Tirso de Molina, I:482
Tiso, Jozef, I:100, 110, 112, 117, 118, 123; II:577; III:28, 32, 173, 174, 183, 192, 204, 213, 219, 235, 236, 238, 239, 240, 242, 254, 255, 256, 303, 306, 307, 327
Tiso, Stefan, III:38
Titian (Tiziano Vecellio), I:499
Tobias sisters, III:399
Tochten, E. (student Zionist leader) II:179
Togman, Esther, III:xi
Toledano, Pinhas, III:586
Tomaschoff, Baruch, I:89, II:97, 283
Tomášek, Václav Jan, I:553
Tomek, V.V. (historian), II:540-42
Torberg, Friedrich, pseud. of Kantor-Berg, Friedrich I:504, 512, 520
Toscanini, Arturo, I:480, 552
Toury, Jacob, I:61
Toynbee, Arnold, II:15
Tramer, Hans, I:522
Traub, Edmund, I:419
Trieger, Gustl, II:608
Trier, Walter, II:478
Trietsch, Davis, II:11, 589
Trifunac, Alexander, I:82
Troller, Norbert, III:127, 128
Trotsky, Leon, II:479
Trunk, Isaiah, III:323, 325, 327
Tuach, George, II:621
Tucholsky, Kurt, I:505
Tuerk, K. (German nationalist), I:31

NAME INDEX

Tugendhat, Albert, I:415
Tuka, Vojtěch, I:96, 99, 116; II:578; III:32, 173, 174, 181, 190, 191, 192, 197, 208, 213, 219, 250, 304, 307, 309, 310
Türk, Heda, III:74
Turnauer, Herbert, I:375
Tusar, Vlastimil, I:168; II:265
Tvrdý, Vojtěch, III:210, 218, 219
Tyrnau, Rabbi Isaac, II:365

Udržal, František, I:104
Uhde, Wilhelm, II:480
Überreich-Urban, Walter, Vilém, III:383, 439
Uhrman, Jiří, I:398
Ujvari, Peter, I:81, 83
Ulberth, Franz, I:240
Ullman, Paul, I:viii, 398, 433
Ullmann, Fritz, II:207; III:50, 71
Ullmann, Robert, I:368
Ullmann, Viktor, I:547; III:127
Ungar, František, I:99
Ungar, Hermann, I:500, 501, 511, 519
Ungar, Markus, I:230-33, 250, 251, 272; II:30
Ungar, Otto, II:490; III:125, 126, 127, 128
Ungar, Rabbi Samuel David II:162, 168, 169, 369
Unger, Zikmund, III:129
Unsdorfer, Rabbi Hillel, II:97
Úprka, Jóža, II:479
Urbach, Emil, I:388
Urzidil, Gertrude, I:490
Urzidil, Johannes, I:470, 490, 511, 516, 522; II:587
Ussischkin, Menahem M., I:98; II:15, 192
Ussoskin, Moshe, III:61
Utitz, Emil, I:471
Utrillo, Maurice, II:481

Vacak, Václav, III:511, 512
Vachek, Emil, I:464
Václav I, King, II:523, 535
Vajansky, Svetozár Hurban. *See* Hurban-Vajánský, Svetozár
Valadon, Suzanne, II:481
Valk, Fritz, II:586
Vámbery, Armin, I:81
Vámoš, Gejza, I:106; II:465

Van Gogh, Vincent, II:480, 487
Vaněura, Bohumil, I:110, 122
Vantoch, Lev, I:389
Vantoch, Max, I:389
Vantoch, Ota, I:389
Varadik, K. (medical officer), III:380
Varlez, Louis, I:120
Váross, Marian, II:499
Vartíková, Marta, III:545, 547, 548
Vašek, Anton, III:202, 206, 246, 247, 248, 249, 307, 308, 326, 327
Vašek, Vladimír. *See* Bezruč, Petr
Vašina, Imrich, II:604, 610
Vatutin, General (Red army), III:402
Veesenmayer, Edmund, III:37, 219
Veit, Arthur, I:399
Vepřík, Josef, I:386
Verdi, Giuseppe, I:471, 480, 492, 557
Veselý, Aleš, II:491
Veverka, Ferdinand, I:225
Victor Emmanuel III, King, III:37
Videky, Alexander, I:414
Vielgut, Oskar, I:376
Viertel, Berthold, I:491
Viest, Rudolf, III:351
Viks, Adolf, III:279
Villon, François, I:499
Vishniak, Marc, I:264
Vlasov, Andrej Andreevich, III:232
Vlček, Jaroslav, I:467
Vogel, James, I:412
Vogel, Karel, II:485, 487
Vogel, Richard, I:417
Vogel, Zdeněk, I:417
Vohralík, Václav, I:200
Vohryzek (Vernon), František, II:214; III:444, 445
Vohryzek, Viktor, I:351, 524; II:149, 151
Vojtašák, Ján, III:195, 254, 256
Volavka, Vojtěch, II:479
Volavková, Hana, I:11; II:520, 525; III:10, 14, 64, 73, 149, 527, 574, 580, 581, 582, 583, 584
Vondra, Václav, III:64
Vondráček, Felix, J., I:120
Voskin-Nahartabi (dean of School of Religious Studies, Prague), I:314
Voskovec, Jiří, II:488; III:125
Votitz, Josef, I:426
Vrba, Rudolf, III:37, 151, 223, 248, 328. *See also* Rosenberg, Walter

Vrchlická, Eva, II: 489
Vrchlický, Jaroslav, pseud. of Frida, Emil Bohumil, I:464, 482, 533
Vuk, Václav, III:434
Vyhlídal, Jan, I:463
Vyshinsky, Andrei, III:566
Vyskočil, Josef, I:83

Wach, Antonín, II:472
Wachsman, Alois, II:488
Wachtel, Charles, I:375
Waern, Inge, II:586
Wagenbach, Klaus, I:65
Wagner, Richard, I:471, 475, 480, 552, 555
Wagner, Wilhelm, II:37, 176
Wahrmann, Moritz, I:73
Waldes family, III:96
Waldes, Georg, I:435
Waldes, Harry, I:435
Waldes, Jindřich, I:405, 409, 434, 435; II:486
Waldes, Milo, I:435
Waldes, Sigmund, I:435
Waldhauser, Antonín, II:474
Waldmeier, Josef, I:488
Waldstein, Emil, I:157, 526; II:142, 256, 259, 262
Waldstein, Wally, II:142
Waley, Frank R., III:586
Wallerstein, Konrad, I:544
Wanis, Paul, I:357
Warburg, M.M., I:365
Ward, E.W.F. (British official in Mauritius), II:629
Warschauer, Frank, I:522; II:587
Wasser, Bedřich, II:204
Wasserman, Jacques, I:398
Wavell, Sir Archibald, III:363
Weber, Rabbi Koloman, I:93, 98, 273, 274; II:160, 161, 164, 165, 272
Weber, Walter, II:180
Wechsberg, Joseph, I:503, 512, 520, 525
Wechsberg, P. (radio operator), III:387, 413
Wedding, Alex, pseud. of Weisskopf, Margarete, I:497; II:585
Wehle family, I:2
Wehle, Gottlieb, I:26
Wehle, Dr. Kurt, III: 9, 10, 14, 65; III:488, 491, 526, 527, 528, 544, 545, 546, 564

Wehli (Wehle), Methuselah, II:474, 475
Weidmann, František, III:38, 39, 40, 50
Weigl, Hans, II:40
Weigner, Emil, I:377
Weigner, Gustav, I:377
Weihs, Friedrich, I:352, 357, 535
Weil, Bedřich, I:370
Weil, Gusti, I:380
Weil, Jiří, I:450, 465; II:16, 129, 582
Weil, Robert, III:63
Weil, Siegfried, I:399
Weiler, Gershon, I:522
Weill, Kurt, I:493
Weinberger, Adolf, I:413
Weinberger, Emanuel, II:105
Weinberger, Hans, I:413
Weinberger, Jaromír, I:507, 540, 541, 554; II:465
Weinberger, Philipp, I:87
Weinberger, Rabbi Samuel Levi, II:166
Weiner, Armin, I:379; II:229, 231
Weiner, Bedřich, II:151
Weiner, Emil, I:377
Weiner, Erich, III:130
Weiner, Gustav, I:339, 344
Weiner (Weiner-Kral), Imro, II:505-08, 516
Weiner, Karel, III: 364-366
Weiner, Lewis, III: x, xii, xx, 582
Weiner, Matěj, I:108; II:286, 296, 303, 304
Weiner, Richard, I:441, 442, 452, 455
Weiner-Kral, Imro. See Weiner, Imro
Weingarten, Shemuel Hakohen, I:94, 124, 154, 531
Weininger, Otto, I:479, 489; II:454
Weinmann family, III:26
Weinmann, Edmund, I:374, 398
Weinmann, Hanuš, J., I:398
Weinmann, Jacob, I:34
Weinmann, Ota, I:373
Weinreb, Schemuel, II:97
Weisel, Georg Leopold, I:42, 67
Weisel, Vilém, I:427
Weiskopf, Franz Karl, I:496, 497, 511, 517; II:585
Weiskopf, Margarete. See Wedding, Alex
Weiss, Bernard, I:87, 88, 91; II:37
Weiss, Dov Berthold, I:118; II:35
Weiss, Ernst, I:486, 494, 495, 511, 517
Weiss, Fritz, II:585

NAME INDEX

Weiss, Jehuda, II:285
Weiss, Josef, I:426
Weiss, Josef Meir, II:358, 376
Weiss, Martin, III:279
Weiss, Max, II:168
Weiss, Oswald, I:398
Weiss, Yehuda, I:54
Weiss, Zelig, I:529
Weiss-Kubinčan, Arnold, II:505, 516
Weissenstein, Emanuel, I:413
Weissenstein, Gustav, I:367
Weissenstein, Wilhelm, I:367
Weisskopf, Hynek, I:416
Weissmandl, Rabbi Michael Ber, II:169, 170; III:35, 38, 205, 206, 221, 223, 234, 248, 252, 314
Weisz, Josef, I:426
Weizmann, Chaim, I:98, 159, 168, 225, 243; II:14, 49, 52, 53, 63, 70, 71, 83, 84, 94, 99, 100, 258, 416, 638; III:482, 483, 484, 560
Weizsäcker, Ernst, Freiherr von, III:67, 246
Wellemin (president of Prague Lodge B'nai B'rith), II:237
Wels, Ota, I:406, 433
Weltsch, Felix, I:54, 58, 121, 471, 486, 487, 489, 522, 525; II:40, 47, 48, 50, 52, 175, 178, 466, 587; III:564
Weltsch, Robert, I:54, 243, 471, 525, 535; II:20, 59, 140, 177, 258, 446
Wengraf, Arthur, I:366
Werfel, Franz, I:461, 468, 471, 472, 480, 482, 489, 490-94, 500, 504, 510, 511, 522; II:433
Werich, Jan, II:488; III:125
Werner, Egon, II:186
Werner, Ludwig, II:186
Werner, Siegmund, II:35
Wertheimer, Jakob, I:390; II:137
Wetzler, Aladar, I:528
Wetzler, Alfred, III:37, 151, 223, 317, 318
Wetzler, Pali, I:528
Wetzler-Verný, Vlado, I:117
Weyr, František, I:161, 253, 264
Wieder, Alter Baruch, I:537
Wien, Josef, II:57
Wiener, Eugen, I:368
Wiener (Alcantara), Josef, II:200
Wiener, Oskar, I:57, 357, 470, 478, 510, 514, 522

Wierer, Rudolf, I:329
Wiesenberger, Rabbi (Košice), III:582
Wiesenthal, Simon, III:290
Wiesmeyer, Emil, I:132; II:231
Wiesmeyer, Wilhelm, II:396
Wiesner, Adolf, II:469, 476, 477
Wiesner, Helena, II:477
Wilensky, Itzhak, II:63
Wilhelm II, Emperor, I:45
Willner, Arthur, I:550
Wilson, Woodrow, I:155, 157, 164, 170, 218, 223, 228, 247; II:254-56; III:474
Wimmer, Paul, I:522
Winder, Ludwig, I:489, 511, 516
Windischgraetz, Count Alfred, I:24
Winkelsberg, Tony, II:142
Winter, Arnošt, II:247
Winter, Gustav, I:447, 448, 523; II:246
Winter, K.E. (journalist), II:586
Winter, Lev, II:246
Winter, Ludvík, I:378
Winter, Walter, III:404
Winternitz, Enoch, II:544
Winternitz, Jaromír, II:94
Winternitz, Joshua, II:477
Winternitz, Olga, II:142
Winternitz, Richard, I:367
Winterstein, Eugen, I:117
Winterstein, Felix, II:38
Winterstein, Ladislav, III:550
Winterstein, Vojtěch (Albert), I:117; III:205, 504, 524, 527, 528, 534, 545, 546, 547, 548, 549, 550
Wise, Rabbi Isaac M., I:2
Wise, Rabbi Stephen S., II:255; III:468, 474, 483, 491, 492, 495, 560
Wishniak, M. *See* Vishniak, Marc
Wiskemann, Elisabeth, I:31, 65, 83, 438
Wisliceny, Dieter, III:174, 188, 189, 190, 197, 205, 206, 213, 222, 223, 249, 250, 255, 305, 310, 313
Wister, Theodor, I:88; II:36, 267
Witt, Zikmund, II:247
Wittler, Ota, II:201
Wittler, Pavel, II:201
Wodička, Rudolf, II:35
Wohlstein-Voldan (member of Central Jewish Office), III:251
Wolf, Erika, III:49, 73
Wolf, Hugo, I:544
Wolf, Jakub, II:200
Wolf, Leo, II:224

Wolf, Lucien, I:177, 264
Wolf, Walter, II:205
Wolfenstein, Alfred, II:587
Wolff, Kurt, I:491
Wolfner family, III:96
Wolfram (Nazi official), III:30
Wolfssohn, David, II:15, 20
Wollner, Max, I:367
Wright, James, A., II:638
Wronkow, Ludwig, II:585
Wronkow, Sonja, II:585
Wünsche, Marion, II:586
Wurm, Otto, II:217

Yablon, Ralph C., III:586
Yahil, Chaim (Hoffman, Heinrich), I:294, 312; II:32, 40, 74, 85, 91, 93, 94, 573; III:62
Yechiel, Zvi, II:609
Yitzhak, Rabbi, II:521

Zador, Heinrich, II:38, 40, 49, 50
Zaitschek, Alois, II: 66, 67
Zaitschek, Viktor, II:91
Žalud, Josef, I:344
Zander, H.A. (Maccabi), II:202
Zangwill, Israel, I:535
Zanker, Arthur, I:499, 500, 511, 518
Západotocký, Antonín, III:41, 521, 522, 524, 529
Zapper, Miss (member of Jewish National Council, 1918), II:256
Zappert (goldsmith), III:573
Zatko, Peter, III:191, 210, 247
Zavrel, Lotte Bloch. See Bloch-Zavřel, Lotte
Zdekauer, Karel Wolf, I:427
Zeisel, Eugen, II:79
Zeisel, Samuel, II:66, 67
Zelenka, František, II:488, 489; III:16, 124, 125, 149, 571, 572, 574, 575, 576, 577
Zelenka, Robert, I:409
Zelenka, Rudolf, I:426
Zelmanovits, Leo, II:49, 50, 179, 287, 296, 304, 311, 373, 453, 456, 457, 459, 460, 461, 463, 464, 473, 474, 488, 489, 492, 495; III:451

Zeman, Antonín. See Stašek, Antal
Zemánek, Dr. (union of employees of Jewish Religious Congregations), II:79
Zemánek, Vilém, I:543, 554
Zemlinsky, Alexander, I:547, 548, 552, 555; II:479
Zeyer, Julius, I:439, 464
Zíbrt, Čeněk, II:153
Ziegler, Ignaz, I:346
Ziemke, Karl, III:18
Zimert (Gestapo commissioner), III:265
Zipper-Vogel, Erwin, II:71
Žižka, Jan, III:403
Zlocisti, Theodor, I:535
Znojemský (Czechoslovak consul), III:334
Zoff, Otto, I:499, 511, 518
Zohn, Harry, I:xii, 23, 55, 61, 65, 71, 411, 461, 481, 541, 551, 552, 560
Zollschan, Ignatz, II:60
Zrzavý, Jan, II:486
Zucker, Alois, II:150
Zucker, Arnošt (Ernest), I:411, 413, 418, 419
Zucker, Herbert, I:418, 419
Zucker, Hermann, II:585
Zucker, Josef, I:418, 525
Zucker, Otto, I:419; II:296, 309, 313; III:12, 31, 38, 41, 43, 45, 107, 108, 110, 131, 136, 138, 139, 146, 147
Zuckerman, Zivia Lubetkin, III:203
Zuckermann, Hugo, I:480, 481, 511
Zunz, Leopold, I:2
Zweig, Arnold, II:180, 463, 464
Zweig, Egon, II:186
Zweig, Fritz, I:542, 545
Zweig, Gustav, II:36, 256, 259, 260
Zweig, Hans, II:67
Zweig, Markus, I:382
Zweig, Max, I:502, 511, 520
Zweig, Paul, I:398
Zweig, Stefan, I:479, 481, 489, 500, 507; II:463
Zweigenthal, Josef, I:426
Zweigenthal, Oskar, II:181, 284
Zwergbaum, Aaron, I:xix; II:599
Zwicker, Julius, I:412
Zygelboim, Samuel M., III:464

PLACE INDEX, VOLUMES I-III*

Akron (Ohio), II:216
Aden, II:615
Agde, III:345, 347, 350, 355
Aix-en-Provence, II:517
Aleppo, III:364
Alexandria, II:531; III:348, 360, 362, 367, 368
Amschelberg, See Kosova Hora
Amsterdam, I:385, 426, 431; II:209
Ankara, III:19
Ansbach, II:160
Antwerp, II:196, 202, 210
Archangelsk, III:267
Argent, III:352
Arlington (Vermont), I:433
Artushovka, III:398
Athens, II:613, 647, 654
Atricourt, III:351
Auschwitz (Oswiecim), I:450, 451, 479, 496, 508, 547, 548; II:247, 252, 488; III:31, 47, 50, 127, 128, 133, 138, 139, 140, 141, 146, 148, 149, 150, 151, 193, 202, 223, 234, 248, 265, 270, 272, 278, 284, 290, 291, 293, 294, 295, 296, 297, 298, 299, 300, 301, 303, 308, 309, 310, 311, 314, 317, 318, 319
Auspitz. See Hustopeče
Aussig. See Ustí nad Labem
Austerlitz. See Slavkov
Avlon, III:353
Az Sumeiriya, III:356, 357

Bábaszék, II:519
Baden (near Vienna), II:213

Baldock (Herts.), I:489
Balovany, III:230
Bamberg, II:534
Bánovce nad Bebravou, II:328, 331; III:300
Bánská Bystrica, I:79, 91, 424; II:189, 190, 192, 198, 207, 224, 301, 317, 328, 519; III:231, 232
Bánská Štiavnica, I:416
Barcelona, I:409
Barco, I:501
Bardejov, I:79, 93, 111; II:109, 329, 562
Bardia, III:365
Basel (Basle), I:79, 504, 534; II:46, 68, 71, 77, 109, 111, 186, 196, 197, 571
Bat Galim, III:361, 366, 367
Bat Yam, II:643
Beau-Bassin, II:616, 618, 625, 626
Běchovice, II:200, 203
Beckov, II:559, 561
Bečov (Hochpetsch), I:402
Beirut, III:345, 348, 356, 367
Bělá, I:44
Biela Cerkev, III:26
Belgrade (Beograd), II:175, 209, 611; III:345, 358
Belsen. See Bergen-Belsen
Belzec, III:30, 281, 285, 286, 309
Benešov, I:343, 373, 428; II:220, 482; III:24
Beograd. See Belgrade
Beregszász. See Berehovo
Berehovo (Beregszász), I:82, 136, 217; II:72, 338, 362, 410; III:390, 400

Compiled by Zdenka Münzer

653

PLACE INDEX

Bergen-Belsen, I:504; III:38, 272, 274
Berlin, I:102, 118, 167, 313, 326, 341, 345, 346, 368, 425, 471, 473, 475, 476, 478, 481, 484, 495, 496, 497, 499, 500, 502, 508, 541, 543, 549, 550, 551; II:6, 36, 58, 100, 101, 110, 114, 116, 122, 140, 167, 175, 186, 188, 191, 192, 196, 206, 210, 214, 219, 222, 223, 243, 257, 280, 355, 372, 385, 387, 478, 479, 505, 510, 513, 517, 519, 566, 583, 585, 586, 587, 606; III:17, 38, 42, 48, 50, 119, 125, 132, 135, 137, 141, 149, 190, 242, 263, 264, 276, 280, 297, 300, 303
Bern, III:318
Beroun, II:203; III:31
Bet Alpha, I:20
Beverly Hills (Calif.), I:492
Béziers, III:345
Bialystok, III:134
Biberach, II:591
Biela Cerkev, III:409, 410, 423
Bielsko, III:267, 332, 333
Bílenec (Bielenz), I:41
Birkenau (part of Auschwitz), III:150, 272, 277, 295, 296, 297, 299, 300, 301, 309, 317, 318, 325
Blankenberghe, II:518
Blansko, II:191, 196
Blatná, II:517
Blechhammer, III:301
Bleistadt. See Olovi
Bodenbach. See Podmokly
Böhmisch Krumau. See Český Krumlov
Böhmisch Leipa. See Česká Lipa
Bohumin (Oderberg), I:199, 403, 499; II:190, 328, 555
Bohušovice, III:33, 50, 110, 275
Boissy, III:352
Boleráz, I:388
Bologna, II:209
Bombay, I:549
Bory (part of Plzeň), I:406
Boskovice, I:25, 46, 315, 350, 352, 418, 500; II:6, 23, 33, 79, 164, 187, 190, 262, 555
Brandýs nad Labem, I:428
Bratislava (Pressburg, Pozsony), I:7, 77, 79, 80, 86, 87, 88, 89, 91, 93, 94, 95, 97, 98, 102, 103, 104, 111, 115, 116, 117, 214, 225, 273, 317, 320, 326, 343, 369, 370, 375, 386, 388, 396, 403, 404, 408, 411, 414, 421, 424, 425, 426, 429, 430, 431, 434, 474, 528, 535, 536; II:24, 35, 36, 37, 39, 40, 65, 67, 73, 86, 87, 97, 98, 103, 104, 105, 109, 112, 118, 133, 142, 158, 160, 161, 162, 163, 164, 165, 167, 168, 171, 172, 176, 180, 183, 187, 189, 190, 198, 200, 204, 205, 208, 209, 210, 211, 223, 226, 227, 232, 241, 263, 267, 272, 278, 283, 284, 285, 306, 313, 319, 321, 328, 329, 331, 355, 360, 363, 365, 367, 370, 373, 375, 377, 379, 380, 382, 383, 384, 385, 387, 388, 395, 402, 455, 498, 501, 503, 504, 506, 511, 514, 517, 518, 519, 553, 559, 561, 562, 571, 590, 594, 599, 600, 602, 603, 605, 606, 607, 609, 611, 612, 647, 655, 658; III:42, 50, 172, 184, 187, 190, 193, 196, 204, 208, 223, 235, 239, 247, 250, 285, 304, 305, 306, 308, 318, 418, 465, 509, 510, 542, 566
Bratislava-Patronka, III:38
Břeclav, II:79, 187, 190, 328
Breslau, I:313, 326, 345, 346, 347, 533; II:196, 223, 372
Brest-Litovsk, III:287
Brisbane, I:545
Brno (Brünn), I:4, 7, 8, 36, 40, 41, 57, 59, 102, 216, 339, 345, 348, 368, 379, 382, 394, 403, 412, 413, 419, 420, 424, 428, 431, 443, 472, 474, 475, 477, 478, 480, 494, 498, 501, 502, 524, 527, 534, 535, 536, 539, 546, 548, 552, 557; II:9, 21, 22, 23, 31, 35, 37, 42, 50, 54, 55, 57, 59, 61, 62, 64, 65, 67, 69, 73, 75, 77, 79, 81, 82, 86, 87, 91, 92, 93, 98, 103, 104, 107, 109, 118, 119, 132, 133, 142, 175, 180, 181, 182, 183, 187, 188, 189, 190, 191, 192, 193, 195, 196, 197, 198, 199, 204, 205, 208, 210, 211, 212, 213, 216, 223, 224, 226, 227, 230, 231, 236, 238, 239, 241, 245, 246, 249, 250, 256, 259, 260, 262, 265, 266, 267, 268, 274, 278, 284, 296, 317, 328, 331, 382, 394, 475, 519, 554, 556, 571, 587, 601, 602, 605, 646, 647; III:21, 30, 33, 39, 42, 44, 92, 105, 110, 126, 127, 130, 132, 141, 147, 273, 360, 418, 517

PLACE INDEX

Brockton (Mass.), III:590
Bronowice, III:363
Brooklyn (N.Y.), II:358
Broumov, I:411; III:514
Brünn. *See* Brno
Brussels, I:365, 384, 385, 412; III:381
Brüx. *See* Most
Buchenwald, I:451; II:251; III:128, 265, 294
Buchs, II:571
Bučovice, I:554
Budapest, I:17, 80, 82, 99, 102, 114, 128, 274, 286, 345, 361, 364, 387, 429, 473, 504; II:139, 158, 159, 203, 209, 210, 263, 354, 372, 376, 381, 387, 402, 436, 497, 498, 499, 500, 502, 505, 508, 509, 511, 512, 517, 518, 519, 611, 655; III:42, 50, 138, 207, 234, 316, 318
Budějovice (Budweis), I:297, 393, 424; II:22, 63, 217, 227, 230, 236, 241, 381, 485; II:23, 128, 264, 285
Budweis. *See* Budějovice
Budyně nad Ohří, III:590
Bukovec, III:232
Buštěhrad, I:427
Buština, III:350
Buzuluk, III:267, 340, 390, 391, 392, 393, 394, 395, 396, 405, 410
Bystřice, III:51
Bytča, I:229, 329
Bzenec, I:62; II:54

Cairo (Egypt), III:369
Cape Town, II:621, 633, 634, 651, 652
Caracas, I:387
Carlsbad. *See* Karlovy Vary
Čáslav, I:50, 390; III:31
Čemerné, III:38
Čenkov, I:404
Cernachov, III:409
Czernowice, II:222; III:413, 415
Červený Kameň, II:559
Česká Kamenice (Kamnitz), I:393
Česká Lípa (Böhmisch Leipa), I:31, 32, 477; II:142; III:41, 264
Česká Třebová, I:411
České Budějovice. *See* Budějovice
Český Krumlov (Böhmisch Krumau), I:375, 392

Český Těšín (Teschen, Cieszyn), I:202, 231, 392, 547; II:165, 329, 337, 555, 579; III:267
Cheb (Eger), I:424, 480; II:22; III:384
Chelmno, III:30, 271, 277, 281, 285
Chicago (Ill.), I:377, 400, 426, 432, 454, 542
Chlumec nad Cidlinou, II:226
Choceň, I:394, 411; III:31
Cholmondeley, III:374, 375, 377
Cholon, II:643. *See also* Holon
Chomútov (Komotau), I:417, 480, 481; II:22, 117, 187, 189, 190, 219, 262
Chotěboř, I:44
Chrást, I:23, 396, 474
Christianstadt, III:301
Chrudim, I:420
Chust (Hust), I:136, 142, 217; II:167, 168, 328, 359, 369, 410, 554; III:318, 423
Cieszyn. *See* Český Těšín
Cincinnati (Ohio), II:223
Cinvald (Zinnwald), II:207
Cologne, I:541, 546
Constantinople. *See* Istanbul
Coulommiers, III:352
Cracow. *See* Krakow
Croydon, I:500
Curepipe, II:622

Dachau, I:448; III:25, 272, 294, 472
Danzig, II:90, 93, 94, 610, 630, 632, 654; III:335, 345
Děčín (Tetschen), II:117
Degeš, III:215
Degheile, III:363
Derna, III:365
Derinská Nová Ves, III:215
Dessau, I:503, 547; II:218, 487
Diosek Velký, I:383, 387, 388, 504
Diviaky, II:331
Dobrá, I:34, 35
Dobřany, I:376
Dobříš, I:40, 420; II:22, 36, 37, 203, 262; III:21
Dobšiná, I:377
Dolni Hamry, I:402
Dolní Kounice, I:69, 353
Dolný Kubín, I:79; II:505, 519, 561
Domažlice (Tauss), I:556

Dresden, I:409, 475; II:477, 517; III:96, 138
Duchcov (Dux), I:427, 428
Dukla, III:26, 422, 423
Dunaszerdahely. *See* Dunajská Streda
Dunajská Streda (Dunaszerdahely), I:388, 528; II:161, 163, 164, 165, 166, 167, 171, 328
Dunkirk, II:510, 653; III:383, 384
Dusina, II:305
Dušníky, I:473
Düsseldorf, II:517, 518; III:290
Dux. *See* Duchov
Dvůr Králové n.l. (Königinhof), I:41, 45, 424; II:483

Eger. *See* Cheb
Eidelstedt, III:301
Eilat, II:643
El Alamein, III:367, 368
Elbogen. *See* Loket
Erfurt, II:525
Erida, III:280
Ersekujvár. *See* Nové Zamky
Es Zib, III:365, 367
Evian, III:265

Fairfield (Conn.), I:483
Falknow. *See* Sokolov
Fayetteville, III:590
Felixstowe, III:379
Fil'akovo (Fülek), I:404
Flarau, II:532
Florence, II:548, 549
Fontfroid, II:523
Fort Capuzzo, III:366
Frankfurt am Main, I:409, 481; II:156, 163, 171, 204, 221, 222, 367, 514, 533, 584
Františkovy Lázně (Franzensbad), I:378; II:556, 587
Franzensbad. *See* Františkory Lázně
Freiburg, I:477
Frýdek-Místek, II:109; III:24, 265
Frýdlant nad Ostravicí, I:428
Fryštát, II:109, 337
Fülek. *See* Fil'akovo
Fünfkirchen. *See* Pécs

Gabelsdorf. *See* Libeč
Gablonz a.N. *See* Jablonec nad Nisou

Galanta, II:164, 165, 167, 369, 514, 519; III:509, 542
Galgocz. *See* Hlohovec
Gardner (Mass.), II:371
Gaja. *See* Kyjov
Gbely, I:375
Gdansk. *See* Danzig
Gdynia. *See* Danzig
Gedera, III:358, 359, 362
Gemer, I:377
Geneva, I:118, 396, 609; II:115, 290, 608; III:42, 300, 316, 469
Ghent, I:120, 442; II:518
Gien, III:351, 352
Giraltovce, II:559
Giurgiu, II:611
Göding. *See* Hodonín
Goslar, II:533
Gottenhof, III:278
Gottvaldov (Zlín), I:419, 431; II:227
Graslitz. *See* Kraslice
Graz, I:473; II:387
Great Yarmouth, III:379
Grossrosen, III:301
Grosswardein. *See* Nagyvárad
Grottau. *See* Hradek n.N.
Guta, II:163

Haifa, I:62, 68; II:14, 139, 613, 614, 615, 641, 643, 647, 654; III:339, 358, 359, 360, 366, 367, 368
Hain, II:583
Halle an der Saale, I:353
Hamburg, I:365, 430, 489, 491, 541; II:202; III:42, 273, 301
Handlová, III:229
Hannsdorf. *See* Hanušovice
Hanušovice (Hannsdorf), I:388; II:559
Havana, I:435
Havlíčkův Brod (Německý Brod), I:71, 417, 420; III:23, 31, 264
Heidelberg, I:501
Heiligenkreuz, II:534
Heinrichstal. *See* Jindřichov
Helleran, I:404
Heřmanův Městec, I:40, 50; II:220
Heydebreck, III:297
Hlinsko, I:416; III:31
Hlohovec (Galgocz), II:190, 260, 285, 328
Hloubětín, I:390, 398

Hlubočepy, II:199
Hluboczek Wielki, III:337
Hochpetsch. *See* Bečov
Hodonín (Göding), I:375, 466; II:23, 79, 187, 190, 215, 262, 555; III:35
Hohenelbe. *See* Vrchlabi
Holesŏv, I, 350; II:262
Holešovice (Prague), III:32
Holice, I:420
Holič, II:561, 562; III:255
Holon, III:490
Horažďovice, I:71
Hořice (Höritz), I:25, 57, 476
Höritz. *See* Hořice
Horná Štubňa, III:231
Horni Bříza, I:376
Horní Planá (Oberplan), I:375
Horodyszec, III:338
Hořovice, I:404
Horšův Týn, II:219
Hostomice, I:44; II:202; III:589
Hradec Králové, I:419, 424, 548; II:40, 285, 328; III:36, 611
Hrádek n.N. (Grottau), I:410
Hranice (Mährisch Weisskirchen), I:57, 476; II:105, 349
Hronec, I:404
Hronov, I:454
Hroznětín (Lichtenstadt), I:64
Hrušov, II:190
Hull (England), I:396
Humenné, I:72, 81, 82, 101, 111, 528; II:167
Humpolec, I:65, 542; II:227
Huncovce (Hundsdorf), II:376, 558, 561
Hunsdorf. *See* Huncovce
Husiatyn, III:338
Hust. *See* Chust
Hustopeče (Auspitz), I:428

Iglau. *See* Jihlava
Ilava, II:561; III:215
Ischl, Bad, I:497
Istanbul (Constantinople), III:49, 251, 313, 316, 339
Ithaca (N.Y.), I:540
Ivančice (Eibenschütz), I:69; III:31, 126
Izbica, III:281, 282, 285, 286

Jablonec nad Nisou (Gablonz a.N.), I:40, 397, 398, 542, 545; II:40, 207; III:38, 613
Jáchymov (Joachimsthal), I:371, 372, 378, 432, 433
Jagala, III:279
Jägerndorf. *See* Krnov
Jaffa, II:6
Janegg. *See* Jenikov
Janowice, III:281
Jaroměř, I:419; III:38, 613
Jasina, I:136; II:331, 554
Jelšava, I:377
Jeníkov (Janegg), I:361, 490
Jerusalem, I:69, 94, 97, 530, 544; II:2, 132, 157, 161, 232, 366, 367, 369, 376, 387, 492, 530, 594, 600, 643, 646, 647, 652, 655, 658; III:38, 248
Jeseníky, III:337
Jezreel Valley, I:20
Jičín, I:543
Jihlava (Iglau), I:36, 417, 419, 420, 424, 497, 499; II:23, 35, 79, 109, 187, 190, 555; III:21, 24, 306
Jindřichov (Heinrichstal), I:393
Jindřichův Hradec, I:343
Jinonice, I:408
Joachimsthal. *See* Jáchymov
Johannesburg, II:495, 639
Josefova Huť (Josefshütte), I:393
Josefshütte. *See* Josefova Huť
Josefův Důl, I:410
Jung Bunzlau. *See* Mladá Boleslav
Júr pri Bratislave, III:187, 215, 306
Jutěnin (Muttersdorf), I:70

Kaiserwald, III:278
Kalbasy, III:538
Kalegi-Liiva, III:279
Kaliště, I:540; II:443
Kalymnos, III:172
Kamenec Podolsk, III:315, 338
Kamenice, I:402
Kamnitz. *See* Česka Kamenice
Kandalakša, III:342
Kaposvár, II:519
Karlovy Vary (Karlsbad, Carlsbad), I:54, 94, 96, 112, 132, 376, 377, 378, 379, 390, 431, 478, 499, 502, 503, 542, 544, 549; II:22, 28, 31, 39, 40, 60, 61, 73, 75, 99, 165, 188, 189, 190,

Karlovy Vary (*Cont.*)
  191, 195, 230, 231, 236, 237, 238, 241, 285, 329, 556, 587; III:486
Karlsbad. *See* Karlovy Vary
Karlsruhe, II:387
Karviná, I:372, 388; II:337; III:26
Kaschau. *See* Košice
Kasejovice, II:262
Kassa. *See* Košice
Katowice, III:265, 267, 333, 334
Kaufering, III:272
Kayat Beach, III:361
Kbely, I:431
Kežmarok, I:79, 393; II:24, 165, 655
K'far Maccabi, II:192, 194
K'far Masaryk, I:312; II:435
Kharkov, III:398, 402
Kierling, I:484
Kijew, III:26, 339, 407, 408
Kiriat Shmoneh, II:643
Kisgajár, II:519
Kiviyli, III:280
Kladno, I:34, 373; II:221; III:26, 35
Klášterec nad Ohří (Klösterle an der Oder) I:376
Kláštor pod Znievom, I:73
Klatovy, I:418, 419, 424; II:220, 262, 490; III:21
Klösterle au der Oder. *See* Klášterec nad Ohří
Klosterode, II:533
Kočkovice, I:377
Kodaň, I:44, 420
Kojetín, II:23
Kolín, I:8, 25, 31, 57, 344, 350, 388, 394, 424, 479, 480, 526; II:79, 186, 215, 221, 445, 485, 608; III:420
Kolinec, I:418
Kolšteyn, I:375
Komárno, I:113, 114, 304, 430; II:162, 167, 365, 508, 509, 519
Komarow, III:285
Komotau. *See* Chomútov
Königinhof. *See* Dvůr Králové n.L.
Konskawola, III:310
Kopčany, I:539
Kořenov, II:207
Kosiče (Kaschau, Kassa), I:74, 79, 80, 81, 86, 88, 91, 94, 96, 99, 101, 103, 114, 304, 391, 424, 426, 428, 431, 528; II:24, 25, 37, 98, 105, 142, 163, 167, 190, 209, 213, 214, 224, 226, 241, 247, 285, 306, 313, 328, 329, 354, 375, 495, 498, 502, 504, 508, 517, 519, 553; III:316, 317, 318, 542, 569, 582
Kosino, I:136
Kosova Hora (Amschelberg), I:57, 482
Kovno (Latvia), III:30, 276, 278
Krakow, III:334, 336, 393, 418
Královo Pole, I:428
Kralupy nad Vltavou, I:375, 394, 405
Kraslice (Graslitz), II:337
Krásná Lípa (Schönlinde) I:416
Krásno nad Bečvou, I:398
Krasnogorsk, III:406
Kremnice, II:207, 262
Krnov (Jägerndorf), I:389, 542
Kroměříž, I:479; II:187, 190
Krosno, III:418, 422
Kujbyshev, III:340, 404
Kutná Hora, I:17, 44, 71; II:22
Kutno, III:271
Kyjov (Gaya), I:39, 59, 496; II:23, 190, 262, 555; III:31, 348
Kyselka (Kysibl), I:379
Kysibl. *See* Kyselka

Lab, III:187, 215
Lány, I:373
Le Cateau, II:518
Leamington Spa, III:177
Lednice, I:413
Leipzig, I:491, 546; II:110, 222
Leitmeritz. *See* Litoměřice
Letňany, I:406, 407; II:216
Levoča, II:314, 559
Ležáky, III:34
Libeč (Gabelsdorf), I:414
Liberec (Reichenberg) I:40, 65, 68, 70, 340, 412, 424, 425, 431; II:190, 230, 236, 238, 241, 285
Lichtenstadt. *See* Hrozňetín
Lidice, II:514; III:464
Lieszná, III:336, 363
Lille, III:345
Limassol, II:613
Linz, II:571
Lipiany, II:112, 559
Lipník nad Bečvou, I:46, 68, 372; II:262
Liptov, I:106; II:513
Liptovský Hrádok, III:38

PLACE INDEX

Liptovský Mikuláš, I:72, 74, 77, 89, 91, 92, 108, 419; II:262, 296, 328, 331, 518, 519, 559; III:171, 317, 318
Liptovský Svatý Mikuláš. *See* Mikuláš
Lisbon, III:469
Litoměřice (Leitmeritz), I:298, 419; II:109, 116, 262, 273, 284, 285, 328; III:31
Little Neck (N.Y.), III:590
Liverpool, III:355, 369
Lobositz. *See* Lovosice
Loděnice, II:493
Locarno, I:502
Lodz, I:479, 495; II:89, 239, 489; III:30, 31, 32, 50, 105, 138, 268, 269, 270, 271, 272, 273
Loket (Elbogen), I:44
London, I:11, 168, 223, 226, 364, 365, 369, 392, 400, 402, 409, 426, 433, 447, 455, 465, 480, 481, 483, 497, 503, 549, 550, 553; II:1, 8, 9, 13, 16, 30, 36, 113, 114, 120, 142, 143, 146, 147, 175, 192, 207, 212, 245, 247, 250, 268, 387, 492, 510, 513, 517, 572, 590, 620, 621, 628, 633, 634, 635, 636, 652, 655; III:7, 20, 355, 363, 367, 369, 372, 386, 389, 397, 398, 403, 404, 450, 463, 464, 531, 584, 586
Los Angeles (Calif.), I:498; II:203
Loštice, III:590
Louka, II:533
Louny, II:534
Lovosice (Lobositz), I:386, 387, 415, 428, 431
Lublin, III:50, 202, 265, 267, 271, 272, 275, 280, 281, 282, 283, 284, 285, 304, 311, 464
Lublin-Majdanek. *See* Majdanek
Lubochňa, II:207
Lučenec, I:101, 114, 387, 404, 424; II:97, 328, 515, 519
Lucerne, II:80, 93, 121
Lwow, III:340, 341, 392, 393
Lydda, II:654
Lysá nad Labem, II:221

Machnowka, III:418
Magdeburg, II:535
Mährisch Aussee. *See* Úsov
Mahrisch Ostrav. *See* Ostrava
Mährisch Schönberg. *See* Sumperk
Mahrisch Trübau. *See* Moravská Trebová
Mährisch Weisskirchen. *See* Hranice
Majdanek, II:30; III:203, 248, 271, 272, 280, 281, 282, 284, 285, 288, 309
Malé Bronowice, III:336
Malé Svatonovice. *See* Svatonovice
Malé Uherce, III:230
Malý Trostinec, III:286, 287, 288
Mannheim, III:119
Mantov, I:402
Marburg, II:525
Mardjayun, III:364
Marianské Lázně (Marienbad), I:378, 431, 485; II:165, 168, 238, 262, 556, 587
Marienbad. *See* Marianské Lázně
Marmaros Siget, III:317
Marseille, III:345, 347, 348, 354, 355
Martin (Turčansky Svätý Martin), I:73, 85, 87, 91, 99, 392, 417; II:285, 498, 519, 559
Matějovce (Matzdorf), I:404
Matzdorf. *See* Matejovce
Maulbronn, II:533
Mauritius, II:599, 600, 618, 620, 621, 626, 628, 630, 635, 636
Mauthausen, I:445; II:239; III:272, 294
Medlánky, II:68
Meersburg, I:57, 476
Mělník, I:421, 544, 545, 546
Merkelsgrün. *See* Merklín
Merklín (Merkelsgrün), I:376
Mersin, III:339, 359
Michalovce, I:74, 109; II:167, 369, 385
Michelstein, II:533
Michle (Prague) I:380; III:585
Mies. *See* Stříbo
Mikuláš (Liptovský Svätý Mikuláš), I:72, 74, 77, 89, 91, 92, 108, 419; II:262, 296, 328, 331, 518, 519, 559
Mikulov (Nikolsburg), I:57, 69, 70, 350, 474, 475; II:xix, 187, 190, 197, 328, 381, 472, 547, 548, 549, 550, 551, 555; III:565, 568
Milan (Milano), I:498, 541
Milano. *See* Milan
Mittenberg, II:525
Mimoň (Niemes), I:394
Minsk, III:30, 31, 105, 268, 269, 273, 274, 286, 287

Mirogorod, III:398
Miroslav (Misslitz), II:109, 187
Mírov, I:496
Mischdorf, III:62
Misslitz. *See* Miroslav
Mladá Boleslav (Jung Bunzlau), I:23, 25, 31, 71, 375, 404, 406, 408, 410, 428, 435, 474; II:202, 212, 220; III:38, 44, 567, 613
Mnichovo Hradiště (Münchengrätz), I:23, 420, 473
Mníšek, II:518
Mohelnice, I:408
Monovice, III:294
Montigny sur Aube, III:351
Montpelier, III:355
Montreal (Canada), I:388, 432
Montreux III:352
Moravská Ostrava. *See* Ostrava
Moravská Třebová (Mährisch Trübau), I:415
Moravské Budějovice, I:498
Morristown (N.J.), III:590
Mortemer II:532
Moscow I:497; II:246, 501, 552, 572; III:267, 285, 339, 369, 392, 397, 404, 413, 484, 531
Most (Brüx), I:32, 374, 428; II:22, 40, 190, 262, 337; III:26
Mount Kisco (N.Y.), II:170, 369
Mouraux, III:352
Mukačevo (Munkács), I:129, 136, 142, 144, 148, 150, 216, 217, 274, 304, 308, 314, 315, 391, 528, 529, 537; II:36, 40, 54, 75, 93, 113, 142, 162, 165, 183, 213, 233, 270, 284, 285, 287, 292, 295, 296, 297, 305, 313, 326, 328, 329, 331, 355, 356, 358, 359, 366, 369, 371, 372, 375, 339, 385, 402, 408, 409, 410, 416, 425, 426, 427, 428, 430, 518, 553, 554, 587, 590, 602; III:316, 317, 318, 401, 490
Münchengrätz. *See* Mnichovo Hradiště
Munich, I:115, 478, 499, 503; II:147, 221, 222, 233, 399, 476, 477, 478, 480, 487, 499, 517, 518, 519, 568, 571, 601; III:20, 332
Munkács. *See* Mukačevo
Muttersdorf. *See* Jutěnin
Myjava, II:164
Mytilene, II:612

Náchod, I:31, 50, 339, 410, 411, 425; II:220, 226, 227, 262, 328; III:514
Nagybánya, II:519
Nagyvárad (Grosswardein), III:50
Nahariya, II:642, 643
Námestovo, II:373, 561, 562
Narbonne, III:345
Narva, III:280
Natanya, III:550
Německý Brod. *See* Havlíčkův Brod
Neratovice, I:388, 428
Neštědice (Nestersitz), I:402
Nestersitz. *See* Neštědice
Neuengamme, III:294
Neusiedel. *See* Novosedly
Neutra. *See* Nitra
New York (N.Y.), I:viii, 10, 11, 364, 365, 367, 369, 374, 375, 377, 382, 383, 388, 392, 394, 396, 398, 401, 402, 409, 413, 417, 427, 433, 434, 435, 454, 455, 480, 490, 492, 493, 496, 498, 499, 500, 501, 504, 541, 552; II:8, 10, 13, 112, 120, 132, 172, 220, 235, 241, 387, 477, 511, 512, 517, 519, 552, 628, 655
Niemes. *See* Mimoň
Nikolsburg. *See* Mikulov
Nisko, III:24, 25, 106, 265, 266, 267
Nitra (Neutra), I:79, 81, 88, 89, 96, 105, 388; II:24, 37, 39, 73, 160, 162, 163, 164, 165, 166, 167, 168, 169, 170, 190, 260, 329, 369, 553, 554; III:215, 306, 348
Nováky, III:214, 215, 226, 227, 228, 229, 230, 231, 257, 306, 308, 313
Nové Benátky, I:376
Nové Město nad Metují, I:389
Nové Mesto nad Váhom, I:72, 80, 81, 91, 404; II:24, 40, 190, 321, 328, 503, 518, 559, 561; III:215, 228
Nové Zámky (Érsekujvár), I:89, 91, 94, 114, 414; II:39, 164, 165, 167, 287, 376; III:509, 548
Novochopersk, III:404, 405, 406, 407
Novosedly (Neusiedel), I:393
Nový Burluk, III:402
Nový Bydžov, I:31, 62, 64, 419
Nový Jičín, I:417; II:190, 284, 328
Nuremberg, III:5
Nymburk, I:389; II:221, 223; III:24
Nýřany, I:404
Nyrsko, I:418

PLACE INDEX

Oberdöbling, I:473
Oberplan. *See* Horní Planá
Oderberg. *See* Bohumin
Odessa, III:339
Olmütz. *See* Olomouc
Olomouc (Olmütz), I:36, 386, 388, 390, 424, 425, 426, 473, 541, 542; II:23, 37, 39, 40, 61, 79, 81, 82, 109, 186, 187, 199, 200, 213, 224, 238, 241, 262, 284, 302, 328; III:21
Olovi (Bleistadt), I:398
Olšany, I:393
Opava (Troppau), I:281, 326, 340, 389, 424; II:23, 35, 36, 37, 39, 40, 98, 109, 186, 230, 241, 328, 479, 555; III:39
Oran, III:345
Oranienburg, III:272, 284, 472
Oránky, III:340
Orava, I:106
Osek (Ossek, Ossegg), I:35; II:533
Osov, III:289
Ossegg. *See* Osek
Ossek. *See* Osek
Ostrava (Moravská Ostrava, Mährisch Ostrau), I:36, 40, 95, 102, 115, 177, 222, 230, 252, 271, 275, 321, 322, 326, 340, 348, 373, 400, 403, 408, 425, 428, 431, 503, 525, 535; II:23, 28, 35, 36-38, 40, 50, 59, 76, 79, 82, 86, 87, 93, 98, 103, 107, 109, 114, 115, 186, 187, 190-92, 196, 202, 205, 223, 224, 236, 238, 241, 247, 250, 256, 260, 266, 268, 278, 280, 283, 284, 293, 295, 296, 300, 306, 311, 317, 328, 329, 331, 395, 397, 399, 486, 555, 579, 587, 590; III:24, 25, 26, 39, 47, 105, 146, 265, 266, 294, 335, 386, 396, 418
Ostrov (Schlackenwerth), I:376
Oswiecim. *See* Auschwitz
Oxford, I:2, 501; II:1

Palestine, II:100, 103; III:524
Panenské Břežany, III:35, 264
Panino, III:393
Pardubice, I:65, 375, 425, 427, 524; II:39, 190, 203, 214, 219, 220, 226, 482; III:15
Paris, I:158, 169, 170, 171, 173, 175, 176, 177, 364, 365, 369, 373, 378, 383, 403, 406, 409, 427, 431, 432, 440, 447, 495, 496, 497, 498, 547; II:30, 101, 208, 210, 212, 224, 246, 261, 264, 397, 475, 476, 477, 480, 483, 484, 485, 486, 501, 506, 508, 510, 511, 512, 513, 514, 518, 519, 572, 576
Parkáň, II:328
Paterson (N.J.), I:382
Pečovská Nová Ves, II:562
Pécs (Fünfkirchen), I:475
Pécsvárad, II:518
Peking, I:497; II:585
Pelhřimov, III:264
Pelsöc, II:519
Perečín, I:396
Pest. *See* Budapest
Petřvald, III:332
Pezinok, II:261, 190
Philadelphia, I:353, 403, 413; II:9
Piaski, III:282
Pieštány, I:87, 88, 90, 91, 93, 274, 307, 378; II:37, 160, 162, 164, 165, 167, 171, 197, 259, 260, 292
Pilsen. *See* Plzeň
Pisa, I:482
Písek, I:65, 246, 418, 419; II:22, 533
Plymouth, III:355
Plzeň (Pilsen), I:31, 34, 40, 64, 71, 275, 290, 297, 326, 373, 376, 381, 393, 402, 404, 405, 424, 425, 489; II:22, 59, 190, 195, 219, 230, 235, 236, 237, 241, 262, 285, 328, 556; III:21, 24, 33, 39, 384
Podbořany (Podersam), I:478; II:328
Poděbrady, I:65, 390, 483, 500; II:215; III:517
Podersam. *See* Podbořany
Podhořany, II:328
Podivín, II:190
Podmokly (Bodenbach), I:377, 428; II:40, 142
Pohořelice, II:190, 555
Polina, II:359
Polná, I:17, 378, 420
Pommerle. *See* Poverly
Poprad, II:28, 270, 558; III:193, 247, 308
Port-Louis, II:616, 618, 622, 629, 636, 641, 654
Port Vendres, III:354
Postelberg. *See* Postoloprty
Postoloprty (Postelberg), II:262; III:52

Považská Bystrica, I:100; II:519
Poverly (Pommerle), I:402
Požáry, II:608
Poznaň, I:52; III:371
Pozsony. *See* Bratislava
Prachatice, I:479
Prague*
Praskolesy, I:44
Přerov, II:23, 262
Prešov, I:79, 81, 82, 86, 88, 89, 91, 94, 101, 119, 304, 528; II:24, 37, 39, 75, 162, 163, 165, 167, 213, 273, 285, 328, 331, 380, 553, 655; III:318, 538
Pressburg. *See* Bratislava
Příbor, II:445
Příbram, I:69, 389; II:203, 221; III:21
Prievidza, III:37, 612
Priluky, III:407
Priorki, III:407
Přívoz, I:428; II:187
Prosnice, II:367
Prossnitz. *See* Prostějov
Prostějov (Prossnitz), I:22, 24, 25, 26, 35, 46, 58, 62, 68, 417, 418, 502; II:23, 35, 37, 39, 40, 67, 79, 81, 93, 107, 108, 109, 118, 186, 190, 198, 199, 200, 224, 226, 241, 256, 259, 260, 262, 284, 328, 445, 555
Púchov, I:377
Pyšely, II:219, 283

Ra'anana, II:194
Raasiká, III:279
Radotín, I:404
Radvaň n Hr., III:225
Rafiah, II:641
Rájec, II:559; III:37, 612
Rakovník, I:411
Rakow, III:338
Ramat Gan, II:642, 643
Raná, II:216
Rataje, I:63
Ravensbrück, I:123; III:315
Regensburg, II:519, 523, 524
Reichenberg. *See* Liberec
Rejnovice, III:283
Rembertów, III:283
Revúca, I:73

Riga, I:543; III:30, 105, 269, 276, 278, 279
Rimavská Sobota, I:114; III:542
Rjeka (Sušak), II:646
Rochlice, I:412
Rokycany, III:384, 390
Rokytnice, I:474
Rome, I:44, 392; II:212, 549; III:313, 465
Rose Hill, II:622, 629
Rosh Pinah, III:364
Rosice (u Brna), I:373
Roudnice nad Labem, I:27, 57, 69, 70, 403, 427, 474; II:211; III:31
Rozhanovce, II:561
Rožňava, I:100, 114
Rožnov pod Radhoštem, I:416
Rozvadov, III:24
Ruda, III:410
Rumburk, I:411
Ružomberok, I:111, 392; II:224, 328
Ruzyně, I:431
Rybár Pole, I:410
Rychnov nad Kněžnou, I:552
Rýmařov, II:475

Sabinov, II:331, 553
Sachsenhausen, III:50, 234, 294, 315
Sadagora, III:414, 415
Šahy, I:114
St. Louis (Mo.), I:23
Saint Martin, II:626
St. Montaine, III:352
St. Petersburg (Fla.), I:541
Šaľa, II:167
Salaspils, III:278
Saloniki, III:348
Salzburg, II:518; III:173, 238
Šamorín, II:511, 519
San Diego (Cal.), I:432
Sanary-sur-mer, I:492
São Paulo, III:290
Sarafand, III:347, 358, 360
Sarajevo, II:484
Sarid, II:591
Šariš, III:220, 306
Saris-Zemplin. *See* Šariš
Sarna, III:333

---

*The city of Prague is not included in this index because of its frequent occurrence throughout these three volumes. For subjects related to Prague, including its Jewish religious and communal institutions, see Subject Index.

PLACE INDEX 663

Šaštín-Stráže, II:190, 561
Satov, I:489
Savannah (Ga.), I:370
Sawina, III:283
Schlackenwerth. See Ostrov
Schönlinde. See Krásná Lípa
Schüttenhofen. See Sušice
Schwarzheide, III:301
Sečovce, II:561
Semily, II:227
Senica, I:81, 415; II:561, 562
Sered, II:167, 190, 285, 558, 646; III:214, 215, 228, 234, 306, 308, 313, 314, 315
Sète, III:352, 354
Sevluš, I:136, 142, 217; II:36, 276, 328, 356, 410, 554; III:38, 613
Sezemice, I:420
Shanghai, I:401; III:366
Sidi Bashir, III:366
Sidi Bel Abbès, III:345
Skirotawa, III:277, 278
Sklené, III:230
Skuteč, I:420
Slatina, I:129; II:519
Slavkov (Austerlitz), III:590
Sliač, II:501, 519
Slovenská L'upča, II:37
Snina, III:424, 509
Sniatyn, III:413
Sobibor, III:148, 275, 281, 283, 289, 290, 309, 310
Sobrance, II:518
Sokolov (Falknov), III:26
Sokolovo, III:26, 398, 401, 402, 403, 405, 414, 423
Sosnowiec-Bedzin, III:170, 188, 221
Southampton, III:355
Southwold, III:379
Spišská Nová Ves, I:100, 425; II:518, 553
Spišské Podhradie, II:162, 559
Stalingrad, III:132
Stará Paka, II:220
Staré Mésto, I:375
Stettin, I:373, 430
Štítnik, II:517
Stockholm, III:469
Strakonice, I:35, 418, 541
Strasbourg (Strassburg), II:525
Strassburg. See Strasbourg
Strážnice, II:190, 367

Střešovice (Prague), III:22
Stříbo (Mies), I:373; II:262
Štubianské Teplice, II:304, 328
Stupava, I:117; II:162, 164, 560, 561
Stutovo. See Stutthof
Stuttgart, I:551
Stutthof, III:278, 280, 301
Suchdol, II:219, 475
Sudetenland, III:3, 4
Šumperk (Mährisch Schönberg), I:415
Šurany, II:165, 190
Sušak. See Rjeka
Sušice (Schüttenhofen), I:44, 396
Suzdal, III:363
Svalava, II:410
Svatoňovice (Malé Svatoňovice), I:373
Svätý Júr. See Júr pri Bratislave

Tábor, I:31, 381; II:246, 534
Tachau. See Tachov
Tachov (Tachau), I:70, 339, 350, 367
Talin, III:280
Taormina, II:495
Tarnopol, III:338
Tatranská Polianka, II:500
Tauss. See Domažlice
Tbilisi (Tiflis), III:388
Teheran, III:366
Tel-Aviv, I:449, 498, 502, 503, 508, 542, 544; II:13, 89, 141, 197, 204, 210, 235, 238, 512, 642, 643, 646, 647, 655; III:348, 359, 463
Teplice-Šanov (Teplitz-Schönau), I:22, 31, 32, 70, 297, 315, 340, 398, 403, 417; II:22, 37, 39, 40, 91, 109, 117, 174, 190, 195, 207, 219, 230, 236, 238, 241, 250, 262, 285, 328, 329, 543
Teplitz-Schonau. See Teplice-Sanov
Teresinov (Theresiental), I:415
Terezín (Theresienstadt), I:446, 450, 547, 548, 556, 557; II:182, 209, 239, 246, 248, 249, 250, 469, 477, 488, 489, 490, 491; III:37, 62, 73, 75, 102, 104, 106, 107, 108, 110, 111, 114, 115, 116, 117, 118, 119, 120, 122, 123, 124, 125, 126, 127, 128, 130, 131, 132, 133, 134, 135, 136, 137, 139, 140, 141, 142, 143, 144, 145, 146, 147, 148, 149, 150, 151, 220, 236, 264, 268, 269, 270, 272, 274, 275, 276, 278, 279, 280, 281, 282, 283, 284, 285, 286, 287, 288, 289,

Terezín (*Cont.*)
  290, 291, 292, 293, 294, 295, 296, 297, 299, 300, 303, 315, 469, 502, 515, 517, 518, 579
Teschen. *See* Český Těšín
Tetschen. *See* Děčín
Tewfik, III:369
Theresienstadt. *See* Terezín
Tietsack, III:301
Tiflis. *See* Tbilisi
Timoshenkovo, III:398
Tirnau. *See* Trnava
Tisovec, I:375
Tisnov, II:533, 534
Tobruk, II:635; III:365, 366, 368, 369
Topoľčany, II:162, 153, 165; III:424, 509, 538
Toronto (Canada), I:374, 413
Toruň, I:140, 216, 217
Trautenau. *See* Trutnov
Trawniky, III:282, 286
Třebíč, I:69, 70, 419; II:262, 534
Treblinka, III:30, 203, 281, 283, 289, 290, 309
Třeboň, III:285
Trenčianské Teplice, I:378; II:162, 296, 331, 517
Trenčín, I:390, 425; II:217, 227, 328, 377, 517, 559
Treves. *See* Trier
Trier (Treves) II:387
Trieste, I:367, 429, 430; III:42
Trnava (Tirnau), I:79, 80, 81, 89, 91, 111, 115, 383, 388, 424; II:24, 162, 164, 165, 171, 190, 262, 289, 292, 328, 329, 365, 369, 553, 554, 558, 559, 561; III:197
Trnovany (Turn), I:550
Trnovo nad Teresvou, I:130
Troppau. *See* Opava
Trstená, II:560
Truški, III:410
Trutnov (Trautenau), I:45, 388, 414, 426; II:54, 108, 109, 207, 241, 328, 582
Tucson (Arizona), I:500
Tulcea, II:611; III:360
Tuln a.d. Donau, II:519
Turčansky Svätý Martin. *See* Martin
Turn. *See* Trnovany
Turnov, III:31
Turnu-Severin, II:611
Tužany nad Váhom, II:517

Uherské Hradiště, I:394; II:23, 37, 109, 186, 187, 190, 197, 219, 224, 284, 302, 331, 555; III:590
Uherský Brod (Ungarisch Brod), II:54, 190, 377, 555; III:21
Uherský Ostroh, I:394; II:39, 362
Uhlířské Janovice, I:63
Ujazdow, III:275
Ulič, III:538
Ungarisch Brod. *See* Uherský Brod
Ungvár. *See* Uzhorod
Unhošť, I:390
Uničov, I:428
Unterhaus (near Gera), II:517
Úpice, I:414
Úsov (Mährisch Aussee), I:71
Úštěk, I:382
Ústí nad Labem (Aussig), I:35, 290, 374, 386, 394, 426, 547; II:37, 40, 109, 190, 255, 586; III:26, 612
Ústí nad Orlicí, II:217
Uzgorod. *See* Užhorod
Užhorod (Uzgorod, Ungvar), I:98, 103, 129, 135, 136, 146, 216, 217, 274, 307, 425, 431, 528, 537; II:37, 51, 54, 75, 86, 105, 107, 213, 285, 297, 328, 331, 358, 359, 362, 369, 371, 375, 387, 406, 519, 554; III:316, 317, 418

Valašská Belá, III:231
Varnsdorf (Warnsdorf), I:411; III:509, 523, 524, 529
Vasilkovo, III:409
Vatican, III:210, 242, 250, 310, 313, 318, 465
Vaucelles, II:532
Vážec, II:517
Velím, I:389
Velké Meziříčí, I:21
Velké Popovice, I:380
Velké Šurany. *See* Šurany
Veľky Berezný (Velikij Bereznyj), I:152; II:329
Veľky Meder, II:167
Veľky Šariš, I:82
Venice, II:549
Verbo. *See* Vrbové
Veseloje, III:404
Vézelay, II:533

PLACE INDEX 665

Vienna, I:17, 19, 23, 24, 26, 57, 59, 76, 80, 102, 111, 112, 115, 116, 128, 158, 163, 286, 333, 343, 345, 346, 360, 362, 364, 365, 367, 368, 369, 373, 376, 387, 412, 415, 421, 427, 429, 431, 440, 471, 473, 474, 475, 476, 477, 479, 482, 492, 496, 498, 499, 503, 504, 528, 536, 541, 543, 546, 550; II:xviii, 7, 21, 22, 23, 58, 80, 83, 89, 103, 104, 108, 109, 110, 114, 120, 138, 142, 163, 164, 165, 167, 171, 175, 180, 186, 187, 190, 191, 196, 202, 204, 206, 208, 223, 235, 236, 254, 273, 280, 339, 370, 372, 382, 399, 402, 468, 475, 477, 478, 479, 487, 489, 503, 509, 517, 518, 519, 553, 554, 555, 576, 587, 607, 608, 610; III:22, 48, 50, 105, 119, 146, 151, 250, 266, 278, 288, 303, 317, 359, 360, 571, 611
Vilbert-Rozay, III:351
Vimperk (Winterberg), I:418
Vitkov, III:266
Vitkovice, I:373, 374, 401, 402, 430; II:190; III:26
Vlašim, I:428; II:217
Voroshilovgrad, III:392
Vranov, I:101
Vratislavice, I:416
Vratimov, I:393
Vrbove (Verbo), II:163, 167, 561
Vrchlabí (Hohenelbe), I:45
Vrchovina, I:129
Vrútky, I:98; II:118
Vsetín, III:20, 21, 612
Vtáčnik (mountain), III:227
Vyhne (near Bratislava), III:170, 214, 215, 229, 306, 313
Vyškov, II:262
Vyšné Hágy, II:486
Vyšší Brod, II:533, 534, 537

Walkenried, II:533
Walton on Naze, III:379
Wannsee, III:276
Warnsdorf. *See* Varnsdorf
Warsaw, I:431; II:89, 121, 210, 216, 579; III:138, 248, 283
Wartburg, II:533

Washington, D.C., I:370, 393, 497; II:647; III:590
Weddel, III:301
Weimar, I:497, 503
Westerbork (Holland), III:120
Wieprzerp, III:281
Wimbledon, II:212
Winterberg. *See* Vimperk
Worms, II:523, 533, 544
Wrocanka, III:418
Wülzburg, I:546
Würzburg, I:547

Zagreb, II:212
Zakopané, II:192, 197
Žalhostice, I:419
Zám, II:518
Žamberk, II:227
Zamosc, III:266, 285
Žatec, I:382, 404; II:227, 241; III:559
Zborov (near Bardejov), II:517, 564
Zbraslav, I:416, 494
Zdice, II:220
Zemianské Kostol'any, III:227, 230
Zemplin, I:122
Žhitomir, III:409
Žilina, I:85, 92, 101, 110, 112, 117, 391, 392, 412, 426, 528; II:39, 40, 193, 198, 202, 208, 212, 213, 217, 224, 273, 285, 306, 307, 328, 329, 331, 355, 382, 505, 553, 554; III:193, 215, 221, 247, 303, 306, 308, 317
Zinnwald. *See* Cinvald
Zlatá Koruna, I:396
Zlaté Moravce, II:164
Zlíchov, I:398
Zlín. *See* Gottvaldov
Znaim. *See* Znojmo
Znojmo (Znaim), I:353, 390, 425; II:40, 187, 190, 328, 555, 608; III:348, 359
Zohor, III:38, 187, 215, 306
Zurich, I:227, 274, 499, 502; II:46, 74, 93, 159, 196, 571, 583
Zveňigorodka, III:411
Zvíkov, II:533
Zvolava, I:217
Zvolen, I:88, 89, 401; II:37
Zwardón, III:197

SUBJECT INDEX, VOLUMES I-III*

A-Juden ("A-Jews"; individuals officially belonging to the Jewish faith), III:503, 511, 521
Academy of Fine Arts (Prague), II:471, 472, 474, 476, 481, 495
Achei Zion (Zionist society), II:24
Actors, Jewish, I:542, 548. *See also* Theater, Jews in
Adult education, Jewish I:344
Afike Jehuda (organization for the dissemination of Jewish knowledge), I:5-6, 344
Afike Yehuda. *See* Afike Jehuda
Aged, Jewish homes for, II:231; III:517
Agrarian party, Czechoslovak, I:97, 98, 107, 131, 136; II:269, 272; III:3, 15
Agrarian Reform Law (Slovakia). *See* Land Reform Act (Slovakia, 1919)
Agriculture, Jews in, I:39, 76, 89, 129, 379-80; II:591
Agudah. *See* Agudath Israel
Agudat Israel. *See* Agudath Israel
Agudat Shofte HaHakhra'a HaYehudit (ASHY: Jewish League of Soccer Referees), II:198-99
Agudath Dovrei Ivrith (Hebrew-Speaking Union), I:141; II:403
Agudath Israel, I:251 (n. 62); II:353; Founding Conference (1912), II:155; Kenessiah Gedolah (1st, 1923), II:160, 164; (2nd, 1929), II:165; (3rd, 1937), II:168; press, I:528; II:162, 163, 166, 167; in Slovakia, II:155-72, 353, 370; women's and girls' groups, II:165-66, 167; World Organization,

III:455; youth movements, II:162, 165, 168; and Zionism, II:156, 157, 158-59, 161; during Holocaust, II:169; III:142; after Holocaust, III:506, 534, 542
Ahavat Zion Society (Slovakia and Hungary), I:79; II:22, 24, 176
Ahdut HaAvoda (Zionist party), II:58, 59
Air force, Czech, II:217; during World War II, I:432, 435 (n. 16); III:384-89
Aktion Gitter ("Operation Bars"; mass arrests in 1939), III:19-20
Aktion Reinhard ("Operation Reinhard" in Lublin region), III:280-81
Aliya, First, Second and Third, II:116 (n. 96)
Aliya Bet (illegal immigration to Palestine), II:594, 600-03, 607, 608, 609; III:xxxii, 171, 555. *See also* "Illegal boats"
Allgemeine Jüdische Rundschau (Mizrahi newspaper), II:24
Allgemeine Jüdische Zeitung (newspaper, founded 1933), I:528
Alliance Israelite Universelle, II:261, 393
Almanacs and calendars, Jewish, I:7, 39, 45, 341-42, 344, 524, 525, 526, 529, 533, 535; II:151 (footnote)
Ältestenrat der Juden (Council of Jewish Elders), III:36; in Prague, III:xxxvi, 49, 50, 51, 52, 88, 500-01, 513, 577; of Slovak Jews in Konskalowa, Lublin region, III:310;

* *Compiled by Gertrude Hirschler*

Ältestenrat der Juden (*Cont.*)
  in Terezín, III:xxxix, 106, 111, 114-17, 118, 119, 130, 131, 137, 140, 141, 144, 145, 147 (note 6), 299, 302. *See also* Judenrat
Altneuschul (Old-New Synagogue), I:8, 14, 331, 337, 338; II:450, 472, 520-46, 588; III:21, 570, 572, 574-75, 580 (note 3), 582-83 (note 17), 590
Altschul (Old Synagogue, Mikulov), II:547-51
Altschul (Old Synagogue, Dušní ulice, Prague), I:331, 341, 342; II:542, 545; III:580 (note 3)
Aluf Tefila (prayer book), I:340-41
American Central Jewish Relief Committee, I:98
American Jewish Committee, III:517
American Jewish Congress, I:164, 228; II:255; III:468, 492-93 (note 63)
American Jewish Joint Distribution Committee (JDC), I:88, 91, 96, 130; II:144, 163, 320, 397, 399; III:7, 40, 41-42, 49, 50, 170, 172, 222, 234, 251 (note 72), 514, 516, 517, 525, 535, 541, 542
American Zionist Federation, I:167. *See also* Zionist Organization of America
Anglo-American Committee of Inquiry on Palestine, Rada representatives testify before, III:524
Anglo-American Conference on Refugees (Bermuda, 1943), III:470
Anglo-Jewish Association, I:177; II:261
Anti-Jewish discrimination, pre-Nazi era, I:204, 207; II:265, 323, 395, 437; during Holocaust, III:77-80, 83-84, 86-87, 166, 176, and *passim*
Anti-Jewish legislation, during Nazi era, I:117; II:578; III:xxix, xxx, 22, 24, 34-35, 43, 75-103, 165-66, 167, 174, 175, 176, 198-200, 245 (note 20), 304 and *passim*. *See also* Aryanization; Jewish Code
Anti-Semitism, I:25, 26, 463; II:16, 455-59, 461-63; III:474; *pre-1918*, I:17, 18, 34, 36, 37, 44, 45, 60, 77-78; *1918-39*, I:73, 86, 91-92, 107, 109-10, 111, 115-16, 117, 133, 137, 139, 151-52, 167-69, 207, 220, 244, 246-47 (notes 42 and 43), 248 (note 45), 273; II:232, 243-44, 260, 263, 264, 265, 268, 271, 280-81, 283, 289-90, 296, 304, 307, 315, 316, 317, 321, 324, 325, 329, 335, 336, 338, 409; II:10; *1939-1945*, Vol. III passim; *1945-1948*, III:424, 445-56 (note 288), 484-85, 508-11, 512, 522, 529 (note 34), 533, 535, 536, 538-39, 540-41; after Communist takeover in 1948, II:251-52; a-S themes in Czech literature, I:460-64, 465, 466. *See also* Armed Forces, Czechoslovak, World War II, anti-Semitism in; Slanský trials
Anti-Zionism and anti-Zionists, I:527, 529, 531; II:413; Arab, II:100; British, II:100. *See also* Agudath Israel, Assimilationists, Hasidim and Hasidism
Arab Refugees. *See* Refugees, Arab in Middle East
Arab Riots (1929), II:89, 237
Arabs in Palestine, III:357
Arbeitsgemeinschaft sozialistischer Zionisten. *See* Working Association of Socialist Zionists
Architects, Jewish, II:485-86
Arijský boj ("The Aryan Struggle"; anti-Semitic sheet), III:15
Arlosorovia (Zionist students' organization), II:176, 180, 183
Armed Forces, Czechoslovak, and Jews in; before World War II, I:434 (note 10); during World War II, II:510, 600, 635-36; III:286, 331-448, 457, 469, 514; anti-Semitism in World War II, II:636; III:18-19, 337, 338-39, 347, 349, 350, 358, 362-63, 365, 367, 368, 370, 372-76, 377-78, 381, 384-85, 386, 388, 394, 404, 407, 412, 414-15, 422, 443 (note 224), 444 (note 246), 449-52; in England, II:635, 636; III:225, 347, 359, 369, 370, 371-80, 406, 415, 416; in France, III:225, 339, 343-56, 372, 478; in Middle East, II:635, 636; III:225, 338, 339-40, 347, 356-70, 406, 415, 478; in Poland, III:334-38, 339, 340; in USSR, III:xxxiv, 25-26, 225, 267, 347, 368, 379, 389-424, 453; registration of Czechoslovak Jews in Palestine for draft into, III:xxx, xxxi, 346-47, 359, 366, 462, 463, 476-81; in

Armed Forces (*Cont.*)
  liberation of Czechoslovakia, III:422-24; in liberation of Belgium and France, III:381-84; list of Jews killed in, III:427-34; list of Jewish recipients of Soviet decorations, III:433; Jewish chaplains in, before and during World War II, I:347; III:350, 367, 372-73, 374, 375, 379-80, 381, 425, 513-14; women in, III:390, 394-95, 398, 399, 400, 405, 407, 411, 413, 416, 418-19, 421. *See also* under names of units
Arrow Cross party (Hungarian Fascists), III:316, 341
Art, religious, II:379-81, 470-71, 563; III:567, 570, 571, 572, 573-74, 575, 578-79. *See also* Museums, Jewish; State Jewish Museum, Prague
Artia (Czech government agency in charge of cultural properties), III:585
Artists, Jewish, Historic Lands, II:469-96; Slovakia, II:497-519; Nazi discrimination against Jewish artists, III:88. *See also* Holocaust, art and artists in
Aryanization, II:606; III:xxxi, xxxii, 16, 22, 23, 26-28, 75, 166-68, 174, 175, 177-78, 179, 211, 251 (note 73), 306, 535, 539, 540; abolished in Czechoslovakia by Presidential Order No. 5/1945, III:536
Aschrei Zion (Zionist organization), II:22
Ashkenazi ritual, I:336. *See also* Nusakh Ashkenaz
Assanierung (Prague slum clearance project), I:42
Assimilation and assimilationists, I:22-23, 50, 58, 60, 76, 91, 134, 136, 149, 150, 173, 268, 269, 272, 294-95, 319, 321, 324, 333-34, 335, 457, 482, 523, 524; II:21, 25, 29, 113, 141, 148, 149, 150, 151, 152, 161, 179, 180, 182, 263, 276, 315, 406, 464-66; III:10, 11, 38, 112, 124, 131, 504-05. *See also* Czech-Jewish movement
Associated Jewish Parties, I:90, 95
Association des Juifs de Tchécoslovaquie en France (1939), III:344, 350
Association for the Advancement of Jewish Religious Ritual (Prague), I:331
Association of Jewish Participants in the Czechoslovak Resistance Campaign *(Sdružení židovských účastníků československého odboje)*, III:565 (note 11)
Association of Jewish University Students in Czechoslovakia, II:180
Association of Political Zionists *(Gemeinschaft politischer Zionisten)*, II:42, 54, 129
Athletics. *See* Sports; Sports clubs
Atlantic, S.S., II:599, 611-14, 626, 632; III:361
Attorneys, Jewish, I:207, 427; III:84
Aufbau (German-language Jewish weekly, New York), II:628
Aufbaukommando(s) (construction detail([s]), Terezín), III:xxxiv, 31, 47, 110, 127, 133, 269
Auftakt, Der (German-language musical magazine, Prague), I:551-52
Ausgleich. *See* Constitutional Compromise (1867)
Austro-Hungarian monarchy, I:155-56, 157, 210, 214, 268, 332, 336, 362, 542; II:394
Auswanderungsfond für Böhmen und Mähren (Emigration Fund for Bohemia and Moravia), III:27, 30, 82, 88
Autonome orthodoxe Landeskanzlei für die Slowakei. *See* Autonomous Orthodox Regional Bureau for Slovakia
Autonomous Orthodox Jewish Religious Congregations, Hungary, Slovakia and Subcarpathian Ruthenia, I:93, 281, 301, 306, 307, 313; II:158, 160, 162, 352, 359, 377; III:169-70, 204, 534
Autonomous Orthodox Regional Bureau for Slovakia *(Ústredná zemská ortodoxní kancelár pro Slovensko; Autonome orthodoxe Landeskanzlei für die Slowakei)*, Bratislava, I:273-74; II:162, 267, 272, 353; III:244 (note 7), 245 (note 19)
Autonomous Orthodox Regional Bureau, Užhorod, II:359
Autonomy, Jewish cultural, I:219

Avoda (Palestine settlement society, founded in Prague, 1920), II:591

B-Juden ("B-Jews;" Jews according to the Nuremberg laws; Jews baptized, or of "non-Mosaic faith" or without official Jewish religious affiliation), III:43, 46, 503, 504, 511, 521

Balfour Declaration, I:88, 218; II:10, 13, 14, 26, 84, 159, 180, 589; III:482-83

Bargiora (Zionist students' couleur organization, Prague), II:176

Bar Kochba sports clubs, II:222 (note 35); in Berlin, II:186, 191, 196, 206, 210, 222 (note 35); in Czechoslovakia, II:208, 210, 226 (note 53). *See also* Sports clubs

Bar Kochba Zionist students' society, Bratislava, II:183; Prague, I:2, 19-20, 54, 60; II:20, 21, 36, 42, 56, 59-60, 62, 70, 109-10, 111, 140, 177-78, 179, 322, 323, 591, 596

Barissenblätter (news bulletin of Barissia organization), II:174

Barissia (*Jüdische Akademische Verbindung Barissia;* Barissia Jewish Students Association), II:20-21, 22, 110, 114, 174-75

Barissia-Jordania Jewish Academic and Technical Clubs, II:322, 323

Beau Bassin internment camp (Mauritius), II:618 ff.

BEBCA. *See* Böhmische Escompte Bank

Beer Textile Factory, Varnsdorf, III:522. *See also* Varnsdorf incident

Ben Guria (Zionist students' organization, Bratislava), II:176-77, 183

Besitzfähigkeit (right of Jews to own landed property, 19th century), I:39

Betar. *See* B'rit Trumpeldor

Bet(h) (Ha)Midrash (plu.: Batey Midrash, prayer or study hall), I:337, 340; II:366, 367, 371-72, 374, 375, 415

Beth Jacob (Zionist society, Trnava), II:25

Beth Jacob Schools (for Orthodox Jewish girls), II:165, 166-67, 172 (note 31), 370

Bikkur Holim (Visitors of the Sick), I:75; II:393

Binyan HaAretz (Zionist group), II:60, 116

Birth records, I:290, 291

Blätter für die jüdische Frau ("Jewish Woman's Pages," in *Selbstwehr*), II:143

Blau-Weiss (Blue-White). *See Te(c)helet Lavan.*

Blood libel. *See* Ritual murder trials

B'nai Akiva (youth group of Mizrahi movement), II:412; III:542

B'nai B'rith, I:5, 6, 271, 312, 527; II:229-33, 234-35, 236, 239, 240-42, 261, 373, 395, 397, 455; III:6; Joseph Popper Lodge, New York, I:10; II:235, 242; III:61 (note 11), 499 (footnote)

B'nai Zion (Zionist youth group, Bratislava), II:387 (note 58)

B'ne Emuna (Orthodox congregation of Teplitz-Schönau), I:340

Board of Deputies of British Jews, II:261; III:459, 461

Bodleian Library, Oxford, I:2

Böhmische Elegien (poems by Moritz Hartman, 1845), I:22

Böhmische Escompte Bank (BEBCA; Discount Bank of Bohemia), III:26

B'riha ("Flight"; underground Zionist organization, 1945-48), III:xl, 514, 531, 541, 554-55

Brill-Schul (synagogue, Bratislava), II:363, 379-80, 385 (note 46)

B'rit Trumpeldor (Betar; Revisionist Zionist youth organization), II:51, 72, 104, 105, 412, 591, 594; III:11, 172

B'rith Hachayal (Revisionist Zionist group, Bratislava), II:105

B'rith HaTzohar (Brith HaTziyonim HaRevisionistim; Union of Zionist Revisionists), II:99. *See also* Revisionism and Revisionists

B'rith Nashim Leumiyoth (Revisionist Zionist women's organization), II:105

B'rith Yeshurun (religious wing in Revisionist movement), II:105

British Broadcasting Corporation (BBC), Czech broadcasts from, during World War II, III:17-18

British Committee for Refugees from Czechoslovakia, III:38
British Mandatory Government (Palestine), II:100, 101-02, 103, 590; III:12, 171. *See also* Palestine Mandate
British Military Auxiliary Pioneer Corps, Czech soldiers join, III:375, 379
Brno, Conference (November 1947), II:246
Broadcasting, Jews in, I:544-46
Brundibár (children's opera composed in Terezín), I:547, 556 (note 13); III:125
Bund (Socialist organization), II:579; III:464
Burial brotherhood(s). *See* Hevra Kadisha
Business and industries, Jews in, I:40, 76, 129, 361-62; III:507; Airplanes, aeronautics and aviation, I:405-08, 430-31; II:215-16; alcohol manufacturing, I:40; automotive industries, I:404-05; banking and finance, I:361, 363, 364-66; III:26; beer, I:40, 380-81; butchering, I:129; chemical, I:394-95; clothing, I:416, 417, 418, 419, 420-21; commerce, I:424-26; communications, I:408-09; cork, I:421; distilleries, I:387; economic analysis and reporting, I:369-70; engineering, I:402-03; explosives and matches, I:395-96; fertilizer manufacturing, I:40; films, I:422; foodstuffs, I:386-87, 389, 390; forestry and lumber, I:391-92; furniture, I:394; glass, I:40, 397-400; III:26; hatmaking, III:26; health resorts, I:378-79; hosiery, III:26; insurance, I:366-69; knitting, I:417; land ownership, I:76, 89, 208-09; II:305; leather, I:419; malt and hops, I:381-82; metals, I:400-02, 404; mining, I:40, 372-75, 376, 377; III:26; navigation and ships, I:429-31; oil, I:375; pharmaceuticals, I:397; plywood, I:394; porcelain and ceramics, I:376-77; pulp and paper products, I:392-93; railroads, I:427-29; rubber, I:421; rugs, I:416-17; scientific research, I:371-72; shoes, I:419-20; shop ownership, I:129; skilled labor, I:129; starch, I:388; stocks and commodities, I:426; sugar production, I:40, 382-86; taverns, I:129; textiles, I:40, 41, 409-16; III:26; typewriters and business machines, I:403, 434; unskilled labor, I:129; water power, I:379; wholesale business, I:41-43; wine and liquor, I:389-90; yeast, I:387-88

Camp News (Mauritius), II:600
Cantors *(hazzanim)*, I:339, 345, 347; II:363, 372
Cartels and syndicates, I:423
Catholic Church and Catholics, I:44, 77-78, 268, 492, 550; II:244; and anti-Semitism, I:463; II:304; III:15, 183, 195, 208, 211-12, 219, 227, 237-38, 239, 240, 241-43, 252 (note 85), 254 (notes 100, 104), 255-56 (notes 112, 113), 319; in France, saved Jewish children during Holocaust, III:511. *See also* Vatican
Čechoslovák (official organ of Czechoslovak government-in-exile, World War II), III:377
Cemeteries, Jewish, I:vii, 7, 8, 14, 75, 117-18, 275, 293, 338, 349, 350; II:377-78, 522, 558-64, 588; III:572; desecrated after World War II, III:509; restored after World War II, III:515-16, 542
Census, population (1930), I:102-03; II:281; III:506, 508, 509, 520, 521
Center for the Emigration of Austrian Jews (organized by Adolf Eichmann), II:576
Central Association to Aid Refugees (Prague, 1930's), II:567; III:6
Central British Fund (CBF; refugee aid organization, London), III:517
Central Committee for the Social Welfare of the Jews in Slovakia. *See* Ústredný výbor pre sociálnu starostlivosť Židov na Slovensku
Central Council of National Jews from Czechoslovakia *(Ústřední rada národních Židů Československa,* London), III:373, 456, 457, 459, 463
Central Economic Office. *See* Ústredný hospodársky úrad *(ÚHÚ)*

Central European nations, Declaration of Independence of. *See* Declaration of Independence of Central European Nations
Central Federation of Jewish University Students, Prague, II:322-24
Central Jewish Museum, Prague (name during Holocaust), III:xxxv, 570-71, 573, 574, 575, 576, 577. *See also* State Jewish Museum, Prague
Central Jewish Office for the Region of Slovakia. *See Židovská Ústredná Úradovňa pre krajinu Slovensku*
Central Office for Jewish Emigration. *See Zentralstelle für jüdische Auswanderung*
Central Union of Jewish Religious Congregations in Slovakia (after Holocaust). *See Ústredný Sväz židovských náboženských obcí na Slovensku (ÚSŽNO)*
České Listy (poems by Siegfried Kapper, 1846), I:22
Československá Associace Footbalová (ČSAF: Czechoslovak Soccer Association), II:199
Československá samostatná brigáda. See Independent Czechoslovak Brigade
Československá samostatná obrněná brigáda. See Independent Czechoslovak Armored Brigade
Československý národní výbor. See Czechoslovak National Council (World War II)
Českožidovské listy (Jewish newspaper), I:524
Chapayev Partisan Fighters' Brigade, III:229
Chaplains, Jewish. *See* Armed Forces, Czechoslovak, and Jews in
Charity, Jewish, I:289, 294, 311; II:144, 237, 393. *See also* under names of organizations.
Charles University, Prague, II:214, 232; chair for modern Hebrew at, I:316
Chevra Kadisha. *See* Hevra Kadisha
Chmielnicki revolt and pogroms (1648), II:349, 356
Church and state, separation of, in post-1918 Czechoslovak Republic, I:335-36

Citizenship laws, II:285-86; III:13
Civil party (or "Citizens' party"; Subcarpathian Ruthenia). *See Občanská strana*
Civil rights, restoration after World War II, III:508
Civil service, Jews in, II:314-15; III:xxix, 14, 84, 507
Collaborators, Fascist, in Slovakia, punishment of, III:541
Comité des délégations Juives auprés de la Conférence de la Paix (Committee of Jewish Delegations at the Peace Conference; after World War I), I:169-70, 174, 224, 230-32; II:30, 261-62, 264, 330
Comité des Réfugiés de Tchécoslovaquie (France, 1938), III:343-44
Comité National Tchéco-Slovaque pour les Réfugiés provenant d'Allemagne (Czechoslovak National Committee for Refugees from Germany; 1930's), II:299 (footnote)
Comité pour les droits des Juifs (Committee for Jewish Rights; Paris Peace Conference), I:228
Committee for Jewish Rights. *See Comité pour les droits des Juifs*
Committee of Jewish Delegations at the Peace Conference. *See Comité des délégations Juives auprés de la Conférence de la Paix*
Committee to Aid the Jews of Subcarpathian Ruthenia, II:144
Communism and Communists, I:496; III:333, 343, 461; *1918-1939,* I:102, 112, 113, 131; II:81, 121 (note 189), 567, 572, 585; *1945-1948,* III:xxxix, xl, xli, 484, 505, 506, 511, 521, 522, 534-35, 536, 538, 539, 540, 555; after Communist takeover in 1948, I:451; II:251; III:424, 519-20, 525, 535, 541, 543, 557, 558, 560, 562, 563, 565 (note 11), 575: and anti-German resistance (World War II), III:36, 224, 403, 532; anti-Semitism and, I:450; II:251; in Czechoslovak armed forces (World War II), III:375, 381, 390, 393, 394-95, 409; and Czechoslovak government-in-exile, III:461; Jews accused of C. sympathies, I:109, 226-27; II:326;

Communism and Communists (*Cont.*)
III:368; and Jews, II:81; III:112,
341-42, 455, 505, 534; party
organization of Czechoslovak C.'s in
Moscow, III:392, 396-97, 402, 405,
406, 453; in Protectorate of Bohemia
and Moravia, III:14; in Slovak
puppet state, II:577

Composers, Jewish, I:540-41, 546-47,
548-49, 550, 551, 555. *See also*
Music, Jews in

Compulsory Education Law (1884),
I:75

Concentration camps, I:446, 448, 545,
546, 547, 548, 551; III:xxxv, 188-89,
214, 220, 222, 223, 226, 227, 229,
234, 239, 240, 272, 278, 279-82, 283,
284, 285, 288, 289, 290, 291, 293,
294, 295, 296, 297-99, 300-01, 302,
303, 308-09, 310-11, 314-15, 317, 318-
19, 342, 471, 510, 513. *See also*
Labor camps and labor centers; also
in name and place index

Concentration centers (Slovakia),
III:188, 214, 308; difference from
concentration camp, III:214

Concentration points (Slovakia),
III:214-16

Conductors, Jewish, I:542, 543, 545,
549, 555. *See also* Music, Jews in

Conference of European Zionist
Federations (Karlovy Vary, August
12, 1947), III:486-87

Conference of Jewish National
Councils (Paris, 1919), II:261

Conference of Zionist Students (Prague,
1920's), II:324-26

Confraternitaet (Jewish fraternal lodge),
II:240

Congregation Law (1890), I:49

"Congress" Congregations, I:93. *See
also* Neolog congregations

Congress of Czechoslovak Jews. *See*
Congress of Czechoslovak National
Jewry

Congress of Czechoslovak National
Jewry, First (Prague, 1919), I:169,
215, 222, 270; II:35, 258-59; Second
(Brno, 1920), II:267

Congress of Hungarian Jews (Budapest,
1868), I:73, 74, 75, 300; II:351, 352,
354, 359

Congress of Nationalities (Philadelphia,
1918), I:164-65

Conjoint Foreign Relations Committee
(of Board of Deputies of British
Jews), II:261

Conservative Jewish party (political
faction, *Židovská konzervativná
Strana*), I:91; II:270

Constitution of Czechoslovak Republic
(1920), extracts from, I:237-38

Constitutional Compromise (1867),
I:73, 79-80

Conversion of Jews and Jewish
converts, I:448; II:245; III:11, 183,
195, 198-99, 535

Copenhagen office (headquarters of
World Zionist Organization), I:157,
159, 168, 245-46 (note 41); II:36, 114

"Couleur" students' organizations,
II:21, 173, 174, 175, 176

Council of Jewish Elders. *See*
Ältestenrat der Juden

Council of Jewish Religious
Congregations in Bohemia and
Moravia (after World War II). *See*
Rada Židovských náboženských obcí v
Čechách a na Moravě

Cremation and burial urns, I:290, 293

Crusades and Jewish settlement in
Slovakia, II:348

Cultural life, Jewish, Subcarpathian
Ruthenia, I:139-46; after Holocaust
in Czechoslovakia, III:515. *See also*
Holocaust, cultural life in; Terezín,
cultural activities in

Currency Liquidation Fund Law
(1947), III:520

Customs, religious. *See* Minhagim

Czech and Slovak Legion (Poland,
World War II), III:337-38, 339, 340

Czech Assistance Action (following
liberation of Terezín), III:145

Czech Brethren's Protestant Church,
Synod of *(Synoda Českobratrské
Cirkve Evangelické)*, III:512

Czech Committee to Boycott Nazi
Germany, II:8

Czech-Jewish movement (Svaz Čechů-
Židů), I:33, 46, 50, 269, 270, 271,
272, 292, 294-95, 312, 319, 323, 324,
333, 448, 457, 523; II:113, 140, 148-

Czech-Jewish movement (*Cont.*)
54, 267, 276; III:10, 38, 71 (note 161), 344, 455, 458, 504-05, 506
Czech language, used by Jews in Czechoslovakia, I:18-19, 31-33, 35, 36, 212, 216, 295, 297-98, 331, 334
Czech Legion, World War I, I:440-41; III:3, 349; World War II, III:362, 365, 391
Czech literature. *See* Literature, Czech, Jews in
Czech National Democrats, II:272
Czech Philharmonic *(Česká Filharmonie)*, I:543, 546
Czech Realist party (Progressive party), II:64
Czech Refugee Trust Fund (England), III:70 (note 158)
Czech Scrolls. *See* Torah Scrolls, sent from Czechoslovakia to England
Czech Social Democrats. *See* Czechoslovak Social Democratic party
Czech Technical College (Brno), II:182, 183
Czech University of Prague, II:174, 178
Czecho-Slovakia (rump state following Munich agreement), I:113, 118, 324; III:xxix, 3-5, 11, 12, 13, 76
Czechoslovak, The (periodical, London, World War II), II:628
Czechoslovak Agrarian party. *See* Agrarian party, Czechoslovak
Czechoslovak Armored Brigade (England, World War II), II:636
Czechoslovak Bar Association, I:207
Czechoslovak Brigade (organized in Buzuluk, World War II), III:25-26
Czechoslovak Committee for the World Jewish Congress, II:333-35
Czechoslovak Friends of the Hebrew University in Jerusalem, II:232
Czechoslovak-Hungarian Trade Treaty, I:103
Czechoslovak Jewish Representative Committee (in U.S.), I:9-10; III:516
Czechoslovak League against Anti-Semitism, III:10
Czechoslovak Legion. *See* Czech Legion
Czechoslovak National Assembly, I:167, 169

Czechoslovak National Council (London, World War II), III:xxx, 17, 346, 351, 450, 453, 456
Czechoslovak National Socialist party (*not* a Nazi movement), II:245, 256
Czechoslovak Social Democratic party, I:107, 112, 133, 136, 202; II:33, 34, 78, 245-46, 247, 248, 249, 256, 258, 272, 281, 286-87, 292, 295; III:343
Czechoslovak-Soviet Treaty (1935), I:107
Czechoslovak Zionist Central Committee, II:73
Czechoslovak Zionist Conventions, 7th (Brno, 1926), II:274; 8th, II:276; 11th (1934), I:316; 12th (Moravská Ostrava, 1935), II:300
Czechoslovak Zionist Territorial Conferences, 1st (Prague, 1919), I:88, 271; II:36-37, 38, 124; 2nd (Brno, 1921), II:31, 34, 37, 60, 85, 124, 591; 3d (Moravská Ostrava, 1922), I:95; II:116, 124; 4th (Moravská Ostrava, 1923), II:124; 5th (extraordinary, Brno, 1924), II:124; 6th (Olomouc, 1924), II:61-62, 124; 7th (Brno, 1926), II:66, 67, 69, 124; 8th (Brno, 1928), II:73, 120, 124; 9th (Brno, 1929), II:74-75, 105, 124; 10th (Moravská Ostrava, 1932), II:44, 124; 11th (Moravská Ostrava, 1934), II:44, 124; 12th (Moravská Ostrava, 1938), II:40, 124, 399
Czechoslovak Zionist Territorial Federation *(Zemský svaz sionistický)*, II:31, 33, 34, 35, 38, 41, 42, 43, 44, 45, 50, 51, 53, 55, 60, 63, 64, 69, 70, 71, 73, 74, 75, 83, 84, 85, 88, 91, 92, 94, 97-98, 104, 106, 113, 120, 577, 588, 600; III:25
Czechoslovak Zionist Territorial Union. *See* Czechoslovak Zionist Territorial Federation
Czechs and Germans, Jews caught in struggle between (1848-1918), I:21-71

Darkei Teshuvah ("Paths of Repentance," Orthodox Jewish organization, Subcarpathian Ruthenia), II:428
Davar (Hebrew newspaper), I:140
Death marches, III:285-86

Deborah (Zionist girls' clubs, Slovakia), I:79
Declaration of Independence of Central European Nations, I:164
Decorations awarded to Jews, III:233; See also Armed Forces, Czechoslovak, and Jews in; list of Jewish recipients of Soviet decorations
Demec (underground group, World War II), III:224
Democratic faction (in Zionist movement), II:94-95
Democratic Refugee Relief Committee (Czechoslovakia, 1930's), II:567, 578
"Department B" (of Jewish Religious Congregation in Prague during Holocaust), III:513
"Department 14" (in Slovak Ministry for Internal Affairs), III:xxxiv, 175, 206, 217, 307
Department for Jewish Affairs (Czechoslovakia, 1946), III:523-24
Department for Special Tasks. See Oddelenie pre zvláštné úkony
Department of State, U.S., III:319, 468
Deportations (during Holocaust), III:xxxiii, xxxiv, xxxv, xxxvi, xxxviii, 24-26, 28-37, 45, 46-47, 48, 49, 50-52, 55-60, 89-90, 117-18, 120, 133, 134, 141, 187, 189-200, 201-03, 216, 217-18, 219, 222, 225, 234, 235, 239, 242, 263, 269, 290-95, 308-12, 313-15, 318-22, 464-65, 576-77; question of Jewish resistance to, III:203-07; slowdown in, III:xxxi, 132, 200, 207-13, 312-13. See also Concentration camps; Ghettoization; Terezín; under names of death camps
Derech (Hebrew newspaper), I:140
Deutsch-demokratische Freiheitspartei (Czechoslovakia, pre-Hitler), II:247-48
Deutsche Partei (ethnic Germans in Slovakia), III:304
Deutsche Technische Hochschule (German Technical University; Prague), II:281, 325
Dietary laws. See Kashrut
Dispensrabbiner, I:283
"Documentary Action" (Holocaust evidence-gathering agency, Slovakia), III:542
Dovrei Ivrith, II:403
D'ror (Zionist movement), III:542
Dueling fraternities (Schlagende Verbindungen), II:21
Dušegubka (plural: dušegubky; "soul-destroyers," sealed vans in which ghetto inmates were killed by exhaust fumes), III:274, 287, 288
Dušní ulice Synagogue (Prague). See Altschul (Old Synagogue, Dušní ulice, Prague)

East Africa scheme, II:10, 12, 13, 16
East Slovak Museum (Košice), II:502
East Slovak Republic (1918), I:86
Economy, Jews and, I:37-43, 94-95, 126-34, 205-10, 359-438; II:327-28, 408; elimination of Jews from, III:xxix, 21-22. See also Business and Industries, Jews in; Anti-Jewish discrimination; Anti-Jewish legislation during Nazi era
Education, Jews and; Jewish and modern Hebrew, I:49, 50, 141-42, 143, 144-46, 149, 270, 272, 296, 334; II:137, 138, 302, 308, 369-71, 400-49, 552; III:516; secular, I:37, 43, 49-50, 75-76, 142-43. See also Adult education, Jewish; Religious instruction of Jewish students at public schools; Religious instructors; Schools, Jewish; Yeshivoth; under names of Jewish educational institutions
Egyenlöseg ("Equality," Hungarian-language Jewish newspaper), I:80, 81
Eichmann trial, III:203
Einsatzgruppen (SS mobile killing squads), III:28, 271, 273, 277, 278, 286, 287
El Al Zionist High School Society (Bratislava), II:176
Elections, local, II:262, 268, 316, 317; parliamentary, I:xxi, 107, 135, 136, 201, 269, 271, 279, 296
Elections Tribunal, II:273
Electoral Union of the Polish and Jewish Parties (Subcarpathian Ruthenian election list, 1929), II:279

Elementary School Law, Imperial (1869), I:50
Emancipation Law (Hungary, 1867), I:73
Emancipation of Jews, I:12-17, 27, 30, 73-76
Emigdirekt (Emigration-Direction, organized in Berlin, 1921), II:397; III:7
Emigration, I:104-05, 114; II:181, 334; III:53, 88-89, 169, 542-43; to Palestine (Israel), I:96-97, 104-05, 112, 114, 411, 498, 499, 502, 503, 508, 542, 544; II:140-41, 145, 146-47, 168, 231, 235, 238, 379, 589-98, 642-44; III:12, 41, 42, 43, 171-73, 475, 476, 542, 554-55; to U.S., I:2-3, 26, 96-97, 374, 375, 377, 413, 433 (note 7), 434 (note 8), 490, 498, 499, 500, 501, 542, 548, 549, 522; II:235, 247, 250; to other countries, I:115, 413, 433 (note 5), 435 (note 11), 502, 503, 549; II:247; III:38, 42. *See also* Aliya; Aliya Bet; B'riha; "Illegal boats" to Palestine; Refugees, Jewish
Emunah Verein jüdischer Handelsangestellter (Emunah Federation of Jewish Commercial Employees; Brno), II:23, 24
Ethnic Germans. *See Volksdeutsche*
"Etzion base" (military airfield, Žatec), III:559-61
"Europa Plan" (proposal for ransoming of Jews), III:222
Evangelical Church (Slovakia), III:xxx, xxxii, 212
Evian Conference on Refugees (1938), II:314, 333-35; III:265

Familiantengesetz (law permitting only eldest son in a Jewish family to marry), I:22; II:348-49
"Family camp" (Auschwitz-Birkenau), III:xxxvii, xxxviii, 295-98, 299, 300, 301, 302, 303, 325 (note 51)
"Family purity" laws, I:335. *See also* Mikvah
Federation of Artists, Architects, Painters and Sculptors, I:207
Federation of Congregations in Slovakia (founded 1927), I:307
Federation of Czech Physicians, I:207

Federation of Czechoslovak Jews (England), III:70 (note 158)
Federation of Jewish Congregations (Bohemia, 1918), I:157
Federation of Orthodox Jews from Czechoslovakia (*Federace orthodoxních Židů z Československa,* London), III:455
Ferialverbindungen (Vacation societies organized by Zionist students), II:23
"Final Solution," III:xxxiii. *See also* Wannsee Conference
First Czechoslovak Field (Infantry) Battalion (World War II, Buzuluk), III:267, 340, 346, 389-98
First Independent Czechoslovak Army Corps (World War II, USSR), III:412-22
First Independent Czechoslovak Brigade (World War II, USSR), III:403-12
Fond národní obnovy (National Rehabilitation Fund), III:519
Fond pre podporu vysťahovalectva Židov. See Fund for Jewish Emigration
Fond pre správu poľnohospodárskych majetkov (Fund for the Administration of Agricultural Property, Slovakia, organized 1942), III:179, 211
Forced labor assignments, Slovakia, II:646 (note 15); III:186-89, 190, 221, 239, 306, 307, 316. *See also* Labor battalions; Labor camps and labor centers
Foreign Legion, French, III:344-45, 364, 450
Foreign Office, British, II:15, III:470
Fourteen Points (Woodrow Wilson), I:155, 242 (note 1); II:254
Fourth Tactical Group (in Slovak uprising), III:229
Frankist movement, II:357
Fraternal Orders. *See* Lodges and Fraternal Orders, Jewish
Free loan and charity fund. *See Gemilut Hesed*
Freemasons, II:567; III:7, 15
Freiwillige Schutzstaffel (FS: Volunteer Defense Squadron, Slovakia), I:114; III:175, 193, 194, 245 (note 17), 304, 308, 314

Freizügigkeit (freedom of Jews to move), I:27, 35
FS. *See Freiwillige Schutzstaffel*
Fund for Jewish Emigration *(Fond pre podporu vysťahovalectva Židov)*, Slovakia, III:18-81, 501. *See also* National Administration of the Assets of the Fund for Jewish Emigration
Fund for the Administration of Agricultural Property. *See Fond pre správu poľnohospodárských majetkov*

Gabella tax, I:313
Gegenwartsarbeit (Zionist cultural and political activities in the Diaspora), II:20, 23, 30
Gemeinschaft politischer Zionisten. See Association of Political Zionists
Gemilut Hesed (Free loan and charity fund), I:75
General Zionists, II:40, 44-45, 46, 48, 49, 51, 52-54, 70, 74, 75, 84, 115, 121, 127, 128, 129; III:542. *See also* Zionism and Zionists
German Aid Committee (for anti-Nazi refugees from Sudetenland), III:8
German language, used by Jews in Czechoslovakia, I:17-18, 36, 43, 46, 80, 100, 210, 216, 297-98, 315, 331, 334, 346, 469; II:274, 314; III:12, 39, 349, 509, 540
German literature, Jews of Czechoslovakia in, I:468-522
German National party (Prague), II:271
German nationality, Jews of, III:505, 520
German occupation of Austria, I:111-12, 322; II:312, 399, 566, 570, 583; of Belgium, III:xxxii; of Czechoslovakia, I:112, 524, 536; II:8, 147, 169, 177, 238, 239, 554, 574, 575, 592, 596; III:20, 39, 262, 332, 343, 344, 449, 502, 568; of Denmark and Norway, III:xxxi; of France, III:xxxvi; of Holland, III:xxxi; of Hungary, III:219, 220, 222-23; of Poland, II:169; III:xxx; of Slovakia, III:233-34; of Sudetenland, I:258 (note 144), 324; II:317-19, 507, 571, 574, 592; III:xxviii, 4, 7, 8, 262

German Social Democratic party in Czechoslovakia, II:249, 250, 251, 294; III:344, 351
German Socialist Medical Association, II:250
German Socialist movement (in Czechoslovakia), II:250
German University (Prague), I:6, 18, 19, 23, 104, 107, 548, 550, 551; II:174, 248, 271, 281, 322, 323, 324
German Workers' and Economic Union (northwestern Bohemia), II:280
"Germanization," pre-Nazi era, I:18, 342; II:149, 150; Nazi era, II:316; III:22, 34
"Germanization Schools." *See* "Normal Schools"
Germans, Jews regarded as, in Bohemia and Moravia after World War II, III:509
Geschichten aus dem Ghetto (Tales from the Ghetto, by Leopold Kompert, 1846, 1848, 1860), I:23, 474
Gestapo, III:19, 23, 38, 42, 119, 128, 150 (note 26), 222, 236, 264, 266, 571
"Ghent system" (unemployment relief scheme), I:97
Ghettoization (in Holocaust), III:141, 268-76, 277-79, 282, 286. *See also* Deportations; Terezín
Girls' Club (Zionist), II:138, 139, 140, 141, 591
Gordonia (Zionist youth movement), II:542
"Gottwald Brigade" (soldiers and pioneers in Israel from Czechoslovakia), II:562, 565 (note 11)
Government-in-exile, Czechoslovak (World War II), II:510, 633, 634; III:xxxviii, 17, 19, 223, 252 (note 85), 339, 358, 360, 361, 367, 371, 377, 389, 390, 397, 398, 413, 418, 423; and Holocaust, III:464-72; and Jews, III:449-95, 532; and Zionism, III:454, 455, 457, 458-60, 462-63, 474-84, 552
Government-in-exile, Polish (London), III:223, 464, 468

SUBJECT INDEX

"Great Anathema" (Rebbe of Mukačevo vs. Belz Hasidim), I:308; II:297. *See also Herem*
Grenzbote (German-language newspaper, Bratislava), III:255 (note 107), 310
Grosszähmung (Nazi dragnet operation in Bohemia and Moravia, 1942), III:34
Grynszpan affair, III:76. *See also Kristallnacht*

HaAretz (Hebrew newspaper), I:140
Habans pottery works, II:562
HaBima (Yiddish theater troupe, Slovakia and Subcarpathian Ruthenia), II:554, 555-56
Habimah (Israeli theater), I:97, 508, 509
HADEGA (German public purchasing agency for Jewish-owned precious metals and jewelry), III:xxxi, 27, 81, 82
"Hagana" (group of illegal immigrants to Palestine from Czechoslovakia), II:611, 612, 613
Haganah (defense force of pre-Israel Palestine Jewish community), III:363, 542, 554, 555, 556, 558, 559, 560, 561, 562
Hagibor (sports club), I:294; II:198, 200, 201-02, 203, 204, 205, 206, 208, 209, 210, 219, 220; III:52
Hagibor-Hamakabi (sports club magazine), I:527; II:202
Hagshamah (Zionist concept: "materialization"), II:425
Haint (Yiddish newspaper, Poland), I:140
Hakhnasat Kalla (organizations providing dowries for brides without financial means), II:393
Hakhshara(h) (plu.: *Hakhsharoth*; training centers for future pioneers in Israel), II:36, 51, 55, 66, 67, 71, 72, 139, 146, 268, 593, 601, 607, 608; III:41, 171, 244 (note 12), 516
Hakoah Sports Club, II:200, 206
HaKokhav (The Star; Hebrew monthly, founded 1935), I:529
Halle. See Jüdische Akademische Lese- und Rede-Halle

Halutz (plu.: *Halutzim*; pioneers in Israel), II:36, 137, 194, 303, 397, 601, 602, 606; III:36, 41, 228
Halutziut (pioneering in Israel), II:90, 313 (footnote), 430
Hamaabar Labogrim (HaShomer HaTza'ir monthly, Žilina), I:528
HaMaggid (Hebrew magazine), I:81
HaMakabi (official organ of Makkabi sports organization), II:194
HaMayan (The Fountain; Hebrew magazine, Bratislava), II:377
Hanoar Hatzioni (Zionist youth movement), II:412
HaOlam ("The World"; Hebrew magazine, Palestine), I:81, 140
HaOr (Czech Yiddish theater company), II:553, 554
HaOved (Zionist organization), III:542
HaPo'el Hamizrahi (labor wing of Mizrahi movement), II:171, 592
HaPo'el Hatza'ir (Labor Zionist movement), II:28, 32, 33, 37, 39, 42, 52, 53, 55-64, 65, 68, 69, 76, 80, 83, 85, 88, 89, 116, 117, 126, 590
HASAG (Hugo Schneider Aktiengesellschaft; munitions plant), III:271
Hashachar (high school society of Bar Kochba Zionist students' society, Prague), II:111 (note 20)
HaShomer (Socialist Zionist monthly, Bratislava, founded 1926), I:528
Hashomer (Socialist Zionist movement, Slovakia and Subcarpathian Ruthenia), I:96, 98; II:412, 591
HaShomer Hatza'ir (Socialist Zionist movement), I:528; II:28, 34, 43, 51, 87-88, 92, 412, 424-25, 430, 592, 601, 608, 644; III:35, 207, 224-25, 228, 232, 542, 564 (note 8)
HaShomer-Kadimah (Zionist organization, Slovakia and Subcarpathian Ruthenia), I:98; II:72, 412
Hasidism and Hasidim, I:350, 449; in Historic Lands, I:339; Slovakia, I:75, 330; II:369; in Subcarpathian Ruthenia, I:150, 330, 529; II:162, 313-14, 350, 355-56, 357-59, 360, 362-63, 369, 370, 406, 411, 425-30. *See also* Rebbes, Hasidic

Haskalah (Enlightenment), I:486
Hatchiya Libanonia (Zionist students' *couleur* organization, Prague), II:176
HaTehiyah (Zionist organization, Subcarpathian Ruthenia), I:141; II:403
HaTehiyah Libanonia. *See* Hatchiya Libanonia
HaTikvah (Jewish student organization, Brno and Prague), II:183
Hatikvah (Zionist and Israeli anthem), III:298
HaTzefira (Hebrew magazine), I:81
HaTzohar. *See* B'rith HaTzohar
Haver (honorary title awarded for contributions to Jewish life), II:373
Hazzanim. See Cantors
Hazmonea (Zionist students' *couleur* organization, Prague), II:176
Hebrew gymnasium, Mukačevo, I:20, 144, 314; II:142, 233, 274, 295, 297-98, 371, 415-19, 422, 426, 428, 429, 602
Hebrew gymnasium, Tel Aviv. *See* Herzliyah Gymnasium, Tel Aviv
Hebrew gymnasium, Užhorod, I:146; II:274, 371
Hebrew language, and Czechoslovak Republic, III:551; instruction in, I:296, 334; II:137, 138; laws restricting use of, I:241, 342; recognition as language of Jewish national minority, I:211, 212, 219, 275; II:90, 198, 281; use by Jews in Czechoslovakia, I:213
Hebrew University, Jerusalem, I:94, 97, 530; II:232, 376, 594; III:425, 518
Hebrew University and National Library, Jerusalem, II:232
Hechalutz. *See* HeHalutz
Hechalutz Hatzair (Zionist youth organization), II:435
Heder (cheder; plu.: hedarim; old-style one-room Hebrew schools), I:49, 146; II:370, 404
HeHalutz (Hechalutz; Zionist pioneering youth organization), II:39, 51, 63, 71, 88, 115, 117, 120, 143, 146, 296, 430-31, 594, 601, 608, 609, 610; III:35-36, 41, 49, 52, 223, 470, 552

HeHalutz Haklal Tzioni (General Zionist HeHalutz), II:51
Helios, S.S., II:610 ff.
Henlein party. *See* Sudetendeutsche Partei (SDP)
Herder Union. *See* Johann Gottfried Herder Union
Herem (ban, excommunication, anathema), I:145; II:358, 554
Hermann Göring Werke (German industrial concern), III:26
Herut party, III:436 (note 78). *See also* Revisionism and Revisionists
Herzliah Gymnasium, Tel Aviv, I:20; II:414
Hevra Kadisha (burial brotherhood), I:289-90, 293, 337, 349, 350; II:377-79, 393, 450, 470; III:568, 573; in Mauritius, II:626
Hevrat Shas (Talmud study association), I:75
HIAS (Hebrew Immigrant Aid and Sheltering Association), II:397; III:7
HICEM (acronym: HIAS, ICA, Emigdirekt), I:112, 115; II:397, 399, 647; III:7, 40, 170
Hiddush HaAdam ("renewal" of man; Zionist concept), II:56
High Synagogue (Hoch-Schul; Prague), I:337; III:47, 571, 580 (note 3)
Hilfsverein der deutschen Juden, II:14, 393
Hilsner ritual murder trial. *See* Ritual murder trials, Hilsner
Histadrut (Israel's general labor federation), II:71, 409, 418, 431
Histadrut Ole Czechoslovakia (Federation of Immigrants from Czechoslovakia in Israel), II:590-91. *See also* Hitahdut Ole(i), Czechoslovakia
Historical Surveys, Historic Lands *(pre-1918),* I:12-20; Slovakia *(1848-1938),* I:72-124; Subcarpathian Ruthenia *(1918-1938),* I:124-54
Historiography, Jewish, I:1-11, 312
Hitahdut. *See* Hitahdut 'Olamit shel HaPo'el Hatza'ir uTze'ire Zion
Hitahdut 'Olamit shel HaPo'el Hatza'ir *uTze'ire Zion* (Labor Zionist organization), II:32-33, 42, 51, 52, 58, 61, 62, 63, 64, 65, 67, 68, 69, 70,

Hitahdut (*Cont.*)
71, 72, 84, 85, 88, 89, 91, 92, 126, 127, 128
Hitahdut Ole(i) Czechoslovakia (Union of Immigrants from Czechoslovakia in Israel), II:591, 643; III:480, 481
Hlinka Guard (HG, Hlinkova Garda), I:114; II:455, 604, 605; III:xxx, xxxiv, 175, 182, 193, 194, 196, 212, 217, 226, 227, 245 (note 17), 246 (note 39), 304, 308, 314, 424
Hlinka party. *See* Slovak People's party
Hlinkova Garda. *See* Hlinka Guard
Hlinkova slovenská ludová strana. See Slovak People's party
Hoch-Schul. *See* High Synagogue
Holič factory (ceramics), II:562
Holocaust; I:9; II:145; III:passim; aftermath, I:364; III:484-87, 499-550, 554; art and artists in, II:488-91, 495, 496; III:126-29, 272; cultural life in, III:215-16, 272-73; literature of, I:445, 450-51, 465; III:124; memorials, III:542, 576, 578, 582 (note 16); music of, I:547, 556-58 (notes 13 and 14); III:124, 125, 272; survivors and rehabilitation of, III:xl, 516, 517, 518-19, 525, 531, 532-33; theater, III:124-25
Horsemanship. *See* Sports, Jews in
"Hort" (mutual assistance association, Prague and Brno), II:239-40
Hotels, kosher, I:348; III:514
House of Commons, British, II:574, 632, 638; III:319, 469
House of Representatives, U.S., II:639
Hover. See Haver
Hoveve Zion (pre-Herzlian Zionist movement), I:79
Hradčany Palace, *III:20, 30, 78, 562, 577*
Hungarian Jewish Congress. See Congress of Hungarian Jews (Budapest, 1868)
Hungarian language, used by Jews in Czechoslovakia, I:18, 73, 80, 100, 210, 212; II:311-12, 411; III:349, 540
Hungarian Social Democrats (Czechoslovakia), II:247
Hungarian Zionist Organization, I:79; II:19, 24, 25, 97, 436
Hungarization. *See* Magyarization

ICA. *See* Jewish Colonization Association
IHUD (United Socialist Zionists), II:88-94
"Illegal boats" to Palestine, II:599, 600, 607, 610, 611-14, 615, 626, 632; III:11, 171-72, 305, 359-61. *See also* Aliya Bet
Illustrierte Welt, Die (German-language Jewish family paper, Prague, 1935-39), I:525
IMI pockets (miniature Jewish National Fund box), II:114 (note 52)
Indemnification of war victims in Czechoslovakia, III:516
Independent Czechoslovak Armored Brigade *(Československá samostatná obrněná brigáda)*, III:380-84
Independent Czechoslovak Brigade *(Československá samostatná brigáda)*, III:376-80
Industrial Revolution, I:22, 32
Industrialization, I:360
Institute for the History of Contemporary Jews, III:425
Intelligentsia, Jewish, in Bohemia and Moravia, II:440-54
Interdenominational Law of 1925, I:302
International Brigade (Spanish Civil War), I:496; III:350, 375, 390, 401
International Federation of Private Employees, II:247
International Red Cross, III:xxxviii, xxxix, 18, 136-37, 142-43, 144, 145, 222, 235-36, 325 (note 53)
International Women's League for Peace and Freedom, II:583 (footnote)
Internment camp (in Svatobořice), III:35
Irgun Z'vai Leumi, III:436 (note 78)
Israel, Czechoslovak political and military support of, III:541-42, 551-66
Israel air force, founded with Czechoslovak help, III:559-60
Israel armed forces, Jews from Czechoslovakia in, II:644; III:542
Israeli Legation, Prague, II:529; III:562, 564 (note 9)

Israelitisches Familienblatt (Mizrahi organ, Czechoslovakia, founded 1926), I:528

Jaldut (children's monthly, Prague), I:526
Jan Žižka Partisan Brigade, III:231
JDC. *See* American Jewish Joint Distribution Committee
Jeschurun Federation of Jewish Religious Congregations in Slovakia (founded 1928), I:93, 306-07, 316, 317, 318; II:350, 352, 355, 373, 377; III:204, 244 (note 7), 534
Jewish Agency, I:316; II:53, 84, 89, 593, 596, 597, 615, 638, 641, 643, 653-54; III:xxxvi, 12, 38, 223, 313, 357-58, 359, 373, 379, 460, 462, 469, 470, 476, 477, 478, 480, 481, 486, 535, 543, 552, 553
Jewish Aid Committee (for refugees, Prague), III:6
Jewish Brigade group (World War II), II:637; III:477
"Jewish Clauses" (of Polish "Model Treaty" re Jewish minority rights), I:172
Jewish Code (*Judenkodex,* Slovakia, September 1941), III:xxxiii, xxxiv, 181-84, 210, 212, 218-19, 238, 246 (note 27), 263, 306
Jewish Colonization Association (ICA), I:131; II:393; III:7
Jewish Committee of Aid for Refugees from Germany, II:397; III:6
Jewish Communist party of Czechoslovakia (1920's), II:81
Jewish Cultural Society of Slovakia, I:101-02
Jewish Democratic party. *See* Conservative Jewish party
Jewish Economic party *(Židovská hospodářská strana),* I:91, 98, 202; II:272
Jewish Farmers' party (*Židovská agrární strana;* Subcarpathian Ruthenia), I:136
Jewish Historical Society of England, and Oskar K. Rabinowicz, II:1, 9, 17
Jewish Hospital, Bratislava (1930), I:101

Jewish Ladies Aid Committee for Subcarpathian Ruthenia, II:330
Jewish Legion, II:6, 100, 102, 103
Jewish Museum Association (Czechoslovakia), I:311
Jewish Museum Society (Slovakia), I:101
Jewish National Committee (Slovakia), II:264
Jewish National Council (*Národní rada židovská;* post-World War I), I:87, 88, 90, 95, 134, 156-57, 158, 159-60, 161, 166, 167, 168, 169, 173-74, 218-21, 222, 224, 227-29, 231, 245 (note 41), 248 (note 45), 269-70, 275, 505; II:31, 32, 33, 78, 85, 98, 142, 253, 256, 257, 258, 260, 262, 263, 264, 265-66, 267, 268, 270, 271, 272-73, 275, 276, 278, 319-20, 321, 395
Jewish National Fund (JNF: Keren Kayemet), I:96; II:36, 55, 66, 83, 98, 105, 119, 138, 141, 143, 175, 177, 178, 181, 194, 268, 411, 434, 597; III:42, 542
Jewish national minority, I:90, 94, 100, 110, 134, 138, 144, 145, 155-265, 267, 270, 275, 333; II:29, 30, 149, 254-55, 257, 259-60, 291, 305-06, 338-39; struggle for recognition, I:155-77; and government-in-exile, III:472-75, 506
Jewish National party. *See* National Jews (political party)
Jewish National Soldiers, Councils. *See* Jewish Soldiers' Councils
Jewish Office. *See* Ústredňa Židov (ÚŽ)
Jewish party *(Židovská strana),* I:87, 89, 90, 91, 97, 98, 99, 102, 107, 108, 110, 112, 116, 131, 132, 133, 135, 136, 137, 138, 152, 160, 201-02, 269, 274, 275, 319-20, 531; II:31, 32, 33, 34, 85, 98, 143, 144, 176, 253-346, 351, 353, 418, 429, 430; III:169, 244 (note 8), 344, 456, 457, 458, 460, 462, 463, 464, 501
Jewish People's Association. *See* Jüdischer Volksverein
Jewish People's Council. *See* Jüdischer Volksrat
Jewish Press Bureau (Bratislava), II:263, 319-22

SUBJECT INDEX

Jewish Refugee Relief Committee (Prague, 1930's), II:299
Jewish Religious Congregation, Berlin, III:50, 118-19
Jewish Religious Congregation (Jüdische Kultusgemeinde), Vienna, III:50, 118-19
Jewish Religious Congregations *(Kultusgemeinden)*, Czechoslovakia, I:47-48, 160, 220, 270, 271; II:79; III:23, 32, 37, 265, 513; history of *(1918-38)*, I:267-329; Federations of, I:297, 298; III:274; laws regarding structure and status, I:276-91; II:332-33; Provincial Union of, Moravia and Austrian Silesia, I:221-22; Supreme Council of Federations of, Bohemia, Moravia and Silesia *(Nejvyšší Rada)*, I:310, 312, 313, 317, 344, 346-47; II:150, 307; III:6, 7, 13, 37, 399, 513; Bratislava, III:50; Brno, II:181; III:37, 108; České Budějovice, III:264; Moravia, II:258, 278; Moravská Ostrava, I:271, 321-22; III:37; Pelhřimov district, III:264; Prague *(pre-1939)*, I:42, 269, 279, 284, 291-95, 338, 344; II:333, 567; (1939-45), III:xxxi, xxxvi, 15, 21, 24, 25, 29, 30-31, 32, 33, 37, 38, 39, 42, 43, 44, 46, 48, 49, 50, 147 (note 5), 265, 269, 499, 500, 502, 503, 569, 571; *(after 1945)*, III:272, 501, 502, 504-05, 506, 512, 581 (note 10); Slovakia, I:73-75; III:50, 175, 209. *See also* Jeschurun Federation of Jewish Congregations in Slovakia; *Rada Židovských náboženských obcí v Čechách a na Moravé*
Jewish Religious Congregations, Hungary, III:50
Jewish Restitution Successor Organization (JRSO), III:519
Jewish Sick Relief Organization *(Židovská péče o nemocné*, Prague), II:398
Jewish Social Service Center (of Supreme Council of Federations of Jewish Religious Congregations of Bohemia, Moravia and Silesia), I:311-12
Jewish Socialist Council (1918), II:78

Jewish Soldiers' Councils (defense against anti-Semitism, 1918), I:168, 247 (note 43), II:258. *See also* Self-defense, Jewish
Jewish State Museum. *See* State Jewish Museum, Prague
Jewish State party, II:34, 107-08, 128, 129
Jewish Teachers' Association for Bohemia (1919), II:79
Jewish Theological Seminary, Breslau, I:313, 345, 346, 347
Jewish Town Hall *(Židovská radnice)*, Prague, I:14, 247 (note 43), 295, 486; II:324; III:38, 39, 500; Synagogue, I:247 (note 43)
Jewish Vacation Association (free vacations for needy), II:394, 398
Johann Gottfried Herder Union (B'nai B'rith youth organization), II:233-34
Joint. *See* American Jewish Joint Distribution Committee (JDC)
Joint Committee of Jews from Czechoslovakia in England, III:70 (note 158)
Joint Distribution Committee. *See* American Jewish Joint Distribution Committee (JDC)
Joint Youth Federation (Federation of Jewish youth organizations in Slovakia), I:95
Joseph Popper Lodge. *See* B'nai B'rith, Joseph Popper Lodge, New York
Journalism, Czech, Jews in, I:441, 446-48, 523. *See also* Press, Jews in, and under titles of Jewish newspapers
Jud Süss (anti-Semitic film), III:305
Judaea (organization of Slovak students at schools in Bohemia and Moravia), II:183
Judaica (German-language Jewish periodical), Bratislava, I:7; II:167, 168, 172, 376
Jude, Der (first Jewish newspaper in Slovakia, Yiddish, Košice, 1866), I:80
"Judea-Holič" Students' Association (Zionist, Slovakia), I:79
Judenälteste ("Jewish Elder," chairman of Ältestenrat der Juden), Minsk, III:273; Prague, III:50, 52; Terezín, III:xxxvii, 130, 135, 141, 147 (note 6), 297, 300

Judenkodex. *See* Jewish Code
Judenpatent (Francis II, 1797), I:342
Judenrat, Lodz, III:270. *See also* Ältestenrat der Juden
Jüdische Akademische Lese- und Rede-Halle (Jewish Academic Reading and Lecture Hall), Brno, II:21, 22, 111 (note 19), 179, 181, 182; Prague, II:21, 174, 179-81, 263; Vienna, II:110 (note 10)
Jüdische Akademische Verbindung Barissia. *See* Barissia
Jüdische Akademische Verbindung Veritas. *See* Veritas
Jüdische Arbeiter, Der (German-language Po'ale Zion organ, Vienna), II:81, 82
Jüdische Herold, Der (German-language weekly of Agudath Israel, Dunajská Streda), I:528; II:163
Jüdische Jugendblätter (German-language Zionist youth journal), II:177
Jüdische Korrespondenz (German-language Orthodox periodical, Vienna), II:163
Jüdische Nachrichten (German-language Orthodox weekly, Prešov), I:528; II:163
Jüdische Presse (German-language organ of Agudath Israel, Bratislava, Vienna), I:528; II:162, 163, 166, 167
Jüdische Revue (German-language periodical, Subcarpathian Ruthenia, 1926-38), I:537
Jüdische Rundschau (German-language Zionist periodical, Bratislava), II:35-36
Jüdische Selbstverwaltung, Theresienstadt (autonomous Jewish administration in Terezín ghetto), III:517. *See also* Ältestenrat der Juden, in Terezín.
Jüdische Sozialist, Der (German-language Labor Zionist newspaper), II:80, 82
Jüdische Stimme, Die (Yiddish-language Zionist weekly, Subcarpathian Ruthenia, founded 1929), I:529
Jüdische Tradition (German-language weekly of Agudath Israel, Košice), II:163

Jüdische Volksstimme (German-language weekly, Brno), I:7, 525, 535; II:24, 104, 105
Jüdische Volkszeitung (German-language weekly, Slovakia), I:88, 100-01, 528; II:273, 321-22
Jüdischer Bürgerverein (*Židovský občiansky spolok;* Jewish Citizens' Union, Piešťany), I:87
Jüdischer Frauenverein (Jewish Women's Association), II:137-39
Jüdischer Soldatenrat (Jewish militia unit founded by Veritas, Brno), II:175. *See also* Jewish Soldiers' Councils; Self-defense, Jewish
Jüdischer Volksrat (Jewish People's Council), Brno, II:175, 259
Jüdischer Volksverein (Jewish People's Association; first Zionist association in Prague), II:137, 140
Jüdisches Familienblatt (German-language Zionist-oriented paper, Slovakia), I:101
Jüdisches Nachrichtenblatt-Židovské Listy (Nazi-censored bilingual organ of Prague Jewish Religious Congregation, founded 1939), III:42-43
Jüdisches Volksblatt (German-language Zionist weekly, Moravská Ostrava), I:525
Jüdisches Weltblatt-Organ für alle jüdischen Interessen (German-language journal, Bratislava, founded 1878), I:80
JULAG (Judenarbeitslager; labor camp for Jews), III:275. *See also* Labor camps and Labor centers
Jung Juda (monthly), I:7, 525
Jungzionistische Organisation, II:57
J.V. Stalin First Partisan Brigade, III:231

Kadimah (Zionist organization, Subcarpathian Ruthenia), I:98, 141; II:403, 411
Kameri (Chamber) Theater, Tel Aviv, III:562
Kapo(s), III:294, 298; defined, III:293 (footnote)
Kapper Club (*Spolek akademiků Čechů-Židů Kapper;* academic club), II:149,

SUBJECT INDEX 683

Kapper Club *(Cont.)*
153, 179, 180; III:39. *See also* Czech-Jewish movement
Karpathendeutsche Partei (Carpatho-German party in Slovakia and Subcarpathian Ruthenia), I:107
Kartell Sozialistischer Akademiker (Socialist Students' Corps, Prague, 1934), II:183, 184
Karussel (cabaret production in Terezín), III:125
Kashrut (dietary laws), I:268, 285, 335, 348; II:97, 364; III:514
Kehilla (Jewish community), II:349
Kenessiah Gedolah. *See* Agudath Israel, Kenessiah Gedolah
Keren HaTorah (fund for support of yeshivoth, Agudath Israel), II:164, 172 (note 31)
Keren HaYesod (Palestine Foundation Fund), I:157-58, 316; II:38, 39, 52, 55, 66, 70, 83, 98, 105, 143, 229, 597; III:38, 42, 477, 485-86, 542
Keren HaYishuv (fund for religious settlement work in Palestine, Agudath Israel), II:164
Keren Kayemet. *See* Jewish National Fund
Keren Tel Hai (Revisionist fund), II:105
Kibbutzim set up in Israel by Jews from Czechoslovakia, II:591; III:542
Kindergartens, Jewish (Prague), I:139
Kitzur Shulhan Arukh ("Code of Jewish Law," based on Shulhan Arukh), II:375
"Klaus" Synagogue (Prague), I:337; III:47, 57, 572-73, 580 (note 3)
Kloiz (small place of prayer and study), II:366, 404. *See also* Shtibel
Komenský University, Bratislava, I:104; II:183
Kongressgemeinden, I:287, 300. *See also* "Congress" Congregations; Neolog congregations
"*Kongrua*" (State contribution to salaries of clergy in recognized religious congregations), I:93
"*Kongrua*" (conformist) congregations, I:287
Kongruagesetz (Conformist Church Law; 1926), I:285, 288, 299, 311; III:275
Kristallnacht, III:xxix
Kristallnacht-type pogrom in Trnava, I:115
Kultusgemeinden, Jüdische or *Israelitische,* I:47, 74, 161, 340; II:157, 158, 175, 258; III:118-19; defined, III:268 (footnote). *See also* Jewish Religious Congregation, Berlin; Jewish Religious Congregation, Vienna; Jewish Religious Congregations, Czechoslovakia
Kupat Eretz Yisrael (fund for support of old Orthodox community in Palestine, Agudath Israel), II:161; defined, II:170 (note 12)
Kvutza Biberach (group of young Palestine pioneers from Czechoslovakia), II:591
Kvutzat Mosahake Kadur Regel Yehudit (KMKRY: Jewish Soccer Union), II:198-99

Labor battalions, III:186-87, 214, 226
Labor Bonds (issued by Czechoslovak government, 1930's), I:317
Labor camps and labor centers, Hungary, III:415, 416; Slovakia, III:187-88, 214-16, 227-28, 234, 306, 313; Soviet Union, III:267, 340-43, 416, 440 (note 163)
Labor Zionists, III:563. *See also* Mapai; Po'ale Zion; Socialist Zionists; and under names of organizations
Labour party (England), II:83
Land Reform Act (Slovakia, 1919), I:89; III:178-79
Landeskanzlei (Autonomous Orthodox Jewish Religious Congregations), Budapest, I:305; II:158, 159; Slovakia, II:160, 170, 171. *See also* Autonomous Orthodox Jewish Religious Congregations; Autonomous Orthodox Regional Bureau for Slovakia
Landesmassafond (Zemská podstata), I:48, 312-13
Landespolitik (Zionist cultural and political work in individual Diaspora

Landespolitik (Cont.)
countries), II:23-24, 30, 32, 33, 34, 59, 73, 84, 98, 112, 290, 300. See also *Gegenwartsarbeit*
Landowners, Jewish. See Business and industries, Jews in
Landräte (German administrative bodies in Bohemia), III:23
Language Code (1920), I:193-94, 196, 199, 212; excerpts from, I:239-40, 242
Language Laws (1897), I:44
Lateran Council (1215), II:521
Law of Exchanges (1927), I:212-13
Law of Nationalities, Czechoslovak, I:186-87
Law on the Protection of Minorities (part of Czechoslovak Constitution, 1920), I:198, 204
League for Human Rights of Czechoslovakia, II:566-67
League for a Working Eretz Yisrael. See *Liga für das arbeitende Eretz Israel*
League of Nations, I:97, 103, 104, 162, 178, 184, 229, 252 (note 68), 384, 447; II:103, 248, 299, 568, 569-70, 573, 575; III:7, 468
Left Center. See *Linkes Zentrum-Arbeitendes Eretz Israel* (Zionist party list)
Lese- und Redehalle jüdischer Hochschüler in Prag. See Jüdische Akademische Lese- und Rede-Halle, Prague
Letters of exemption. See Yellow passes
Letters of protection. See Yellow passes
Lex Dérer (1926), II:286
Lex Perek (Moravia, 1906), I:192
Liberal Jews, I:74, 148, 290, 331, 340; II:159
Liberal party (Slovakia, pre-1918), I:77-78
Liberale Kommission für die Überwachung und Regulierung der Angelegenheiten der Kultusgemeinde (Liberal Commission for the Supervision and Regulation of the Affairs of the Religious Congregation; 1861), II:353

Libraries, Jewish, II:331, 374-75; III:571, 581 (note 10)
Lidové Noviny (Czech newspaper), I:523; II:245
Lidumilný spolek (Charity Association), Prague, II:393
Liga für das arbeitende Eretz Israel (League for a Working Eretz Yisrael), II:72, 73, 82, 88, 128
Linkes Zentrum-Arbeitendes Eretz Israel (Left Center), II:64, 68, 70, 71, 74, 85, 127
Listy Židovské mládeže (Zionist students' newspaper), I:526; II:179
Literary life of Czech Jews, I:56-58, 81-82; II:444-45
Literature, Czech, Jews in, I:438-53, 454-57; Jewish themes in, I:448-50, 456-67
Literature, German. See German literature, Jews of Czechoslovakia in
Literature, Jewish, religious, II:373-77
"Little School Law" (1922), I:182-83
Liturgy, Jewish, I:336, 338, 340-41. See also Prayer books
Loan and savings societies, Jewish (Subcarpathian Ruthenia), I:130
Locarno, Treaties of, I:97; II:248
Lodges and fraternal orders, Jewish, II:229-42
Lord Mayor's Fund, London, II:146; III:8
L'udová strana (People's party; pre-1918 Slovak clerical party), I:77-78

Maccabaea (later Bar Kochba Zionist students' society), I:59; II:109, 177
Maccabea (sports group, Bratislava), II:189, 200, 204, 208-09
Maccabi (sports organization), I:115, 344; II:21, 112, 176, 186, 187, 188-98, 199, 200, 202, 206, 207, 213, 219, 222, 312, 601, 608, 609; III:542; Congress (Žilina, 1937), I:110; II:193; ideology, II:193-94; youth camp, II:191, 196
Maccabi Aid Committee (England), III:70 (note 158)
Maccabi HaTza'ir, II:192, 194, 592, 601, 608; III:228, 542
Maccabi-Hehalutz organization (Prague), II:604, 609

"Maccabi-Hehalutz Transport," I:601-03, 606, 607, 609 ff., 631, 642. *See also* Aliya Bet
Maccabia (sports event), in Antwerp (1930), II:196, 210, 223, 225; in Palestine, (First, 1932), II:192, 197, 592; (Second, 1935), II:192, 197, 204, 210, 592; in Poland (1933), II:192; in Prague (1933), II:213
Maginei Degel Hatorah ("Defenders of the Banner of Torah," Orthodox Jewish organization, Subcarpathian Ruthenia), II:428
Magyar language. *See* Hungarian language
Magyar National party, I:91
Magyar Nemzeti-Ōslakó Party (Hungarian Rights party, Subcarpathian Ruthenia), I:136
Magyar party (Slovakia), I:102
Magyar Rabbik (Hungarian-language rabbis' monthly, Trnava, 1905-10), I:81
Magyar Zsidó Szemle (Hungarian-language Jewish periodical, Slovakia), I:81
Magyarization, I:106, 139-40, 226; II:401, 402
Maisel Synagogue. *See* Maislová ulice Synagoga (Prague)
Maislova ulice Synagoga (Prague), I:338, 342; III:573
Makkabi Association of Jewish University Students (Prague), II:322, 324
Makkabi HaTza'ir. *See* Maccabi HaTza'ir
Makkabi sports organization. *See* Maccabi (sports organization)
Makkabi Weltverband. *See* World Maccabi Union
Malvazinka Synagogue (Prague), III:590
Mánes Society of Artists (founded 1884), II:476, 477
Mapai (Mifleget Po'ale Eretz Yisrael), II:89; III:542
Mapilim ("The Daring," Zionist youth group), II:424-25
Marriage, civil, I:304-05
Marshall plan, III:557
Masaryk University, Brno, II:182, 245

Matica Slovenská. *See* Slovak Academy
Matteotti Fund, II:576
Medina Iwrit-Judenstaat (Revisionist Zionist paper, Prague, 1934-39), I:527; II:7, 113
Mehalke Tarn'golim (Prague; served chicken soup on Sabbath to poor and sick), II:393
Mein Kampf, quoted, II:461
Meisl Synagogue. *See* Maislová ulice Synagoga (Prague)
Melamed (plu.: *melamdim;* instructors in *heder*), II:404-05
Mensa Academica Judaica, II:176, 201, 222, 394
"Meshek Minimum" (Palestine pioneering group of Maccabi members), II:608
Michle Synagogue (Prague), III:585
Mifleget Po'ale Eretz Yisrael. *See* Mapai
Migration, within Historic Lands, I:27, 28, 33, 35, 39
Mikvah (plu.: mikvaot(h); ritual bath), I:288, 301, 339, 340; II:357; III:542
Minhag (plu.: *minhagim;* customs), I:331, II:364-66, 380, 385
Minorities, pre-1918, I:12, 14
Minorities, national. *See* National minorities
Minorities Protection Treaty. *See* Treaty for the Protection of Minorities
Mischlinge (Jewish "half-castes"), III:76-77, 87, 182, 502
Mixed marriages, and Hitler era, III:18, 36, 51, 77
Mizrahi (religious Zionist movement), I:79, 93-94, 141, 273; II:24, 25, 28, 32, 36, 41-42, 51, 82, 83, 94-99, 106, 112, 126, 127, 128, 129, 158, 171, 287, 296, 351, 353, 382, 603; III:542
Mizrahi Hehalutz, II:591
Mobile killing squads. *See* Einsatzgruppen
Mo'etzet Gedole HaTorah (Council of Torah Sages, Agudath Israel), II:156, 164, 168
Moment (Yiddish newspaper, Poland), I:140
"Monism" (Revisionist concept), II:102

Moravod Company (drainage project, Slovakia), III:187-88
More tzedek ("righteous teacher"; title accorded to non-ordained Jewish clergy), II:372
Morgenpost (Yiddish weekly, Subcarpathian Ruthenia, 1924), I:528
Mossad (Aliya Bet headquarters), II:608, 609
Munich agreement, I:112, 115, 207, 258 (note 144), 318, 324, 445; II:147, 233, 315 (footnote), 319, 399, 568, 571, 575, 601; III:xxviii, 3, 7, 8, 10, 11, 18, 75-76, 262, 303, 343, 348, 349, 449, 452, 492 (note 63)
Munich pact. *See* Munich agreement
Munkaczer Humorist (Yiddish weekly, Mukačevo, 1924-25), I:529
Museums, Jewish, Mikulov, I:312; III:568; Prague, I:312, II:474; III:515, 519, 567-58; taken over by Czechoslovak State, III:579; Prešov, I:101; II:380; III:568. *See also* Central Jewish Museum, Prague; State Jewish Museum, Prague
Music, Hasidic, II:358-59
Music, Jews in, I:539-58; III:125, 272. *See also* Composers, Jewish; Musicians, Jewish; Musicologists, Jewish; Opera, Jews in; Singers, Jewish
Music, liturgical, I:342; II:363
Musicians, Jewish, I:539-40, 544, 545, 547, 548-49, 550, 553, 554
Musicologists, Jewish, I:550-52

Narodné Noviny ("National Paper"; Slovakia), I:99
Národní Politika (newspaper, quoted), III:10
Národní rada židovská. *See* Jewish National Council
Národní Souručenství (Committee of National Solidarity; replaced Czech parliament in 1939), III:20
Národní správa majetkových podstat Vystěhovaleckého fondu a Majetkového úřadu. *See* National Administration of the Assets of the Fund for Jewish Emigration
Národní správa Židovské Rady Starších. *See* National Administration of the Council of Jewish Elders
Národny správca. *See* "National managers"
Národní Výbor (National Council of the Czech Republic, 1918), I:159, 160, 165-66, 215, 218, 221, 248 (note 45), 270; II:31, 256, 257, 259
Národní Výbor (London, World War II). *See* Czechoslovak National Council (London, World War II)
Národní Výbor k likvidaci Židovské Rady Starších. *See* National Committee for the Liquidation of the Council of Jewish Elders
Naše vojsko (daily news bulletin of Czechoslovak armed forces in England, World War II), III:377
Nástup ("Roll Call," weekly of Slovak people's party), I:108
National Administration of the Assets of the Fund for Jewish Emigration *(Národní správa majetkových podstat Vystěhovaleckého fondu a Majetkového úřadu)*, III:501
National Administration of the Council of Jewish Elders *(Národní správa Židovské Rady Starsích)*, III:501
National Aryan Cultural Union, III:15
National Committee for the Liquidation of the Council of Jewish Elders *(Národní Výbor k likvidaci Židovské Rady Starších)*, III:501
National Congress of the Jews in the Czechoslovak State. *See* Congress of Czechoslovak National Jewry
National Coordinating Committee (Refugee aid, Czechoslovakia, 1930's), II:567; III:6-7
National Council of the Czech Republic, 1918. *See Národní Výbor* (National Council of the Czech Republic, 1918)
National Council of Czechoslovak Women, II:144, 147
National Federation of Slovak Jews *Sväz Židov na Slovensku)*, I:87-88, 89, 90, 94; II:262, 263, 264, 267, 270, 273, 319-22
National Guard, Jewish unit in (1848 Revolution), I:25-26

National Jewish Council. *See* Jewish National Council
National Jews (political party), II:270, 285, 302, 313
National Labor party, III:4
National League *(Jiří Stříbrný,* anti-Semitic party), II:317
"National managers" *(národný správca),* III:537, 539, 546 (note 29)
National minorities, non-Jewish, I:112, 113, 114, 134, 139, 140, 161-62, 203-05; II:139-40, 249, 336, 337, 433-34, 577; rights in Czechoslovak constitution (1920), I:178-200, 403; government-in-exile and, III:452-53, 456; post-1945 Czechoslovak government and, III:533
National Minority Law (1868), I:139
National Socialist Czech Workers party (Fascist party), III:15
National Theater *(Národní dívadlo),* I:543; II:475, 488
National Unity party *(Strana Národního Sjednocení),* I:208; III:4, 5, 15, 21, 28
Nationalism, Czech, I:16, 18, 21-71; II:6, 140, 245, 429; German (in "Historic Lands"), I:18, 21-71, 113; II:139-40, 429, 433-34; Hungarian, I:99, 105, 113; II:272, 423-24, 433-34; Ruthenian, I:135; Slovak, I:73, 104, 105, 107, 108, 111, 112
Nazi party (Nationalsozialistische deutsche Arbeiterpartei), I:202, 545; II:9; III:288; influence on German national minority, I:205; in Sudeten area, I:105, 258 (note 144); III:452; propaganda in Czechoslovakia, II:291-92
Nazism, II:152, 153, 212, 249, 423-24; III:238, 454 *et passim*
Nebenregierung. See Working Group
Nedělní Listy (Sunday News, quoted), II:314-15
Nejvyšví Rada (Supreme Council of Federations of Jewish Religious Congregations of Bohemia, Moravia and Silesia). *See* Jewish Religious Congregations *(Kultusgemeinden),* Czechoslovakia
Neolog congregations in Slovakia, Subcarpathian Ruthenia and Hungary, I:75, 103, 287, 300, 301, 302, 303, 305, 306, 307; II:159, 351, 352, 353-54, 355, 356, 359, 363, 372, 373, 375, 377, 380
"Néppárt." See L'udová strana
Netzach (Zionist youth movement), II:601
Neue Freie Presse (daily, Vienna), I:17-18, 80, 546
Neue Weg, Der (German-language Labor Zionist paper), II:82
Neue Weg, Der (German-language weekly), I:369
Neuschul (synagogue, Prague), III:567
New Zionist Organization, II:33, 43, 53, 594. *See also* Revisionism and Revisionists
Newspapers, Jewish, I:80, 88, 100-01, 213, 272, 525-26, 527-29, 530; II:7, 22, 24, 35, 80, 162-63; III:42; non-Jewish, I:17-18, 23, 25, 26, 62 (note 9), 80, 99, 108, 109, 110, 112, 117, 224; II:245, 315-16. *See also* Press; under names of newspapers
Nieuw Zeeland, S.S., II:615
NKVD (Soviet secret police), III:267, 389-90, 396, 421
Nora, S.S. (boat with Czech weapons to Israel), III:558
"Normal schools" (Germanization schools), I:43, 49-50
Nováky group (resistance fighters), III:229, 230-31, 232
"November pillages" (anti-Semitic excesses, Slovakia, post-World War I), I:86
N'she Agudath Israel (women's organization of Agudath Israel), II:165-66
Numerus clausus (Jewish quota), in bar association, I:207; at high schools, II:437; at institutions of higher learning, II:323, 395; III:87, 415
Numerus nullus (no Jews admitted), at high schools, II:437
Nuremberg Laws, I:317; II:298-99; III:xxxiii, 6, 60, 76, 306, 457, 500, 502; Jews defined in, III:xxix, 91 (note 8), 183
Nusakh Ari, II:362
Nusakh Ashkenaz (Ashkenazic prayer service), II:361, 362

Nusakh Sepharad (Sephardic prayer service), II:362

Občanská strana ("Civil party"), Subcarpathian Ruthenia, I:136
Occupations of Jews, I:38, 39-40, 126-27, 206; II:338-39; III:68 (note 115), 507, 508. *See also* Business and industries, Jews in; Professions, Jews in
Oddelenie pre zvláštné úkony (Department for Special Tasks in *Ústredňa Židov*), III:184, 185, 206
"Old Czech" party, I:44, 45
Old-New Synagogue. *See* Altneuschul
Omladina (youth movement of *L'udová strana*), I:109
Opera, Jews in, I:541, 554
Operation Nahshon (Israel), III:558
Opora Lodge, II:240
"Optants" (persons who left Soviet Subcarpathian Ruthenia after World War II to settle in Czechoslovakia), III:506-07
Ordnungspolizei (regular German police), III:273
Organ, use of, in synagogues, II:354, 355, 380
Organization of Victims of Racial Persecution at the Hands of the Fascist Regime *(Sdruženie fašistickým režimom rasove prenásledovaných;* SRP), Slovakia, III:504, 512, 533, 534, 535, 536
Orphanages, Jewish, I:101, II:231, 394; III:517
ORT *(Obshczestvo Rasprostranenya Truda),* I:130; III:40, 517; defined, III:528 (note 25)
Or Tamid Religious Society (Prague), I:341
Orthodox Jews, I:56, 300, 301, 318, 331-32, 335, 340; II:157, 158, 380, 464, 466; III:455; autonomous congregations, I:103, 287, 288, 302, 305-06, 307; II:159, 353; Bohemia and Moravia, I:319, 245-46 (note 41); Slovakia, I:74-75, 93, 303, 307-08, 319, 330, 333, 347, 348; Subcarpathian Ruthenia, I:135-36, 142, 145, 150, 303, 308, 319, 330, 333, 347, 348; II:413, 420-21; in Czechoslovak armed forces (World War II), III:394; and Czechoslovak government-in-exile, III:458; in Holocaust, III:169-70, 244 (note 10), 534; and Jewish party, I:273-74; II:292, 351; and liberal Jews, I:290; political behavior, I:292, II:258, 269, 313; and Zionists, I:98, 273-74; II:352-53, 410-11. *See also* Agudath Israel; Autonomous Orthodox Religious Congregations; Hasidism and Hasidim; Rebbes, Hasidic; Religious life
OSE *(Obshczestvo Zdravookhranenya Evreyev),* III:517, 542; defined, III:528 (note 25)
Osma ("The Eight"; modern artists' group), II:481, 501
Österreichisches Zentralorgan (weekly newspaper), I:23, 25, 26
Osvobozené divadlo (Liberated Theater), II:488
Otzar Hachaim (Orthodox monthly, Humenné), I:528

Palestine Foundation Fund. *See* Keren HaYesod
Palestine Mandate (1922), II:589, 601. *See also* British Mandatory Government
Palestine (Emigration) Office(s), II:28, 83, 98, 268, 589, 590, 592, 595, 597; III:xxxiii, 38, 41, 108, 170-71, 542
Palmah (commando troops), III:560
Parachutists, Palestine, III:xxxviii, 231-32
Partisans, III:225-26, 229-33, 286. *See also* Resistance, anti-Nazi; Underground; also under names of units
Patent of Toleration (1782). *See Toleranzedikt*
Patria, S.S., II:613, 614; III:11, 361, 364, 365
Patronka (internment camp, Bratislava), II:603, 604, 605, 607, 610, 612
Peace Conferences (after World War I), I:156, 158, 159, 164, 169-77, 223, 228; II:30, 264, 319; III:474
Peace treaties (after World War I), I:185, 229-30

SUBJECT INDEX 689

Pentecost uprising (1848), I:24
People's party. *See* L'udová *strana*
Permanent Court of International Justice, I:178
Pester Lloyd (German-language newspaper, Budapest), I:80
Petition Committee "We Remain Faithful" (PVVZ-*Petiční výbor Věrni Zůstaneme;* home front resistance organization), III:17
Physicians, Jewish, I:378-79, 440, 482; III:14, 243 (note 2)
Pinkas Synagogue (Prague), I:337; II:520; III:47, 570, 573, 575-76, 580 (note 3); Holocaust memorial, III:576, 578, 582 (note 16)
Pioneers and Helpers (WIZO publication, London), II:143
Po'ale Agudath Israel (labor wing of Agudath Israel), II:168
Po'ale Zion (Socialist Zionist workers' party), I:116, 157, 222, 269; II:24, 30, 32, 33, 34, 43, 51, 53, 56, 57, 58, 71, 72, 73, 74, 75, 76-87, 88, 89, 90, 91, 92, 93, 94, 98, 106, 113, 119, 121, 123, 127, 262, 266, 267, 280, 313; III:108; Left, II:80, 81; Right, II:80; World Conferences (1907), II:77; (1919), II:80; (1920), II:80; (1931), II:89
Pod pokličkou ("garret weddings," secret weddings in defiance of anti-Jewish marriage restrictions), I:27
Podkarpatské Hlasy ("Subcarpathian Voices," newspaper in Subcarpathian Ruthenia), II:277
Poets, Jewish, I:22-23
Polina, Shohet of (Hasidic mystic figure), II:359
Polish Middle-class party, II:279, 280
Polish Social Democratic Workers party, II:279, 280
Political life, Jewish, I:134-39, 296. *See also* Jewish party; under names of other Jewish organizations
Political life, Jews in, II:243-52; III:505
Poverty, among Jews in Subcarpathian Ruthenia, II:356
Prager Presse (German-language newspaper), I:552, II:584
"Prager Richtung" ("Prague Orientation" in Zionism), II:20

Prager Tagblatt (German-language newspaper), I:551; II:584; III:8
"Prague Circle," I:472
Prague League against Anti-Semitism, I:110
Prague Radio Symphony Orchestra, I:545
Prague Transfer Committee, III:12
Prague uprising (May 5, 1945), III:500
Prayer books, I:336, 340, 341, 343; II:365-66, 376
Press, Jews in, I:523-31; emigré press from Austria and Germany in Czechoslovakia (1933-38), II:585, 586. *See also* Journalism, Jews in; under titles of Jewish newspapers
Press Bureau, Jewish, Bratislava, II:263; Stockholm, II:257
Pressburger Jüdische Zeitung (German-language newspaper, Bratislava), II:24
Přítomnost ("The Present," periodical), II:315
Privilegium de non tolerando Judaeos, I:32
Professions, Jews in, I:76, 92, 124, 129, 150, 371-72, 378-79, 402, 427, 440, 482; II:339, 451, 485-86; discriminated against, during Nazi occupation, III:84-85; exempted from deportation in Slovakia, III:211. *See also* under professional classifications
Progressive party. *See* Czech Realist party
Protocols of the Elders of Zion, cited in Slovak nationalist press, I:107
Publishing houses, Jewish, I:532-38; II:163, 321
PVVZ. *See* Petition Committee "We Remain Faithful"

Quakers (refugee aid in Czechoslovakia), II:7

Rabbinical Conference of Michalovce (1865), I:74; II:359
Rabbinical scholars, I:80-81; II:373, 375-76, 521; III:515
Rabbinical seminaries, I:313, 317-18, 345, 346, 347; II:372. *See also* Yeshivoth

Rabbis and rabbinate, I:52-53, 272, 282-88, 299, 301, 303, 306, 310-11, 312, 313-14, 315, 322, 323, 337, 338, 339, 345-47; II:359, 371-73, 374; III:204, 209, 239, 513-14, 573-74
Rada Narodowá (National Council of Polish government-in-exile), III:464
Rada Židovských náboženských obcí v Čechách a na Moravě (Council of Jewish Religious Congregations in Bohemia and Moravia [after World War II]), III:424, 499 (footnote), 504, 505, 506, 507, 512-13, 515, 516, 517, 518, 519, 520, 521, 522-23, 524, 525, 527 (note 19), 528 (note 26), 529 (note 34), 535, 543
Radical Zionists, II:28, 39, 42, 53, 54, 71, 75, 108, 118, 127, 128
Rebbes, Hasidic, I:348, 350, 529; II:162, 168, 357, 358, 364-65, 366, 372, 425-30. *See also* Hasidism and Hasidim
Red army, III:272, 283, 284, 392, 397, 416
Red Cross, Czechoslovak, II:138, III:8; Danish, III:xxxvi, xxxvii, 135; German, III:18; Swedish, III:135, 143
"Red Help" (Moscow), III:7
Rede- und Lesehalle. *See* Jüdische Akademische Lese- und Rede-Halle
Refugee Aid Office (Prague), II:147
Refugee children, day camps for (Prague, post-1945), III:516
Refugees, Arab, in Middle East, II:15
Refugees, Jewish, from Austria and Germany to Czechoslovakia, I:112, 133, 316-17, 322, 325; II:145, 146, 250, 291, 299, 301, 315-16, 396-97, 399, 565-70, 572, 582-88; III:5, 6-9; from Eastern Europe to Czechoslovakia (World War I), I:339; II:169, 265-66, 394, 395; (after World War II), III:514, 515, 541; from Czechoslovakia (post-1939), II:570-71, 574-79; from Czechoslovakia to England, I:115; II:146, 576; III:38, 343, 451-52, 454-55; to France, III:343-44, 373; to Palestine and Israel, I:114-15; II:589-98, 599-654; from Czechoslovakia to Poland, II:578-79; III:38, 332-34, 335, 345; in Soviet labor camps, III:340-43; return to Czechoslovakia from Palestine after World War II, II:641, 642, 645
Registration of Jews. *See* Anti-Jewish legislation during Nazi era
Rehabilitation of Holocaust survivors, III:502, 503, 512, 516, 518, 519, 525
Reichsbürgergesetz (Reich Citizenship Law, 1943), III:35, 245 (note 18)
Reichsfluchtsteuer (Reich emigration tax), II:577
Reichssicherheitshauptamt (RSHA; Central Office of Reich Security), III:xxxix, 23, 37-38, 132, 140, 142, 147 (note 3), 189, 190, 235, 263, 297, 303
Reichsvereinigung der deutschen Juden (representative body of German Jewry), III:42, 245 (note 18)
Reichsvereinigung der Juden in Deutschland. *See* Reichsvereinigung der deutschen Juden
Rekhesh (Haganah's arms acquisition unit), III:555, 562
Religious articles, I:348 ff.
Religious communities. *See* Jewish Religious Congregations *(Kultusgemeinden)*, Czechoslovakia
Religious freedom, under Czechoslovak Constitution (1920), I:183-84
Religious instruction, of Jewish students at public schools, I:182-83, 290, 303, 343, 344; II:370; of Jewish students after public school hours, III:542
Religious instructors, I:345-46, 347; training courses for, I:314-15
Religious life, I:41-42, 51-53, 147-51, 267, 271, 272, 330-57; II:347-92; during Holocaust, III:50, 129-30; after Holocaust, III:513-14, 542. *See also* Hasidism and Hasidim; Kashrut; Orthodox Jews; Sabbath observance, etc.
Religious literature. *See* Literature, Jewish, religious
"Repatriation" of Jews from Czechoslovakia to Soviet Subcarpathian Ruthenia by USSR, III:506-07. *See also* "Optants"

Rescue activities. *See* Rescue Committee (Istanbul); *Vaadat Ezra VeHatzalah;* "Working Group"
Rescue Committee (Istanbul), III:251 (note 72), 313, 316
Resistance, anti-Nazi, III:16-17, 18, 479, 540; Czech participation in, abroad, III:449; in "family camp," III:298, 300; Slovak Jews in, III:224-33; Treblinka revolt, III:xxxvii, 289-90. *See also* Partisans; Slovak uprising; Underground
Responsa, I:336; II:349, 374, 376
Restaurants, kosher, I:348; III:514, 542
Restitution (after 1945), III:519-23, 535-36, 537-38, 539-40, 541
Restitution Law of 1946, III:519, 538
Révai Nagy Lexikona (Révai's Great Encyclopedia), I:82
Revisionism and Revisionists (Zionist party), I:527; II:6, 7, 28, 34, 39, 42-43, 51, 53, 69, 71, 75, 82, 99-108, 113, 115, 118, 127, 128, 600; III:436 (note 78), 542
Revolution of 1848, I:15, 21-22, 23-26, 27, 72
Revolutionary National Assembly (Council; 1918-20), II:246, 290
Ribbentrop-Molotov pact (1939), III:xxx, 340, 343, 371, 461
Ritual baths. *See* Mikvah
Ritual murder trials, Hilsner, I:17, 44, 152; III:9; Starý Simeri, I:152; II:289; Tisza-Eszlár, I:77
Ritual slaughter, I:275, 285, 288, 290; II:313, 372, 386 (note 47). *See also Shehitah*
Domobrana (Home Guard; Fascist semi-military organization in Slovakia, 1920's), I:96
Royal Air Force, British, III:560; Czechs and Czech Jews in, III:384, 386, 387, 388
Rozvoj ("Development," Czech-language weekly, official organ of Czech-Jewish movement), I:524, 530; II:153, 276
RSHA. *See* Reichssicherheitshauptamt
Rudé Právo (Communist paper, Prague), I:523; III:403
Runciman mission, I:112, 323; III:5

"*S bohom Praho*" ("Goodbye Prague"; slogan of Slovak separatists, 1938), I:111
SA ("*Sturmabteilung*"; Storm Troops), II:605
Sabbath observance, I:250 (note 59), 251 (note 64), 273, 275, 335; II:97, 163, 287, 331, 364; during Holocaust, III:116, 572
Šalda Committee, II:567, 583; III:6
Salzburg conference (July 28, 1940), III:xxxii, 173, 181, 238, 304
Sanatorium, Jewish (Tatra mts.), III:517
Sanhedrin. *See* Rabbinical Conference of Michalovce (1865)
Schlagende Verbindungen. See Dueling fraternities
Schnorrers (mendicants), I:42-43
School for (of) Applied Arts, Bratislava, II:501, 506
School of Religious Studies, Prague, I:314, 315
School system in Czechoslovakia, statistics for 1924, I:255-56 (note 112)
Schools, Jewish, I:72-73, 75, 100, 117, 141, 144, 145, 213-17, 270, 274, 295, 314, 343; II:83, 137, 139, 142, 165, 166-67, 172, 176, 233, 262-63, 295, 297-98, 308, 309, 321, 331, 371, 415-19, 422, 426, 428, 429, 602. *See also* Education, Jews and
Schoolteachers, Jewish, I:129
Scientists, Jewish, I:371-72, 402
SD. *See* Sicherheitsdienst
SDP. *See* Sudetendeutsche Partei
Sdružení uprchlíků z Československa. See Comité des Refugiés de Tchécoslovaquie
Sdružení židovských účastníků československého odboje. See Association of Jewish Participants in the Czechoslovak Resistance Campaign
Second Jewish World Relief Conference (Karlovy Vary, August, 1924), I:132
"Section Seven" (provincial department of Jewish Religious Congregation of Prague during Holocaust), III:569
Security Police. *See* Sicherheitspolizei

Selbstwehr (German-language Zionist weekly, Prague), I:7, 90, 98, 231, 304, 325 (note 3), 525; II:22, 47, 52, 68, 81, 91, 114, 115, 116, 143, 145, 194, 205, 276-77, 324-39, 587
"Selection" (in concentration camps), III:271, 272, 274, 275, 277, 279, 280, 281, 282, 283, 285, 286, 289, 291, 293, 294, 295, 300-01, 308, 311, 314, 317
Self-Aid Association of Jews from Bohemia, Moravia and Slovakia (England), III:70 (note 158), 371 (footnote)
Self-defense, Jewish, (before 1918), I:26; (1918), I:168, 247 (note 43); II:258; in post-1945 Slovakia, III:539. See also Jewish Soldiers' Council; Jüdischer Soldatenrat
Selihot (Selichoth; penitential compositions and elegies), II:365, 543-44
"Shalom (Peace) Battalion," III:368
Shehitah, I:301, 316; II:1, 7, 169, 271; III:244 (note 10, 514)
Shnorrer. See Schnorrers
Shohet (plu.: *shohetim;* ritual slaughterers), I:339, 345; II:355, 356, 357, 364
Shomre HaDat ("Guardians of the Faith"; Orthodox Jewish organization, Slovakia), I:74
Shomre Shabbos (employment agency for Sabbath observers), II:163
Shomrei Torah Society ("Guardians of the Torah," Orthodox Jewish organization, Mukačevo), II:427, 428
Shtibel, II:366. See also *Kloiz*
Shulhan Arukh, I:74, 275, 287, 306, 323; II:160, 349, 373, 375
Sicherheitsdienst (SD; intelligence branch of SS), III:44, 77, 189, 233, 279, 288
Sicherheitspolizei (SIPO; German security police), III:197, 201, 219, 235, 268
Sinai (Union of Orthodox Jews in Bohemia), I:245 (note 41)
Singers, Jewish, I:548
Skupina výtvarných umělců (Czech sculptors' group), II:482
Skoda Works, I:400, 402, 405

Slánský trials (1951-52), II:251-52; III:440 (note 163), 441 (note 174), 564 (note 8), 565 (note 11), 566 (note 12)
Slobodárna (*Slobodáréň a nocláháreň;* shelter for "illegal" Jewish refugee transports in Bratislava), II:603-06, 607, 609, 610, 611
Slovák (political daily), I:99, 108; II:297
Slovak Academy (Matica Slovenská), I:73
Slovak Bar Association, I:207-08
Slovak Democratic party, III:532-38
Slovak Fascist party, II:307-08; III:539
Slovak language, used by Jews in Czechoslovakia, I:100, 108; II:311-12; III:540
Slovak National Council (1918), I:87; after World War II, III:532, 533, 536, 537
Slovak National Museum, Bratislava, II:562
Slovak National party (*Slovenská Národná Strana,* pre-1918), I:78, 104; II:577
Slovak People's party *(Hlinkova slovenská l'udová strana),* I:100, 104, 105, 107, 108, 109, 110, 112; II:297, 303-04, 577, 604 (footnote); III:179, 183, 188, 193, 194, 195, 208, 209, 210, 237, 254 (note 100), 303, 305, 539; youth movement of, I:109
Slovak University, II:183. See also Komenský University
Slovak uprising (August-October, 1944), III:xxxviii, 213, 227, 229-33, 313-14, 418, 424, 532
Slovakia, autonomous Nazi puppet state (1938-45), I:112, 113, 118; II:577-78, 606, 607; III:xxix, 14, 165-261, 262-63, 303-15, 341, 344, 347, 464-65, 508, 535-36; Germans occupy, III:233-34
Slovenská Národná strana. See Slovak People's party
Slovenská Pravda ("Slovak Truth"; newspaper), I:109
Slovensko (newspaper), I:224
Směr Praha ("Direction Prague"; publication of Czechoslovak army, World War II), III:395

Soccer. *See* Sports, Jews in
Social Association of Slovak Jews (relief organization, 1923), I:96
Social Democratic party of Germany (SOPADE), II:567
Social Democratic Relief Committee (Czechoslovakia), II:567; III:6
Social Democrats, I:363; II:23, 576, 577; III:6, 8, 333, 505
Social Institute of Jewish Religious Congregation of Greater Prague (founded 1935), I:294, 312; II:397-98
Social life, Jewish, I:53-55, 147-53
Social services and social work, Jewish, II:393-400; Agudath Israel, II:163; B'nai B'rith, II:231, 233; "Hort," II:239; Jewish party, II:300, 301; Société, II:236; Zionists, II:398-99, after Holocaust, III:517
Socialist Zionists, I:527; II:55-94; III:244 (note 8), 563. *See also* Po'ale Zion; Labor Zionists; under names of Labor Zionist organizations
Société (Fraternal order), II:235-38, 239
Society for the Advancement of the Science of Judaism (Prague, founded 1896), I:344
Society for the History of Czechoslovak Jews (New York), I:10; III:589, 591
Society for the Study of the History of the Jews in the Czechoslovak Republic (Prague, founded 1928), I:5-7, 9, 311, 526-27; yearbook, 1:6-7, 526-27
Society for the Study of the History of the Jews of Bohemia, Moravia and Silesia, II:231-32
Sokol (sports organization), II:185; III:5, 386
Sonderbehandlung ("special treatment;" Nazi euphemism for murder of Jewish deportees), III:282, 297
Sonderkommando ("special detail"; concentration camp inmates assigned to disposing of corpses of Jews killed in gas chambers, III:288, 294, 298, 309, 317
SOPADE. *See* Social Democratic party of Germany
Soup kitchens, kosher, III:514, 542
Soviet-Czechoslovak agreement (June 29, 1945), III:506

Španěláci ("Little Spaniards"; veterans of International Brigade of Spanish Civil War), III:350
Spanish Civil War, I:496; III:350, 375, 390, 401
Společenský Klub (Czech social club), II:243
Spolek Sionistických akademiků v Brně (Society of Zionist University Students in Brno), II:182
Sports, Jews in, II:185-228; and Zionism, II:185-86, 193, 195; aviation, II:216-17; field hockey and ice hockey, II:205-06; fencing, II:213-14; gymnastics, II:186, 190, 191, 192, 193, 195-98; horsemanship, II:214-15; rowing and canoeing, II:211; skating and skiiing, II:206-07; soccer, II:198-99; swimming, II:207-11; table tennis, II:212-13; tennis, II:211-12; track and field activities, II:200-05
Sports clubs, I:294, 295, 344; II:186-94, 200; journal, I:527, II:202. *See also* Maccabi; under names of sports organizations
SRP. *See* Organization of Victims of Racial Persecution at the Hands of the Fascist Regime *(Sdruženie fašistickým režimom rasove prenásledovaných)*
SS ("Schutzstaffel"; Elite Guard), II:605; III:xxxvii, 22-23, 32, 34, 44, 45, 47, 50, 106, 107, 108, 109, 110, 111, 112, 114, 116, 117, 118, 119, 121, 123, 126, 132, 133, 134, 135, 137, 138, 139, 140, 141, 142, 143, 144, 145, 148 (note 11), 149 (note 18), 151 (note 35), 189, 233, 264, 266, 270, 271, 273, 274, 275, 277, 278, 279, 282, 283, 284, 285, 286, 287, 288, 289, 290, 291, 293, 294, 296, 297, 298, 300, 302, 308, 310, 311-12, 316, 317, 325 (note 51), 579
Starosta (head of *Ústredňa Židov*), III:175, 245 (note 19)
State Council. *See Státní rada*
State Jewish Museum, Prague, I:9; II:469, 474, 495 (note 30); III:47, 128, 129, 515, 518, 567-83, 585; *See also* Museums, Jewish, Prague

Statistical tables, I:29, 129, 204, 206, 227; II:124, 125, 332-33; III:29, 37, 40, 51, 53-60, 177, 201, 202, 273, 319, 320-22
Státní rada (State Council; of Czechoslovak government-in-exile, World War II), III:xxxii, xxxiv, xxxvi, 371, 373, 375, 376-77, 385, 424, 454-64, 466, 468-69, 471, 472, 479, 492 (note 63), 501
"Status quo ante" congregations in Slovakia, Subcarpathian Ruthenia, and Hungary, I:75, 79, 93, 103, 287, 300, 301, 305, 306; II:351, 352, 353, 354, 355, 359, 372, 375, 377
Strana Národního Sjednocení. See National Unity party
Students' Legion (1918), I:23-24, 25
Stürmer, Der (Julius Streicher's Nazi party sheet), I:117; III:5
Sudetendeutsche Partei (SDP; Sudeten German party), I:105, 107, 258 (note 144), 317, 546
Sunday rest law, I:94-95, 103-04; II:287, 289, 306-07, 313
Svaz Čechů Židů. See Czech-Jewish movement
Sväz Slovenských Židov (Slovak assimilationist movement), I:91
Sväz Židov na Slovensku. See National Federation of Slovak Jews
Svaz Židů z Československa ve Francii. See Association des Juifs de Tchécoslovaquie en France
Svůj k svému ("Each His Own;" anti-Semitic slogan against Jewish retail traders), I:38, 40
Synagogues, I:8, 42, 74, 101, 289, 311, 336-40, 341, 342; II:354-55, 360-63, 380, 547-51; III:21, 52, 516, 542, 567, 568, 570, 571, 580 (note 3); Liberal, I:337, 338-39; Neolog, II:361; Orthodox, I:337; II:354, 355, 361. *See also* under names of synagogues
Synoda Českobratrské Církve Evangelické. See Czech Brethren's Protestant Church, Synod of

Talmud, II:531; and paganism, II:458; anti-Semitic attacks on I:449; II:307-08

Talmud Tora(h) (religious schools), I:214, 275, 303-04, 334, 340; II:361, 369-70
Tarbut Society (Hebrew culture organization), I:141-42, 143; II:143, 308, 409, 418
Taxation of Jews, prior to 1918, I:22, 27, 72, 313; during Nazi era, II:577; III:85-86, 89, 181, 192, 535-36
Teachers' Seminary, Brno, I:308
Technion (Haifa), II:14, 594
Te(c)helet Lavan (*Blau-Weiss*, Blue-White, Jewish scouting movement), I:527; II:21, 92, 112, 123, 177, 183, 591, 592, 601
Tel Chai Fonds (Tel Hai Fund), II:6
Tel Hai (Betar monthly), I:528
Terezín ghetto, art in, III:126-29; "beautification" project, III:xxxvi, xxxvii, xxxix, 134-37, 142-43, 150 (note 33); burial of dead in, II:491; III:130, 149 (note 23); cabaret in, III:125; cultural activities in, III:116, 118, 123-29; daily life, III:120-23; deportations to, II:246; III:xxxiv, xxxix, 32, 33, 113, 117-18, 133-34, 141, 148-49 (note 16), 264, 269, 275, 315; deportations from, III:xxxiv, xxxv, xxxvi, xxxix, 111, 112, 126, 127, 133, 135, 138, 139, 140, 276-89, 291, 293, 294, 295, 296, 297, 299, 300, 302; escapes from, III:135, 150 (note 30); executions in, III:xxxiv, 110; ghetto leadership, III:xxxvii, xxxix, 119-20; ghetto police, III:115; history, III:xxxiii, 104-64; Jewish assets from, III:517-18, 520, 525; liberation and aftermath, II:469; III:xl, 143-46; liquidation of ghetto, III:138-42; music in, I:547, 556-58 (note 14); III:116; preservation of historic sites in, after Holocaust, III:515; religion and morals in, III:129-32; SS propaganda film on, III:137-38
Theater, Jews in, I:541-43; II:488. *See also* Holocaust, theater in; Yiddish theater
Theodor Herzl (Zionist) Student Society (Prague), I:341-42, 526; II:20, 23, 177, 178-79, 182, 324

SUBJECT INDEX

Tisza-Eszlár ritual murder trial. *See* Ritual murder trials, Tisza-Eszlár
Többens (armaments factory), III:286
Toleranzedikt (Patent of Toleration, 1782), I:14-15, 22, 342, 469
Toleranzpatent. *See Toleranzedikt*
Tora VaAvoda (religious labor Zionist movement), II:129
Torah scrolls, sent to Prague during Holocaust, III:570; sent from Czechoslovakia to England (1964), III:584-610; synagogues and other institutions having scrolls from Czechoslovakia, III:587, 589-91, 592-609
Totenkopfverbände ("Death's Head Units," SS), III:266
Trade union movement, II:247, 250-51
Trade Unions, Central Federation of (post-1945), III:521, 522, 523, 529 (note 34)
"Transfer of Funds" Agreement *(Ha'avara),* II:595-97; III:12, 38
Transports. *See* Deportations (during Holocaust)
Treaty for the Protection of Minorities, I:85, 180-81, 183, 189-90, 193, 194, 197, 200-01, 212, 215, 231, 232, 251; II:264, 267, 323. *See also* Treaty of St. Germain
Treaty of Brno (on citizenship and minorities), I:187
Treaty of St. Germain (1919), I:178, 184, 185, 186, 239, 242; excerpts from, I:232-36. *See also* Treaty for the Protection of Minorities
Treaty of Trianon (1920), I:85, 99, 139
Trefort decree (1888), I:276, 301, 305
Tři roky druhé světové války (Three Years of World War II), book by Beneš, III:424
Tribuna (Czech daily, friendly toward Czech-Jewish movement), I:272, 369; II:151, 152
Tribuna (post-1945 weekly newspaper of Slovak Jews, founded 1947), III:515, 542
Turks, invasion of Hungary by (1526), II:348
Tvorba (Communist paper), I:523
Tze'ire Zion (Zionist organization), II:28, 32, 42, 57, 58, 83, 89, 126, 590

Tzemah David (historical chronicle, 1592), I:3
ÚHÚ. *See Ústredný hospodársky úrad*
Uj Szó ("New Word;" Hungarian-language Zionist weekly, Mukačevo), I:529
Umschulungslager (vocational retraining camp, Nazi period), III:24, 41, 263-64. *See also* Vocational guidance and reorientation
Underground, III:xxxviii, 224, 225-26, 227-28, 229, 453, 531, 576. *See also* Resistance, anti-German; Slovak uprising; "Working Group"
Underground, Jewish, in Palestine, III:554, 556. *See also* Haganah; Irgun Z'vai Leumi
Underground rescue activities. *See* Vaadat Ezra VeHatzalah; "Working Group"
Union of Czech Jews, I:449
Union of Former Political Prisoners (Czechoslovakia, post-1945), III:520
Union of Jewish Medical Students at the German University in Prague, II:322, 323
Union of Orthodox Rabbis of the United States and Canada, III:142
United Jewish party (Subcarpathian Ruthenia), I:136
United Nations, III:483, 558; and national minority groups, I:162; Palestine resolution and partition plan supported by Czechoslovakia, III:524-25, 552-53, 556, 557, 558
United Nations Relief and Rehabilitation Administration. *See* UNRRA
United Nations Special Commission on Palestine (UNSCOP), Czechoslovakia represented on, III:552, 564 (note 1)
United States of America, contribution of Czech-born Jews to life in, I:2-3, 26-27, 542, 548-49, 552
Universal Declaration of Human Rights, II:569
Universität, Die (Revolutionary poem by August Frankl), I:23, 474
University of Bratislava, I:102, 113
University of Prague, I:19, 23
University of Vienna, I:23

UNRRA (United Nations Relief and Rehabilitation Administration), III:423, 514, 517, 541
UNSCOP. *See* United Nations Special Commission on Palestine
Upper Nitra Partisan Brigade, III:229, 230
Urania (Prague), I:544
Uranus, S.S., II:610 ff.
ÚSC. *See Ústredný Sväz Cionistický* (Central Zionist Union), Slovakia
Ústredňa štátnej bezpečnosti (Slovak counterpart of Gestapo), III:222, 251 (note 73)
Ústredňa Židov (ÚŽ; Jewish Office), Slovakia, III:xxxii, 175, 180, 184, 185-86, 194, 196, 198, 203-04, 205, 206, 216, 234, 245 (note 18), 247 (note 39), 251 (note 74), 306, 312, 314
Ústřední zemská orthodoxní kancelář pro Slovensko. See Autonomous Orthodox Regional Bureau for Slovakia
Ústredný hospodársky úrad (ÚHÚ; Central Economic Office), Slovakia, III:xxxii, 174, 175, 177, 180, 181, 184, 185, 188, 190, 205, 208, 245 (note 19), 305-06
Ústredný Sväz Cionistický (ÚSC; Central Zionist Union), Slovakia, III:533, 534, 542
Ústredný Sväz židovských náboženských obcí na Slovensku (ÚSŽNO; Central Union of Jewish Religious Congregations in Slovakia), III:503-04, 507, 512, 516, 517, 524, 525, 533-34, 535, 543
Ústredný výbor pre sociálnu starostlivosť Židov na Slovensku (Central Committee for the Social Welfare of the Jews in Slovakia), III:172
Usury laws (Austria, 1882), I:39
ÚSŽNO. *See Ústredný Sväz židovských náboženských obcí na Slovensku*
ÚŽ. *See Ústredňa Židov*

V boj ("The Struggle"; underground newsletter), III:333
Va'ad HaAliya (Central Emigration Department, Berlin), II:590
Va'ad HaIr Ashkenazi (Ultra-orthodox community of Jerusalem), II:161, 170 (note 11)
Va'ad Leumi, II:593
Vaadat Ezra VeHatzalah (Jewish Committee for Help and Rescue; Budapest), III:207, 234, 316, 318
Varnsdorf incident, III:522, 523, 524. *See also* Beer Textile Factory, Varnsdorf
Vatican, I:100, III:xxxiv, xxxvi, 217-18, 235, 239, 242, 250 (note 65), 256 (note 114), 310, 313, 318, 464-65
Verband Zionistischer Akademiker (Association of Zionist Academicians), II:174
Verein der jüdischen Hochschüler in Prag Bar Kochba. *See* Bar Kochba Zionist students' society, Prague
Veritas (Zionist students' organization; Brno), I:59; II:22, 111 (note 19), 175-76
Věstník židovské náboženské obce pražské (monthly bulletin of the Jewish Religious Congregation of Prague, pre-1939), I:527
Věstník židovské náboženské obce v Praze (bulletin of the Jewish Religious Congregation of Prague, after World War II), I:529; III:511, 515, 521
Vienna Award (November, 1938), I:112, 113-14; II:435, 577; III:xxix, 262, 303, 315, 537
Vilna troupe, II:552, 555
Vítkovice (Witkowitz) Iron Works, I:373-74, 401, 402; III:26, 27
Vocational guidance and reorientation, II:145, 146, 293, 300, 302, 313 (footnote), 327-28, 330, 397, 399, 602; III:13, 24, 40-41, 87, 185-86, 244 (note 12), 263-64
Völkischer Beobachter (German Nazi party organ), I:110
Volksdeutsche (Ethnic Germans), I:104, 107, 109, 114, 469; II:609; III:5, 11-12, 27, 254 (note 105)
Volksverband der Juden für die Slovakei (People's Federation of the Jews in Slovakia), I:528
Volksverein Zion (People's Zion Society), Prague, II:22

SUBJECT INDEX

Východ ("The East;" Slovak newspaper), I:99

Wannsee Conference (January, 1942), III:xxxiv, 48, 49, 113, 114, 276-77
War crimes trials, III:289, 290, 302, 303
War of Independence, Israel, II:644; III:394, 531
War Refugee Board, U.S., III:318, 471
War Veterans (organized before World War II), II:314
Wehrmacht (German army), III:265, 270, 286
Weissberger case (anti-Semitic trial), II:290
Welt, Die (Zionist organ), II:112
Welthilfskonferenz (Karlovy Vary, 1924), I:132 (footnote)
Weltshpiegel, Der (Yiddish newspaper, Poland), I:140
Westminster Abbey (Czech Torah scroll lent to), III:587
Westminster Synagogue, London, III:586, 587, 588, 589, 592, 607
White House, Czech Torah scroll in, III:590-91
White Paper (British, 1922), II:100; (1939), II:601
Wirtschaftsverwaltungshauptamt (WHVA; Central Office of Economic Administration, Berlin), III:280
WIZO. *See* Women's International Zionist Organization
WJC. *See* World Jewish Congress
Women's International Zionist Organization, I:97, 525; II:34, 43-44, 141-47, 169, 597; III:6, 205, 542, 562-63
Women's League for Peace and Freedom, II:144
Women's Zionist Organization of Czechoslovakia, II:137-38
Working Association of Socialist Zionists (Arbeitsgemeinschaft sozialistischer Zionisten), II:33, 69-76, 86, 87, 88, 91, 92, 93, 119 (note 151), 123 (note 238)
"Working Eretz Israel" (party list, for 17th Zionist Congress), II:91
"Working Group" (underground rescue committee), II:169-70; III:xxxv,
xxxvii, xxxviii, 203, 205-07, 220, 221-23, 227, 234, 312-13, 314, 317
World Federation of Hungarian Jews, II:246
World Jewish Congress (WJC), I:9; II:80-81, 261, 290, 304, 382, 444, 445; III:xl, 223, 343, 451, 457, 459, 461, 462, 464, 465, 466, 467, 468, 470, 471, 475, 482, 484, 492-93 (note 63), 516, 520, 535, 538, 543, 590; London conference of British section (May 12, 1946), III:484-85
World Maccabi games. *See* Maccabia (sports event)
World Maccabi Union (Makkabi Weltverband), II:188, 206, 207
World Union of General Zionists, II:49
World War I, Czech Jews in, I:60
World Union of Zionists-Revisionists, II:6, 101, 105. *See also* Revisionism and Revisionists
World Zionist Executive, II:36, 53, 63, 66, 71, 83, 84, 92, 100, 114, 116, 267, 276
World Zionist Organization, I:157-58, 166, 167, 168, 169, 177, 223-24, 225-26, 229; II:20, 26, 30, 32, 33, 34, 41, 43, 49, 55, 63, 68, 69, 71, 81, 85, 87, 91, 94, 95, 100, 101, 102, 106, 107, 108, 117, 127, 157, 258, 266, 267, 276; III:170-71, 459, 477
Writers and thinkers, Jewish, I:55-59, 80-82; II:153; III:16. *See also* Literary life of Czech Jews; Literature, Czech, Jews in
WVHA. *See* *Wirtschaftsverwaltungshauptamt*

Yad Vashem Memorial Authority, Jerusalem, II:600; III:542 (and in source notes throughout Vol. III)
Yedidut Lodge (former Société members in Tel Aviv), II:238
"Yellow passes" (*Žltá legitimácia;* letters of exemption or protection, Slovakia), III:197-98, 200, 211, 214, 234, 238, 248 (note 46)
Yellow star (Jewish badge), III:xxxiii, 77, 79, 134, 183, 184, 316
Yeshiva Farm Settlement (Mt. Kisco, New York), II:170, 369

Yeshiva of Bratislava. *See* Yeshiva of Pressburg
Yeshiva of Dunajská Streda (Dunaszerdahely), II:368
Yeshiva of Galanta, II:368
Yeshiva of Huncovce (Hunsdorf), I:304; II:368
Yeshiva of Hunsdorf. *See* Yeshiva of Huncovce
Yeshiva of Hust, II:369
Yeshiva of Košice, II:368
Yeshiva of Mukačevo, II:369, 372
Yeshiva of Nitra, II:170, 369
Yeshiva of Poneviezh, II:164
Yeshiva of Pressburg (Bratislava), I:214, 304; II:367-68, 372
Yeshiva of Šurany, II:368
Yeshiva of Trnava, II:368, 369
Yeshiva of Užhorod, II:369
Yeshivoth (sing.: Yeshiva), I:49, 142, 145, 146, 150, 214, 275, 304; II:164, 355-69, 372, 374, 594; III:542. *See also* under names of yeshivoth
Yiddish language, I:140, 146, 486; press, I:523, 524, 527, 528; used by Jews in Czechoslovakia, I:80, 211, 212, 213, 241; II:90, 170 (note 3) 281, 372, 411; III:349, 395, 417-18. *See also* under names of Yiddish newspapers and periodicals
Yiddish theater, I:485; II:552-57
Yiddishe Post (first Zionist periodical in Subcarpathian Ruthenia, 1920-22), I:528
Yiddishe Volksblatt, Dos (Yiddish-language anti-Zionist publication), I:529
Yiddishe Zeitung (Yiddish-language organ of Mukačevo Hasidim), I:529
Yiddishe Wort-Zsidó Szó (Hungarian-Yiddish weekly, Košice), I:528
YIVO (Yiddish Scientific Institute), II:377
Yom HaNo'ar (Day of Youth, sports event), II:199, 204, 205
Young Czech party, I:45
Youth Aliyah, I:112; II:237, 592-93; III:xxix

Z Buzuluku do Prahy (*From Buzuluk to Prague;* memoirs of Ludvík Svoboda), III:390

ZAM. *See* Zionist Association of Mauritius
Zbrojovka munitions plant, Brno, III:554, 556, 566 (note 12)
Zefirah (Zionist youth organization, Brno), II:23
Zeitschrift für die Geschichte der Juden in der Tschechoslowakei, I:7, 527
Zemská podstata. See Landesmassafond
Zemský svaz sionistický. See Czechoslovak Zionist Territorial Federation
Zensuswahlrecht (suffrage based on census figures), I:47
Zentralamt für die Regelung der Judenfrage in Böhmen und Mähren (Central Office for the Settlement of the Jewish Problem in Bohemia and Moravia), III:xxxv-xxxvi, 35, 52, 86, 88, 89, 141-42, 146-47 (note 3), 571
Zentralstelle für jüdische Auswanderung (Central Office for Jewish Emigration), II:602; III:xxx, xxxi, xxxv, 23, 27, 29, 30, 32, 35, 37-38, 40, 41, 44, 45, 46, 47, 52, 77-78, 79, 82, 83, 84, 85, 86, 88, 89, 93-94 (note 33), 95 (note 58), 105, 106, 134, 135, 138, 140, 141, 146-47 (note 3), 148 (note 16), 151 (note 40), 263, 264, 265, 268, 360, 569, 571, 572, 581 (note 6)
Židovská agrární strana. See Jewish Farmers' party (Subcarpathian Ruthenia)
Židovská hospodářská strana. See Jewish Economic party
Židovská konzervatívna strana. See Conservative Jewish party
Židovská péče o nemocné. See Jewish Sick Relief Organization, Prague
Židovská radnice. See Jewish Town Hall, Prague
Židovská strana. See Jewish party
Židovská stravovna (Jewish free-meal kitchen), II:394, 398
Židovská Ústredna Úradovna pre krajinu Slovenskú (ŽÚÚ; Central Jewish Office for the Region of Slovakia), I:115; II:647; III:xxviii, 169, 170, 171, 172-73
Židovské listy pro Čechy, Moravu a Slezsko ("Jewish News for

SUBJECT INDEX

Židovské listy pro Čechy (Cont.)
Czechoslovakia, Moravia and Silesia"; Zionist fortnightly, 1913-14), I:526; II:22
Židovské L'udové Noviny (newspaper), I:100; II:22
Židovské Noviny (Jewish newspaper, Slovakia), I:117
Židovské besídky (story almanac for Jewish children; Kolín), I:526
Židovské zprávy (Jewish weekly; Prague), I:272, 444, 526, 530; II:22, 29, 144, 179, 194, 205
Židovský občianský spolok. See Jüdischer Bürgerverein
Zigeunerschul (synagogue; Prague), III:567, 578
Žilina manifesto, I:112
Zion (Zionist youth organization, Brno), II:23
Zionism and Zionists, II:11, 440, 446-47, 466; history of, in Czechoslovakia, II:19-136; in Historic Lands (before 1918), I:19-20, 20-24, 58, 59, 60; in Slovakia, I:78-79, 87, 115; II:24; III:171; in Subcarpathian Ruthenia, I:137, 140, 141, 143, 151; II:402, 404, 406, 408, 411-12, 430-31, 433; in Czechoslovak Republic (1918-39), I:173, 334, 335, 339, 341, 343, 443; II:80, 81, 82, 89, 143, 268, 274; and government of Czechoslovak Republic, I:165; II:222, 229, III:551; and Czechoslovak government-in-exile, III:454, 455, 457, 458-60, 462-63, 474-84, 552; during Holocaust, III:xxxii, 35-36, 38, 39, 42, 112, 130, 131, 170-71, 344, 631; World War II in Czech armed forces, III:363, 378-79; and post-1945 Czechoslovak Republic, III:485-86, 504, 505, 506, 514, 534, 535, 552; after Communist takeover, III:486-87, 543; assimilationists and, I:134, 145; II:148-49; Max Brod and, I:506; lodges and fraternal orders and, II:239; Jewish education and, I:143, 145; II:355; Jewish party and, II:267, 288, 313, 351; Jewish Religious Congregations and, I:271, 281, 292; II:295, 298; Franz Kafka and, I:486-87; in literature, I:444; Orthodoxy and, I:93, 145; II:156, 157, 158-59, 161, 352-53, 404, 553, 554; political behavior, I:149; press, I:523, 525, 527, 528, 529; II:22, 35-36, 264; Oskar K. Rabinowicz and, II:5, 8, 10, 11, 12, 15, 16; sports and, II:185-86, 193, 195; women's movement, II:137-47. *See also* Czechoslovak Zionist Territorial Conferences; Czechoslovak Zionist Territorial Federation; under names of Zionist organizations and parties; Zionist Congresses
Zionist Actions Committee, I:79; II:7, 28, 39, 111, 112
Zionist Activists, II:101
Zionist Association of Mauritius, II:639-40, 641
Zionist Central Committee in Czechoslovakia, II:31, 35, 60, 73, 275
Zionist Conference (Vienna, October 14, 1918), I:156-57
Zionist Conference (Luhačovice, Summer, 1946), III:505
Zionist Conference (Piestany, January, 1949), III:543
Zionist Congresses, II:158, 424; elections to, II:125, 126-30, 417; technical organization of, II:130-32; 1st (Basel, 1897), I:79; II:109, 110; 2nd (Basel, 1898), I:271; II:77, 120, 186; 4th (London, 1900), II:30; 5th (Basel, 1901), II:94; 6th (Basel, 1903), II:186; 7th (Basel, 1905), II:111; 11th (Vienna, 1913), II:109, 112, 114, 187; 12th (Karlovy Vary, 1921), I:94; II:28, 31, 32, 61, 63, 80, 83, 99, 188, 195; 13th (Karlovy Vary, 1923), I:96; II:28, 61, 189, 195; 14th (Vienna, 1925), II:62, 64-65, 83, 89, 103, 106, 122, 196; 15th (Basel, 1927), II:54, 64, 68, 69, 70, 71, 85, 86, 91, 196; 16th (Zurich, 1929), II:46, 64, 74, 86, 91, 105, 106, 120; 17th (Basel, 1931), II:14, 49, 91, 100, 106, 197; 18th (Prague, 1933), II:28, 92, 106, 107, 197, 203; 19th (Lucerne, 1935), II:54, 93; 20th

Zionist Congresses (*Cont.*)
(Zurich, 1937), II:54, 93, 99, 108;
21st (Geneva), I:118; II:44
Zionist Executive. *See* World Zionist
Executive
Zionist Federation (London), III:482
Zionist Federation of Bohemia, I:157
Zionist Federation of Slovakia (after
1938), I:115; III:xxxi, 171
Zionist Organization. *See* World
Zionist Organization
Zionist Organization of America, I:165,
244 (note 35), 245 (note 37), 248
(note 45); II:257, 259
Zionist Realists, II:33, 62, 64-69
Zionist-Revisionists. *See* Revisionism
and Revisionists
Zionist Revisionist Union, II:33, 99.
See also Revisionism and
Revisionists
Zionist Socialists. *See* Socialist Zionists
Zionist Students' Association (Prague),
II:281
Zionist students' organizations, II:173-
84. *See also* under names of
organizations
Zionist Territorial Conferences. *See*
Czechoslovak Zionist Territorial
Conferences
Zionist Territorial Federation. *See*
Czechoslovak Zionist Territorial
Federation
Zionist women's movement, II:137-47
Zionist World Executive. *See* World
Zionist Executive
Zionist World Organization. *See* World
Zionist Organization
Žltá legitimácia. See "Yellow passes"
Zsidó Néplap ("Jewish People's Paper";
Hungarian-language Zionist paper),
I:101, 528-29; II:105